SO-ADG-196

History of Madness

Praise for this new edition:

'One of the major works of the twentieth century is finally available in English. This comprehensive translation finally overcomes one of the great divisions within the world of reason; an occasion to revisit *Madness and Civilization* as it was written.' **Paul Rabinow, University of California, Berkeley**

'With this beautiful and moving book, Michel Foucault transformed our understanding of the processes that had made psychiatry possible – the process which had brought its object, mental illness, into existence, and which inscribed it into our modern imagination as pathology, negativity, incompetence and deficiency. In studying the history of madness in this way, Foucault also taught us crucial lessons about the assembling of what we have come to call 'civilization'. Now, at last, English speaking readers can have access to the depth of scholarship that underpinned Foucault's analysis: I have no doubt that this long awaited translation will have a transformative effect on a new generation of readers.' **Nikolas Rose, London School of Economics**

Reviews of the original French edition:

'A thick manuscript arrived: a philosophy thesis on the relations between madness and unreason in the classical age, by an author I did not know. I was dazzled when I read it.' **Philippe Ariès**

'This magnificent book . . . requires a mind that is capable of being in turn a historian, a philosopher, a psychologist, and a sociologist . . . never simply one of these . . . This is not a method that could be offered as an example; it is not within the reach of just anybody. Something more than talent is necessary.' **Fernand Braudel, Annales**

TAVISTOCK PUBLICATIONS

READER'S REPORT   From:...... R. D. Laing

Date...... 29/4/65

Author... Michel Foucault

Title... Madness & Civilisation

Series... Existentialism and Phenomenology

This is quite an exceptional book
of very high calibre - brilliantly
written, intellectually rigorous, and
with a thesis that thoroughly shakes the
assumptions of traditional psychiatry

Michel
Foucault

History of Madness

Edited by Jean Khalfa

Translated by Jonathan Murphy and Jean Khalfa

LONDON AND NEW YORK

First published 2006 by Routledge
First published in paperback 2009 by Routledge
2 Park Square, Milton Park, Abingdon, Oxon, OX14 4RN

Simultaneously published in the USA and Canada by Routledge
711 Third Avenue, New York, NY 10017

Routledge is an imprint of the Taylor & Francis Group, an informa business

First published in French as 'Folie et Déraison: Histoire de la
folie à l'âge classique' Librarie Plon, Paris, 1961.

This edition is a translation of 'Histoire de la Folie à l'âge classique'
© Editions GALLIMARD, Paris, 1972

Appendices 'Mon corps, ce papier, ce feu' and 'La folie, l'absence d'œuvre'
© Editions GALLIMARD, Paris, 1972

Appendix 'Reply to Derrida' from Michel Foucault, *Dits et Ecrits* Vol II
© Editions GALLIMARD, Paris, 1994

This English Translation © 2006, 2009 Routledge

Introduction and Editorial Matter © 2006, 2009 Jean Khalfa

Foreword © 2006, 2009 Ian Hacking

Typeset in Joanna by RefineCatch Limited, Bungay, Suffolk
Printed and bound in the United States of America by Edwards Brothers, Inc.,
Lillington, NC

All rights reserved. No part of this book may be reprinted or reproduced or
utilised in any form or by any electronic, mechanical, or other means, now
known or hereafter invented, including photocopying and recording, or in any
information storage or retrieval system, without permission in writing from
the publishers.

British Library Cataloguing in Publication Data
A catalogue record for this book is available from the British Library

Library of Congess Cataloging-in-Publication Data
Foucault, Michel, 1926–1984.
[Histoire de la folie à l'âge classique. English]
History of madness / Michel Foucault ; edited by Jean Khalfa ; translated by
Jonathan Murphy and Jean Khal.—Pbk. ed.
p. cm.
Includes bibliographical references and index.
1. Psychiatry—History. 2. Mental illness. I. Khalfa, Jean. II. Title.
RC438.F613 2009
616.89009—dc22
2008053339

ISBN 10: 0–415–27701–9 (Hbk)
ISBN 10: 0–415–47726–3 (Pbk)
ISBN 10: 0–203–64260–0 (eBook)

ISBN 13: 978–0–415–27701–3 (Hbk)
ISBN 13: 978–0–415–47726–0 (Pbk)
ISBN 13: 978–0–203–64260–3 (eBook)

Biography of Michel Foucault

Michel Foucault was born in Poitiers on 15 June 1926, the son of a doctor. He finished his secondary education in Paris at the Lycée Henry IV in 1946 and went on to study philosophy at the prestigious École Normale Supérieure, attending in particular the lectures of Maurice Merleau-Ponty and working with Jean Hyppolite, on Hegel, and with Louis Althusser. Despite suffering from sporadic bouts of depression and a suicide attempt in 1948, Foucault secured degrees in philosophy in 1948 and in psychology in 1950. He passed his *agrégation* in philosophy in 1951. He joined the French Communist Party in 1950 and quit in 1952.

Lecturing at the École Normale Supérieure and working as a psychologist at the Hôpital Sainte-Anne, in the early 1950s, he became dissatisfied with the confines of French academic life and held diplomatic and academic posts in Sweden (where he met and worked with Georges Dumézil), Poland and Germany, whilst working on his thesis *Folie et Déraison: Histoire de la folie à l'âge classique*. Initially rejected by Gallimard, it was published in 1961 by the great historian Philippe Ariès at Librairie Plon, the publisher of Claude Lévi-Strauss. It was hailed as 'magnificent' by Fernand Braudel. Several other now famous works followed, including *The Birth of the Clinic, The Order of Things*, and *The Archaeology of Knowledge*. In 1968, Foucault was appointed to a chair at the new, experimental, University of Vincennes and, in 1970, was elected to a prestigious chair at the Collège de France where he taught the History of Systems of Thought.

While producing a very large and influential body of research during the 1960s and 1970s, Foucault threw himself into political and social activism. He campaigned in particular on behalf of homosexuals and for prison reform. In 1975 he published one of his most famous works, *Discipline and Punish: Birth of the Prison*. Foucault travelled to North America in the late 1970s and early 1980s, teaching annually at the University of California at Berkeley. Freely experimenting with LSD and the liberal sexual environment, he lived what he termed 'limit experiences'. During that period, in addition to many articles (published posthumously in four volumes), he wrote the three volumes of his *History of Sexuality*.

Fatally ill with AIDS, Michel Foucault died in Paris on 25 June 1984 in the Salpêtrière Hospital at the age of fifty-seven. After his death, the French prime minister issued a tribute and memorial homages featured on the front pages of all the national press. In his obituary, Georges Dumézil wrote, 'Foucault's intelligence literally knew no limits.'

Contents

PART THREE

APPENDICES

ANNEXES

FOREWORD

Ian Hacking

Thank goodness this enormous book is finally available in English. A masterpiece needs no foreword, so I shall hardly go beyond the title. The original one is a bit like Alice's Cheshire Cat, of which nothing is left but the grin. It starts out as *Madness and Unreason: History of Madness in the Classical Age*, and fades away so that we are left with our present *History of Madness*. I shall go through the steps. It is a gradual disappearing act, and I shall point you in the direction of the disappeared 'unreason', not to explain it, but to encourage you to notice it. In the tale of the titles and of unreason, there are all the signs of Foucault changing his mind about madness.

The exact title in 1961 was *Folie et Déraison. Histoire de la folie à l'âge classique.* Very often only the first word of a French title is capitalised. In 1961 the second noun, *déraison*, was also given a capital letter. Daniel Defert, Foucault's longtime intellectual colleague, companion, and posthumous editor, laid emphasis on the *exact* title of the original. He does so in his incredibly valuable date list, far richer than any ordinary chronology, at the beginning of *Dits et écrits*, the collection of Foucault's published essays, interviews, speeches and prefaces.

'Unreason' was right up there alongside 'Madness'. The big book of 1961 was severely abridged, and appeared as a paperback in 1964. Half of the first preface was suppressed. On the cover we see only *Histoire de la folie*. On the title page the full 1961 title appears in block letters, but with *Folie et Déraison* in smaller print than the subtitle. Fading, like the cat. This version was translated into many languages, while only an Italian publisher did the unabridged book. For the 1965 English version, Foucault restored a little material that he had cut from the 1964 French abridgement. For a moment, a flicker more of the cat's face came back. For here are the most vivid assertions about Unreason to be found in the entire work. They will hardly make sense out of context, so I refer you to the pages in question which were suppressed and then restored (pp. 225–250). You will find sentences like this: 'How can we avoid summing up this experience by the single word Unreason? By that we mean all that for which reason is at once nearest and most distant, fullest and most empty.'

In 1972 Foucault published a second edition of the entire book, plus three appendices, but with a substitute preface. The French title had become what was formerly the subtitle, History of Madness in the Classical Age.

What is the déraison that dropped from the title but was still all over the text? Unreason is not identical to madness but something that contrasts with it. For example,

> in the anxiety of the second half of the eighteenth century, the fear of madness grew at the same rate as the dread of unreason, and for that reason the twin obsessions constantly lent each other mutual support.
>
> (p. 362)

Later we read that since the end of the eighteenth century 'the life of unreason' no longer manifests itself except in the flashes of lightning found in works like those of 'Hölderlin, Nerval, Nietzsche and Artaud' which resisted 'through their own strength that gigantic moral imprisonment'. Standard French history and iconography of psychiatry represents Pinel casting off the chains of madmen soon after the Bastille had fallen, so that is a story of liberating the mad. Here we are told that the new 'moral' treatment of insanity was also the imprisonment of unreason that had flashed so openly on the canvasses of Hieronymus Bosch.

Casual reference books diagnose Hölderlin as a schizophrenic poet, Nietzsche as a philosopher suffering from dementia caused by terminal syphilis, and Artaud as a bipolar (manic-depressive) playwright. Nerval killed himself: we say suicide is caused by severe depressive illness. It is a central thesis of this book that, far from these being inevitable ways of conceiving of four very strange men, it requires a specific organization of thought to categorise them — and so many other people — in terms of mental disorder. Foucault does not pander to the thought that genius and mental disturbance are of a piece. The art of these men, as he shouts at the end of the book, is the exact opposite of insanity: '*Where there is an œuvre, there is no madness*' (p. 577).

Alongside madness there is *also* unreason. It had much fuller play in the Renaissance, an unreason that Foucault evokes by the ship of fools and the paintings of Bosch, especially *The Temptation of Saint Anthony*. (Foucault is marvellous with paintings: look how much he draws from Goya at the end of the book, and one knows the *tour de force* on Velasquez that open *The Order of Things*.) He even says that in the early days of confining the mad, the experience of unreason smothered something else, the consciousness of madness (p. 362).

But then two distinct obsessions emerged, he tells us, madness and unreason. The fear of one and the dread of the other were tamed in the asylum. The life of unreason could break through the resulting silence only in the voices of those who were classified among the mad but who, through their art, rose above madness to act as standards to which the sane and classifying world is unable to answer.

A romantic fantasy lurks here, the purity of the possessed, those who not only speak the truth in paradox, like the fools in Shakespeare, but who are also themselves the truth.

The fantasy leaps out at you from the 1961 preface, in words suppressed in 1964: 'a madness whose wild state can never be reconstituted; but in the absence of that inaccessible primitive purity . . .' (p. xxxiii). There it is: the *inaccessible primitive purity*. That is what made the book so attractive to the British anti-psychiatric movement. So much is clear from the end of David Cooper's preface to the English (as opposed to the American edition) version of 1967 — and it was Cooper who had coined the neologism 'anti-psychiatry' in 1962.

By 1964, half the preface was cut, and by 1972 it had all gone. In a new, splendidly brief, and seemingly transparent preface, Michel Foucault speaks, as was then his wont, of a book being an event, which if it lives, lives through repeated doublings and simulacra. It has its own life, free of the author.

Doublings: I suggest that you hold in your hands two distinct books. The main text of each is the same. It is all too easy to compare these two books to the two *Don Quixote* invented by Borges, the one written by

Cervantes, the other, identical in words, written much later by an imagined Pierre Menard. Despite the words being the same, so much has happened that the meaning is different.[1]

One of these books is governed by an idea of déraison, in which there lurks a dream of madness in the wild, as something prediscursive, inaccessible, pure. The other book is what the first became, stripped of romantic illusion.

The 1961 preface promised an archaeology of a silence – and not an archaeology of psychiatry, that 'monologue of reason about madness'. What Foucault named 'archaeology' shows, in part, how a discourse becomes possible. He did not show how the psychiatric monologue became possible: he merely recorded that it came into being.

The silence was silence about unreason. That causes us difficulty. Unreason is still a word, but it is no longer part of daily language. Much the same goes for French déraison (p. 156). From the very first paragraph of this foreword you will have been wondering what it means. Rightly so. Madness is the visible grin, unreason the cat that has faded away.

'Archaeology of a silence' – that is from the part of the 1961 preface that remained in 1964, but then disappeared. Once Foucault's idea of archaeology had matured, it appears that an archaeology can only be of what is said. If so, the second book (of the two identical texts) is no longer an archaeology of silence. It is the work of an author who is no longer obsessed by the fear of madness and dread of unreason. He has made peace with both, and has moved on to the greatest of his archaeologies, *The Order of Things* (1966).

INTRODUCTION

Jean Khalfa

Foucault's *History of Madness* has yet to be read. *Madness and Civilisation*, the English translation of *Histoire de la Folie*, was based on an abridged French edition from which roughly 300 pages had been removed, together with most of the scholarly apparatus (about 800 footnotes and the bibliography).[1] Most interpretations and criticisms made of the book in the English-speaking world were therefore based on a partial perspective. Additionally, because of the historical circumstances of its appearance, the book was largely confined to debates surrounding the anti-psychiatric movement: the Introduction to the English edition was written by David Cooper, and the reader's note R.D. Laing had written for Routledge (reproduced here) was used for the back cover. It is true that Foucault did not mark his distance from such readings, perhaps because his desire was, he said,

> that this object-event, almost imperceptible among so many others, should recopy, fragment, repeat, simulate and replicate itself, and finally disappear without the person who happened to produce it ever being able to claim the right to be its master, and impose what he wished to say, or say what he wanted it to be.
>
> (1972 Preface)

Rereading it today, and in the way it requests that historical events should be understood, that is by referring them to the conditions of their genesis and not to their aftermath, it appears much more complex than these readings implied.

First, it is without doubt an analysis of the history of madness considered as a cultural, legal, political, philosophical and then medical construct, from the Renaissance to the beginning of the nineteenth century. But it is also a reflection on the notion of history and on the methodology of the historian, a reflection influenced by Nietzsche's criticism of historical teleologies.[2] The book, from this point of view, shows how a non-teleological approach to historical phenomena can denaturalise what is to us most familiar by unearthing its long forgotten and often unpalatable origins through the study of forgotten archives, traces of a reality often very removed from what was to become the dominant narrative. From a philosophical point of view, this book is the moment when Foucault's thought starts to look beyond phenomenology and towards structuralism, moving from a theory of forms of consciousness to a description of historical systems of thoughts. Most of its vocabulary is phenomenological and its avowed object is a particular *experience*, that of the other as mad: 'To try to recapture, in history, this degree zero of the history of madness, when it was undifferentiated experience, the still undivided experience of the division itself' (1961 Preface). Yet the idea is that specific structures of power determine this experience differently at different moments. Finally this book also marks the rejection of a particular conception of philosophy as irreducible to the material circumstances of its production. This is what is at stake in the violent debate with Derrida on Descartes' exclusion of the insane (Foucault's texts on this topic are reproduced in the appendices to the present edition).

MADNESS

As a history, the thesis of this book is that whether madness is described as a religious or philosophical phenomenon (an experience of inspiration, a loss of mind, etc.), or as an objective medical essence (as in all the classifications of types of madness that have been developed by psychiatry), these conceptions are not discoveries but historical constructions of meaning. When comparing the conceptions of madness prevailing in different civilisations, Foucault realised that there could be a history of madness itself, in other words that it was a 'phenomenon of civilisation, as variable, as floating as any other phenomenon of culture' and, as a consequence, that 'curing the mad is not the only possible reaction to the phenomenon of madness'. There is a moment in history when madness started to be perceived as a disease, as an object of scientific inquiry and if this transformation is interesting from the point of view of the history of psychiatry and of medicine in general, it is perhaps more important in what it tells us about what must have changed in a society as a whole for such a transformation to occur. In other words, Foucault does not look at madness from the point of view of the classical historian of a scientific discipline, here psychiatry, who would trace the development of a science from inchoate early notions towards its modern, rational state. Rather he is interested in decisions, limits and exclusions which took place at particular points in time and indicate shifts in the way certain phenomena were experienced. These shifts often coincided or overlapped with other transformations coming from different parts of a society, but made their way into ruptures of which we are no longer aware precisely because what they excluded (an earlier experience of madness) has disappeared. So the history of madness is not the history of a disease (of what we now consider to be such, of its treatments and of the institutions developed to deal with it). Rather, and in order to grasp what is no longer directly accessible, it is the history of the gesture of *partage*, division, separation, through each of its moments, incarnations or *figures*, to use the Hegelian vocabulary so present throughout the book (and still so dominant in French philosophy at the time of its writing) to describe a process of division through which a reality splits into radically different parts until a new realisation takes place, a synthesis which in itself is a new reality.

Foucault distinguishes three periods in the separation between madness and reason (or in the construction of madness as unreason, as the title of the first French edition, of 1961, made clear: *Folie et Déraison. Histoire de la folie à l'âge classique*). First, the *Renaissance* when the conversation between reason and madness which dominated in the Middle Ages is subtly transformed into a reflection on wisdom; then the radical separation of reason and madness in what he calls the *Classical Age*, that is, roughly, the seventeenth century and a large part of the eighteenth, when most of the social institutions of confinement are created – a period he calls tragic because it stages a contradiction without any hope of a reconciliation; and finally the *modern experience of madness* where madness is now perceived as factual or positive, an object of science, as a disease or a series of diseases, a period which starts at the end of the eighteenth century and which, Foucault indicates, has already been transformed in some respects by a new, literary experience of madness, obvious in late romantic works (Nerval) and in Part of the avant-garde of the twentieth century (Roussel, Artaud).

The main thesis of the book, as a work of history, is that the passage from one phase to the other is not a progression from obscure or inhuman conceptions to a final understanding of the truth about madness (as a disease, the object of a medicine of the soul, a 'psychiatry'). In fact each phase reflects for Foucault a different mode of production of society itself through a different system of exclusion. Thus, for him, the modern medical positivism which developed from the end of the eighteenth century is based on an attempt at objectifying madness which, when looked at in detail, in particular in the institutions it accompanies, is a new mode of social control. This is not to say that for Foucault the construction of modern Western society could be conceived simply as based on an exclusion of madness. He will later on consider many other types of ruptures and exclusions. But studying madness allows one to recognise deeper and much larger transformations.

In the first phase, the Renaissance, Foucault focuses initially on the works of artists, to show that madness was perceived as a sort of know-ledge, akin to some religious experience, that of a possible chaos of the world, obvious in particular in depictions of the apocalypse. The mad would be those who have the tragic experience of possible worlds which constantly menace the real one and of the essential frailty of human institutions. Able to perceive forces which, from the inside, threaten the great organisation of the world and of humanity, the mad seem to reveal and belong to the limits of our world. This experience is what the proliferation of images relating to madness during the Renaissance attempts to convey. But at the same time Foucault notes that another form of consciousness of madness seems to emerge, in texts this time, and it is no longer tragic but critical. The role of madness is to indicate a discrepancy between what men are and what they pretend to be, a great theme in humanist writing, for example Montaigne, Rabelais or Erasmus. Wise is the man who can see that there is a madness in all claims by reason to have found an absolute truth. From a Christian point of view, human reason is madness compared to the reason of God, but divine reason appears as madness to human reason. So here there is still a presence of unreason within reason, but both are looked at from a superior point of view, that of a wisdom which would understand the limits of reason, while earlier madness was experienced, so to speak, from the inside. A first, embryonic division between two forms of experience of madness has thus occurred.[3]

The classical experience of madness (seventeenth and eighteenth centuries) is very different. Now madness is perceived as unreason, that is, the absolute opposite of reason. This is the time when the mad are locked up instead of being sent out of the cities to live at their limits, when the movement towards the exclusion of the irrational by society meets 'le grand renfermement', the moment when, from the middle of the seventeenth century onwards, places of confinement are created all over Europe. Foucault insists that these institutions were not perceived as medical establishments and that what happened inside them was unrelated to the medical knowledge and practices of the time. In them the mad were locked up with the blasphemous and the unemployed, with prostitutes and other deviants, and were considered as having freely chosen the path of mistake, against truth and reason. The perspective was ethical, not medical: they were made to reverse this choice by a meticulously described system of physical constraints and rewards. But, as in the first phase, in the Renaissance, alongside these institutional developments, another movement occurs. While for the powers which had organised their internment the mad were guilty because they had made the choice to *reject nature*, for medical doctors, madness was becoming a *natural object*: the mad were no longer perceived as an aberration but as a phenomenon worthy of scientific study. Foucault envisages several reasons for this development but an important one, important precisely in that it gives its full role to the contingent in history, is that the mad, because they were now locked up, could precisely be an object of observation (which of course raises the question: why did they become the object of the medical gaze while prostitutes, vagrants, etc. became the object of other disciplines in the making, for instance sociology or criminology).

The division or *partage* between reason and madness has clearly taken place, there is no longer a surface of contact between them as there was during the Renaissance and this division parallels the social division instituted by the house of confinement. Of course there are many ways to interpret the social causes of this great movement of confinement of all those who did not work: regulation of the number of the unemployed and of prices (the workhouses where people were barely paid served to keep prices down); getting rid of undesirable characters through means that side-stepped the normal judiciary procedures (internment could be decreed by royal *lettres de cachet* and the Hôpital Général, an institutional space of legal exception, was beyond the reach of judicial authorities); fulfilment of the charitable purposes of the church, etc. Such explanations of confinement by its social function are true for Foucault who declared that social sensibility to madness changed as a function of the rise of mercantilism and the bourgeois family, but they refer to specific decisions which always presuppose a specific form of awareness or the experience of the other and of a group as un-reasonable, as fundamentally alien to the norm. Here however, what really interests Foucault is that the act of exclusion is in fact contemporary to or even predates and in a sense produces the alienation. Suddenly a new figure becomes perceptible and this perception will in turn have new effects.

The third, modern phase emerges at the end of the eighteenth century with the end of the Hôpitaux Généraux and the creation of institutions exclusively dedicated to the care of the mad. Madness has now become the exclusive object of a medical perception.

The lunatic asylum or psychiatric hospital is the result of a synthesis between the newly perceived need to cure the mad whom their family cannot afford to treat at home and the old need to protect society. But this synthesis of a space of cure and a place of exclusion is soon forgotten in its historical origin and becomes perceived as natural: the mad are now locked up *in order to be cured*. At first, internment was perceived confusedly as a reflection of the nature of madness viewed as a loss of the natural freedom of man. Now it is the only space where the necessary treatments to protect this freedom and restore it can be administered. Madness, which has been alienated by society, is now defined as psychological alienation, an alienation of the self from itself and the space of confinement a space where the self can gather itself again. So in important respects, for Foucault, the medical liberation of the mad by 'philanthropists', for instance Tuke in England and Pinel in France, famous for having removed their chains, this sudden and 'real' understanding of madness, is a myth, based, like all myths, on the forgetting of historical origins. The transformation of the exclusion space into a medical space made it possible for madness to become an object of scientific observation and experimentation. To objectify the mad was to master them, since they were defined as the product of natural causalities, and in practice it clearly became a new way of exerting a power upon them (of which the invention of the straitjacket is a model, analysed in depth by Foucault). In the end the asylum, where man could be systematically observed and studied, was one of the birthplaces of the idea of the 'human sciences'. But Foucault's target here is not scientific truth in itself but the claims to scientificity of disciplines which take as natural an object that they have in fact shaped in ways and for reasons that are often largely exterior to the object itself. In that, his approach is similar to that of Maurice Merleau-Ponty in his criticism of behaviourism as a false science in *The Structure of Behaviour*, or to that of Georges Canguilhem in his studies on the construction of scientific concepts.[4]

HISTORY

Foucault describes the book as a 'history of the conditions of possibility of psychology': the first dimension of the *History of Madness* was to trace the origins of our conception of human beings as psychological subjects from the moment when a radical separation between madness and reason had taken place, the classical age, and when the possibility of a science of this new object appears. This clearly shows the aims of the particular brand of historiography that Foucault named, in this book, the 'archaeology of knowledge'. What we spontaneously see as the final elimination of archaic and largely incomprehensible visions of the mad by the modern medical truth was not the fruit of a linear progress. Rather, it resulted from a complex series of transformations where the evolution of structures of social control gave rise to new forms of consciousness which in turn produced new structures of control. So, however Hegelian the vocabulary (and however prophetic or apocalyptic the tone sometimes is), Foucault constantly rejected the idea that the trajectory of madness was determined from the beginning and attempted to avoid the illusions born from a retrospective gaze which necessarily *naturalises* the present.[5]

But in addition to this historical analysis of madness and its institutions, and to a reflection on Western historiography, the book also contains the germs of a reflection on history in general. The reason is that the exclusion of madness coincided for Foucault with the birth of a certain conception of historical time as unified, directed and *meaningful*, as opposed to the chaotic violence, the monotonous repetition of a meaningless fury, the paradoxical 'tale told by an idiot'. The history of madness was thus also implicitly a history of the conditions of the possibility of history taken in this sense. It saw in the exclusion of the mad through the construction of madness as unreason one of these conditions, a dimension particularly emphasised in the first preface:

> *The necessity of madness* throughout the history of the West is linked to that decisive action that extracts a significant language from the background noise and its continuous monotony, a language which is transmitted and culminates in time; it is, in short, linked to *the possibility of history*.

PHILOSOPHY

A third dimension of this book is that it marks the passage between two philosophical perspectives. The vocabulary of the phenomenological approach is still common here, in particular in the first preface and what is at stake is described as a particular *experience* (this word is perhaps the most common in the book).[6] But there are several experiences or forms of experience of madness and they are historically very different even though they interfere and overlap. They are not used as indicators of the structures of a transcendental subjectivity but, rather, described as historically constructed, as forms of culture. In fact, when reading the book closely it is soon obvious that the means through which these 'experiences' are accessed by Foucault, the archives, the different types of documents which form the material of the historical inquiry become its real object. When he mentions an experience, he never does anything other than to point to a difference in historical configurations of practices, beliefs and institutions. Thus, when writing about 'the two major forms of the experiences of madness that were juxtaposed throughout the classical age [and] both follow their own chronological index', he notes that 'the formulations that justify confinement are not presentiments of our [modern] diseases, but represent instead an experience of madness that intersects with our pathological analyses, but which could never coincide with them in any coherent manner'. The purpose of history is therefore no longer to extract the real meaning of documents which would have so far remained obscure (here, to decipher, behind the crude descriptions of the registers of confinement, archaic ways of seeing the reality analysed by modern taxonomies of mental diseases) but to see rather how those specific descriptions articulate with certain norms or principles (in particular moral and religious) of their time. Rather than simply seeking to identify an obsessional neurosis behind the description of the 'deranged mind inventing its own devotion', the aim is to understand the moral order against which this disturbance is perceived as madness. The Introduction to Foucault's major methodological text, The Archaelogy of Knowledge, noted that the passage to an archaeological analysis applied to the history of ideas, thought or science, 'has broken up the long series formed by the progress of consciousness, or the teleology of reason, or the evolution of human thought':

> Thus, in place of the continuous chronology of reason, which was invariably traced back to some inaccessible origin, its founding opening, there have appeared scales that are sometimes very brief, distinct from one another, irreducible to a single law, scales that bear a type of history peculiar to each one, and which cannot be reduced to the general model of a consciousness that acquires, progresses and remembers.
>
> (p. 8)

A spectacular consequence of this shift from an analysis of experience to an analysis of structures and practices is the connection established by Foucault at the beginning of the second chapter of the first part of the History of Madness, between the refusal by Descartes to consider the possibility of his own madness as a legitimate reason for doubting the reality of the world and of his own existence, and the invention of vast houses of confinement roughly at the same time. These would be two aspects of the same 'event'. One of the questions Descartes asks, in his systematic exploration of the reasons for scepticism, is: how do I know that I am not mad? But instead of examining the question, Descartes dismisses it in an exclamation all the more astonishing when coming from a philosopher who defined the two causes of error as prejudice and precipitation: 'But such people are insane, and I would be thought equally mad if I took anything from them as a model for myself' (Metaphysical Meditations, 1641. The French translation, reviewed and approved by Descartes, is even stronger. It can in turn be translated as: 'I would be equally mad if I took anything from them as a model for myself'). Foucault seems to have been the first modern reader of Descartes to note this gap in an otherwise watertight argument.[7] He sees the a priori exclusion of madness from the process of thought, where the mad, as in-sane, are characterised solely by what they lack, as symptomatic of the parallel formation of modern rationalism and of institutions of confinement, both forming the two sides of what he calls 'the classical event'.

This connection established between the detail of an argument within the canonical exposition of Descartes' philosophy – an extraordinarily methodical and meticulous metaphysical meditation, and a large-scale historical-social transformation, drew the attention of Jacques Derrida who published in 1964 a critique of *Madness and Unreason*, under the title 'Cogito and history of madness',[8] initiating a violent debate which led Foucault to clarify his basic assumptions. In substance Derrida raised two objections.

First, he rejected Foucault's reading. If Descartes moves so quickly from the argument of madness to the argument of the dream – an essential moment in the consideration of sceptical arguments since the experience of the dream shows that there is no criterion we could use, 'within' the field of consciousness, to assert the reality of an existence 'exterior' to this field – it is because the experience of the dream is common and perhaps universal, as opposed to the experience of madness. The voice which excludes the mad from the field of rational inquiry would thus not be that of the philosopher but of the layman, in the hypothetical dialogue which would be contained in this 'meditation'. This man would never consider as serious the argument of madness but would easily be shaken, as any philosophy teacher knows, by the argument of the dream. So, for Derrida, the strength of madness as a radical questioning of beliefs in whatever exists, in its proximity therefore to the sceptical moment of philosophy, is here, in Descartes, triumphant in the hyperbole of the dream itself. Far from indicating a gesture of exclusion, the substitution of the argument of the dream, claims Derrida, is the 'hyperbolic exasperation of the hypothesis of madness'.

The second important point of Derrida's critique is of a much more general nature. He sees in what he calls 'the hyperbolic audacity of the Cartesian Cogito, its mad audacity', a fundamental move, which is the essence of philosophical thought itself. 'It is the [. . .] point of certainty from which the possibility of Foucault's narration, as well as of the narration of the totality, [in fact] the project of thinking this totality by escaping it, is embedded.' That audacity in Descartes comes from beyond Descartes, and it should not be pinned down to any particular moment in history because it is the condition, says Derrida, of all histories or all narration. This audacity is Philosophy or, more precisely, the initial excess or extravagance of the philosophical gesture when it questions the totality of what exists, and therefore can ask the question of the nature and meaning of being (whatever the answer is, theological or not). By doing that, he adds, this initial gesture opens up a space at the same time for madness and for reason, and also for history, as history is always a meaning imposed onto the infinite multiplicity of the real. In other words, what Foucault attributes to a moment in time (the division reason/unreason, the idea of history as a meaningful whole) is in fact the initial philosophical gesture, without which Foucault could not have written his book, for this gesture of freedom which questions the totality of being as such, as in the first of Descartes' *Metaphysical Meditation*, is in excess of, or takes place before a discursive practice has started, before a book has been written to answer it, and therefore cannot be totally reduced to the historical conditions under which books are written or thoughts expressed. Ignoring that would be a sign on the part of Foucault of what Derrida calls a 'historicist totalitarianism', which would reduce all thought to the conditions of its production and would therefore *ipso facto* endanger its own claim to truthfulness.[9]

Foucault, responded in 1972, in the second edition of the book, by then called *History of Madness*, in two ways. First he removed the Preface of 1961, on which Derrida had concentrated his more general attack, and second he added to the book an important appendix, 'My body, this paper, this fire', which is a systematic rebuttal of Derrida's argument, so violent in tone that the two writers stopped communicating for ten years. We publish here both prefaces and this text together with a second appendix Foucault inserted in the 1972 edition (at the insistence of Gilles Deleuze), which reformulates and develops some of the themes of the first Preface: 'Madness, the absence of an œuvre'. This text was originally published in May 1964. The present edition also contains an earlier and different version of Foucault's answer to Derrida, published in the Japanese journal *Paideia* in February 1972.

There is little doubt that on the textual analysis of Descartes Foucault has no difficulty countering Derrida's argument. The meditation as a type of discursive practice is radically different from the dialogue and it is only through distortions of the text that Derrida can claim otherwise.[10] In particular he does not see that in the movement of the meditation, the very act of thinking about the dream, the particular steps of this thought as events within the meditative process, are an essential element in blurring the border between dream and reality and operate a transformation of the meditating subject himself. In other words Derrida fails to see that in Descartes' text meditation is action as much as demonstration (as the Cogito itself will again demonstrate in the *Second Meditation*). Hence the violent conclusion:

> it was not at all on account of their inattentiveness that classical scholars omitted, before Derrida and like him, this passage from Descartes. It is part of a system, a system of which Derrida is today the most decisive representative, in its final explosion: a reduction of discursive practices to textual traces; the elision of events that are produced there, leaving only the marks for a reading; the invention of voices behind the text, so as not to have to examine the modes of implication of the subject in discourses; the assignation of the originary as said and not-said in the text in order to avoid replacing discursive practices in the field of transformation where they are carried out.

Foucault goes on to say that the very statement of an a priori irreducibility of the opening of a critical (philosophical) thought to the historical conditions of its emergence is itself a discursive practice, reducible to the conditions of its emergence:

> I would say that it is a historically well-determined little pedagogy, which manifests itself here in a very visible manner. A pedagogy which teaches the student that there is nothing outside the text, but that in it, in its interstices, in its blanks and silences, the reserve of the origin reigns; that it is never necessary to look beyond it, but that here, not in the words of course, but in words as crossings-out, in their *lattice*, what is said is 'the meaning of being'. A pedagogy that inversely gives to the voice of the masters that unlimited sovereignty that allows it to indefinitely re-say the text.

In its defence of the methods of the new historiography of ideas, with its insistence on 'thresholds, mutations, independent systems, and limited series', *The Archaeology of Knowledge* explains the violence of Foucault's reaction and the importance of Descartes in this debate:

> If the history of thought could remain the locus of uninterrupted continuities, if it could endlessly forge connections that no analysis could undo without abstraction, if it could weave around everything that men say and do, obscure synthesis that anticipate for him, prepare him, and lead him endlessly towards his future, it would provide a privileged shelter for the sovereignty of consciousness.
>
> (p. 12)

But then Foucault's answer does not explain in this book how it is possible for a thought that claims to be doing an archaeology of systems of thoughts, which thus must study accurately the conditions of its own production and the constraints that bear on its own exercise, a thought therefore that can neither postulate for itself an absolute origin (say in the act of institution of a *ratio*), nor a detachment from its own time – how it is possible for such a thought to explain the freedom within which it operates and the truthfulness of the structures it constructs when studying history. Must philosophy postulate the transcendence of thought to history? This is the question of this book since as a history of modern conceptions of madness it also opens up the possibility of a history of forms of rationality. One could read a large part of Foucault's later work as an attempt to address this question.

opposition between "madness" and "Reason"

PREFACE TO THE 1961 EDITION

Pascal: 'Men are so necessarily mad, that not being mad would be being mad through another trick that madness played.'' And that other text, by Dostoevsky, from *A Writer's Diary*: 'It is not by locking up one's neighbour that one convinces oneself of one's own good sense.'

We need a history of that other trick that madness plays — that other trick through which men, in the gesture of sovereign reason that locks up their neighbour, communicate and recognise each other in the merciless language of non-madness; we need to identify the moment of that expulsion, before it was definitely established in the reign of truth, before it was brought back to life by the lyricism of protestation. To try to recapture, in history, this degree zero of the history of madness, when it was undifferentiated experience, the still undivided experience of the division itself. To describe, from the origin of its curve, that 'other trick' which, on either side of its movement, allows Reason and Madness to fall away, like things henceforth foreign to each other, deaf to any exchange, almost dead to each other.

It is, no doubt, an uncomfortable region. To pass through it we must renounce the comforts of terminal truths and never allow ourselves to be guided by what we might know of madness. None of the concepts of psychopathology, even and above all in the implicit play of retrospection, can be allowed to play an organising role. The gesture that divides madness is the constitutive one, not the science that grows up in the calm that returns after the division has been made. The caesura that establishes the distance between reason and non-reason is the origin; the grip in which reason holds non-reason to extract its truth as madness, fault or sickness derives from that, and much further off. We must therefore speak of this primitive debate without supposing a victory, nor the right to victory; we must speak of these repeated gestures in history, leaving in suspense anything that might take on the appearance of an ending, or of rest in truth; and speak of that gesture of severance, the distance taken, the void installed between reason and that which it is not, without ever leaning on the plenitude of what reason pretends to be.

Then, and only then, will that domain be able to appear, where men of madness and men of reason, departing from each other and not yet separate, can open, in a language more original, much rougher and much more matutinal than that of science, the dialogue of their rupture, which proves, in a fleeting fashion, that they are still on speaking terms. There, madness and non-madness, reason and unreason are confusedly implicated in each other, inseparable as they do not yet exist, and existing for each other, in relation to each other, in the exchange that separates them.

In the midst of the serene world of mental illness, modern man no longer communicates with the madman: on the one hand is the man of reason, who delegates madness to the doctor, thereby authorising no relation other than through the abstract universality of illness; and on the other is the man of madness, who only communicates with the other through the intermediary of a reason that is no less abstract, which is order, physical and moral constraint, the anonymous pressure of the group, the demand for conformity. There is no common language: or rather, it no longer exists; the constitution of madness as mental illness, at the end of the eighteenth century, bears witness to a rupture in a dialogue, gives the separation as already enacted, and expels from the memory all those imperfect words, of no fixed syntax, spoken falteringly, in which the exchange between madness and reason was carried out. The language of psychiatry, which is a monologue by reason *about* madness, could only have come into existence in such a silence.

My intention was not to write the history of that language, but rather draw up the archaeology of that silence.

*

The Greeks had a relation to a thing they called ὕβρις (hubris). The relation was not solely one of condemnation: the existence of Thrasymachus, or that of Callicles, is proof enough of that, even if their discourse comes down to us already enveloped in the reassuring dialectics of Socrates. But the Greek Logos had no opposite.

European man, since the depths of the Middle Ages, has had a relation to a thing that is confusedly termed Madness, Dementia or Unreason. It is perhaps to that obscure presence that Western Reason owes something of its depth, as with the threat of hubris, the σωφροσύνη (sophrosyne) of Socratic speechmakers. In any case, the Reason–Unreason relation constitutes for Western culture one of the dimensions of its originality: it accompanied it long before Hieronymus Bosch, and will follow it long after Nietzsche and Artaud.

But what then is this confrontation below the language of reason? Where might this interrogation lead, following not reason in its horizontal becoming, but seeking to retrace in time this constant verticality, which, the length of Western culture, confronts it with what it is not, measuring it with its own extravagance? Towards what region might it take us, which was neither the history of knowledge nor history plain and simple, which was commanded neither by the teleology of the truth nor the rational concatenation of causes, which only have value or meaning beyond the division? A region, no doubt, where it would be a question more of the limits than of the identity of a culture.

We could write a history of limits – of those obscure gestures, necessarily forgotten as soon as they are accomplished, through which a culture rejects something which for it will be the Exterior; and throughout its history, this hollowed-out void, this white space by means of which it isolates itself, identifies it as clearly as its values. For those values are received, and maintained in the continuity of history; but in the region of which we would speak, it makes its essential choices, operating the division which gives a culture the face of its positivity: this is the originary thickness in which a culture takes shape. To interrogate a culture about its limit-experiences is to question it at the confines of history about a tear that is something like the very birth of its history.[3] There, in a tension that is constantly on the verge of resolution, we find the temporal continuity of a dialectical analysis confronted with the revelation, at the doors of time, of a tragic structure.

At the centre of these limit-experiences of the Western world is the explosion, of course, of the tragic itself – Nietzsche having shown that the tragic structure from which the history of the Western world is made is nothing other than the refusal, the forgetting and the silent collapse of tragedy. Around that experience, which is central as it knots the tragic to the dialectic of history in the very refusal of tragedy by history, many other experiences gravitate. Each one, at the frontiers of our culture, traces a limit that simultaneously signifies an original division.

In the universality of the Western *ratio*, there is this division which is the Orient: the Orient, thought of as the origin, dreamt of as the vertiginous point from which nostalgia and promises of return are born, the Orient offered to the colonising reason of the Occident, but indefinitely inaccessible, for it always remains the limit: the night of the beginning, in which the Occident was formed, but in which it traced a dividing line, the Orient is for the Occident everything that it is not, while remaining the place in which its primitive truth must be sought. What is required is a history of this great divide, all along this Occidental becoming, following it in its continuity and its exchanges, while also allowing it to appear in its tragic hieratism.

Other divisions must also be told: in the luminous unity of appearance, the absolute division of dreams, which man cannot prevent himself from questioning in search of his own truth – be it that of his destiny or that of his heart – but which he only questions beyond an essential refusal that constitutes it and pushes it into the derision of the oneiric. It will also be necessary to write the history of sexual prohibitions, and not simply in terms of ethnology: and speak, in our culture itself, of the continuously mobile and obstinate forms of repression, not to write a chronicle of morality or tolerance, but to reveal, as a limit of our Occidental world and the origin of its morality, the tragic division of the happy world of desire. Finally, and firstly, we must speak of the experience of madness.

The following study will only be the first, and probably the easiest, in this long line of enquiry which, beneath the sun of the great Nietzschean quest, would confront the dialectics of history with the immobile structures of the tragic.

*

What then is madness, in its most general but most concrete form, for anyone who immediately challenges any hold that knowledge might have upon it? In all probability, nothing other than the *absence of an œuvre*.

What place could the existence of madness have in becoming? What is its wake? Quite probably very narrow; a few mildly worrying lines, which leave the great reasonable calm of history unchanged. What weight might they have, in the face of the few decisive words that wove the becoming of Western reason, these vain words, these dossiers of indecipherable delirium, juxtaposed by chance to the words of reason in prisons and libraries? Is there any place in the universe of our discourses for the thousands of pages where Thorin, an almost illiterate lackey and 'frenzied madman', transcribed, at the close of the seventeenth century, his fugitive visions and the roaring of his terror?[4] All that is merely fallen time, the poor presumption of a passage refused by the future, a thing in becoming which is irreparably less than history.

It is that 'less than' that we must investigate, immediately freeing it of any association with the pejorative. From its originary formulation, historical time imposes silence on a thing that we can no longer apprehend, other than by addressing it as void, vanity, nothingness. History is only possible against the backdrop of the absence of history, in the midst of a great space of murmurings, that silence watches like its vocation and its truth: 'I will call desert this castle that you were, night this voice, absence your face.'[5] An obscure, equivocal region: pure origin, as it is from there that the language of history would be born, slowly conquering so much confusion with the forms of its syntax and the consistency of its vocabulary – and ultimate residue, a sterile beach of words, sand that has run its course and is immediately forgotten, keeping nothing, in its passivity, other than the empty imprints of abstracted figures.

The great œuvre of the history of the world is indelibly accompanied by the absence of an œuvre, which renews itself at every instant, but which runs unaltered in its inevitable void the length of history: and from before history, as it is already there in the primitive decision, and after it again, as it will triumph in the last word uttered by history. The plenitude of history is only possible in the space, both empty and peopled at the same time, of all the words without language that appear to anyone who lends an ear, as a dull sound from beneath history, the obstinate murmur of a language talking to itself – without any speaking subject and without an interlocutor, wrapped up in itself, with a lump in

its throat, collapsing before it ever reaches any formulation and returning without a fuss to the silence that it never shook off. The charred root
of meaning.

That is not yet madness, but the first caesura from which the division of
madness became possible. That division is its repetition and intensification, its organisation in the tight unity of the present; the perception
that Western man has of his own time and space allows a structure of
refusal to appear, on the basis of which a discourse is denounced as not
being language, a gesture as not being an *œuvre*, a figure as having no
rightful place in history. This structure is constitutive of what is sense and
nonsense, or rather of that reciprocity through which the one is bound to
the other; it alone can account for the general fact that in our culture there
can be no reason without madness, even though the rational knowledge
that we have of madness reduces it and disarms it by lending it the slender
status of pathological accident. *The necessity of madness* throughout the history
of the West is linked to that decisive action that extracts a significant
language from the background noise and its continuous monotony,
a language which is transmitted and culminates in time; it is, in short,
linked to *the possibility of history*.

This structure of the experience of madness, which is history through
and through, but whose seat is at its margins, where its decisions are
made, is the object of this study.

Which means that it is not at all a history of knowledge, but of the
rudimentary movements of an experience. A history not of psychiatry, but
of madness itself, in all its vivacity, before it is captured by knowledge. We
need to strain our ears, and bend down towards this murmuring of the
world, and try to perceive so many images that have never been poetry, so
many fantasies that have never attained the colours of day. But it is, no
doubt, a doubly impossible task, as it would require us to reconstitute the
dust of this concrete pain, and those insane words that nothing anchors in
time; and above all because that pain and those words only exist, and are
only apparent to themselves and to others in the act of division that
already denounces and masters them. It is only in the act of separation,
and from it, that we can think of them as dust that has not yet been
separated. Any perception that aims to apprehend them in their wild state
necessarily belongs to a world that has captured them already. The liberty
of madness can only be heard from the heights of the fortress in which it
is imprisoned. There, freedom 'has only the morose registry of its prisons,

and its wordless experience as a persecuted thing; all we have is its description as an escaped convict'.[6]

To write the history of madness will therefore mean making a structural study of the historical ensemble – notions, institutions, judicial and police measures, scientific concepts – which hold captive a madness whose wild state can never be reconstituted; but in the absence of that inaccessible primitive purity, the structural study must go back to that decision that both bound and separated reason and madness; it must tend to discover the perpetual exchange, the obscure common root, the originary confrontation that gives meaning to the unity and the opposition of sense and senselessness. That will allow that lightning flash decision to appear once more, heterogeneous with the time of history, but ungraspable outside it, which separates the murmur of dark insects from the language of reason and the promises of time.

*

Should we be surprised that this structure was above all visible during the 150 years that preceded and prepared the formation of a psychiatry considered by us as positive? The classical age – from Willis to Pinel, from the fury of Oreste to the *Quinta del Sordo* and *Juliette* – covers precisely that period when the exchange between madness and reason modifies its language, in a radical manner. In the history of madness, two events signal this change with singular clarity: in 1657, the founding of the Hôpital Général, and the Great Confinement of the poor; and in 1794, the liberation of the mad in chains at Bicêtre. Between these two singular and symmetrical events, something happened, whose ambiguity has perplexed historians of medicine: blind repression in an absolutist regime, according to some, and, according to others, the progressive discovery, by science and philanthropy, of madness in its positive truth. In fact, beneath these reversible meanings, a structure was taking shape, which did not undo that ambiguity but was decisive for it. This structure explains the passage from the medieval and humanist experience of madness to the experience that is our own, which confines madness in mental illness. In the Middle Ages, and up until the Renaissance, the debate between man and madness was a dramatic debate that confronted man with the dark powers of the world; and the experience of madness was absorbed in images that spoke of the Fall and the End of All Things, of the Beast, of Metamorphosis, and of all the marvellous secrets of Knowledge. In our time, the experience of madness is made in the calm of a knowledge which, through knowing it too much, passes it over. But in the movement from the one experience to the other, the passage is made through a world without images or positivity, in a sort of silent transparency that allows a great immobile structure to appear, like a wordless institution, a gesture without commentary, an immediate knowledge; this structure is neither that of drama nor of knowledge; it is the point at which history freezes, in the tragic mode that both founds it and calls it into question.

At the centre of this attempt to re-establish the value of the classical experience of madness, in its rights and its becoming, there is therefore a motionless figure to be found: the simple division into daylight and obscurity, shadow and light, dream and waking, the truth of the sun and the power of midnight. An elementary figure, which only accepts time as the indefinite return of a limit.

Another effect of that figure was to lead man into a powerful forgetting; he was to learn to dominate that great division, and bring it down to his own level; and make in himself the day and the night, and order the sun of the truth to the pale light of his truth. Having mastered his madness, and having freed it by capturing it in the gaols of his gaze and his morality, having disarmed it by pushing it into a corner of himself finally allowed man to establish that sort of relation to the self that is known as 'psychology'. It had been necessary for Madness to cease being Night, and become a fleeting shadow within consciousness, for man to be able to pretend to grasp its truth and untangle it in knowledge.

In the reconstitution of this experience of madness, a history of the conditions of possibility of psychology wrote itself as though of its own accord.

*

In the course of writing this book, I sometimes had recourse to material that had been already gathered together by other authors. I did this as little as possible, and only in cases when I was unable to gain access to the document itself. Beyond any reference to a psychiatric 'truth', the aim was to allow these words and texts, which came from beneath the surface of language, and were not produced to accede to language, to speak of themselves. Perhaps, to my mind, the most important part of this work is the space I have left to the texts of the archives themselves.

For the rest, it was necessary to ensure that I remained in a sort of relativity without recourse, never looking for a way out in any psychological *coup de force*, which might have turned over the cards and denounced some unrecognised truth. It was necessary to speak of madness only through that other 'trick' that allows men to not be mad, and that other trick could only be described, for its part, in the primitive vivacity that engages it in an indefinite debate regarding madness. A language without support was therefore necessary, a language that entered the game, but was to authorise the exchange; a language that constantly corrected itself to proceed, in a continuous movement, to the very bottom. The aim was to keep the *relative* at all costs, and to be *absolutely* understood.

There, in that simple problem of elocution, the greatest difficulty that faced the enterprise hid and expressed itself: it was necessary to bring to the surface of the language of reason a division and a debate that must of necessity remain on the near side of it, as that language only has meaning well beyond them. What was required was therefore a language that was quite neutral (fairly free from scientific terminology, and social or moral options), in order to approach most closely these primitively tangled words, and so that that distance through which modern man shores himself up against madness might be abolished; but a language that remained sufficiently open for the decisive words through which the truth of madness and of reason are constituted to find their place without being betrayed. Of rules and methods, I retained only one, summed up in a text by Char, where the definition of the most pressing and the most contained truth can be read: 'I removed from things the illusion they produce to protect themselves from us, and I left them the part that they concede us.'[7]

*

In this task, which was inevitably a slightly solitary one, many came to my assistance and have a right to my gratitude. First of all M. Georges Dumézil, without whom the work would never have been begun – neither begun in the course of a Swedish night, nor finished in the stubborn, bright sun of Polish liberty. I must also thank M. Jean Hyppolite, and above all M. Georges Canguilhem, who read this work in a still unformed state, advised me when things were not simple, saved me from many errors, and showed me the value of being heard. My friend Robert Mauzi, a great authority on the eighteenth century, provided much of the knowledge that I was lacking.

I should also name many others who appear not to matter. Yet they know, these friends from Sweden and these Polish friends, that there is something of their presence in these pages. May they pardon me for making such demands on them and their happiness, they who were so close to a work that spoke only of distant sufferings, and the slightly dusty archives of pain.

*

'Companions in pathos, who barely murmur, go with your lamp spent and return the jewels. A new mystery sings in your bones. Cultivate your legitimate strangeness.'[8]

Hamburg, February 5, 1960.

PREFACE TO THE 1972 EDITION

I really ought to write a new preface for this book, which is old already. But the idea I find rather unattractive. For whatever I tried to do, I would always end up trying to justify it for what it was, and reinsert it, insofar as such a thing might be possible, in what is going on today. Perhaps that would be possible, perhaps not, I might do it with varying degrees of success, but it would not be an honest course of action. And above all, that wouldn't be in keeping with what should be, regarding a book, the preserve of the person who wrote it. A book is produced, it is a minuscule event, an object that fits into the hand. But at that moment, it takes its place in an incessant game of repetitions, for its doubles, both near and far, start to multiply; each reading gives it for an instant an impalpable, unique body; fragments of it pass into circulation and are passed off as the real thing, purporting to contain the book in its entirety, and the book itself sometimes ends up taking refuge in such summaries; commentaries double the text still further, creating even more discourses where, it is claimed, the book is itself at last, avowing all that it refused to say, delivering itself from all that which it so loudly pretended to be. A reissue in another place and in another time is yet another of these doubles, something which is neither totally an illusion, nor totally an identical object.

The temptation is great for the person who wrote the book to lay down the law regarding these flickering simulacra, and prescribe a form for them, to give them the ballast of an identity, imposing a unique mark that would give them all a certain constant value. 'I am the author: look at my face or my profile; this is what all these doubled figures that are going to circulate under my name should look like; those who stray from it are worthless; and it is from their degree of resemblance that you should measure the value of the others. I am the name, the law, the soul, the secret, and the balance in which these doubles should be weighed.' So speaks the Preface, the first act in which the monarchy of the author is established, a declaration of tyranny: my intention should be your precept; you must bend your reading, your analyses, your criticisms to what I was trying to do, and take note of my modesty: when I speak of the limits of my enterprise, I mean to set a boundary for your freedom, and if I claim that I feel I was not up to the task, it is because I don't want to leave you the privilege of substituting my book with the fantasy of a different one, close to it, but more beautiful than the book itself. I am the monarch of the things that I have said, and I keep an eminent sovereignty over them; that of my intention, and the meaning that I wished to give to them.

My desire is that a book, at least for the person who wrote it, should be nothing other than the sentences of which it is made; that it should not be doubled by that first simulacrum of itself which is a preface, whose intention is to lay down the law for all the simulacra which are to be formed in the future on its basis. My desire is that this object-event, almost imperceptible among so many others, should recopy, fragment, repeat, simulate and replicate itself, and finally disappear without the person who happened to produce it ever being able to claim the right to be its master, and impose what he wished to say, or say what he wanted it to be. In short, my desire is that a book should not create of its own accord that status of text to which teaching and criticism will all too probably reduce it, but that it should have the easy confidence to present itself as discourse: as both battle and weapon, strategy and shock, struggle and trophy or wound, conjuncture and vestige, strange meeting and repeatable scene.

For these reasons, when I was asked to write a new preface for this book, which is being reissued, I could only answer that the previous one should be removed. That would be the honest course. We should not try to justify the old book, nor reinsert it into the present; the series of events to which it belongs, and which are its true law, are far from being over. As for novelty, we should not pretend to discover in it a secret reserve or a richness that initially escaped detection; its only novelty is the things that have been said about it, and the events in which it has been caught up.

I will add only two texts: one, already published, where I expand on a phrase I ventured rather blindly: 'madness, the absence of an œuvre'; the other, unpublished in France, where I try to address a remarkable criticism by Derrida.

'But you have just written a preface.'

'At least it's short.'

Michel Foucault

Part One

1

STULTIFERA NAVIS

At the end of the Middle Ages, leprosy disappeared from the Western world. At the edges of the community, at town gates, large, barren, uninhabitable areas appeared, where the disease no longer reigned but its ghost still hovered. For centuries, these spaces would belong to the domain of the inhuman. From the fourteenth to the seventeenth century, by means of strange incantations, they conjured up a new incarnation of evil, another grinning mask of fear, home to the constantly renewed magic of purification and exclusion.

From the High Middle Ages until the end of the crusades, leprosaria had sprung up and multiplied across the surface of Europe. The exact figure is unknown, but according to Mathieu Paris, there were some 19,000 of these cities of the damned spread throughout Christendom.[1] In the years leading up to 1266, when Louis VIII ordered a set of statutes to be drawn up for the lazar houses, there were more than 2,000 such institutions in France. They numbered forty-three in one diocese in Paris alone, and Bourg-la-Reine, Corbeil, Saint-Valère, and the sinister Champ Pourri (Rotten Row) all figure on the list. Charenton, a name that would resonate down the centuries, is there too. The two largest houses – Saint-Germain and Saint-Lazare – were on the immediate outskirts of Paris, and their names too will crop up in the history of another sickness.[2] From the turn of the fifteenth century, a new emptiness appears: Saint-Germain becomes a home for young offenders the following century, and before Saint Vincent, Saint-Lazare counted only one leper, 'Le Sieur Langlois, a practitioner in the civil court'. The leprosarium in Nancy, which had been one of the largest in Europe, had only four inmates during the regency of Marie de Médicis. The *Mémoires* of Catel recount that there were twenty-nine hospitals in Toulouse at the end of the medieval period, seven of which were leprosaria, but at the beginning of the seventeenth century the number had shrunk to three – Saint-Cyprien, Arnaud-Bernard and Saint-Michel.[3] Festivities were widespread to celebrate the disappearance of leprosy: in 1635 for instance, the inhabitants of Reims processed solemnly to thank God for delivering their town from its plight.[4]

By that time, the French crown had already been reorganising the immense fortune the leper houses' lands' represented for more than a century. François I had ordered a census and an inventory of all such institutions on 19 December 1543 'to put an end to the great disorder apparent in leper houses', and in his turn Henri IV decreed in 1606 that the accounts of such institutions be revised 'and that revenue accruing from this review be used for the upkeep of poor gentlemen and invalid soldiers'. Another such overview was ordered on 24 October 1612, with the idea that this time the surplus revenue be used to feed the poor.[5]

In fact the leprosaria question wouldn't be settled in France before the close of the seventeenth century, and the economic importance of the question would be at the base of many a conflict. In 1677, there were still forty-four leprosaria in the province of Dauphiné alone.[6] On 20 February 1672 Louis XIV transferred control of all military and hospital orders to the orders of Saint-Lazare and Mont-Carmel, which were entrusted with the administration of all the remaining leprosaria in the kingdom.[7] Twenty years later the 1672 edict was revoked and, by means of series of measures that came into force from March 1693 to July 1695, the goods of the leper houses were redistributed among other hospitals and institutions for the succouring of the afflicted. The few lepers who still inhabited the 1,200 leprosaria that remained were grouped together in Saint-Mesmin near Orleans.[8] These new orders were first brought into force in Paris where Parliament transferred the revenue in question to the Hôpital Général, and the example was soon being followed in the provinces. In Toulouse, all leprosy possessions were redirected to the hospital for Incurables in 1696, revenue from Beaulieu in Normandy was transferred to the main hospital in Caen, and in Voley, the money was transferred to the Sainte-Foy hospital.[9] Together with Saint-Mesmin, only Les Ganets near Bordeaux retained its former status.

For their million-and-a-half inhabitants in the twelfth century, England and Scotland had opened 220 leper houses. But even by the fourteenth century they were beginning to empty: when Edward III ordered an inquiry into the state of Ripon hospital in 1342, it emerged that there were no more lepers, and the foundation was charged with the care of the poor instead. By 1434, in the hospital founded in the late twelfth century by Archbishop Puisel, there were only two remaining beds reserved for lepers, and they were often unoccupied.[10] In 1348 the great leper house of Saint-Alban had only three inhabitants; Romenall hospital in Kent was abandoned twenty-four years later as no more lepers could be found. In Chatham, the Saint Bartholomew leper house founded in 1078 had been one of the biggest in the country: by the time of Queen Elizabeth it had only two inmates, and it was finally closed altogether in 1627.[11]

The same regression of the disease was witnessed in Germany, although there the process was slightly slower. As in England, the Reformation hastened the transfer of control of the leper houses to local city authorities, who converted them into houses for the poor or hospitals, as was the case in Leipzig, Munich and Hamburg. In 1542, all possessions of the leper houses of Schleswig-Holstein were handed over to hospitals. In Stuttgart, a magistrate's report indicated in 1589 that no leper had been recorded in the city's lazar house for more than fifty years. In Lipplingen, the lazar house was peopled with the insane and the incurably ill from an early stage.[12]

This strange disappearance was probably not the long-sought-after result of obscure medical practices, but rather a spontaneous result of segregation, and the consequence, with the coming of the end of the crusades, of cutting the cord that led to the main source of infection in the Middle East. Leprosy retreated, and the lowly spaces set aside for it, together with the rituals that had grown up not to suppress it but to keep it at a sacred distance, suddenly had no purpose. But what lasted longer than leprosy, and persisted for years after the lazar houses had been emptied, were the values and images attached to the leper, and the importance for society of this insistent, fearsome figure, who was carefully excluded only after a sacred circle had been drawn around him.

If lepers were socially excluded and removed from the community of the visible church, their existence still made God manifest, as they showed both his anger and his bounty: 'Dearly beloved', says a ritual from a church in Vienne in the south of France, 'it has pleased God to afflict you with this disease, and the Lord is gracious for bringing punishment upon you for the evil that you have done in this world.' And as he was dragged out of the church by the priest and his acolytes *gressu retrogrado*, the leper was assured that he was God's witness: 'however removed from the church and the company of the Healthy, you are never separated from the grace of God'. Brueghel's lepers watch from afar, but forever, as Christ climbs Mount Calvary accompanied by a whole people. Hieratic witnesses of evil, their salvation is assured by their exclusion: in a strange reversal quite opposed to merit and prayers, they are saved by the hand that is not offered. The sinner who abandons the leper to his fate thereby opens the door to their salvation. 'Thus be patient in your sickness, for the Lord does not underestimate your ills, nor separate you from his company. If you have patience, so shall you be saved, like the leper who died outside the door of the rich man, and was carried straight up to Heaven.'[13] Abandonment is his salvation, and exclusion offers a different form of communion.

Once leprosy had gone, and the figure of the leper was no more than a distant memory, these structures still remained. The game of exclusion would be played again, often in these same places, in an oddly similar fashion two or three centuries later. The role of the leper was to be played by the poor and by the vagrant, by prisoners and by the 'alienated', and the sort of salvation at stake for both parties in this game of exclusion is the matter of this study. The forms this exclusion took would continue, in a radically different culture and with a new meaning, but remaining essentially the major form of a rigorous division, at the same time social exclusion and spiritual reintegration.

*

But let's not get ahead of ourselves.

The role that leprosy had played was first taken by venereal disease. Such diseases were the natural heir to leprosy in the late fifteenth century, and the disease was treated in several leper hospitals. Under François I, an attempt was made to confine it to the hospital of the Parish of Saint-Eustache, and then in the parish of Saint-Nicolas, both of which had served as lazar houses. Twice more, under Charles VIII and again in 1559, various buildings and outhouses at Saint-Germain-des-Prés previously used for lepers were converted for venereal diseases.[14] Soon the disease was so common that the construction of special buildings was being considered 'in certain spacious areas in towns and suburbs, segregated from passers-by'.[15] A new leprosy was born, which took the place of the former, but not without difficulty or conflicts. For lepers too have their fears.

Lepers were far from overjoyed at being forced to share their space with these newcomers to the world of horror: 'Est mirabilis contagiosa et nimis formidanda infirmitas, quam etiam detestantur leprosi et ea infectos secum habitare non permittant' ('This astonishing and contagious disease is much to be feared: even the lepers themselves reject it in horror, and refuse to permit those who have contracted the disease to keep their company').[16] But despite their longstanding right to stay in these segregated areas, there were too few of them to make their voices heard, and the venereal, more or less everywhere, had soon taken their place.

Yet in the classical age it was not venereal diseases that would take over the role that leprosy had played in medieval culture. Despite these initial measures of exclusion, venereal disease was soon classed as simply another disease once more, and despite the reservations of the population sufferers were soon being treated in hospitals. They were taken in at the Hôtel-Dieu in Paris,[17] and despite several attempts to expel them, they soon blended in with the other sick.[18] In Germany, special houses were built for them not to ensure their exclusion, but so that appropriate treatment could be given, and the Fuggers in Augsburg set up two such hospitals. The city of Nuremberg appointed a special physician who claimed to able to 'control the French malady'.[19] The major difference with leprosy was that venereal diseases became a medical affair very early on, to be dealt with exclusively by doctors. Treatments sprang up on all sides: the order of Saint-Côme followed the Arab example and used mercury,[20] whereas in the Hôtel-Dieu in Paris treatment relied mainly on theriac. Then came the great vogue for gaiac, more precious than American gold, if Ulrich von Hutten and Fracastor's Syphylidis are to be believed. Sweat cures were practised everywhere. In the course of the sixteenth century, venereal diseases took their place among other ills requiring medical treatment. The place of venereal diseases was fixed in a whole network of moral judgements, but that horizon brought only minor modifications to the essentially medical apprehension of the disease.[21]

Curiously, it was only under the influence of the world of confinement in the seventeenth century that venereal disease became detached to some extent from this medical context, and like madness entered a space of social and moral exclusion. It is not in venereal disease that the true heir of leprosy should be sought, but in a highly complex phenomenon that medicine would take far longer to appropriate.

That phenomenon is madness.[22] But only after a long latency period of almost two centuries did that new obsession take the place of the fear that leprosy had instilled in the masses, and elicit similar reactions of division, exclusion and purification, which are akin to madness itself. But before madness was brought under control towards the mid-seventeenth century, and before ancient rituals were resuscitated in its honour, it was linked obstinately to many of the major experiences of the Renaissance.

A brief overview of this presence and some of the essential figures is now in order.

*

The simplest of these figures is also the most symbolic.

A new object made its appearance in the imaginary landscape of the Renaissance, and it was not long before it occupied a privileged place there; this was the Ship of Fools, a strange drunken boat that wound its way down the wide, slow-moving rivers of the Rhineland and round the canals of Flanders.

This *Narrenschiff* was clearly a literary invention, and was probably borrowed from the ancient cycle of the Argonauts that had recently been given a new lease of life among mythological themes, and in the states of Burgundy at least now had an institutional function. Such ships were a literary commonplace, with a crew of imaginary heroes, moral models or carefully defined social types who set out on a great symbolic voyage that brought them, if not fortune, at the very least, the figure of their destiny or of their truth. Symphorien Champier for example composed successively a *Ship of Princes and Battles of the Nobility* in 1502 and a *Ship of Virtuous Ladies* the following year; there is also a *Ship of Health*, together with Jacop Van Oestvoren's *Blauwe Schute* of 1413, Brant's *Narrenschiff* of 1497 and Josse Bade's *Stultiferae naviculae scaphae fatuarum mulierum* of 1498. Naturally, Bosch's painting belongs to this same oneiric flotilla.

But among these satirical and novelistic ships, the *Narrenschiff* alone had a genuine existence, for they really did exist, these boats that drifted from one town to another with their senseless cargo. An itinerant existence was often the lot of the mad.[23] It was common practice for towns to banish them from inside the city walls, leaving them to run wild in the distant countryside or entrusting them to the care of travelling merchants or pilgrims. The custom was most common in Germany. In Nuremberg during the first half of the fifteenth century the presence of sixty-two madmen was recorded, and thirty-one were chased out of town. There were twenty-one more enforced departures over the fifty years that followed, and this was merely for madmen arrested by the municipal authorities.[24] They were often entrusted to the care of the river boatmen. In Frankfurt in 1399, boatmen were given the task of ridding the city of a madman who walked around naked, and in the earliest years of the following century a criminal madman was expelled in the same manner from Mainz. Sometimes the boatmen put these difficult passengers back ashore earlier than they had promised: one Frankfurt blacksmith returned twice from being expelled in such manner, before being definitively escorted to Kreuznach.[25] The arrival in the great cities of Europe of these ships of fools must have been quite a common sight.

It is hard to pin down the precise meaning of the practice. It is tempting to think of it as a general means of expulsion used by the municipalities to punish vagabondage among the mad, but that hypothesis doesn't quite fit the facts as this was a fate that only befell certain madmen, as some were treated in hospitals, even before the construction of special houses for the insane began. In the Hôtel-Dieu in Paris they had specifically allocated bunks in some dormitories reserved for them,[26] and in most of the great cities of Europe throughout the Middle Ages and the Renaissance there was always a special place reserved for the detention of the insane, like the Melun Châtelet[27] or the famous Tour aux Fous in Caen.[28] In Germany there were countless *Narrtürme*, like the gates of Lübeck or the Hamburg Jungpfer.[29] So the mad were not systematically run out of town. It could be argued that only foreign madmen were expelled, and that each town only took responsibility for its own citizens who had lost their wits, and indeed in the accounts of various medieval cities there are records of funds put aside for the mad, and donations made in favour of the insane.[30] But the problem is not so simple, for there were centres where the insane, more numerous than elsewhere, were certainly not indigenous. To the fore here were centres of pilgrimage like Saint-Mathurin de Larchant, Saint-Hildevert de Gournay, Besançon and Gheel; such trips were organised and even paid for by cities and hospitals.[31] And it may be that these ships of fools, which haunted the imagination of the Early Renaissance, were in fact ships of pilgrimage, highly symbolic ships filled with the senseless in search of their reason; some went down the rivers of the Rhineland towards Belgium and Gheel, while others went up the Rhine to Besançon and the Jura.

But there were other towns, like Nuremberg, which were certainly not places of pilgrimage, yet which contained a higher than average number of madmen, far more than the city itself could have furnished. These madmen were lodged and paid for out of the city coffers, but were not cared for: they were simply thrown into prison.[32] It may be the case that in some big cities – where there were markets and many people who came and went – the mad were brought in considerable numbers by merchants and river boatmen, and that there they were 'forgotten', thereby cleansing their home town of their presence. Perhaps these places of 'counter-pilgrimage' became confused with places where the insane really were taken as pilgrims. The concern with cure and exclusion fused within the sacred space of the miraculous. It is possible that the town of Gheel developed in this manner – a place of pilgrimage that became a place of confinement, a holy land where madness awaited its deliverance, but where it seems that man enacted the ancient ritual of division.

This constant circulation of the insane, the gesture of banishment and enforced embarkation, was not merely aimed at social utility, or the safety of citizens. Its meanings were closer to rituals, and their trace is still discernible. So it was for instance that the insane were barred entry to churches,[33] while ecclesiastical law allowed them to partake of the sacraments.[34] The church took no sanctions against priests who lost their reason, but in Nuremberg in 1421 a mad priest was expelled with particular solemnity, as though the impurity was multiplied by the sacred nature of the character, yet the town paid the money that was to serve for his viaticum.[35] On occasions, the insane were publicly whipped, and in a sort of simulated hunt were chased out of town while being beaten with sticks.[36] All of which indicates that the departure of the mad belonged with other rituals of exile.

So the ship of fools was heavily loaded with meaning, and clearly carried a great social force. On the one hand, it had incontestably practical functions, as entrusting a madman to the care of boatmen meant that he would no longer roam around the city walls, and ensured that he would travel far and be a prisoner of his own departure. But there was more: water brought its own dark symbolic charge, carrying away, but purifying too. Navigation brought man face to face with the uncertainty of destiny, where each is left to himself and every departure might always be the last. The madman on his crazy boat sets sail for the other world, and it is from the other world that he comes when he disembarks. This enforced navigation is both rigorous division and absolute Passage, serving to underline in real and imaginary terms the *liminal* situation of the mad in medieval society. It was a highly symbolic role, made clear by the mental geography involved, where the madman was *confined at the gates of the cities*. His exclusion was his confinement, and if he had no *prison* other than the *threshold* itself he was still detained at this place of passage. In a highly symbolic position he is placed on the inside of the outside, or vice versa. A posture that is still his today, if we admit that what was once the visible fortress of social order is now the castle of our own consciousness.

Water and navigation had that role to play. Locked in the ship from which he could not escape, the madman was handed over to the thousand-armed river, to the sea where all paths cross, and the great uncertainty that surrounds all things. A prisoner in the midst of the ultimate freedom, on the most open road of all, chained solidly to the infinite crossroads. He is the Passenger *par excellence*, the prisoner of the passage. It is not known where he will land, and when he lands, he knows not whence he came. His truth and his home are the barren wasteland between two lands that can never be his own.[37] Perhaps this ritual lies at the origin of the imaginary kinship common throughout the culture of the West. Or perhaps it was this kinship that called for and then fixed the ritual of embarkation whose origins are lost in the mists of civilisation. But one thing is certain: the link between water and madness is deeply rooted in the dream of the Western man.

In the medieval romance of *Tristan et Iseut*, Tristan is put ashore by the boatmen on the coast of Cornwall, disguised as a madman. On his arrival at the castle of King Mark, he is recognised by no one, and no one knows where he has come from. But his conversation is too strange, distant and familiar, and he is too aware of the well-kept secrets of this world not to have come from another very close by. He is not from dry land, with its solid cities, but from the unceasing restlessness of the sea, whose unknown paths reveal such strange truths, that fantastic plain, the flipside of the world. Iseut is the first to realise that this madman is a son of the sea, and that he's been put ashore by unrepentant sailors, making him a harbinger of bad luck: 'Damn the sailors who brought this madman, would that they had thrown him in the sea!'[38] she cries. The theme reappears many times throughout the ages. For the mystics of the fifteenth century, it was the idea of the soul as bark, tossed on the sea of infinite desires, surrounded by sterile attachments and ignorance on all sides, and distracted by the meretricious sparkles of knowledge, in the midst of the great unreason of the world – a boat at the mercy of the great madness of the sea, unless he drops anchor on the solid ground of faith, or spreads its spiritual sails so that so that the breath of God might bring it home to port.[39] In the late sixteenth century, De Lancre blamed the demoniacal calling of a whole people on the sea; the uncertain furrow of the wake, the exclusive trust placed in the stars, the secret knowledge that passed from mariner to mariner, the distance from women and the ceaselessly shifting plain of the surface of the sea made men lose faith in god, and cast off the shackles of their attachment to their homeland, thereby opening the door to the Devil and the ocean of his ruses.[40] The classical era was content to blame the English melancholy on the influence of a marine climate: the cold, wet, fickle weather and the fine droplets of water that entered the vessels and the fibres of the human body made a body lose its firmness, predisposing it to madness.[41] And finally, ignoring the huge literary tradition that stretches from Ophelia to the Lorelei, it is perhaps enough to quote the anthropo-cosmological analyses of Heinroth, where madness is the manifestation in man of an obscure, aquatic element, a dark, disordered, shifting chaos, the germ and death of all things as opposed to the luminous, adult stability of the mind.[42]

So the ship of fools resonates in the Western imagination with immemorial motifs. But why then, towards the fifteenth century, do we get this sudden formulation of the theme in literature and iconography? What made the silhouette of the ship of fools and its mad cargo loom so large against familiar landscapes? Why, from the old alliance of water and madness, was this ship born, and what made it appear at that very moment?

*

The ship is a symbol of a sudden unease that appears on the horizon of European culture towards the end of the Middle Ages. Madness and the figure of the madman take on a new importance for the ambiguousness of their role: they are both threat and derision, the vertiginous unreason of the world, and the shallow ridiculousness of men.

The first thing of interest is a literature of stories and morality tales. Its origins, no doubt, were far distant, but at the end of the Middle Ages it became a considerable mass: a long series of 'follies' which as in the past stigmatised vices or faults but blamed them not on pride, a lack of charity or the neglect of Christian virtues but on a great unreason which could be blamed on no one in particular but which dragged everyone along in its wake in a sort of tacit agreement.[43] The denouncing of madness became a general form of moral critique. In farces and *soties*, the character of the Fool, Idiot or Simpleton took on an ever-greater importance.[44] He was no longer familiar and ridiculous, but exterior to the action,[45] and took centre stage as the harbinger of truth, playing the complementary, inverse role of the figure of the fool in tales and satires. If madness drags everyone into a blindness where all bearings are lost, then the madman by contrast brings everyone back to their own truth: in comedy, where everyone deceives someone else and lies to themselves, he is a comedy of the second degree, a deception that is itself deceptive. Reasoning has no place in his sottish language, but his words bring a reason that comically undoes the comedy. To lovers he speaks of love,[46] he teaches the truth about life to the young,[47] and the sad reality of things to the proud, the insolent, and those who bear false witness.[48] Even the old feasts of fools, so popular in Flanders and northern Europe, became theatrical events, and were organised into social and moral criticism, whatever they may have contained of spontaneous religious parody.

In high culture too Folly was at work, at the heart of reason and truth. In Van Oestvoren's *Blauwe Schute* and Brant's *Narrenschiff* madness takes all mankind aboard the foolish ship and whisks it off on a communal odyssey. The evil reign of madness is railed against by Murner in *Narrenbeschwörung*, and madness joins forces with love in Corroz's satire *Contre Fol Amour*, and competes with love in a rhetorical joust to see who came first, and who makes the other possible and dictates his conduct at will, as in Louise Labé's *Débat de folie et d'amour*. Madness too made an appearance in the academic arena, becoming a self-reflexive object of discourse. Madness was denounced and defended, and proclaimed to be nearer to happiness and truth than reason itself. Wimpfeling wrote *Monopolium Philosophorum*,[49] and Judocus Gallus brought out *Monopolium et societas, vulgo des*

Lichtschiffs.[50] Against the backdrop of these serious games, two great humanist texts stand out: Flayder's *Moria Rediviva* of 1527, and Erasmus' *Praise of Folly* from 1509. Facing this sea of words, with their tireless dialectics and their endless variations and repetitions, stands a long dynasty of images, from Hieronymus Bosch's *The Cure of Madness* and *The Ship of Fools* to Brueghel's *Mad Meg.* Engravings and woodcuts show what literature and the theatre have already taken up: the interwoven themes of the Festival and the Dance of the Mad.[51] From the fifteenth century onwards, the face of madness never ceased to haunt the imagination of the West.

The succession of dates speaks for itself. The Dance of Death in the Innocents' cemetery in Paris probably dates from the early years of the fifteenth century, while the example in the Chaise-Dieu was probably made around 1460, and in 1485 Guyot Marchand published his *Danse macabre.*[52] There is no doubt that this sixty-year period was dominated by grinning death's head imagery. In 1492, Brant wrote the *Narrenschiff*, and five years later it was translated into Latin. At the very end of the century Bosch painted his *Ship of Fools. The Praise of Folly* is from 1509, and the order of succession is clear.

Until the second half of the fifteenth century, or perhaps slightly beyond it, the death theme reigns supreme. The end of mankind and the end of time are seen in war and the plagues. Hanging over human existence is an order and an end that no man can escape, a menacing presence from within the world itself. Suddenly, as the century drew to a close, that great uncertainty spun on its axis, and the derision of madness took over from the seriousness of death. From the knowledge of that fatal necessity that reduces man to dust we pass to a contemptuous contemplation of the nothingness that is life itself. The fear before the absolute limit of death becomes interiorised in a continual process of ironisation. Fear was disarmed in advance, made derisory by being tamed and rendered banal, and constantly paraded in the spectacle of life. Suddenly, it was there to be discerned in the mannerisms, failings and vices of normal people. Death as the destruction of all things no longer had meaning when life was revealed to be a fatuous sequence of empty words, the hollow jingle of a jester's cap and bells. The death's head showed itself to be a vessel already empty, for madness was the being-already-there of death.[53] Death's conquered presence, sketched out in these everyday signs, showed not only that its reign had already begun, but also that its prize was a meagre one. Death unmasked the mask of life, and nothing more: to show the skull beneath the skin it had no need to remove beauty or truth, but merely to remove the plaster or the tawdry clothes. The carnival mask and the cadaver share the same fixed smile. But the laugh of madness is an anticipation of the rictus grin of death, and the fool, that harbinger of the macabre, draws death's sting. In the High Renaissance, the cries of Mad Meg conquer the *Triumph of Death* that decorates the Late Medieval walls of the Camposanto in Pisa.

The substitution of the theme of madness for that of death is not the sign of a rupture, but rather of a new twist within the same preoccupation. It is still the nothingness of existence that is at stake, but this nothingness is no longer experienced as an end exterior to being, a threat and a conclusion: it is felt from within, as a continuous and unchanging form of life. Whereas previously the madness of men had been their incapacity to see that the end of life was always near, and it had therefore been necessary to call them back to the path of wisdom by means of the spectacle of death, now wisdom meant denouncing folly wherever it was to be found, and teaching men that they were already no more than the legions of the dead, and that if the end of life was approaching, it was merely a reminder that a universal madness would soon unite with death. This much was prophesied by poets like Eustache Deschamps:

> We are cowardly, ill-formed and weak
> Aged, envious and evil-spoken.
> I see only fools and sots
> Truly the end is nigh
> All goes ill.[54]

The terms of the argument were therefore now reversed. It was no longer the end of time and the end of the world that would demonstrate that it was madness not to have worried about such things. Rather, the rise of madness, its insidious, creeping presence showed that the final catastrophe was always near: the madness of men brought it nigh and made it a foregone conclusion.

The bond between madness and nothingness was tied so tight in the fifteenth century that it would last for a very long time indeed, so much so that it will still be found at the heart of the experience of madness in the classical age.[55]

*

In various guises, in literary forms and visual representations, this experience of the senseless seems extremely coherent. Text and painting constantly answer each other and swap roles, now as commentary, now as illustration. The *Narrentanz* or dance of fools is a theme found time and again in popular balls, theatrical performances and engravings, and the last part of the *Praise of Folly* is built on the model of a long dance where the professions and orders file past and form the eternal round of unreason. It is likely that in the Lisbon *Temptation*, many of the fantastical figures who cover the canvas are borrowed from traditional masques, and some of them may even be transposed from the *Malleus Maleficarum*.[56] Bosch's *Ship of Fools* is a direct transposition of Brant's *Narrenschiff*, whose title it bears, and it seems to illustrate in precise fashion the 27th canto, which stigmatises *potatores et edaces* – drunkards and gluttons. It has even been suggested that Bosch's painting was originally part of a whole series of pictures illustrating the principal cantos of Brant's poem.[57]

In fact we should not be taken in by this continuity in themes, nor should we suppose more than history allows.[58] It would no longer be possible to do an analysis of the subject along the lines of those done by Emile Mâle for previous ages, particularly where the theme of death is concerned. The beautiful unity between word and image, between that which was figured in language and said by plastic means, was beginning to disappear, and they no longer shared a single, unique signification that was immediately discernible. Although it was still the case that the vocation of the Image was essentially to *say*, and its role was to transmit something that was consubstantial with language, the time had nonetheless come when it no longer said exactly the same thing. By its own means painting was beginning the long process of experimentation that would take it ever further from language, regardless of the superficial identity of a theme. Language and figure still illustrate the same fable of madness in the moral world, but they are beginning to take different directions, indicating, through a crack that was still barely perceptible, the great divide that was yet to come in the Western experience of madness.

The rise of madness on the Renaissance horizon is first noticeable in this decay of Gothic symbolism, as though a network of tightly ordered spiritual significations was beginning to become undone, revealing figures with meanings only perceptible as insane. Gothic forms lived on, but little by little they fell silent, ceasing to speak, to recall or instruct. The forms remained familiar, but all understanding was lost, leaving nothing but a fantastical presence; and freed from the wisdom and morality it was intended to transmit, the image began to gravitate around its own madness.

Paradoxically, this liberation was the fruit of a luxuriant growth in meanings, a multiplication of signification, as the web of connections between objects became ever more complex. Meaning created links so numerous, so rich and involved that only esoteric knowledge could possibly have the necessary key. Objects became so weighed down with attributes, connections and associations that they lost their own original face. Meaning was no longer read in an immediate perception, and accordingly objects ceased to speak directly: between the knowledge that animated the figures of objects and the forms they were transformed into, a divide began to appear, opening the way for a symbolism more often associated with the world of dreams. One book demonstrates well this mad proliferation of meanings at the end of the Gothic age: the *Speculum humanae salvationis* or *Mirror of Human Salvation*, which together with the traditional symbolism of the Church Fathers draws up a whole network of connections between the Old and New Testaments, not so much of the order of prophecy as of a world of imaginary equivalence.[59] The Passion of Christ is no longer simply prefigured by the sacrifice of Abraham, but calls up all the prestige of torture and innumerable dreams associated therewith, so that Tubal, the blacksmith, and Isaiah's wheel take their place around the cross, going beyond all the lessons about sacrifice to form a fantastical tableau of pain and relentlessly tortured bodies. The image becomes overburdened with supplementary meanings, and constrained to deliver them up. But dreams, senselessness and unreason could slip all too easily into this excess of meaning. Symbolic figures easily became nightmarish silhouettes. A case in point was the traditional German image of wisdom as long-necked bird that circulated widely in engravings. The bird's thoughts, which start in its heart and finish in its head, travel slowly up the neck and thus have all the time necessary to be carefully considered and judged.[60] But the symbol became too heavily charged with meaning as its values were emphasized. The long path of reflection became a still where arcane thoughts were concentrated into a quintessence of knowledge. The neck, which in early versions simply belonged to a *Gutemensch*, became infinitely lengthened to symbolize not only wisdom but the real mediations of learning, and the symbolic man became a fantastical bird whose long neck folds round on itself repeatedly – a senseless being halfway between animal and object, glorying more in imaginative possibilities than in any rigorous meaning. Symbolic wisdom wound up a prisoner of the madness of dreams.

The world of images therefore underwent a fundamental change. The obligation for multiple meanings freed it from rigorous order. The profusion of diverse meanings lurking beneath the surface of the image meant that its visible face became ever more enigmatic. Its power was no longer that of instruction but more of fascination. This is well demonstrated by the changes undergone in the representation of the gryllos, a familiar figure in the Middle Ages in English psalters and in Chartres and Bourges. It originally taught how in men ruled by their desires the soul became a prisoner of the beast. These grotesque faces found on the bellies of monsters belonged to the world of the grand platonic metaphor, denouncing the abasement of the spirit in the madness of sin. But in the fifteenth century, the gryllos, a symbol of human madness, became a preponderant figure in the innumerable *Temptations*. The hermit's tranquillity is assailed not by objects of desire but by demented forms locked into their own secrets, who have risen up from dream and sit on the surface of a world, silent and furtive. In the Lisbon *Temptation* facing Saint Anthony sits one such figure born of madness, its solitude, its penitence, and its deprivation: a thin smile spreads across its disembodied face, the pure presence of worry in the guise of an agile grimace. This nightmarish silhouette is both the subject and the object of the temptation, captivating the hermit's glance: both of them are prisoners of a mirroring interrogative process, where response is indefinitely suspended, in a silence broken only by the restive growl of the monsters that surround them.[61] The gryllos no longer recalls, even in a satirical mode, the spiritual vocation of man forgotten in the madness of desire. The gryllos is madness made Temptation: all that there is in him of the impossible, fantastical and inhuman, all that indicates that which goes against nature or the seething mass of a senseless presence immanent in the earth is the source of his strange power. For men of the fifteenth century, the fearsome freedom of dreams and the fantasies born of madness held a power of attraction stronger than the pull of the desires of mortal flesh.

The strange fascination that lurks in these images of madness can be explained in a number of ways.

First of all, men seemed to discover in these fantastical figures one of the secret vocations of their nature. In the thought of the Middle Ages, the legions of the animals that Adam had named once and for all had symbolic human values.[62] But in the early Renaissance, that process of signification underwent a reversal. The beasts were let loose, and they made their escape from the world of legend or moral instruction and took on a fantastical life of their own. In an astonishing reversal, it was mankind that began to feel itself the object of the animals' gaze, as they took control and showed him his own truth. Impossible animals, the fruit of mad imaginings, became the secret nature of man, and in images of the Last Judgement, when man appears in the hideous nudity of his fallen state, he has taken on the monstrous face of a delirious animal. Screech owls with toad-like bodies mingle with the naked bodies of the damned in Thierry Bouts' Hell, the work of Stefan Lochner pullulates with winged insects, cat-headed butterflies and sphinxes with mayfly wingcases, and birds with handed wings that instil panic, while in Grünewald's *Temptation* there prowls a beast of prey with gnarled, knotty claws. The animal realm has moved out of range of all domesticating human symbolism, and while it fascinates mankind with its disorder, its fury and its plethora of monstrous impossibilities, it also serves to reveal the dark rage and sterile folly that lurks in the heart of mankind.

At the opposite pole to this nature of darkness, madness also exerts a fascination because it is knowledge. And that is because these absurd figures are in reality the elements that make up a difficult, hermetic, esoteric knowledge. These strange forms belong from the outset to the great secret, and Saint Anthony is tempted by them because he has fallen prey not to the violence of desire but rather to the far more insidious vice of curiosity, tempted by the lure of this knowledge which is just beyond his reach, offered and withdrawn at the same instant by the smile on the face of the gryllos. His instinctive pulling backward is the movement that prevents him from stepping over the line into the territory of forbidden knowledge, for he already knows, as Jérôme Cardan was later to say, that 'wisdom, like all precious materials, must be ripped from the entrails of the earth' – and that desire is what his Temptation is.[63] This is the inaccessible, fearsome knowledge that the madman, in his innocent foolishness, already possesses. While men of reason and wisdom see only fragmentary figures that are all the more frightening for their incompleteness, the madman sees a whole, unbroken sphere. For him, the crystal ball empty for others is filled with invisible knowledge. In Brueghel's *Flemish Proverbs*, the sick man who attempts to enter the crystal ball is an object of ridicule, but it is the same iridescent bubble of infinite knowledge that swings around on that derisory but infinitely precious lantern slung over the shoulder of Mad Meg. And the same ball figures on the reverse of the *Garden of Earthly Delights*. The tree, another symbol of knowledge (like the forbidden fruit tree, the tree of promised immortality or the tree of sin) once planted in the middle of the earthly paradise, is uprooted and forms the mast of the ship of fools, as can be seen in the engraving that illustrates Josse Bade's *Stultiferae Naviculae*, and doubtless it is the same tree that sways around above Bosch's *Ship of Fools*.

So what, precisely, is the knowledge that madness brings? Most probably, as it is forbidden knowledge, it predicts both the reign of Satan and the end of the world, ultimate happiness and supreme punishment, omnipotence on earth and the descent into hell. The *Ship of Fools* passes through a landscape of delights where all is offered to desire, a paradise regained of sorts, as men once more become strangers to necessity and want, yet without a return to a state of innocence. This false happiness is the diabolical triumph of the Antichrist, the End that is ever nigh. True, there was little new in the apocalyptic dreams of the fifteenth century, and yet these images are of a different nature from all that went before. In the vaguely fantastical iconography of the fourteenth century, where castles could be knocked down like houses of cards, and the beast was always the traditional dragon that the Virgin could keep at a safe distance, the coming of the kingdom of God was always visible. But the following century brought a vision of the world where knowledge and wisdom were destroyed. This was the great Sabbath of nature, where the mountains were washed away, bones poked up from graves and the earth vomited up its dead; the stars fell from the sky, the earth caught fire and all life died away as the reign of death began.[64] This end was neither a passing moment nor a promise, but the coming of a night in which the ancient season of the world finally passed away. The four horsemen of the apocalypse in the Dürer engraving have indeed been sent by God, but they are no angels of Triumph or reconciliation, nor heralds of serene justice; they are bloodthirsty warriors out for mad vengeance. The world is sliding into universal Fury, and the victor will be neither God nor the Devil, but Madness itself.

The fantastic images that madness inspired were no fugitive appearance that quickly vanished from the surface of things: man was fascinated by madness on all sides. By a strange paradox, that which was born of the most singular delirium was already hidden, like a secret inaccessible truth, buried in the bowels of the earth. When the arbitrary nature of madness was exhibited, man encountered the sombre necessity of the world: the animal that haunted nightmares and visions born of ascetic deprivation was man's own nature, revealed in the unpitying truth of hell. The vain images of blind foolishness turned out to be the truth of the world, and in this grand disorder, this mad universe, the cruelty that lay in the day of judgement began to appear. These mad images are an expression of hidden Renaissance worries about the menacing secrets of the world, and it was those fears that gave the fantastic images such coherence and lent them such power.

*

During this same period, literary, philosophical and moral aspects of madness were in an altogether different vein.

The Middle Ages had placed madness or folly in its hierarchy of vices. From the thirteenth century onwards it was common to see Folly enlisted in the wicked soldiery of the Psychomachia.[65] In Paris and Amiens, madness is there among the twelve evil soldiers who fight against their antithesis for dominion over the human soul: Faith and Idolatry, Hope and Despair, Charity and Avarice, Chastity and Lust, Prudence and Folly, Patience and Anger, Sweetness and Harshness, Concord and Discord, Obedience and Rebelliousness, Perseverance and Inconstancy. During the Renaissance, Folly left that modest place and took centre stage.[66] In the work of Hugues de Saint-Victor, the old Adam genealogical tree of vices had pride as its root,[67] but now it was Madness that led the joyful choir of human weaknesses. The uncontested leader, Madness, leads the troupe, naming her partners and ordering the dance:

> This one – you see how she raises her eyebrows – is obviously Philautia (Self-love). The one you see here, with smiling eyes and clapping hands, is Kolakia (Flattery). This one, dosing and half asleep, is Lethe (Forget-fulness). This one, leaning on her elbows with her hands clasped, is Misoponia (Laziness). This one, wreathed with roses and drenched with sweet-smelling lotions, is Hedone (Pleasure). This one, with the restless glance and the rolling eyes, is Anoia (Madness). This one, with the smooth complexion and the plump, well-rounded figure, is Tryphe (Luxury). You also see two Gods among the girls: one is called Comos (Rowdiness), the other Negreton Hypnon (Sweet sleep).[68]

Madness now has an absolute privilege, and reigns over all the negative aspects of the human character. It also controls indirectly all the possible aspirations to good, the ambition that creates wise politicians, the greed that causes wealth to grow, and the indiscreet curiosity that fires the research of philosophers and men of science. Louise Labé repeats it after Erasmus, and Mercury implores the Gods on her behalf: 'Don't let this beautiful Lady who has given you such pleasure slip away.'[69]

But this new dominion has little in common with the dark kingdom mentioned above, which linked madness to the powerful tragic forces that controlled the world.

This literary Folly is an attraction, but hardly a fascination. It governs all that is facile, joyous or light-hearted in the world. It is a madness that causes men to make merry and rejoice, just as it gave the classical gods 'Spirit and Youthfulness, Bacchus, Silenus and that quiet guardian of gardens'.[70] Madness was a shiny, reflective surface, with no dark secrets lurking below.

Undoubtedly, it did have links with some of the darker byways of knowledge. The first canto of Brant's *Narrenschiff* tells of books and bookmen, and in the engraving that illustrates the passage in the Latin edition of 1497, perched on his throne and surrounded by books, a Master with his doctoral bonnet can be seen, and behind his hat is a fool's cap sown with bells. In his great dance of the mad, Erasmus reserved pride of place for the learned. After the grammarians come the poets, the rhetoricians and the writers; then the lawyers and the philosophers 'venerable with their beards and robes', followed at last by a hurried multitude of theologians.[71] But if knowledge is important for madness, it is not because madness might hold some vital secrets: on the contrary, it is the punishment for useless, unregulated knowledge. If it is the truth about knowledge, then all it reveals is that knowledge is derisory, and that rather than addressing the great book of experience, learning has become lost in the dust of books and in sterile discussions, knowledge made mad by an excess of false science.

> O vos doctores, qui grandia nomina fertis,
> Respicite antiquos patris, jurisque peritos.
> Non in candidulis pensebant dogmata libris,
> Arte sed ingenua sitibundum pectus alebant.[72]
>
> (Oh ye men of science, who bear great names,
> Look back at the ancient fathers, learned in law.

They did not weigh dogmas in shining white books,
But fed their thirsty hearts with natural skill.)

As in the theme so long familiar in popular satire, madness appears here as the comic punishment of knowledge and its ignorant presumption.

For in a general manner madness here is not linked to the world and its subterranean forms, but rather to man and his frailties, his dreams and illusions. The dark cosmic forces at work in madness that are so apparent in the work of Bosch are absent in Erasmus. Madness no longer lies in wait for man at every crossroads; rather, it slips into him, or is in fact a subtle relationship that man has with himself. In Erasmus, the mythological personification of Madness is no more than literary artifice. Here, rather than madness, there are only follies, human forms of madness: 'I considered that as many statues have been set up for me as there are men who display, sometimes unwillingly, a living image of me.'[73] When he turns his attention to even the wisest and best-governed cities, 'wherever you look they abound in so many forms of folly, and they think up so many new ones from day to day, a thousand Democritus's would not be enough to laugh at them.'[74] Madness is only in each man, as it lies in the attachments that men have to themselves, and the illusions that they entertain about themselves. Philautia or self-love is the first among the figures that Folly leads on its dance, but that is because these two forms are linked to each other above all others; an attachment to oneself is the first sign of madness, and it is through that attachment to oneself that man takes error for truth, lies for reality, violence and ugliness for beauty and justice:

> One man who is uglier than any monkey is quite confident that he is as handsome as Nereus. Another, as soon as he can draw three lines with a compass, immediately thinks he is another Euclid. Another, who sounds like an ass playing a harp, and who sings no better than the bird that gives the hen uxorious nips, still thinks he is another Hermogenes.[75]

In this imaginary adhesion to the self, madness is born like a mirage. From now on, the symbol of madness was to be a mirror, which reflected nothing real, but secretly showed the presumptuous dreams of all who gazed into it to contemplate themselves. Madness here was not about truth or the world, but rather about man and the truth about himself that he can perceive.

In that respect, madness now opens out onto an entirely moral universe.

Evil was no longer a punishment or the end of time, but merely a fault or flaw. In Brant's poem, 116 cantos are devoted to drawing a portrait of the insane cargo aboard the boat. There are misers, liars, drunkards, those given to debauchery or disorder, adulterers, and those who read scripture awry. In his Latin preface, Brant's translator Locher outlined the project that lay behind the work, and the desire to show 'quae mala, quae bona sint; quid vitia, quo virtus, quo ferat error' (what evil there may be, what good; what vices; whither virtue, whither vices might lead), and this by berating, in the measure appropriate to the evil in each case, 'impios, superbos, avaros, luxuriosos, lascivos, delicates, iracundos, gulosos, edaces, invidos, veneficos, fidefrasos' (the unholy, the proud, the greedy, the extravagant, the debauched, the voluptuous, the quick-tempered, the gluttonous, the voracious, the envious, the poisoners, the faith-breakers)[76] – in short, every possible irregularity invented by man himself.

In the domain of literature and philosophy, the experience of madness in the fifteenth century takes on above all the appearance of a moral satire. There is little there to recall the overwhelming threat of invasion that haunted the imagination of the painters. On the contrary, care was taken to neutralise that threat: literature and philosophy are quite simply talking of a different experience. Erasmus turns attention away from that madness 'sent up from the underworld by the avenging Furies whenever they dart forth their serpents', for the Folly that he set out to praise was of a different order. His concern is with the 'most desirable' form that 'occurs whenever a certain pleasant mental distraction relieves the heart from its anxieties and cares and at the same time soothes with the balm of manifold pleasures'.[77] A world of calm, without secret, that is easily mastered and fully displays its naïve reductions to the eyes of the wise, who keep their distance easily through laughter. Whereas Bosch, Brueghel and Dürer were earthly spectators pulled into the madness that they saw seething around them, Erasmus observes it from a distance that ensures that he is never drawn in. Like an Olympian God he observes it from on high, and if he sings its praises, it is because his laughter is the inexhaustible good humour of the gods themselves. For the madness of man is a sight for divine eyes:

> In brief, if you could look down from the moon, as Menippus once did, and see the innumerable broils of mortals, you would think you were looking at a great cloud of flies or gnats quarrelling among themselves,

warring, plotting, plundering, playing, frisking, being born, declining, dying. It is downright incredible what tumults, what tragedies can be stirred up by such a tiny creature, so frail and short-lived.[78]

Madness is no longer the familiar strangeness of the world, but a spectacle well known to the observer from outside; not a figure of the *cosmos*, but merely of the order of the *aevum*.

*

That then, somewhat hastily reconstructed, is the schema of the opposition between the cosmic experience of madness in the proximity of fascinating forms, and a critical experience of the same madness, as seen from across the unbridgeable gap of irony. Doubtless, in reality, the opposition was neither as clear-cut nor as immediately discernible. For a long time the two threads were intertwined, and there were constant exchanges between them.

The theme of the end of the world, and of the great final violence, was also a part of the critical experience of madness such as it was formulated in literature. Ronsard speaks of the struggles of these last days, in the void left by the departure of Reason:

> Justice and Reason have flown back up to Heaven
> And in their place, alas, reign brigandage
> Hatred, rancour, blood and carnage.[79]

Towards the end of Brant's poem, an entire chapter is taken over with the apocalyptic theme of the Antichrist; a terrible storm carries away the ship of fools on a senseless course that is identical to the End of the World.[80] Conversely, many figures of moral rhetoric are illustrated in a direct manner in the cosmic images of madness: Bosch's famous doctor is far more insane than the patient he is attempting to cure, and his false knowledge does nothing more than reveal the worst excesses of a madness immediately apparent to all but himself. For his contemporaries and for the generations that followed, Bosch was above all a moralist, and his work was a series of moral lessons. His figures were born of this world, but they demonstrated the monstrous contents of the human heart. 'The difference between the paintings of this man and those of others is that others usually portray man as he appears from the outside: Bosch alone dares paint them as they are within,' said Joseph de Siguença.[81] And it was that unsettling irony, that desire of wisdom to denounce all folly, that the same early seventeenth-century commentator saw in almost all of Bosch's paintings, in the clear symbolism of the burning torch (the never-sleeping vigil of contemplative thought) and the owl, whose strange, fixed stare 'keeps watch in the calm and the silence of the night, consuming oil, not wine'.[82]

Despite these crossovers, the division is nonetheless made, and from now on the gap between these two radically different visions of madness will not cease to widen. The paths taken by the figure of the cosmic vision and the incisive movement that is moral reflection, between the *tragic* and the *critical* elements, now constantly diverge, creating a gap in the fabric of the experience of madness that will never be repaired. On the one side is the ship of fools, where mad faces slowly slip away into the night of the world, in landscapes that speak of strange alchemies of knowledge, of the dark menace of bestiality, and the end of time. On the other is the ship of fools that is merely there for the instruction of the wise, an exemplary, didactic odyssey whose purpose is to highlight faults in the human character.

On the one side, Bosch, Brueghel, Thierry Bouts and Dürer line up beside their silent images. For madness unleashes its fury in the space of pure vision. Fantasies and threats, the fleeting fragments of dreams and the secret destiny of the world, where madness has a primitive, prophetic force, revealing that the dream-like is real and that a thin surface of illusion opens onto bottomless depths, and that the glittering surface of images opens the way to worrying figures that shine forever in the darkness. The inverse revelation, no less painful, is that the reality of the world will one day be absorbed into the fantastic Image, at that delirious moment between being and nothingness which is pure destruction. When at last the world will be no more, but night and silence have not yet closed over, and all will flame up in a blinding flash, in the extremity of disorder that will precede the ordered monotony of the end of all things. The truth of the world resides in that last fleeting image. This weave of experience and secrecy, of immediate images and hidden enigmas, is unfurled in fifteenth-century painting as *the tragic madness of the world*.

By contrast, in Brant, Erasmus and the whole humanist tradition, madness is confined to the universe of discourse. There it becomes ever more refined, more subtle, and is slowly disarmed. It changes scale: born in the hearts of men, it rules and disrupts their conduct; when it rules cities, the calm truth of things and nature herself are unaware of its existence. It disappears fast when essential issues like life and death or justice and truth appear. It may hold every man in its control, but its reign is narrow and relative as its mediocre truth is constantly unmasked by the penetrating gaze of the savant. For such men of science, it becomes a mere object, and in the worst possible manner, as it often winds up an object of ridicule: they tamed it by the act of praising it. Even if madness was wiser than science, it would still find itself obliged to bow down before wisdom itself, the condition of its being. Now and then it might *have* the last word, but it never *was* the last word about the truth of the world, for its self-justificatory discourse is bound up with *a critical consciousness of man.*

This conflict between critical consciousness and tragic experience underlies all that was felt and formulated on the theme of madness at the beginning of the Renaissance.[83] But it was short-lived, and a century later, this grandiose structure, which at the beginning of the sixteenth century was so evident and clear-cut, had almost entirely disappeared. Disappearance is perhaps not the best term to describe exactly what happened. Rather, it is a question of the ever-increasing importance that the Renaissance accorded to one of the elements in the system – the vision of madness as an experience within the domain of language, where man was confronted with his moral truth, the laws of human nature and human truth. In short, the critical consciousness of madness was increasingly brought out into the light, while its more tragic components retreated ever further into the shadows, soon to almost vanish entirely. Only much later can a trace of the tragic element be again discerned, and a few pages in Sade and the work of Goya bear witness to the fact that this disappearance was merely an eclipse; the dark, tragic experience lived on in dreams and in the dark night of thoughts, and what happened in the sixteenth century was not a radical destruction but a mere occultation. The cosmic, tragic experience of madness was hidden by the exclusive privileges of a critical consciousness. For that reason the experience of the classical age, and by extension the modern experience of madness, cannot be considered as a total figure, which would thus finally reach its positive truth.[84] It is rather a fragmentary figure that is erroneously taken as complete, an ensemble unbalanced by all that it lacks, or rather all that obscures it. Behind the critical consciousness of madness in all its philosophical, scientific, moral and medicinal guises lurks a second, tragic consciousness of madness, which has never really gone away.

It is that tragic consciousness that is visible in the last words of Nietzsche and the last visions of Van Gogh. It is that same element that Freud began to perceive at the furthest point of his journey, the great wound that he tried to symbolise in the mythological struggle between the libido and the death instinct. And it is that same consciousness that finds expression in the work of Antonin Artaud. If the thinkers of the twentieth century paid more attention, they would find in Artaud's work one of the most pertinent questions of the age, and whose clutches are the most difficult to escape. Artaud never ceased to claim that Western culture lost its tragic focus the moment it finally forgot what he termed the great solar madness of the world, the violent ceremonies which enacted the life and death of 'the great Fire Satan'.

It is only by examining such extreme discoveries that we can finally come to understand that the experience of madness common since the sixteenth century owes its particular face, and the origin of its meaning, to that absence, to that dark night and all that fills it. The linearity that led rationalist thought to consider madness as a form of mental illness must be reinterpreted in a vertical dimension. Only then does it become apparent that each of its incarnations is a more complete, but more perilous masking of tragic experience – an experience that it nonetheless failed to obliterate. When constraints were at their most oppressive, an explosion was necessary, and that is what we have seen since Nietzsche.

*

But how did this pride of place awarded to critical reflection come into being in the sixteenth century? How did it end up being the case that madness was appropriated by reason, so much so that at the dawn of the classical age all the tragic images previously associated with madness suddenly passed into shadow? How ended the movement that caused Artaud to write: 'the Renaissance of the sixteenth century made a clean break with a reality that had laws both natural and superhuman, and the Renaissance humanism that resulted was not an expansion but a restriction for mankind'?[85]

A brief résumé of this evolution is perhaps in order, for a clear understanding of what the classical age did to madness.

1   Madness becomes a form related to reason, or more precisely madness and reason enter into a perpetually reversible relationship which

implies that all madness has its own reason by which it is judged and mastered, and all reason has its madness in which it finds its own derisory truth. Each is a measure of the other, and in this movement of reciprocal reference, each rejects the other but is logically dependent upon it.

In the sixteenth century, this tight-knit dialectic gave a new lease of life to the old Christian theme of the world being madness in the eyes of God. Man believes that he sees clearly, and that he is the measure of all things, while the knowledge that he thinks he has of the world locks him into his complacency: 'If, at midday, we either look down to the ground, or on the surrounding objects which lie open to our view, we think ourselves endowed with a very strong and piercing eyesight', but then if we turn our eyes towards the sun, we are obliged to confess that 'our acuteness in discerning terrestrial objects is mere dimness when applied to the sun'. Yet this almost Platonic conversion towards the sun of being does not reveal truth and the foundation of appearances: it merely lays bare the abyss of our own unreason:

> But should we once begin to raise our thoughts to God … what strangely imposed upon us under the name of wisdom will disgust by its extreme folly; and what presented the appearance of virtuous energy will be condemned as the most miserable impotence.[86]

Rising up in spirit towards God and sounding the bottomless depths into which we find ourselves plunged are one and the same, and in Calvin's experience madness is the measure of man when he is compared to the boundless reason of God.

In its finitude, man's spirit is less a shaft of the great light than a fragment of shadow. The partial and transitory truth of appearances is not available to his limited intelligence; his madness discovers but the reverse of things, their dark side, the immediate contradiction of their truth. In his journey to God, man must do more than surpass himself – he must rip himself away from his essential weakness, and in one bound cross from the things of this world to their divine essence, for whatever transpires of truth in appearances is not its reflection but a cruel contradiction: 'Everything has two faces,' says Sébastien Franck,

> for God is resolved to oppose himself to this world, leaving appearances here and keeping the truth and essence of things to himself. For that

> reason things are the opposite of the way they appear in this world: an
> open Silenus.[87]

The abyss of folly into which men are plunged is such that the appearance of truth that men find there is in fact its complete opposite. But there was more: the contradiction between truth and appearances was present in appearance itself, for if appearance was coherent with itself, at least it would be an allusion to the truth, or some form of hollow echo. So it was rather within things themselves that this reversal was to be found, a reversal that henceforth was to be without a clear direction or pre-established end. The movement was not to be from an appearance towards truth, but towards another one, which negates it, and then towards all that denied or contested that negation, so that the process could never come to an end. Before that great moment of conversion that Calvin and Franck expect, Erasmus finds himself trapped by the myriad tiny conversions that appearances provide him with on their own level. Silenus opened up is not a symbol of the truth that God has removed, but much more and much less – a symbol, on an earthly level, of things themselves, an indication of the contradictions that deprive us, perhaps for all eternity, of the simple path towards truth. All human affairs, he says,

> like the Sileni of Alcibiades, have two aspects quite different from each
> other. Hence, what appears 'at first blush' (as they say) to be death will,
> if you examine it more closely, turn out to be life; conversely, life will turn
> out to be death, beauty will become ugliness; riches will turn to poverty;
> notoriety will become fame, learning will be ignorance . . . in brief, you
> will find everything reversed if you open the Silenus.[88]

All is plunged into immediate contradiction, and man is urged to embrace only his own madness: when measured against the truth of essences and God, human order is nothing but madness.[89]

And in this human order, the movement through which man tries to break free of his earthly bonds becomes just another form of madness. In the sixteenth century, more so than at any other moment, Paul's second epistle to the Corinthians shone with incomparable prestige: 'I speak as a fool.'[90] The renunciation of the world becomes an act of folly, like the total abandonment of the self to the obscure will of God, a mad quest that seemingly has no end, as the mystics had long acknowledged. Tauler wrote of this path, where the madness of the world is renounced for darker and more desolate follies: 'The small vessel drifts off, and as man finds himself in a state of desolation, anguished sentiments, temptations, images and misery in all forms rise up within him.'[91] Nicholas of Cusa describes a similar experience: 'When man abandons the realm of the senses, his soul falls prey to a kind of dementia.' Marching towards God, man is more open than ever to madness, and that haven of truth towards which grace will give him the final push, what else could it be for him than an abyss of unreason? The wisdom of God, when man is blinded by it, is not a reason that has long been concealed by a veil, but depth without measure. There the secret is still fully secret and contradiction contradicts itself, for at the heart of its all surpassing comprehension is this wisdom that seems vertiginous folly: 'Lord, thy counsels are as a great deep.'[92] What Erasmus glimpsed from afar when he dryly noted that God had hidden salvation even from the eyes of the wise and saved the world through folly,[93] Nicholas of Cusa had explored all along, losing the weak reason of man, which is but folly, in the abysmal madness of the wisdom of God:

> It is unutterable in any language, unintelligible to every intellect, and immeasurable by every measure. It cannot be limited by any limit, nor bounded by any boundary. No proportion is proportionate to it. No comparison can be compared to it, nor can it be conformed to any confirmation. It cannot be formed by any formation, and it cannot be moved by any motion . . . because it cannot be expressed in any speech, no limit to such modes of expression can be grasped. This is because that Wisdom by which, in which and from which all things exist is unthinkable in any thought.[94]

So closed a great circle. Compared to Wisdom, the reason of man is nothing but folly: compared to the shallow wisdom of men, the Reason of God is caught up in the essential movement of Madness. On the great scale of things, all things are Madness; on the small scale, the Whole itself is madness. Which means that if madness can only exist in reference to some form of reason, the whole truth of reason is to allow a form of unreason to appear and to oppose it, only to disappear in turn in a madness that engulfs all. In one sense, madness is nothing at all, the madness of men, a nothingness faced with the supreme form of reason that alone delineates being; and the abyss of fundamental madness, nothing, as it is such only for the fragile reason of men. But reason is nothing, as the reason in whose name the folly of human reason is denounced, when it is finally glimpsed, reveals itself to be nothing other than a vertiginous chasm where reason itself must remain silent.

And so, under the powerful influence of Christian thought, the great peril faced by the fifteenth century was kept at bay. Madness was no longer a dark power that threatened to undo the world, revealing fantastical seductions, and no longer showed, in the twilight of Time, the violence of bestiality, or the great struggle between Knowledge and Interdiction. It is caught up instead in the indefinite cycle that attaches it to reason; they deny and affirm each other. Madness is robbed of its absolute existence in the night of the world, and now only exists in relation to reason, and this mutual process of redemption is the undoing of both.

2   Madness then becomes a form of reason. It becomes integral to it, forming either part of its secret strength, one of the moments of its manifestation, or a paradoxical form where reason becomes conscious of itself. In either case madness only has meaning or value in relation to the field of reason.

> The natural, original distemper of Man is presumption. Man is the most blighted and frail of all creatures and, moreover, the most given to pride. This creature knows and sees that he is lodged down here, among the mire and shit of the world, bound and nailed to the deadest, most stagnant part of the universe, in the lowest storey of the building, the farthest from the vault of heaven; his characteristics place him in the third and lowest category of animate creatures, yet, in thought, he sets himself above the circle of the Moon, bringing the very heavens under his feet. The vanity of this same thought makes him equal himself to God.[95]

Such is the worst madness of man: the inability to recognise the misery of his confinement, the weakness that prevents him from ascending to the true and the good, and not knowing which part of madness is his own. His turning his back on unreason is a sure sign of his condition, in that it prevents him from ever using his reason in a reasonable manner. For if reason does exist, it lies precisely in the acceptance of the unbroken circle joining wisdom and folly, in the clear consciousness of their reciprocity and the impossibility of dividing them. True reason is not free of the contamination of madness, but on the contrary, it borrows some of the trails first carved out by madness.

> Be present, then, you daughters of Jove, for a bit, while I show that no one can reach the heights of wisdom, and the very 'inner sanctum', as they themselves say, 'of happiness', except with the guidance of Folly.[96]

But such a path, even when it fails to reach any final wisdom, and when the promised citadel reveals itself to be nothing more than a mirage or a new incarnation of folly, remains the path to wisdom when those who follow it are well aware that it leads to madness. The vain spectacle, the frivolous sounds and the maelstrom of noise and colour that make up the world is only ever the world of madness, and that must be accepted. This artificiality of the world must be welcomed, in the knowledge that that shallowness belongs not only to the spectacle but to the spectator as well, and that to appreciate it what is required is not the serious ear reserved for the truth, but that more light-hearted form of attention more usually reserved for a fairground spectacle or a circus act, blending irony, complicity, a readiness to learn and the secret knowledge that does not allow itself to be taken in:

> give me your attention – not the kind you give to godly preachers, but rather the kind you give to pitchmen, low comedians and jokesters – in short lend me your ears, just as my protégé Midas did long ago to Pan.[97]

Here, in the midst of that colourful, noisy immediacy, in that easy acceptance which is also an imperceptible refusal, the essence of wisdom is to be found more surely than in any lengthy search for the hidden truth. Subtly, through the welcome it reserves for it, wisdom invests madness, besieges it, becomes conscious of it and is able to situate it.

Where else could it be found, other than within reason itself, as one of its forms, and perhaps even one of its resources? For there is no doubt that between certain forms of madness and certain forms of reason, the resemblances are manifold. And worrying: how can a distinction be made between a wise act carried out by a madman, and a senseless act of folly carried out by a man usually in full possession of his wits? 'Wisdom and folly are surprisingly close. It's but a half turn from the one to the other.

That much can be discerned from the actions of men who have lost their wits.'[98] Such a resemblance, despite the fact that it sows confusion among reasonable men, serves reason itself. And by dragging into its movement the great violence that madness brings, reason can attain the greatest heights. Visiting Tasso in his delirium, Montaigne felt disappointment more than pity, but the most powerful emotion he experienced was admiration. 'Is there anyone who does not know how imperceptible are the divisions separating madness from the spiritual alacrity of a soul set free, or from actions arising from supreme and extraordinary virtue?' Montaigne experiences a paradoxical admiration, for in the depths of that madness, reason finds the strangest resources. For if Tasso, 'fashioned in the pure poetry of the atmosphere of antiquity, who showed more judgment and genius than any other Italian for many a long year', now found himself 'in so wretched a state, surviving himself', it was also because

> his agile and lively mind has overthrown him; the light has made him blind; his reason's grasp was so precise and so intense that it has left him quite irrational; his quest for knowledge, eager and exacting, has led to his becoming like a dumb beast; his rare aptitude for the activities of the soul has left him with no activity . . . and no soul.[99]

If madness comes to sanction the efforts of reason, it is because madness was already part of those efforts: the liveliness of images, the violence of passion, the great retreating of the spirit into itself are all part of madness, but are also the most powerful, and therefore the most dangerous, tools that reason can use. There is no reason so strong that it does not put itself at risk in venturing into madness to carry out its task to the full: 'there is no great spirit who is not tempered by a touch of madness . . . many wise men and countless brave poets have ventured into madness, and some have become lost there'.[100] Madness is a hard but essential moment in the labour of reason. Through it, and through its apparent victories, reason makes itself manifest and triumphs. Madness, for reason, was nothing more than a secret life and a source of strength.[101]

Little by little, madness finds itself disarmed and the same steps are displaced: invested by reason, it is as though it is welcomed in and planted within it. Such was the ambiguous role of sceptical thought, or rather of a form of reason that was vividly conscious of the forms that limited it and the forces that contradicted it: it discovered madness as one of its own figures – one way of warding off anything that may have formed an exterior power, irreducible hostility or a sign of transcendence; while by the same token placing madness at the heart of its work and indicating it to be an essential moment in its own nature. Beyond Montaigne and Charron, in that same movement of the insertion of madness into the nature of reason itself, the outline of the thought of Pascal begins to become discernible: 'Men are so necessarily mad, that not being mad would be being mad through another trick that madness played.'[102] That thought is the distillation of the long process of reflection that began with Erasmus: the discovery of a form of madness immanent within reason; and from there a process of doubling – on the one hand a 'mad madness' that turns its back on the madness that properly belongs to reason, and which through that rejection, redoubles its power, and through that redoubling falls into the simplest, most hermetic and most immediate forms of madness; and on the other hand a 'wise madness' which welcomes the madness of reason, listens to it, recognises its right of abode and allows itself to be penetrated by all its vivid power, thereby protecting itself from madness in a manner far more effective than any obstinate refusal, which is condemned to failure in advance.

Now the truth of madness is at one with the victory of reason and its definitive mastery, for the truth of madness is to be interior to reason, to be one of its figures, a strength and a momentary need to be sure of its own powers.

*

Perhaps that provides one explanation for its multiple presence in the literature of the end of the sixteenth and beginning of the seventeenth century, an art which, in its effort to master this reason in search of itself, recognises the presence of madness, its own madness, circumscribes it, gives it power and finally triumphs over it. These are the games of a Baroque age.

But in art as in thought, a whole process is accomplished which will also lead to the confirmation of the tragic experience of madness inside a critical consciousness. But let us ignore that for a moment, and concentrate instead on the lack of distinction between the two that is apparent in figures in Don Quixote, as well as in the novels of Scudéry, King Lear, and in the theatre of Rotrou or Tristan l'Hermite.

Foremost among these and most durable (the eighteenth century still recognised its traces)[103] was *madness through literary identification*. Its features were fixed once and for all by Cervantes, but the theme was taken up time and again. There were direct adaptations (Guérin de Bouscal's *Don Quichotte* first played in 1639; two years later the same author brought out *Le Gouvernement de Sancho Pança*), reinterpretations of a particular episode (Pichou's *Les Folies de Cardenio* are a variation on the theme of the Ragged Knight of the Sierra Morena), or in less direct fashion, satires on fantastical novels (as in the *Julie d'Arviane* episode in Subligny's *La Fausse Clélie*). From writer to reader, the chimera pass, but the fantasy of the one becomes the phantasm of the other, and the writer's ruse is naively taken up as a figure of the real. On the surface, such novels are nothing more than a gentle critique of the fantastical novel form; but on a deeper level they bear witness to a more profound preoccupation with the links in a work of art between the real and the imaginary, and perhaps too between the fantastical imaginings of a creative mind at work and the fascination inside delirium. 'We owe the invention of the arts to deranged imaginations: the *Caprice* of Painters, Poets and Musicians is only a name moderated in civility to express their *Madness*.'[104] A madness where the values of another age, another art and another morality are all called into question, but also where all the forms of human imagination, even the most distant ones, are reflected in a glass darkly, strangely transformed into a common hallucination.

Hard on the heels of this first form comes *the madness of vain presumption*. Here the madman identifies not with a literary model, but with an imaginatively transformed version of his own self, where all the qualities, virtues and powers that he lacks are present. He is the inheritor of Erasmus' *Philautia*. Poor, he finds himself rich, ugly, he sees himself as beautiful, and with his feet in chains he believes himself to be the all-powerful. One example is Cervantes' Osuna graduate, who took himself for Neptune.[105] It is also the destiny of the seven characters in Desmarets de Saint-Sorlin's *Les Visionnaires*,[106] of Chateaufort in Cyrano de Bergerac's *Le Pédant joué* and of M. de Richesource in Saint-Evremond's *Sir Politick*. A vast form of madness, with as many faces as there are characters, ambitions or necessary illusions in the world. Even at its limits, it is the least extreme form of madness, for in every man's heart this madness is the imaginary relation that man has with his own self. The most ordinary faults are born out of this form of madness, and it is the first and ultimate object of any form of moral criticism.

It is also to that moral universe that the *Madness of just punishment* belongs. This form of madness chastises the disorder of the heart with disorder of the spirit. But it has other powers: the punishment it inflicts multiplies of its own accord, in that as it progresses it reveals the truth. The justice of this form of madness lies precisely in its capacity to unveil the truth. Its truthfulness lies in the fact that in the vain delirium of his hallucinations, the guilty party already feels what will be for all eternity the pain of his punishment. In Corneille's *Mélite*, Eraste already sees himself pursued by the Furies and condemned by Minos. Truthfulness also lies in the fact that the crime that was hidden from all becomes apparent in the night of this strange punishment. Madness, through the senseless words that are not mastered, speaks its own meaning through the strange visions revealing the hidden truth: the cries of madness speak for the conscience. So the delirium of Lady Macbeth reveals to those who 'have known what [they] should not' words long uttered only to 'deaf pillows'.[107]

The last form of madness is the *madness of desperate passion*. Love disappointed in its excess, or more commonly a love undone by the inevitability of death, leads inexorably towards dementia. So long as it had an object, mad love was still more love than madness, but left to its own devices it continues in a delirious void. The punishment, perhaps, of a passion too given to its own violence, but a punishment that is also a calming of the pains of love, peopling the irreparable absence with imaginary presences, or finding the disappearing form in the paradox of innocent joys or the heroism of senseless pursuits. If this form of madness leads to death, it is to a death where lovers will be reunited for all eternity. This madness is the last song of Ophelia, Ariste's delirium in *La Folie du sage*, and above all the bittersweet dementia of King Lear.

The madness to be found in the work of Shakespeare leads to death and murder, while the forms we see in Cervantes are linked rather to presumption or the compensations of the imagination. But they are the high models that imitators inflect and weaken. Both in all probability still bear witness to the tragic experience of madness born in the fifteenth century more than they reflect the critical or moral experience of unreason that is nonetheless a product of their era. Through time, they connect with a kind of madness that is in the process of disappearing, and which will live on only under the cover of darkness. But a comparison between their work and what it maintains and the new forms to be found in their contemporaries or their imitators will show what is happening in this early part of the seventeenth century, in the literary experience of madness.

In Cervantes and Shakespeare, madness occupies an extreme position in that it is invariably without issue. There is no going back to truth or reason. It opens only onto a tear in the fabric of the world, and therefore onto death. Madness, in its empty words, is not vanity: the void that fills it is 'disease beyond my practice' as the doctor says of Lady Macbeth, and it is already the plenitude that death brings, a madness that does not need a doctor, but divine forgiveness.[108] The sweet joy that Ophelia finds at the end has little to do with happiness, and her senseless song is as near the essential as 'the cry of women' announcing in the corridors of Macbeth's castle that the queen is dead. The death of Don Quixote takes place in an atmosphere of calm, where links with reason and truth have at last been renewed. The Don's madness has become aware of itself at a stroke, and falls away as stupidity before his very eyes. But the onlookers are unconvinced: 'they were certain that he was in the grip of some new madness'. This indefinitely reversible ambiguity can only be decided by death. Madness dissipated blends seamlessly into the imminence of the end: 'one of the signs that he was really dying was the ease with which he had turned from a madman into a sane man'.[109] But death brings no peace, and madness will triumph again, a truth derisory in its eternity, beyond the end of a life delivered from madness only by its own ending. The senselessness of his life pursues him, and ironically he is immortalised only by his madness, which becomes his imperishable life in death:

> This is a doughty knight's repose;
> So high his matchless courage rose
> That as it's plain enough to see,
> He granted death no victory,
> Not even when in death's last throes.[110]

But early on, madness leaves these extreme regions where Cervantes and Shakespeare had placed it, and in the literature of the early seventeenth century its preferred place is median, forming the core of the action rather than an ending, and is an adventure rather than the ultimate imminence. Displaced in the structures of novels and plays, it now allows both a manifestation of truth and a calm return to reason.

Henceforth it is no longer to be considered in its tragic reality, as the absolute tear in the fabric of this world that opens on to the other, but simply in the irony of the illusions it brings. Madness is no longer a genuine punishment, but an image of a punishment, and therefore a false one: it can only be linked to what is a crime in appearance, or the illusion of a death. Ariste, in *La Folie du sage*, goes mad on hearing the news of his daughter's death, but only because she is not really dead; and when Eraste, in *Mélite*, is pursued by the Furies and dragged before Minos, it is for a double crime that he could have committed, that he would have wanted to commit, but which in fact resulted in no blood being shed. Madness is stripped of its dramatic seriousness, and is no longer a punishment or cause of despair other than as error. Its dramatic function only survives as a false drama, a chimerical form where faults are merely supposed, murders are illusory and disappearances lead inevitably to reunions.

Yet despite this absence of seriousness it is still essential – even more essential than before, in that it brings illusion to its limits, and it is from there that the process of illusion is undone. In the madness to which the error of their ways confines them, characters pick up the thread in spite of themselves. In accusing themselves, they begin to speak the truth regardless of their intentions. Again in *Mélite*, all the clever ploys the hero uses to deceive his companions turn against him, and he is the first victim in that he genuinely believes himself to be guilty of the murder of his rival and his mistress. But in his delirium, he accuses himself of having invented a whole lovers' correspondence, and the truth emerges in and through the madness brought on by the illusion of an ending, a madness which in fact undoes the real imbroglio of which it is both the cause and the effect. In other words, madness is the false punishment for a false ending, but through its own virtues it also reveals the real problem, which can then be brought to a proper conclusion. It covers the secret machinations of truth under the veil of error. It is to this ambiguous yet central function of madness that the author of *L'Ospital des fous* is referring when he shows two lovers who feign madness to throw off their pursuers, taking refuge amongst a group of mad people. In a simulated fit of madness the young girl, dressed as a boy, pretends to believe that she really is a girl – which of course, in fact, she is – thereby asserting, by the process in which two ruses cancel each other out, the truth that will indeed triumph in the end.

Madness is the purest and most complete form of *quid pro quo*: it takes the false for the true, death for life, man for woman, a lover for the Furies, and

the victim for Minos. But it is also the most rigorously necessary form of
quid pro quo within the dramatic structure, for it has no need of an external
element to reach its final conclusion. All that needs to be done is to push
the illusion until it reaches the truth. At the heart of the structure, in its
mechanical centre, it is at once a feigned conclusion that holds within it
the promise of a new beginning, and an initiation to what will be recog-
nized as reconciliation with truth and reason. It marks the vanishing point
where the tragic destinies of the characters apparently converge, and where
the real lines leading to a happy ending all have their origins. Equilibrium
begins in madness, but madness hides that equilibrium in a cloud of
illusion and feigned disorder, camouflaging the rigour of the architecture
beneath a cleverly arranged violent disorder. This unexpected vivacity, this
wind of madness that suddenly shakes gestures or words, breaks the mood or
blows through the curtains when the fabric is in fact stretched tight, is a
typical instance of the Baroque *trompe-l'oeil*. Madness is the great *trompe-l'oeil*
in the tragic-comic structure of pre-classical literature.[111]

Georges de Scudéry was well aware of this, as he shows in the *Comédie des
comédiens*, where by turning the theatre into a theatre he situates his play
inside the illusions of madness. One section of the cast is to take the role of
spectators, while the remainder play the actors. One side must then pretend to take the set for reality, and acting for real life, while acting on a set
that is real enough, and the other must pretend to act and imitate players,
being in fact nothing other than actors playing roles. In this double game
every element is doubled, leading to a constant process of exchange
between reality and illusion, which is also the dramatic sense of madness.
'I don't know', says Mondory in the prologue to Scudéry's play,

> what extravagance has taken hold of my companions today, but it is so
> powerful that I am forced to believe that some spell has robbed them of
> their wits, and the worst of it is that they're trying to make me and you
> lose our reason too. They're trying to convince me that I'm not in a
> theatre, but that this is the city of Lyon, that there's an inn over there and
> a tennis court here, and that some actors, who aren't us but whom we
> nevertheless are, are in the middle of playing a pastoral.[112]

In this extravaganza, theatre develops its truth, which is to be an illusion.
And that, strictly speaking, is what madness is.

*

And so the classical experience of madness comes into being. The great threat that appeared on the horizon in the fifteenth century begins to fade, and the dark power that lurked in the paintings of Bosch begins to lose its violence. The forms live on, now transparent and docile, forming part of the great cortège of reason. Madness has ceased to be an eschatological figure at the edge of the world of mankind and of death, and that darkness into which man stared and made out impossible forms has slowly begun to retreat. A great forgetting falls on the world that was criss-crossed by the free slavery of the ship of fools, and madness is no longer a strange passage from here to the hereafter, no more that fugitive and absolute limit. The ship of fools is solidly anchored in the world of people and things, berthed at the quay. No longer a boat at all, but a hospital.

Scarcely a century after the fashion for those ships, the literary theme of the 'Hospital for the Mad' is born. There each empty head, bound and classified by the true reason of men, speaks of contradiction and irony, in the double language of Wisdom:

> the hospital for the incurably mad, where, point by point, all possible types of madness and all the maladies of the spirit are carefully mapped out, in both men and women, an enterprise that is both amusing and useful, and forms the only path to the acquisition of true wisdom.[113]

There each form of madness has its place ready and waiting, its sign and its protective god. For frenzy and ranting madness, there is the fool strapped to the chair under the watchful eye of Minerva; for the sombre melancholics who haunt the countryside like hungry lone wolves there is Jupiter, the master of animal metamorphoses, and then there are the 'drunkard madmen', 'madmen with no memory or understanding', 'drowsy or half-dead madmen' and 'stale or empty-headed madmen'. . . . A whole world of disorder, where every man has his place, and the *Praise of Reason* is sung in the manner of Erasmus. Already, in these primitive hospitals, *embarkation* has given way to *confinement*.

Tamed, madness still keeps up the appearance of its rule. It has become part of the measures of reason, and of the labour of truth. It plays on the surface of things in the glittering light of day, on all games of appearance, on the equivocation between the real and the illusory, and on the constantly broken and mended thread of the weave that unites and separates truth and appearance. It hides and shows, speaks truth and lies, and is both shadow and light. A central yet indulgent figure, it flickers and shimmers, an already precarious figure of this baroque age.

And it constantly returns, in both fiction and writing for the theatre. The figure of the madman really does stalk through the streets, and François Colletet came across it again and again:

> I see in that avenue
> An innocent followed by children
> . . . Let us admire the wretch
> This poor madman, what could he
> Want with so many rags?
> I have seen so many of these gruff madmen
> Singing their foul ditties in the streets . . .[114]

Madness becomes a familiar silhouette on the social landscape. There was a new, intense pleasure to be had from these brotherhoods of fools, their parties, meetings and speeches. A burning issue of the day was the case of Nicolas Joubert, better known as Angoulevent, who declared himself the Prince of Fools, only to find that his title was contested by Valenti Le Comte and Jacques Resneau. Pamphlets, passionate defences and law cases followed: his lawyer certified him to be 'an empty head, a hollowed-out pumpkin free of all common sense, a reed, a dismembered brain without a single spring or wheel in place'.[115] Bluet d'Arbères, who took the name Comte de Permission, was protected by some of the most noble families in France, such as the Créquis, the Lesdiguières, the Bouillons and the Nemours, and in 1602 he published (or had published for him) works where he claimed to be unable to either read or write, and has never learned but found himself filled with 'inspiration from God and the Angels'.[116] Pierre Dupuis, who is mentioned by Régnier in his sixth satire,[117] is in the words of Brascambille 'an arch-madman in a long coat';[118] and he himself in his *Remontrance sur le réveil de Maître Guillaume* declares that his spirit is so elevated, it is 'in the antichamber of the third degree of the moon'. There are many similar figures in Régnier's fourteenth satire.

The world of the early seventeenth century is strangely hospitable to madness. Madness is there, in the hearts of men and at the heart of things, an ironic sign blurring the distinction between the real and the chimerical, but with barely a memory of the great tragic threat. More a cause of hesitation than genuine confusion, a derisory agitation in society, mobility of reason. But new demands are being born:

> Hundreds of times I walked out with my lantern
> Into the full midday sun . . ."[9]

II

THE GREAT CONFINEMENT

COMPELLE INTRARE

After defusing its violence, the Renaissance had liberated the voice of Madness. The age of reason, in a strange takeover, was then to reduce it to silence.

On the methodical path of his doubt, Descartes came across madness beside dreams and all the other forms of error. Might the possibility of his own madness rob him of his own body, in the manner in which the outside world occasionally disappears through an error of the senses, or in which consciousness sleeps while we dream?

> How could it be denied that these hands or this whole body are mine? Unless perhaps I were to liken myself to madmen, whose brains are so damaged by the persistent vapours of melancholia that they firmly maintain they are kings when they are paupers, or say they are dressed in purple when they are naked, or that their heads are made of earthenware or that they are pumpkins, or made of glass.[1]

But Descartes does not evade the danger of madness in the same way that he sidesteps the possibility of dream or error. However deceptive they might be, the senses can only alter 'things that are barely perceptible, or at a great distance', and however strong the illusion, there is still a residue of truth assuring him that he is 'sitting by the fire, wearing a dressing gown'. Dreams, like the imaginings of painters, can represent 'Sirens and Satyrs, by strange, extraordinary, shapes', but of their own accord, they can never create 'simpler or more universal things' that make fantastical images possible: 'corporeal nature, and its extension, are of this class of things'. The fictitiousness of such things is so slight that they lend dreams their verisimilitude, and they are the inevitable marks of a truth that dreams themselves can never undo. Thus neither sleep peopled with images nor the clear consciousness that the senses are deceived can lead doubt to its most universal point: we might admit that our eyes can deceive us, and 'suppose that we are asleep', but the truth will never slip away entirely into darkness.

Madness is an altogether different affair. If its dangers compromise neither the enterprise nor the essential truth that is found, this is not because this thing, even in the thoughts of a madman, cannot be untrue, but rather because I, when I think, cannot be considered insane. When I think I have a body, can I be certain that my grasp on the truth is stronger than that of the man who believes his body to be made of glass? Assuredly, says Descartes, 'such people are insane, and I would be thought equally mad if I took anything from them as a model for myself'. It is not the permanence of truth that ensures that thought is not madness, in the way that it freed it from an error of perception or a dream; it is an impossibility of being mad which is inherent in the thinking subject rather than the object of his thoughts. If one admits the possibility that one might be dreaming, and one identifies with that dreaming subject to find 'some grounds for doubt', truth still appears, as one of the conditions of possibility for the dream. By contrast, one cannot suppose that one is mad, even in thought, for madness is precisely a condition of impossibility for thought: 'I would be thought equally mad.'[2]

In the economy of doubt, there is a fundamental disequilibrium between on the one hand madness, and dreams and errors on the other. Their position is quite different where truth and the seeker of truth are concerned. Dreams and illusions are overcome by the very structure of truth, but madness is simply excluded by the doubting subject, in the same manner that it will soon be excluded that he is not thinking or that he does not exist. A specific decision has been taken since the *Essays* of Montaigne. When the latter went to meet Tasso, there was nothing to assure him that all thought was not haunted by the ghost of unreason. What of the people, the 'wretched folk taken in by this madness?' Perhaps they were no different from anyone else, and the thinking man was also in danger of falling into such eccentricity. He is to be 'equally pitied', for what reason could make him a judge of madness?

> Reason has taught me that if you condemn in this way anything whatever as definitely false and quite impossible, you are claiming to know the frontier and bounds of the will of God and the power of Nature our Mother; it taught me also that there is nothing in the whole world madder than bringing matters down to the measure of our own capacities and potentialities.[3]

Amongst all other forms of illusion, madness traces what was still in the sixteenth century one of the most commonly taken paths of doubt. Man was never certain that he was not dreaming, and never sure that he was not mad: 'do we not often feel ourselves to be in contradiction with our own better judgement?'[4]

Descartes by contrast has now acquired that certainty, and he grasps it firmly: madness, quite simply, is no longer his concern. It would be an eccentricity for him to suppose that he were eccentric: as a way of thinking, madness implies itself, and thus excludes itself from his project. The perils of madness have been quashed by the exercise of Reason, and this new sovereign rules a domain where the only possible enemies are errors and illusions. The process of Descartes' doubt breaks the spells woven by the senses and steers a clear course through the landscape of dreams, constantly guided by the light of true things. But madness is banished in the name of the man who doubts, and who is no more capable of opening himself to unreason than he is of not thinking or not being.

Montaigne's problematics of madness are thereby modified, in an almost imperceptible but nonetheless decisive manner. Madness is placed in a zone of exclusion, from which it will only escape in part in Hegel's *Phenomenology of the Spirit*. Unreason in the sixteenth century was a sort of open wound, which in theory constantly posed a threat to the link between subjectivity and truth. The path taken by Cartesian doubt seems to indicate that by the seventeenth century the danger has been excluded, and that madness is no longer a peril lurking in the domain where the thinking subject holds rights over truth: and for classical thought, that domain is the domain of reason itself. Madness has been banished. While man can still go mad, thought, as the sovereign exercise carried out by a subject seeking the truth, can no longer be devoid of reason. A new dividing line has appeared, rendering that experience so familiar to the Renaissance – unreasonable Reason, or reasoned Unreason – impossible. Between Montaigne and Descartes an event has taken place, which concerns the advent of a ratio. But the advent of a ratio in the Western world meant far more than the appearance of a 'rationalism'. More secretly, but in equal measure, it also meant the movement whereby Unreason was driven underground, to disappear, indeed, but also take root.

And it is to that other aspect of the classical event that we must now turn our attention.

*

More than one sign gives it away, and they don't all come from a philosophical experience of knowledge. What we need to address is a wide cultural surface. This is signalled quite precisely by a series of dates, and with them an ensemble of institutions.

It is well known that the seventeenth century created vast houses of confinement, but it is less well known that in the city of Paris, one out of every hundred inhabitants found themselves locked up there within a matter of months. It is also recognised that the authorities made use of lettres de cachet and other arbitrary measures of imprisonment, but the juridical thinking behind such practices is less familiar.[5] Since Pinel, Tuke and Wagnitz, we know that the mad underwent this process of confinement for a century and a half, until one day they were discovered in the wards of the Hôpital Général and in the cells of houses of correction, or among the population of the workhouses and Zuchthäuser. But it is rarely the case that their status there is clarified, or that what was meant by this enforced fraternisation between the poor, the unemployed, the criminal and the insane is clearly understood. It was in these spaces of confinement that Pinel and the psychiatry of the nineteenth century met the mad, and – lest we forget – it was there too that they allowed them to remain, while claiming to be their liberators. Since the mid-seventeenth century, madness had been linked to this place of confinement, and to the gesture that designated it as its natural place.

We should begin by addressing the facts in their simplest formulation, since the locking up of the insane is the structure most clearly visible in the classical experience of madness, and because it is that practice of confinement that would suddenly seem so scandalous when the experience came to disappear from European culture.

> I saw them naked and covered in rags, with nothing but straw to protect themselves from the damp cold of the stones on which they lay. I saw them badly fed and deprived of fresh air to breathe and water to quench their thirst, lacking even the basic necessities of life. They were in the charge of gaolers, and entirely at the mercy of their brutish ways. I saw them in cramped, dirty places, deprived of air and light, locked up in dens where men would hesitate to keep the wild animals that governments maintain at great cost in the capitals of Europe.[6]

A single date serves as a reference point here. In Paris in 1656, the Hôpital Général was set up by royal decree. At first glance it looks like a simple process of reform, little more than an administrative reorganisation. Various establishments that already existed were grouped together into one common administration: the Salpêtrière, which had been rebuilt under the previous reign to be used as an arsenal,[7] and Bicêtre, which Louis XIII had wanted to place under the Commanderie de Saint-Louis to make a house of retreat for army invalids.[8] 'House and Hospital, of both the large and the small Pitié, and the Refuge in the faubourg Saint-Victor, the House and the Hospital of Scipion, and the House of the Savonnerie, with all its dependent places, Squares, Gardens and Houses and Buildings, as well as the Houses and Plots at Bicêtre'[9] All were now assigned to the poor of Paris, 'any person of either sex, regardless of their age and origin, quality or birth, and whatever their condition, be they able or unable, ill or convalescent, curable or incurable,'.[10] Their function was to supply food and lodgings to anyone who presented themselves, or was sent there by a royal or judicial decree, and to look after the subsistence and good order of anyone else for whom there was no room, but who might in other circumstances find themselves staying at the Hôpital Général. These duties were entrusted to directors appointed for life, whose powers over inmates extended beyond the confines of the hospital, in effect to anyone within their jurisdiction. 'They are granted full powers where authority, direction, administration, commerce, policing, tribunals, correction and punishment are concerned, over all the poor of Paris, both within the hospital and without.'[11] The directors were also to appoint a physician, who would be paid an annual fee of one thousand pounds, and who was to reside at La Pitié and carry out visits to each hospital house twice a week. One fact is immediately clear: the Hôpital Général was not a medical establishment. It was more of a semi-judicial structure, an administrative entity that was granted powers to deliberate, judge and pass sentence independently of other pre-existing authorities and courts.

> To that end the directors will have the following at their disposal: gallows, iron collars, prisons and dungeons inside the Hôpital Général and dependent buildings, which they may use as they see fit, without there being any recourse to appeal against the judgements they are to promulgate inside the hospital. Judgments made with reference to outside the hospital will be carried in their due form, regardless of any defence or appeals that have been made or are pending and without prejudice to them; no defence or appeal to any higher court will be accepted.[12]

Their sovereignty was thus almost absolute, there was no right of appeal against their jurisdiction, and nothing could prevail against their right of execution. The Hôpital Général was a strange power that the king set up half-way between police and justice, at the limits of legality, and forming a third order of repression. This was the world to which the insane whom Pinel was later to find in Bicêtre and the Salpêtrière belonged.

The Hôpital Général bore no resemblance to any medical idea in either its purpose or functioning. It was rather an instrument of order, of the new bourgeois and monarchical order that was beginning to take shape in the France of that time. It was directly connected to the power of the king, who had placed it under the authority of the civil government. The Royal Almonry, which had previously provided ecclesiastical and spiritual mediation in the politics of assistance, suddenly found itself sidelined. The decree stated:

> It is our intention to be both the curator and protector of this Hôpital Général, and of all the places that depend upon it, as a royal foundation; and nevertheless they will depend in no fashion on the grand Almoner nor on any of our other officers; they will be totally exempt from the superiority, visit and jurisdiction of the Officers of the

general Reformation, or of the grand Almonry, or of any other, to which
we forbid any knowledge or jurisdiction in these matters, in any way
conceivable.[13]

The origins of the project had been parliamentary,[14] and the first two
directors were to be the First President of the Parliament and the Procurator General. But they were quickly joined by the Archbishop of
Paris, the President of the Court of Assistance, the President of the Treasury, the Lieutenant of Police and the Provost of Commerce. Soon, the
'Grand Bureau' saw its role reduced to that of little more than a
deliberative chamber. The real administration and genuine responsibility
had in effect been handed over to controllers who had been co-opted into
the role. They were the true governors, the delegates of royal power and
bourgeois fortune in the world of poverty. The French Revolution
paid homage to them in the following terms: 'Chosen among the high
bourgeoisie . . . they brought disinterested views and pure intentions to
this administration.'[15]

This structure, typical of the monarchical and bourgeois order, which
coincided in France with the move towards a more absolute form of
monarchy, was soon to be found right across the country. A royal edict
dated 16 June 1676 ordered the creation of a Hôpital Général in every city
of the kingdom. Sometimes the decision had already been taken by the
local authorities: the bourgeoisie of Lyon had been running a charitable
establishment that worked along similar lines since 1612.[16] The Archbishop of Tours was proud to announce on 10 July 1676 that his

> metropolitan city had fortunately foreseen the wishes of the King and
> erected a Hôpital Général called La Charité before the Paris hospital had
> come into being, with an organisation which has long been a model for all
> hospitals subsequently created, both within the kingdom and beyond.[17]

La Charité de Tours had indeed been founded in 1656, and the king had
endowed it with 4,000 pounds. The new General Hospitals began to
appear all across France, and on the eve of the Revolution, they were to be
found in thirty-two cities around the country.[18]

Despite being deliberately excluded from the organisation of the
General Hospitals – doubtless on account of some complicity between
the king and the bourgeoisie[19] – the Church was not entirely a stranger
to this movement. It began a reform of its hospital institutions, and

redistributed the wealth of its foundations, and created new institutions whose aims were broadly similar to those of the Hôpital Général. Vincent de Paul reorganised Saint-Lazare, the largest of what were once the Leper Hospitals of Paris. On 7 January 1632, he signed a new contract with the 'Priory' of Saint-Lazare in the name of the Congregationists of the Mission, to receive 'people detained on the orders of his Majesty'. The Order of the Good Sons opened several hospitals of that ilk in the north of the country. The Brothers of Saint John of God, who had been in France since 1602, founded first the Charité de Paris in the faubourg Saint-Germain, and then Charenton, which opened on 10 May 1645.[20] Not far from the capital, it was they again who set up the Charité de Senlis, which opened its doors on 27 October 1670.[21] A few years earlier, the Duchess of Bouillon had donated the buildings and revenues accruing from the leprosarium that had been founded by Thibaut de Champagne in Château-Thierry in the fourteenth century.[22] Also under their control were the Charités of Saint-Yon, Pontorson, Cadillac and Romans.[23] The year 1699 saw the foundation by the Lazarists of the establishment that was later to become the Saint-Pierre Hospital. In the eighteenth century, these were followed by Armentières (1712), Maréville (1714), the Bon Sauveur in Caen (1735) and, shortly before the Revolution, Saint-Meins in Rennes in 1780.

These were curious institutions, and their meaning and status is often difficult to define. Many were in effect still run by religious orders, and yet there were also lay associations that imitated the lifestyle and clothing of the different orders, but were in no manner part of them.[24] In the provinces, the bishop was automatically a member of the General Bureau, but the clergy rarely held a majority, and effective management was mostly in the hands of the bourgeoisie.[25] Yet in each of these houses life was led among highly conventual lines, with readings, religious services, prayers and meditation. 'Communal prayers are held mornings and evenings in the dormitories, and at different hours of the day there are spiritual exercises, prayers and readings from scripture.'[26] And there was more: being vectors of both assistance and repression, these hospitals were intended not only to assist the poor, but also for imprisonment. Almost all of them had cells where prisoners could be detained, and *quartiers de force*, where inmates were imprisoned at the expense of either the king or their family: 'No one, on any pretext whatsoever, is to be allowed into the detainment areas of these religious Charitable hospitals, other than those sent there on the orders of the King or judicial authority.' Often these new houses of confinement were built within the walls of what had previously been the lazar houses, and they inherited their belongings, either through an ecclesiastical decision (as was the case for Saint-Lazare) or by one of the royal decrees of the end of the century.[27] But they were also supported by the public coffers in that they received donations from the king and a proportion of fines collected by the treasury.[28] These institutions were thus places where conflicts were not uncommon, as the ancient privileges of the Church in matters of social assistance and rites of hospitality were mixed with the bourgeois will to bring order to the world of poverty. Together with a desire to assist was a need to repress, a duty of charity and a will to punish. The result was an ambiguous practice whose meaning needs elucidation, best symbolised by the lazar houses, which had been empty since the Renaissance but were now swiftly put to a new use, and found themselves rearmed with mysterious powers. The classical age invented confinement in the way that the Middle Ages had invented the segregation of lepers; and the empty space left by the disappearance of leprosy was now peopled with new characters in the Western world – the 'internees'. The significance of leprosy had gone far beyond a mere medical classification, and the gesture of banishment to these spaces reserved for the damned had had many other functions. The gesture of confinement was equally complex, and it too had social, political, religious, economic and moral meanings. In all probability, they concern certain essential structures of the classical age as a whole.

The phenomenon was truly European in its dimensions. The constitution of the absolute monarchy and the strong Catholic revival at the time of the Counter-Reformation meant that it had a particular character in France, where civic power and the power of the Church found themselves both in competition and complicitous on many issues.[29] In other countries its form was quite different, but the moment was equally precise. The great hospitals, the houses of confinement, the civic and religious institutions for assistance and punishment, for charity and governmental assistance are a fact of the classical age, as universal as that age itself and almost contemporaneous with its birth. In German-speaking countries it was the *Zuchthäuser*, or houses of correction, the first of which preceded the French houses of confinement (with the exception of the Lyon Charité), opening in Hamburg around 1620.[30] Others were created in the second half of the century: Basel in 1667, Breslau in 1668, Frankfurt in 1684,

Spandau the same year and Königsberg in 1691. They continued to multiply in the eighteenth century, first with Leipzig in 1701, then Halle and Cassel in 1717 and 1720, later Brieg and Osnabrück in 1756, and finally Torgau in 1771.[31]

In England, the roots of confinement can be traced back considerably further. A 1575 Act (18 Eliz. c.3) which concerned 'the punishment of vagabonds and relief of the poor' ordered the construction of houses of correction, at least one of which was to be built in each county. Their upkeep was to be paid by a tax, but the public were also encouraged to make donations.[32] It would appear that in that form the measures were hardly ever applied, as within a few years the same function could be carried out by private enterprise. It was no longer necessary to have an official permit delivered to open a hospital or a house of correction, and anyone could do it if they wished.[33] A general reorganisation took place at the beginning of the seventeenth century, and a fine of five pounds was to be levied on any Justice of the Peace who did not have a house of correction in his jurisdiction. There was an obligation to install looms and set up workshops and factories (for milling, spinning or weaving) to help the upkeep of the institution, and ensure that its inmates had work. Who deserved to be sent there was left to the discretion of the judges.[34] In fact these Bridewells were less widespread than might be supposed, and often they were progressively absorbed by an adjoining prison.[35] They were not known in Scotland.[36] But workhouses, by contrast, which date from the second half of the seventeenth century, were far more successful.[37] A 1670 Act (22–23 Car II. c.18) defining the status of the workhouses ordered officers of justice to audit the taxes collected and the management of the funds required for their functioning, and entrusted ultimate control of their administration to a justice of the peace. In 1697, several Bristol parishes united to form the first English workhouse, and to appoint the corporation that would run the institution.[38] Another was set up in Worcester in 1703, and a third that same year in Dublin,[39] followed by Plymouth, Norwich, Hull and Exeter. By the end of the eighteenth century, their number had risen to 126. The 1792 Gilbert Act granted parishes the power to create new workhouses, and the control and authority of the Justice of the Peace was simultaneously reinforced. To keep workhouses from turning into hospitals, it was recommended that internees with contagious diseases should be expelled.

Within a few years, a whole network had spread across Europe. At the end of the eighteenth century John Howard decided to tour them, and he proceded to make a pilgrimage of prisons, gaols and hospitals – the high places of confinement – in England, Holland, Germany, France, Italy and Spain. He was indignant at what he found, his philanthropic instincts shocked that common criminals were locked up with young men who had showed themselves to be spendthrifts, or troubled the peace of their family, with vagrants or with the insane. His reaction was proof perhaps that a certain category of order in the classical age had lost its obviousness; suddenly confinement, which had sprung up with such rapidity and spontaneity across Europe, no longer seemed so obviously right. After 150 years, confinement appeared to be an ill-conceived blend of heterogeneous elements. Yet at its origins, its unity must have been self-evident, justifying the haste with which it was brought into effect. Between the varied forms that it took and the classical age there must be a principle of coherence, which it is wrong to ignore under the scandalous mask of the pre-Revolutionary sensibility. What was the reality targeted by the confinement of an entire sector of the population who almost overnight found themselves locked up and banished far more rigorously than the lepers of the Middle Ages? We do well to remember that within a few years of its opening its doors, the Hôpital Général in Paris was home to more than 6,000 people, which was approximately 1 per cent of the population.[40] For that to happen, a Europe-wide social sensibility must have almost imperceptibly taken shape, probably over many years beforehand, until suddenly it became manifest in the second half of the seventeenth century. It was that sensibility that suddenly isolated the category destined to people these places of confinement. To our eyes, the population designated to fill the space long left empty by lepers seems a strange amalgam, but what appears to us as a confused sensibility was evidently a clearly articulated perception to the mind of the classical age. And it is this mode of perception that needs to be addressed for any understanding of the sensibility to madness of the period we often term the age of Reason. For that act of drawing a line around a space of confinement, of giving it a special power of segregation and assigning madness a new land, however coherent and willful it may appear at first glance, is anything but simple. This complex unity brings together a new sensibility to poverty and the duty to relieve it, new forms of reaction to the economic problems of unemployment and idleness, a new work ethic, and the dream of a city where moral obligations go hand in hand with civic duties, all held together by the authoritarian forms of constraint. Those themes all lurk behind the construction and organisation of these spaces of confinement, and it is they that give meaning to this ritual, and explain in part how madness was perceived, and lived, by the classical age.

*

The practice of confinement demonstrates a new reaction to poverty and indigence, a strange, novel form of pathos, a different relationship between mankind and all that can be inhuman in his existence. In the course of the sixteenth century, the figure of the pauper, and those who could not be responsible for their own existence, gradually assumed a role that the Middle Ages would have failed to recognise altogether.

The Renaissance had stripped poverty of what had previously been a positive, mystical charge. This came from a dual movement of thought that stripped Poverty of its absolute meaning, and stripped Charity of its value. From Luther's point of view, and even more so to Calvin's way of thinking, the specific volitions of God, 'God's singular bounty towards each man', meant that happiness and suffering, poverty and riches or glory and misery no longer spoke in their own right. 'Poverty' was no longer a humiliated Lady, rescued from the mud by a Husband who then proceeded to exalt her: she too had her own place in the world, a place that testified as much to God as that of riches. God was present everywhere, his generous hand as near to abundance as it is to famine, 'according as it is the pleasure of God to nourish one child more liberally, and another more sparingly'.[41] The specific volitions of God concerning the poor no longer spoke of the promise of glories to come, but only of predestination. Gone were the days when God was thought to exalt the poor in a process of inverse glorification – now he humbled them in his anger and hatred, the hatred that he had brought to bear on Esau from even before he was born, dispossessing him of the flocks to which his primogeniture gave him right. Poverty signified punishment: it is 'by his command the heaven becomes hard as iron, the crops are destroyed by mildew and other evils, that storms and hail, in devastating the fields, are signs of sure and special vengeance'.[42] Poverty and riches were now equal signs of the Almighty's omnipotence. The poor could only show that the Lord was not pleased, for their lives bore the signs of his ire; for that reason it was important to 'exhort the poor to patient endurance, seeing that those who are discontented with their lot endeavour to shake off a burden which God has imposed upon them'.[43]

Under such circumstances, it might be wondered what value charitable works could have. It came not from the relief of poverty, as poverty no longer had any intrinsic glory, nor from the action of assistance itself, as the gesture was nothing more than another specific will of God being carried out. It was not the good work itself that provided the justification for such actions, but the faith that connected it to God. 'Men may not be justified before God by their efforts, their merits or their works, but only through Christ and by faith.'[44] Luther's position on good works was well known, and his proclamation on the matter reverberated throughout Protestant thought: 'No, good works are not necessary, and they serve no purpose for sanctity.' But that refusal only has a bearing on the meaning of good works where their relationship with God and salvation were concerned. Like all human actions, they bear the signs of finitude and the stigma of the fall, and in that respect they are nothing more than 'sin and uncleanliness'.[45] But on a human level they had a meaning: inefficacious for salvation, they serve as testimony and an indication of faith. 'Faith is the root from which all good works originate, and cannot, by any means, make us slothful about them.'[46] That serves to explain the common Reformation trend where the property that belonged to the church was turned over to lay charities. In 1525, Michel Geismayer proposed that all monasteries be transformed into hospitals, and the following year at the Diet of Speyer a list of grievances was presented, demanding the abolition of convents and the confiscation of their goods, which were to be used instead for the succouring of the poor.[47] And it was in buildings that had previously been convents and monasteries that the majority of the great asylums of England and Germany were set up. One of the first hospitals for the mad in a Lutheran country (*arme Wahnsinnige und Presshafte*) was set up by the Landgraf Phillip of Hainau in 1533, in a Cistercian monastery that had been dissolved a decade earlier.[48] Cities and States took over poor relief from the Church. Taxes were levied, collections taken up, donations solicited, and legacies encouraged. In Lübeck, in 1601, it was decided that all wills involving substantial sums had to contain a clause in favour of the poor of the city.[49] In England, the use of the Poor Rate became widespread in the sixteenth century, and cities that had set up houses of correction or workhouses were granted the right to levy a special tax, with Justices of the Peace appointing an Administrator – known as the Guardian of the Poor – to manage the finances and share out the benefits.

To say that in Protestant countries the Reformation led to a progressive secularisation of Charity is something of a commonplace. But through this process of taking responsibility for the poor and unable, cities and states prepared the way to a new form of sensibility to poverty. A new form of pathos came into being, which no longer spoke of a glorification of pain, nor of salvation proper both to Charity and to Poverty, but concerned rather the idea of civic duty, and showed the poor and destitute to be both a consequence of disorder and an obstacle to order. The aim therefore was no longer to glorify poverty in the act of relieving it, but quite simply to dispose of it altogether. Bound to poverty as such, Charity too suddenly seemed to be a kind of disorder. But if private enterprise, as a 1575 act demanded in England, helped the state repress poverty, it became part of the social order and acquired meaning.[50] Shortly before the 1662 Settlement Act, the most important text of the seventeenth century regarding the English poor, Sir Matthew Hale had written a *Discourse touching Provision for the Poor*,[51] which was a clear indication of the new manner in which the meaning of poverty was perceived. To Hale, helping to make poverty disappear was 'necessary, and becomes us both as men and Christians'. He recommended that the mission should be entrusted to officers of the peace, who should subdivide counties, group parishes together and set up compulsory workhouses. No one should then beg: 'No man will be so vain, an indeed hurtful to the Publique as to give to such as beg, and thereby encourage them.'[52]

Poverty is no longer part of a dialectic of humiliation and glorification but rather of the relationship of disorder to order and is now locked in guilt. After Calvin and Luther, poverty bore the marks of an immemorial punishment, and became, in the world of state-assisted charity, self-complacency and crime against the good order of the state. From being the object of a religious experience and sanctified, poverty became the object of a moral conception that condemned it. The great houses of confinement were a clear result of that evolution. They were indeed the secularisation of charity, but in obscure fashion they were also the moral punishment of poverty.

By different paths, and not without considerable difficulty, Catholicism too arrived at analogous results, at approximately the time of Matthew

Hale, that of the Great Confinement. One result of the Reformation had been the transformation of convents and monasteries into hospitals, and at the Council of Trent, the Catholic Church hoped to obtain a similar result from its own bishops. The Reformation Decree recommended that: 'bonorum omnium operum exemplo pascere, pauperum aliarumque miserabilium personarum curam paternam gerere'[53] ('the poor should be nourished by the example of good works, and anyone worthy of pity should be treated with paternal attention'). The Church was giving up nothing of the importance that dogma had traditionally accorded to good works, but it sought to give them a more general social bearing, and evaluate them on their contribution to the good order of the state. Shortly before the Council, one of the first entirely profane conceptions of charity in the history of the Catholic Church was put forward by Juan Luis Vives, in which he criticised private aid to the poor, and underlined the dangers of charity, which, he claims, supports evil, and the dangerous proximity between poverty and vice.[54] The problem was to be taken in hand by magistrates:

> As it is disgraceful for the father of a family in his comfortable home to permit anyone in it to suffer the disgrace of being unclothed or in rags, it is similarly unfitting that the magistrates of a city should tolerate a condition in which citizens are hard pressed by hunger and distress.[55]

Vives recommended that magistrates should be nominated in every city, and that they should walk the streets and slums drawing up a register of the poor, and recording their lifestyle and moral outlook, so that the most recalcitrant could be locked up in houses of confinement, and workhouses created for all. Vives was of the opinion that the project could be financed with money from private donors, but that otherwise the more affluent should be taxed. These ideas echoed around the Catholic world, and were taken up and imitated first by Medina, at the time of the Council of Trent,[56] and then in the late sixteenth century by Christoval Perez de Herrera.[57] In 1607, a text appeared in France which was both pamphlet and manifesto, *The Chimera, or the Spectre of Mendicity*, demanding the creation of a hospital for the poor, where they might find 'a life, clothes, a trade and *punishment*'. The author recommended funding the project through taxes on the wealthy, and that anyone refusing to pay should face a fine of double the amount initially requested.[58]

But Catholic thought was reluctant to change, as were the traditions of the Church. These collective forms of assistance met with initial resistance, as they appeared to downgrade the merit of an act of individual assistance, and removed the eminent dignity that was inherent to poverty. The Christian duty of charity was being turned into little more than a civic obligation, and poverty had simply become a crime against public order. These difficulties slowly disappeared, and appeals were made to the universities to address the problem. The University of Paris approved the public forms of organisation that were submitted for its assessment. Public assistance, it was noted, was 'a difficult, but pious, useful and salubrious activity, authorised by the gospels, apostolic scripture, and by our forebears'.[59] Before long, the Catholic world had adopted the mode of perception of poverty that had come to prevail in the world of Protestant thought. In 1657, Vincent de Paul gave his whole-hearted approval to the project to 'group together the poor in one place to look after them, instruct them and keep them occupied. This is a grand design.' He nonetheless hesitated before involving his order, on the grounds that they had as yet no clear evidence that the enterprise had God's blessing.[60] But within the space of a few years, the Catholic Church in France had given its backing to the Great Confinement ordered by Louis XIV. This meant that the poor were no longer recognised as a pretext sent by God to elicit charity, an opportunity for Catholics to work towards their salvation. Catholics, following the example of the Archbishop of Tours, began to see the poor as 'the very dregs of the Republic, not on account of their physical poverty, which properly arouses compassion, but for their spiritual indigence, which is a cause of revulsion'.[61]

The Church had chosen its camp, and in so doing had split the Christian world of poverty, which had previously been sanctified in its totality by the medieval world.[62] On the one side was the realm of Good, where poverty submitted and conformed to the order that was imposed upon it, and on the other the realm of Evil, where poverty rebelled and tried to escape that order. The former accepted internment, and found its repose there; the latter resisted it, and thereby merited its condition.

This reasoning was expounded quite bluntly in a text inspired by the Papal court in 1693, which was translated into French at the close of the century under the title La Mendicité abolie (Begging Vanquished).[63] The author made a distinction therein between the good and bad poor, those of Christ and those of the Devil. Both bear witness to the usefulness of houses of confinement, the former because they gratefully accepted all that the authorities bestowed upon them, 'patient, humble, modest, content with their station and the assistance that the Bureau brings them, and thanking God for his providence'. The Devil's poor by contrast complained about the General Hospital, and the constraints that it imposed upon them. 'Enemies of good order, lazy, deceitful, lascivious and given over to drink, they speak no language other than that of the devil their father, and curse the Bureau's teachers and directors.' Therein lay the justification for depriving them of their freedom, a freedom for which they had no use other than the glorification of Satan. Confinement was thus doubly justified, in a movement of undecidable equivocation, both as reward and as punishment, according to the moral standing of the person on whom it was inflicted. Up until the close of the classical age, this ambiguity of the practice of confinement remained, its strange reversibility implying that its meaning could alter in response to the merits or faults of its victims. The good poor, the deserving, saw it as a gesture of assistance, and a good work from which they drew comfort, while the bad poor – precisely inasmuch as they were bad – turned the gesture into an act of repression. This opposition between the good and bad poor is essential for an understanding of the structure and meaning of confinement. The Hôpital Général classified them as such, and madness too was divided up in similar fashion, so that it too, according to the moral standing it manifested, could fall under the categories of assistance or repression.[64] All internees fell within the scope of this ethical valorisation, and before being objects of knowledge or pity, they were treated as *moral subjects*.

But paupers could only be moral subjects in so far as they had ceased to be the invisible representatives of God on earth. Until the end of the seventeenth century, this was still the main objection voiced by Catholic consciences. Scripture clearly stated, 'inasmuch as ye have done it unto one of the least of these my brethren, ye have done it unto me', and since the earliest times the Church Fathers had glossed that text as meaning that alms should never be refused to a poor man, for fear of refusing them to Christ himself. Naturally, Father Guevarre was aware of these objections, but his answer, which stood for the Church of the classical age, was abundantly clear. Since the creation of the General Hospital and the charitable bureaux, God no longer appeared in a poor man's rags. The fear of refusing a crust to Jesus dying of hunger underpinned a whole Christian mythology of Charity, and had given an absolute meaning to the whole grand medieval ritual of hospitality; but that fear, it emerged, was now ill-founded.

> When a Charitable bureau has been set up in a town, Christ will no longer take the appearance of a poor man who, to maintain his lazy, idle life, refuses to submit to an order established by genuinely holy means for the relief of true poverty.[65]

This time want really had lost its mystical sense. Nothing, in the suffering that it represented, now referred back to the miraculous, fugitive presence of a god. It was stripped of all power of manifestation. If it still presented Christians with an opportunity to carry out an act of charity, then that was only in so far as the gesture could be carried out in accordance with the provisions made by the State. In itself, poverty now only served to demonstrate its own shortcomings, and appears only within the sphere of guilt. Reducing poverty first implied transferring it towards the order of penance.

This was the first of the great shackles with which the classical age was to bind madness. It is commonly noted that in the Middle Ages the madman was seen as kind of holy person, because he was possessed. Nothing could be further from the truth.[66] If the madman was sacred, then it was only in so far as, for medieval charity, he was associated with the obscure powers of poverty. More than any other, he exalted it. The mad were intimately connected to the poor, and the sign of the cross was shaved into their hair. It was under that sign that Tristan presented himself in Cornwall for the last time, safe in the knowledge that he would receive the charity offered to the poor. In the guise of a pilgrim of unreason, with his staff around his neck and the sign of the cross marked on his skull, he was sure to gain admittance to the King's castle:

> no one dared bar the way, and he crossed the courtyard, playing the fool to the great delight of the servants. So he continued steadily, without fear, until he reached the chamber where the king, the queen and all the knights were to be found. King Mark smiled.[67]

If madness, in the seventeenth century, had become a *secular* affair, it was above all because poverty had been downgraded, and appeared now only on a moral horizon. The hospitality that had previously been reserved for the mad would henceforth only be found within the walls of a hospital, and it would be no different from the welcome reserved for the poor. And there madness was to remain until the end of the eighteenth century. A new sensibility had come into being, no longer religious but social. A familiar figure on the human landscape of the medieval world, the madman had come from another world. Now he stood out on the background, a problem of 'police', a matter of social order for individuals of the polity. Once, he was welcomed because he came from without; now he was excluded because he came from within, and the mad were forced to take their place alongside paupers, beggars and vagabonds. An ambiguous welcome awaited them, in the form of this public health measure that put them out of circulation: the mad still wandered, but no longer on the road of a strange pilgrimage – they just troubled the order of the social space. Stripped of the rights and glory that had previously belonged to poverty, madness, with poverty and idleness, was suddenly no more than a moment in the immanent dialectics of the State.

*

Confinement, the signs of which are to be found massively across Europe throughout the seventeenth century, was a 'police' matter. In the classical age the word had a meaning that was quite precise, refering to a bundle of measures that made work possible and necessary to all those who could not possibly live without it. Voltaire was soon to formulate the question, but Colbert's contemparies had voiced it already: 'What? Now you are set up as a body of people, but you still haven't found a way to force the rich to make the poor work? Evidently, you have not even reached the first elements of 'police'.'[68]

Before it developed the medical meaning that we associate with it, or at least attribute to it, confinement was demanded for reasons quite independent of any desire to cure. What really made it necessary was a work imperative. Modern philanthropists like to divine the signs of concern for illness where nothing is to be seen other than the moral condemnation of idleness.

That much was already clear from the earliest moment of the Confinement, in the Royal Proclamation of 27 April 1656 that had set up the Hôpital Général. The task the institution was set was to 'prevent begging and idleness, which are the source of all unrest'. In fact this was the last of the great measures taken since the Renaissance to put an end to unemployment, or at least to begging.[69] In 1532, the Parliament of Paris had decided to arrest all beggars and force them to work in the city sewers, chained up in pairs. The crisis quickly worsened, as on 23 March 1534, an order was given to expel 'poor scholars and indigents' from the city, and the singing of hymns before sacred images in the streets was forbidden.[70] The wars of religion swelled the ranks of these indigents, where peasants thrown off their land met deserters and redundant soldiers, poor students, the sick and the unemployed. When Henri IV besieged Paris, the city had a population of less than 100,000, including more than 30,000 beggars.[71] The new century brought an economic upturn, and it was decided to reintegrate forcibly all the unemployed who had still to find their place in society. A parliamentary act of 1606 decreed that in Paris all beggars were to be whipped in a public place, branded on the shoulder, and then thrown out of the city with their heads shaved. The following year another act created companies of archers to guard the gates of the city and refuse entry to any of the poor who tried to return.[72] The coming of the Thirty Years War cancelled the effects of the economic upturn, and the problem of begging and idleness continued until the middle of the century, as the high taxes levied on manufacturers put a brake on prosperity and created unemployment. These were the times of the great riots in Paris (1621), Lyon (1652) and Rouen (1639). The appearance of new economic structures brought disarray to the world of the workers, as factories became bigger and more widespread, and brotherhoods and guilds saw their powers and rights dwindle. New General Regulations removed the right of assembly for all associations, leagues and groups of workers. In some professions, these guilds managed to reform,[73] only to be harried again by institutional pressure. The parliaments showed a measure of leniency, the Normandy parliament for example refusing to judge rioters in Rouen. Perhaps for that reason the Church intervened, ruling that secret organisations of workers had the same status as witches' covens. A Sorbonne decree of 1655 proclaimed that to join the ranks of these orders was equivalent to sacrilege or mortal sin.

In this secret conflict, which saw the severity of the Church at loggerheads with the indulgence of the parliaments, the foundation of the Hôpital Général, in the early days at least, was a clear victory for the parliaments. It was certainly a novel solution, and the first time that the purely negative measures of exclusion had been replaced by the idea of confinement: the unemployed were no longer simply expelled or hunted down, and responsibility was taken for them by the nation, but at the expense of their individual liberty. Between the confined and society there was an implicit system of obligation: they had the right to be nourished, but they had to accept the physical and moral constraints of confinement.

The 1656 edict addressed a quite undifferentiated mass, made up of a population with no resources and no social moorings, an underclass that had been abandoned, displaced against its will due to economic change. Less than two weeks after it had been signed, the edict was being proclaimed in the streets. Paragraph 9 stipulated that:

> We forbid most formally any person of either sex, regardless of their age and origin, quality or birth, and whatever their condition, be they able or unable, ill or convalescent, curable or incurable, to beg in the city and the faubourgs of Paris, or in the churches, or at church doors, or at the doors of houses, or in the streets, or anywhere else, publicly or in secret, by day or by night, . . . on pain of whipping for the first offence, and galleys for the second, for men and boys, and with banishment for men and women.

On Sunday, 13 May 1657, a solemn mass was sung at Saint-Louis de la Pitié in honour of the Holy Spirit, and on the morning of the 14th, the militia, who in the popular imagination were to become immortalised as the Hospital Archers, went out hunting for beggars for the first time, and brought them back to the different buildings of the Hospital. Four years on, the Salpêtrière was home to 1,460 women and children, while at the Pitié there were 98 boys, 897 girls aged between 7 and 17, and 95 women; at Bicêtre there were 1,615 men; at the Savonnerie, 305 boys aged between 8 and 13, and in Scipio there were 530 pregnant or nursing women and infants. Married couples were not allowed at first, regardless of their situation, and the administration was instructed to feed them in their home, but soon a donation from Mazarin meant that they too could be lodged at the Hospital. In all, between 5,000 and 6,000 people.

Confinement had the same meaning throughout Europe, in these early days at least. It was one of the first responses that the seventeenth century offered to the economic crisis that was affecting the whole of the Western world: wages were falling, unemployment was widespread and the money supply was dwindling, probably as a repercussion of the crisis in the Spanish economy.[74] Even in England, which of all the countries in Western Europe was the least dependent on the system, the same problems had to be resolved. Despite all the measures that had been taken to avoid unemployment and wage falls, poverty was increasing inexorably around the country.[75] In 1622 a pamphlet appeared, the *Grevious Groan for the Poor*, which was attributed to Dekker, and underlined the peril the country faced, while condemning a widespread negligence:

> Though the number of the poor do daily increase, all things yet worketh for the worst on their behalf; [for there hath been no collection for them, no, not these seven years, in many parishes in the land, especially in the country towns; but] many of these parishes turneth forth their poor, yea, and their lusty labourers that will not work, [or for any misdemeanour want work,] to beg, filch and steal for their maintenance, so that the country is pitifully pestered with them.[76]

The fear was that the country might be overrun, and as it was impossible for them to move to another country as on the continent, it was suggested that they might be 'banished and conveyed to the New-Found Land, the East and West Indies'.[77] In 1630, the King set up a royal commission to supervise the vigorous application of the laws concerning the poor. The same year he published a series of 'Orders and Directions' that recommended that all beggars and vagabonds should be pursued, as well as 'any persons that live out of service, or that live idly and will not work for reasonable wages, or live to spend all they have in the ale house'. They were to be punished in accordance with the law, and placed in houses of correction. As for those who had dependants, it was first of all to be verified that they were in fact genuinely married, and that their children were baptised, for 'these people live like savages, neither marry nor bury, nor christen; which licentious libertie make so many delight to be rogues and wanderers'.[78] Despite the recovery that began in England in the middle of the century, the problem had still not been solved by the time of Cromwell, as the Lord Mayor complained that a 'Vermine of the Commonwealth doth now swarme in and about this City, and Liberties disturbing and annoying the inhabitants and passengers, by hanging on coaches, and clamorously begging at the doores of Churches and private Houses.'[79]

For many years to come, houses of correction and the Hôpital Général would serve as places for the authorities to hide the homeless and the unemployed. Each time there was an economic crisis and the number of jobless soared, the houses of confinement assumed once again their primary economic *raison d'être*. In the mid-eighteenth century, France once again found itself in crisis. Rouen was home to 12,000 workers who were forced to beg, Tours had just as many, and the workshops and factories in Lyon too began to close. The Comte d'Argenson, who had charge of the department of Paris and the mounted police, gave an order to arrest all beggars in the kingdom. His police set out to do it in the countryside, and the same was done in Paris, where they could not escape, since they were 'harried from all sides'.[80]

But outside the times of crisis, confinement took on another meaning, and its repressive aspects were soon paralleled by a second use. It was no longer simply a question of hiding away the unemployed, but now also of giving them work which could serve the interests and the prosperity of all. The cycle was clear: in times of high wages and full employment, they provided a low-cost workforce, while in a slump they absorbed the unemployed, and protected society against unrest and riots. It should not be forgotten that the first workhouses in England appeared in Worcester, Norwich and Bristol, which were the most heavily industrialised parts of the country, nor that the first Hôpital Général opened in Lyon, forty years before Paris had one,[81] and that Hamburg, the largest city in Germany, had its *Zuchthaus* from 1620. Its regulations, published in 1622, were very precise. All inmates had to work. A register of the value of their work was kept, and they were paid one quarter of that. For work was not simply to busy idle hands: it also had to be productive. The eight directors of the institution drew up a general plan. The *Werkmeister* gave a task to every inmate, and checked at the end of each week that it had been accomplished successfully. The work rule remained in force until the end of the eighteenth century, as Howard noted that there inmates

> were knitting and spinning; weaving stockings, linen, hair and wool, and rasping logwood and hartshorn; (the task of logwood to a strong man is forty-five pounds *per* day). Some men and horses worked at a fulling-mill; and a smith was in constant employment.[82]

Each institution in Germany had its own speciality: spinning was done above all in Bremen, Brunswick, Hanover, Breslau and Berlin; weaving was the speciality of Hanover. Woodworking went on in Bremen and Hanover.

In Nuremberg, inmates polished glass for lenses, and in Mentz the main task was grinding flour.[83]

When the first houses of confinement opened in England, the country was in the depths of economic recession. The Act of 1610 only recommended that all these institutions be linked to mills, spinning shops and wool-carding workshops, to keep the inmates occupied. But that moral concern was turned into an economic tactic when the Navigation Act was passed in 1651 and the base rate was lowered, as the economic situation improved and commerce and industry began to develop. Now the aim was to use in the best manner possible – i.e. by the cheapest means possible – all of the available workforce. When John Carey published his plans for a workhouse in Bristol, he stressed above all the need for work: 'The poor of both sexes may be employed in beating hemp, dressing and spinning flax, or in carding and spinning wool and cotton.'[84] Worcester specialised in canvas and in making clothes, and had a special workshop for children. All of which did occasionally run into difficulties. The idea was to ensure that workhouses benefited from the proximity of local industries and markets, and it was perhaps also believed that low-cost production would have a stabilising influence on prices. But manufacturers protested.[85] Daniel Defoe remarked that the fierce competition that the workhouses sometimes provided made new paupers in one region while suppressing them elsewhere: 'this is giving to one what you take away from the other; putting a vagabond in an honest man's employment, and putting diligence on the tenters to find out some other work to maintain his family'.[86] Realising the dangers that this competition was creating, the authorities increasingly allowed this obligation to work to disappear. Inmates were no longer allowed to earn even a sufficient amount to pay for their keep, and some were simply sent to prison instead, where at least they would receive free bread. There were few Bridewells where 'any work is done, or can be done. The prisoners have neither tools, nor materials of any kind, but spend their time in sloth, profaneness and debauchery.'[87]

When the Hôpital Général was created in Paris, the aim was that begging would disappear, not that all the inmates should work. But it would seem that Colbert, like his English contemporaries, saw in assistance through work both a remedy for unemployment and a stimulus for the development of manufacturing.[88] Intendants in the provinces were instructed to ensure that charitable houses had some economic significance.

All the poor who are able should do a day's work, both to keep them from the idleness that is the root of all evil and to get them used to working, while enabling them also to earn a portion of their food.

On occasion, there were arrangements whereby local entrepreneurs used an asylum workforce for their own profit. It was stipulated, for example, in a 1708 agreement, that a merchant would deliver wool, soap and coal to the Charité in Tulle, and that in return he would receive carded and woven wool. The profits were shared between the entrepreneur and the hospital.[89] In Paris too, there were several attempts to transform some of the larger buildings in the Hôpital Général into factories. If the author of an anonymous memoir published in 1790 is to be believed, in the Pitié 'all the types of manufacturing done in the capital were tried out', until in desperation 'it was decided that laces should be made there, as that seemed to be the least wasteful enterprise'.[90] Attempts elsewhere were no more successful. There were countless initiatives to help Bicêtre pay its way, including thread and rope manufacture, mirror polishing, and most memorably the great well.[91] In 1781, rather than using horses, an attempt was made to use teams of prisoners working in shifts from five a.m. to eight p.m. to draw up the water. As a reformer noted around the time of the Revolution:

What could have lain behind this strange decision? Was it a wish to save money, or was it simply the need to find some occupation for the prisoners? If it were the latter, would it not have been a better idea to occupy them with something of greater use to the hospital or themselves? If on the other hand it were a question of savings, it must be said that none spring to the eye.[92]

Over the course of the eighteenth century, the economic significance that Colbert had wished for the hospital slowly receded, and the place for obligatory work became a site of privileged idleness. 'Why is there such disorder at Bicêtre?' asked the Revolutionaries of 1789. The answer had already been provided by the seventeenth century: 'Idleness. And the simple remedy is work.'

The classical age used confinement in an equivocal manner, making it play a double role: it was to absorb unemployment, or at least erase its most visible social effects, and it was to keep prices low, when they seemed to be rising too sharply. It acted alternately on the labour market and on the cost of production. In practice, houses of confinement do not seem to have played the role that was expected of them very effectively. While they provided a home for the unemployed, they did little more than mask poverty, and prevent social and political unrest among those who had no work. Placing the unemployed in mandatory workshops created more unemployment nearby or in similar sectors.[93] Any effect on prices was at best artificial, the cost of the products manufactured being out of proportion to that of production when the cost of confinement was included.

*

Measured against their functional value, the creation of these houses of confinement might be seen as a failure. Their disappearance, throughout Europe, as centres for the indigent and prisons for poverty, in the early days of the nineteenth century confirms their ultimate failure showing them to be a transitory remedy that failed to address any real issues, an ill-conceived precautionary social measure produced by the nascent age of industry. Yet within that failure, the classical age had carried out an irreducible experiment. What to modern eyes appears as a clumsy dialectic between prices and production took its real significance from an ethical consciousness of work, where the complexities of economic mechanisms were less important than the assertion of a value.

In this first take-off period of industrialisation, labour did not appear to be linked to problems it might cause. On the contrary, it is seen rather as a general remedy, an infallible panacea that solves all forms of poverty. Labour and poverty face each other in a simple opposition, and the domain of the one is in inverse proportion to that of the other. In classical thought, the power that labour was believed to possess to make poverty disappear came not from its productive capacity but from a sort of moral enchantment. The effectiveness of labour was perceived as deriving from its ethical transcendence. Since the Fall, the punishment of work had the force of penance, and was a means of redemption. What forced man to work was not a law of nature, but the consequences of a curse. The earth was not to blame for that sterility into which it would fall if man remained idle:

> the earth has not sinned, and if she is cursed, it is on account of the
> fallen men who work to render her plentiful: the earth gives no useful

fruit, even the most necessary, other than through the continual arduous efforts of man.[94]

The obligation to work is not linked to any confidence in nature, and it was not even through any obscure faithfulness to man that the earth was to reward man's labours. That theme comes back constantly in the thought of both Catholics and Protestants, showing that labour itself does not of necessity bear fruit. The harvest, and the wealth that it entailed, were not the result of a dialectic of work and nature. Calvin's admonition was as follows: 'Let us not then thinke, that man's care & skill, or his travell and endevour can make the ground fertile: but that the blessing of GOD ruleth all.'[95] The danger that man might toil in vain if God failed to intervene in his bounty was a possibility that Bossuet recognised in his turn: 'The expected harvest, the fruit of our labours, may come to nought, for we are constantly at the mercy of the unpredictable heavens, which may open to drown the tender shoots at any moment.'[96] This precarious enterprise, to which nature was never obliged to respond other than upon a specific will of God, was nonetheless obligatory, not on the level of any natural synthesis, but on the level of a moral one. The poor man who, refusing to 'torment' the soil, expected God to come to his aid on the grounds that He had promised to feed the birds of the air, was disobeying one of the fundamental laws of scripture – 'Thou shalt not tempt the Lord thy God'. The man who desired not to work, said Calvin, 'trieth God's power too far'.[97] It was tantamount to demanding a miracle, while the real miracle was that man was recompensed freely for his labours on a daily basis.[98] Toil was not a law of nature, but it was contained in the state of man since the fall. For that reason idleness was an act of rebellion, and in some senses the worst of all possible revolts: expecting nature to be as bountiful as she had been when man lived in a state of innocence was a denial of Adam's fault. Pride had been man's sin before the fall, but idleness was the ultimate form of pride for fallen man, the derisory pride born out of poverty, and in this world where only weeds and briars grow wild of their own accord, it was the fault *par excellence*. For the Middle Ages, pride (*superbia*) had been the greatest sin, *radix malorum omnium* (the root of all evil). If Huizinga is to be believed, there was a time in the early days of the Renaissance when avarice could claim that privilege, as in Dante's *cicca cupidigia*.[99] But all seventeenth-century texts by contrast agree on the infernal triumph of idleness, and it was idleness that now led the great round of the vices and encouraged all the others. It should be remembered that the edict founding the Hôpital Général stated clearly that one of its aims was to prevent 'begging and idleness, the source of all unrest'. Bourdaloue echoed that condemnation of idleness, the miserable pride of fallen man: 'What then is the disorder of an idle life? Saint Ambrose replies quite unambiguously that it is a second revolt against God.'[100] In the houses of confinement, work therefore took on an ethical significance: as idleness had become the supreme form of revolt, the idle were forced into work, into the endless leisure of labour without utility or profit.

The economic as well as moral demand for confinement was thus the result of a certain experience of work. In the classical world, work and idleness created a dividing line that replaced the exclusion of the lepers in the medieval world. Both literally and in spirit, the asylum took the place of the leprosarium in the landscape of the moral universe as in the physical geography of haunted places. The ancient rites of excommunication were once again renewed, but this time in the world of production and commerce. And in these places where the evil of idleness was condemned, the inventions of a society that read an ethical transcendence into the law of work, madness too one day appeared, eventually making this space its own. The day would come when these barren, idle places would be taken over by the mad, as though in accordance with some obscure, ancient right. The nineteenth century will consider it rational, even necessary that these places be filled with the insane, where 150 years earlier it had seemed normal to lock up paupers, beggars and the unemployed.

The fact that the mad had been caught up in this great proscription of idleness is not without significance. From the outset they had had their place there beside the poor, both good and bad, and those who were idle by choice or necessity. Like the poor, they were subject to the rule of compulsory labour, indeed in many cases the singularity of their condition became perceptible against the uniformity of this constraint. In the workshops where they were expected to blend in with the others, they often signalled themselves through their inability to work and to follow the rhythms of collective life. The need that the eighteenth century discovered to give a specific structure to the lives of the insane, and the great crisis in confinement that was evident on the eve of the Revolution, were linked to the experience of madness that resulted from this general obligation to work.[101] The mad had been locked up from long before the seventeenth century, but it was only then that they found themselves 'confined', grouped together with a population with whom they were believed to have something in common. Up until the Renaissance, the perception of madness had been linked to the presence of imaginary transcendences. From the classical age, and for the first time, madness was seen through an ethical condemnation of idleness in the social immanence now grounded on a community of work. That community of work had an ethical power to exclude, which allowed it to expel, as though to another world, all forms of social uselessness. It was in this *other world*, surrounded by the sacred powers of labour, that madness was to take on the status still familiar to us. If in the classic form of madness there is an element that speaks of an *elsewhere*, of *something else*, it is not because the mad do come from a different heaven, that of the meaningless, still bearing its signs, it is simply that they have crossed the frontiers of the bourgeois order, and become alien to the sacred limits of its ethics.

*

The relationship between the practice of confinement and the constraints of work was not therefore solely a result of economic conditions: a moral perception underpinned it and provided its force. When the Board of Trade published its report on the poor, proposing a means of 'rendering them useful to the public', it clearly stated that the origin of poverty was neither food shortages nor unemployment, but 'the relaxation of discipline and the corruption of morals'.[102] The 1656 edict, among moral condemnations, also contained some unusual threats: 'the libertinage of beggars leads to an abject abandonment bringing crimes of all sorts, which brings the wrath of God down on the State if their wrongdoing goes unpunished'. This 'libertinage' did not simply refer to their refusal to comply with the great obligation to work, but was a moral question:

> The experience of those who worked with such people has shown that many of them of both sexes, as well as their children, are unbaptised, and live in an almost complete ignorance of religion, contempt for the Sacraments and the continual habit of vices of all varieties.

Hence the Hôpital Général was not simply a refuge for the old, the infirm, and those whom sickness prevented from working, and neither was it like a forced labour workshop; it was rather a moral institution destined to punish and castigate a certain 'void' of conscience, which was not serious enough to be brought before a human court, but which the severity of penance alone was insufficient to correct. The Hôpital Général had the status of an ethical institution. Its directors had a moral charge, and for that reason they were granted the judicial and material apparatus of repression. 'They are granted full powers where authority, direction, administration, commerce, policing, tribunals, correction and punishment are concerned', and to that end, they had at their disposal 'gallows, iron collars, prisons and dungeons'.[103]

It is in such a context that the obligation to work is best understood: it was both an ethical exercise and a moral guarantee. It was a moral ascesis, a punishment, and the sign of a certain disposition of the heart. Prisoners who showed the ability and the desire to work could be set free, not so that they might be useful members of society once again but because they had renewed their allegiance to the great ethical pact that underpinned human existence. In April 1684, a new ordinance created a section inside the hospital for young men and women under the age of 25, and it stipulated that work was to occupy the greater part of the day, and was to be accompanied by readings from certain 'pious books'. Rather than stressing the productive nature of their work, the regulation made it plain that this was of a purely repressive nature: 'they should be forced to work for as long as possible, at activities as arduous as their strength and the location of the hospital permit'. Only after these initial stages, where they were given the opportunity to demonstrate a willingness to change their ways, should they be given instruction in a trade 'fitting their sex and inclination'. Any wrongdoing was to be punished by 'curtailing their soup ration, increasing their workload, sending them to prison, or by the use of the other punishments applied in these hospitals, which directors consider reasonable'.[104] A reading of the 'General regulations of what is to be done each day in the Maison de Saint-Louis de la Salpêtrière' makes it clear that the obligation to work was part of an attempt at moral constraint and improvement, which if not the ultimate meaning, provided the essential justification for confinement.[105]

This invention, a place of constraint where moral reform was brought about through administrative placement, was an important phenomenon. For the first time, moral establishments had been founded, where an astonishing synthesis between moral obligations and social laws came into being. From then on, the order of the state outlawed the disorders of the heart. Naturally, this was not the first time in European society that moral shortcomings, even of the most private nature, had been perceived as being an attack on the tacit or written laws of the land. But in the Great Confinement of the classical age, the essential, new event was that the law no longer condemned; instead sinners were locked up in these cities of pure morality, where the law that should govern the human heart was applied without mercy and without compromise, as a rigorous form of physical constraint. A sort of reversibility from the moral order of principles to the physical realm was set, with the implication that one could pass from the former to the latter in a pure manner, without constraint or an abuse of power. The exhaustive application of the moral law was no longer the preserve of accomplished acts, but was present from the very first social synthesis. Morality could be administered like commerce or economics.

In these institutions set up under the rule of absolute monarchy – institutions that for many years remained the symbol of its arbitrary power – the great bourgeois (and latterly republican) idea that virtue too is an affair of state can be discerned, together with the belief that virtue can be established by decree and policed by civil authority. The walls of these houses of confinement contained something like a photographic negative of the city of morals that was beginning to haunt the bourgeois con-sciousness of the seventeenth century; a city for those who had tried to escape from the outset, where the rule of law was kept by force and no appeal was possible, where good was sovereign and threat triumphed, where virtue's only recompense was that it was spared further punish-ment, so much was it believed to be its own reward. This strange republic of good was born in the shadow of the bourgeois city, and it was imposed by force on all those who were believed to have had any truck with the forces of evil. This was the reverse of the grand dream, and the greatest worry for the bourgeoisie of the classical age: the laws of the state and the laws of the human heart identical at last. 'Let our politicians deign to suspend their calculations in order to reflect on these examples,' said Rousseau, 'and learn once and for all that with money one has everything, except morals and Citizens.'[106]

This dream was one of the fundamental principles that lay behind the founding of the house of confinement in Hamburg. It was the task of one of the stewards to ensure that:

all in the house are properly instructed as to moral and religious duties . . . the school master must instruct the children in religion, and encourage them, at proper times, to learn and repeat portions of Scripture. He must also teach them reading, writing and accounts, and a decent behaviour to those that visit the house. He must take care they attend divine service, and are orderly at it.[107]

In England, the rules of the workhouses stressed the importance of watching over the morals of the inmates, and instilling in them a religious education. In Plymouth for example, provisions were made for a school-master to be appointed, who was required to be 'pious, sober and discreet', and every morning and evening at the appointed time it fell to him to lead the prayers. On Saturday afternoons and on feast days he had to address the inmates, encourage them and instruct them in 'the fundamental parts of the Protestant religion, according to the doctrine of the Church of England'.[108] Hamburg or Plymouth, *Zuchthäuser* or work-houses, all over Protestant Europe these fortresses of moral order sprang up, teaching the religion that was the essential foundation of civic peace.

In Catholic lands, the goal was the same but the religious imprint was slightly more marked, as is borne out by the works of Saint Vincent de Paul:

The ultimate purpose for which inmates were removed from the bustle of the world and placed in this solitude as pensioners was to remove them from the slavery of sin, to prevent them from falling into eternal damnation, and to provide them with the means to perfect happiness both in this life and the next. They will learn to love divine providence for that . . . Experience has shown all too often that the source of the disorder so common among the young people of today is a lack of teaching and insubordination to spiritual matters, as they would rather follow their evil inclinations than the holy inspiration that comes from God or the charitable advice of their parents.[109]

The aim therefore was to deliver the inmates from a world which in their weakness was nothing more than an invitation to sin, bringing them back to a solitude where their only companionship would take the form of the daily presence of the guards, who 'would play the role of their guardian angels, teaching them, instructing them, bringing them consolation and salvation'. At the Charité, great care was taken to bring order to lives and consciences, and in the course of the eighteenth century it became increasingly clear that such was the true purpose of these houses of confinement. In 1765, new regulations were drawn up for the Charité at Château-Thierry. They stated that

> the Prior [was] to visit all the prisoners in turn, separately, at least once a week, bringing them consolation and encouraging them to improve their ways, and assuring himself that they are receiving the treatment that they deserve: his assistant should do this every day.[110]

All these morally ordered prisons could equally have borne the motto that Howard had found on the walls at Mentz: 'If even wild beasts can be tamed to the yoke, we should not despair of reclaiming irregular men.'[111] For the Catholic Church, as for Protestant countries, confinement represents an authoritarian model of the myth of social happiness: an order of policing totally transparent to religious principles, and a religion whose demands could be entirely satisfied by the rules of policing, and the constraints it can inflict. The institutions were an attempt to demonstrate that good order could coincide with virtue, and in that sense 'confinement' hides both a metaphysics of the city and a politics of religion, and takes its place, in a tyrannical form of synthesis, in that distance that separates the garden of God from the cities which men, thrown out of paradise, had built with their own hands. The house of confinement of the classical age was the most intensely charged symbol of that form of 'police' and considered itself the civic equivalent of religion for the construction of a perfect city. All the moral themes of confinement are to be found already in de La Mare's *Traité de police*, where religion is seen as 'first and foremost' among matters to be treated by the police.

> If men were sufficiently wise to comply perfectly with its requirements, it would be the sole matter that the police should treat. Then there would be no more corrupted morals, temperance would ward off sickness, hard work, frugality and prudence would ensure that man never wanted for anything, charity would banish vice, and public order would be assured, humility and simplicity would destroy all that is vain or dangerous in the human sciences, good faith would reign in the sciences and the arts . . . the poor would find assistance through voluntary means, and begging

would be banished; we can say without doubt that if the tenets of religion were strictly adhered to, policing would happen of its own accord . . . Hence the law makers have wisely grounded the felicity and the durability of the State on Religion."[112]

Confinement was an institutional creation peculiar to the seventeenth century. It immediately took on a scale that bore no relation to the practice of imprisonment in the Middle Ages. As an economic measure and a social precaution, it was an invention. But in the history of unreason, it signals a decisive event: the moment when madness is seen against the social horizon of poverty, the inability to work and the impossibility of integrating into a social group. It was the moment when it started to be classified as one of the problems of the city. The new meanings assigned to poverty, and the importance accorded to the obligation to work and the ethical values surrounding it were ultimately determining factors in the experience of madness, transforming its meaning.

A new sensibility had been born: a line had been drawn, a threshold established, and its purpose was banishment. The society of the classical age created a neutral zone in its own concrete space, a blank page where the real life of the city was suspended; order was no longer in a free conflict with disorder, and reason no longer attempted to find its way through places that eluded it or refused it entry. Reason reigned in a pure manner, triumphantly, and victory over unchained unreason was guaranteed in advance. Madness was denied the imaginary liberty that still allowed it to flourish at the time of the Renaissance. Not so long ago it was still visible in the light of day, as in *King Lear* or *Don Quixote*, but in the space of less than half a century it found itself a recluse in the fortress of confinement, bound fast to Reason, to the rules of morality and their monotonous nights.

III

THE CORRECTIONAL WORLD

Contained within the confinement walls was not just poverty and madness. There were faces far more varied, and it is not always easy to understand what these silhouettes had in common.

It is clear that confinement, in its primitive forms, worked as a social mechanism, and that the mechanism was extremely widespread, stretching from elementary economic regulation to the great bourgeois dream of a city where an authoritarian synthesis of nature and virtue reigned supreme. From here, believing that the meaning of confinement can be reduced to an obscure social mechanism that allowed society to expel heterogeneous or harmful elements is but a step away. To that way of thinking, confinement was merely the spontaneous elimination of the 'asocial'. The classical age is taken to have neutralised, with sure-footed efficiency – all the more efficacious for being blind – the people who, not without hesitation or danger, we now divide between prisons and corrective institutions, psychiatric institutions and the psychoanalyst's couch. One group of historians (if that isn't too grand a term) set out to defend this view at the turn of the twentieth century.[1] If they had spotted the obvious link between the policing of confinement and political economy, it would have been grist to their mill, and perhaps the only element of their hypothesis worthy of serious consideration. They would have been able to demonstrate the backdrop of social sensibility against which the medical consciousness of madness had begun to take shape, and the extent to which they remained linked together, as it was that sensibility that served as a regulatory element whenever it was necessary to decide between confinement or freedom.

That sort of analysis supposes an immutable continuity in madness, which is supposed to come equipped with its timeless, intricate psychological complexities, whose truth was only gradually discovered. After it had been ignored for centuries, or at least very imperfectly known, the classical age would have dimly perceived it as a rupture in family structures, a social disorder and a danger for the state. And little by little, that first perception became increasingly organised, and slowly perfected itself into a medical consciousness, which came to classify as an ill of nature that which until then was only recognised in an unease within society. The argument would also require a sort of orthogenesis, as man was seen to move directly from social experience to scientific knowledge, progressing from group consciousness to positive science, the former being the raw form of the latter, something like the primitive elements of its vocabulary. Social experience and practical knowledge would be an early form of knowledge, a step on its journey towards perfection.[2] The object of knowledge, to that way of thinking, pre-exists the investigation, since that is what was apprehended before being rigorously circumscribed by positive science: in its atemporal solidity it is shielded from history, locked into its own truth, where it slumbers until facts, in their positivity, reach awareness.

But there is no certainty that madness was content to sit locked up in its immutable identity, waiting for psychiatry to perfect its art, before it emerged blinking from the shadows into the blinding light of truth. Nor is it clear that confinement was above all, or even implicitly, a series of measures put in place to deal with madness. It is not even certain that in this repetition of the ancient gesture of segregation at the threshold of the classical age, the modern world was aiming to wipe out all those who, either as a species apart or a spontaneous mutation, appeared as 'asocial'. The fact that the internees of the eighteenth century bear a resemblance to our modern vision of the asocial is undeniable, but it is above all a question of results, as the character of the marginal was produced by the gesture of segregation itself. For the day came when this man, banished in the same exile all over Europe in the mid-seventeenth century, suddenly became an outsider, expelled by a society to whose norms he could not be seen to conform; and for our own intellectual comfort, he then became a candidate for prisons, asylums and punishment. In reality, this character is merely the result of superimposed grids of exclusion.

The gesture that proscribed was as abrupt as the one that had isolated the lepers, and in both cases, the meaning of the gesture should not be mistaken for its effect. Lepers were not excluded to prevent contagion, any more than in 1657, 1 per cent of the population of Paris was confined merely to deliver the city from the 'asocial'. The gesture had a different dimension: it did not isolate strangers who had previously remained invisible, who until then had been ignored by force of habit. It altered the familiar cityscape by giving them new faces, strange, bizarre silhouettes that nobody recognised. Strangers were found in places where their presence had never previously been suspected: the process punctured the fabric of society, and undid the familiar. Through this gesture, something inside man was placed outside of himself, and pushed over the edge of our horizon. It is the gesture of confinement, in short, which created alienation.

It follows from this that to rewrite the history of that banishment is to draw an archaeology of that alienation. What is to be determined is not the pathological or police category that was targeted, which would be to suppose that alienation pre-existed exclusion, but to understand instead how the gesture was accomplished, i.e. the operations which together, in their equilibrium, composed its totality, and the diverse horizons from which those who suffered the same exclusion originated, to investigate how men of the classical age experienced themselves at the moment when familiar faces began to become strange, and lose their resemblance with that image. If the decree does have a meaning, where modern men have designated their own *alienated* truth in the mad, then it must be in the extent to which the field of alienation where the mad found themselves banished (together with other figures who to our way of thinking had so little in common with them) had already been constituted before it came to be symbolised and peopled by the insane. That field was circumscribed in real terms in the space of confinement, and the form it took should show us how the experience of madness came into existence.

*

Once the Great Confinement had come into being across Europe, who exactly was to be found inside the walls of these cities of exile that sprang up at the gates of towns? Who do we find forming a sort of kinship with the insane, a kinship they would have such problems shaking off at the end of the eighteenth century?

A 1690 survey at the Salpêtrière revealed the presence of some 3,000 inmates. A large proportion were female paupers, vagabonds and beggars. But the different sections had diverse elements, whose presence can only partly be explained through poverty. In Saint-Théodore, 41 prisoners were there due to *lettres de cachet*; the gaol had eight 'common people'; there were 20 'decrepit' women in Saint-Paul, the Madeleine had 91 women who were 'sick, or in a second childhood', Sainte-Geneviève had 80 'girlish old women', Saint-Levège had 72 epileptics, Saint-Hilaire had 80 women who had 'returned to child-hood', Sainte-Catherine had 69 'malformed, damaged simpletons', while women who were simply labelled mad were divided between Sainte-Elizabeth, Sainte-Jeanne and the dungeons, according to whether they were 'weak in the mind', intermittently mad or violent. The House of Correction was home to 22 girls because they were deemed 'incorrigible'.[3]

That is merely one example. The population was just as varied at Bicêtre, so much so that in 1737, an attempt was made to divide them up logically into five 'employments'. The first was for the 'Maison de force', the dungeons, gaols and cells reserved for *lettre de cachet* prisoners; the second and third were for the 'deserving poor' and people paralysed to a greater or lesser degree; the mad and the alienated were reserved for the fourth section, while the final section was for the venereal, convalescents and the children of inmates.[4] When Howard visited the workhouse in Berlin in 1781, he found, 'beggars, idle persons, petty offenders of both sexes . . . poor and criminals . . . aged and infirm'.[5] For 150 years, confinement went its monotonous way throughout Europe; faults were equalised, and suffering was alleviated. From 1650 to the time of Tuke, Wagnitz and Pinel, the Brothers of Saint John of God, the Congregationists of Saint Lazarus, the Guardians of Bethlem, Bicêtre and the *Zuchthäuser* recited the litanies of confinement in their lengthy registers: 'debauched', 'imbecile', 'prodigal', 'infirm', 'of unsound mind', 'libertine', 'ungrateful son', 'dissolute father', 'prosti-tute', 'insane', and so forth.[6] No attempt was made to discriminate between them, and all were cast into the same abstract dishonour. Any feeling of surprise that the sick should be locked up together with the insane, and that madmen and criminals should be confused, was to come later. At this point, confinement was a uniform fact.

To us, the differences are clear, and the undistinguishing consciousness that mixes them together looks like ignorance. But it was a positive fact, and demonstrated, throughout the classical age, an original and irreducible experience. To our eyes it seems a strangely closed domain, oddly silent when we consider that this was the first homeland for modern madness. But it is not to our knowledge that we should refer to understand what we take to be ignorance: rather we must examine that experience, to understand the terms in which it thought of itself, and what it could articulate of it. Only then will we understand how madness blended in with other experiences, and how it slowly became detached from those experiences, while still maintaining that dangerous association.

For confinement did not simply play the negative role of exclusion, but also had a positive organising role. Its practices and regulations constituted a domain of experience that had unity, coherence and function. It brought together in one field characters and values where preceding cultures had seen no resemblance, and it imperceptibly nudged them towards madness, laying the ground for an experience – our own – where they identified themselves as clearly belonging to the realm of mental alienation. For such a *rapprochement* to be carried out, a whole reorganisation of the ethical world was necessary, and a new dividing line was needed between good and evil, the acceptable and the blameworthy, and new social norms were required for social integration. Confinement was merely the visible phenomenon on the surface of this deeper process, and an integral part of the whole of classical culture. There were certain experiences that the sixteenth century had either accepted or refused, formulated or sidelined, which were now taken up by the seventeenth century and grouped together and banished *en masse*, exiling them together with madness, creating a uniform world of Unreason. These experiences can be summed up by saying that they all touch either on sexuality and its relation with the organisation of the bourgeois family, or on profanation in relation to the new conception of the sacred and of religious rituals, or on *libertinage*, i.e. the new relations that were beginning to emerge between free thinking and the system of the passions. Together with madness, these three domains of experience form a homogeneous world in the space of confinement where the meaning of mental alienation as we know it today was born. By the end of the eighteenth century it would seem obvious – in a way that was never really put into words – that certain forms of libertine thought, like those of Sade, had some connection with delirium and madness, and it seemed equally obvious that magic, alchemy, certain sacrilegious practices and also some forms of sexuality were directly linked to unreason and certain types of mental illness. There would come a time when all that would take its place among the major symptoms of madness, and be considered among its most essential manifestations. But for these unities to be constituted as significant to our eyes, the upheavals operated by classicism in the relations between madness and the domain of ethical experience were necessary.

*

From the earliest months of the great confinement, the venereal had their place in the Hôpital Général. Men were sent to Bicêtre, and women went to the Salpêtrière. The medical staff at the Hôtel-Dieu were forbidden to take them in or give them any form of treatment at all. Pregnant women were admitted under exceptional circumstances, on the understanding that they were not to be treated like other patients, with only an apprentice surgeon attending the birth. The Hôpital Général was therefore to admit the 'corrupted', but not without formality: a debt had to be paid to public morality, and patients had to be prepared on the path of punishment and penance for their return to the communion from which sin had caused their expulsion. Entrance to the *grand mal* quarter was refused without the necessary paperwork: and the paper required was not a letter of confession, but a certificate of punishment. Such was the decision, after deliberation, of the administration of the Hôpital Général in 1679: 'Sufferers from venereal diseases will only be admitted after correction has been carried out, and after they have been whipped: this much is to be certified by their referral papers.'[7]

Originally, venereal sufferers had been treated no differently from victims of the other great ills, like the 'hunger, plague and other blights' that in the view expressed by Maximilian in the 1495 Diet of Worms had been sent by God to punish mankind. Such suffering was of universal value, and in no way a sentence meted out for any particular immoral act. In Paris, sufferers of what was known as Naples Sickness were admitted to the Hôtel-Dieu, and as was the case in every other hospital in the Catholic world their only obligation was to make a mandatory confession, as was required from all patients who entered the hospital. However, at the end of the Renaissance they began to be regarded with a new eye. Thierry de Héry was of the opinion that none of the causes usually advanced to explain the origins of the disease, like pestilential air or contaminated water, provided a sufficient explanation:

> For which reason we consider the disease to have its origins in the divine indignation of the creator of all things, who when he considered the libidinous, lascivious, petulant lust of men allowed such ill to reign among them, as a revenge and punishment for the enormous sin of luxury. It was precisely in this manner that God commanded Moses to throw dust up into the air in the presence of the Pharaoh, so that throughout Egypt all the animals and men would be covered with boils.[8]

There were more than 200 inmates of this variety when the decision was taken to expel them in 1590. Suddenly they were proscribed, sent into an exile which rather than being a solely therapeutic isolation was a segregation. Initially they were given shelter in wooden huts near the Cathedral of Notre-Dame, before being exiled on the outskirts of the city in Saint-Germain-des-Prés, but their upkeep was expensive and they brought unrest. They were admitted once again, not without difficulty, inside the confines of the Hôtel-Dieu, before finally being found a more permanent asylum inside the walls of the General Hospitals.[9]

It was only then that the ceremonial became codified, bringing together, in a common intention to purify, whippings, traditional medicine and the sacrament of penance. The intention to punish, and to punish individually, became quite clear. Venereal disease had lost its apocalyptic character, and became instead a local marker of guilt. More explicitly, 'grand mal' patients only required these rites of purification if the origins of their disease were to be found in a disorder of the heart, a sin, understood as the result of a deliberate intention to sin. The regulations of the Hôpital Général left no room for doubt: the prescribed measures were 'of course' reserved for those

> men or women who had contracted the disease through their own dissipation or debauchery, and not for those who had caught it within

the confines of marriage or otherwise, as a wife from her husband, or a wet nurse from a child.[10]

Evil, it appeared, was no longer part of the destiny of the world, but was reflected instead in the transparent law of a logic of intentions.

Once the distinctions had been made, and the first punishments applied, the venereal were accepted into the hospital. And they were crammed inside. In 1781, 138 men occupied 60 beds in the Saint-Eustache quarter of Bicêtre, and in the Miséricorde in the Salpêtrière there were 125 beds for 224 women. Patients in the terminal stages of the disease were simply left to die. 'Grand Remedies' were applied to the others: never more, and rarely less than six weeks of care, starting of course with blood-letting and purging, then a week of baths for two hours per day, then purging again, followed by a full and complete confession to bring this first part of the treatment to a close. Rubbing with mercury could then begin, with all its efficacy. Each course of treatment lasted one month, and was followed by two more purges and one final bleeding to chase out the remaining morbific humours. Fifteen days of convalescence were then granted. After he had definitively made his peace with God, the patient was declared cured and sent away.

This 'therapeutic' demonstrates a rich tapestry of fantasy, and above all a profound complicity between medicine and morality, which give their full meaning to these purification practices. For the classical age, venereal disease was less a sickness than an impurity to which physical symptoms are correlated. Accordingly, medical perception is ruled by ethical perception, and on occasion even effaced by it. The body must be treated to remove the contagion, but the flesh must be punished, for it is the flesh that attaches us to sin. Mere corporal punishment was not enough: the flesh was to be pummelled and bruised, and leaving painful traces was not to be feared, as good health, all too frequently, transformed the human body into another opportunity for sinful conduct. The sickness was to be treated, but the good health that could lead to temptation was to be destroyed.

> Alas, I am not in the least surprised that a saint like Bernard constantly feared perfect health among his brothers: he knew where it led, if the flesh was not mortified in the manner of the apostles, and reduced to servitude through fasting and prayers.[11]

The 'treatment' reserved for the venereal was precisely of that nature, and was medicine that acted both against the disease and against good health – acting for the body but at the expense of the flesh. This is an idea that has important consequences for an understanding of certain treatments that were transposed as cures for madness in the course of the nineteenth century.[12]

For a period of nearly 150 years, the venereal were to be penned in side by side with the insane in a single enclosure, and the result was a certain stigma which for the modern consciousness was the sign of an obscure kinship, leading to similar fates within the same system of punishment. The notorious Petites-Maisons in the Rue de Sèvres in Paris was reserved more or less exclusively for the insane and for the venereal, and this until the end of the eighteenth century.[13] This kinship between the pains of madness and the punishment of debauchery was not some archaic trace in the European consciousness, but came into being on the threshold of modern times, as it was the seventeenth century that was almost entirely responsible for discovering it. By inventing the space of confinement in the imaginary geometry of its morality, the classical age found a homeland and a place of redemption for sins of the flesh and faults committed against reason. Madness found itself side by side with sin, and it is perhaps from there that stems the immemorial linking of unreason and guilt that the alienated today still feel to be their fate, and which doctors discover as a truth of nature. In this artificial space created out of nothing in the mid-seventeenth century, dark alliances were created, which more than 100 years of so-called 'positive psychiatry' have never managed to break, despite the fact that they came into being such a short time ago, in the age of rationalism.

It is strange that rationalism authorised this confusion between punishments and remedies, this quasi-identity between the act of punishment and the act that cures. It supposes a certain treatment at the junction of medicine and morality that was both an anticipation of the torments of eternal damnation and an attempt to bring the patient back to health. The key element is the ruse in medical reasoning that does good while inflicting pain. It is clearly that ruse that lies behind the sentence that Saint Vincent de Paul had printed above the regulations at Saint-Lazare, which was both a promise and a threat for all the prisoners: 'Whereas their temporary suffering will not prevent eternal damnation.' What followed was the religious system of control and repression which, by inscribing the temporal suffering in the order of penance that was always reversible into eternal terms, can and should exempt the sinner from the pains of hell. Human constraints come to the assistance of divine justice by striving to render it unnecessary. Repression thus becomes doubly efficacious, as it cures the body and purifies the soul. In that manner, confinement made possible the whole panoply of moral treatments, or therapeutic punishments, that were later to become the principal activity of the first asylums of the nineteenth century, for which Pinel, before Leuret, provided the formula by stating that it was occasionally 'useful to strongly shake up the imagination of the alienated, and imprint therein a sensation of terror'.[14]

The idea of a link between medicine and morality is no doubt as ancient as Greek medicine. But if the seventeenth century and the order of Christian reason inscribed it in their institutions, it was in a manner as far from that of the Greeks as could be imagined – in the form of repression, constraint, and the obligation to redeem one's soul.

*

On 24 March 1726, the Lieutenant of Police Hérault, assisted by the judges who presided over the Châtelet in Paris, made public a judgement whose terms stated that:

> Etienne Benjamin Deschauffours is declared guilty as charged of committing the crimes of sodomy mentioned in the trial. In reparation for this and other actions, Deschauffours is sentenced to be burnt alive in the Place de Grève, his ashes are to be scattered to the winds, and his goods and worldly possessions confiscated by the King.

The execution was carried out the same day.[15] This was one of the last capital punishments to be handed out in France for sodomy.[16] But consciences of the time were already sufficiently indignant about the severity of the punishment for Voltaire to record it when writing the entry on 'Socratic Love' in his *Dictionnaire philosophique*.[17] In most cases, the punishment, if it was not banishment to the provinces, was confinement in the Hôpital Général or in a house of detention.[18]

Confinement was a singular attenuation of the punishment, when compared to the ancient punishment of *ignis et incendium* – being burnt

at the stake – that the laws still on the statutes prescribed, which recommended that 'anyone who falls into these crimes is to be burnt alive. This
punishment, which has been adopted by our jurisprudence, applies
equally to men and women.'[19] But what gives particular meaning to this
new indulgence towards sodomy is the moral condemnation and the air
of scandal that was beginning to surround homosexuality in its social and
literary expressions. The moment when sodomites were being burnt for
the last time was also the moment when 'erudite libertinage', and a
whole culture of lyrical homosexuality that the Renaissance had tolerated
unquestioningly, began to disappear. It is as though sodomy, which had
previously been condemned in the same manner as magic and heresy,
and in the same context of religious profanity,[20] was now condemned on
purely moral grounds, like homosexuality itself. From now on it was the
homosexual element that became the chief matter of the accusation,
this being compounded by the practice of sodomy, and a scandalised
sensibility came into being regarding homosexual feelings.[21] Two
different experiences blended together, which had previously remained
separate: the sacred prohibitions concerning sodomy, and the amorous
ambiguities of homosexuality. One condemnation now applied to both,
drawing an entirely new dividing line in the field of emotions. What
comes into being is a new moral unity, freed from ancient punishments,
and already close to modern forms of guilt.[22] The homosexuality to which
the Renaissance had accorded a liberty of expression now passed into
silence, moved to the domain of the forbidden, inheriting the ancient
condemnation of the now desacrilised sodomy.

From this point onwards, a new relation between love and unreason
began to take shape. In Platonic culture, love had been divided up inside a
hierarchy of the sublime that likened it, according to its level, either to a
blind madness of the body, or to the great intoxication of the soul where
Unreason is in a position of knowledge. In their different forms, love and
madness shared out between them the different regions of the gnoses.
The modern age, after classicism, made a different choice, and love was
either reasoned or governed by unreason. Homosexuality belonged to
the second group and, little by little, it was forced to take its place in the
stratifications of madness. For the modern age it was firmly inside
unreason, placing within all sexuality an obligation to choose, through
which our era constantly repeats its decision. In the light of its own
ingenuity, psychoanalysis understood that all forms of madness have

roots in troubled sexuality; but to say that is to do little more than note that our culture, by a choice typical of its own form of classicism, placed sexuality on the dividing line of unreason. Since time immemorial, and probably in all cultures, sexuality has been governed by systems of constraint; but it is a comparatively recent particularity of our own culture to have divided it so rigorously into Reason and Unreason. As a consequence and degradation of that, it was not long before it was also classified into healthy or sick, normal or abnormal.

A further aspect of these categories of sexuality were the new views of prostitution and debauchery. In France, it was here that the majority of the inmates of the General Hospitals were recruited. As La Mare explained in his *Traité de Police*,

> What is required is a powerful remedy to deliver the public from this corruption, and no better, more prompt or efficacious remedy could be found than a house of confinement where it could be contained, where such people could be forced to live in a discipline proportionate to their sex, their age or their fault.[23]

The Lieutenant of Police had an absolute right to arrest without procedure any person caught in an act of public debauchery, until the Châtelet sentence was passed, which was without appeal.[24] But such measures were only taken if the scandal was public, or if there was a possibility that the interests of the families concerned would be compromised. The major concern was with ensuring that family inheritances were not squandered, or passed into unworthy hands.[25] In an important sense, confinement and the whole police structure that surrounded it served to control a certain order in family structures, which was at once a social regulator and a norm of reason.[26] Family and its requirements became one of the essential criteria of reason, and it was above all in its name that confinement was demanded and obtained.

The whole era bears witness to the great confiscation of sexual ethics by family morality, although the process of confiscation did not come about without debate or reservations. For a long time the *Précieux* movement resisted, and the moral importance of this resistance was considerable, even if its effects were precarious and short-lived. Their efforts to reinstate the rites of courtly love and maintain its integrity beyond matrimonial laws, and their attempts to create a sentimental solidarity or complicity to outwit the constraints of family were ultimately doomed to failure in the face of the triumph of bourgeois morality. Love was made banal by legal contracts. Saint-Evremond was all too aware of that, while still mocking the Précieux for whom 'love was still like a god . . . stirring no passion in their breast, but filling the role of religion'.[27] The ethical disquiet common to courtly love and its Précieux reincarnation were not long in disappearing, so that Molière could note on behalf of his class and for generations to come: 'Marriage is a sacred, holy thing, and honesty is to start out from there.' It was no longer love itself that was sacred, but the notarised pact of marriage: 'Love should only be made by means of a marriage contract.'[28] The institution of the family traced the circle of reason, and outside it lurked all the perils of insanity, where man might fall prey to unreason in all its fury. 'Oh unhappy earth,' lamented Bossuet, 'continually shrouded in a thick cloak of smoke from the dark vapours of tenebrous passion, hiding the sun and the sky, and constantly bringing down the thunder and lightning of divine justice, punishing the wickedness of humankind'.[29]

Born of and in the family, this new sensibility now dominates Western love, excluding anything that failed to conform to its order or interest as being a form of unreason. This was the time of the threat of Mme Jourdain: 'You are mad, husband mine, with these fantasies', and 'these are my rights that I defend, and all women will be behind me'.[30] Her words were not in vain, and the promises were kept, for the day would come when the Marquise d'Espart could demand the confinement of her husband simply on the appearance of a liaison that went against the interest of the family heritage: for to the eyes of the justice system, such a liaison was tantamount to a husband losing his reason.[31] The most common grounds for confinement were debauchery, prodigality, inadmissible liaisons and shameful marriages. This power of repression belonged neither entirely to the justice system nor to religion. It was directly linked to the king, yet at bottom it is not an illustration of the arbitrary nature of despotism, but rather of the newly rigorous character of the demands of family. Confinement was placed by absolute monarchy at the disposal of the bourgeois family.[32] Moreau openly admits as much in his 1771 Discourse on Justice:

> A family finds a viper in its breast, a cowardly individual who is capable of bringing dishonour. To avoid any such mishap the family swiftly

makes a decision which the courts should follow, and any sovereign has a duty to look favourably on any such family deliberations.[33]

Only under the Breteuil administration at the end of the eighteenth century did society begin to question the principle, while the crown made efforts to distance itself from the demands of the family. A 1784 circular declared that

> If a mature individual dishonours himself by marrying badly, ruins himself with inconsiderate expenditure, gives himself over to debauched excesses and keeps low company, none of these things in themselves seem sufficiently powerful motives to deprive of their liberty persons who are *sui juris* [i.e legally competent to manage their own affairs].[34]

In the nineteenth century, conflicts between individuals and their families became a private affair, and took on the allure of a psychological problem. Throughout the period of confinement, by contrast, such matters had been affairs of public order, calling into question a sort of universal moral structure, and the rigour of the family structure was a matter of civic interest. To attack the family was to flirt with the world of unreason. And thus by becoming the major form of sensibility to unreason, the family one day was to become the place of conflicts from which the various forms of madness spring.

When the classical age locked up those who through sexually transmitted diseases, homosexuality, debauchery or prodigality had demonstrated a sexual freedom that previous ages might have condemned but had never dreamt of assimilating to forms of insanity, it brought about a strange moral revolution, uncovering a common denominator of unreason among experiences that had long remained separate from each other. It banded together a whole group of blameworthy behaviour patterns, creating a halo of guilt around madness. Psychopathology might feign surprise at finding feelings of guilt mixed in with mental illness, but they had been placed there by the obscure groundwork of the classical age. It is still true today that our scientific and medical knowledge of madness rests implicitly on the prior constitution of an ethical experience of unreason.

*

The habitual practices of confinement also reveal a further grouping: those who fell foul of the various categories of profanation.

On the registers of the Hôpital Général there are occasionally to be found notes like the following:

> A furious character with no known religion, who never goes to church and never fulfils a single Christian duty, who swears the holy name of God as an imprecation and claims that God does not exist, and that if he did, he would pursue him sword in hand.[35]

In previous times such fury would have carried all the dangers of blasphemy, and also the prestige attached to profanation, and its meaning would have been understood against the backdrop of the sacred. Uses and abuses of the word had long been too strongly linked to religious prohibitions for such violence not to be thought of as akin to sacrilege. And until the mid-sixteenth century, verbal or gestural violence was still punished with sentences that were religious in character, like the iron collar or the pillory, branding on the lips with a red-hot iron, removal of the tongue, or burning at the stake in the case of a repeated offence. The Reformation and the ensuing religious struggles made blasphemy a more relative matter, and the line of profanation was no longer an absolute frontier. Under the reign of Henri IV, the statutes stipulate vaguely worded fines, followed by 'exemplary and extraordinary' punishments. But the Counter-Reformation and the new religious rigour meant a return to traditional punishments, 'in accordance with the seriousness of the words uttered'.[36] Between 1617 and 1649, there were 34 executions for blasphemy.[37]

But therein lies the paradox. While the severity of the laws was unwavering,[38] between 1653 and 1661 only fourteen people were sentenced for the offence, with seven put to death. And these executions became less frequent still.[39] But the severity of the punishments in force did not diminish the frequency of the offence: right up until the end of the eighteenth century, houses of confinement were filled with 'blasphemers' and people who had carried out acts of profanation. Blasphemy did not disappear: it received a new status outside the legal system, despite the laws in force, where it found itself stripped of its dangerous charge. It became instead an affair of civic order, where extravagance with the word was halfway between a disorder of the mind and an impiety of the heart. One of the great ambiguities of this loss of the sacred was the degree to which violence could be simultaneously interpreted as unreason and irreligion, without any risk of contradiction. The difference between madness and impiety was imperceptible, or there was at least a practical equivalence between the two that justified confinement. The following report was made to d'Argenson at Saint-Lazare concerning one inmate, who had complained several times about being locked up while being neither 'eccentric nor insane'. The guards' reply was that

> he never kneels at the most sacred moments of the mass . . . and he keeps a portion of his Thursday supper for Friday, this last trait revealing that while he may not be mad, he is well on the road to impiety.[40]

A whole new ambiguous region was thus coming into being, which the world of the sacred had abandoned, but which was not yet invested by medical concepts and the various forms of positivist analysis, a somewhat undifferentiated region where impiety, irreligion, and disorders of the mind and heart all reigned. It was neither profanation nor pathology, but a region between their confines, with meanings that were reversible, but invariably subject to an ethical condemnation. This region, halfway between the sacred and the morbid, was characterised above all by a fundamental ethical refusal, and formed the bedrock of what the classical age referred to as unreason. It covered not only excluded forms of sexuality, but also all forms of violence against the sacred which had lost the strict character of profanation. It designated a new series of options where sexual mores were concerned, and new limits to religious constraints.

This new evolution in the regimes of blasphemy and profanation had an almost exact counterpart in suicide. Long considered both a crime and a sacrilege,[41] failed suicide attempts were therefore punishable by death: 'Anyone who has turned his hand against himself should not be spared the fate that he has tried to bring upon himself.'[42] The 1670 ordinance was of the same tenure, likening 'murder of the self' to a crime of 'human or divine lèse majesté'.[43] But here, as was the case for profanation and crimes of a sexual nature, the rigour of the Ordinance seems to have authorised a series of extra-judicial practices where suicide was treated as different from an act of profanation. The mention 'wanted to end it all' is often to be found on the registers of houses of confinement, without any reference being made to the sickness or mental confusion that legislation traditionally accepted as an excuse for such actions.[44] In itself, a suicide attempt indicated a disorder of the soul, to be reduced by constraint. People who had desired to kill themselves were no longer sentenced but were confined instead,[45] and a regime that was both a punishment and an effort to prevent them from repeating the attempt was imposed upon them. In the eighteenth century, it was this group of inmates who were the first to experience the constraining devices that the positivists who followed were to use as a form of therapy: wicker cages with a hole for the head, with the hands bound,[46] or the 'wardrobe' which enclosed the subject up to his neck, with only the head protruding.[47] In such fashion, the sacrilege of suicide found itself annexed to the neutral domain of unreason. The system of repression that sanctioned the action removed all traces of profanation, and by treating it as a form of moral behaviour, progressively nudged it towards the domain of psychology. For Western culture, such as it has evolved over the course of the last three centuries, has founded a science of man by turning the previously sacred into the moral.

Let us momentarily set aside the religious horizon of witchcraft and its development throughout the classical age.[48] Many rituals and practices found themselves emptied of meaning and content, as what had once been magic procedures, beneficial or harmful recipes, and old secrets about elementary alchemy slowly came into the public domain. The once-demonic practice of witchcraft was now treated as a diffuse sort of impiety, a moral failing, and the constant threat of social disorder.

There was no wavering in the rigour of the legislation in the course of the seventeenth century. A 1628 decree introduced a fine of 500 pounds for all sorcerers and astrologers, to be accompanied by corporal punishment. The 1682 edict was more fearsome still:[49] 'Anyone caught practising divination will be expelled from the kingdom immediately', all superstitious practices were to receive exemplary punishments according to the demands of the case, and 'if it is found that there are individuals sufficiently wicked to mix impiety, superstition and sacrilege . . . such people are to be punished by death'. A similar fate was reserved for anyone caught using poison or magic potions, 'whether they brought death or not'.[50] However, two points should be singled out. First of all, sentences for magic and witchcraft became extremely rare in the late seventeenth century, after the affair of the poisons, and while there were a few cases in the provinces, the severity of the punishments rapidly diminished. But such forbidden practices did not disappear, and the Hôpital Général and the houses of confinement admitted a considerable number of people who were mixed up in affairs of magic, divination, witchcraft and sometimes alchemy.[51] It was as if under a severe juridical regime, forces were at work to bring into practice a very different form of social consciousness, which read a completely different meaning into this type of conduct. Curiously, this new significance that enabled perpetrators to escape the full force of the law was already formulated by the legislator himself in the grounds of the edict of 1682. The text is directed against 'all those who describe themselves as soothsayers, magicians and enchanters', on the grounds that 'it is surely the case that on the pretext of horoscopes, divination, magical practices and other similar illusions that these people are in the habit of using, they will have tricked the ignorant or the credulous into joining them unthinkingly'. Further down, the same text singles out

> all those who vainly profess themselves to be sorcerers, magicians, soothsayers and the like, and are condemned by justice both divine and human, and who infect and corrupt the spirit of the people by their speeches and practices, and by the profanation of all that religion holds most holy.[52]

When looked at from that point of view, magic is stripped of the efficacious power of sacrilege: it is no longer profanation, but is reduced instead to mere trickery. Its power is illusion, both in the sense that it is devoid of reality and in that it blinds the weak-willed and the feeble-minded. If it still belonged to the realm of evil, it was no longer due to the manner in which its action demonstrated dark transcendent powers, but because it took its place in a system of errors that had its dupes and artisans, its illusionists and its gullible public. Witchcraft was on occasion the vehicle for real crimes,[53] but in itself it was no longer a criminal gesture or a sacrilegious action. Severed from its sacred power, it became little more than a vector for malicious intent, an illusion of the mind at the service of unquiet hearts. It was no longer judged according to its profanatory illusions, but according to what unreason it revealed.

This was an important change. It broke the unity which previously held together a system of practices and the beliefs not only of those who made use of the arts in question, but also of those who sat in judgement upon them. Henceforth, there would only be on the one hand a system judged from without and labelled an illusion, and on the other a system that was lived from within, but adhered to in what was no longer a moment in ritual, but the event of an individual choice – an error with criminal implications, or a crime that knowingly made use of error. In either case, the continuous chain of evil that magic required was severed, leaving an external world suddenly empty or locked into illusion, and a consciousness imprisoned in the guilt of criminal intentions. The arena where the sacred and the profane had done battle vanished, and was replaced by a world where previously powerful symbols were reduced to the status of tell-tale signs betraying evil intent. The old rituals of magic, profanation and blasphemy became so many empty words, and passed from a domain filled with their effective power to the domain of unreason, a place of mere illusion, where they became guilt-laden markers of insanity. The day would come when the sole import of profanation and its tragic gestures was to serve as an indication of a pathological obsession.

To one way of thinking, magic rites and profanatory patterns of behaviour become pathological from the moment that a culture ceases to recognise their effectiveness. In our own culture at least, this passage to pathology was not operated immediately, but at the term of a transitional period during which efficacy had been neutralised while belief was culpabilised. The transformation of prohibition into neurosis passes through a stage where the process of interiorisation is carried out by moral condemnation, where errors are seen as ethical failings. Within that period, in the system of the world, magical practices no longer belong to the arts of success, but are not yet considered an imaginary compensation on a psychological level for individual failure. During this period they are positioned at the point where error meets moral failing within this region of unreason which is difficult for us to understand. The classical age by contrast had a sensibility precise enough to come up with an original reaction: confinement. For almost two centuries, the signs that for nineteenth-century psychiatry were to become the tell-tale symptoms of illness remained 'between impiety and eccentricity', half-way between the profanatory and the pathological, precisely where unreason came into its own.

*

The work of Bonaventure Forcroy had a certain echo in the closing years of the reign of Louis XIV. While Bayle was drawing up his *Dictionary*,

Forcroy was one of the last witnesses of *libertinage érudit*, or one of the first *philosophes*, in the meaning that the eighteenth century was to give to the term. He wrote a biography of Apollonius of Tyana, entirely directed against the Christian miracle, and later addressed a memoir to the Doctors of the Sorbonne entitled *Doubts about Religion*. These numbered seventeen, and in the last one Forcroy wondered if Natural Law was not 'the only true religion'. The figure of the philosopher of nature was represented as a second Socrates and another Moses, 'A new reforming patriarch for humankind, the institutor of a new religion'.[54] Under other conditions, 'libertinage' of this sort would have led to the stake, as it had done for the Italian philosopher Vanini, who was executed for heresy in Toulouse in 1619, or to the Bastille, as it had for countless other authors of impious books in the eighteenth century. But Forcroy was neither burnt at the stake nor imprisoned in the Bastille. He was confined instead for six years at Saint-Lazare, and once freed, given the order to retire to his native town of Noyon. His fault was not judged to be religious, and no one accused him of having written a seditious book. If he was confined, it was because something else had been discerned in his book: a certain closeness of immorality and error. The fact that his book was an attack on religion demonstrated a moral wantonness that was neither heresy nor a lack of belief. The report drawn up by d'Argenson expressly notes that the libertinage of his thought was nothing other than the result of a looseness of mores that he could not express or satisfy by other means: 'Alone in his studies, he occasionally fell into boredom, and had therefore drawn up his own moral and religious system, mixed with magic and debauchery.' If he was sent to Saint-Lazare rather than Vincennes or the Bastille, it was so that, through the rigorous moral system he would find there, he might once again find the conditions that would lead him back to the path of truth. And after six years, that result was achieved: he was finally freed when the priests of Saint-Lazare, his guardian angels, testified that he showed 'some docility and would now almost accept the sacraments'.[55]

In its repression of thought and control of expression, confinement was not simply a more convenient version of the customary condemnations. It had a precise meaning, and was used to a particular purpose, bringing the lost back to the truth by moral constraints. As such, it bore witness to an experience of error that should be understood above all as a question of ethics. To be libertine was no longer a crime, but became instead a fault, or more precisely it gave a new meaning to the idea of fault. Previously, libertinage was a form of unbelief, and as such bordered questions of heresy. But when judgement was passed on Fontanier in the early years of the seventeenth century, people might have felt indulgent to his overly free thinking and his libertine ways, but he was burnt at the stake in the Place du Grève as a former Protestant who had been a novice with the Capucines, before converting to Judaism, and, it was said, Islam.[56] In those days, a disordered life was a sign of religious infidelity, not a cause of it, and it was not that disorder itself for which people were principally condemned. In the latter part of the century, by contrast, what was denounced was a new relationship to disbelief, seen as barely more than the consequences of a licentious lifestyle. Condemnation was carried out on precisely those grounds, as the danger was a moral sickness of the spirit rather than a peril for religion. Belief had become part of the social order, and it was looked after accordingly. What was feared for in atheists or people guilty of impiety was the weakness of their sentiments, the disorder that reigned in their lives rather than the force of their disbelief, and confinement accordingly functioned as a process of moral reform whose aim was to strengthen their attachment to the truth. There was a whole quasi-pedagogical side to the houses of confinement that made them a stronghold of truth, where any moral constraints necessary were applied to ensure that the light of truth would be perceived by all the inmates. 'I have yet to see a sober, chaste, well-balanced and moderate man declare that there is no God; what he would say would at least be sincere, but such a man cannot be found.'[57] Until Holbach and Helvétius, the classical age would remain steadfast in the belief that such men did not exist, and for all that period, men were convinced that by turning anyone who spoke against God into a sober, chaste and moderate individual, any interest that he might have in proffering such opinions would disappear, and he would be led to recognise that God did exist after all. This was one of the major meanings of confinement.

The use that was made of it demonstrates a curious thought process, where certain forms of free thinking and certain aspects of reason became associated with unreason. In the early seventeenth century, libertinage was not exclusively an emergent form of rationalism, but was equally important as a concern about the presence of unreason inside reason itself: a scepticism applied not to human knowledge and its limits, but to reason in its entirety. 'All our life can be taken for a fable, our knowledge for foolishness, our certainties for fairy tales – the whole world can be seen as a farce and an unrelenting comedy.'[58] No firm division could be made between sense and madness, as both existed together in an indecipherable unity, the one often passing for the other: 'Nothing is so frivolous that it is not in some sense of the highest importance, and there is no form of madness, if taken far enough, that would fail to pass for wisdom.' This sudden awareness of the compromised nature of reason did not throw into question the search for order, provided it was a moral order, the possibility of happiness through reason ruling the heart in a happy equilibrium. The seventeenth century broke that unity by bringing about the great divide between reason and unreason, of which confinement was no more than the institutional expression. The 'libertinage' of the early part of the century, which drew its inspiration from concerns about the proximity and often confusion of reason and unreason, therefore disappeared, to continue in two radically different incarnations until the end of the eighteenth century. One was an effort of reason towards a rationalism, where all unreason was merely a form of the irrational, while in the other the unreason of the heart bent the discourse of reason to its own unreasonable logic. In the eighteenth century, enlightenment and libertinage were juxtaposed but not identical, and the division brought about by confinement meant that they rarely communicated. When the Enlightenment triumphed, libertinage was forced underground, and was never really formulated before Sade's *Justine* and above all *Juliette*, a formidable pamphlet written against the *philosophes*. It was the first real expression of a form of experience which until that point had only been treated as a police offence within confinement.

Libertinage was therefore forced into the domain of unreason. Outside of a certain superficial use of the term, the eighteenth century saw no coherent philosophy of libertinage, and the only systematic use of the term was on the register of the centres of confinement. What it came to designate was not exactly free thinking, nor wanton behaviour, but rather a state of servitude where reason was the slave of desire and a servant of the heart. Nothing could be further from that conception of libertinage than the idea of a free choice made in a reasoned manner, all spoke instead of the bondage into which reason had been forced, to the flesh, to money and the passions, and when Sade, for the first time in the eighteenth century, tried to come up with a coherent theory of a form of libertinage that until then had led a secret existence, it was exactly that slavery that was exalted: any libertine who wished to enter the *Society of the Friends of Crime* had to agree to commit any actions 'to which the slightest passing whim might lead him, no matter how revolting it might be'.[59] The libertine was obliged to place himself at the heart of such servitude, convinced that 'men are not free, but bound by the laws of nature, and slaves to those primary laws.'[60] Libertinage, in the eighteenth century, was the use of reason alienated in the unreason of the heart.[61] For that reason there was no paradox for classical confinement in placing side-by-side libertines and those who professed religious error, like Protestants or the inventors of any new religious system. All were treated in the same fashion and obliged to follow the same regime, for in all cases the refusal of truth was the result of the same moral abandonment. It is impossible to tell whether the following note by d'Argenson, concerning a woman from Dieppe, applies to a libertine or a Protestant:

> I have no doubt that this woman who glories in her own obstinacy is a very bad subject. But as all the accusations against her are scarcely sufficient for her case to be taken to court, I feel it would be more fitting for her to be interned for a spell at the Hôpital Général, where she might find punishment for her faults, and the desire for conversion.[62]

In this way, unreason annexed a new domain, where reason serves the desires of the heart, and its use is indistinguishable from the disorder that results from immorality. The unfettered discourse of madness comes to appear in this enslavement to the passions, and it is there, in that moral assignation, that one of the great themes of madness was to be born: the idea of a madness that results not from fantasy being given free reign, but from the constraints of the heart, the passions, and finally human nature itself. Senselessness long bore the mark of the inhuman: suddenly it became apparent that there was a form of unreason inherent to man, when he was too faithful to his own inclinations, an unreason that was like the abandoning of man to himself. This unreason was to slowly take the form the evolutionists of the nineteenth century conceived, the truth of man, but seen from the point of view of his feelings, his desires, the crudest and most irresistible parts of his nature. Unreason lurked in dark regions inaccessible to any moral conduct that might lead man towards the truth. This opened the way to a mode of thinking that classed unreason as one form of natural determinism. But it should be remembered that it had its origins in the ethical condemnation of libertinage, and in that strange evolution that considered a certain form of free thinking as a model, a first experience of the alienation of the mind.

*

The world of confinement was home to a strange parade. In the second half of the seventeenth century the venereal, the debauched, the dissolute, blasphemers, homosexuals, alchemists and libertines found themselves on the wrong side of a dividing line, and were thrown together as recluses in asylums destined, in a century or two, to become the exclusive preserve of madness. Suddenly a new social space was opened and defined. It was not exactly a place of poverty, although it was born out of a great concern about indigence, nor was it exactly a place of illness, although the day would come when sickness would take it over. It was rather the result of a singular sensibility, unique to the classical age. What is at stake here is not a negative gesture of exclusion, but a whole ensemble of operations that slowly gave shape over a century and a half to a realm of experience where madness would recognise itself, before gradually taking it over entirely.

Confinement had little institutional unity, other than that which resulted from its 'police' character. It had no medical, psychological or psychiatric coherence either, as is clear when looked at from a point of view that excludes the possibility of anachronism. But it only seems arbitrary when examined from the point of view of political criticism. This new range of operations that served to reposition the limits of morality, establish new prohibitions, attenuate opprobrium and lower the threshold of scandal did, without doubt, possess its own implicit coherence, but it was a form of coherence that was neither that of rights nor that of science – it was the more secret coherence of a *perception*. What confinement and these labile practices demonstrate, as though it were written into the surface of these institutions in filigree, was the manner in which the classical age perceived unreason. The Middle Ages and the Renaissance had felt the menace of insanity at all the weak points of the world. They feared its lurking presence beneath the thin veneer of appearances, and their evenings and nights were haunted by presentiments that resulted in the spectacular bestiaries and apocalypses of their imagination. Being so present and pressing the world of the insane was not easily perceived: it was intimated, felt and recognised before it was really there at all, and banished to a world of dreams and literary and pictorial representation. To feel its presence so close was not to perceive it, but was rather a certain means of experiencing the world in its entirety, a certain tonality of each perception. Confinement, by contrast, isolated unreason, removing it from the landscapes where it had been permanently present and elusive all at once. It also delivered it from the abstract ambiguities which, up until Montaigne, and until libertinage érudit, necessarily implicated it in the game of reason. The movement of confinement displaced unreason, removing it from a landscape where it had been everywhere present, and firmly localised it. Freed from dialectical ambiguities, it is now circumscribed in its concrete presence, within the distance necessary for it to become an object of perception.

But against what horizon was it perceived? Obviously that of a social reality. From the seventeenth century onwards, unreason was no longer a fear that floated over the world, and it lost its place as a natural dimension of the adventures of reason. It appeared as a new kind of human fact, a spontaneous mutation in the field of social species. That which had previously been considered an inevitable peril for things and the language of men, their reason and their land, now took the form of a social type. Or rather, social types, as unreasonable men were characters whom society recognised and isolated: the debauched and the dissolute, homosexuals, magicians, libertines and suicides. Unreason began to be considered as a certain distance from a social norm. It might be objected at this point that the Ship of Fools and the great embarkation that figured in the iconography and texts of the fifteenth century were also peopled with characters, and were a symbolic prefiguration of confinement; and that the punishment might have been different, but the sensibility was already in place. But there were important differences. The characters aboard the stultifera navis were abstract, moral types: gluttons, sensualists, the impious and the proud personified. If they were forcibly transformed into an insane crew and obliged to set sail without any destination, it was because they were designated by a consciousness of evil in its most universal form. From the seventeenth century, a man of unreason was a real individual picked from a real social world, judged and sentenced by the society of which he was part. The key point was that madness was suddenly invested in a social world, and was granted there its own privileged and quasi-exclusive place almost from one day to the next (across the whole of Europe in the space of fifty years), a clearly delimited terrain where it could be observed and denounced by all. Gone were the days when it sneaked through alleyways and hid in familiar places: now madness, and all those who were its incarnation, could be instantly exorcised through measures of order and precautions of police.

All of which adds up to a first approximation of the classical experience of unreason. It would be absurd to look for the cause in confinement, as it was precisely confinement itself, with all its strange modalities, that signalled an experience that was in the process of being constituted. For these men of unreason to be singled out in their own land, that first alienation must have already taken place, wrenching unreason away from its own truth and confining it in the space of the social world. At the base of so many of these obscure alienations that cloud our perception of madness there must at least be that: the recognition that when society one day decided that the mad were 'alienated', it was in society that unreason first alienated itself, and it was in society that unreason exiled and silenced itself. The word 'alienation', in this context at least, is not entirely metaphorical. What it designates is that movement whereby unreason ceased to be an experience in the adventure that any human reason is, and found itself instead avoided and enclosed in a quasi-objectivity. As a force, it could then no longer feed into the secret life of the spirit, nor accompany it as a constant threat. It was placed at a distance – a distance that was not merely symbolised, but effectively realised on the surface of the social sphere by the closing off of houses of confinement.

This process of distancing and objectification was not a deliverance for knowledge, an unveiling or a pure opening of avenues of learning. It is more reminiscent of the process whereby lepers were banished from the medieval community. It repeats it, even, but lepers had a visible badge of evil: the new outlaws of the classical age were marked by the more secret stigma of unreason. So if it is true to say that confinement defined an area of possible objectivity, that area was already qualified with the negative associations of banishment. Objectivity became the homeland of unreason, but as punishment. People who claim that madness became an object of calm scientific psychiatric study when freed from the ethical and religious associations with which it had been saddled by the Middle Ages should be brought back to this decisive moment when unreason was made into an object and thrown into an exile where it was to remain mute for centuries. They should have this original sin constantly before their eyes, and be ceaselessly reminded that it was only this obscure condemnation that opened the way for a discourse about unreason, reduced to silence at last, whose neutrality is proportionate to its own forgetfulness. Is it not important for our culture that unreason could only become an object of knowledge after it had been subjected to a process of social excommunication?

Furthermore, if confinement reveals the process whereby reason takes a distance from unreason, and severs their kinship, it also manifests the enslavement of unreason to something other than knowledge, and inserts it in a dark network of obscure complicities. It was precisely that servitude that was slowly to give unreason the concrete and indefinably complicitous face of madness that is now familiar from our own experience. Inside the walls of the institutions were the debauched and the venereal, alchemists, libertines, those who 'were claimed to be witches' and, as we shall see, the insane. Associations became more common and similarities were found, and to the eyes of those for whom unreason was becoming an object, an almost homogeneous field came into being. Out of guilt, sexual pathos, magic and age-old incantatory rituals, delirium and the laws of the human heart, a hidden network of associations emerged, forming the secret foundations of our modern experience of madness. To this domain thus structured, the tag of unreason was to be applied, as men were labelled 'fit for confinement'. That unreason, which the thought of the sixteenth century had considered to be the dialectical point of the reversal of reason, was thus given a concrete content. It was linked to a whole shift in ethics involving questions about the meaning of sexuality, the line between love, profanation and the limits of the sacred, and the links between morality and truth. All these experiences, from divergent horizons, were the depths under the simple gesture of confinement. That surface phenomenon hid a system of underground operations all oriented in the same sense: creating in the ethical world a homogeneous division so far unknown. In approximate terms, it can be said that until the Renaissance the world of ethics, beyond the great division between Good and Evil, kept its equilibrium in a sort of tragic unity, that of destiny and of providence and divine will. That unity was now to disappear, broken by the definitive split between reason and unreason. A crisis in the world of ethics therefore came into being, and to the great struggle between Good and Evil was juxtaposed the irreconcilable conflict between reason and unreason, multiplying images of the split. Figures like Nietzsche and Sade bear witness to that. Half the world of ethics thus fell into the domain of unreason, bringing an immense content of eroticism, profanation, magic, ritual, and bodies of visionary knowledge secretly moved by the laws of the heart. At the moment when it was sufficiently freed to become an object of perception, unreason found itself caught up in a whole system of concrete servitude.

In all probability, it is that system of servitude that explains the strange temporal fidelity of madness. Even today, there are obsessional gestures that seem like magic rituals, delirious patterns that are placed in the same light as ancient religious illuminations, and in a culture where the presence of the sacred has been absent for so long, a morbid desire to profane sometimes surfaces. This persistence seems to be an indicator of the dark memory that accompanies madness, condemning its inventiveness to be nothing more than repetition, and often designating it as the spontaneous archaeology of cultures. Unreason would be the great memory of peoples, their greatest faithfulness to the past, where history is always indefinitely contemporary. All that remains is to invent the universal element within which such persistence takes place. But that illusion of identity is a trap: continuity is actually a phenomenon of discontinuity, and if such archaic patterns of behaviour have survived, it is only in so far as they have been altered. The problem of reappearance only exists for the backward-looking glance; if one follows the warp of history, it becomes apparent that the real problem is the transformation of the field of experience. These patterns of behaviour have been eliminated, but that is not to say they have disappeared – they have rather been given a new place of exile and predilection. They are no longer to be found in the field of everyday experience but in the domain of unreason instead, where they have slowly come to belong to the sphere of illness. This survival is not to be explained by the properties of a collective unconscious, but rather by the structure of the domain of experience that is unreason, and by its modifications.

Unreason thus comes to the fore with the whole network of meanings that classicism had placed within its bounds, a field of experience too secret ever to be formulated in clear terms, and from the Renaissance to the modern era too reprehensible to be granted a right of expression, but of sufficient importance to have sustained the institution of confinement, and forced a reconsideration of the conception and practices surrounding madness and a thorough readjustment of the world of ethics. The character of the madman such as it appears in the classical era, and the manner in which the nineteenth century constituted mental alienation as one of the immemorial truths of its positivism, should be seen in the light of that readjustment. In it madness, which the Renaissance had managed simultaneously to experience as non-wisdom, disorder of the world, eschatological threat and illness, found its equilibrium, and a unity that would lay it open to the perhaps illusory grip of positivist thought. In this manner, but through a moral interpretation, it was placed at the distance necessary for objective knowledge, and encountered the guilt that explained such a fall into nature and a moral condemnation that singled out a determinism of the heart, its desires and its passions. By annexing to the domain of unreason, alongside madness, religious and sexual prohibitions and the freedom of thought and of emotion, classicism shaped a moral experience of unreason, which still today forms the bedrock of our 'scientific' knowledge of mental illness. Posited at a distance, and disarmed of its sacred overtones, madness reaches an appearance of neutrality which is compromised from the outset since it depends on an initial statement of condemnation.

If the new unity was decisive for the advancement of knowledge, it was also a key factor that allowed an image of a certain 'existence of unreason' to be constituted, which had a correlative where punishment was concerned in what might be termed 'correctional existence'. The practice of confinement and the existence of men destined for confinement are almost inseparable, and mirror each other with a sort of reciprocal fascination that serves to produce this correctional existence, as though there was a style of existence before confinement which made it inevitable in the end. It is neither exactly the existence of criminals nor of the sick, but in the same way that modern men take flight into neurosis or take refuge in a life of crime, it is probable that this existence of unreason sanctioned by confinement exerted a power of fascination on men of the classical age. That, perhaps, is what is to be perceived vaguely in the physiognomy clearly common to the faces of all the internees, confined for the 'disorder of their ways or their mind', as the texts inform us with such enigmatic confusion. Our actual positive knowledge is scant assistance, and leaves us incapable of deciding whether they were victims or patients, criminal or insane; they all partook in a similar form of existence, which might possibly lead to illness or crime but was different from them at the outset. This existence might have been libertinage, debauchery, dissipation, blasphemy and madness, but all internees had a particular mode of shaping a common form of being: an experience of unreason.[63] We moderns are beginning to understand that beneath the surface of madness, crime, neurosis and social inadequacy lurks something resembling a common experience of anguish. Perhaps, for the classical world, in the economy of evil there also lurked a common experience of unreason. If that were the case, it would be against that horizon that madness was identified, in the 150 years that separate the Great Confinement and the 'liberation' brought about by Pinel and Tuke.

One thing is for sure: it was from that moment of liberation that men ceased to experience and understand what unreason was – and from that moment the laws of internment suddenly lost their obviousness. That moment can be symbolised by a strange meeting between the only man who formulated the theory of these existences of unreason and one of the first men who had wanted to turn madness into a positive science, i.e. to silence unreason by listening only to the pathological voices of madness. This confrontation took place in the early years of the nineteenth century, when Royer-Collard wished to expel Sade from Charenton and turn it into a hospital. Royer-Collard, the philanthropist of madness, wanted to protect his hospital from the presence of unreason, for he understood that what the eighteenth century had placed in houses of confinement as a matter of course would have no place in the asylums of the nineteenth century: its place instead was prison. 'There is one man in Charenton,' he wrote to Fouché, the chief of police, on 1 August 1808,

> whose audacious immorality has made him all too well known, and his continuing presence in the hospital entails serious problems. I refer of course to the author of the scurrilous novel *Justine*. This man is not insane (*aliéné*). His only delirium is that of vice, and it is not in a centre dedicated to the medical treatment of insanity that vice of that sort can be repressed. The individual suffering from it must be submitted to the severest form of sequestration.

Royer-Collard no longer understood correctional existence. Having looked for its meaning in illness, and failing to find it there, he reverts to an idea of pure evil, which has no reason for existence other than its own unreason, which he terms the delirium of vice. The day of that letter to Fouché, classical unreason ended, leaving its own enigma, and that strange unity that grouped together so many diverse faces was definitively lost to us.

IV

EXPERIENCES OF MADNESS

From the creation of the Hôpital Général in Paris, and the opening of the first houses of correction in England and Germany, up until the end of the eighteenth century, the classical age was a time of confinement. Dissolute fathers, prodigal sons, *débauchés*, blasphemers, libertines and suicides were all locked up in houses of confinement. And out of these complicities and strange rapprochements, a profile of the age's experience of unreason begins to emerge.

But in each of these cities there was also a whole population of madmen. One in ten of all arrests made for the Hôpital Général in Paris concerned 'the insane', 'demented men', 'alienated men' or people 'driven quite mad'.[1] No difference seems to have been made between these men and the rest of the population, and looking down the register, it would seem that they were chosen by the same sensibility and excluded by the same gesture as the others. Archaeologists of medicine might quibble over whether people confined for 'irregular behaviour' were ill or not, or whether a person who mistreated his wife and several times attempted to put an end to his existence was criminal or insane. Posing that problem means accepting the deformation imposed by our own retrospective glance. We find it easy to believe that the most general and undifferentiated forms of confinement were applied because the observers had failed to recognise the *nature* of madness, missing its positive signs. But by doing that, we prevent ourselves from understanding that what we see as a failure of recognition contained in fact an explicit consciousness. For the real problem is precisely to determine the content of that judgement which, without using our distinctions, expelled equally those we might have treated and those we might have wanted to condemn. The goal here is not to find the error that led to such confusion, but to follow the continuity that our own way of thinking has broken. After 150 years of confinement, people began to imagine that among these imprisoned faces they noticed singular grimaces, cries that signified a different kind of anger and demanded an alternative form of violence. But throughout the classical age, there was only one confinement, and all the measures that were taken, from one extreme to the other, hide a common, homogeneous experience.

That experience can be summed up and almost symbolised in a single word that constantly recurs in all the registers of confinement. 'Frenzy' (fureur) and the adjective 'frenzied' (furieux) were, as we shall see, technical terms in case law and medicine, and indicated quite precisely a particular form of madness. But in the vocabulary of confinement, the words said both much more and much less, alluding to the forms of violence that escape the rigorous definition of crime and its juridical assignation, denoting an undifferentiated region of disorder – a disorder of the spirit, or a disordered way of life, a whole obscure region of menacing rage that did not yet form grounds for a possible condemnation. To our way of thinking this might appear a confused concept, but it was sufficiently clear to the classical age to dictate a moral and police imperative to confine. One of the powers that classical reason gave itself in its experience of unreason was the possibility of confining subjects by noting not that they were ill or criminal but simply that they were 'frenzied'.

This power had a positive meaning. When the seventeenth and eighteenth centuries confined madness together with debauchery and libertinage, the point is not that they had failed to diagnose an illness, but that they understood it in radically different terms.

*

There are of course real dangers of oversimplification here. The world of madness was not uniform during the classical age. And while it would not be untrue to say that the mad were treated purely and simply as prisoners of the police, it would not be telling the whole truth either.

Some had a special status. In Paris, one hospital reserved the right to treat paupers who had lost their reason. Whenever there was still hope that a madman might be cured, he could be admitted to the Hôtel-Dieu. There he was given the usual treatment, consisting of bleeding, purges, and in some case vesicants and baths.[2] It was already an old tradition, as there had been beds reserved for the mad at the Hôtel-Dieu since the Middle Ages. Those known as the 'fantastical and frenetic' were locked up in closed couchettes, which had two windows through which they could be observed, and receive food.[3] At the end of the eighteenth century, when Tenon wrote his *Mémoires sur les hôpitaux de Paris*, these madmen were grouped together in two rooms. The men were placed in the Saint-Louis ward, where there were two single beds and ten beds for four people. Such promiscuity was a source of worry for Tenon (this was an age when medical imagination considered heat to be a source of evil, while the cool fresh air of the countryside was thought of as having physical and moral healing powers): 'How can the air in the beds be fresh, when three or four madmen are squeezed in to roll around and fight there?'[4] The women did not exactly have a room of their own, but a thin division had been put in place in the large chamber reserved for the fevered, where there were eight small beds, and six beds for four people. If after a few weeks the disease had not been cured, men were transferred to Bicêtre and women to the Salpêtrière. This meant that for the whole of Paris and its environs there was a sum total of seventy-four beds for all the mad who were considered curable – seventy-four beds that were effectively a waiting room for confinement, which signified a fall from the world of illness, medicine and possible cure.

London too had a place reserved for those whom the British called lunatics – the Bethlem Royal Hospital. The institution had been founded in the mid-thirteenth century, and it is known that in 1403 there were six madmen who were kept bound in irons and chains; by 1598, that figure had grown to twenty. When the hospital was extended in 1642, twelve new rooms were built, eight of which were reserved for the insane. After a refurbishment in 1676, the hospital had room for between 120 and 150 people. By then it was exclusively reserved for the mad, as is shown by the two Cibber statues.[5] Lunatics who were considered incurable were not admitted until 1733, at which date two special buildings were constructed to house them.[6] Inmates received treatment on a seasonal basis: the major medication was administered to all on an annual basis in the spring. T. Munro, who was a physician at Bethlem from 1783, outlined the treatment in a statement to a special committee of the House of Commons:

> Patients are ordered to be bled about the latter end of May, according to the weather, and after they have been bled, they take vomits, once a week for a certain number of weeks; after that we purge the patients. That has been the practice invariably for years long before my time; it was handed down to me by my father, and I do not know any better practice.[7]

It would be wrong to think that the confinement of the mad in the seventeenth and eighteenth centuries was an unproblematic police matter, or that it demonstrated a uniform insensitivity to the pathological character of alienation. Even inside the monotonous function of confinement, madness had a varied function, and it already jarred in the world of unreason that surrounded it and haunted it with its universality. While it was true to say that in certain hospitals the mad had a special place that assured them a quasi-medical status, the majority resided in houses of confinement, and led in effect a correctional existence.

However rudimentary the medical care given to the insane in Bethlem or the Hôtel-Dieu might appear, that treatment was still the reason for, or at least the justification behind, their presence in those hospitals. There was no question of any such treatment in any of the buildings of the Hôpital Général. The regulations called for the presence of a single physician who was to reside in the Pitié, and whose duty was to do his rounds twice a week in all of the buildings of the hospital.[8] What resulted was a remote medical surveillance that was not supposed to treat the internees in general, but concentrate instead on any who had fallen ill, which demonstrates that internees who were confined on account of their madness were not considered ill because of that madness. In a late eighteenth-century *Essay on the Physical and Medical Topography of Paris*, Audin Rouvière explained that

> Epilepsy, cold humours and paralysis are enough to gain entry to Bicêtre, but no attempt is made to cure them with any remedy . . . so a child of

10 or 12 admitted there for convulsions that were reputed to be of an epileptic nature caught among true epileptics an illness that he did not have, and in the long career that should lie before him on account of his youth, his only hope of a cure is the often imperfect efforts of Mother Nature.

As for the mad, 'They are judged incurable when they arrive at Bicêtre, and they receive no treatment there . . . despite this lack of treatment, some of them still manage to recover their wits.'[9] This absence of medical care, with the exception of the prescribed visit, meant that there was little practical difference between the Hôpital Général and a prison. The regulations in force there were more or less identical to the ordinance passed in 1670 for good order in prisons:

> It is our wish that prisons should be safe and so disposed that the health of prisoners is not adversely affected. We enjoin gaolers and door-keepers to visit prisoners locked in dungeons at least once a day, and to warn the procurator if any are ill, so that they may be visited by the prison physicians or surgeons, if such persons exist.[10]

If there was a doctor at the Hôpital Général, it was not because of a consciousness that sick people were locked up there, but rather on account of a concern that inmates might catch and spread a contagious illness. 'Gaol fever' was feared above all. In England, cases were often cited of prisoners who had infected their judges at trial, and of others who brought home illness from a prison and infected a family on their release.[11] Howard notes that:

> Air which has been breathed is made poisonous to a more intense degree, by the effluvia from the sick, and what else in prisons is offensive . . . air, corrupted and putrified, is of such a subtile and powerful nature, as to rot and dissolve heart of oak . . . .[12]

Palliative care is added to the practice of confinement to limit some of its effects: cure was neither the meaning nor the aim.

Confinement did not constitute a first step towards a hospitalisation of madness, in all its morbid aspects. It is more usefully considered as a homogenisation of the insane and the other prisoners, as is demonstrated by the strange, juridical formulae used, which did not so much entrust the insane to the good offices of the hospitals as pass custodial sentences to be served there. The register at Bicêtre has many entries like the following: 'transferred to the Conciergerie by virtue of a parliamentary decree that condemned him to perpetual detention at Bicêtre, to be treated there like the other insane'.[13] Being 'treated like the other insane' did not mean undergoing medical treatment,[14] it meant following the corrective regime, doing the same exercises, and following the rules laid down in its pedagogy. One set of parents who had placed their son in the Charité at Senlis on account of his 'frenzy' and 'disordered mind' asked for him to be transferred to Saint-Lazare, 'having had no desire to see their son die when they asked for him to be confined, but only wishing that he would mend his ways and recover the wits that he seemed to be losing'.[15] Confinement was intended to be a punishment, and if it was given a term, it was not to coincide with a cure, but with an acknowledged process of repentance. One tonsured clerk, an organist called François-Marie Bailly, was transferred in 1772 by order of the king from the prison of Fontainebleau to Bicêtre, so that he might be locked up there for three years. That sentence was followed by a new one from the Provosty on 20 September 1773, 'so that the Bailly might be kept among the weak-minded, until such time as resipiscence come about'.[16] The time that gave a rhythm and limit to confinement was only ever the time necessary for a moral conversion or a return to wisdom, the time necessary for a punishment to have the desired effect.

It was not therefore surprising that houses of confinement had the appearance of prisons, and that often the one was taken for the other, so much so that at times the mad were placed in both almost indiscriminately. When a committee was set up to study the condition of the 'Poor lunatics of England' in 1806, it found 1,765 madmen in the workhouses and 113 in houses of correction.[17] There were doubtless many more in the course of the eighteenth century, as Howard noted the following as an instance that was far from rare:

In some few gaols are contained idiots and lunatics. These serve as sport to idle visitants at assizes, and other times of general resort. Many of the Bridewells are crowded and offensive, because the rooms which were designed for prisoners are occupied by the insane. Where these are not kept separate, they disturb and terrify other prisoners. No care is taken of them.[18]

In France it was just as common to come across the mad in prisons, in the Bastille first of all, but also in the provinces, in the Hâ fort in Bordeaux, in the house of correction in Rennes, and in the prisons of Amiens, Angers, Caen and Poitiers.[19] In most of the general hospitals the insane were kept with the other inmates, and no distinction was made between them and their fellow internees, with only the most agitated being kept in special cells reserved for their use:

> In all the hospices and hospitals, there are reserved for the insane run-down, damp buildings quite unsuited to their presence, together with a few cells built specially for the more frenzied amongst them; the quiet or incurable mad are mixed in together with the poor and the indigent. In a small number of hospitals where prisoners are kept in what is known as the secure section, the mad live together with the prisoners and are subject to the same regime.[20]

Such are the facts, in purely schematic form. When put together, some common factors seem to emerge, as though there were two different experiences of madness juxtaposed in the seventeenth and eighteenth centuries. Physicians of the period that followed were struck by the inhumanity of the treatment that the mad received, and everywhere they noted the same misery and the same inability to alleviate it. They could see no distinction between the work at Bicêtre and the rooms of the Hôtel-Dieu, or between Bethlem and a workhouse. And yet there clearly was an irreducible difference: some establishments only took in the mad to the extent that they were theoretically curable, while others took them in order to rid society of them, or with the idea of correcting them. The first group was no doubt less widespread and more restricted: there were fewer than eighty madmen at the Hôtel-Dieu, whereas there were hundreds or perhaps even a thousand at the Hôpital Général. But regardless of how unequal the distribution of the two practices might be, they are nonetheless two distinctly different experiences. The experience of madness as sickness, however limited it might be, cannot be denied. Paradoxically, it was contemporaneous with a different experience where madness was part of confinement, punishment and correction. That juxtaposition is the core of the problem, but it also helps an understanding of the place of the madman in the classical age, and in outlining the manner in which the mad were perceived.

*

It is tempting to take a simple approach here. What if that juxtaposition was merely a sign that slow progress was being made, and that paradoxes were inevitable during this period of change? To that way of thinking, the mad in the Hôtel-Dieu and the lunatics of Bethlem had already been granted the status of medical patients. Better still, there before anywhere else, the mad had been identified and isolated, and in their favour a hospital treatment had been instituted that already seemed to prefigure what the nineteenth century defined as treatment suitable for mental patients. The others, who were to be found indiscriminately in the Hôpital Général, the workhouses, prisons and houses of correction, could then be thought of as a series of patients whose sickness was yet to be identified by a medical science still in its infancy at that moment. Age-old superstitions and concern by the rising bourgeoisie would have condemned the mad to a definition of insanity that assimilated it to criminals and asocials. Medical historians are much given to recognising the solid medical categories of the diseases of the mind in confinement registers, and in the approximate terms used in reports, as though they were timeless facts of knowledge. Those termed 'illuminated' and 'visionaries' are considered to correspond to the people we think of as suffering from hallucinations: 'visionary imagining he sees celestial apparitions', 'visionary who has revelations', and those described as 'imbeciles' are deemed cognitively deficient or suffering from some form of organic or senile dementia – 'imbecilic after horrible debauchery with wine', 'an imbecile who is always talking, comparing himself to the Pope or a Turkish emperor', 'imbecile with no hope of return'. Sufferers from such delirium are characterised by the picturesque or absurd aspect, as in 'a man pursued by people who wish to kill him', 'institutor of crackpot projects', 'man continually electrified, who receives ideas transmitted by other people', or 'madman who wants to submit reports to Parliament'.[21]

Perhaps doctors find it a great support and a comfort to know that under the sun of madness there have always been hallucinations, that there has always been delirium in the discourse of unreason, and that restless hearts have ever been filled with the same anguish.[22] Mental medicine finds the guarantee of its eternity here, and if doctors ever suffered from their conscience, they would doubtless be reassured to find that the object of their quest was there all the while, shining out through different times. And for anyone worried about the meaning of confinement and the way in which it fitted into the history of medical institutions, it is a great relief to consider that, after all, the people who were locked up were just lunatics, and that behind this obscure practice what we consider an immanent medical justice was hidden. All that was lacking for the insane who were confined was the label 'mental patient' and the medical status already given to those who were more obviously ill and better recognised. This way of thinking is a short cut to an easy conscience where the justice of history and the eternity of medical science are concerned, as a continuity emerges between medicine and pre-medical practices, and history is justified by an infallible, pure, spontaneous social instinct. Add to those postulates a sure belief in progress, and the path is traced out between confinement – a silent diagnosis carried out by nascent, unformulated medical science – and hospitalisation, whose early incarnation in the eighteenth century anticipates this progress and symbolically announces its end.

Unfortunately, things are much more complicated. The history of madness cannot serve as a justification or as a supportive science in the pathology of mental illness. In the reality of its historical becoming, madness did make possible at a certain moment a knowledge of alienation according to a style of positivity that isolated it as mental illness, but that knowledge is not the truth of this history, nor does it secretly animate it from the beginning. If it was believed for a while that such a history had its end in it, it was because it had not been acknowledged that madness as a domain of experience could never be exhausted by a medical or para-medical knowledge. Yet the fact of confinement itself could serve as a proof of that.

We need to start further back in history, and examine the character of the madman before the seventeenth century. There is a tendency to believe that the mad were individuated as a result of a process of medical humanitarianism, as if the figure of their individuality was never anything other than pathological. In fact, in the Middle Ages, long before the medical status that came with positivism, the mad had already acquired a sort of personal density, although perhaps more as character types than pathological cases. The disguise of the madman that Tristan adopted and the 'dervé' who appears in Adam de la Halle's Jeu de la Feuillée had already sufficiently individual values to constitute roles and take their place in highly familiar landscapes. Madmen had no need of medical diagnoses to accede to their own individual kingdom: the circle drawn around them by the Middle Ages sufficed. But that individuality was neither stable nor immobile, and was undone and reorganised to a certain degree in the course of the Renaissance. From the end of the Middle Ages onwards, the mad were treated with a certain degree of medical humanism, perhaps as a result of Oriental and Arab thought. The Arab world seems to have built some early hospitals specifically for the insane. There may have been one such institution in Fez in the seventh century,[23] there may also have been one in Baghdad towards the end of the twelfth century,[24] and there certainly was one in Cairo in the course of the century that followed. A sort of spiritual therapy was carried out there, involving music, dance, and theatrical spectacles and readings of marvellous stories. The therapy was directed by physicians, and they decided when to bring it to a close in the event of success.[25] It may not be a coincidence that the first hospitals for the mad in Europe were founded in Spain around the beginning of the fifteenth century. It is surely important too that the Brothers of Mercy, who were familiar with the Arab world as they specialised in buying back captives, were the founders of the hospital in Valencia in 1409, after the funds were provided by wealthy laymen and merchants like Lorenzo Salou.[26] In 1425, it was the turn of the Saragossa hospital, whose wise order was to be so admired nearly four centuries later by Pinel. Its doors were open to patients of all creeds, all governments and all nationalities, as was promised by its motto urbis et orbis ('of the city and of the world'). Life there followed the rhythm of a garden, with the usual seasonal concentration on harvests, trellising and grape and olive picking.[27] There were also similar hospitals in Spain, in Seville (1436), Toledo (1483) and Valladolid (1489). All these hospitals had a medical character, unlike the Dollhäuser that already existed in Germany,[28] or the well-known Charité in Uppsala.[29] At around the same time similar institutions of this new type began to open all around Europe, like the Casa di maniachi in Padova (around 1410), and the Bergamo asylum.[30] In hospitals, space began to be reserved especially for the mad. The presence of the mad is documented at Bethlem hospital from the early fifteenth century; it had been founded in the mid-thirteenth century and confiscated by the crown in 1373. At this time too in Germany, special places put aside for the mad were referred to in contemporary literature: first the Narrhäuslein in Nuremberg,[31] then in 1477 a building for the insane and the 'disobedient sick' (ungehorsame Kranke) was constructed in the hospital at Frankfurt;[32] and in Hamburg mention is made of a cista stolidorum (literally, 'the basket for fools'), also known as custodia fatuorum (the prison for the insane) in 1376.[33] A further proof of the particular status that the mad had acquired by the end of the Middle Ages was the strange development of the colony at Gheel, a centre of pilgrimage from the tenth century onwards, and a village where the mad constituted one third of the population.

Part of the social fabric of the Middle Ages and a familiar figure on the horizon, the madman was considered in a different fashion during the Renaissance, and grouped together in something resembling a new specific unity, isolated by a practice that was no doubt ambiguous as it isolated him from the world without exactly granting him a medical status. The mad became the objects of a particular form of solicitude and hospitality, reserved for them alone and none other in that precise fashion. By contrast, what characterised the seventeenth century was not that it advanced quite rapidly along a path that led to a recognition of the madman, and hence to the scientific knowledge that might emerge therefrom, but quite the opposite. The seventeenth century began to distinguish them less clearly, and reabsorbed them instead into an undifferentiated mass. The individual features of insanity, unique for centuries, began to be erased. In comparison with the mad of the Narrtürme and the first asylums in Spain, the madman of the classical age, locked up with venereal sufferers, the debauched, libertines and homosexuals, lost the marks of his individuality, and faded into a general apprehension of unreason. This was a strange evolution for a sensibility which seemed to lose the capacity to make distinctions and reverted to a less refined form of perception. The perspective became more uniform. It was as though, in the asylums of the seventeenth century, the figure of the madman simply faded away among many others, so much so that the trace of the mad almost disappears until the moment of reform that immediately preceded the Revolution of 1789.

There are many signs of this 'involution' in the seventeenth century, even in the course of its development. The change can be vividly distinguished by an examination of the establishments that were originally intended to house the mad more or less exclusively. When the Brothers of

Charity set up in Charenton on 10 May 1645, it was with the intention of building a hospital reserved for sick paupers, including the mad. Charenton differed little from the other Charité hospitals, which began to appear all across Europe after the founding of the Order of Saint John of God in 1640. But some time before the end of the seventeenth century, new buildings were added for prisoners who were confined, lettres de cachet inmates, prisoners who needed punishment, and the mad. In 1720, mention is made for the first time in a capitulary of a 'house of reclusion' which had clearly been there for some time, as that year, in addition to the sick, it contained a total of 120 inmates: a whole population in which the mad became an undifferentiated group.[34] The evolution was even more rapid at Saint-Lazare. If the first hagiographers are to be believed, Saint Vincent de Paul hesitated for a while before taking over this former lazar house for his Congregation. The argument that finally convinced him was the presence in the 'priory' of some madmen, who he felt were in need of assistance.[35] If we exclude from this account the wilfully apologetic intention and the retrospective attribution of humanitarian sentiments, it is possible, and even probable, that there was a desire to avoid certain difficulties arising from the attribution of this lazar house and its considerable attendant goods, which was still the property of the Knights of Saint-Lazare, by converting it into a hospital for the 'poor insane'. But soon it was turned into a 'Gaol for Persons Detained by Order of His Majesty',[36] and its inmates suddenly found themselves prisoners rather than patients. Pontchartrain was well aware of this, and he wrote a letter to Lieutenant d'Argenson on 10 October 1703 to point it out:

> As you know, the men of Saint-Lazare have long been accused of using too harsh a regime to look after their charges, and even of preventing those who were sent there for being simple-minded or corrupt in their ways from informing their families of improvements in their ways, in order to keep them there for a longer period.[37]

It is indeed a prison regime that is invoked by the author of a contemporary manuscript entitled A Summary and Faithful Relation of the Atrocious Conditions in the Prison of Saint-Lazare:

> The serving brothers, or the guardian angels of the mad take them out for a walk in the courtyard of the house after dinner on working days, and

walk them around stick in hand the way they would a flock of sheep, and if any of them stray away from the main group or fail to keep up with the others, they are beaten with batons so harshly that some of them are permanently disabled, others had their heads broken and have died from the blows they received.[38]

This might simply seem a logical consequence of the confinement of the mad, since it escaped all medical control and by necessity became some form of punishment. But as it was not simply the structures and organisations that were involved, the process seems to have been something more than mere administrative inevitability, and was in fact linked to the consciousness of madness that was beginning to develop. The shift occurs within this consciousness, where asylums for the insane were no longer seen as hospitals and increasingly considered to be houses of correction instead. When a new gaol was built in the Charité at Senlis in 1675, it was indicated immediately that the new building was for 'libertines and the mad, and anyone else that the King's government should choose to confine there'.[39] It was therefore in a very deliberate manner that the mad went from the register of the hospital to the correctional centre, and the signs that marked them apart were slowly erased as they were enveloped in a moral experience of unreason of a totally new sort. A single account will serve as an illustration of this. Bethlem hospital was rebuilt in the second half of the seventeenth century, and in 1703, Ned Ward had one character in his novel *London Spy* remark:

> 'In truth,' said I, 'I think they were mad that built so costly a college for such a crack-brained society,' adding, it was a pity so fine a building should not be possessed by such as had a sense of their happiness.[40]

What happened between the end of the Renaissance and the height of the classical age was therefore not simply an evolution of the institutions: it was a change in the consciousness of madness, and thereafter it was the asylums, houses of confinement, gaols and prisons that illustrated that new conception.

If there was a paradox behind this situation where the mad were to be found in hospital wards and in houses of confinement and prisons, it was not due to any ongoing progress that might have been underway, where the mad were gradually moved from prisons to hospitals and incarceration was replaced by treatment. In fact the mad who were in hospitals in the classical age were something of a throwback, recalling the period between the end of the Middle Ages and the early Renaissance when the mad were acknowledged as such and isolated, even if they did not have a precise medical status. By contrast the mad of the Hôpital Général, the workhouses and *Zuchthäuser* demonstrate an experience of unreason that is rigorously contemporary with the classical age. If it is true that there is a chronological slippage between these two ways of dealing with the insane, hospitals did not belong to the most recent geological stratum, but rather represented a form of archaic sedimentation. The proof of that is that hospitals were increasingly attracted towards centres of confinement as though by a gravitational pull, becoming so assimilated that it was soon almost impossible to distinguish between them. From the day when Bethlem, the hospital for curable lunatics, was opened to hopeless cases in 1733, there was no longer any notable difference between the London hospital and the French Hôpital Général, or any other house of correction. Saint Luke's hospital, which was built to complement Bethlem in 1751, demonstrated the same pull towards the correctional style. When Tuke visited it in the last years of the century, he noted his impressions in his diary:

> The superintendent has never seen much advantage from the use of medication ... Thinks confinement or restraint may be imposed as a punishment with some advantage, and, on the whole, thinks fear the most effectual principle by which to reduce the insane to orderly conduct.[41]

The traditional manner of examining confinement, where the elements that resemble imprisonment are blamed on the past, and the aspects that point towards the psychiatric hospitals are seen as intimations of the future, is a permutation of the data. In fact the mad were placed in institutions specially designed for them, perhaps as a result of the influence of Arab thought and science, and some of those institutions, particularly in southern Europe, were sufficiently similar to hospitals for us to say that some of the mad were effectively treated as patients, in part at least. Certain hospitals did maintain that status for the mad throughout the classical age, until the great reform. But in contrast with those institutions the seventeenth century created a new experience, where previously unknown relations between madness and social and moral viewpoints were developed, the like of which had not been seen before.

The point here is not to establish a hierarchy, nor to demonstrate that the classical age was a step backwards in comparison to the sixteenth century and the knowledge it had developed of madness. We shall see that medical texts from the seventeenth and eighteenth century are enough to prove the contrary. What matters here is to remove all chronology and historical succession from the perspective of a 'progress', to reveal in the history of an experience, a movement in its own right, uncluttered by a teleology of knowledge or the orthogenesis of learning. The aim here is to uncover the design and structures of the experience of madness produced by the classical age. That experience is neither progress nor a step backward in relation to any other. It is possible to talk of a loss of the power of discrimination in the perception of madness, and to say that the face of the mad began to be erased, but this is neither a value judgement nor even a negative statement about a deficit of knowledge. It is a manner, still very exterior, of approaching the experience of madness in its positive reality, an experience which stripped the madman of the precise individuality an status that the Renaissance had given him, which prepared for him, beyond the field of our customary experience, a new face, where the naïvety of our positivism believed that it could recognise the nature of all madness.

*

This juxtaposition of hospitalisation and confinement should alert us to the specific chronology of these institutions, and demonstrate quite clearly that the hospital was not the imminent destiny of houses of correction. It is nonetheless true that in the overall experience of unreason in the classical age, both structures remained in place: although one was newer and more vigorous, the other was never totally replaced. That duality must exist also in the social perception of madness, in the synchronic consciousness that apprehends it, both as separation and as balance.

The recognition of madness in canon law as in Roman law was linked to a medical diagnosis, and medical consciousness was necessary for any judgement of insanity. In *Quaestiones medico-legales*, drawn up between 1624 and 1650, Zacchias summed up all Christian jurisprudence that related to the question of madness.[42] For all cases of '*dementia et rationis laesione et morbis omnibus qui rationem laedunt*' ('when reason is tainted by madness, injuries, or any sickness of the reason'), Zacchias categorically stated that only a doctor was competent to decide if an individual was mad, and to determine the degree to which he still had the use of his reason. It is clearly significant that a century-and-a-half later, this rigorous obligation that an expert in canon law took to be a self-evident truth had evaporated, as can be seen in Kant,[43] and that at the time of Heinroth and then Elias Régnault it had become the centre of a polemic.[44] Medical participation in the assessment of sanity was no longer considered self-evident, and a new series of arguments had to be produced. To Zacchias, the situation had been perfectly clear. A lawyer could recognise a madman by his speech, if he was incapable of giving order to it, and he could also recognise him by his actions, if his gestures were incoherent or his decisions absurd. The emperor Claudius might have been judged mad for example, simply for favouring Nero rather than Britannicus as his heir. But these opinions were mere presentiments, and it took a physician to turn them into certainties. A physician's experience makes use of a whole system of signals. In the sphere of the passions, a continuous sadness without apparent cause indicated melancholy; where the body was concerned, taking the temperature meant that frenzy could be distinguished from all apyretic forms of excitement. A physician could carefully weigh up the subject's life history and all the judgements that had been made about him since childhood before deciding whether or not some form of illness was involved. But the task of the physician did not end there: it was merely the starting point for a much more subtle task. It was then necessary to ascertain which faculties had been affected (memory, imagination or reason), in which manner and to what degree. Reason was diminished in *fatuitas*, and superficially affected by the passions; frenzy and melancholy affected it profoundly, while with mania, raving and the morbid forms of sleep, reason was almost entirely destroyed.

By carefully examining each question in order, a physician could examine human behaviour and determine the extent to which it was affected by madness. There were cases, for example, where love was a form of alienation. A judge might suspect as much before calling for a medical opinion if a subject demonstrated an excessive concern with his appearance, and was constantly looking out for new clothes or new perfumes, or if he was spotted out of his way in a street where a beautiful woman lived. But such signs merely sketched out a probability, and even taken together were usually not sufficient for an indisputable decision. The indubitable marks of truth were to be uncovered by a physician. Was a subject sleeping badly, and had he lost his appetite? Did he have sunken eyes, and was he given to long bouts of sadness? If so, it was undoubtedly because his reason had already been corrupted, and he was struck down with the melancholy of love, which Hucherius described as the 'atrabilious sickness of a soul that has lost its reason, deceived by a phantom and a false estimation of beauty'. But if, when the patient caught a glimpse of the object of his desire, his eyes became haggard, his pulse began to race and he fell into an agitated state, he was to be considered no longer responsible for his actions, in the manner of all those who suffered from a mania.[45]

The power of decision was entrusted to medical opinion, as only a physician had the capacity to understand the world of madness; a physician alone could tell a sane person from a madman, or a criminal from a man no longer responsible for his actions. But the practice of confinement was structured in a totally different manner, and in no manner was it ordered in accordance with a medical decision. It was a product of a different consciousness altogether. The case law of confinement was complex where the mad were concerned. If the texts are to be believed, it would appear that a medical opinion was always required: at Bethlem hospital, for instance, up until 1733 a medical certificate declaring that the madman could be treated was required, guaranteeing that his idiocy was not congenital, and that he was not suffering from a permanent affliction.[46] At Petites-Maisons the opposite was required, i.e. a certificate that stated that the patient had been treated in vain, and that the disease was therefore incurable. Families who wished to confine a relation with the insane at Bicêtre had to apply to a judge, who 'sanctioned a visit by a doctor and a surgeon, who drew up a report and submitted it to the Clerk of the Court'.[47] But the reality behind those administrative precautions was quite different. In England, it was the Justice of the Peace who took the decision to decree confinement, either because he had been petitioned to do so by the subject's entourage, or because he believed it necessary for the good order of his district. In France, confinement was sometimes decreed by court sentence, when a subject was convicted of a crime or tort.[48] The commentary on the criminal ordinances of 1670 allowed for madness as an element of justification, whose proof was only to be admitted after complete consideration of the case. If, after all the necessary information regarding the accused had been gathered, it was agreed that his mind was indeed disturbed, the judges then made a decision on whether the accused was to be kept with his family or sent to a place of confinement or a gaol, 'to be treated there like the other insane'. It was very rare for magistrates to have recourse to a medical opinion, despite the fact that after 1603, in all large towns, there had been appointed 'two men of the medical and surgical arts of high reputation, probity and experience, to make visits and draw up legal reports'.[49] Up until 1692, all confinements at Saint-Lazare were made on the order of a magistrate, and regardless of any medical certificate, carried the signatures of the First President, the Civil Lieutenant, the Lieutenant of the Châtelet or the General Lieutenants of the province; if it concerned men of the cloth, the orders were signed by the bishops and the chapters. The situation became both simpler and more complicated at the end of the seventeenth century. In March 1667, the new post of Lieutenant of Police was created.[50] Many confinements, particularly in Paris, were made at his request, providing that the request was countersigned by a minister. After 1692, the most frequent procedure was clearly the *lettre de cachet*. The family or entourage made a request to the king, who accepted it and granted it after it had been signed by a minister. Some such demands were accompanied by medical certificates, but those cases were the least common.[51] Normally the family, the neighbours or the parish priest were asked for their opinion. The grievances or apprehensions of close relatives carried the most weight in the writ that requested confinement. Care was taken to obtain the consent of the entire family, or to uncover the rivalry or conflict of interest that lay behind any absence of unanimity.[52] But it did also happen that more distant relations and even neighbours could obtain a measure of confinement against the wishes of the family.[53] In the seventeenth century, like crime, public order and scandal, madness had effectively become a matter of social sensibility, and accordingly it could be judged by the most spontaneous and primitive forms of that sensibility.[54]

What determined and isolated the fact of madness was not so much medical science as a consciousness susceptible to scandal. In that respect, men of the Church were in a position even more privileged than that of the civil authorities to make judgements regarding madness.[55] When in 1784 Breteuil decided to limit the use of *lettres de cachet*, and began to have them phased out, he did everything possible to ensure that so far as possible confinement did not take place prior to the judicial process of interdiction.[56] That measure was taken to guard against arbitrary writs from families or orders from the king. But the change was not introduced to transfer the balance of power to the more objective world of medicine: in fact the aim was that the power of decision should pass to a judicial authority that had no recourse to medical expertise. Interdiction required no medical expertise, and was a matter to be agreed between the families and the judicial authorities.[57] Confinement, and the judicial practices that had grown up around it, had in no way enabled a more rigorous medical grip on insanity. On the contrary, it seems that the tendency was increasingly to dispense with the medical controls that had been planned by the regulations of certain hospitals in the seventeenth century, and increasingly to turn decisions about where madness began and ended into purely social issues. It was therefore not surprising that at the turn of the nineteenth century, the question of medical competence in the diagnosis of madness was still being debated. Zacchias, the inheritor of the whole tradition of Christian law, had considered that medical science had all the necessary authority: within 150 years Immanuel Kant contested that view, and Régnault rejected it altogether. Classicism, and more than a century of confinement, had clearly not been without their effects.

Judging by the results, it does seem that there was a gap between a juridical theory of madness, which was sufficiently elaborate to discern, with the help of medical science, the limits and forms of madness, and a repressive social practice which understood it in a far less sophisticated manner, almost a police practice, and used the varieties of confinement that were already in place for repressive purposes, neglecting to follow the subtle distinctions that were provided for in judicial arbitration. That gap may at first glance appear normal, or at least extremely common, as the legal consciousness is usually more elaborate and subtle than the social mechanisms or institutions that put it into practice. But the gap takes on its significance when it is considered that the judicial consciousness of madness had been evolving over an extremely long period of time, and that it had been constituted throughout the Middle Ages and the Renaissance through canon law and the remnants of Roman law, long before the practice of confinement was put in place. That judicial consciousness did not anticipate the practices: they belonged to different worlds.

The one is the result of a certain experience of the person as a subject of law, and concerns an analysis of the forms and obligations of this subject, while the other is the result of a certain experience of the individual as a social being. In one case, what is to be examined are the changes that madness necessarily brings to a system of obligations, while in the other, the moral aspects of madness are the core of the issue and justify exclusion. As subjects of law, men are progressively absolved of their responsibilities as alienation takes its toll, but as social beings, madness brings them to the fringes of culpability and condemnation. The law constantly refined its analysis of madness, and in that sense it is correct to say that the medical science of mental illness grew out of a judicial experience of alienation. Already in the case law formulations of the seventeenth century, some of the more subtle distinctions of psychopathology were already apparent. Zacchias, for example, inside the ancient category of *fatuitas* (imbecility), made distinctions that seem to anticipate Esquirol's classification, and what would later be known as the psychology of cognitive deficiency. The first in his hierarchy of decreasing competence were fools (*sots*), who could bear witness, make a will and marry, but could not take holy orders or have charge of anything, 'for they are like children approaching puberty'. Next came imbeciles proper (*fatui*). They could be given no responsibility, as, like children under seven, their mind had not reached the age of reason. The stupid (*stolidi*) were worth no more than stones: no legal act could be authorised by them, with the possible exception of a will, providing they were at least capable of recognising their parents.[58] Under pressure from legal concepts, and the necessity to define ever more clearly the legal person, the analysis of alienation became further refined, and seemed to prefigure still distant medical theories.

The differences that emerge between that conceptual analysis and the practice of confinement are profound. A term like 'imbecility' only operates in a system of approximate equivalences which excludes any precise value. On the register of the Charité in Senlis, mention is made of a 'madman turned imbecile', another 'a man once mad, but now weak-minded and imbecile',[59] while the lieutenant d'Argenson confined a man 'of a rare variety, combining two opposed features: a semblance of good sense for many things, and the appearance of an animal for others'.[60] Even more curious is a comparison between a jurisprudence like that of Zacchias and the extremely rare medical certificates that accompanied confinement dossiers. It is as though none of the case law analysis ever entered into the judgement. Regarding imbecility, one entry signed by a doctor states:

> We have seen and visited the person named Charles Dormont, and after examining his bearing and the movement of his eyes, taking his pulse and watching his behaviour, interrogating him in diverse manners and weighing up his replies, we are unanimously convinced that Dormont has lost his wits and fallen into a total and absolute dementia and imbecility.[61]

Reading that text, one has the impression that it has two meanings, and almost two levels of medical elaboration, according to whether it is involved in the context of the law, or as part of the social practice of confinement. In the one instance it assesses the mental faculties of a subject of the law, and thereby lays the groundwork for a psychology that blends a philosophical analysis of the faculties and a juridical analysis of the ability to make and honour contracts in an ambiguous unity, and in that respect it concerns the delicate structures of civil liberty. In the other, it measures social behaviour, and paves the way for a dualist pathology that will divide everything into binary oppositions – normal and abnormal, healthy and sick – to create two radically different domains separated by the simple formula 'good for confinement'. A rough structuring of social freedom.

The eighteenth century saw numerous attempts to adapt the ancient juridical notion of a 'subject of the law' to the contemporary experience of man in society. The political thought of the enlightenment postulated a fundamental unity between the two, and a constant possibility of resolving any practical conflicts that might emerge. Such notions quietly led to an elaboration of the notion of madness, and the organisation of the relevant practices. The positivist medicine of the nineteenth century inherited these *Aufklärung* ideas, and took it as an established and proven fact that the alienation of legal subjects should coincide with the madness of social man in a unified pathological reality, which could be analysed in legal terms as well as perceived by the most immediate forms of social sensibility. Mental illness, which medicine took as an object, was slowly constituted as a mythical unity between a legally irresponsible subject and a man who troubled the social order, all under the influence of the political and moral thought of the eighteenth century. That new unity was already apparent shortly before the Revolution, when in 1784 the minister Breteuil decided that the confinement of the mad should be preceded by a more careful judicial procedure that involved interdiction and an examination of the extent to which the person in question could be considered responsible before the law. 'With regard to people for whom confinement is requested after they have lost their wits,' he wrote to the regional intendants of justice, 'justice and prudence require that the King's orders be carried out only when the judgement that was passed proposes an interdiction.'[62] These liberal gestures in the last years of the absolute monarchy were continued by the Civil Code that came into operation after the Revolution, where interdiction was an indispensable requirement for confinement.

The moment when the jurisprudence of alienation becomes the necessary condition for confinement is also the moment when Pinel and the psychiatry that was beginning to emerge claim to treat the mad as human beings for the first time. What Pinel and his colleagues felt to be a discovery for both philanthropy and science was at bottom little more than the reconciliation of the divided consciousness of the previous century. Building the confinement of social man into the interdiction of the juridical subject meant that for the first time the alienated were recognised as being both incapable *and* mad: their eccentricity, which was immediately perceived by society, limited their juridical existence but did not obliterate it altogether. By that fact, the two meanings of medicine were reconciled − the one which attempted to delineate the delicate structures of responsibility, and the other which only helps bring the social decree of confinement.

All of which was of the utmost importance for subsequent developments in the medicine of the mind. In its positivist incarnation, this was little more than the combination of the two experiences that classicism had juxtaposed without ever joining them together: a social, normative and dichotomous experience of madness that revolved entirely around the imperative of confinement, formulated in a style as simple as 'yes or no', 'dangerous or harmless', and 'good or not good for confinement', and a finely differentiated, qualitative, juridical experience, well aware of limits and degrees, which looked into all the aspects of the behaviour of the subject for the polymorphous incarnations that insanity might assume. The psychopathology of the nineteenth century (and perhaps our own too, even now) believes that it orients itself and takes its bearings in relation to a *homo natura*, a normal man pre-existing all experience of mental illness. Such a man is in fact an invention, and if he is to be situated, it is not in a natural space, but in a system that identifies the *socius* to the subject of the law. Consequently a madman is not recognised as such because an illness has pushed him to the margins of normality, but because our culture situates him at the meeting point between the social decree of confinement and the juridical knowledge that evaluates the responsibility of individuals before the law. The 'positive' science of mental illness and the humanitarian sentiments that brought the mad back into the realm of the human were only possible once that synthesis had been solidly established. They could be said to form the concrete *a priori* of any psychopathology with scientific pretensions.

*

All that which, after Pinel, Tuke and Wagnitz, pricked the conscience of the nineteenth century, has tended to mask how polymorphous and varied the experience of madness was in the classical age. Historians have been fascinated by this undiagnosed disease, madmen in chains, and the population confined by means of *lettres de cachet* or the orders of the Lieutenant of Police. The different experiences intertwined within these seemingly monolithic practices, at first sight so rudimentary, went unseen. In fact madness during the classical age received two different types of hospitality – one in hospitals proper, the other in centres of confinement. It was identified by two different means, one which came from the world of law and borrowed its concepts, and one which belonged to spontaneous forms of social perception. In the many different forms of sensibility to madness, medical consciousness was not inexistent, but it was not *autonomous*, and indeed was far from underpinning the other forms of experience. It had its place in certain hospital practices, and it was present in the juridical examination of alienation, although the role it played was far from essential. Yet its place in the economy of these experiences was important, and it provided an important intersection between them. It was through medicine that the rules of juridical analysis and the practice of placing the mad in medical establishments were coordinated. But it had comparatively little impact on the world of confinement, and the social attitudes it expressed.

Two independent spheres of experience thus came into being, and it would appear that throughout the classical age, the experience of madness was lived in two different ways. It was as though the legal subject was surrounded by a halo of unreason; he was both defined and controlled by the judicial recognition of his irresponsibility and incapacity, by the decree of interdiction and the definition of his disease. A different halo of unreason, or so it seems, surrounded man as a social being, defining and controlling him in the consciousness of scandal and the practice of confinement. These two domains did on occasion intersect, but they never fully overlapped and they defined two essentially different forms of alienation.

One was taken to be a limitation of subjectivity, and was a line drawn around an individual showing the limits of his powers and designating the areas where he could not be held responsible. In this alienation the subject was dispossessed of his liberty by a double movement – the natural movement of his madness, and the juridical movement of interdiction, which brought him under the power of an Other – other people in general, effectively represented by a guardian. The other form of alienation was the sudden consciousness, within his own society, that a madman was a stranger in his own land. Rather than being freed from his responsibility, he was made to feel guilty by association and kinship with other bearers of guilt: he became the Other, the Outsider, the Excluded. The strange concept of 'psychological alienation', which is thought to have its roots in psychopathology, however enriched with ambiguities from other domains of reflexion, is little more than the anthropological confusion of these two different experiences of alienation, the first of which concerns those who have fallen under the power of the Other, and are chained to their liberty; while the second is the individual turned Other, excluded from the fraternal resemblance between men. The one is close to the determinism of a disease, while the other takes on the appearance of an ethical condemnation.

When the nineteenth century decided that unreason should be treated in hospital, and that confinement should be a therapeutic process aimed at curing the sick, the decision came about through a coup that reduced to a confused unity, which it is difficult for us to disentangle, these diverse themes of alienation and the multiple faces of madness, which classical rationalism had always allowed to appear.

V

THE INSANE

The two major forms of the experience of madness to be found side by side throughout the classical age follow their own chronologies. That is not say that one is a developed form of experience, and the other a confused emergent consciousness – both are clearly articulated into a coherent practice – but rather that one was inherited, and was one of the most fundamental facts in Western unreason, while the other was an invention of the classical world. It is that second experience that we will examine here.

Despite the reassuring pleasure that historians of medicine may feel when they recognise in the great ledgers of confinement what they consider to be the timeless, familiar face of psychotic hallucinations, cognitive deficiencies, organic consequences or paranoid states, it is impossible to draw up a coherent nosological map from the descriptions that were used to confine the insane. The formulations that justify confinement are not presentiments of our diseases, but represent instead an experience of madness that occasionally intersects with our pathological analyses, but which could never coincide with them in any coherent manner. The following examples are taken at random from entries on confinement registers: 'of unsound mind', 'obstinate plaintiff', 'has obsessive recourse to legal procedures', 'wicked cheat', 'man who spends days and nights deafening others with his songs and shocking their ears with horrible blasphemy', 'bill poster', 'great liar', 'gruff, sad, unquiet spirit'. There is little sense in wondering if such people were sick or not, and to what degree, and it is for psychiatrists to identify the paranoid in the 'gruff', or to diagnose a 'deranged mind inventing its own devotion' as a clear case of obsessional neurosis. What these formulae indicate are not so much sicknesses as forms of madness perceived as *character faults* taken to an extreme degree, as though in confinement the sensibility to madness was not autonomous, but linked to a moral order where madness appeared as a disturbance. Reading through the descriptions next to the names on the register, one is transported back to the world of Brant and Erasmus, a world where madness leads the round of moral failings, the senseless dance of immoral lives.

And yet the experience is quite different. In 1704, a priest named Bargedé was confined in Saint-Lazare. He was seventy years old, and he was locked up so that he might be 'treated like the other insane'. His principal occupation was

> lending money at high interest, beyond the most outrageous, odious usury, for the benefit of the priesthood and the Church. He will neither repent from his excesses nor acknowledge that usury is a sin. He takes pride in his greed.'

It was totally impossible 'to find any feeling of charity in him'. Bargedé was insane, but not in the manner of the insane on the *Ship of Fools*, who were mad to the extent that they were carried away by the brute force of madness. Bargedé was insane not because he had lost the use of his reason, but because he, a man of the church, practised usury, showed no charitable inclinations and felt no remorse, and was therefore marginal to the moral order to which he belonged. What becomes apparent in this judgement is not an inability to name a particular form of sickness, nor a tendency to condemn madness from a moral point of view, but the fact, essential for an understanding of the classical age, that madness then became perceptible in the form of ethics.

It is almost as though, paradoxically, rationalism could conceive of a form of madness where reason itself was not affected, but where the madness was apparent from the moral disorder of a life and an evil will. For in the final analysis, madness was a question of the quality of the will more than it was of the integrity of reason. It is curious to note that a century before Sade's case caused Royer-Collard such intense soul-searching,[2] Lieutenant d'Argenson too wondered about a similar case, the only difference being the genius of Sade:

> A sixteen-year-old woman, whose husband is called Beaudoin . . . publicly proclaims that she will never love her husband, and that there is no law ordering that she should do so, that everyone is free to use their own heart and body as they please, but that it is a sort of crime to give the one without the other. [. . .] I have spoken to her on two occasions, and despite the fact that over the course of the last few years I have become accustomed to hearing impudent and ridiculous opinions, I couldn't help but be surprised by the reasoning that the woman employs to support her system. Marriage, to her way of thinking, is no more than a first attempt.[3]

Sade was left to die in Charenton in the early nineteenth century; in the early years of the eighteenth century, men still hesitated before locking up a woman whose only crime, it must be admitted, was that she had too much spirit. Pontchartrain, who was minister at the time, refused d'Argenson permission even to place her in the Refuge for a few months. 'That would be excessive,' he wrote. 'Give her a stiff talking to.' Yet for d'Argenson, there is little difference between her and the other insane: 'On hearing such impertinence, I was strongly tempted to consider her mad.' We are on the way here to what the nineteenth century would term 'moral madness', but what is even more important is the emergence of the theme of a form of madness that rests entirely on 'bad' will, on an *ethical mistake*. Throughout the Middle Ages, and for a long period during the Renaissance, madness had been linked to Evil, but through the form of imaginary transcendences: henceforth, they would communicate by the more secret means of individual choice and bad intent.

The apparent indifference that the classical age demonstrates to the line between madness and error, alienation and evil, should not be surprising. It results not from any primitive state of knowledge, but is a conscious choice that was arrived at in a lucid manner. Madness and crime were not mutually exclusive, but neither were they confused in one nebulous concept. They were linked within the same consciousness, treated equally reasonably, according to individual circumstances, with either prison or hospital. During the Spanish Wars of Succession, a man calling himself

Count d'Albuterre, whose real name was Doucelin, was sent to the Bastille. He claimed that he was the heir to the throne of Castille:

> But however intense his madness, his cleverness and evil intentions go further still: he swears that the Holy Virgin appears to him every eight days, and that God often speaks to him face to face ... I think ... that this prisoner should be locked up in hospital for all his life as a highly dangerous madman, or that he should be abandoned in the Bastille like a wicked man of the first order; I would even go so far as to say that this last course of action is the safer and therefore to be preferred.[4]

There was no mutually exclusive relation between madness and crime, but rather an implication that bound them together. The degree of insanity or criminality might vary, but even the most extreme forms of madness were haunted by evil intentions. Again with regard to Doucelin, d'Argenson later noted that 'the more he appears docile, the more it should be believed that there is much affect and malice in his eccentricities'. In 1709, he noted, 'he is much less keen to deny the hallucinations, and slightly more imbecile'. This complementarity comes through strongly in another report by d'Argenson regarding Thadée Cousini, a 'bad monk' who had been placed in Charenton. In 1715, 'his impiety continues when he reasons, and he is absolutely imbecile when not reasoning. Although the peace now means that he could be freed as a spy, his mental state and the honour of religion forbid any such action'.[5] Here we find ourselves at the opposite extreme from the fundamental rule of law that states, 'true madness excuses anything'.[6] In the world of confinement, madness neither explains nor excuses anything: it enters into complicity with evil to multiply it and render it more insistent and dangerous, lending it ever-new faces.

Of a slanderer who is mad, we would say that his slander is a form of delirium, as we have become accustomed to considering madness to be a sort of ultimate, innocent truth about man: but in the seventeenth century, a deranged mind taken together with slander meant a greater sum total of evil. One man locked up in the Charité at Senlis was charged with 'slander and weak-mindedness', and it was said of him that he was 'of a violent, superstitious and unpredictable turn of mind, as well as a great liar and slanderer'.[7] In frenzy, one of the most common entries on the confinement register, wickedness was never explained away by the violence of madness, but was taken together with it to form a kind of unity of totally unchained evil. D'Argenson asked that one woman be confined in the Refuge, 'not simply for her disorderly behaviour, but because of her madness, which often approaches frenzy, and will lead her either to kill her husband or to do away with herself at the first available opportunity'.[8] The process is as though the psychological explanation was added to the moral condemnation, whereas to the modern way of thinking the former obliterates the latter.

Involuntary madness, which possessed men despite their best intentions and conspired spontaneously with wickedness, differed little in its secret essence from the madness simulated by lucid subjects, and it was believed that there was a fundamental similarity between them. The law, by contrast, attempted to make as rigorous a distinction as possible between feigned and authentic alienation, as a person was not sentenced in the normal manner if he 'was *genuinely* suffering from madness'.[9] But that distinction was not made for confinement, where real madness was worth no more than its feigned counterpart. In 1710, a young man of twenty-five who claimed to be called Don Pedro de Jesus, and a son of the King of Morocco, was locked up in Charenton. Until then, he had been taken for a madman, but it was not long before he was suspected of simulating his condition. Within a month of his confinement he demonstrated that 'he was in his right mind, and agreed that he was not the son of the King of Morocco, but maintained that he was the son of the governor of a province, and refused to give up that illusion' Real madness and feigned dementia were side by side, as though advantageous lies filled any gaps left by the chimera of unreason. 'I think,' d'Argenson wrote to Pontchartrain, 'that it would be fair to punish him for his deception and his feigned madness by sending him back to the Bastille.' In fact he ended up in Vincennes, and five years later the hallucinations seemed to have taken over from the deception. He eventually died there among the prisoners. 'His reason is quite disturbed, and he talks nonsense. He is given to bouts of frenzy, the last of which was nearly the end of one of his comrades: so many good reasons for his detention to continue.'[10] Unintentional madness or the intention to appear insane are treated in the same fashion, perhaps because they are dimly perceived as having a common root in evil, or at least in a perversion of the will. Accordingly, passage from the one to the other was thought to be simple, and it was commonly thought that people went mad simply as a result of desiring to do so. Regarding one man who was 'sufficiently mad to want to talk to the king, without ever having told any minister what he had to say to him,' d'Argenson wrote:

> he has played the madman for so long, in Bastille and Bicêtre, that he has effectively lost his mind. He still wishes to have a private conversation with the King, and when pressed on the issue, he explains himself in terms that do not have even a semblance of reason.[11]

These examples demonstrate how the experience of madness such as it was expressed through the practice of confinement (and no doubt also formed by that practice) differs from the other experience of madness, embodied in the legal consciousness since Roman law and the juridical writing of the thirteenth century. For men of the law, madness essentially attacked the faculty of reason, and altered the will, thus making it innocent: 'Madness or eccentricity is an alienation of the spirit, an unhinging of reason which prevents us from being able to distinguish between the true and the false, and which by its continual agitation of the spirit removes the subject's power of assent.'[12] The essential issue therefore was to ascertain the reality and degree of the madness in question. The deeper the insanity, the more innocent the subject's will. Bouchet reports several sentences 'decreeing that men who had killed even close relatives in a fit of frenzy should not be punished'.[13] By contrast, in the world of confinement, it mattered little if the faculty of reason had been affected or not; if that was the case, and the will was thought to be enslaved, then it was in any case an example of the bending of the will, which was never wholly innocent, since it did not belong to the order of consequences. This accusing of the will in the experience of madness such as it was conceived of in the world of confinement is obviously never explicit in the texts that survive, but is clearly apparent from the motivation behind confinement and the different modes that were used. There is an obscure connection between madness and evil, where the evil is no longer the swarming chaos that lies beneath the surface of the world as it was at the time of the Renaissance, but the individual power given to man in his will. Madness, thus, takes root in the world of morality.

*

But madness was something other than the pandemonium of all the faults and crimes committed against morality. The classical experience of madness and its refusal of the condition was not simply a question of moral rules, but involved a whole ethical consciousness. It was that consciousness, and not some scrupulous sensibility, that eyed madness with such caution. If men of the classical age perceived the tumult of madness, it was not from the banks formed by a pure and simple reasonable consciousness: they looked down on it from the great height of an act of reason that inaugurated an ethical choice.

Taken in its simplest form, and seen from the outside, confinement would seem to indicate that classical reason had conquered the power of madness, and that a clear dividing line was drawn at the level of the social institutions themselves. From some points of view, confinement looks like a successful exorcism. But the moral perception of madness that can be discerned in the forms that confinement took betrays a divide that was still far from being clear-cut. It proves that unreason in the classical age was not expelled to the margins of reasonable consciousness sure of its power, but rather that the opposition it presented to reason took place in a space of freedom and choice. The unimportance of any rigorous distinction between moral failings and madness indicates a deeper region in the classical consciousness, that of a decisive option, akin to a more essential, more responsible form of will within the subject. Obviously, that consciousness is never made explicit in the literature of confinement and its justifications. But it did not remain silent throughout the seventeenth century. Philosophical thought gave it one formulation that allows it to be approached from another angle.

The decision by which Descartes, in the progression of doubt, side-stepped the possibility that he was mad was noted above. While other forms of error and illusion encircled the region of certainty, and at the same time liberated a certain form of truth, madness was excluded without a trace, leaving not even a scar on the surface of thought. Madness was simply of no use in the process of doubt's movement towards truth. The time has come now for us to ask why, and to see whether Descartes turned away from the problem because of its insurmountable nature, or whether this refusal of madness as an instrument of doubt has meaning on the level of the history of culture – revealing a new status accorded to unreason in the classical world. It would seem that if madness does not appear in the economy of Descartes' doubt, it is because it is simultaneously always present and always excluded from the doubting project and the will that controls it from the outset. The path that leads from the initial project of reason to the first foundations of science runs alongside a precipice of madness. What stops it tumbling into that abyss is an ethical decision made at the outset, a resolute will to stay awake and to do nothing other than 'devote [oneself] solely to the search for truth'.[14] Reason is perpetually threatened by the temptation to fall asleep or to give in to illusions, and the solution is to reiterate constantly the need to fix one's eyes on the truth:

> a kind of laziness brings me back to normal life. I am like a prisoner who is enjoying an imaginary freedom while asleep; as he begins to suspect that he is asleep, he dreads being woken up, and goes along with the pleasant illusion as long as he can. In the same way, I happily slide back into my old opinions and dread being shaken out of them.[15]

Madness can be brushed aside on the path of doubt, as doubt, in so far as it is methodical, is wrapped in the will to stay awake, which at every instant is a refusal of the temptations that madness offers. Just as the thought that doubts supposes both the thought and the thinking man, the will to doubt has already excluded the involuntary charms of unreason and the Nietzschean possibility of the mad philosopher. Long before the Cogito, there is an archaic implication of the will and of the choice between reason and unreason. Classical reason does not encounter ethics at the end of the quest, in the shape of moral laws; ethics, as a choice made against unreason, are present from the earliest moment of a concerted thought process, and indefinitely prolonged throughout the process of reflection, indicating the path of a freedom that is the very initiative of reason.

In the classical age, reason is born inside the space of ethics. And it is doubtless that which lends such an unusual style to the recognition – or non-recognition – of madness at that time. All madness hides an option, in the same way that all reason is the result of a freely accomplished choice. That much is discernible in the insistent imperative of Cartesian doubt; but the choice itself, the constitutive movement of reason where unreason is freely excluded, is apparent throughout Spinoza's thought, and the unfinished efforts of the *Treatise on the Emendation of the Intellect*. Reason asserts itself first of all as a decision made against the unreason of the world, in the clear consciousness of the 'hollowness and futility of every-thing that is ordinarily encountered in daily life'. The quest should therefore be for a good 'whose discovery and acquisition would afford . . . a continuous and supreme joy, to all eternity'. Spinoza is postulating a sort of ethical wager, which is won when it is discovered that the exercise of freedom is accomplished in the concrete fullness of reason, which, by its union with nature taken in its totality, is access to a higher form of nature. 'What that nature is we shall show in its proper place; namely, the knowledge of the union which the mind has with the whole of Nature.'[16] The freedom of the wager culminates in a unity where it disappears as a choice to reappear as a necessity of reason. That final step, however, is only possible against a backdrop of conquered madness, and madness appears as a constant peril until the end, In the nineteenth century, reason attempts to situate itself in relation to unreason on the grounds of positive necessity, and not in the free space of choice.From that moment on the refusal of madness was no longer an ethical exclusion, but a distance that had already been granted. It was no longer necessary for reason to divide itself from madness, but to recognise itself as always anterior to it, even if it does on occasion lose its way within it. But throughout the period in which classicism maintained a fundamental choice as the condition for the exercise of reason, madness is revealed in the light of freedom.

When the eighteenth century confined a woman as insane because she had a 'deranged mind inventing its own devotion' or a priest because no sign of charity could be found in him, the judgement that sentenced that form of madness did not mask a moral presupposition, but simply made manifest the ethical division between madness and reason. It took a 'moral' consciousness, such as the term was understood in the nineteenth century, to object to the inhuman treatment the mad had received in the previous age – or to be amazed that they had not been treated in hospital at a time when so many physicians were writing learned treatises about frenzy, melancholy and hysteria. But in fact medicine as a positive science could have no purchase on the ethical division that had given birth to all possible reason. The peril of madness, for the classical age, was not the faltering, human pathos of reason incarnated, but the region where the eruption of liberty brought reason into being, together with the true face of man In Pinel's time, when the fundamental relationship between ethics and reason would be reversed into a secondary relation between reason and morality, and madness would be seen as an involuntary avatar that had affected reason from the outside, only then could the situation of the mad in the dungeons of hospices be discovered with horror. Only then was it a source of indignation that 'innocent' men had been treated as 'guilty'. That did not mean that madness had at last found a human status, or that the evolution of mental pathology was emerging for the first time from its barbarous prehistory, but it did indicate that man's originary relation to madness had changed, and that madness was seen as mere reflection on the surface of the self, as an accidental sickness. And from that new point of view, it suddenly seemed inhuman to leave the insane to rot in gaols and houses of confinement, as men no longer understood that for men of the classical age the possibility of madness was contemporaneous with a choice constitutive of reason, and consequently of man himself. So much so that in the seventeenth and eighteenth centuries there had been no question of treating madness in a 'humane' manner, for by its nature it was inhuman, forming the other option in a choice whereby man could gain the free exercise of his rational nature. There was no misunderstanding, confusion or error in placing the mad alongside the criminal, simply the resolution to let madness speak the language proper to it.

*

For men of the classical age, this experience of choice and liberty, contemporaneous with reason, established with obvious clarity an unbroken continuity that stretched all the way through unreason: behavioural disturbances and disturbances of the mind, madness both true and feigned, delirium and lies all sprang from the same soil, and all were treated in the same fashion.

Yet it should not be forgotten that the 'insane' as such did have a place apart in the world of confinement. Their status cannot simply be summed up as being comparable to that of their fellow prisoners. In the general sensibility towards unreason there was a particular modulation for madness properly speaking, and it related to all those who were termed, with no precise semantic distinctions, insane, deranged, alienated, eccentric and demented.[17]

The particular form of this sensibility outlines the face of madness in the world of unreason. It concerns first of all the place of scandal. In its most general form, confinement was explained, or at least justified, by a will to avoid scandal. It thereby signalled an important change in the consciousness of evil. The Renaissance had let unreason in all its forms come out into the light of day, as public exposure gave evil the chance to redeem itself and to serve as an exemplum. In the fifteenth century, Gilles de Rais, accused of having been and of being still 'a relapsed heretic, a sorcerer, a sodomite, an invoker of evil spirits, a diviner, a killer of the innocent, an apostate, an idolater, and a man who refused to see the error of his ways',[18] ended up admitting his crimes 'which were enough to send 10,000 people to their deaths' in an extra-judicial confession. He made his confession again in Latin in court, and then asked of his own accord

> that the confession might be translated into the common language, so that everyone attending the court, most of whom did not understand Latin, might understand, and that for his shame the publication and confession of the aforementioned crimes might obtain more easily the remission of his sins, and the favour of God, and the absolution for the sins he had committed.[19]

In the civil trial, the same confession was required before the assembled public: 'he was told by the judge that he should repeat his case in full out loud, and that the shame that he would feel would be an alleviation of the torments that he would experience in the next world'. Until the seventeenth century, evil, in all its violence and inhumanity, could only be compensated for and punished if it was brought out into the open. Only the light in which confession and punishment are enacted can make up for the darkness in which evil was born. There was a cycle of accomplishment of evil, which necessarily involved public manifestation and avowal before reaching the completion that eradicated it.

Confinement, by contrast, betrays a consciousness where inhumanity can provoke nothing but shame. Certain aspects of evil had a power of contagion, and such scandalous force that publicity risked causing them to multiply infinitely. Only oblivion could suppress them. Regarding a case of poisoning, Pontchartrain prescribed not a public trial but sequestration in an asylum:

> As the investigations involved a whole part of the city of Paris, the King did not feel it necessary to conduct the trial of so many people, some of

whom fell into their crimes unwittingly, and others simply because it was so easy to do. His Majesty's decision was facilitated by the conviction that some crimes must absolutely be put out of sight and forgotten.[20]

Together with the fear that others might be inspired to similar actions, the honour of a family and of religion was often sufficient for a subject to be confined. Regarding a priest who was to be sent to Saint-Lazare: 'a priest of this sort cannot be hidden too carefully, for the honour of religion and that of the priesthood'.[21] Quite late in the eighteenth century, Malesherbes defended confinement as a right for families who wish to avoid dishonour. 'Despicable acts are not tolerated by society . . . It appears that the honour of all good families requires that those who make their parents blush through vile and abject behaviour should be removed from society altogether.'[22] Inversely, when the danger of scandal had passed, and the honour of the family or the church could no longer be sullied, an inmate could once more be set free. After spending many years in confinement, and never being authorised to leave despite repeated requests, the Abbé Bargedé was finally freed once his infirmity and old age meant that scandal was no longer possible. 'His paralysis continues,' wrote d'Argenson. 'He can no longer write or even sign his name, so I think that it would be justice and charity to set him free.'[23] All forms of evil that resembled unreason were to be hidden from view. Classicism felt a sense of shame before all that was inhuman that was quite unknown in the Renaissance.

There was, however, an exception to this process of locking evil away from public view, which directly concerned the mad.[24] Putting the insane on show was doubtless an ancient practice that dated back to the Middle Ages. Some of the German *Narrtürme* had special windows with bars so that the chained madmen inside could be observed from the outside. The mad were often a spectacle at the city gates. Strangely, the custom did not disappear at the moment of the great confinement, but in fact became more developed still, taking on an almost institutional nature in London and Paris. As late as 1815, if a report presented to the House of Commons is to be believed, Bethlem Hospital showed its lunatics every Sunday for one penny. The annual revenue from those visits amounted to almost 400 pounds, which means that an astonishing 96,000 visitors came to see the mad each year.[25] In France, right up until the Revolution, the visit to Bicêtre to see the insane was a major Sunday pastime for the bourgeois of the left bank. In *Observations d'un voyageur anglais*, Mirabeau recounts how the mad were shown at Bicêtre 'like strange beasts, to anyone willing to hand over their shilling'. People went to see the gaolers show off the mad as if they went to see a mountebank training monkeys at the fair in Saint-Germain.[26] Some of the gaolers were widely known for their skill in making their charges perform dances or feats of acrobatics in response to a few cracks of the whip. The only modification that had come into practice by the end of the eighteenth century was that the insane themselves were to serve as guides to the mad, as though madness itself had to bear witness to its true nature.

> Let us not slander human nature. The English traveller is right to consider the task of acting as a guide to the mad as beyond the most hardened elements of humanity. We have said so ourselves. But there is a remedy for all things. It is the mad themselves who, in their intervals of lucidity, are entrusted with the task of showing off their companions, who in their turn will eventually return the favour. So the guards of these unfortunates enjoy the benefits that the spectacle procures them, while never having to develop themselves the strength of insensibility, an insensibility that is probably beyond their reach.[27]

Madness here was erected as a spectacle above the silence of the asylums, and it became, for the joy of all, a public scandal. Unreason was hidden away discreetly in houses of confinement, but madness was a continued presence of the world stage, more strikingly than ever before. During the Empire period (1803–1815), things were taken to greater extremes than anything seen in the Middle Ages or the Renaissance. In a previous age, the strange Brotherhood of the Blue Ship staged shows where madness was imitated,[28] but under the Empire it was insanity itself, madness in flesh and blood that took centre stage. In the early years of the nineteenth century, Coulmier, the director of Charenton, organised the notorious spectacles where the mad played the roles of actors, or that of an audience watched by a real audience:

> The mad who watched these theatrical representations were themselves an object of attention for a public that was on occasion frivolous, inconsequential and mean-spirited. The unusual behaviour of these unfortunates and their posture often provoked mockery and laughter, and the insulting pity of the audience.[29]

Madness became pure spectacle, in a world where Sade extended his sovereignty, which was offered as an amusement for a self-assured reason. Up until the early nineteenth century, and until the indignation of Royer-Collard, the mad remained monsters – literally things or beings worthy of being put on show in public.

Confinement hid unreason, thereby demonstrating that it was something to be ashamed of; but it put madness on show, pointing it out at arm's length. The concern with unreason was the avoidance of scandal, but madness became an organised pageant. This is indeed a strange contradiction. The classical age enveloped madness in the overall experience of unreason, and it blurred the features that had been distinguished during the Middle Ages and the Renaissance in a generalised apprehension where it rubbed shoulders with unreason in all its forms. But at the same time it marked madness out with a particular sign – indicating not illness, but an exalted form of scandal. There is little in common between the organised parading of madness in the eighteenth century and the freedom with which madness came to the fore during the Renaissance. The earlier age had found it everywhere, an integral element of each experience, both in images and in real life dangers. During the classical period, it was also on public view, but behind bars. When it manifested itself it was at a carefully controlled distance, under the watchful eye of a reason that denied all kinship with it, and felt quite unthreatened by any hint of resemblance. Madness had become a thing to be observed, no longer the monster within, but an animal moved by strange mechanisms, more beast than man, where all humanity had long since disappeared. 'I can conceive of a man without hands, feet or head (for it is only experience that teaches us that the head is more important than the feet). But I cannot conceive of a man without thought: that would be a stone, or a brute.'[30]

*

In his *Report on the Section for the Insane*, Desportes described the state of one cell at Bicêtre at the end of the eighteenth century: 'The unfortunate inmate had no furniture other than a straw mattress, and had his feet, body and head pressed up against the wall, unable to sleep without being soaked by the water that ran down the walls.' At the Salpêtrière, what made survival even more difficult was the fact that in the winter when the Seine rose, the cells down by the sewers were slowly flooded with water, becoming even more insalubrious than usual:

> and to make matters worse, the cells are invaded by hordes of rats, who run all over the patients confined there at night, biting them anywhere they can. Mad women have been found with bites all over their feet, hands and faces; these bites are sufficiently dangerous to have proved mortal for several inmates.

These were the dungeons traditionally reserved for the most agitated and dangerous prisoners. If they were calmer and there was nothing to be feared from them, they were herded into larger cells. Godfrey Higgins, one of Tuke's most active disciples, paid the sum of 20 pounds for the right to visit York Asylum as a volunteer inspector. In the course of his visit he discovered a door that had been carefully hidden, behind which was a room no more than eight feet by eight feet (six square metres), where thirteen women were kept each night. During the day they were kept in a second chamber scarcely larger than the first.[31]

If on the other hand the insane were particularly dangerous, they were kept in place by a system of constraints which was probably not intended to be punitive by nature, but which was intended to fix a physical limit in the event of a fit of rage. Chaining the mad to walls and beds was common practice. At Bethlem, mad women were chained by the ankles to the wall of a long gallery, and had no clothing other than a sackcloth dress. In another hospital at Bethnal Green, a woman subject to violent fits of excitement was kept in a pigsty, her legs and arms bound, whenever she began to rave. Once the fit passed, she would be tied to her bed again, covered with a blanket, and when she had permission to take a few steps, an iron bar was placed between her legs, and her ankles shackled to the bar, and linked to her handcuffs by a short chain. Samuel Tuke wrote of a laborious system that had been put in place in Bethlem to control one raving madman. He was tied to a long chain that went over a wall and allowed the guard to control his movements, as though keeping him on a leash from the outside. He had an iron collar around his neck attached to another ring by a short chain, the second ring going round a thick vertical iron bar that went from the floor to the ceiling. When Bethlem was reformed, a man named Norris was found to have spent twelve years in the cell living under those conditions. He was freed, and died within a year of his release.

The violence of these practices demonstrates quite clearly that they were not governed by a consciousness of the need to punish, or by the duty to correct behaviour. The notion of resipiscence is quite foreign to the whole system. What haunts the hospices is an image of bestiality. Madness here took its face from the mask of the beast. The men chained to the walls of the cells were not seen as people who had lost their reason, but as beasts filled with snarling, natural rage, as though madness at its furthest point was liberated from the moral unreason where its milder forms languished, and was revealed in all its immediate, animal violence. That model of animality slowly came to dominate the asylums, and explained their cage-like, menagerie aspects. Describing the Salpêtrière at the end of the eighteenth century, Coguel had this to say:

> The frenzied madwomen are chained like dogs to the doors of their cells, and separated from visitors and their gaolers by a long corridor with iron bars: their food, and the straw that they sleep on is passed under the bars, and part of the filth that surrounds them is pulled out by rakes.[32]

In the hospital at Nantes, the menageries resembled individual cages for wild animals. Esquirol wrote that he had never seen

> such an array of locks, bolts and iron bars to close the doors of cells . . . Even the tiny openings beside the door are barricaded with locks and bars. Near the opening, a chain was set into the wall, with a clog-shaped iron vessel at its other extremity, in which food was passed through the gaps between the bars.[33]

When François-Emmanuel Fodéré arrived at Strasbourg hospital in 1814, he found a kind of human stable, which had been set up with great ingenuity. For the mad 'who misbehaved or soiled themselves', there were two cages at either end of the room, which had just enough room for an average-sized man. The cages had a floor raised about six inches off the floor, covered with straw, 'where the unfortunates lay down, naked or half-naked, to eat their food or relieve themselves'.[34]

What is in place here is clearly a safety mechanism to guard against the violence of the insane in their moments of frenzy. Their raving is first seen as presenting a danger to society. But the key point is that these fits of madness are seen as a kind of animal freedom. The negative fact that 'the mad were not treated as human beings' was the result of a very real thought process, in that this apparently inhuman indifference betrayed a deep-seated worry which since antiquity, and above all since the Middle Ages, had given the animal world its familiar strangeness, its menacing marvels, and the weight of all the fears it inspires. Yet this animal fear that accompanied the perception of madness with all its imaginary landscapes no longer had the meaning that it had had for previous centuries. Metamorphosis into an animal was no longer an indication of the power of the devil, nor a result of the diabolical alchemy of unreason. The animal in man was no longer the indicator of a beyond, but had become in itself his madness, with no reference to anything other than itself, his madness in a natural state. The animality that raged in madness dispossessed man of his humanity, not so that he might fall prey to other powers, but rather to fix him at the degree zero of his own nature. Madness, in its ultimate form, was for the classical age a direct relation between man and his animality, without reference to a beyond and without appeal.[35]

1   The day would come when this animal presence in madness would be considered from an evolutionary perspective as a sign – or even the essence – of sickness. But in the classical age the opposite was the case, and man's bestiality demonstrated with singular power that *a madman was not sick*. The mad were protected by their animality from all that was fragile, precarious and delicate in man. The animal solidity of madness, and the thick skin that was inherited from the animal kingdom, was a carapace for the insane against hunger, heat, cold and pain. It was common currency until the late eighteenth century that the mad could put up indefinitely with the miseries of existence. Hence there was no need to protect them, cover them or even provide warmth for them. When Samuel Tuke visited some workhouses in the southern counties in 1811, he found cells where the daylight went straight through barred windows on the doors of the cells. The women inside were entirely naked. 'The temperature was extremely low, and the previous evening the thermometer had registered 18 below. One of these poor unfortunates was sleeping on the straw without any cover.' The ability that the insane possessed to tolerate like animals the worst excesses of the weather was still accepted as medical dogma by Pinel, who repeatedly admired

the constancy and facility with which the mad of both sexes can tolerate prolonged extremes of cold. During the month of Nivôse in year III, there were days when thermometers registered 10, 11, and even 16 below zero, but one inmate at Bicêtre could still not keep his woollen blanket on, and instead remained seated on the frozen floor of his cell. In the morning, as soon as his door was opened, he would run out into the courtyard in his shirt, and taking up fistfuls of snow and ice, rub them on his chest and watch them melt with glee.[36]

The animal ferocity of madness was a barrier against sickness for the mad, granting them a sort of invulnerability like the one that nature, in her bounty, provided for the animal world. Curiously, the troubled reason of men brought the bounties of nature within the grasp of the mad, by means of this return to bestiality.[37]

2   For that reason, at these extremities, madness had less than ever to do with medicine, and precious little to do with correction either. Unchained bestiality could only be *tamed* or *trained*. The theme of the madman as a wild animal owes its fullest development to the eighteenth century, to the pedagogy that was sometimes imposed on the mad. Pinel quotes the case of a 'well-known monastic institution in one of the southern parts of France' where the insane were ordered very clearly to change their ways. If they refused to go to bed or to eat, 'they were warned that their obstinacy would be punished the following morning by ten lashes with a bullwhip'. But if they cooperated, 'they were allowed to take their meals in the refectory, beside the teacher'. The slightest mistake there was greeted with a sharp rap on the knuckles.[38] This strange dialectical movement explains all the 'inhuman' aspects of confinement. The free animality of madness could only be tamed, and not so that the beast might become human again, but to restitute man to what is exclusively animal in him. Madness unveiled a secret of animality which is its truth, and in which, in some sense, it is resorbed. In the middle period of the eighteenth century, a Scottish farmer named Gregory had his moment of fame when he claimed to have the ability to cure mania. Pinel noted the colossal stature of the man:

his method was to employ the mad for the most menial tasks possible around the farm, using some as beasts of burden and others as domestic servants, reducing them to obedience with a flurry of blows if they ever stepped out of line.[39]

In this reduction to animality, madness found its truth and its cure. When the madman became a beast, the animal presence in him removed the scandal of madness, not because the beast had been silenced but because all humanity had been evacuated. If a human being became a beast of burden, the absence of reason followed the order of wisdom. Madness was cured when it was alienated in a thing that was nothing other than its own truth.

3   The moment would come when the idea of a mechanistic psychology would be derived from this animal nature of madness, together with the idea that the different forms of madness can be compared to the great structures of animal life. But in the seventeenth and eighteenth centuries, the animal face of madness was far from entailing a determinism of its manifestations. On the contrary, madness was a *space of unpredictable liberty* where frenzy was unleashed. The only form of determinism possible was through the hoped-for effects of constraint, punishment and training. Animality did not lead so much towards the grand laws of nature and life as it did towards the myriad forms of the Bestiary. Unlike the examples from the Middle Ages, however, which used symbolic figures to recount the metamorphoses of evil, the classical Bestiary was more abstract. Evil no longer stalked through its pages in fantastical guises; all it displayed was the extreme form, the truth without content of the beast. The rich fauna of the imagination were removed, leaving only a generalised air of threat and menace, the mute danger of a sleeping animal, who might at once abolish reason in violence and truth in insane fury. Despite efforts to draw up a positivist zoology, this fear of bestiality as the natural form of madness constantly haunted the hell of the classical age. The origins of the savage treatment meted out to the insane in confinement are to be found in this imagery.

In the Middle Ages, before the early days of the Franciscan movement (and for a long time afterwards despite that movement), the human conception of the animal world was of a reservoir of the dark power of evil. The naturalist positivism of our age reflects it in terms of hierarchies, order and evolutionary development. The classical age was a transitional period in that respect. Animality was still seen as a negative force, but natural nonetheless. This is the moment when man only experienced his relation with animality in the absolute peril of madness, which would transform human nature into natural homogeneity. That conception of madness is the proof that even in the eighteenth century man's relationship with his nature was neither simple nor immediate, but that it passed through the most rigorous forms of negativity.[40]

It was probably essential for Western culture to link its perception of madness to imaginary forms of the relation between men and animals. It had never been absolutely clear that animals were part of the fullness of nature, its wisdom and good order; this was a late idea that had long remained on the surface of the culture, and it may not have even filtered through into the deeper regions of the imagination. Closer examination reveals that animals were more often thought of as being part of what might be termed a counter-nature, a negativity that menaced the order of things and constantly threatened the wisdom of nature with its wild frenzy. The work of the French poet Lautréaumont is proof of that. Did the fact that, after Aristotle, men had spent two thousand years thinking of themselves as reasonable animals necessarily imply that they accepted the possibility that reason and animality were of a common order? Or that the definition of man as a 'rational animal' provided a blueprint for understanding man's place in natural positivity? Independently of whatever Aristotle had meant exactly with that definition, it might be the case that for the Western world 'rational animal' meant the manner in which the freedom of reason took off from a space of unchained unreason and marked itself off from it, ultimately forming its opposite. From the moment when philosophy became anthropology, and men decided to find their place in the plentitude of the natural order, the animal world lost that power of negativity, and assumed the positive form of an evolution between the determinism of nature and the reason of man. At that point, the meaning of the term 'rational animal' underwent a radical change, and the unreason that it had designated as the origin of all reason vanished entirely. From then on, madness had to follow the determinism of a humanity perceived as natural in its own animality. In the classical age, while it was true that the scientific and medical analysis of madness, as we shall see, sought to inscribe madness within a mechanism of nature, the everyday practices that affected the insane were proof enough that madness was still thought of as the counter-natural violence of the animal world.

*

Whatever 'rational animal' meant, confinement constantly stressed the *animality of madness*, while attempting to avoid the scandal linked to the *immorality of the unreasonable*. This demonstrates clearly the distance that sprang up in the classical age between madness and other forms of unreason, despite the fact that from some points of view they seemed to merge or be taken for each other. If a whole side of unreason was reduced to silence, but madness was allowed to express the scandal of its unreason as it desired, what could have been expected from madness, which unreason itself was not allowed to transmit? What was the meaning of the frenzied ravings of the insane, which was not to be found in the more intelligible opinions of the other inmates? Why was madness thought of as being especially significant?

After the seventeenth century, unreason in its widest sense was no longer considered to teach anything much at all. The reversibility of reason, which had been such a real danger for the Renaissance, was forgotten, and its scandal disappeared. The great theme of the madness of the Cross that had seemed so intimately linked to the Christian experience of the Renaissance began to disappear in the seventeenth century, despite Pascal and Jansenism. Or rather, it continued, but in a different, almost inverse form. It no longer demanded that human reason relinquish its pride and its certainties to lose itself in the great unreason of sacrifice. When classical Christianity spoke of the madness of the Cross, it was to expose false reasoning and bring the eternal light of the truth out into the open: the madness of God made man was wisdom that the men of this world failed to recognise, ruled as they were by unreason. 'Jesus on the Cross was the scandal of the world, and it looked like ignorance and madness to the eyes of that century.' But when the world converted to Christianity, and the divine order became clear through the twisting course of history and the madness of men, it became apparent that Christ was 'the highest form of wisdom'.[41] The scandal of faith, and the abasement of Christians, which was still very real for Pascal and which kept for him the value of a manifestation, soon lost all meaning for Christian thought, and served only to show the blindness of these scandalised consciousnesses. "Do not allow your cross, which has brought the universe into submission, to be treated as madness and scandal by the proud." Christians themselves banished Christian unreason to the margins of reason, which was taken as the wisdom of God made man. After Port-Royal, Western culture had to wait two centuries before Christ found once more the glory of his madness in Dostoevsky and Nietzsche, when scandal regained its power of manifestation, and unreason ceased being nothing more than the public shaming of reason.

But just as Christian reason was divesting itself of the madness that had so long been part of it, the mad were granted a singular power of demonstration, in their abolished reason and animal fury. It was as though scandal had been expelled from those higher regions above, where man related to the divine through the Incarnation, only to reappear with renewed force and teach an important lesson in the region where man was related to nature and his own animality. The lesson to be learned now came from the lower depths of madness. The cross was no longer to be considered in all its scandal; but it should not be forgotten that all through his life, Christ had honoured madness. He had sanctified the mad as he had sanctified the sick who were cured, sinners who were forgiven, and the poor, who were promised eternal riches. Saint Vincent de Paul recalled for those whose task it was to watch over the demented in houses of confinement that they should never forget that their saviour had chosen 'to be surrounded by lunatics, diabolical men and madmen, by the tempted and the possessed'.[42] These men who were controlled by inhumanity, next to those who represent eternal Wisdom, presented a perpetual opportunity for glorification, as in their very proximity they were praising the reason that they had been denied, and at the same time, led to humility, in the recognition that reason was only provided by the grace of God. But there was more. Christ had wanted not only to be surrounded by lunatics, he had also wanted to pass himself off as a madman, experiencing in his incarnation all the miseries to which the flesh was heir. Madness therefore became an ultimate limit, the last degree of God made man, before the deliverance and transfiguration on the Cross:

> O my Saviour, you wanted to be the scandal of the Jews, and the madness of the gentiles; you wished to appear beside yourself, yes Lord, it was your wish to appear insane as it says in the Gospel, where it is noted that people thought you had gone mad. *Dicebant quoniam in furorem versus est* ('since he is said to wander in the direction of madness'). The apostles sometimes looked at their saviour as a man who had fallen into anger, in order to show them that he could sympathise with all our infirmities and sanctify our afflictions, the better to understand them, and also to teach them and us compassion for all those who fall into such infirmities.[43]

By coming into this world, Christ accepted to take on all the signs of the human condition, and even the stigmata of fallen nature. From misery to death, the path of the Passion was also the path of the passions, of wisdom forgotten and of madness. And because it was one of the forms of the Passion – the ultimate one, before death – madness was seen in those who suffered from it as an object commanding respect and compassion.

Respecting madness did not mean uncovering an involuntary mechanism, or an accidental slide into illness, but it did mean recognising the lower limit of human truth, a limit that was not accidental but essential. Just as death was the term of human life from a temporal point of view, so madness was the term from the point of view of animality, and just as death itself had been sanctified by Christ's death, madness too, in its most bestial form, received a measure of sanctity. On 29 March 1654, Saint Vincent de Paul told Jean Barreau, a fellow Congregationist, that his brother had been confined in Saint-Lazare as a madman:

> We must also honour our Lord in the state in which he found himself when men thought he had lost his wits, *quoniam in frenesim versus est*, and sanctify this state in all those in whom it is God's Will that it is to be found.[44]

Madness is the lowest point of humanity to which God gave his consent in the Incarnation, showing that there was no form of inhumanity in man that could not be saved. The lowest point of the fall was thus glorified by divine presence, and for the seventeenth century, this was a lesson that was contained in all madness.

It should now be clear how it came to be possible for the scandal of madness to be exalted, while other forms of unreason were so carefully hidden from view. Unreason meant nothing more than immorality and the possibility of a contagious fault, while madness showed men how close to the animal world their fall could take them, as well as teaching them how far divine forgiveness could reach when it consented to save mankind. For the Christianity of the Renaissance, the value contained in the teaching of unreason and all its scandal was in the madness of God-made man. For classicism, the incarnation itself was no longer mad, but what was mad was the incarnation of man in the beast, the lowest point of his fall and therefore the most obvious sign of original sin. And as the ultimate object of divine pity, it was also a symbol of universal salvation and innocence refound. Henceforth the lessons of madness, and the force of its teaching, were to be sought in the darker regions of human consciousness, where man intersected with the material world, where the ultimate fall meets absolute innocence. The Church's concern with the insane, during the classical period, as demonstrated by Saint Vincent de Paul and his Congregation, by the Brothers of Charity and all the other religious orders who turned their attention to madness, showing it to the world, are a sure sign that what the Church found there was a difficult but essential theme: the guilty innocence of the animal in man. That is the lesson that should be read into and understood from these spectacles where the ravings of the mad or the beast in man were exalted. Paradoxically, this Christian consciousness of madness prepared the moment when madness was treated as a fact of nature. What that 'nature' had meant to the classical age was quickly forgotten – not a domain ever open to objective analysis, but a region where what came into being was the scandalous possibility for humanity of a form of madness that was both its ultimate truth and the form of its abolition.

*

All these facts, these strange practices that grew up around madness, these habits that exalted it and tamed it, and reduced it to an animal state while simultaneously obliging it to exemplify redemption, meant that madness was placed in an odd relation to unreason. Inside the centres of confinement, madness rubbed shoulders with unreason in all its forms, which enveloped it and defined its most general truth; and yet at the same time it was singled out as unique, as though it were a part of unreason filled with an energy all its own, moving spontaneously towards its most paradoxical extremity.

All of which would be unimportant if the concern here were with a purely positivist history of madness. It was not thanks to the confinement of libertines or the fear of bestiality that the progressive realisation of the pathological reality of madness was made; rather, it is thanks to a process of disengagement from everything that linked madness to the moral concerns of the classical age that its medical truth was established. Or so positivism would have us believe, conveniently redrawing the map of its own development, as though the history of knowledge was a slow, objective process of erosion, where the fundamental structures of truth slowly emerged; as though the claim that the objectivity of medicine can define the essence and the secret truth of madness was not a postulate. One could equally see the teaming of madness and pathology as a kind of confiscation, a sort of avatar that was carefully prepared in the history of our culture, but not determined in any sense by the essence of madness itself. The links that seemed so obvious in the classical age between madness and libertinage, which were consecrated by the practice of confinement, suggest that madness then had a face which is now entirely invisible to us.

Our age has fallen into the habit of conceiving of madness as a fall into a kind of determinism where all forms of liberty are slowly eroded, so much so that now all we can see there are the natural regularities of a determinism, the chain of its causes, and the discursive movement linking its various forms. The threat that madness poses for modern human beings is a return to the monotonous world of beasts and things, all freedom curtailed. But it was not against that horizon of *nature* that the seventeenth and eighteenth centuries recognised madness, but rather against the backdrop of *unreason*. Madness was not a mechanism, but a freedom to roam among the monstrous forms of animality. Today we have lost the freedom to understand unreason other than in its adjectival form. We can use the word '*unreasonable*' to describe someone's speech or behaviour, and in the eyes of non-specialists, it could be an indicator of madness with all its pathological conditions. The unreasonable is only one possible way in which madness might transpire. But for the classical age unreason had the value of a noun, and had a substantive function. It was in relation to unreason alone that madness could be understood. Unreason lay beneath it, or rather defined the space of its possibility. For men of the classical age, madness was not the natural condition, the psychological and human root of unreason, but rather its empirical form, and the mad, a humanity sliding down towards animal frenzy, revealed the backdrop of unreason that menaced man and enveloped from afar each form of his natural existence. Unreason was no slide towards determinism, but opened instead onto an endless night. More than any other mode of thinking – more so than our positivism, to be sure – classical rationalism was on guard against the subterranean peril of unreason, the threatening space of absolute liberty.

Men of our age, after Nietzsche and Freud, find within their consciousness a black spot that threatens all truth, and are able to identify, thanks to what they have learnt, a place through which unreason might rise up and challenge the sovereignty of higher forms of consciousness. But men of the seventeenth century discovered in the immediacy of thought present to itself the certainty in which reason expresses itself in its primordial form. This is not to say that in their experience of truth, men of the classical age were more distant from unreason than we are ourselves. It is true to say that the Cogito, 'I think therefore I am', is an absolute beginning, but it should not be forgotten that the evil genius has preceded it. And the evil genius is not just the symbol that sums up in a systematic way the dangers of psychological events such as images from dreams and errors of the senses. Half-way between man and God, the evil genius has an absolute meaning: he is both the possibility of unreason and the sum of all its powers. More than the refraction of human finitude, it designates the peril that beyond man might prevent him in a definitive manner from reaching the truth, a major obstacle threatening not so much the individual mind as reason itself. The brilliant light of the truth of the Cogito should not be allowed to obscure the shadow of the evil genius, nor to obfuscate its perpetually threatening power; until the existence and the truth of the outside world have been secured, he haunts the whole movement of Descartes' *Meditations*. Under conditions like these, how could the classical age reduce unreason to a mere psychological event, or even some human pathos? For the classical age, it was rather the element in which the world was born to its own truth, the domain where reason will have to assert itself. Accordingly, madness could never form the essence of unreason for the classical age, even in its most primitive formulations, and no psychology of madness could ever claim to tell the truth about unreason. Madness had to be squarely placed against the free unreason for its real dimensions to be understood.

If libertines, blasphemers, the debauched and the prodigal were thrown together with those whom we would described as mentally ill, it was not because too little account was taken of the innocence or determinism of madness, but simply because unreason was given pride of place. When the time came to deliver the mad and free them from their shackles, it was not an indicator that the old prejudices had been done away with; it simply meant that eyes were suddenly closed, and that the watch that had long been kept over unreason was slowly abandoned. Classical rationalism can be thought of as being closely linked to that watch. In the confusion that reigned in centres of confinement, dissipating only in the early nineteenth century, it seems to us that the psychological profile of the madman was little understood. It is rather that a deep kinship with all forms of unreason was recognised in his condition. Confining the insane with heretics or the dissolute was one way of glossing over the fact of madness, but it did reveal the perpetual possibility of unreason, and it was that threat in its most abstract and universal form that the practice of confinement attempted to dominate.

What the fall of man was to sin, so was madness to the other faces of unreason. It was the principle, the original movement, the highest form of guilt in instantaneous contact with the greatest innocence, the constantly repeatedly model of all that was to be shamefully forgotten. If madness was an exemplary form in the world of confinement, on show at a time when all other forms of unreason were reduced to silence, that was because it carried within it the power of scandal. It traversed the whole gamut of unreason, forming a bridge between its two extremes, between the moral failing, the relative choice, the faltering of the will, and animal rage, freedom chained to frenzy and the initial, absolute fall; the shore of clear liberty, facing the opposite shore of dark freedom. Madness summed up the whole of unreason in a single point – the guilt of day and the innocence of the night.

There lies the major paradox of the classical experience of madness. Madness was caught up and enveloped in the moral experience of an unreason that was proscribed by internment in the seventeenth century, but it was also linked to the experience of an animal unreason that formed the absolute limit of the incarnation of reason, and the scandal of the human condition. Placed under the sign of all minor forms of unreason, madness was linked to ethics and the moral valorisation of reason, but when seen as part of the animal world and its rampant unreason, it was its monstrous innocence that came to the fore. What resulted could be called a contradictory experience, far distant from the juridical definitions of madness, whose concern was with finding a way between responsibility and determinism, weighing up guilt and innocence, distant too from the medical analyses of the time that saw madness as a natural phenomenon. Yet despite these contrasts in the practice and the concrete consciousness of the classical age there is this singular experience of madness which holds together the whole domain of unreason, as though in a flash of lightning: based on an ethical choice and yet indissolubly linked to the fury of the animal world. Positivism never really solved the dilemma, even if it did simplify it. It placed the theme of the innocent, animal side of madness within a theory where mental alienation was seen as a patho-logical mechanism of the natural world, while simultaneously keeping the mad confined in the manner invented by the classical age, thereby main-taining them – without admitting as much – within the power of instru-ments for moral constraint and for the mastering of unreason.

The positivist psychiatry of the nineteenth century, like our own, may no longer have used the knowledge and practices handed on from the previous age, but they secretly inherited the relationship that classical culture as a whole had set up with unreason. They were modified and displaced, and it was thought that madness was being studied from the point of view of an objective pathology; but despite those good inten-tions, madness was still haunted by an ethical view of unreason, and the scandal of its animal nature.

Part Two

INTRODUCTION

One simple truth about madness should never be overlooked. The consciousness of madness, in European culture at least, has never formed an obvious and monolithic fact, undergoing metamorphosis as a homogeneous ensemble. For the Western consciousness, madness has always welled up simultaneously at multiple points, forming a constellation that slowly shifts from one place and form to another, its face perhaps hiding an enigmatic truth. Meaning here is always fractured.

But what form of knowledge, after all, is sufficiently singular, esoteric or regional to be given only at a single point, in a unique formulation? What learning could be so well – or so badly – understood to be known only in a single time, in a uniform manner, in a single mode of apprehension? What figure of science, however coherent or tight it might be, does not allow more or less obscure forms of practical, moral or mythological consciousness to gravitate around it? If it were not experienced in a random order, and recognised only through profiles, all truth would soon fall dormant.

It may be though that a degree of non-coherence is more essential to the experience of madness than it is to any other. Perhaps dispersal is a fundamental part of this experience, bringing us closer to the primordial facts than a diversity of modes of elaboration one could arrange along an evolutionary schema. And whereas in most other forms of knowledge, the object is slowly seized in the convergence of its profiles, here divergence might be inscribed in the structures themselves, authorising only a broken, fragmentary consciousness of madness from the outset, in a debate that could not end. It may be that some concepts or a certain arrogance of knowledge occasionally masks this primary dispersion in a superficial manner; one example is the effort the modern world makes to only speak of *madness* in the serene, objective terms of *mental illness*, blotting out its *pathetic* values in the hybrid meanings of *pathology* and *philanthropy*. But the meaning of madness for any age, our own included, can never be covered entirely by the theoretical unity of a project: it lies instead in its torn presence. And when the experience of madness attempted to surpass itself and to find its balance by projecting itself on the plane of objectivity, nothing could efface the dramatic values that were given at the outset of its own debate.

This debate constantly recurs, and each time, in various different guises but equally difficult to recognise, the same forms of consciousness recur, obstinately irreducible.

1 *A critical consciousness of madness*, which identifies madness and designates it against a backdrop of all that is reasonable, ordered and morally wise. This consciousness is wholly invested in its own judgement, even before any concepts have been worked out, and it does not so much *define* as *denounce*. Madness is experienced as an opposition that is immediately felt, a blatant aberration; an abundance and plethora of proofs show it to be 'empty-headed and topsy-turvy'.[1] From this still initial starting point, the consciousness of madness is self-assured, that is, confident that it itself is not mad. But this consciousness has launched itself into difference, without measure or concept, into the heart of the conflictual region where madness and non-madness exchange their most primitive language, and the opposition becomes reversible: in the absence of a fixed point of reference, madness could equally be reason, and the consciousness of madness a secret presence, a strategy that belongs to madness itself:

> Men on a river, on a vessel afloat
> Oft see the land move, not their boat.[2]

But as madness does not possess the certainty that it is not mad, there is in it a madness more general than any other, which assimilates to madness the most obstinate wisdom:

The more I pare myself down, the more one thought holds sway:
The world and its brother have all lost their way.[3]

This wisdom may be thin, but it reigns supreme. It presupposes and requires a perpetual doubling of the consciousness of madness, which disappears beneath the surface of madness, only to reappear again on the other side. It relies on the values, or rather on the single, immediately stated value of reason, which it abolishes only to regain it immediately in ironic lucidity, feigning despair at this abolition. This critical consciousness claims to be so rigorous as to carry out a radical self-critique, and to risk all in an absolute combat whose outcome is uncertain, while secretly ensuring its own survival in advance, recognising its own rationality in the simple fact of accepting the risk. In one sense, reason's engagement is total in this simple and reversible opposition to madness, but it is only total on account of the secret possibility of total disengagement.

2 *A practical consciousness of madness*, where the process of disengagement is neither virtual nor a result of some virtuoso dialectics. It emerges as a concrete reality in the existence and the norms of a group. But more than that, it is given as a choice, an inescapable choice as one is either in one group or the other, within or without. But this choice is a false one, as only those who are inside the group have the right to decide who is to be considered an outsider, accusing them of having made the choice to be there. The merely critical consciousness that those outsiders have somehow *deviated* rests on the consciousness that they have *chosen a different path*, and there it finds its justification, at the same time becomes brighter and obscure, turning into unmediated dogma. This is not the troubled consciousness of being engaged in the difference and homogeneity of madness and reason, but rather the consciousness of the difference between madness and reason, a consciousness only possible *inside* the confines of the homogeneity of a group considered to be the bearers of the norms of reason. Although it is social, normative and has a solid base from the outset, this practical consciousness of madness is still dramatic, and while it implies solidarity inside the group, it also demonstrates the urgency of the division.

The ever-perilous freedom of dialogue is muted in this division. All that remains is the calm certainty that madness should be reduced to silence. It is an ambiguous form of consciousness, serene in the confidence that it is the keeper of the truth, but worried at recognising the obscure power of madness. Against reason, madness now seems disarmed, but in the struggle against order, and against all that reason can show of itself in the laws of men and things, it reveals itself to have strange powers. It is that order that the consciousness of madness feels to be under threat, together with the division that it operates. But from the outset, the risk is limited, even falsified – no real confrontation will take place. Instead, what is exercised is the absolute right, with no compensation, that the consciousness of madness grants itself from the outset, by considering itself to be homogeneous with the group and with reason itself. Ceremony is more important than debate, and what this consciousness of madness demonstrates is not the dangers of a real struggle between madness and reason, but only the immemorial rites of an exorcism. This form of consciousness is at once the most and the least historic; it considers itself to be an instantaneous defensive reaction, but the reaction does nothing more than reactivate the age-old anguishes of horror. The modern asylum, when one considers the obscure consciousness that justifies it and makes it necessary, is anything but purified from the heritage of the lazar house. The practical consciousness of madness, which seems to define itself only by the transparency of its finality, is without doubt the densest form of that consciousness, its schematic ceremonies heavy with ancient drama.

3 *An enunciatory consciousness of madness*, which allows for immediate pronouncements, without any detours through the world of knowledge: 'that man is mad'. Here there is no question of qualifying or disqualifying madness, but only of pointing at it as a kind of substantive existence: there before us, the object of our gaze, is someone who is undeniably, indisputably mad. Madness here has a simple, obstinate and immobile existence, and no identification of its quality or judgement on its nature is required. This consciousness is not concerned with values, peril or risk, but is on the level of being. It is nothing more than a monosyllabic nod that categorises at a glance. In a sense, this is the most serene form of the consciousness of madness, as it is at bottom nothing but a simple perceptive apprehension. As it avoids any detour through knowledge, it also avoids the worries of a diagnosis. This is the ironic consciousness of the interlocutor in Diderot's *Le Neveu de Rameau*, or the consciousness at peace with itself, scarcely over its suffering, that recounts the dreams in Nerval's *Aurélia*, half-way between bitterness and fascination. However simple it may be, this consciousness is not pure: it experiences a perpetual backwards movement, as it at once supposes and proves that it is not madness

through the simple fact that it is an immediate consciousness of it. Madness is only there, present and designated as an irrefutable self-evident truth, as long as the consciousness that designates it has already rejected it, having defined itself in a relation of opposition towards it. It is only consciousness of madness against the backdrop of a consciousness sure of its own sanity. However free of prejudice it might be, however distant from all forms of constraint and oppression, it remains a way of having taken control of madness already. Its refusal to qualify madness always supposes a certain qualitative consciousness of itself as something other than madness, and it is a simple perception only in so far as it is this surreptitious opposition: 'If others had not been foolish, we should be so',[4] said William Blake. But no mistake should be made about this apparent anteriority of the others' madness: its ancient appearance is mainly due to the manner in which, beyond all possible memories, the consciousness of not being mad has spread a veil of atemporal calm. 'The hours of folly are measur'd by the clock, but of wisdom: no clock can measure.'[5]

4 *An analytical consciousness of madness*, unfolding all its forms, all its phenomena and modes of appearing. Doubtless the totality of these forms and phenomena can never be present at the same time to this consciousness. Since long ago, and forever perhaps, madness disguises most of its powers and truths in the unfamiliar, but it is in this analytical consciousness that it rejoins the tranquillity of the familiar. While it may be true that the phenomena and causes of madness will never be truly mastered, it still is the rightful property of the gaze that dominates it. Madness here is the totality of its phenomena, even if only virtual. It presents no dangers, and no longer implies a division; it requires no more distance than any other object of knowledge. It is this form of consciousness that founds the possibility of an objective knowledge of madness.

Each of these forms of consciousness is self-sufficient, and supportive of all the others. A solidarity due to the secret reliance of each upon the others: there can be no knowledge of madness, however objective its pretensions, however much it claims to rest exclusively on scientific knowledge, that does not, despite everything, suppose the prior movement of a critical debate, where reason confronted madness, facing it both as a simple opposition and in the peril of immediate reversibility. This knowledge also supposes a practical division as an ever-present virtuality structural to its horizon, whence the group confirms and reinforces its values by this exorcism of madness. Inversely, it can also be said that there is no critical consciousness of madness that does not attempt to found itself or surpass itself in an analytical knowledge that would quell the disquiet of the debate, where the risks would be under control and the distances would be definitively established. Each of these four forms of the consciousness of madness thus relies on one or several of the others as constant points of reference, as justifications or as presuppositions.

But none can be totally absorbed into any other. However close they may be, their relationship can never reduce them to a unity that would abolish them in a tyrannical, definitive and monotonous form of consciousness. By their nature, their meaning and their basis, each has its own autonomy. The first instantly cordons off a region of language that acts as a meeting point for opposites like sense and nonsense, truth and error, wisdom and inebriation, daylight and fascinating dreams, the limitations of judgement and the infinite presumption of desire. The second, an heir to great ancestral horrors, unwittingly, unwillingly and silently reinvents the ancient mute rites that purify and reinvigorate the obscure consciousness of the community, enveloping a whole history that never speaks its name; despite the self-justification that it provides on occasion, it remains closer to the immobile rigour of ceremony than to the incessant labour of language. This is not of the order of knowledge, but of recognition, a mirror, as in the *Neveu de Rameau* or remembrance, in Nerval and Artaud, always at bottom a reflection on itself even when it thinks it examines the other, or any otherness within the self. What it keeps at a distance, in its immediate enunciation, in this purely perceptive discovery, was its deepest secret, and in the simple existence of madness, which is there like an object offered and disarmed, it unknowingly recognises the familiarity of its own pain. In the analytical consciousness of madness, the drama is appeased, and the dialogue silenced. Gone are the ritual and the lyricism, as phantasms acquire their own truth. The perils of the counter-natural become the signs of a nature, and techniques of suppression are all that is called for where once horror was invoked. Here the consciousness of madness can only find its equilibrium in the form of knowledge.

*

Ever since the tragic experience of the insane disappeared with the Renaissance, each historical figure of madness has implied the simultaneity of these four forms of consciousness, with their dark conflicts and their constantly ruptured unity; at each moment what comes together and falls apart is the equilibrium of a dialectical consciousness of the experience of madness, a ritual division, a lyrical recognition and finally a knowledge of it. The successive faces that madness takes on in the modern world receive what is most characteristic in their traits from the proportion and links that result from these four major elements. None of them disappears entirely, but on occasion one is more privileged than another, so that the others may fade into the background, leading to tensions and conflicts that operate below the level of language. It also happens that links are established between these different forms of consciousness, constituting large areas of experience that have their own structure and autonomy. These movements sketch the outline of a historical becoming.

If we were to adopt a long timescale, from the Renaissance to modern times, it is probable that a vast movement would be discernible, where the dominant consciousness of madness moved from critical forms to analytical ones. The sixteenth century privileged the dialectical experience of madness, and more than any other period was open to all that was infinitely reversible between reason and the reason of madness, to all that was close, familiar and akin in the presence of a madman, and to the aspects of his existence that allowed illusion to be denounced so that the ironic light of truth might shine forth. Brant, Erasmus, Louise Labé, Montaigne, Charron and finally Régnier all share a common concern, a critical vivacity and the same consolation in the smiling embrace of madness. 'That reason is thus a strange beast', noted Régnier.[6] Medical experience itself created concepts and measures in keeping with the indefinite movement of this consciousness.

The nineteenth and twentieth centuries by contrast centred their interrogation on the analytical consciousness of madness, even presuming that this was the only domain of experience that would reveal the total, final truth about madness, and considering other forms of experience to be nothing more than approximations, rudimentary explorations or archaic elements. And yet the Nietzschean critique, all the values invested in the partitions operated by the asylums and the great process of experimentation that Artaud, following Nerval, ruthlessly carried out on his self, are proof enough that all the other forms of consciousness are still present at the heart of our culture. The fact that their only formulation now is a lyrical one is not proof that they are dying away, nor that they are merely the prolongation of an existence that knowledge has long surpassed, but demonstrates quite simply that when kept in the shadows they still flourish in the most original and free forms of language. Their power of contestation is perhaps more vigorous as a result.

In the classical age, on the other hand, the dominant experience of madness was of division, defining two autonomous domains of madness. One side saw the critical and practical consciousness of madness, and the other the forms of knowledge and recognition. A whole region became isolated, grouping together the practices and decisions through which madness was denounced and offered for exclusion. All elements within it that were uncomfortably close to reason, and which threatened reason with their derisive similarity, were violently separated and rigorously reduced to silence. Such were the perilous dialectics of the reasonable consciousness, the salutary division contained in the gesture of confinement. The importance of confinement lies not in its value as a new institutional form, but in the manner in which it summarises and demonstrates one of the two halves of the classical experience of madness, where the dialectical concern of consciousness and the ritualised dividing of society are organised into the coherence of a social practice. In the other region, by contrast, madness becomes manifest, attempting to voice its truth and denounce its situation, and express itself through all of its possible forms, looking for a nature and a positive mode of presence in the world.

Having tried in the previous chapters to analyse the domain of confinement and the forms of consciousness that the practice involved, our intention in what follows is to recreate the domain of recognition and knowledge of madness that was proper to the classical age. Who, with such instantaneous confidence, was recognised as mad? How did madness manifest itself in signs that could not be denied? How did it come to hold on meaning as a nature?

Doubtless this separation into two domains of experience is characteristic of the classical age, and is of sufficient importance in itself to hold our attention for a little longer.

It might be claimed that there was nothing extraordinary in this division, nothing that could be strictly tied to a particular period of history. The lack of coincidence between the practices of exclusion and protection and the more theoretical experience that we have of madness is certainly a fairly constant fact in Western experience. Even today, the extreme care which our good conscience takes in defining the grounds of a separation of the mad in purely scientific terms shows quite clearly how much we fear their inadequacy. But what characterises the classical age is both the absence of that fear and of any aspiration towards unity. For a century and a half, madness had a rigorously divided existence. The concrete proof of that stands out before our eyes: confinement, as we have seen, was never in any sense a medical practice, and the rite of exclusion it leads to does not open onto a space of positive knowledge. In France it was only with the great circular of 1785 that some medical order penetrated confinement, and with a decree from the Assembly that the sanity of each internee had to be assessed on an individual basis. Inversely, before Haslam and Pinel, there was practically no medical experience born of or in the asylum; knowledge of madness became part of the general corpus of medical knowledge, where it figured as simply one chapter among others, with no indication of the particular mode of existence of madness, or the meaning of its exclusion.

This division without appeal made the classical age an *age of the understanding* for the existence of madness.[7] There was no possibility of dialogue, no confrontation between a practice that mastered all that went against nature and reduced it to silence, and a form of knowledge that tried to decipher the truths of nature. The gesture that expelled all that man would not recognise remained outside the discourse in which a truth comes to knowledge. The different forms of experience developed to their own ends, the one in a practice without commentary, the other in a discourse without contradiction. Entirely excluded on one side, entirely objectified on the other, madness was never *made manifest* on its own terms, in its own particular language. It was not alive with contradiction but rather lived split between the two terms of a dichotomy. For as long as the Western world was entirely devoted to the age of reason, madness remained subject to the division of understanding.

Therein, no doubt, lies the reason for the profound silence that gives the madness of the classical age the appearance of sleep: such was the force of the feeling of obviousness that surrounded these concepts and protected them from each other. Perhaps no other age was ever so insensitive to the pathetic nature of madness, despite the profound gash in the fabric of life at the time. This was because this very tearing meant that it was not possible to appreciate madness as a unique point, a focus, at once imaginary and real, reflecting the questions human beings ask about themselves. In the seventeenth century, even if people had been convinced of the injustice of a confinement, the essence of reason would not have been compromised; and inversely, uncertainty about the nature of madness, or where to draw its limits, was not felt as an immediate threat to society or the man in the street. The excessive nature of the division ensured the calm of both forms of interrogation. No recurrence risked bringing them into contact with each other, creating the spark of a fundamental question, from which there was no returning.

*

And yet astonishing coincidences do appear repeatedly on all sides. When examined carefully, these two rigorously separated domains show some very close structural analogies. We identify quite easily, in the following pages, the consequences or causes of the retreat of madness brought about by the practices of confinement and the disappearance of the madman as a recognised social type – or, to be more neutral and exact, the corresponding forms, in the scientific and theoretical reflections on madness. What we described on the one hand as an event will reappear, on the other, as a form of conceptual development. However separate the two domains may appear, everything of importance in the first domain finds its counterpart in the second. Which is to say that the division can only be thought of in relation to the forms of unity whose appearance it authorises.

It might be thought that what we are doing here is little more than admiring the unity of theory and practice. Yet it seems to us that the division operated during the classical age between forms of the consciousness of madness does not correspond to the distinction between theory and practice. The scientific or medical knowledge of madness, even when it acknowledges the impossibility of a cure, is always virtually engaged in a system of operations intended to efface the symptoms or master the causes; on the other hand the practical consciousness that separates the mad from the rest of society, condemning them and making them disappear, is necessarily mixed with a certain political, legal and economic conception of the individual in society. Consequently, the division is of a different order. What we find on one side, under the great rubric of internment, is the moment, as theoretical as it is practical, of the division itself, the re-enactment of the ancient drama of exclusion, the form of the appreciation of madness in the gesture of its suppression: the part of madness that manages to express itself in its concerted annihilation. What we shall meet now is the theoretical and practical unveiling of the truth of madness on the basis of a being which is non-being, since this madness only expresses itself visibly through signs such as error, fantasy, illusion, and vain language devoid of meaningful content; our concern now will be with the constitution of madness as nature from the basis of the non-nature that is its being. Until now, our concern was with the dramatic constitution of a being on the basis of the violent suppression of its existence: now the concern will be with the constitution, in the serenity of knowledge, of a form of nature on the basis of the unveiling of a non-being.

But as well as the constitution of this nature, the intention is to describe the single experience that provides the basis both for the dramatic forms of the division and the calm movement of this constitution. It is this single underlying experience, visible here and there, explaining and justifying the practice of internment and the cycle of knowledge, which constitutes the classical experience of madness; and this is the experience that we can describe with the term 'unreason'. Its secret coherence stretches out beneath the great divide that we have just evoked; for unreason is both the reason for the division and the reason for the unity that is be found on both sides of the divide. Unreason is the explanation for the presence of the same forms of experience on *both sides* of the divide, but also for the fact that they are only ever found on one side *and* on the other. The unreason of the classical age is that unity and that division all at once.

It might be asked why we have waited so long before evoking it. Why name unreason at last, in the context of the constitution of a nature, with regard to science, medicine and 'natural philosophy', while only alluding to it indirectly or by paralipsis when speaking of economic and social life, different forms of poverty and unemployment, and institutions concerned with politics and policing? Is this not a means of privileging conceptual becoming over the real movement of history?

An adequate reply to such a question might be to note that in the bourgeois reorganisation of the world during the mercantilist era, the experience of madness was never presented head-on, but was only ever visible in profile or in a silent manner. It would therefore have been quite hazardous to define it using perspectives which are so incomplete in this case while they are so clearly constitutive of other more visible, more readily legible figures. It was enough during the first part of our research merely to evoke its presence, and to promise a fuller explanation later on. But when the philosopher or physician is presented with the problem of the relations between reason, nature and illness, then madness presents the full depth of its volume. The disparate mass of experiences that make up madness find here their point of coherence, it finally reaches the possibility of an expression through language. A singular experience appears at last. The simple, heterogeneous outlines, which until now were merely sketched, suddenly fall into place, and each element can interact with the other according to the law that is its own.

This experience is neither practical nor theoretical. It is part of the fundamental experiences in which a culture risks all its values – allowing them to face contradiction. While forewarning them against it. A culture like that of the classical age, which had so many values invested in reason, risked both the most and the least in madness. The most, in that madness was the most immediate contradiction to everything that justified its existence; the least in that it disarmed it entirely, and rendered it totally powerless. This maximal and minimal risk accepted by classical culture in madness is precisely what the word 'unreason' expresses: the simple, immediate converse of reason, encountered at once; and this empty form, without content or value, purely negative, where all that figures is the imprint of a reason that has taken to its heels, but which will always remain, for unreason, its *raison d'être*.

I

THE MADMAN IN THE GARDEN OF SPECIES

We must now interrogate the other side. Not the consciousness of madness involved in the gestures of segregation, with their unchanging rituals or their interminable critical debates, but that consciousness of madness that plays the game of division for its own ends, the consciousness that describes the madman and unfolds madness.

What was a madman anyway? What were the mad, with their enigmatic madness among men of reason, the reasonable men of an eighteenth century still in its infancy? How could the madman be recognised, he who a century earlier was still so easily discernible on the social landscape, but was now forced to wear a uniform mask for his many faces? How could he be singled out without error, in his everyday proximity that with those who were not mad, and in the inextricable mix of the characteristics of his madness and the obstinate signs of his reason? These are questions asked by the voice of wisdom rather than science, by the philosopher rather than the doctor, and by the attentive troupe of critics, sceptics and moralists.

For their part, physicians and savants would interrogate madness itself, and the natural space that it occupied, treating it as another ill among many, the upsets of the body and the soul, a natural phenomenon that developed both in nature and against it.

What we have then is a double system of interrogations that seem to look in two directions: a philosophical question, more critical than theoretical, and a medical question that implies an entire movement of discursive knowledge. One of these questions concerns the nature of reason, and the manner in which it authorises the division into the reasonable and the unreasonable; the other concerns what there is of the rational or the irrational in nature and in the fantasies of its variations.

Two different ways of interrogating nature when examining reason, and reason through nature. If luck were to have it that in trying both, a common response emerged from their difference, and a single and unique structure were to be discernible, it would doubtless be extremely close to what was essential and general in the experience that the classical age had of madness, and we would be led to the very limits of what must be understood as unreason.

*

The irony of the eighteenth century enjoyed taking up the old sceptical themes of the Renaissance, and Fontenelle is in a tradition of philosophical satire still close to Erasmus when, in the prologue to his *Pygmalion*, he has madness say:

> My dominion is constantly strengthened
> Men of today are madder than their fathers;
> And their sons in turn will be madder still
> Their grandchildren will see more chimera
> Than their eccentric grandparents.[1]

And yet the structure of the irony is no longer that of Régnier's fourteenth *Satire*. It no longer depends on the universal disappearance of reason from the world, but instead on the fact that madness has grown sufficiently subtle to have lost all visible, assignable form. It is as though, by a distant and derived effect of confinement upon thought, madness has withdrawn from its former, visible position, and all that previously made up its real plenitude has been effaced, leaving its place empty, and rendering its certain manifestations invisible. There is in madness an essential aptitude for mimicking reason, which in the end masks its own unreasonable content; or rather, the wisdom of nature is so profound that it manages to use madness as another path for reason, making it a short-cut to wisdom, avoiding its own forms with an invisible prescience: 'The order that nature wished to establish in the world follows its own course: all that can be said is that everything that nature does not obtain from our reason, it obtains through our madness.'[2]

The nature of madness is also at the same time its useful wisdom; its *raison d'être* is to approach reason so closely, and be so consubstantial with it that the two form an indissoluble text, where all that can be discerned are nature's ends: the madness of love is necessary for the preservation of the species, the delirium of ambition is required for the good order of political bodies, and insane greed is necessary for wealth to be created. Such individual, egotistical disorders are part of a greater wisdom, whose order surpasses individuals:

> As the madnesses of men are of the same nature, they are sufficiently well suited to each other to strengthen the bonds that make up human society, as can be seen from the desire for immortality, false glory and many other principles that underlie so much that goes on in the world.[3]

Madness in Bayle and Fontenelle takes a similar role to the one played by sentiment, according to Malebranche, in fallen nature – an involuntary vivacity that goes straight to a point that reason will take much longer to attain by indirect and arduous paths. Madness is the side of order that goes unperceived, which ensures that man, despite himself, is the instrument of a wisdom whose end he does not understand. Madness measures the distance that exists between foresight and providence, between calculation and finality. And it masks a profound, collective reason that masters time itself.[4] Since the seventeenth century, madness had undergone an imperceptible shift in the order of reasons. Previously on the side of the 'reasoning that banished reason', it had now slipped into the position of a silent reason that expedites the slow rationality of reasoning, smudging its well-ordered lines and risking its way beyond its ignorance and apprehensions. The nature of madness was to be a secret reason, existing only through and for reason, having no presence in the world other than the one granted it in advance by reason, already alienated within it.

But then how was it possible to assign a fixed place to madness, and to draw an outline for it that did not have the same features as reason itself? A hasty and involuntary form of reason, it could be allowed nothing that would show it to be irreducible. When Vieussens the Younger explained that the 'oval centre' in the brain was 'the seat of the functions of the spirit', because 'arterial blood there became sufficiently refined to become the animal spirit', and that consequently 'the health of the spirit in its material form depends on the regularity, the equality and the free passage of the spirits through these tiny canals', Fontenelle refused to recognise all that was immediately perceptible and decisive in a criterion so simple, which would allow an immediate division into the mad and the non-mad. Even if the anatomist was right to link madness to a disorder of these 'tiny fine vessels', such a disturbance might be found in anyone: 'there can be no head so healthy it does not have some minute blocked vessel somewhere in the oval centre'.[5] He admitted that the demented, the furious, the maniacal and the violent could be immediately identified, but this was not because they were mad, or inasmuch as they were, but only because their delirium was of a particular type that added its own particular indicators to the imperceptible essence of all madness: 'the frenzied are simply mad in a different fashion'.[6] But outside of such differentiations, the general essence of madness lacked any recognisable form: the mad, in general, had no tell-tale sign, but blended in with the rest of society, and madness was present in everyone, not as one side of a dialogue or conflict with reason, but to serve it obscurely in ways that could not be admitted. *Ancilla rationis* – the handmaid of reason. Long afterwards, despite being a physician and a naturalist, Boissier de Sauvages would still acknowledge that madness 'was never directly perceptible to the senses'.[7]

Despite the apparent similarities in the use of scepticism, the mode of presence of madness in this early eighteenth century had never been more different from anything it had been in the Renaissance. Previously, madness had made its presence manifest through innumerable signs, threatening reason with immediate contradiction, and showing the indefinite reversibility of things in its tightly structured dialectics. Things were now still equally reversible, but madness had become a more diffuse presence, devoid of obvious signs, exterior to the world of the senses, in the secret reign of a universal reason. It was at once plenitude and total absence: inhabiting all regions of the world, it spared no wisdom, no order, and escaped detection by the senses. It was present everywhere, but never in that which made it what it is.

Yet this retreat operated by madness, this essential gap between its presence and its manifestation, did not mean that it had withdrawn from the world of evidence to an inaccessible domain where its truth remained hidden. Paradoxically, having no unmistakeable signs nor positive presence, it presented itself with a sort of calm immediacy, on the surface of the world, with no possible distance for doubt. Only it did not offer itself then as madness but rather as a recognisable type, as the madman. 'Anyone whose reason is healthy can easily identify another whose reason is not, just as a shepherd can always single out the similarly unhealthy sheep in his flock.'[8] There was a degree of obviousness about the madman, an immediate assessment of his features, which seems correlative to the non-determination of madness itself. The less precise madness was, the easier the mad were to recognise. We may not know where madness begins, but we know with a knowledge that brooks no argument what a madman is. Voltaire was astonished that while we have no idea how a soul can reason wrongly, or how something could be changed in its essence, 'it is conducted to Colney Hatch in its bodily garment' without hesitation.[9]

How does this unquestioning recognition of the madman function? By a marginal perception, a sidelong glance, accompanied by a sort of instantaneous process of reasoning, both indirect and negative all at once. Boissier de Sauvages attempted to explain this perception, which could simultaneously involve such certainty and confusion:

> When a man acts in accordance with healthy reason, it is enough to pay attention to his gestures, movements, desires, his speech and his reasoning to discern the link that exists between these actions, and for it to be apparent how his actions combine towards a common end.

By the same token, when a madman is observed,

> To reveal the hallucination or the madness with which he is taken, he does not have to produce faulty syllogisms: the hallucination or the error in his mind is immediately discernible from the disparity that exists between his actions and the behaviour of normal men.[10]

The process is an indirect one in that there is no perception of madness other than by reference to an order of reason, and to the consciousness that we have when confronted with a man of reason, which can assure us of the coherence, the logic and the continuity that underlies his speech; that consciousness lies dormant until madness erupts, appearing all of a sudden, not because it has taken on a positive form but precisely because it is a kind of rupture. It suddenly emerges like a discordance, i.e. it is entirely negative; but it is within that negative character itself that it is assured to be instantaneous. The less madness shows itself in its positive forms, the more the madman, against the continuous weave of reason – which is almost forgotten due to its familiarity – appears abruptly as irreconcilable difference.

This first point is worth dwelling on. The hasty, presumptuous certainty with which the eighteenth century recognised the madman, while simultaneously admitting its incapacity to define madness itself, is clearly an important structure. The madman has an immediately precise, obvious, concrete character, while madness has a confused, distant, almost imperceptible outline. This is not so much a paradox as a natural relation of complementarity. The madman is too immediate to the senses for the general discourses of madness to be recognised in him. He only appears as a kind of punctual existence, an individual yet anonymous form of madness, where he can be singled out without any risk of error, but which disappears as soon as it is perceived. Madness, on the other hand, is indefinitely out of reach, a distant essence only really of interest to nosographers.

Both this direct evidence of the madman against the backdrop of a concrete reason, and the infinite retreat of madness to outer limits barely accessible to discursive reasoning, are the result of a certain absence of madness itself. Absence of a madness that is not linked to reason by any deep finality, of a madness caught in a real debate with reason and which, in the vast region that stretches from perception to discourse, from recognition to knowledge, would be a concrete generality, a living species that multiplied in all its manifestations. A certain absence of madness is discernible throughout this entire experience of madness. A gap has appeared, which leads perhaps to the essential.

For what appears to be absence from the point of view of madness might be the birth of something else, a point where a whole other experience comes into being, in the silent labour of the positive.

*

The madman is not manifest in his being, but if there is no doubt about his existence, it is because he is *other*. At the time of which we are speaking, that alterity was not perceived as an immediate difference, on the basis of some certainty of the self. Faced with the insane who thought 'that their heads were made of earthenware, or that they were pumpkins, or made of glass', Descartes knew immediately that he was not of their number, noting: 'such people are insane'. The inevitable recognition of their madness appeared spontaneously, in a relationship between the self and others – the subject measured the difference against his own self: 'I would be thought equally mad if I took anything from them as a model for myself.' In the eighteenth century, this consciousness of alterity hides a totally different structure under the apparent identity, and is formulated not from a basis of certainty but from a general rule. It implies an exterior relation, going from others to that singular Other that is the madman, in a confrontation where the subject is neither compromised nor even called upon to provide any form of evidence: 'We call madness that disease of the organs of the brain that necessarily prevents a man from thinking and acting like others.'[11] The madman is the other in relation to the others, the other, in the sense of an exception, amongst others, in the sense of the universal. All forms of interiority are therefore banished: the madman is self-evidently mad, but his madness stands out against the backdrop of the outside world, and the relation that defines him, exposes him wholly, through objective comparisons, to the gaze of reason. Between the madman and the subject who notes 'that man is mad', a gulf emerges, which is no longer simply the Cartesian void of 'I am not that man', but is filled instead with the plenitude of a double system of alterity. It is a distance filled with boundary markers, which can thus be measured and can vary: the madman is different to a greater or lesser degree in a group of people which in turn is more or less universal. The madman becomes relative, the better to be stripped of his powers: once that uncanny presence within, perilously close in the thought of the Renaissance, lurking in the heart of reason, he is now expelled to a different realm, where the danger he presents is disarmed. Doubly so, in that what he now represents is *the difference from the Other in the exteriority of others*.

This new form of consciousness inaugurated a new relation between madness and reason. It was no longer a continuous dialectic, the way it had been in the sixteenth century, and it was no longer a simple, permanent opposition as it had been in the rigorous division in force at the outset of the classical age, but became instead a complex, strangely knotted collection of links. On the one hand madness existed *in relation to* reason, or at least in relation to the 'others' who, in their anonymous generality, were supposed to represent it and grant it the value of an exigence; and on the other hand it existed *for* reason, in that it appeared in the consideration of an ideal consciousness, which perceived it as difference from the others. Madness now had a double mode of *facing* reason – it was at once *on the other side*, and *offered to its gaze*. On the other side in that it was immediate difference, pure negativity that betrayed itself as nonbeing in a manner that could not be denied; it was the total absence of reason, immediately perceived as such against the backdrop of *the structures of the reasonable*. And, as an object before the gaze of reason, madness was a singular individuality whose individual characteristics, behaviour, language, and gestures were each different from those to be found in a normal person. Through these particular aspects, madness unveiled itself to reason, taken not as a term of reference but as a principle of judgement; madness was thereby caught up in *the structures of the rational*. What characterised madness after Fontenelle was the permanence of a double relation to reason, this implication, in the experience of madness, of reason taken as a norm, and of reason defined as the subject of knowledge.

It could easily be objected that at any given period in history there was always a double apprehension of madness in that same fashion: a moral one against the backdrop of the reasonable, and another, objective and medical, against a backdrop of rationality. Leaving aside the great problem that is the madness of the ancient Greeks, it is true to say that by the time of the Romans, the consciousness of madness was caught in this duality. Cicero evokes the paradox of the sicknesses of the soul and their cure: when the body is ill, the soul can recognise it, know it and form judgements about it, but when the soul is sick the body can do nothing for it, and can tell us nothing about it: 'the soul is called upon to make judgements on its own state, when it is precisely the faculty of judgement that is unwell'.[12] It would be impossible to escape such a contradiction, were it not that there were two rigorously different points of view regarding the sicknesses of the soul. First of all was a form of philosophical wisdom, which could distinguish the mad from the reasonable, assimilating all forms of non-wisdom to madness – *omnes insipientes insaniunt* (all those who lack reason are insane)[13] – and could by teaching or persuasion dissipate the sicknesses of the soul: 'there is no need, as there is for the body, to look outside the self, and we must employ all of our resources and all our forces to ensure that we are in a state to cure ourselves',[14] and second there was a form of knowledge that could recognise in madness the effect of violent passions, irregular movements of black bile, and all 'that order of causes that spring to mind when thinking of Athamas, Alcmeon, Ajax and Orestes'.[15] Two forms of madness corresponded almost exactly to those two forms of experience: *insania*, which was 'a broad term', particularly 'with the addition of foolishness', and *furor*, a far more serious matter that Roman law had recognised since the law of the Twelve Tables. Because it was opposed to all that is reasonable, *insania* could never affect the wise; *furor*, by contrast, an event of both the body and the soul that reason was capable of reconstituting in knowledge, could at any time affect the spirit of the philosopher.[16] Latin tradition therefore recognised two forms of madness – one in the form of the reasonable and the other in the form of the rational – which even Cicero's moralism could not reduce.[17]

What happened in the eighteenth century was a slippage between perspectives, thanks to which the structures of the reasonable and the rational became interwoven, ultimately creating a weave so tight that for a long period it was impossible to make any distinction between them. They progressively formed a unity in relation to a single form of madness, perceived all together in its opposition to the reasonable, and in what it manifested of itself to the rational. The madman, who was the outsider *par excellence*, pure difference, 'other' to the power of two, became in this very distance the object of rational analysis, fullness offered to knowledge and evident perception, the one precisely to the extent that he was the other. From the first half of the eighteenth century onwards – and it is this that lent this period such a decisive weight in the history of unreason – the moral negativity of the madman began to be nothing other than the positivity of what could be known about him. The critical distance, the pathos of refusal, of non-recognition, this absence of characteristics all became the space in which the various characters of madness serenely appear, slowly forming a positive truth. And it is doubtless that same movement that is to be found in the enigmatic definition of madness in the *Encyclopédie*:

> To stray unwittingly from the path of reason, because one has no ideas, is to be an *imbecile*; knowingly to stray from the path when one is prey to

a violent passion is to be *weak*; but to walk confidently away from it, with the firm persuasion that one is following it, that, it seems to me, is what is called genuinely *mad*.

This is a strange definition, close, in its dryness, to the older philosophical and moral traditions. And yet half-hidden within it is the whole movement that renewed thinking about madness; the superimposition and the forced coincidence between a definition in the negative terms of distance (madness is always a distance from reason, a gap that has been instituted and measured), and a definition in terms of the plenitude of characters and traits that re-establish in a positive form the relationship with reason (confidence and persuasion, a system of belief that implies that the difference between madness and reason is also a resemblance, the opposition disappearing in a sort of illusory fidelity, the gap being filled with a group that is merely appearance, but the semblance of reason itself). So much so that the previous simple opposition between the powers of reason and of insanity is now replaced by a more complex and elusive opposition; madness is the absence of reason, but an absence that takes on a positive form, a quasi-conformity, an almost identical resemblance that is never totally convincing. The madman leaves the path of reason, but by means of the images, beliefs, and forms of reasoning that are equally to be found in men of reason. The madman therefore is never mad to his own way of thinking, but only in the eyes of a third person who can distinguish between reason and the exercise of reason.

Mixed up together in the perception of madness constructed in the eighteenth century then are extremes of the positive and of the negative. The positive is nothing other than reason itself, even if it wears an aberrant appearance; the negative is the fact that madness is nothing other than a vain simulacrum of reason. Madness is reason, with the addition of a thin layer of negativity; it is what is closest to reason, and most irreducible, reason marked with an ineradicable sign: Unreason.

Let us now pick up the threads of the argument. What was the obviousness of the madman that we witnessed above, against the paradoxical backdrop of the absence of madness? It was nothing other than the close proximity of reason, filling all that was positive in the mad, whose evident madness was a sign, affecting reason, but ultimately introducing nothing positive from the outside.

And what of the interweaving of the structures of the rational and the reasonable? In a similar movement typical of the perception of madness in the classical age, reason immediately recognises the negativity of the madman in the unreasonable, while recognising itself in the rational content of all forms of madness. It recognises itself as content, as nature, as discourse, in the end as the *reason* of madness, while simultaneously measuring the unbridgeable gap that exists between reason and the reason of the mad. In that sense the madman can be entirely invested with reason, mastered by it since it secretly inhabits him, but reason always ensures that he is other; if it has any grip on the mad, it is only as an *object*. This status as object, which will later be the foundation of the positive science of madness, is inscribed from the moment of the creation of this perceptual structure that we are currently analysing: an acknowledgement of the *rationality* of the content, as part of the movement that simultaneously denounces all that is *unreasonable* in its manifestation.

There lies the primary and most apparent paradox of unreason: an immediate opposition to reason, whose only content can be nothing other than reason itself.

*

The incontestable evidence of 'that man is mad' was not grounded in any theoretical mastery concerning the nature of madness.

Inversely, when classical thought wished to interrogate madness in its very nature, it did not start out by considering madmen, but rather by thinking in terms of illness in general. The answer to a question such as 'What is madness, ultimately?' was to be deduced from an analysis of the disease, without the madman ever having to speak about himself, in the concrete detail of his existence. The eighteenth century perceived the madman, but deduced madness. And what was perceived in the madman was not so much madness as the inextricable coexistence of reason and unreason. The idea that the age formed of madness was built up not from the multiple experiences of the mad, but from the logical and natural domain of illness, a field of rationality.

Given that classical thought was moving away from the tendency to view disease in purely negative terms (as finitude, limitation and lack), the general notion of disease was caught in a double temptation: to no longer be considered simply as negation (hence the tendency to suppress notions like the idea of "morbiffick matter"), and to be detached from a meta-physics of disease, which became quite pointless if what was desired was an understanding of the real, positive and full nature of illness (hence the tendency to exclude from medical thought notions of illness due to absence or lack).

In the early seventeenth century, the table of diseases drawn up by Plater still accorded an important place to a negative conception of disease. There were those who were ill due to not giving birth, not conceiving, not sweating, or lacking vital movement.[18] But Sauvages subsequently noted that a lack could be neither the truth nor the essence of a sickness, nor even its nature properly speaking: 'It is true that the suppression of certain evacuations often causes sickness, but it does not therefore follow that one should call that suppression a disease.'[19] He advanced two reasons. First of all, a lack was never a principle of order, but of disorder, and of infinite disorder, for its place was in the open, constantly renewed space of negation, where elements are not as numerous as real things, but as innumerable as logical possibilities: 'If types like this took on a concrete existence, the number of types would grow to infinity.'[20] And then secondly, by their very multiplication, sicknesses, paradoxically, would become indistinguishable, for if the essential nature of illness was in a suppression, a suppression that has no positive content cannot give disease its own individuated face; it acts in the same manner upon all the functions to which it is applied in a kind of logical act that is also entirely empty. Disease therefore would be the poor indifference of negation acting on the richness of nature: 'absence and lack are nothing positive, but neither do they imprint any idea of sickness on the mind'.[21] To give a particular content to disease, it was therefore important to examine the real, observable and positive phenomena in which it was apparent: 'The definition of a disease should be the enumeration of symptoms that can be used to identify its type and species, that distinguish it from all other forms.'[22] Where it was clear that there was a suppression, it should be recognised that there was not the illness itself, but only its cause, and it was therefore the positive effects of the suppression that should be examined: 'Even if the idea of the disease is a negative one, as in soporific sicknesses, it is better to define the disease in terms of its positive symptoms.'[23]

It also fell to this search for positive elements to unshackle disease from its invisible and secret associations. Those aspects of evil that still lurked within it were exorcised, and its truth could now be displayed on the surface, in the order of positive signs. Willis, writing in *De morbis convulsivis*, still spoke of 'morbiffick matter' – hidden, anti-natural, foreign substances that were the vehicle of sickness and the vector of the pathological event. In some cases, notably where epilepsy was concerned, the morbific substance was so obscure, so inaccessible to the senses and even to proof, that it still had the mark of transcendence upon it, and could easily be confused with the work of the devil: 'In this Distemper, no marks at all, of the morbiffick matter appears, or are so very obscure, that we may have deservedly suspected it, to be an inspiration of an evill Spirit.'[24] But at the end of the seventeenth century, morbific substances began to disappear. Sickness, even when it contained elements that were difficult to decipher, and when the greater part of its truth remained hidden, was no longer to be characterised in such terms: there was always now a singular truth within it on the level of the most apparent phenomena, on the basis of which it was henceforth to be defined:

> If a general or a captain only specified in a description the hidden marks that his soldiers carried on their body, or some other hidden means of identification not visible to the naked eye, however hard one looked for deserters, they would never be found.[25]

Knowledge of disease was therefore to be first of all an inventory of what was immediately manifest in perception, all that was most evident in truth. In this way medicine adopted, as its first approach, the symptomatic method, which 'takes the characteristics of a disease from the invariable phenomena and the obvious symptoms that accompany it'.[26]

To the 'philosophical way' that is 'the knowledge of principles and causes', which is 'still highly curious, and vital in helping to make the distinction between the dogmatic and the empirical', what is now to be preferred is the 'historical way', which is more sure and more necessary; it is 'simple and easy to acquire', and at bottom is nothing other than 'a knowledge of the facts'. If it is 'historical', it is not so in the sense that it attempts to establish, going back to the earliest causes, the development, the chronology and the length of a given illness, but in a more etymological sense it seeks to *see*, close up and in detail, and recreate an exact portrait of the disease in question. For this there was no better model than those painters who, 'when drawing a portrait, are careful to include even the signs and the tiniest natural things that they see on the skin of the face of the person that they are depicting'.[27]

A whole world of pathology is organised in the light of these new norms. But nothing in it seems to announce a perception of the madman such as we analysed it above: the perception there was purely negative, keeping inexplicit the manifest and discursive truth of madness. How could madness take its place in this world of disease where truths announce themselves in observable phenomena, when its own concrete appearance in the world is always with its sharpest profile, the one most difficult to grasp? The instantaneous, punctual presence of a madman, who is most clearly perceived as mad when he masks the unfolded, discursive truth of madness.

But there is more still. Behind the greatest concern of the classifiers of the eighteenth century is a metaphor as recurrent and as persistent as a myth, where the disorders of diseases are transferred to the order of the vegetal. 'It is necessary,' said Sydenham, 'that all sicknesses should be reduced to certain and definite Species, with the same diligence we see it is done by Botanick Writers in their Herbals.'[28] Gaubius' recommendation was that 'the huge number of human diseases should be placed in a systematic order, in the manner of writers on natural history . . . presenting classes, types and species, each with its own particular, constant and distinct characteristics'.[29] The theme took on its full significance with Boissier de Sauvages: the order defined by botanists becomes the principle of organisation for the whole world of pathology, and diseases are divided up into an order and in a space that is that of reason itself.[30] The project of a garden of species – pathological as well as botanical – belongs to the wisdom of divine providence.

Previously, disease was merely permitted by God, who destined it for men as a form of punishment. But suddenly he was organising its forms, and dividing up its varieties himself. He cultivated it. From now on there was also to be a God of sickness, the same one as He who protects the species, and there was no medical record of this careful gardener of illnesses ever passing away . . . If it was true that on man's side, sickness was a sign of disorder, finitude and sin, on God's side, the side of the creator, i.e. the side of their truth, diseases were a reasoned vegetation. And accordingly, it now fell to medical thought to escape these pathetic categories of punishment, and move instead to genuinely pathological ones, where sickness found its eternal truth:

> I think the chief reason why we still want an exact History of diseases is, because most suppose that they are only the confused and disordered Effects of Nature in defending her self; and that he labours to no purpose, who endeavours a just Narration of their Senses. [However, when creating diseases or in maturing morbific humours, the Supreme Being subjected himself to laws no less binding than for producing plants or animals.][31]

Henceforth, it will be enough for the image to be followed through to its term. Disease, in the least of its manifestations, will be invested with divine wisdom, and discernible on the surface of phenomena will be the providence of divine reason. Sickness will be a work of reason, and reason at work. It will follow an order, and the order will be secretly present as the organising principle behind every symptom. The universal will animate the particular:

> And he shall exactly consider those phenomena that accompany a Quartan Ague, viz, that it most commonly comes about Autumn, that it keeps a certain order, repeating its periodical revolutions, as certainly as a clock strikes unless the order of it be disturbed by some extrinsic thing; that it begins with shivering, and a notable Sense of Cold, which is succeeded by a sensible heat, which at length ends in large sweats . . . He that shall exactly weigh all these things, may as reasonably believe, that this disease is a Species, as a Plant is so.[32]

Sickness, like the plant, is the living rationality of nature: 'Symptoms are to sickness what leaves and supports (fulcra) are to plants.'[33]

In comparison to the first 'naturalisation' to which the sixteenth century bore witness, this second naturalisation was more demanding. What was at stake was no longer a quasi-nature, filled with all that was unreal, imaginary, phantasmatic, an illusory and tempting nature, but a nature that was the fixed and immobile plenitude of reason. A nature that was the totality of reason present in each of its elements.

This was the new space into which madness, like disease, was to fit.

*

A further paradox, in this history that is hardly lacking in paradoxes, is the manner in which madness was integrated without any apparent difficulty into these new norms of medical theory. The space of classification opens unproblematically to the analysis of madness, and madness immediately finds its place there. None of the classifiers appears to have been daunted by the problems madness might have posed.

Might it be that this space without depth, this definition of madness solely through the plenitude of its phenomena, this rupture with the kinship of evil, this refusal of negative ways of thinking – simply comes from a different vein, from a different level to all that we know about the classical experience of madness? Are there not two different systems juxtaposed here, but which belong to two different universes? Is the classification of types of madness an artifice of symmetry, or an astonishing leap towards the classifications of the nineteenth century? If our desire is to analyse the classical experience in all its depth, should we not leave these efforts towards classification at a surface level, and follow instead, in its meandering slowness, all that experience indicates about itself, its negative aspects so commonly linked to the idea of evil, and the whole ethical world of the reasonable?

But to neglect the place that madness genuinely did occupy in the domain of pathology would be a postulate and therefore an error of method. The insertion of madness into the nosologies of the eighteenth century, however contradictory it may appear, should not be left in the shadows. There is surely a meaning to it. This curious opposition between a perceptive consciousness of the mad, which in the eighteenth century was singularly sharp, probably for being extremely negative, and a discursive knowledge of madness that fitted easily into the positive, well-ordered plane of all possible diseases, has to be accepted for what it was – i.e. for all that it said, and all that it kept hidden.[34]

We should therefore start by comparing a few examples of the classification of various forms of madness.

Earlier, Paracelsus had drawn up an influential classification. There were the *Lunatici*, whose sickness had the moon at its origin, and whose behaviour, in its apparent irregularity, was secretly ordered by its phases and movements. The *Insani* owed their condition to heredity, unless they had contracted it, just before their birth, in their mother's womb; the *Vesani* were deprived of reason and sense through the abuse of alcohol or through bad food, and the *Melancholici* were inclined towards madness by some vice in their nature.[35] This classification had an undeniable coherence, where the order of causes was logically articulated in its totality: first came the outside world, then heredity and birth, followed by problems caused by food and last of all internal disturbances.

But it was precisely classifications of that sort that classical thought refused. For a classification to be valid, it was first of all necessary that each disease be determined above all by the totality of the form of the others; secondly, it was the disease itself which determined its diverse variants, and not external determinants. Finally, if a disease could not be known exhaustively, then it should at least be identifiable in an unmistakable manner from its own manifestations.

The path towards that ideal can be followed from Plater to Linnaeus or Weickhard, and what becomes apparent is a language where the divisions of madness are to be formulated on the basis of its own nature, and the natural totality that is formed by all possible diseases.

Plater (1609 – *Praxeos Tractatus*)

The first book of the 'Lesions of the Functions' is devoted to lesions of the senses: among them a distinction is made between external and internal senses (*imaginatio, ratio, memoria*). They can be affected separately or together, and they may be diminished, totally abolished, perverted or exaggerated. Inside that logical space, particular diseases are defined sometimes by their causes (divided into internal or external), sometimes by their pathological context (health, sickness, convulsion, rigidity), or sometimes by associated symptoms (such as fever or its absence).

1 *Mentis imbecillitas* (feebleness of the mind):
   * general: *hebetudo mentis* (dullness of the mind);
   * particular: of imagination: *tarditas ingenii* (a natural slowness of mind);
      of reason: *imprudentia* (imprudence);
      of memory: *oblivio* (absence of memory).
2 *Mentis consternatio* (disturbance of the mind):
   * non-natural sleep:
      in the healthy: *somnus immodicus, profundus* (immoderate or deep sleep);
      in the sick: *coma, lethargus, cataphora*;

- stupor: with resolution (apoplexy); with convulsion (epilepsy); with rigidity (catalepsy).
3 *Mentis alienatio* (alienation of the mind):
  - innate causes: *stultitia* (foolishness);
  - external causes: *temulentia* (drunkenness), *animi commotio* (a commotion of the spirits);
  - internal causes: without fever: *mania, melancholia*;
                      with fever: *phrenitis, paraphrenitis*
4 *Mentis defatigatio* (mental exhaustion):
  - *vigiliae; insomnia.*

Johnston (1644 – *The Idea of Practical Physick*)

Diseases of the brain are part of organic, internal maladies that are particular and non-poisonous. They are divided into troubles:

- of the external senses: *cephalalgia*
- of the common sense: over great and extraordinary watchings
- of the sleepy and drowsy coma, or *cataphora*
- of the imagination: the vertigo
- of the imagination, and the ratiocination,[36] when they are hurt: of memory, delirium or dotage, phrensie, melancholy, madness, rabies or raging madness
- of the internal senses: waking coma, lethargy
- of the animal motion: lassitude, or Literness, restlessness or unquietness, Rigor or extreme stiffness, Tremor, or trembling, the palsy, spasm or convulsions
- of the excretions of the head: catarrh.

There are also composite sicknesses where many symptoms mingle, such as 'incubus or the night-hag, catalepsis, epilepsie or falling sickness, Carus, and apoplexy'.[37]

Boissier de Sauvages (1763 – *Methodical Nosology*)

Classes
I: Vices
II: Fevers

III: Phlegmasia
IV: Spasms
V: Shortness of breath
VI: Weaknesses
VII: Pains
VIII: Madnesses
IX: Flux
X: Cachexia

Class VIII: Madnesses, or sicknesses that trouble reason.
Orders:
1: *Hallucinations*, which affect the imagination. Types: vertigo, double vision, blunders, tinnitus, hypochondria, somnambulism
2: *Strangeness (morositates)* affecting the appetites. Types: depraved appetite, animal hunger, raging thirst, antipathy, homesickness, panicky terror, satyriasis, uterine frenzy, Saint Vitus' dance, hydrophobia
3: *Delirium*, affecting judgement. Types: transports of the brain, dementia, melancholy, demonomania, mania in general
4: *Abnormal forms of madness.* Types: amnesia, insomnia.

Linnaeus (1763 – *Genera Morborum*)

Class V: Mental Maladies

I – *Ideal*: delirium, transport, dementia, mania, demonomania, melancholy
II – *Imaginative*: tinnitus, visions, vertigo, panicky terror, hypochondria, somnambulism
III – *Pathetic*: depraved tastes, bulimia, polydipsia, satyriasis, erotomania, nostalgia, Saint Vitus dance, rage, hydrophobia, cacosity, antipathy, anxiety

Weickhard (1790 – *Der Philosophische Arzt*)

I Sicknesses of the spirit (*Geisteskrankheiten*)

1. Weakness of the imagination;
2. Overactive imagination;
3. Attention deficit (*attentio volubilis*);

4. Obstinate and persistent reflection (*attentio acerrima et meditatio profunda*);
5. Absence of memory (*oblivio*);
6. Errors of judgement (*defectus judicii*);
7. Idiocy, slow wittedness (*defectus, tarditas ingenii*);
8. Eccentric liveliness and instability of the spirit (*ingenium velox, praecox, vividissimum*);
9. Delirium (*insania*).

II Sicknesses of the feelings (*Gemütskrankheiten*)

1. Excitement: pride, anger, fanaticism, erotomania, etc.
2. Depression: sadness, envy, despair, suicide, 'court sickness' (*Hofkrankheit*), etc.

*

All this patient labour of classification, if it indicates a new structure of rationality that was in the process of taking shape, has left no trace of itself. Each of these distributions was abandoned as soon as it was proposed, and those that the nineteenth century would try to put into place were to be of an entirely different order: an affinity in the symptoms, identical causes, temporal succession, and a progressive evolution from one type towards another – each forming a family that grouped together as much as possible the multiplicity of manifestations. The effort then was to discover the great unities, and to bring together connected forms, and the concern was no longer with covering the totality of the pathological space, and discerning the truth about a disease from its place in a table. The classifications of the nineteenth century supposed the existence of great species – mania, paranoia, dementia praecox – not the existence of a logically structured domain where diseases were defined in relation to the totality of the pathological. It is as though these classifications had been an entirely empty activity, unfurling itself to find nothing at all, constantly being corrected in vain, a ceaseless activity that never succeeded in becoming real work. These classifications ultimately functioned as little more than images, whose value lay in the vegetal myth that they contained within them. The clear and explicit concepts they contained remained devoid of any real efficacy.

But this lack of efficacy – which is quite strange when one considers the work that went into it – is really the reverse of a problem. Or rather, it is itself a problem. It poses the question of the obstacles met by these classificatory activities when they were applied to the world of madness. What were the resistances that meant that these classifications had no purchase on their object, and that prevented new pathological concepts from emerging and stabilising through all these species and classes? What was there in the experience of madness that prevented it from fitting into a coherent nosographic plane? What depth, what fluidity? What particular structure meant that it constantly eluded this project that was essential to the medical thought of the eighteenth century?

*

The classificatory activity came up against solid resistance, as if to indicate that the project to divide up the various forms of madness according to their signs and manifestations contained within it a sort of contradiction, as though the relationship between madness and its visible forms was neither one of essence, nor one of truth. That much becomes apparent when one follows the thread of the classifications from their general order through to the detail of the diseases that were classed: there is always a moment where the great positivist theme – classification in accordance with visible signs – is rerouted, or finds an obstacle in its path. A separate principle surreptitiously creeps in, altering the sense of the organisation and placing between madness and its perceptible figures either a series of moral denunciations or a system of causes. Madness alone cannot speak for its manifestations, and forms an empty space where all is possible, except a logical ordering of that possible space. The origin and significance of the order are thus to be sought outside that order. These heterogeneous principles will necessarily tell us a lot about the experience of madness in the medical thought of the eighteenth century.

In principle, a classification should only examine the powers of the human spirit in the disorders to which it is prey. But let us take one example. Thomas Arnold, taking his inspiration from Locke, perceived the possibility of madness according to the two major faculties of the mind. One form was related to 'ideas', i.e. the quality of representative elements, and the truth content that they were intended to convey; the other was related to 'notions', the reflective activity that had constructed them and the architecture of their truth. 'Ideal insanity', the first type, included forms of madness that were frenzied ('phrenitic'), incoherent, maniacal and sensitive (related to hallucinations). But when madness brought its disorder to the notions, it could present itself in nine different ways: 'delusive, whimsical, fanciful, impulsive, scheming, vain or self-important, hypochondriacal, pathetic and appetitive'. Thus far the coherence was preserved. But the content of pathetic madness had sixteen variants: 'amorous, jealous, avaricious, misanthropic, arrogant, irascible, abhorrent, suspicious, bashful, timid, sorrowful, distressful, nostalgic, superstitious, fanatical or desponding'.[38] The slippage in perspectives is clear. The classification starts out as an investigation into the powers of the mind, and the original experiences through which it has the potential of truth. Little by little, as the reality of the concrete differences that make up the world of insanity are approached, we get further from the unreason that problematises reason in its general form, and we reach the surface where madness takes on the traits of real men. But then it diversifies into so many 'characters', and nosography takes on the appearance, or very nearly, of a gallery of 'moral portraits'. Just when the experience of madness hopes to join the concrete reality of man, it finds that it has approached morality instead.

Arnold is not the only one to do this, and Wieckhard's classification follows a similar pattern.[39] There again in the eighth class, the class of sicknesses of the mind, we start out with the distinction between imagination, memory and judgement, but moral characterisations quickly take over. Vitet's classification even makes room, beside simple defects, for vice and sin. The memory of them is still vivid in Pinel's entry on 'Nosography' in the *Dictionnaire des Sciences médicales*:

> What can we say about a classification where theft, baseness, wickedness, displeasure, fear, pride, vanity and so forth are classed as sick afflictions of the mind. These are of course forms of mental sickness, and often incurable diseases, but their true place is in the *Maxims* of La Rochefoucauld, or in the *Characters* of La Bruyère, not in a work on pathology.[40]

The quest was for the morbid forms of madness, and all that was found were deformations in morality. On the way, the notion of disease itself was altered, moving from a pathological significance to a purely critical value. The rational activity that distributed the signs of madness was secretly transformed into a reasonable conscience that enumerated and denounced them. It suffices to compare the classifications of Vitet or Weickhard with the lists to be found on confinement registers to confirm that the same function is at work in both places: the motives for confinement can be superimposed exactly on the themes of the classification even though their origins are entirely different, and none of the nosographers of the eighteenth century ever had any contact with the world of the General Hospitals or the houses of confinement. But as soon as thought, in its scientific speculation, tried to relate madness to its concrete faces, it necessarily met this moral experience of unreason. Between the classificatory project and the known and recognised forms of madness, the foreign principle that slipped in was unreason.

Not all nosographies are caught in the slide towards such moral characterisations, but none are entirely pure, and if it is not morality that plays a diffractive, distributive role, it is the organism and the realm of corporeal causes that takes its place.

The project of Boissier de Sauvages was a simple one. Yet one can easily discern the difficulties that he met in establishing a solid symptomatic basis for mental illness, as though madness were constantly in flight from its own truth. If one sets aside the class of 'abnormal forms of madness', the three principal orders are formed by hallucinations, strangeness and delirium. On the surface, each is defined, in the full rigour of the method, on the basis of its most manifest signs: hallucinations are 'sicknesses whose principal symptom is a depraved and erroneous imagination',[41] 'strangeness' should be understood as 'a depravity of taste or of the will',[42] and delirium as a 'depravity of the faculty of judgement'. But as the analysis progresses, these characteristics slowly lose the sense of symptoms, and increasingly clearly take on the meaning of causes. From the introductory content page itself, hallucinations are already considered as 'errors of the soul occasioned by the vice of organs situated outside the brain, which allow the imagination to be seduced'.[43] But the world of causes is invoked above all when what is required is a distinction between the different signs, i.e. when it is required of them that they should be something other than a sign of recognition, when what is needed is a justification for the logical division into species and classes. At that point delirium is differentiated from hallucinations in that its origin is to be found in the brain alone, and not in the other organs that also form part of the nervous system. If what is required is a distinction between 'essential deliria' and 'passing deliria that accompany fevers', it is enough to recall that the latter are the result of a passing change in the fluids, whereas the former are an often-definitive depravity of the solid elements.[44] At the general and more abstract level of the Orders, the classification remains faithful to the symptomatic principle, but as soon as one nears the concrete forms of madness, the physical cause becomes once more the essential element in distinctions. In its real life, madness is wholly inhabited by the secret movements of its causes. It has no truth of its own, and no nature either, as it is torn between the powers of the mind that give it an abstract and general truth and the more obscure work of organic causes that give it a concrete existence.

In any case the organisation of sicknesses of the mind is never carried out at the level of madness itself. It can never bear witness to its own truth, and there must be an intervention either by moral judgement or by an analysis of the physical causes. It is either a question of passion, and moral faults, with all the associated elements of liberty, or of the rigorously determined mechanics of animal spirits and the nervous system. But that antinomy is only apparent, and it did not exist for the thought of that age. To the classical way of thinking there was a whole region where morality and mechanics, freedom and the body, passion and pathology found both their unity and their measure. It is imagination, which is prey to errors, illusions and presumptions, but in which are equally summed up all the mechanisms of the body. And in fact all that is unbalanced, hetero-geneous and obscurely impure in the temptations of classification, is the result of an 'analytics of the imagination' intervening secretly in their workings. It is there that the synthesis is carried out between madness in general, which was the object of analysis, and the figure of the mad-man, already familiar to perception, whose diverse nature is subsumed as much as possible under a few major categories. This is the place of the experience of unreason, just as we saw it above intervene in the practices of confinement – an experience where man is equally, and in a somewhat paradoxical fashion, singled out and absolved of his guilt, but condemned for his animal nature. This experience was transcribed, when reflected, in terms of a theory of the imagination to be found at the heart of all classical thought concerning madness. Doctors and philo-sophers of the classical age were united in describing the imagination, troubled and straying from its rightful path, half-way between error and sin on the one hand, and corporeal disturbances on the other, as delirium.

Beyond the descriptions and the classifications, a general theory of passion, imagination and delirium can thus be discerned, the site of the real links between madness in general and the mad in particular, and the place where madness and unreason are now related. This was the place where an obscure power of synthesis united unreason, madness and the mad in a single experience. In that sense it is possible to talk of a *transcendence of delirium* subsuming, commanding from above the classical experience of madness, which means that attempts to analyse madness simply in terms of symptoms inevitably come to nought.

*

Another factor to be acknowledged was the resistance of some of the major themes that had taken shape long before the period of classification, which survived in almost immobile, identical forms until the beginning of the nineteenth century. While on the surface the names of the illnesses changed, as well as their place, the divisions between them and the manner in which they were connected, a little more deeply, a small number of hulking shapes lurked in the conceptual shadows, few in number but wide in application, and their obstinate presence meant that classificatory activities were in vain. These notions are more distant from the conceptual activity and the theory of medicine but close to the real work that thought was invested in. They are to be found in Willis' work, and it was on their basis that he was able to elaborate the great principle of maniacal and melancholic cycles; and they reappeared at the other end of the century when the time came to reform the hospitals and give a medical significance to the practice of confinement. They were at one with the work of medicine, imposing their immovable characterisations more through an imaginary cohesion than by a strictly conceptual definition. They remained in place thanks to obscure affinities that lent each one its own indelible imprint. Their trace can be found long before Boerhaave, and survived long after Esquirol.

In 1672, Willis published *De Anima Brutorum* [On the Soul of Brutes], the second part of which deals with 'diseases which belong to the corporeal soul and its subjects, viz, the brain and nervous stock.' His analysis takes up the great illnesses long familiar to medical tradition, like 'frenzy', a state of fury associated with fever, which is to be distinguished in its brevity from 'delirium'. 'Mania' [Willis' translator into English simply

used the term 'madness' here] is a form of frenzy without fever. 'Melancholy' includes neither fury nor fever, but is characterised by sadness and
fear bearing upon a small number of objects, and could often be reduced
to a single preoccupation. 'Stupidity' is the fate of anyone 'lacking memory, judgement or imagination'. If Willis' writings were important in the
definition of various different mental illnesses, it was in so far as the work
was done within these major categories. Willis does not restructure the
nosological space, but isolates forms that have a tendency to unify, even to
blend different realities. Thus he almost goes so far as to propose a notion
of melancholic mania: 'both of which are so much akin, that these
Distempers often change, and pass from one to the other. These two, like
smoke and flame, mutually receive and give place one to another.'[45] In
other cases he manages to make a distinction where previously confusion
reigned. The distinction is more practical than conceptual, a relative
division by degrees, and the fundamental identity of the notions is not
really called into question. This is the case for the great family of all those
suffering from stupidity; first come those who are not capable of mastering literature or any of the liberal sciences, but who are sufficiently able
to learn the mechanical arts; then come those who are simply capable
of becoming farmers; then those who are capable of learning to
subsist in life and learn the right habits, then the lowest rank of all, who
barely understand anything and hardly act intentionally at all.[46] The real
work is not what he did on new classes of illness, but on the traditional
families where images were more numerous, and the familiar faces more
easily recognised.

In 1785, when Jean Colombier and François Doublet brought out
their Instruction sur la manière de gouverner les insensés, more than a century had
passed since Willis. The great nosological systems have been built, but
it would appear that almost nothing remains of those monuments.
Doublet is clearly writing for doctors and heads of medical establishments,
and his aim is to aid with diagnosis and therapy. The only classification
that he knows is the one that was already common currency at the time of
Willis: frenzy, invariably accompanied by inflammation and fever; mania,
where fury is not a sign of the brain being affected; melancholia that
differs from mania in two ways − 'firstly, in that melancholic delirium
invariably has a single object, known as the point of melancholy, and
secondly in that the delirium . . . is always pacific'. To that can be added
dementia, taking the place of Willis' category of stupidity, and grouping

together any atrophy of the faculties. In the early part of the nineteenth century, when the Minister of the Interior asked Giraudy for a report on the hospital at Charenton, what he received distinguished between cases of melancholy, mania and dementia; the only important modification was that hypochondria was isolated, and was only represented by 8 out of 476 internees, and that a distinction was beginning to be made between idiocy and dementia. John Haslam's Observations on Madness and Melancholy takes no account of the incurable, and hence excludes idiots and the demented, and only recognises two images of madness: mania and melancholia.

As is apparent from such classifications, the nosological framework was remarkably stable, despite the numerous attempts that were made in the eighteenth century to modify it. When the great psychiatric syntheses and the systems of madness began to fall into place, the great taxonomy of unreason could be revisited: among the forms of madness, Philippe Pinel counts melancholia, mania, dementia and idiocy, to which he also adds hypochondria, somnambulism and hydrophobia.[47] Jean-Etienne Esquirol adds nothing other than the new family of monomania to the traditional pattern of mania, melancholia, dementia and imbecility.[48] The recognisable faces of madness remain unchanged throughout this period of nosological construction, and the division into species along the lines of the vegetal world was not sufficiently convincing to undo the primitive solidity of these forms. From one end of the classical age to the other, the frontiers of the world of the mad remain unchanged. It would be given to another century to discover general paralysis, to divide up the neuroses and psychoses, and to build the edifice of paranoia and dementia praecox, and to another still to pin down schizophrenia. This patient work of observation was not a characteristic of the seventeenth or eighteenth centuries. They identified fragile families in the garden of species, but those notions did little to change the solidity of the quasi-perceptive experience taking place in any case. Medical thought rested calmly on unchanging forms, which pursued their silent existence. The hierarchical, well-ordered nature of the classifiers was in truth only subsidiary to these primitive, essential forms.

Let us go over these terms once again, as their particular acceptation in the classical age risks being hidden by the permanence of the words themselves, which are still in common usage today. Their entries in Diderot and d'Alembert's Encyclopédie are important reference points here, precisely because they did not aspire to originality.

- The encyclopaedia notes that in opposition to *frenzy*, which was a fevered delirium, *mania* is a delirium without fever, in its essence at least. It includes 'all long-term sicknesses in which the patient loses not only his reason, but also fails to perceive the world as it is, and does things which are or seem to be ridiculous, extraordinary, or without motive'.
- *Melancholy* is also a form of delirium, but a 'particular delirium, which fixes on a small number of objects with great determination, without fever or fury, in which respect it differs from frenzy or mania. This delirium is usually linked to an insurmountable sadness, a black humour, misanthropy and a marked preference for solitude'.
- *Dementia* is opposed to both melancholy and mania: the latter are but the 'depraved exercise of memory and understanding', while the former is a rigorous 'paralysis of the mind' or 'an abolition of the faculty of reason'; the fibres of the brain are no longer impressionable, and the animal spirits are no longer capable of causing them to react. D'Aumont, who wrote the entry, saw a less pronounced form of dementia in *fatuité* (conceitedness), which he took to be a simple weakening of the faculties of understanding and memory.

With the exception of a few modifications in detail, what takes shape here and persists are certain essential connections in classical medicine, much more solid than nosographic links, perhaps because they have their roots in experience rather than theory, and because frenzy and the heat of fevers, mania and furious agitation, melancholy and the quasi-insular isolation of delirium, dementia and the disorders of the spirit had long had their place in the popular imagination and in dreams. The nosological systems sparkled briefly against this backdrop of the qualitative depth of medical perception. But they have no true place in the real history of madness.

*

A third obstacle remains. This is constituted by resistance and developments contained within medical practice.

For a long time, and throughout the realm of medicine, therapeutics had been a relatively autonomous domain. In any case, never, since antiquity at least, had its practices been entirely in line with the concepts of medical science. More than any other disease, and right up until the end of the eighteenth century, madness maintained around it a whole body of practices that were archaic in their origins, magical in their significance, and extra-medical in their system of application. The terrifying powers hidden within madness stoked the secret life of these practices.

But at the close of the seventeenth century, a single event reinforced the autonomy of these practices, and gave them a new turn and a new possibility for development. This event is the definition of upsets initially known as 'vapours', which take on such an important extension in the eighteenth century under the name of 'nervous illnesses'. Very early on, thanks to the force of expansion of their concepts, they revolutionise the nosographic space, and soon take it over almost completely. William Cullen, in *The Practice of Physic*, writes:

> I propose to comprehend, under the title of Neuroses, all those preternatural affections of sense or motion which are without pyrexia, as part of the primary diseases; and all those which do not depend on a topical affection of the organs, but upon a more general affection of the nervous system, and of those powers of the system upon which sense and motion more especially depend.[49]

This new world of vapours and diseases of the nerves had its own dynamics. The forces at work, the classes, species and genus to be discerned there no longer coincided with the forms familiar to nosographers of the past. It would appear that what opens up is a whole new pathological space as yet unknown, which escapes the usual rules of analysis and medical description:

> Philosophers invite doctors to venture deep into this labyrinth, and they ease the way by getting rid of the metaphysical claptrap of the schools, explaining in an analytical manner the principal faculties of the soul, and showing their intimate connections to the movements of the body, going back to the first principles of their organisation.[50]

There are also innumerable projects for the classification of the vapours. None of them rely on the principles that had guided predecessors like Sydenham, Sauvages or Linnaeus. Viridet distinguishes between them in accordance with the mechanism of the illness and its location: 'general vapours come into being throughout the body', 'particular vapours come into being in a particular part'; the former are the result of 'a suppressing of the free flow of animal spirits', while the latter are produced by 'a ferment in or near the nerves' or by 'a contraction of the nervous cavity, through which the animal spirits circulate'.[51] Beauchesne proposes a purely aetiological classification, according to temperament, predisposition and alterations to the nervous system: first of all 'sicknesses due to organic matter and lesions' which are to be found in 'bilious and phlegmatic temperaments', and then hysterical nervous diseases, to be identified by 'a melancholic bilious temperament and lesions to the womb', and finally sicknesses characterised by 'a softening of solid matter and a degeneration of the humours', where the causes are 'a phlegmatic, sanguine temperament, unhappy passions and so forth'.[52] Right at the end of the century, in the great discussion that followed the works of Tissot and Pomme, Pressavin gave diseases of the nerves their greatest extension. They now included all the upsets that the major functions of the organisms are prey to, and a distinction is to be made between them in accordance with the particular function that was disturbed. When the nerves related to feelings are attacked, a diminishment in their activity leads to drowsiness, stupor and coma, while an increase in their activity means itching, tickling or pain. The motor functions might suffer in the same manner, and their diminishment means paralysis or catalepsy, while an increase brings erethism and spasms. Convulsions meanwhile are due to irregular activity, either too weak or too strong, a pattern that is to be found for example in epilepsy.[53]

By their nature, admittedly, these concepts are foreign to traditional classifications. But what makes their originality is that unlike the notions to be found in nosography, they are immediately linked to a practice, or rather from the moment of their formulation they are infused with therapeutic themes, for they are constituted and organised by images that are from the outset common to patients and to practitioners: the vapours that rose up from the hypochondrium, the stretched nerve tissue, 'worn and frayed', or impregnated with damp, the burning ardour that dries out organs. They are indeed explanatory schema, but they are also ambiguous themes where the patient's imagination gives form, space, substance and language to his or her own suffering, and where the physician's imagination immediately projects an outline of the interventions necessary for the restoration of health. In this new world of pathology, ridiculed and scorned since the nineteenth century, something important is happening, and for the first time, no doubt, in the history of medicine. A theoretical explanation happens to coincide with a double projection: the patients' idea of their sickness and the suppression of the disease by the physician. Diseases of the nerves make possible a complicity in the cure. A whole world of symbols and images is coming into being, where for the first time doctors enter into a dialogue with their patients.

From this point on, throughout the eighteenth century, what develops is a form of medicine that has the doctor–patient relationship as its constitutive element. It is this pairing, with the imaginary figures on which it relies, that lies behind a complete reorganisation of the world of madness along new lines. Cures by heat or cold, by relaxation or by invigoration, this whole work of imaginary realisations shared by doctors and patients allow pathological forms to emerge, which the existing classifications are increasingly incapable of assimilating. But it is inside these forms – even if they too have now passed into oblivion – that the real work of the advancement of learning is done.

*

Let us turn our attention once more to our point of departure. On the one side is a consciousness that believes the mad can be recognised immediately, without even the mediation that a discursive knowledge of madness would be; and on the other is a form of knowledge that claims the ability to unfold, along the plane of its virtualities, all forms of madness, complete with all the tell-tale signs that manifest its truth. Between the two is nothing, a void, an absence, almost tangible in its obviousness, of what madness as a general and concrete form would be, as a real element in which the mad would recognise themselves, the deeper ground where the signs of insanity should grow in all their surprising particularity. Mental illness, in the classical age, does not exist, if what is understood by that is the natural homeland of the insane, the mediation between the madman who is perceived and the dementia that is analysed, the link, in short, between the madman and his madness. The madman and his madness are strangers to each other; each has their own truth, a truth kept hidden away and so to speak confiscated within themselves.

Unreason is first and foremost that – that deep division, typical of an age of the Understanding, which alienates the one from the other, making strangers of the madman and his madness.

Unreason, therefore, can be first apprehended in this void. Confinement perhaps was the institutionalised version. As an undifferentiated space of exclusion, did confinement not reign between the mad and their madness, between immediate recognition and a truth that was permanently deferred, covering the same ground in social structures as unreason in the structures of knowledge?

But unreason is more than the void in which it is beginning to become discernible here. The perception of the madman had no content other than reason itself and as to the analysis of madness among the species of illness, it had as a principle nothing other than the order of reasons of a natural wisdom; so much so that in place of a positive plenitude of madness, nothing other than reason was ever found, madness becoming the paradoxical absence of madness and the universal presence of reason. The madness of madness is to be secretly reason. And that non-madness, as the content of madness, is the second essential point that must be made about unreason. Unreason is that the truth of madness is reason.

Or rather, a quasi-reason. And there lies the third fundamental characteristic, which we shall investigate in full in the pages that follow. If reason is the content of the perceptions of the madman, that is not to say that it is not affected by a certain negativity. An agency is working here that gives unreason its distinctive style. However much a madman is mad with regards to reason, in it and through it, however much he is reason, to *become an object of* reason, that distance still forms a problem, and the work of negativity can never be simply the void of a negation. We have also seen the obstacles that appeared in the path of the efforts to 'naturalise' madness and treat it in the natural historical style applied to plants and diseases. Despite repeated efforts, madness never fitted completely into the rational order of species. The problem was that other deep forces were at work. Forces that are foreign to the theoretical plane of concepts, and which ultimately provide sufficient resistance to overturn it completely.

What then are the forces at work here? What is the power of negation that is discernible here? In this classical world, where reason seems to be the content and truth of all things, including madness, what are these secret instances that resist? Here and there, in the cognition of madness and the recognition of the madman, is it not the same virtue that is insidiously deployed, playing tricks upon reason? And if it is the same virtue, can we define its essence, and therefore the active force of unreason, the secret kernel of the classical experience of madness?

But we must proceed with care here, examining one detail at a time. Progress with the respect of a historian, from what we know already, from the obstacles that lay in the path of the naturalisation of madness, and in its projection onto a rational plane. Piece by piece, we must analyse them, after the sketchy enumerations that have been made so far. We must look first at the transcendence of passion, imagination and delirium, as constituent forms of madness; then at the traditional figures that articulated and elaborated the domain of madness throughout the classical age; and finally at the confrontation between doctor and patient in the imaginary world of therapeutics. Perhaps it is there that the positive forces of unreason are to be found, in the work that is both the correlative and a compensation for the non-being that it is, for the ever-deeper void and absence of madness.

Our aim will be to describe this work and the forces to be found within it not as the evolution of historical concepts on the surface of *knowledge*, but rather, by cutting into the historical depth of an *experience*, to try to identify the movement through which a knowledge of madness finally became *possible*: a knowledge that is our own, from which Freudianism has failed to detach us completely, as such was not in fact its vocation. In that knowledge, mental illness is at last present, and unreason has finally departed, other than in the eyes of those who wonder what the stubborn and repetitive presence of a madness that necessarily comes with its own science, medicine and doctors, a madness totally enclosed within the pathos of a mental illness, might signify in the modern world.

II

THE TRANSCENDENCE
OF DELIRIUM

'We call madness that disease of the organs of the brain . . .'[1] The problems of madness prowl around the materiality of the soul.

In this illness that nosologies are so quick to describe as sickness, how is the soul concerned? As a segment of the body attacked by disease like any other? As a general sensibility linked to the whole of the organism, and suffering with it? Or an independent, spiritual principle, only lacking power upon its transitory and material elements?

These are philosophers' questions and a delight to the eighteenth century, questions that are indefinitely reversible, and where each answer multiplies the ambiguity.

There is first of all the weight of a tradition, the tradition of theologians and casuists, and also the tradition of lawmakers and judges. Provided he expresses a few of the external signs of penitence, a madman can receive confession and absolution; even if there is every indication that he is out of his mind, one has the right and the duty to suppose that the Spirit has illuminated his mind in ways that are not perceptible or material, ways that 'God uses sometimes through the ministry of the Angels or by an immediate inspiration'.[2] It also mattered if a madman was in a state of grace when the madness first struck. If so, the madman will doubtless be saved, regardless of his actions while mad: the soul remains in the background, protected from disease, and preserved from evil by the disease itself. The soul is not sufficiently engaged in madness to sin on its account.

Judges follow the same reasoning when they refuse to see the actions of a madman as a crime, and when deciding on placing him under guardianship always suppose that madness is only a temporary incapacity, the soul being no more affected here than it is inexistent or fragmentary in the child. Provided there is no interdiction, the madman, even incarcerated, is not stripped of his citizenship, and the Parliament of Paris formally pronounced that the *de facto* proof of alienation constituted by confinement in no way changed the legal capacity of the subject.[3]

The souls of madmen are not mad.

And yet for anyone who philosophises about the exactness of medicine, and on its successes and failures, is the soul not both more and less than this free prisoner? Must it not be part of matter, as it is affected in the free exercise of its functions and in its most essential capacity – judgement itself – by and through matter? And if the whole tradition of the lawmakers is correct in establishing the innocence of a madman, it is not that his secret liberty is protected by its powerlessness, but rather that the irresistible force of the body affects liberty sufficiently to suppress it entirely: 'This poor soul . . . is then not master of its own thoughts, but is constrained to be forever attentive to the images formed within it by traces in its brain.'[4] But reason restored demonstrates even more clearly that the soul is nothing but organised physical matter; for madness is only ever destruction, and how could it be proved that the soul has really been destroyed, rather than simply bound in chains or hidden, or pushed aside? Nursing the soul back to strength, making it whole again, giving it strength and freedom again by the simple means of a dosage of the correct matter – this is proof enough that the soul has virtue and perfection in matter, as it is the addition of matter that causes it to pass from accidental imperfection to its perfect nature: 'Can an immortal being admit the transposition of parts, and suffer that something be added to the simplicity of its whole, from which nothing can possibly be taken away?'[5]

This dialogue, as old as the confrontation in Stoic thought between humanism and medicine, is taken up again by Voltaire, in an attempt to pin the matter down. Doctors and learned men seek to maintain the purity of the soul, and attempt to convince the madman that his madness is limited to the phenomena of the body. Whether he likes it or not, the madman must have a region of himself of which he is unaware, where a healthy soul is promised eternal life:

> My friend, although you have lost your common sense, your soul is as spiritual, as pure, as immortal as ours. But our souls are well housed, and yours badly, the windows of its house are blocked up, it lacks air, it suffocates.

But the madman has his good moments, or rather, in his madness, he is at times the very moment of truth – although devoid of sense, he has more common sense and reasons less awry than those who have all their wits. From the depths of his reasoning madness, i.e. from the heights of his mad wisdom, he knows that his soul is affected, and he reworks the paradox of Epimenides in the opposite sense, saying that he is mad to the bottom of his soul, and in saying so speaks the truth.

> My friends, as usual you take for granted the matter at issue. My windows are as open as yours since I see the same objects and hear the same words: it must therefore follow that my soul uses its senses awry, and that my soul makes bad use of my senses, or that my soul is itself only a vitiated sense. In a word either my soul is mad in itself, or I have no soul.[6]

Voltaire's Epimenides is twin-headed in his prudence, seeming to say: either all Cretans are liars, or I am, while actually meaning both at once – that madness has reached the deepest part of his soul, and consequently that his soul as a spiritual being does not exist. This dilemma suggests the process of reason that it conceals. We shall follow that path, which is not as simple as it first appears.

From the one side madness cannot be likened to a troubling of the senses: the windows are intact, and if one has difficulty seeing inside the house, that is not because they have been boarded up. Voltaire here leaps over a whole field of medical argument. Under the influence of Locke, many doctors sought the origins of madness in a problem of the senses. If one saw devils and heard voices, this could not be the fault of the soul – the soul did nothing more than receive what the senses imposed upon it.[7] To that, Sauvages, amongst others, replied that a cross-eyed person who sees double is not mad, but anyone who sees double and believes that he is looking at twin objects really is insane.[8] This was a problem of the soul, and not of the eye; it was not because of the poor state of the window, but a result of the sickness of the inhabitant. Such is Voltaire's opinion. The prudent course was to resist any primitive form of sensualism, and to avoid a situation where an overly direct and simplistic application of Locke ends up protecting the very soul sensualism aimed at restricting in its powers.

But if a problem of the senses is not the cause of madness, it is still its model. An affected eye prevents acute vision, and an affected brain, the organ of the spirit, will necessarily confuse the soul itself in the same manner:

> This reflection may arouse the suspicion that the faculty of thinking, given by god to man, is subject to derangement like the other senses. A lunatic is a sick man whose brain is in bad health, just as the man who has gout is a sick man with pains in his feet and hands. He thought with his brain as he walked with his feet, without knowing anything about his incomprehensible ability to walk, nor of his no less incomprehensible ability to think.[9]

Between the brain and the soul, the relationship is the same as between the eye and sight, and from the soul to the brain the same as the project of walking to the legs that bend. In the body, the soul does nothing more than form relationships analogous to those that the body itself has already established. It is the sense of the senses, the action of the action. And just as walking is prevented by a paralysis of the leg, and vision affected by a problem with the eye, the soul can be affected by lesions in the body and above all in the privileged organ that is the brain, the organ of all organs – both of all the senses and of all the actions. The soul is as engaged with the body as sight is with the eye, or action with the muscles. Take away the eye, and it emerges that 'my soul is mad in itself', in its own substance, in the essential core of its nature, and that 'I have no soul', other than the one defined by the exercise of the organs of my body.

In short, Voltaire concludes from the fact that madness is not a problem of the senses that soul, by its very nature, is no different from any other of the senses, and that the brain is its organ. He has subtly slipped from a clearly defined medical problem of the age (the genesis of madness as a result of a hallucination of the senses, or of a delirium of the spirit, which we might characterise in our language as a peripheral or a central theory) to a philosophical problem which cannot in principle or in fact be superimposed upon it – the question of whether or not madness proves the material nature of the soul. For the first question, Voltaire feigns a rejection of any sensualist response, but the better to impose it as a solution to the second problem – this last-minute reprieve for sensualism showing that he had given up on the first question, the medical question of the role of the sense organs in the origin of madness.

In itself, stripped of the polemical intentions that it conceals, this superimposition is significant. For it does not belong to the medical problems of the eighteenth century, but joins the sense–brain, periphery–centre issue, which is fully in line with medical considerations then, to a critical analysis that relies on a dissociation between the soul and the body. The day would come when doctors considering the problem of origins, of causal determination, and of the seat of madness would answer in terms of materialism, or not. But these values would only be recognised in the nineteenth century, precisely when the problematic as defined by Voltaire would be accepted as self-evident. Then, and only then, would it be possible to have a spiritualist and a materialist psychiatry, one conception of madness that reduced it to the body, and another that left a place for the immaterial elements of the soul. But Voltaire's text, precisely where it is contradictory and illogical, in the ruse that he quite deliberately employs, is not representative of the experience of madness in the eighteenth century, and of all that was vital, dense and solid therein. The text has more of an ironic inflection, slanted towards something that reaches beyond the time of that experience, towards the least ironic position possible concerning the problem of madness. It indicates and makes discernible, in another dialectical and polemical form, in the still empty subtlety of concepts, what would be unquestionably obvious in the nineteenth century: either madness is the organic disturbance of a material principle, or it is the spiritual troubling of an immaterial soul.

The fact that through these complex detours, Voltaire has drawn up this simple set of problems from the outside does not mean that they were essential to the thought of the eighteenth century. The questioning of the division between the body and the soul was not born from the depths of classical medicine, but is a problem imported at a fairly recent date, out of time, from the point of view of a philosophical intention.

What medicine of the classical age admitted unproblematically, the foundation upon which it progresses without asking itself any questions, was a different form of simplicity, more complex for us, as since the nineteenth century we are used to thinking the problems of psychiatry in terms of an opposition between body and mind (an opposition that is merely attenuated and eluded by notions like 'organo-' or 'psychogenesis'), it was the simplicity that Tissot presented as a defence against the abstract chimera of the *philosophes*, the beautiful, discernible unity of body and soul, which precedes all the dissociations unknown to medicine:

> Searching for the causes of the influence of the mind on the body and body on the mind is a matter for metaphysics; medicine ventures less far, but perhaps sees more clearly as a result: it ignores causes and observes only phenomena. Experience shows that a certain state of the body necessarily produces certain movements of the soul, which in turn modify the body; experience shows that when the soul is busy thinking, a certain part of the brain is in a state of tension; its research goes no further than that, and it seeks to look no further. The union of mind and body is so strong that it is difficult to conceive of the one acting without the consent of the other. The senses transmit the motive of thought to the mind by causing the fibres of the brain to vibrate, and while the soul reacts the organs of the brain are in movement to some degree, in a state of varying degrees of tension.[10]

One rule of method should be applied immediately: whenever medical texts in the classical age speak of madness, *vesaniae* (hallucinations, or troubles of the reason), or even in an explicit manner of 'mental illness' and 'illness of the spirit', what is being referred to is neither a series of psychological troubles nor of spiritual facts that would stand in opposition to the domain of organic pathology. We should always bear in mind the fact that Willis classified madness as a disease of the head, and placed hysteria among the convulsions, and that Sauvages put blunders, vertigo and tinnitus in the class of *vesaniae*. And there are countless other anomalies too.

Physicians with an interest in the history of medicine love to play at trying to identify the real diseases that lurked behind these classical descriptions. When Willis spoke of hysteria, did he not also include epileptic phenomena? When Boerhaave spoke of mania, was he not describing paranoia? And is Diemerbroek's melancholy not strongly reminiscent of an obsessional neurosis? Fine sport to be sure,[11] but this is not history. Perhaps from one century to another the same name does not refer to the *same diseases* — but this is because fundamentally it is not the *same* disease that is in question. To speak of madness in the seventeenth and eighteenth century is not, in the strict sense, to speak of 'a sickness of the mind', but of something where both the body and the soul *together* are in question. That, more or less, is what Zacchias meant when he proposed a definition that remains more or less valid for the whole of the classical age: *Amentiae a proprio cerebri morbo et ratiocinatricis facultatis laesione dependent* (All forms of madness depend on a disease of the brain, and damage done to the faculty of reason).[12]

Leaving aside therefore a set of problems that were added at a fairly recent date to the experience of madness, we shall now endeavour to sketch out the structures that rightly belong to it, beginning with the most exterior ones (the cycle of causality), moving on to the more interior and less visible ones (the cycle of passion and image), and finally attaining, at the heart of that experience, that which made it what it was, the essential moment of delirium.

*

The distinction between remote causes and immediate ones, familiar in all the classical texts, may not appear to be of great importance at first glance, offering only a fragile structure to organise the world of causality. In fact its importance is considerable, as what lies behind this apparently arbitrary distinction is a highly rigorous structuring power.

When Willis speaks of immediate causes of mania, he understands by that a double alteration of the animal spirits. First come the mechanical alterations, which affect the strength and trajectory of movement. In a maniac the spirits move with considerable violence, and can therefore force their way into unknown regions where they should not venture, and these new paths result in an eccentric flow of ideas, sudden and inexplicable movements, and a redoubled strength that seems to far exceed the patient's natural force. There is also a chemical alteration, where the spirits take on a more acid nature that makes them more corrosive and more penetrative, lighter and less heavy with matter. The result is a spirit as quick and impalpable as a flame, giving maniac behaviour its characteristically lively, unpredictable and ardent quality.[13]

Such are the immediate causes. They are indeed so close that they seem little more than a qualitative transcription of all that is most visible in the manifestations of the sickness. The agitation, disorder and unfevered heat that seem to animate the maniac, lending him a characteristic profile that is simply and immediately perceptible, are transferred by this analysis of immediate causes from the exterior to the interior, from the domain of perception to the domain of explanation, from visible effects to the invisible movement of causality.[14] But paradoxically, that which was originally a quality, once it becomes invisible, is transformed into an image. The ardent quality becomes the flame-image, disorder in gesture and speech solidifies into the inextricable confusion of imperceptible furrows. And values that were at the limits of moral judgement, where one could see and touch, became things beyond the limits of touch and sight; without even a change in vocabulary, ethics becomes a form of dynamics. As Sydenham notes,

> The strength and constancy of mind, as long as it is confined in the body, much depends on the firmness of the spirits that are subservient to it; which indeed are made of the finest matter, and are placed in the confines of material beings; and as the frame of the mind, if it be lawful to call it so, is much more curious and delicate than the structure of the body, for it consists in the harmony of the most excellent and almost divine faculties; so if the constitution is any way vitiated, by so much the greater is the ruin, by how much it was more excellent and more exquisitely composed when it was whole. This truly is the condition of those most miserable and dejected people we have described.[15]

Between these immediate causes and their effects a sort of immediate qualitative communication is established, without interruption or intermediary, and what is formed is a system of simultaneous presence, which is a perceived quality on the side of the effect, and an invisible image for the cause. The circulation is perfect from the one to the other, as the image is induced from all that is familiar to perception, and the symptomatic singularity of the patient is deduced from the physical properties attributed to the causal image. In fact the system of immediate causes is little more than the other side of the empirical recognition of symptoms, a kind of causal valorisation of the qualities involved.

Little by little, in the course of the eighteenth century, this tight circle, this game of transpositions that turned around itself, reflecting itself in an imaginary element, begins to open up, and stretches out into a more linear structure, where the essential element is no longer a communication of quality, but purely and simply the fact of antecedence. The effect of this is that it is no longer in the imaginary elements but inside an organised perception that causes are to be identified.

Already, in the pathology of nerve fibres, most important of all was the need to see the immediate cause, and to ensure that it had a recognisable existence inside perception. Not that quality and image were banished from this new structure of immediate causality, but it did require them to be present in a visible organic phenomenon, which could be presented, without a risk of error or circular return, as the antecedent fact. Sydenham's French translator took him to task for not making the link between the vigour of the soul and the strength of the animal spirits more apparent:

> To which we could add that the idea we have of our spirits is neither clear nor satisfactory . . . the strength and steadfast nature of the soul, to use the terms our author uses, seem principally to depend on the structure of solids, which have the elasticity and suppleness necessary to allow the soul to perform its duties with ease and vigour.[16]

With the physiology of fibres, a whole material network is in place that can serve as a perceptual support for the designation of immediate causes. In fact, if the support itself is visible in its material reality, the alteration that serves as an immediate cause of madness is not strictly speaking perceptible: the most that it might be is an impalpable, almost moral quality, inserted in the tissue of perception. Paradoxically, it is a purely physical modification, usually a mechanical alteration of the fibre itself, but which affects it below the threshold of any possible perception, in the infinitely minute determination of its functioning. Physiologists who see the fibre in question know that it is not possible to observe or measure any tension or relaxation at that level. Even when stimulating the nerves of a frog, Morgagni could detect no contraction, and this was merely a confirmation of the opinions of Boerhaave, Van Swieten, Hoffmann and

1. Hieronymus Bosch (c. 1450–1516), *The Stone Cutter* (The Cure of Folly), 1475–1480. Museo del Prado, Madrid, Spain

2. Hieronymus Bosch (c. 1450–1516), *The Ship of Fools*, 1484/90 or 1510/16, Musée du Louvre, Paris

3. Albrecht Dürer (1471–1528), *Melancholia* (engraving), 1514

Haller, the adversaries of the nerve-cord theory and of the pathologies of tension and rest. But physicians and practitioners saw too, and what they saw was quite different: they saw a maniac, with his muscles in a state of contraction, a rictus grin, jerky, violent gestures, reacting with great energy to the smallest stimulus; they *saw* the nervous system in a state of maximal tension. Between these two forms of perception, that of the modified thing, and that of the altered quality, a conflict reigns, obscurely, in the medical thought of the eighteenth century.[17] Slowly, the first group carry the day, but not without absorbing the values of the second group. These famous states of tension, dryness and withering that the physiologists did not see were seen by practitioners like Pomme with their own eyes, and heard by their ears. They thought they were triumphing over the physiologists, whereas ultimately all they were doing was allowing the triumph of the structure of causality that they were seeking to impose. Hunched over the body of a female patient, Pomme heard the vibrations in the irritated nervous system, and after dipping it in water for twelve hours a day for ten months, he saw the dessicated elements peel away and fall into the bath, 'membranous strips like strips of wet parchment'.[18]

Perceptive and linear structures were now beginning to carry the day. Qualitative communication was no longer sought, and gone were the descriptions of the circle that moved back from the effect and its essential values to a cause that was little more than a transposition of its meaning. The search was now on for the simplest possible *perceptible event*, which might determine sickness in the most direct manner. The immediate cause of madness had to be a visible alteration in the organ closest to the soul, i.e. the nervous system, and in so far as it was possible the brain itself. The proximity of the cause was no longer required in a unity of meaning, or a qualitative analogy, but in the most rigorously possible anatomical proximity. The cause would be found when it was possible to assign, situate and perceive the anatomical or physiological disturbance – regardless of its nature, form or the manner in which it affected the nervous system – which was closest to the junction of the soul and the body. In the seventeenth century, the immediate cause implied a simultaneity and a structural resemblance; by the eighteenth century, it began to imply an unmediated antecedence and an immediate proximity.

It is in this spirit that developments in anatomical research on the causes of madness are to be understood. Bonet's *Sepulchretum*, published for the first time in 1679, still only gave qualitative descriptions, where the pressure of imagination and the influence of theoretical themes weighed heavily on perception, determining its meaning in advance. During post mortems, Bonet had seen the brain of a maniac as dry and brittle, while that of a melancholic was damp and congested with humours. In dementia, the cerebral substance was very rigid or excessively relaxed, but in both cases devoid of elasticity.[19] Nearly fifty years later, the analyses of Meckel still belong to the same world where quality was all – for maniacs, dryness, for melancholics, heaviness and damp. But those qualities were now to be perceived, by a perception purified of all sensible apperception through the use of rigorous measurement. The condition of the brain no longer represents the other version, the perceptible translation of madness, but has become instead, as pathological event, the essential alteration that leads to madness.

The principle behind Meckel's experiments is quite simple. From the brain and cerebellum he cut cubes of tissue of '9, 6 and 3 lines, according to the Paris standard, in all directions'. He observed that a six-line cube taken from the brain of a subject who had died in a normal state of health, who had never suffered from any serious illness, weighed 1 dram and 5 grains, while a section from the brain of a young man who had died of consumption only weighed 1 dram and 3 and ¾ grains, and one from his cerebellum weighed 1 dram and 3 grains.[20] In the case of an old man who had died of pleurisy, the weight of the brain was normal, but the cerebellum was lighter. The first conclusion he drew was that the weight of the brain was not constant, but varied according to different pathological states. Second, as the brain weighed less in diseases of exhaustion like consumption, as did the cerebellum in sicknesses where the humours and fluids flowed into the body, the density of those organs should be attributed 'to the fullness of the little canals to be found there'. Modifications of the same order were to be found in the insane. Doing a post mortem on a woman who had been 'constantly maniacal and stupid uninterruptedly for 15 years', Meckel noted that the 'ashy substance' in her brain was too pale, and that the medullar substance was extremely white: 'this was too tough to be cut into pieces, and so elastic that no imprint of the finger would remain there; it closely resembled the white of a hard-boiled egg'. A six-line cube cut into the medullar substance weighed 1 dram and 3 grains; the corpus callosum was even less dense, and a cube taken from the cerebellum, like the brain, weighed 1 dram and

3 grains. Other forms of alienation brought different effects. One young woman who had been 'intermittently mad' died in a frenzy, and her brain seemed dense to the touch; the arachnoid membrane covered a reddish serum, but the medullar substance itself was dry and elastic, weighing 1 dram and 3 grains. It was therefore necessary to conclude that 'the dryness of the medullar canals can cause upsets in the brain, and consequently perturb reason', and inversely, that 'the brain is all the more effective in the uses for which it is intended when the medullar canals secrete the nervous fluid correctly'.[21]

The theoretical horizon against which Meckel's work should be set, and his hypothesis that madness was the result of perturbations in a nervous fluid secreted by the brain, are of little import. What is essential for the moment is the new form of causality that is apparent in his analyses. This causality is no longer caught up with the symbolism of qualities in the tautology of transposed meanings as it still was in the work of Bonet. What we have instead is linear causality, where the alteration of the brain is an event considered in itself, a phenomenon with its own local, quantifiable values that can be recorded within an organised perception. Between this alteration and the symptoms of madness there was no other connection, no system of communication other than extreme proximity, a result of the fact that the brain was the organ closest to the soul. Disturbances of the brain therefore were to have their own structure – an anatomical structure offered to perception – and troubles of the mind had their own singular manifestation. Causality juxtaposed them, it did not transpose qualitative elements from the one to the other. Meckel's post-mortems were not the result of a materialist methodology: he believed neither more nor less than his predecessors and contemporaries that madness was determined by an organic attack. But he did place the body and the soul in an order of causal proximity and succession in which there was no reversibility, no transposition, and no qualitative communication.

This structure emerges more completely in the work of Morgagni and Cullen. In their analyses, the cerebral mass no longer plays the simple role of a privileged point of application for causality; instead it becomes in itself a heterogeneous, differentiated causal space that develops its own anatomical and physiological structures determining in a game of spatial configuration the various forms of madness. Morgagni observes that often, in the case of mania or fury, when the brain has an extraordinarily hard, firm texture, the cerebellum by contrast maintains its customary suppleness, and that in extreme cases, quite unlike the brain itself, it is 'unusually soft and flaccid'. Sometimes the differences are to be found in the interior of the brain itself: 'while a part of cerebrum was harder and firmer than ordinary, other parts of it were preternaturally soft'.[22] Cullen systematises these differences, making the different parts of the brain the principal aspects of the organic disturbances of madness. For the brain to be in a normal state, its state of excitement needed to be homogeneous in the different parts, either in a state of elevated excitement (for the waking state) or in a lesser degree of excitement or collapse (for sleep). But if excitement and collapse are unevenly spread around the brain, and if they combine and form a heterogeneous network of excited sectors and sectors that are sleeping, the result is dreams if the subject is asleep, and fits of insanity if he is awake. There are therefore chronic forms of madness when these states of unequal excitement and repose are constantly maintained by the brain, solidified in some sense into its very substance. For that reason the anatomical examination of the brain of the mad revealed hard, congested parts, and other softer parts that were in a state of more or less total relaxation.[23]

The evolution that the notion of an immediate cause went through in the classical age, or more exactly the meaning that causality took on inside that notion, are now clear. This restructuring paved the way for the materialism and organicism of the age that followed, and in any case the effort to understand the mechanisms of the brain in terms of cerebral localisations. But in that period, it implies no such project. There was simultaneously much more and much less involved here. Much less than the sudden eruption of a materialism, but much more in that what was undone was the type of causality that had organised the relationship of the soul to the body since the seventeenth century. It was removed from the closed cycle of qualities, and placed in the open perspective of a simpler yet more enigmatic chain of events that put the cerebral space and the system of psychological signs in an order of invariable succession. On the one hand, all signifying communication was interrupted; but on the other, the whole of the body was no longer called upon to form the structure of the immediate cause; only the brain, which, as it was the organ that *approached* the soul most closely, and even only certain privileged sectors within it, grouped together the aspects that were known as immediate causes, a term soon to be forgotten.

*

The fate of the remote cause went through an exactly opposite evolution during this same period. At the outset it was defined only in terms of antecedence, a slightly arbitrary relationship of juxtaposition that did little more than group together coincidences, factual intersections and immediate pathological transformations. Ettmüller gives a good example when he lists the causes of convulsions: nephritic colic, the acid humours of melancholy, birth during a lunar eclipse, neighbouring metal mines, the anger of newborn children, autumn fruits, constipation, medlar stones in the rectum, and in a more immediate fashion, the passions and those of love in particular.[24] Remote causes gradually gain ground, spreading to new regions and taking on an incalculable multiplicity. Soon the whole organic domain was involved, and it seemed that there was no disturbance, no inhibited or excessive secretion, no deviant mode of functioning that could not be registered as a remote cause of madness. Whytt noted in particular the importance of wind, phlegm and mucus, intestinal worms, 'aliments improper in their quality or quantity, scirrhous or other obstructions of the viscera of the lower belly, violent afflictions of the mind'.[25] Any event in the soul, provided it was of sufficient violence or intensity, could now become a remote cause for madness: 'Passions of the soul, a mind filled with contention, enforced study, deep thought, anger, sadness, fear, intense and prolonged sorrow, love scorned . . .'[26] Anything in the outside world, in all its variations and excesses, its violence and its artificiality could bring on madness, air that was too warm, too cold or too damp,[27] the climate under certain conditions,[28] life in society, 'a love of science or a devotion to letters, both of which are increasingly widespread, a growing luxury that makes life too soft for masters and their servants',[29] the reading of novels, theatrical spectacles, and anything that excited the imagination.[30] In short, there was almost nothing that could not be ascribed as a cause in this ever-increasing circle. The world of the soul, the body, nature and society constituted an immense reservoir of causes presenting writers of the eighteenth century with an endless array of possibilities, where little observation or organisation were needed, and it sufficed to follow one's own theoretical preferences or some moral choices. Dufour, in his *Traité de l'entendement*, drew up a summary list of the recognised causes of his day:

> The obvious causes of melancholy are all those elements that immobilise, wear out or trouble these spirits; great, sudden frights, violent

movements of the soul resulting from transports of joy or intense affection, lengthy, deep meditation on a particular object, intense love, lack of sleep, and all excessive exercise of the worried mind, particularly at night; solitude, fear, hysterical affection, anything that impedes growth, healing, the circulation, the various secretions and excretions of blood, particularly in the spleen, the pancreas, the omentum, the stomach, the mesentery, the intestines, the breasts, the liver, the uterus, the haemorrhoidal vessels; consequently the hypochondriac illness, acute diseases imperfectly cured, principally frenzy and causus, all medications or excretions, when over-abundant or interrupted, and consequently sweat, milk, menstrual fluid, lochia, ptyalism and scabies. Dispermatism commonly produces what is known as erotic delirium or erotomania; cold, earthy foodstuffs, anything that is difficult to digest, hard, dry or astringent, similar drinks and raw fruit, floury substances that have not fermented, any long-lasting intense heat that burns the blood, dark, stagnant bog air, being dark-skinned, hairy, dry, tall, male, being in the prime of life, or having a cast of mind that is lively, penetrating, deep or studious.[31]

At the end of the eighteenth century, this almost indefinite extension of the remote causes of madness became accepted as fact, and at the moment of the great reform of confinement, was one of the rare bodies of knowledge that was transmitted without theoretical alteration – the new practice within asylums directly matched the polyvalence and heterogeneity of causal reasoning about the genesis of madness. Analysing the mad in Bethlem hospital between 1772 and 1787, Black indicated the following aetiologies:

a hereditary disposition, drunkenness, excessive study, fevers, the consequences of childbirth, obstructions of the viscera, bruises and fractures, venereal disease, small pox, ulcers that dry too quickly, upsets, worries and misfortunes, love, jealousy, excessive devotion or belonging to a Methodist sect, pride.[32]

A few years later Giraudy reported to the Minister of the Interior about the situation at Charenton in 1804, where he had received 'reliable information' that had allowed him to determine the cause of illness in 476 cases:

One hundred and fifty are ill as a result of powerful afflictions of the soul, such as jealousy, disappointment in love, excessive joy, ambition, fear, terror or intense sadness; 52 have inherited their condition; for 28 it is a result of masturbation; 3, a syphilitic virus; 12, the abuse of the pleasures of Venus; 31, the abuse of alcoholic beverages; 12, the abuse of their intellectual faculties; for 2 it is the result of worms in the intestine; one the consequences of scabies; for 5 it is the result of herpes; 29 of milky metastasis; and 2, sunstroke.[33]

The list of remote causes of madness never ceases to grow. The eighteenth century enumerates them without any order, privileging no single one above the others, in a disorganised multiplicity. And yet that world of causality may not be quite as anarchic as it appears. The multiplicity might seem to stretch on indefinitely, but not in a heterogeneous or chaotic space. One example should allow us to grasp the organising principle that groups together the variety of causes and guarantees their secret coherence.

In the sixteenth century, lunacy was a constant theme that was never questioned. It was still frequent in the seventeenth century, but started to disappear, and by 1707, the year in which Le François asked the question 'Estne aliquod lunae in corpora humana imperium?' (Does the moon have any influence over the human body?), after lengthy discussions, the university decided that their reply was in the negative.[34] In the course of the eighteenth century the moon was rarely cited among the causes of madness, even as a possible factor or an aggravation. But right at the end of the century the idea reappears, perhaps under the influence of English medicine, which had never entirely forgotten the moon,[35] and Daquin,[36] followed by Leuret[37] and Guislain,[38] all admitted the influence of the moon on the phases of maniacal excitement, or at the least on the agitation of their patients. But what is important here is not so much the return of the theme as the possibility and conditions necessary for its reappearance. It reappears entirely transformed, filled with a new significance that it did not formerly possess. In its traditional form, it designated an immediate influence, a direct coincidence in time and intersection in space, whose mode of action was entirely situated in the power of the stars. But in Daquin by contrast, the influence of the moon acts through a whole series of mediations, in a kind of hierarchy, surrounding man. The moon acts on the atmosphere with such intensity that it can set in motion a mass as heavy as the ocean. The nervous system, of all the parts that make up the human organism, is the part most sensitive to atmospheric variations, as the slightest variation in temperature, humidity or dryness can have serious effects upon it. The moon therefore, given the important power that its trajectory exerts on the atmosphere, is likely to act most on people whose nervous fibres are particularly delicate:

> Madness is an exclusively nervous disease, and the brain of a madman must therefore be infinitely more susceptible to the influence of the atmosphere, which itself undergoes considerable changes of intensity as a result of the different positions of the moon relative to the earth.[39]

At the end of the eighteenth century, as it had been more than a century previously, lunacy was considered to be 'beyond reasonable doubt'. But in a totally new way. It is no longer simply the expression of a cosmic power, but rather a sign of the peculiar sensitivity of the human organism. If the phases of the moon can have an influence on madness, that is because man is entirely surrounded by a group of elements to which he is sensitive to some degree, without being conscious of it. The sensitivity of the body and the milieu to which it is sensitive have now come between madness and remote causes, forming a quasi-unity, a system of belonging that organises the ensemble of the remote causes of madness in a new homogeneity.

The system of causes therefore underwent a double evolution in the course of the eighteenth century. Immediate causes constantly grew closer together, instituting a linear relation between the soul and the body, which takes the place of the former cycle of the transposition of qualities. Meanwhile remote causes seemed constantly to expand and separate, in appearance at least, but beneath the apparent chaos a new unity was forming, a new form of liaison between the body and the outside world. During the same period, the body became both an ensemble of different localisations for systems of linear causality and the secret unity of a particular sensibility that picked up on the most diverse, distant and heterogeneous influences from the world that surrounded it. The medical view of madness reflects this new division. On the one hand there is the phenomenon of the soul affected by some accident or upset that befalls the body, and on the other there is the phenomenon of the body and soul linked in the same sensibility, the whole human being, affected by any variation in the influences of his milieu. A localised attack in the brain, and a general disturbance of sensibility. There is now the possibility, and the obligation, to look at once for the cause of madness in the anatomy of the brain and in the dampness of the air, the change of season, or the exaltation in reading novels. The precision of the immediate cause is no contradiction to the diffuse generality of the remote cause. Both the one and the other are no more than the different extremes of a single movement – the phenomenon of passion.

*

Passion is to be found among the remote causes, on the same plane as the others.

But deep down it has quite a different role, and if, in the experience of madness, it belongs to the cycle of causality, it is also at the origin of a second cycle, which is perhaps of a more essential nature.

Sauvages sketched out the fundamental role played by passion, transforming it into a more obstinate, invariant cause of madness, the form that somehow seemed most deserved:

> The wandering of our spirit is the result of giving in blindly to our desires, and of not knowing how to refrain from giving free reign to our passions or moderate them. The result is the delirium of love, antipathy, depraved tastes, the melancholy that sadness causes, the fits brought on by a refusal, excessive eating and drinking, the incommodities and the corporeal vices that bring madness, which is the worst of all diseases.[40]

Here we are still in the moral precedence of passion, and what is at stake in a confused fashion is the question of its responsibility. But what is really targeted through that denunciation is the radical link between the phenomena of madness and the very possibility of passion.

Before Descartes, and long after his influence as a philosopher and physiologist had waned, passion remained the interface between the body and the soul, the point of contact between their activity and their passivity, which also served as the place and the reciprocally imposed limit of their communications.

The medicine of humours perceived this unity as a form of reciprocal causality.

> The passions necessarily cause certain movements in the humours: anger agitates the bile, sadness, melancholy, and the movements of the humours are sometimes so violent that they overturn the entire economy of the body and even bring death. The passions also increase the quantity of the humours, anger causing bile to proliferate, and sadness melancholy. The humours that are agitated by certain passions dispose those in whom they abound to the same passions, and to thinking about objects that ordinarily excite them, so bile disposes one to anger and causes one to think about those that one dislikes. Melancholy disposes to sadness, and causes thoughts about unfortunate things, and well-tempered blood brings joy.[41]

The medicine of animal spirits replaces this vague determinism of a 'disposition' with the rigour of a mechanical transmission of movement. If the passions are only possible in a being that has a body, and a body which is not entirely penetrated by the light of its spirit and the immediate transparency of its will, this is to the degree that in us, independently and usually despite ourselves, the movements of the mind obey a mechanical structure, that of the movement of the spirits.

> Before seeing the object of their passion, the animal spirits are spread throughout the body in order to preserve all the parts in general, but when a new object appears this whole economy is thrown into jeopardy. Most of the spirits are forced into the muscles in the arms, the legs, the face and all the exterior parts of the body in order to give it the specific disposition of the dominant passion, and give it the countenance and movement necessary for the acquisition of the good, or flight from the evil that has appeared.[42]

Passion therefore deploys the spirits that dispose us to passion, so that under the effects of passion, and in the presence of its object, the spirits circulate and are dispersed around the body, and become concentrated in a particular spatial configuration that privileges the trace of the object in the brain and its image in the soul, thereby forming in the corporeal space a sort of geometrical figure of the passion which in fact is its expressive transposition, but which also constitutes its essential causal nature, given that all the spirits being grouped around the object of passion, or at least of its image, the mind in its turn will no longer be able to divert from it the movement of its attention, and consequently will enter the throws of passion.

One step further, and the whole system tightens into a unity where the body and soul communicate immediately in the symbolic values of shared qualities. This is what happens in the medicine of solids and fluids, which dominates the medical practices of the eighteenth century. Tension and relaxation, hardness and softness, rigidity and rest and swelling and desiccation are all qualitative states of the mind as well as of the body, and ultimately refer to an indistinct and mixed situation regarding the passions, imposing its common forms on the flow of ideas and feelings, the state of the nerve fibres and the circulation of the fluids. The theme of causality here appears to be too discursive, and the elements that it groups together are too disparate for any useful schema to be applied. 'Are active passions like anger, joy and envy' the causes or consequences of 'the excessive force, the overwhelming tension, the undesirable elasticity of the nervous fibres, or the overactive movements of the nervous fluid'? And inversely, is it not the case that 'the languorous passions like fear, down-heartedness, boredom, loss of appetite, the chill that accompanies homesickness, bizarre appetites, stupidity and memory loss', can also be followed or preceded by the 'softness of the brain matter and the nervous fibres that distribute it amongst the organs, or a diminution or inertia in the fluids'?[43] There is no sense in attempting to situate passion in a causal succession, or half-way between the corporeal and the spiritual; it indicates, at a deeper level, that body and soul are in a perpetual metaphorical relationship, where qualities do not need to be communicated because they are already shared, and where the facts of expression have no need to acquire a causal value, for the simple reason that body and soul are always the immediate expression of each other. Passion is no longer situated exactly at the geometrical centre of the ensemble of the body and soul, but slightly precedes them, in a place where they are not yet in opposition, the region where their unity and their distinctiveness are both grounded.

But on that level, passion is no longer simply a cause of madness, nor even one of the privileged ones: passion is more like the general condition of its possibility. If it is true to say that there exists in the relations between the soul and the body a domain where cause and effect, determinism and expression are still so tightly interwoven that in practice they form a single movement which will only be undone later on; if it is also true that preceding the violence of the body and the quickness of the soul, and before the softness of the fibres and the relaxation of the spirit, there are some sort of qualitative *a priori* that are not yet divided and which latterly impose the same values on both the organic and the spiritual, then it can be understood that there might be diseases like madness which from the outset affect both the body *and* the soul, diseases where the disturbance of the brain is of the same quality, origin, and ultimately nature as the disturbance of the soul.

The possibility of madness is offered in the very fact of passion.

It is true that since long before the classical age, and for a series of centuries that has probably not yet come to an end, passion and madness have been kept in close proximity. But the classical age did have a genuinely original approach here. Moralists in the Greek and Latin tradition had thought it quite fair that madness should be the punishment for passion, and to confirm it they declared that passion was a provisional or attenuated form of madness. But the classical age created a relation between passion and madness that was neither wishful thinking, nor pedagogical threat nor moral synthesis. There was a break with tradition in that the terms of the argument were reversed, and henceforth the chimera of madness were to be based on the nature of passion, and the *determinism of the passions* was nothing other than the *freedom offered to madness* to penetrate the world of reason. If the unquestioned union between body and soul showed in passion the finitude of man, it also simultaneously opened man to an infinite movement that was his undoing.

The reason is that madness is not simply one of the possibilities presented by the union of body and soul, and is not purely and simply one of the consequences of passion. Grounded in the unity of the body and the soul, it turns against that union and calls it into question. Madness, made possible by passion, threatens, in its own movement, the condition of possibility of passion. It is one of those forms of unity where the laws are compromised, perverted and twisted, demonstrating that the unity clearly exists, but that it is also fragile and destined to disappear.

There comes a moment when, as passion pursues its course, the laws are suspended as though of their own accord, and where the movement suddenly stops, without there being any physical shock or absorption of the force, or where the movement spreads and multiplies throughout, only stopping when excitement is at its highest peak. Whytt allows that a strong emotion can provoke madness just as a physical jolt can start movement, for the simple reason that emotion is both a shock for the soul, and a shaking of the nervous fibres: 'Thus doleful or moving stories, horrible or unexpected sights, great grief, anger, terror and other passions, frequently occasion the most sudden and violent nervous symptoms.'[44] But – and this is where madness properly speaking begins – it also happens that the movement can be checked by its own excess, bringing a form of immobility that sometimes goes as far as death. It is as though in the mechanics of madness rest is not the same thing as an absence of movement, but can also be a brutal rupture within the self, a movement which due to the effect of its own violence reaches its own contradiction and the impossibility of carrying on.

> Some of the more violent passions have, all at once, occasioned a fit of tetanus or catalepsy; so that the person has appeared more like a statue than to any thing alive; nay, excessive fear, grief, joy, and shame have been sometimes followed by sudden death.[45]

Inversely, it also happens that movement, passing from the soul to the body and the body to the soul, becomes infinitely propagated in a sort of space of disquiet, certainly closer to where Malebranche placed souls than where Descartes situated bodies. Imperceptible movements, often brought on by a relatively minor external event, slowly accumulate, grow and then explode into violent convulsions. Lancisi had already stated that the Roman nobility often suffered from the vapours – bringing hysterical falls and hypochondriacal crises – because, in the life they led at court, 'their spirit was constantly torn between fear and hope, and never had a moment's rest'.[46] For many doctors, the life of cities, at court and in salons, leads to madness through this cumulative multiplicity of excitement, which is prolonged and constantly repeated, and never dies down in intensity.[47] But in the image, given sufficient intensity, and in the events that constitute its organic counterpart, there is a certain force which if multiplied, can lead to delirium, as though movement, rather than losing force through being communicated, could drag other forces along in its wake and draw supplementary strength from the complicitous elements. This is how Sauvages explains the birth of delirium. A certain impression of fear is linked to a swelling in or pressure on a certain fibre in the medulla. That fear is limited to a recognisable object, just as the swelling or pressure is strictly localised. But as the fear persists, the soul begins to take more notice, isolating it and detaching it ever more from all that is foreign to it. That isolation in effect gives it strength, and the soul, by concentrating too closely upon it, progressively begins to associate a whole series of more or less remote ideas with it:

> It joins to that simple idea all those others that are wont to nourish and augment it. For example, a man sleeping who dreams he is accused of a crime soon joins satellite ideas to that theme, and dreams of guards, judges, executioners and the gibbet.[48]

Being weighed down with these new ideas, and dragging them in its wake, gives an additional strength to the idea, which soon means that it can resist the strongest efforts of the will to fight against it.

Madness, which finds its first possibility in the fact of passion and in the unfolding of that double process of causality which, originating in passion itself, spreads towards the body and towards the soul, is at the same time a suspension of passion, a rupture of causality, the liberation of the elements of that unity. Madness partakes of the necessity of passion and at the same time of the anarchy that passion brings, which although triggered by passion moves far beyond it, and goes so far as to challenge all that passion supposes. It culminates by being a movement of the nerves and muscles of such violence that nothing in the course of images, ideas or will seems to correspond to it any longer. This is certainly the case for mania, when it suddenly intensifies into convulsions, or when it definitively degenerates into continuous fury.[49] Inversely, when the body is at rest or in a state of inertia, it can also engender and encourage an agitation of the soul, without interruption or appeasement, as is the case for melancholy, where external objects no longer have the effect that they have on the mind of a healthy man; in a melancholic, 'impressions are weak, and rarely draw the attention. The mind of the melancholic is almost entirely preoccupied with the vivacity of his own ideas'.[50]

In fact this dissociation of the external movements of the body and the course of ideas is neither an indication that the unity of the body and soul has come undone, nor that in madness each of them develops their own autonomy. Admittedly, unity is compromised, in its rigour and totality, but it cracks along lines which, without destroying it, divide it into arbitrary sections. For when the melancholic becomes focused on one delirious idea, it is not solely the soul which is involved, but the soul with the brain, the soul with the nerves and their origin and fibres, a whole segment of the unity of the soul and body, which breaks away from the ensemble, and above all from the organs through which the perception of the real is operated. The same phenomenon is to be observed in convulsions and agitation. The soul is not excluded from the body, but is dragged along so quickly by it that it cannot retain its representations, and becomes separated from its memories, its will, its deeply held convictions, and thus ends up isolated from itself and from all that remains stable in the body, carried along by the most mobile fibres. Nothing in its behaviour is then adapted to reality, truth or wisdom. However much the vibration of the fibres imitates the events occurring in perception, the patient can no longer discriminate:

> The rapid and disordered pulsing of the arteries, or any other disturbance of any order, transmits the same movement [as perception] to the fibres, and they represent as present objects that are absent, and make the chimerical appear real.[51]

In madness, the totality of body and soul is broken up. Not according to the elements that constitute it metaphysically, but according to figures that envelop segments of the body and ideas of the soul in a derisory form of unity. These fragments isolate man from himself, and above all from reality. As they detach themselves, they form the unreal unity of a phantasm, and by virtue of their autonomy impose themselves on truth. 'Madness is no more than a disordering of the imagination.'[52] In other words, beginning with passion, madness is still only a vigorous movement in the rational unity of the body and the soul. It is the level of the unreasonable, but that movement quickly escapes the rationality of the mechanical, and in its violence, stupor and insane propagation becomes an irrational movement, and at that point slipping away from the weight of truth and its constraints, the Unreal emerges.

And that brings us to the third cycle that we must now examine. This is the cycle of chimeras, of phantasm and error. After passion, it is the turn of non-being.

*

We should now turn our attention to what is actually said in these fantastical fragments.

An image is not madness. Even if it is true to say that in the arbitrary world of the phantasm, alienation finds its first opening onto its vain liberty, madness itself only begins further on, at the moment when the mind binds itself to this arbitrary power, and becomes a prisoner of this apparent freedom. At the moment we are emerging from a dream, we might note, 'I'm seeing myself dead.' But that statement denounces and measures the illusions of the world of dreams, and indicates that we are not mad. Madness begins when a subject states as an affirmation that he is dead, and gives truth-value to the still-neutral content of the image 'I am dead.' Just as the consciousness of truth is not carried away by the simple presence of the image, but is in the act that limits, confronts, unifies or dissociates the image, so madness proper only begins in that act that lends a value of truth to the image. There is an original innocence in imagination: 'Imaginatio ipsa non errat quia neque negat neque affirmat, sed fixatur tantum in simplici contemplatione phantasmatis' [The imagination does not err because it neither denies nor affirms, but it is fixed to a great degree on the simple contemplation of an image],[53] and only the mind can turn all that is given in the image into an abusive truth, i.e. error, or recognised error, which is another form of truth:

> A drunken man might believe that he sees two candles where in fact there is only one. A man with a squint, whose mind is cultivated, will immediately recognise his error, and know that he is only seeing one.[54]

Madness therefore goes beyond the image, and yet is deeply embedded in it, for it solely consists of allowing the image to take on the value of total and absolute truth. The act of a reasonable man who, rightly or wrongly, judges an image to be true or false, goes beyond the image, and measures it against that which it is not. The madman, by contrast, never steps over the image that appears. He allows himself instead to be totally caught up in its immediate vivacity, and only gives his approval in so far as he is entirely absorbed in it. 'Many people, not to say all of them, fall into madness by being overly preoccupied by a single object.'[55] Inside the image, trapped within it and incapable of escaping, madness is still more than the image, forming an act of secret constitution.

So what is this act? It is an act of belief, an act of affirmation and negation, a discourse that sustains the image while working it, turning it over, distending it through reasoning, and organising it around a particular segment of language. A man who imagines that he is made of glass is not mad, for any sleeper might have that image in a dream. But he is mad if, thinking that he is made of glass, he concludes that he is fragile and in danger of breaking, and that therefore he should avoid contact with hard surfaces, remain immobile, and so forth.[56] That is the reasoning of a madman, although we should note in passing that there is nothing absurd or illogical in the reasoning itself. On the contrary, the strictest figures of logic are clearly being correctly applied. Zacchias had no problem finding the full rigour of logic in the reasoning of the mad. One madman who was starving himself to death applied the following syllogism: 'The dead do not eat. I am dead. Therefore I must not eat.' One who suffered from persecution mania could produce an infinitely extended induction: 'A, B and C are my enemies. They are all men. Therefore all men are my enemies.' An enthymeme is at play in the following: 'Most of the people who have lived in this house are dead. I have lived here. Therefore I am dead.'[57] The marvellous logic of the mad seems to mock that of the logicians, as it shadows it so closely, or rather because it is exactly the same, and at the heart of madness, at the basis of so many errors, absurdities, aimless words and gestures, what is sometimes to be found is the deeply buried perfection of a discourse. 'Ex quibus,' concludes Zacchias, 'vides quidem intellectum optime discurrere' [from these things you truly see how best to discuss the intellect]. The ultimate language of madness is that of reason, but wrapped up in the prestige of the image, confined to the space of appearances that it defines, both forming outside the totality of images and the universality of discourse a singular, erroneous organisation, whose dogged particularity makes up madness. Madness itself is never entirely within the image, which in itself is neither true nor false, neither reasonable nor mad, any more than it is in the reasoning, which is simple form, revealing nothing other than the indubitable figures of logic. And yet madness is there in both, in a particular figure of their relation.

Let us take an example from Diemerbroek. A man was suffering from a profound melancholy. Like all melancholics, his mind was caught up with one particular idea, and the idea for him was a never-ending cause of sadness. He accused himself of having killed his son, and in his excessive remorse, he said that God had placed a demon by his side, to tempt him as Christ had been tempted. He could see the demon, and conversed with him, heard his reproaches and replied to them accordingly. He could not understand that the people around him refused to admit this presence. This then is madness – this remorse, this belief, this hallucination and these discourses, a whole constellation of convictions and images that add up to a delirium. Diemerbroek sought the 'causes' of this madness, and how it had come about. And this is what he learnt: the man had taken his son swimming, and he had drowned. From that point on he felt responsible for the death. The development of the madness can thus be reconstituted as follows. Judging himself to be guilty, the man thinks that murder is execrable to God Almighty, and so it comes into his imagination that he is damned for all eternity. As he knows that the worst of damnation is being handed over to Satan, he tells himself that 'one of Satan's horrible minions is by his side'. He doesn't see the demon yet, but:

> As the idea never leaves him, he holds it to be a very truthful one, and he imposes a certain image of the demon on his brain; that image is offered to his soul by the action of the brain and the spirits with such clarity that he becomes convinced that he is continually seeing the real demon.[58]

There are therefore in madness, such as it is analysed by Diemerbroek, two levels. The first is the one that is obvious to all eyes: a groundless sadness in a man who wrongly accuses himself of having killed his own son, a deranged imagination that conjures up demons, and a disjointed reason that converses with a ghost. But on a deeper level there is also to be found a rigorous organisation that follows the faultless structure of a discourse. The logic of that discourse calls up a set of extremely solid beliefs, and progresses by a chain of judgements and reasoning, and is a sort of reason in act. In short, beneath the obviously disordered delirium reigns the order of a secret delirium. In this second delirium, which is, in a sense, pure reason, reason that has slipped off the external rags of dementia, the paradoxical truth of madness is to be found. And this doubly so, as what is to be found there is both that which makes madness true (faultless logic, well organised discourse, and the flawless flow within the transparency of a virtual language), and that which makes it truly mad (its own nature, the rigorously particular style of all its manifestations and the internal structure of delirium).

But at a deeper level still, that delirious language is the ultimate truth of madness in that it is its organising form, the determining principle in all its manifestations, whether it be those of the body or those of the mind. For if Diemerbroek's melancholic converses with his demon, it is because his image has been profoundly engraved in the ever-ductile matter of the brain by the movement of the spirits. But in its turn, that organic figure is just the converse of the worry that had long obsessed the patient. It is like a sedimentation in the body of an infinitely repeated discourse about the punishments that God has reserved for sinners guilty of murder. The body and the traces that it hides, the soul and the images that it perceives here are nothing more than the relays within the syntax of delirious language.

Lest we be reproached for basing this whole analysis on a single observation from a single author, an observation privileged because it deals with a melancholic delirium, confirmation can be found elsewhere of the fundamental role of delirious discourse in the classical conception of madness, in a different author, at another moment, and with regard to a radically different illness. This second case is an example of 'nymphomania' observed by Bienville. The imagination of a young girl, 'Julie', had been inflamed by precocious reading, and stoked by the conversation of a serving girl 'initiated into the secrets of Venus . . . whom the mother had considered to be a paragon of virtue, but who had been a dear and voluptuous handmaid to the pleasures of the daughter'. Yet against what for her were new desires, Julie struggled with all the impressions she had received from her education, and against the seductive language of novels, she opposed the lessons learnt from religion and virtue, and however vivid her imagination became, she did not fall into illness, as long as she had 'the strength to follow her own reasoning, where it was neither licit nor honest to obey so guilty a passion'.[59] But the guilty discourses and the dangerous reading multiplied, and at every turn they made the agitation of the fibres more vibrant, thereby weakening them; and then the fundamental language that had enabled her to resist slowly began to fade:

> Nature alone had *spoken* until then, but soon illusion, chimera and extravagance played their role, and she finally came to acquire the unfortunate strength that led her to approve a new, dreadful maxim in herself: that there is nothing so beautiful or sweet as to give in to one's amorous desires.

That fundamental discourse opened the doors of madness: once the imagination was set free, appetites could only grow, and the fibres were stretched to an ultimate degree of irritation. Delirium, in the lapidary form of a moral principle, leads straight to convulsions that can be life-threatening.

At the end of this last cycle, which began with the liberty of the phantasm and closes with the rigour of delirious language, four conclusions become apparent.

1　In *classical madness, there are two forms of delirium.* One is a unique form, symptomatic, particular to certain sicknesses of the mind and especially to melancholy; so that one can say that there are sicknesses with or without delirium. In any case this particular delirium is always manifest, and is an integral part of the signs of madness, immanent to its truth and forming only one of its sections. But there is also a different form of delirium that is not always apparent, which is not formulated by the sufferers themselves in the course of their disease, but which cannot fail to exist in the eyes of anyone searching for the origins of madness, and attempting to formulate its enigma and its truth.

2　*This implicit delirium exists in all alterations of the mind,* even in places it might least be expected. Wherever it is a question of silent gestures, wordless violence and inexplicable behaviour, there is no doubt for classical thought that there is an underlying delirium, where each particular sign is attached to the general essence of madness. Regarding the 'delirious', Robert James' *Medicinal Dictionary* expressly invited readers to consider them as follows:

> We conclude therefore that [the delirious] are to be esteemed as labouring under a disorder of reason, who have some one of the voluntary actions excessive or deficient, contrary to Reason, and all due Decorum; as when the Hand, for example, is employed after a ridiculous manner in fruitless picking of Motes or catching of flies; or when anything is done by the Patient contrary to his usual Custom, and without a Cause, as when he talks too much or little, contrary to his usual Custom, or talks obscenely, or utters his words after an incoherent and broken manner, or fetches his breath slower than necessity requires, or exposes his pudenda to the Bystanders. We call those delirious, also, whose mind, thro some default of the Senses, is incapable of receiving ideas, or is regardless of them when received; among whom are certainly to be

reckoned those who labour under some unusual Deficiency of the Senses without a Cause, or employ them in any unusual Manner; as when the Patient is either deprived of some voluntary action, or puts it to an ill Use.[60]

3 *Understood in this fashion, discourse covers the entire spectrum of madness.* Madness, in the classical sense, does not designate a certain change in the mind or the body, but the existence of a *delirious discourse* that underlies the alterations of the body and the strangeness in behaviour and speech. Thus the simplest and most general definition that can be given for madness is delirium itself: 'Delirium – from *Deliro*, to rave, or talk idly; which is derived from *Lira*, a Ridge or Furrow of Land. Hence *Deliro* properly imparts, to deviate from the Right, that is, right Reason.'[61] Suddenly it becomes less surprising that eighteenth-century nosographers often class vertigo as a form of madness, and more rarely so hysterical convulsions: behind the latter it is often impossible to find the unity of a discourse, while in vertigo what can be discerned is the delirious affirmation that the world really is spinning.[62] Delirium is the necessary and sufficient condition for an illness to be considered as madness.

4 *Language is the primary and ultimate structure of madness.* It is the constituent form, since it is on language that all the cycles in which it reveals its nature rely. The fact that the essence of madness can ultimately be defined in the simple structure of a discourse does not bring it back to a purely psychological nature, but instead gives it a grip on the totality of the body and soul. This discourse is the silent language in which the spirit addresses itself in its own truth, and at the same time visible articulation in the movements of the body. The parallelism and complementarities, all the immediate forms of communication that we have seen manifest themselves in madness between the soul and the body, depend on this language and its powers. The movement of passion that is followed through until it reaches breaking point and turns on itself, the eruption of the image, and the agitation of the body that was the visible concomitant – all that we were trying to exhume was already secretly animated by this language. If the determinism of passion is surpassed and undone in the fantasy of the image, and if the image in its turn took over the whole world of beliefs and desires, it was because the delirium of language was already present in the form of a discourse that liberated passion from its limits, and clung to the liberated image with the constraining weight of its affirmation.

It is in that delirium, which is both body and soul, language and image, and grammar and physiology, that all cycles of madness end and begin. The rigorous meaningfulness of delirium organised these cycles from the outset. Delirium is both madness itself, and beyond each of its phenomena, the silent transcendence that constitutes it, in its truth.

*

One last question remains. In the name of what can this fundamental language be regarded as delirium? Allowing that it is the truth of madness, in what sense is it true madness, and the originary form of the insane? Why should it be in this discourse, which we have seen in forms so faithful to rules of reason, that so many tell-tale signs of the absence of reason will be found?

This is a key question, but one to which the classical age had no direct answer. Attacking the issue head on is not the most effective path to truth, and what must be investigated are the experiences to be found in close vicinity to the essential language of madness, that is dream and error.

The dream-like character of madness is one of the constant themes of the classical age. It is doubtless a theme that is inherited from a very archaic tradition, to which Du Laurens, at the end of the sixteenth century, still bears witness. To his way of thinking, melancholy and dreams have the same origin, and have equal value in relation to truth. There are 'natural dreams' that represent, in the waking state, things that have passed through the senses or through the understanding, but which are altered by the subject's temperament; and in similar fashion there is a form of melancholy whose sole origin is in the physical constitution of the patient, and which affects to his mind the importance, the value and, so to speak, the colour of real events. But a different form of melancholy allows the future to be predicted, enables people to speak in tongues, and to see beings that are normally invisible. That melancholy has its origins in supernatural intervention, the same force that brings dreams that foretell the future to the mind of the dreamer, announcing events and causing him to see 'strange things'.[63]

But in fact the seventeenth century only maintained the tradition of the resemblance between sleep and madness the better to break it, revealing new, more essential links. Links where dreams and madness are no longer understood simply in terms of their remote origins or their imminent value as signs, but are compared instead in their phenomena, their development and their very nature.

Dreams and madness then reveal themselves to be made of the same substance. Their mechanism is identical, and Zacchias identifies in the progress of sleep the movements that bring dreams into being, but which might equally in a waking state bring on madness.

In the first moments of sleep, the vapours that rise up from the body to the head are multiple, turbulent and dense. They are so dark that they provoke no images in the mind, but their turbulence brings disorder to the nerves and muscles. The same is true for maniacs and the frenzied. Their fantasies are few, they have a limited number of erroneous beliefs and scarcely any hallucinations, but they have trouble mastering their intense agitation. Going over the evolution of sleep again, we see that after the initial period of turbulence, the vapours rising up to the brain begin to clear, and their movement becomes more organised, and at this point fantastical dreams begin, containing miracles and countless impossible things. Dementia corresponds to this stage, where sufferers are convinced of many things 'quae in veritate non sunt' [that in truth do not exist]. Finally the agitation of the vapours is calmed entirely, and the sleeper begins to see things more clearly. Through the transparent, now limpid vapours, memories of the previous day appear, representing the world as it really was, with perhaps a small number of metamorphoses, as is the case in melancholics who see things the way they really are, 'in paucis qui non solum aberrantes' [in particular those who are not distraught].[64] There is a constant analogy to be found between the progressive developments of sleep, and what each stage brings to the quality of the imagination, and different forms of madness, because the mechanisms are shared. Both involve the same movement of vapours and the animal spirits, the same liberation of images, the same correspondence between the physical qualities of phenomena and the psychological or moral value of sentiments. 'Non aliter evenire insanientibus quam dormientibus' [here there is no difference between the mad and the sleeping].[65]

What is important in Zacchias' analysis is that madness is not compared to dreams in their positive phenomena, but rather to the totality formed by sleep and dreams, i.e. to an ensemble that includes images, fantasies, memories and predictions, as well as the great void of sleep, the night of the senses, and the whole negativity that separates man from his waking state and the concomitant truth of the senses. While tradition was content to compare the delirium of the mad and the vividness of dream images, the classical age assimilates delirium to the indissoluble nexus of the image and the night of the spirit against which it gains its freedom. That whole, transported in its entirety to the waking state, is what constituted madness. That is the manner in which the definitions of madness that obstinately return in the classical age should be understood. The dream, as a complex figure of the image and of sleep, is almost invariably present. Either in a negative manner, as when the notion of waking is all that distinguishes a madman from a man asleep,[66] or in a positive manner, as when delirium is defined as a modality of dream, with waking being the specific difference: 'Delirium is the dream of waking persons.'[67] The ancient idea that dreams are a transitory form of madness is reversed. It is no longer dreams that borrow their worrying power from madness, thereby showing how much reason is fragile or limited, but madness that takes its fundamental nature from dream, demonstrating by that similarity that it is a liberation of the image in the night of the real.

Dreams deceive, bring confusion, and are illusory. But they are not erroneous. For that reason madness is more than a waking dream, and flows over into error. While it is true that in dreams the imagination creates 'impossibilia et miracula' [wonders and impossible things], and that it assembles life-like figures 'irrationali modo' [in an irrational manner], Zacchias remarks that 'nullus in his error est ac nulla consequenter insania' [there is no error in such things, and therefore no insanity].[68] Madness begins when images, which are so close to dreams, are compounded by the affirmation or the negation that are essential to mistakes. It is in that sense that the Encyclopédie proposed its famous definition of madness: abandoning reason 'to walk confidently away from it, with the firm persuasion that one is following it, that, it seems to me, is what is called genuinely mad'.[69] With dreams, error is the other element always present in the classical definition of insanity. In the seventeenth and eighteenth centuries, the madman is not so much the victim of an illusion, of a hallucination of the senses or a movement of his mind. He is not misled, he is making a mistake. While the mind of the madman is led on by the arbitrary, oneiric nature of images, on the other hand, and at the same time he locks himself into a cycle of erroneous consciousness. As Sauvages noted,

> We call mad those who are currently deprived of reason or who persist in some notable error; and it is that constant error of the soul that is

manifested in its imagination, in its judgements and desires that constitutes the character of this class.[70]

Madness begins where man's relationship to the truth becomes cloudy and unclear. And it takes its general meaning and particular form from the nature of that relationship and of its destruction. Dementia, according to Zacchias, who uses the term in the most general sense to mean madness, 'in hoc constitit quod intellectus non distinguit verum a falso' [is where the intellect cannot distinguish truth from falsehood].[71] But this rupture, if it can only be understood as a negation, has positive structures that lend it singular forms. To different forms of access to the truth correspond different types of madness. For that reason Crichton for example draws distinctions inside the order of vesaniae[72] first of all between the category of deliria, which alter the relation to truth that takes form in perception ('a general derangement of the mental faculties, in which diseased perceptions are mistaken for realities'), and the category of hallucinations, which alter representation: 'an error of mind in which ideal objects are mistaken for realities, or in which the real objects are falsely represented'; finally there is also the category of dementia which, without destroying the faculties that provide access to the truth, still sap their strength or weaken their powers.[73] But madness can also be analysed starting from truth itself, and the different forms that it takes. In that way the Encyclopédie makes a distinction between 'physical truth' and 'moral truth'. Physical truth is the correct relation between sensations and physical objects, and one form of madness was defined by an inability to accede to this form of truth. This was a kind of madness of the physical world, including illusions, hallucinations, and troubles linked to perception: 'it is madness to think that one hears the angels singing in concert, the way certain enthusiasts do'. Moral truth, on the other hand, was 'seeing a correct relation between moral objects, or between those objects and ourselves'. To lose the ability to discern those relations was a form of madness, such as the madness of character, of conduct and of the passions:

> The deformations of our mind are therefore genuinely forms of madness as are the illusions of self-love, and all our passions when they lead to blindness, for blindness is the distinctive characteristic of madness.[74]

Blindness is perhaps one of the words that get closest to the essence of classical madness. It refers to that near-sleep night that surrounds the images of madness, lending them an invisible sovereignty in their solitude; but it also refers to ill-founded beliefs, misjudgements and the whole backdrop of errors inseparable from madness. In its constituent powers, the fundamental discourse of delirium thereby reveals the manner in which it is not after all a discourse of reason, despite the formal analogies and the rigour in its meaning. It spoke, but in the night of blindness; it was more than the loosely structured disorder of dreams as it *deceived itself*, but it was more than an erroneous proposition, as it was still covered by the global cloak of *darkness* that envelops sleep. Delirium as the principle of madness was a system of erroneous propositions inside the general syntax of dreams.

Madness is precisely the point of contact between the oneiric and the erroneous, covering in all its various forms the surface where they meet, which joins and separates them at the same time. With error, it shared truthlessness and arbitrariness of affirmation or negation, while from dreams it borrowed the welling up of images and the colourful presence of the phantasm. But whereas error is simply non-truth, and dreams neither affirm nor judge, madness fills the void of error with images, and binds fantasies together through the affirmation of falsehood. In one sense therefore it is a form of plenitude, joining the figures of night to the powers of daytime, and the activity of the waking mind to the forms of fantasy, tying dark content to the forms of clarity. But is that plenitude not also the *ultimate emptiness*? The presence of images offers nothing but phantasms framed by the night, figures from the recesses of the world of sleep, detached from any reality familiar to the senses. However vivid they are, however rigorously they exist within the body, these images are nothingness since they represent nothing. The erroneous judgement is a judgement in appearance only, and affirming nothing real or true, it does not affirm at all, entirely caught up in the non-being of error.

Joining vision and blindness, image and judgement, phantasm and language, sleep and waking, day and night, madness at bottom is *nothing*, for all that it unites in them is the negative. But its paradox is that it *manifests* this *nothingness*, causing it to overflow with signs, words and gestures. It is an inextricable unity of order and disorder, of the reasonable being of things and the nothingness of madness. For madness, if it is nothing, can only show its face by emerging from itself and assuming an appearance within the order of reason, thereby becoming its own opposite. The paradoxes of the classical experience then become more explicable: madness is always absent, in perpetual, inaccessible retreat, with no phenomenal or positive character, and yet it is present and perfectly visible in the unmistakably singular appearance of the madman. Examined close up, this most insane of disorders reveals ordered species, rigorous mechanisms in both body and soul, and a language articulated along the lines of a visible logic. All is reason in what madness has to say about itself, despite being a negation of reason. To sum up, *a rational grip on reason is always possible and necessary, precisely because madness is non-reason.*

How can we avoid summing up this experience by the single word *Unreason?* By that we mean all that which for reason is at once nearest and most distant, fullest and most empty, and that which presents itself in familiar structures (authorising a form of knowledge, soon claiming to be a positive science), and something that always holds back in relation to reason, in the inaccessible reserve of nothingness.

*

If our intention now is to reveal classical unreason on its own terms, outside of its ties with dreams and error, it must be understood not as a form of reason that is somehow diseased, lost or mad, but quite simply as *reason dazzled.*

Dazzlement[75] is night at noon, the darkness that reigns at the heart of all that is excessive in the radiance of light. Dazzled reason opens its eyes to the sun and sees *nothing*, i.e. it *does not see*,[76] for in dazzlement the general retreat of objects into the darkness has as its immediate correlative the suppression of vision itself. At the very instant when objects disappear into light's secret night, sight sees itself at the moment of its disappearance.

To say that madness is dazzlement is to say that the madman sees the day, the same day that rational men see, as both live in the same light, but that when looking at that very light, nothing else and nothing in it, he sees it as nothing but emptiness, night and nothingness. Darkness for him is another way of seeing the day. Which means that in looking at the night and the nothingness of the night, he does not see at all. And that in the belief that he sees, he allows the fantasies of his imagination and the people of his nights to come to him as realities. For that reason, delirium and dazzlement exist in a relation that is the essence of madness, just as truth and clarity, in their fundamental relation, are constitutive of classical reason.

In that sense, the Cartesian progression of doubt is clearly the great exorcism of madness. Descartes closes his eyes and ears the better to see the true light of the essential day, thereby ensuring that he will not suffer the dazzlement of the mad, who open their eyes and only see night, and not seeing at all, believe that they see things when they imagine them. In the uniform clarity of his closed senses, Descartes has broken with all possible fascination, and if he sees, he knows he really sees what he is seeing. Whereas in the madman's gaze, drunk on the light that is night, images rise up and multiply, beyond any possible self-criticism, since the madman *sees* them, but irremediably separated from being, since the madman sees *nothing*.

Unreason is to reason as dazzlement is to daylight. This is not a metaphor, as we find ourselves here at the heart of the great cosmology that animates all of classical culture. The 'cosmos' of the Renaissance, so rich in communication and internal symbolism, was entirely dominated by the relational presence of stars, but this had now disappeared, and 'nature' had not yet been promoted to its status as universality, nor received the lyrical celebration of men, leading them along the rhythm of its seasons. What the classical age retained of the 'world', its premonition of what was to be 'nature', was an extremely abstract law that nevertheless engendered the most vivid and concrete of oppositions, that between *day and night*. The fatal time of the planets had gone, and the lyric cycle of the seasons had not yet begun. The age was that of the universal, but absolutely divided time, divided between darkness and light. This form is totally mastered by thought within a mathematical science – Cartesian physics is like a mathesis of light – but it simultaneously traces the great tragic caesura within human existence, which dominates the theatrical time of Racine and the painterly space of Georges de la Tour in the same imperious fashion. The circle of day and night is the law of the classical world: the most restricted but most demanding of the necessities of the world, the most inevitable but the simplest of the legislations of nature.

This was a law that excluded all dialectics and all reconciliation, consequently laying the foundations for the smooth unity of knowledge as well as the uncompromising division of tragic existence. It reigns on a world without darkness, which knows neither effusiveness nor the gentle charms of lyricism. All is waking or dreams, truth or error, the light of being or the nothingness of shadow. It prescribes an inevitable order, a serene division as the necessary condition for truth, on which it definitively places its seal.

And yet at both ends of that order, two symmetrical and inverse figures demonstrate that there are limits which could be surpassed, while simultaneously signalling the importance of never going beyond them. Tragedy is one. The rule of the unity of the theatrical day has a positive effect, requiring that the time of tragedy be balanced around the singular but universal alternation between day and night. The whole of tragedy was to take place in that unity of time, for at bottom tragedy was the confrontation between the two irreconcilable kingdoms bound together by time itself. In the theatre of Racine, the day is constantly overshadowed by night, which it brings, so to speak, to light: the night of Troy and the massacres in *Andromaque*, the night of the desires of Nero in *Britannicus*, the Roman night of Titus in *Bérénice*, and the night of *Athalie*. These great swathes of night are the shadowy quarters that haunt the day without ever being reduced by it, and only disappear in the new night of death. These fantastical nights in their turn are haunted by a light that is the infernal reflection of day: the fires of Troy, the torches of the praetorian guard, and the pale light of dreams. In classical tragedy, day and night mirror one another, reflecting each other indefinitely and giving this simple couple a sudden depth that envelops in a single movement the whole of the life of man and his death. In the same fashion, in de la Tour's *Madeleine at the Mirror*, shadow and light face each other, dividing and unifying a face and its reflection, a skull and its image, waking and silence; and in *The Image of Saint Alexis*, the pageboy with the torch uncovers in the shadow of the vault the body of the man who was his master, a luminous, serious young man discovering the misery of men, a child bringing light to death.

Facing the hieratic language of tragedy is the confused murmur of madness. There again the great law of division has been broken, and shadow and light blend in the fury of madness just as they do in the disorder of tragedy. But in a different mode. The tragic character found in the night the dark truths of daytime, the night of Troy being the truth of Andromaque just as the night of Athalie presaged the truth of the day that was already on the way. Night, paradoxically, unveiled, and was *the most profound light of being*. The madman, by way of contrast, in daylight, finds only the inconsistency of the figures of the night, and through him light is darkened by all the illusions of dreams. His day is nothing but *the most superficial night of appearances*. This is why tragic characters more than any other are engaged in being and are carriers of its truth, since, like Phèdre, they throw the secrets of the night into the face of the unpitying sun, while the mad are entirely excluded from being. How could it be any other way, when they lend the illusory reflection of daylight to the non-being of night?

It is understandable then that tragic heroes, unlike the baroque characters who had preceded them, could never be mad, and that inversely madness could never take on the tragic value we have known since Nietzsche and Artaud. In the classical epoch, tragic characters and the mad face each other without any possible dialogue or common language, for the one can only pronounce the decisive language of being, where the truth of light and the depths of night meet in a flash, and the other repeats endlessly an indifferent murmur where the empty chatter of the day is cancelled out by the deceptive lies of the shadows.

*

Madness is equinox between the vanity of fantasies of the night and the non-being of judgements of the light.

And that, which we have learnt piecemeal through the archaeology of knowledge, is something we were also told by a single tragic fulguration, in the last words of Andromaque.

It was as though at the moment when madness disappeared from tragic action, at the moment when tragic heroes were to be separated for more than two centuries from men of unreason, what was required of madness was one last role. The curtain that falls on the last scene of *Andromaque* also falls on the last of the great tragic incarnations of madness. But in that presence on the edge of its own disappearance, in that madness that is slipping away forever, what is announced is what madness was and would remain throughout the classical age. For is it not precisely at the instant of its disappearance that madness can best proffer its truth, its truth of absence, truth which is that of the day at the limits of night? This had to be the *last* scene of the first great classical tragedy; or equally the first time that the classical truth of madness is pronounced, in a tragic movement that is the *last one* on the pre-classical stage. In any case, this truth was instantaneous, as its appearance could be nothing other than its disappearance: a lightning bolt can only stand out in gathering darkness.

Oreste, in his fury, goes through a triple circle of night, three concentric incarnations of *dazzlement*. Day has just risen on the palace of Pyrrhus; night is still discernible, bordering the light with shadow and imperiously marking its limits. On this feast day morning, the crime has been committed and Pyrrhus has closed his eyes on the day that was dawning, and a fragment of shadow is thrown onto the steps of the altar, at the threshold of light and darkness. The two great cosmic themes of madness are therefore present in diverse forms, as presage, backdrop and counterpoint to the fury of Oreste.[77] It can then begin: in the unpitying clarity that will denounce the murder of Pyrrhus and the treachery of Hermione, in the early light where all is revealed in a truth that is both so young and so old at the same time, here is a first circle of shadow, a dark cloud into which, all around Oreste, the world begins to retreat. Truth slips away in this paradoxical darkness, this morning twilight where the cruelty of the truth will slowly metamorphose into the rage of fantasy:

'But what is this thick night that suddenly surrounds me?'

It is the empty night of *error*, but against the backdrop of that first darkness a flicker comes into being: the deceptive lure of images. The nightmare begins, not in the clear light of day but in scintillating darkness, the light of storms and murder:

'O Gods! What rivers of blood flow around me!'

And now begins the dynasty of *dreams*. In this night, fantasies take wing, and the Fates appear and impose their will. That which makes them precarious also brings them sovereignty, and they triumph easily in the solitude in which they succeed each other. Nothing challenges them, and images and language intersect in apostrophes that are invocations, presences that are at once affirmed and rejected, desired and feared. But all these images converge towards a second darkness, which is the night of punishment and eternal vengeance, of death within death itself. The Erinyes are recalled to their shadows, their place of birth and truth, i.e. the nothingness that is their own.

'Have you come to carry me off into the eternal night?'

This is the moment when it becomes clear that the images of madness are nothing but dream and error, and that if the unfortunate sufferer who is blinded by them invokes them, it is the better to disappear with them into the annihilation for which they are destined.

Once again, therefore, we cross a circle of night. But that is not enough to bring us back to the clear reality of the world. We accede, beyond what is manifested of madness, to delirium, the essential constitutive structure that had secretly supported madness from the outset. That delirium has a name: Hermione. She appears here no longer as a hallucinated vision, but as the ultimate truth of madness. It is significant that she intervenes at this moment of the frenzy, not among the Furies, nor preceding them as a guide, but behind them, and separated from them by the night into which they have dragged Oreste, and into which they have now vanished. The point is that Hermione intervenes as a constitutive figure of delirium, as the truth that reigned secretly since the beginning, to which the Furies were ultimately little more than handmaidens. We find ourselves here at the opposite pole to Greek tragedy, where the Furies themselves were the final destiny and truth that had lain in wait for the hero since the beginning of time, using his passion as their instrument. Here the Eumenides are merely figures in the service of delirium, which is the first and last truth, already discernible in passion, and now standing naked before us. This truth reigns supreme, pushing all images aside:

> 'But no, retreat! Let Hermione carry out her will'

Hermione, who has been present from the beginning, has always torn at Oreste, lacerating his reason, parcel by parcel; she for whom he who has become 'a parricide, an assassin, an outlaw', finally reveals herself as the culminating truth of his madness. And delirium, in its rigour, has no option but to announce, as an imminent decision, a truth long considered commonplace and derisory:

> 'I bring her my heart that it might be devoured.'

Oreste made this savage offering days, even years previously, but only now does he present it as the term of his madness. For madness can go no further than this. Once its truth has been uttered in this essential delirium, it can do nothing but sink back into that third night from which there is no return, the night where one is ceaselessly devoured. Unreason can only appear for an instant, at the moment when language sinks back into silence, when delirium itself falls still and the heart is at last devoured.

In the tragedies of the early seventeenth century, madness too provided the dénouement, but it did so in liberating the truth. It still opened onto language, to a renewed form of speech, that of explanation and of the real regained. The most it could ever be was the penultimate moment of tragedy. Not the closing moment, as in *Andromaque*, where no truth appears, other than, in Delirium, the truth of a passion that finds its fullest, most perfect expression in madness.

The movement proper to unreason, which classical learning followed and pursued, had already accomplished its entire trajectory in the concise language of tragedy. After which silence could reign, as madness disappeared into the ever-withdrawn presence of unreason.

*

What we know now about unreason enables a better understanding of the nature of confinement.

The gesture that banished madness into the dull, uniform world of exclusion is neither the sign of a pause in the evolution of medicine nor an indicator of a halt in the progress of humanitarian ideas. Its exact meaning comes from the simple fact that in the classical world madness was no longer the sign of another world, and became instead a paradoxical manifestation of non-being. In the final analysis, confinement was not overly concerned with suppressing madness or removing from the social order a figure which could not find its place there, and its essence could not really be described as the exorcism of any danger. It only manifested what madness is, in its essence: the unveiling of non-being. Making manifest that manifestation, it also suppressed it, as it restored it to the truth of its emptiness. Confinement was a practice that corresponded most fully to madness when experienced as unreason, i.e. as the empty negativity of reason: madness was considered to be nothing at all. That is, on the one hand madness was immediately perceived as difference, which explains why the mad were confined not on the recommendation of a doctor of medicine, but in response to a spontaneous and collective judgement carried out by men of good sense.[78] On the other, confinement could have no purpose other than correction (i.e. the suppression of that difference, or the accomplishment of the nothingness that was madness in death), which provides one explanation for the desires for death that are so often to be found on confinement registers, written in the guardians' hand, and which are not so much signs of barbarism, savagery, inhumanity or perversion as the precise expression of the meaning of confinement – an operation whose aim was to return nothingness to nothingness.[79] On the surface of phenomena, in a hasty moral synthesis, confinement sketches the outline of the secret and distinctive structure of madness.

Is it confinement that roots its practices in this deep intuition? Is it because madness, under the effects of confinement, really had disappeared from the classical horizon, that it ultimately came to be considered as non-being? The answers to these questions echo each other in a perfect circularity. It probably serves no purpose to lose oneself in these endless, circular interrogations. It is more useful to see how classical culture formulates the general structure of its experience of madness. That experience is discernible, with the same meaning and the same internal logic, in the order of speculative thought as well as in the order of the institution, in discourse as well as in decrees, in words as well as in watchwords – in all the places where a significant element can take on for us the value of language.

III

FIGURES OF MADNESS

Madness, therefore, was negativity. But a form of negativity that offered itself in a plenitude of phenomena, part of the well-ordered riches in the garden of species.

The discursive knowledge of madness unfolds in the limited space defined by this contradiction. Behind the calm order of medical analyses a difficult relationship is at work, where historical becoming comes into being: this is the relation between *unreason*, as the ultimate meaning of madness, and *rationality* as the form of its truth. How madness, always situated in the originary regions of error, and always held back in relation to reason, might yet lay itself entirely open to reason and entrust her with all its secrets: this is the problem that the knowledge of madness at once manifests and hides.

This chapter will not be concerned with the history of different notions of psychiatry in their relationship to contemporary observations, knowledge, or theories about madness; we shall not look at psychiatry in the medicine of the spirits or the physiology of solids. But taking up in turn the great figures of madness that remained constant throughout the classical age, we shall try to see how they took their place inside the experience of unreason, how each of them took on a particular cohesiveness, and how they came to manifest the *negativity* of madness in a *positive* manner.

Once that positivity had been acquired, it was not of the same nature, level or strength for the different forms of madness. For the concept of *dementia* it was thin, frail and transparent, still quite close to the negativity of unreason; while in *mania* and *melancholy* it acquired a greater density through a whole system of images. The most consistent form of positivity, and the most remote from unreason (and the most dangerous for it), was the form to be found at the limits of moral and medical thoughts. It elaborated a sort of corporal space that was as much ethical as it was organic, and thus gave content to the notions of *hysteria* and *hypochondria*, and all that which before long would come to be known as *nervous illnesses*: that positivity was so distant from all that constituted the centre of unreason, and fitted so poorly with its structures, that it ended up by calling unreason into question, and caused it to crumble at the close of the classical age.

I DEMENTIA

Dementia was recognised by most physicians in the seventeenth and eighteenth centuries under diverse names covering a more-or-less identical domain — *dementia, amentia, fatuitas, stupiditas,* or *morosis*. Recognised, and isolated with relative ease among the other more morbid varieties, but rarely defined in its concrete or positive content. For two centuries it retained this negative identity, which constantly prevented it from taking on a characteristic shape. In one sense, of all the sicknesses of the soul, dementia was the one that remained closest to the essence of madness. But of madness in general, madness experienced in the full force of its negativity, as disorder, the decomposition of thought, error, illusion, non-reason and untruth. It was this form of madness, as the simple converse of reason and pure contingency of the mind, that one eighteenth-century author defined very well, showing how no positive form would ever exhaust or limit its extension:

> The symptoms of madness vary *ad infinitum*. In it can be found in every-thing that has been seen or heard, anything that has been thought or meditated upon. It can bring together things that seem far distant. It can recall things that seem long forgotten. Remote images rise up, ancient aversions thought to have disappeared reappear, desires become more intense, but all is disturbed. In their confusion, ideas

resemble the letters of a printing press thrown together without purpose or understanding. What results has no coherent sense at all.'

Dementia is close to madness conceived of in the full negativity of its disorder.

Dementia is thus in the mind both pure chance and total determinism, where any effect can be produced because any cause can provoke it. There is no disorder in the organs of thought that cannot bring on one of the aspects of dementia. It has no symptoms of its own as such, but is rather the open possibility of all the possible symptoms of madness. For Willis, the essential characteristic is *stupiditas*,[2] but within a few pages, *stupiditas* becomes the equivalent of *dementia: stupitas sive morosis* . . . ['stupidity, or morosis, or foolishness'] and stupidity then becomes purely and simply 'a defect of the intellect and judgment', the ultimate impairment of reason in its higher functions. Yet that defect itself does not come first, for the rational soul troubled by dementia is not enclosed in the body without some mixed element forming a link between the two. In that mixed space between the rational soul and the body, which is extended yet punctual, corporeal yet thinking, the *anima sensitiva sive corporea* [sensitive or corporeal soul] is to be found, bearing the intermediary and mediating powers of imagination and memory; it is they who furnish the spirit with ideas, or at least with the elements it uses to build them, and whenever their functioning – their bodily functioning – is disturbed, the *intellectus acies* [acuity of the mind] 'is defective or hindered; forthwith the eye of the intellect, as if covered with a vail, is wont to be much dulled, or wholly darkened'.[3] In the organic and functional space that it inhabits and whose living unity it ensures, the corporeal soul has its seat, and there too are the instruments and organs of its immediate action. The seat of the bodily soul is the brain (and more particularly the corpus callosum for imagination, and the white matter for memory), and its immediate organs are formed by the animal spirits.[4] Thus, in cases of dementia, either the brain itself was affected or the spirits were disturbed, or there was a combined disturbance of the seat and the organs, i.e. the brain and the spirits. If the brain alone is the cause of the illness, then its origins can be sought in the dimensions of the cerebral matter, which was either too small to function correctly, or too abundant, and therefore less solid and, so to speak, of lower quality, *mentis acumini minus accomodum* ['less adapted to the acuity of the spirit']. It sometimes happens that the shape of the brain too is to blame: if it lacks the spherical (*globosa*, 'globous') shape necessary for an equitable reflection of the animal spirits whenever any depression or swelling has occurred then the spirits are sent off in erratic directions, and their path can no longer transmit a true and faithful image of things and give the rational soul the sensitive idols of the truth. The result is dementia. In an even more subtle manner, for the rigour of its functioning, the brain must maintain a certain level of warmth and dampness, a sensible quality of physical consistency and texture. If it becomes too damp or too cold – as is often the case with children and old people – the first signs of *stupiditas* begin to appear. Those signs are also apparent when the texture of the brain becomes too coarse, as though impregnated with a heavy terrestrial influence. Such heaviness of the cerebral substance, might it not in turn be attributed to a heaviness of the air and a certain roughness of the local soil, which would explain the legendary stupidity of the Batavians?[5]

In *morosis*, sometimes only the animal spirits are affected, perhaps because they themselves have been slowed by some similar heaviness, causing them to become roughly shaped and irregular in their dimensions, as though some imaginary gravitational force had dragged them down to the slowness of the earth. In other cases, they might have become aqueous, inconsistent or voluble.[6]

Disturbances of the animal spirits or of the brain might be isolated in the early stages, but this situation never persists for long. Disturbances invariably combine, and either the quality of the spirits declines as a consequence of the vices of the cerebral matter, or the cerebral matter itself is modified on account of the imperfection of the spirits. When the spirits are heavy and their movements too slow, or when they are excessively fluid, the pores of the brain and the channels that they pass through become blocked or take on vitiated forms. On the other hand, if the brain itself is defective, the spirits can no longer travel through it in the normal fashion and consequently the result is a defective diathesis.

We would look in vain, in this analysis of Willis, for an exact portrait of dementia, for the tell-tale signs that indicate its presence or its particular causes. It is not that his description lacks precision, but that dementia seems to cover the domain of all the possible alterations in any of the domains of the 'nervous stock': the spirits or the brain, softness or hardness, heat or chill, exaggerated heaviness or excessive lightness, or a deficiency or abundance of matter. All the possible pathological metamorphoses are gathered around the phenomenon of dementia to furnish virtual explanations.

Dementia does not organise its causes or localise them, nor does it specify their qualities in accordance with the figure of its own symptoms. It is the universal effect of any possible deterioration. In some manner, dementia is madness, minus the particular symptoms of any specific form of madness, a sort of watermark that shows madness in the purity of its essence, in its general truth. Dementia is anything unreasonable in the orderly mechanics of the fibres and spirits of a well-ordered brain.

But at that level of abstraction, no medical concept is elaborated; it is too distant from its object, and formulated in purely logical dichotomies, it slips over virtualities, it works to no effect. Dementia, as a medical experience, does not crystallise.

*

Towards the middle of the eighteenth century, dementia is still a negative concept. From the medicine of Willis to the physiology of solids, the shape of the organic world has changed, yet the analysis remains of the same type; the sole concern regarding dementia is with hunting down the various forms of 'unreason' that the nervous system might display. At the beginning of his article on 'Démence' in the *Encyclopédie*, Aumont explains that reason considered in its natural existence is nothing other than the transformation of sense impressions, and that communicated by the fibres, they reach the brain, which then changes them into notions by the internal movements of the animal spirits. Unreason or rather madness appears whenever these transformations are no longer carried out along the normal paths, and are exaggerated, diminished or abolished altogether. Their total abolition is pure madness, the paroxysm of madness, madness as if at the peak of intensity of its truth, in other words dementia. The question then is how it comes about, and how it is that all of a sudden the whole work of the transformation of impressions is abolished. Like Willis, Aumont groups all possible disorders of the nervous stock around unreason. There are disturbances brought about by intoxications of the system, by opiates, hemlock or mandragora; Bonet, after all, in his *Sepulchretum*, reported the case of a young girl who had lost her reason after being bitten by a bat. Certain incurable illnesses like epilepsy have exactly the same effect. But more frequently the cause of dementia is to be sought in the brain, which might have suffered as the result of a blow, or might have a congenital malformation so that its volume is too limited for the fibres to function correctly and for the spirits to circulate in the required manner. The spirits themselves might be at the origin of the dementia if they are fatigued, languishing or lacking strength, or if they have become thickened or serous and viscous. But the most common cause of dementia is to be found in the state of fibres that have lost the capacity to receive and transmit impressions. The vibration necessary for sensation to operate simply fails to happen, and the fibre remains immobile, doubtless because it is too flaccid or too stretched, and has become rigid. In some cases, it cannot vibrate in unison because it is too calloused. Whatever the cause, the necessary 'springiness' has disappeared. The reasons behind that inability to vibrate might be the passions, innate causes or a whole variety of illnesses, from vaporous afflictions to old age. The whole domain of pathology was traversed to find the causes and an explanation of dementia, but the symptomatic figure was slow in coming: observations accumulated, causal chains stretched out, but we would seek the specific profile of the disease in vain.

When François Boissier de Sauvages set out to write the entry on *Amentia* for his ten-volume *Nosologie Méthodique*, he lost the thread of his symptomatology, and could no longer be faithful to the 'botanical spirit' that he hoped would preside over his work. He could only distinguish between the different forms of dementia according to their causes: *amentia senilis*, caused by 'the rigidity of the fibres making them insensible to object impressions'; *amentia serosa*, caused by an accumulation of serous fluid in the brain – a butcher had noted that mad ewes 'neither ate nor drank', and that their cerebral matter 'was entirely changed to water'; *amentia a venenis*, brought on in particular by opium; *amentia a tumore*; *amentia microcephalica* – Sauvages himself had seen 'this type of dementia in a young girl in the hospital in Montpellier: she was called the Monkey on account of her tiny head, and because of her resemblance to that animal'; in a general manner, nothing weakened reason more than the drying out of the fibres, and *amentia a siccitate* was observed whenever the fibres became desiccated, frozen or coagulated, as demonstrated by the case of three young women who had been riding in a cart in the depths of winter, and were taken with dementia. Bartholin returned them to their wits 'by wrapping up their heads in the fleece of a freshly skinned sheep'. Then there was *amentia morosis*, Sauvages being uncertain as to how it should be distinguished from serous dementia; *amentia ab ictu*; *amentia rachialgica*; *amentia a quartana*, due to quartan fever; and *amentia calculosa*, for one practitioner had found in the brain of a demented man 'a fish-shaped calculus swimming in the fluid in the ventricle'.

In a sense, there is no clear symptomatology for dementia. It has no form of delirium, hallucination or violence of its own, and there is none that can be associated with it by a necessity of nature. Its truth consists in a juxtaposition, with on the one side the accumulation of possible causes, whose level, order and nature can be as different as possible, and on the other a series of effects whose only common characteristic is that they demonstrate a lack or a defect in the functioning of the faculty of reason, which is unable to relate to the reality of things and the truth of ideas. Dementia is the most general and negative empirical form of unreason all at once – non-reason as a presence perceived in its most concrete form, but which cannot be assigned in its positive dimensions. Dufour tries to pin down this presence constantly in flight from itself in his *Traité de l'entendement humain*. He goes through the whole multiplicity of possible causes, drawing up a list of all the partial determinisms that have been suggested regarding dementia: a hardening of the fibres, a dryness of the brain as in the theories of Bonet, a softness or serosity of the encephalum as in Hildanus, the use of henbane, stramonium, opium and saffron (according to the observations of Rey, Bautain, and Barère), the presence of a tumour, of encephalitic worms, and malformations of the skull. These are positive causes, but they only ever lead to the same negative result – a rupture between the mind and the outside world and truth:

> Sufferers from dementia are negligent and indifferent to many things; they sing, laugh and amuse themselves equally with good or evil. They do experience hunger, cold and thirst, but remain unaffected; and they feel too the impressions that objects make on their senses, but seem little concerned with them.[7]

The fragmentary positivity of nature is thus superimposed on the general negativity of unreason, but without any real unity. As a form of madness, dementia is only lived and considered from the outside; it is a limit where reason is abolished in an inaccessible absence. Despite the constancy of the description, the notion has no power of integration, and the being of nature and non-being of unreason do not find their unity here.

*

Yet the notion of dementia does not disappear in an undifferentiated mass. It is in fact limited by two groups of neighbouring concepts, the first of which is already quite ancient, while the second is a novel concept that comes into being during the classical age.

The distinction between dementia and frenzy is a traditional one. It is a distinction easily drawn on the level of signs, as frenzy is invariably accompanied by a fever, whereas dementia is an apyretic disease. The fever that characterises frenzy means that both its immediate causes and its nature can be identified: it is an inflammation, excessive body heat, a painful burning of the head, a violence in gesture and speech, and a generalised ebullition of the whole individual. Cullen still characterises it in terms of that qualitative coherence at the end of the eighteenth century:

> The symptoms by which this disease may most certainly be known are, a vehement pyrexia, a violent, deep-seated head-ach, a redness and turgescence of the face and eyes, an impatience of light or noise, a constant watching, and a delirium impetuous and furious.[8]

Its distant origins had given rise to endless discussions, all of which centre round the theme of heat. The two main questions were whether frenzy was a result of changes in the brain or a quality acquired from outside, and whether it was provoked by excessive movement or by an immobilisation of the blood.

In the polemic between La Mesnardière and Duncan, the former suggests that as the brain is a damp, cold organ filled with liquids and fluids, it is inconceivable that it might become inflamed. 'Such an inflammation is no more possible than the sight of fire burning in a river without artifice.' Duncan's apologist in France does not deny that the primary qualities of the brain are opposed to those of fire, but believes that it has a local vocation that goes against its substantial nature: 'placed as it is above the gut, it receives the vapours from cooked food and the exhalations of the whole body'. In addition, it is surrounded and penetrated by 'an infinite number of veins and arteries that enclose it and can easily disgorge themselves into its substance'. Furthermore, the soft and cold qualities that characterise the brain mean that it is easily penetrated by outside influences, particularly those that are opposed to its primary nature. While warm substances resist the cold, cold substances can warm up, and the brain, because it is 'soft and damp', is 'consequently capable only of limited resistance against the excess of other qualities'.[9] The opposition of qualities then becomes the very reason for their substitution. But increasingly, the brain comes to be considered as the primary seat of frenzy. One exception worthy of note is a thesis put forward by Fem, where frenzy is due to difficulties brought on by overburdened viscera, which 'communicate their disorder to the brain through the nerves'.[10] But for the great majority of writers in the eighteenth century, frenzy has its cause and seat inside the brain, which becomes one of the centres of organic heat. James' *Dictionary* places its origins inside the 'membranes of the brain',[11] and Cullen goes so far as to think that the cervical matter itself could become inflamed. To his mind, frenzy is 'an inflammation of the parts contained in the cavity of the cranium, and may affect either the membranes of the brain, or the substance of the brain tissues'.[12]

That excessive heat is easily explained within a pathology of movement. But there was one type of heat that was physical, and another that was chemical. The physical type is due to an excess of movements, which are too numerous, too frequent or too rapid, bringing on a warming of various parts that are in constant friction:

> The remote causes of phrenzy are all those which directly stimulate the membranes or the substance of the brain; and particularly all those which increase the impetus of the blood in the vessels of the brain. Among these, the exposure of the naked head to the direct rays of a very warm sun, is a frequent cause. The passions of the mind, and certain poisons, are among the remote causes.[13]

By contrast, warmth of the chemical variety is brought on by immobility, as the body becomes engorged with substances that accumulate and begin to ferment and rot, giving off great heat as they fester: 'A Phrenitis is a Madness accompanied with a Fever, and arising from an inflammatory Stagnation of the Blood in the Vessels of the Brain.'[14]

While the notion of dementia remains abstract and negative, frenzy is clearly centred around precise qualitative themes that integrate its origins, causes, location, signs and effects in an imaginary cohesiveness, in the almost tangible logic of body heat. It is ordered by a dynamic of inflammation, and the fire of unreason courses through it, as a fire in the fibres or an excitement in the vessels, a flame or an ebullition: the variation matters little. Discussions centre round an overarching theme that has the power to integrate all these themes – unreason, a violent flame of the body and the soul.

*

The second group of concepts related to dementia concern stupidity, imbecility, idiocy and foolishness. In practice, dementia and imbecility are treated as synonymous.[15] For Willis, the term *morosis* includes both acquired dementia and the stupidity that could be noted in children from the first months of their life, affecting memory, imagination and judgement in all cases.[16] Yet the distinction between ages slowly became established, and was a certainty in the eighteenth century:

> Dementia is a sort of inability to form judgements and to reason in a healthy manner: it has been given different names, according to the age during which it becomes apparent: in childhood it is known as *silliness* or *foolishness*, but when it affects a person who is of an age to reason it is known as *imbecility*; when it comes on at an advanced age, it is known as *senility*, *dotage* or a *return to childhood*.[17]

Those distinctions have little value, other than in chronological terms, as neither the symptoms nor the nature of the disease vary according to the age at which they first become apparent. All that could be concluded was that 'people in a demented state occasionally demonstrate some of the virtues of the learning they once possessed, which the stupid cannot do'.[18]

Slowly, the difference between dementia and stupidity became more pronounced, not simply in terms of chronological distinctiveness but also as an opposition in the world of actions. Stupidity acted upon the very domain of sensation: an imbecile was insensible to light and noise, while a demented person was merely indifferent. The first type receives nothing from the outside world: the second ignores what is given to him. One is refused the reality of the outside world; for the second, its truth is of no importance. That was more or less the distinction that was taken up by Sauvages in his *Nosologie*: to his way of thinking dementia

> differs from stupidity in that the demented are perfectly receptive to impressions of objects, while the stupid are not: but the former pay no attention to these impressions, and look upon them with sovereign

indifference, taking no heed of any consequences that might derive from them, and have no concern for them.[19]

What difference, then, was to be established between stupidity and a congenital infirmity of the senses? If dementia was taken as a trouble of the judgement, and stupidity as a deficiency of the senses, was there not a risk that a blind man or a deaf mute might be mistaken for an imbecile?[20]

An article in the *Gazette de médecine* in 1762 took up the problem from the point of view of the observation of animals. Speaking of a young dog, the author noted that:

> Everyone insists that the dog is blind, deaf, dumb, and has no sense of smell, either since birth or as the result of an accident shortly after, so that he is in a vegetative state, and might well be regarded as being half-way between an animal and a plant.

There could be no question of dementia regarding an animal that was not destined to possess reason in the full sense of the word. Was the problem therefore limited to the sensory organs? The response to that question was far from clear:

> The dog has quite beautiful eyes that seem to react to light, yet constantly bumps into furniture and injures himself in that manner; he can hear noises, and high-pitched noises like the sound of a whistle disturb and frighten him, yet he could never be taught to answer to his name.

It was therefore neither sight nor hearing that were affected, but rather the organ or faculty that organises the sensations into perceptions, turning a colour into an object, or a sound into a name.

> This general defectiveness of the senses does not appear to originate in any of the external organs, but rather in the internal organ that modern physicians call *sensorium commune*, and the ancients sensitive soul, which receives and combines the images transmitted by the senses, so that this animal has never been able to give shape to a perception, and sees without seeing, and hears without understanding.[21]

What is closest to sensation in the soul or in the activities of the spirit is paralysed under the effects of imbecility, whereas in dementia what is affected is the functioning of reason, inasmuch as it is free and detached from sensation.

And at the end of the eighteenth century, imbecility and dementia would be distinguished not so much on the basis of the precocity of their opposition, nor with regard to the faculty they affected, but by qualities that were theirs alone, and secretly directed their manifestations. For Pinel, the difference between imbecility and dementia is essentially the difference between immobility and movement. In idiocy, what was observed was a general paralysis, a somnolence 'of all the functions of understanding and moral affections', with the mind frozen in a sort of stupor. In dementia, by contrast, the essential functions of the mind do think, but they think in a void, and consequently are extremely mercurial. Dementia is like a pure movement of the mind, devoid of any form of consistency, a perpetual flight that time cannot immobilise in the memory: 'a rapid, or rather, quickly alternating, succession, an uninterrupted flow of ideas and isolated actions, inconsequential and disordered emotions, with no memory of any preceding state'.[22] With these images, the concepts of imbecility and stupidity became fixed, and as a result dementia slowly emerged from its negativity, and began to be considered from within a certain intuition of time and motion.

But putting aside these adjacent categories of frenzy and imbecility, which are organised around qualitative themes, it can be said that the concept of dementia remains on the surface of experience – close to the general idea of unreason, and far distant from the real centre where the concrete figures of madness are born. Of all the medical concepts of alienation, dementia is the simplest, and the least affected by myth, moral valorisation and dreams of the imagination. Yet despite all that, it is the most secretly incoherent, in that it eludes the clutches of these forms of classification. In it, nature and unreason remain on the surface of their abstract generality, and do not manage to take shape in the depths of the imagination, unlike the notions of mania and melancholy.

II MANIA AND MELANCHOLY

In the sixteenth century, the notion of melancholy was caught between a certain definition in terms of symptoms and an explanatory principle hidden in the term used to designate it. Where the symptoms were concerned, there were all the delirious ideas that an individual could form about himself:

> Some of them believe that they are beasts, of which they take on the voice and the gesture. Others think that they are vessels made of glass, and for that reason flee passers-by, fearing they might be broken into pieces; others fear death, but still often end up killing themselves. Others believe themselves to be guilty of crimes, so much so that they tremble with fear whenever they see someone approach, thinking that they will be arrested and taken away to prison, where justice will put them to death.[23]

These delirious ideas are isolated, and do not compromise reason in its entirety. Sydenham noted that melancholics were 'people who are very prudent and judicious; and who must excell, for deep Thought and Wisdom of Speech . . . so that Aristotle was in the Right, when he said, That melancholy People are most ingenious.'[24]

This clear, coherent ensemble of symptoms was designated by a single word, melancholy, which implied a whole system of causality. 'I would ask you to look most carefully at the thoughts of melancholics, their words, visions and actions, and you will come to see how all their senses are depraved by a melancholic humour spread throughout the brain.'[25] In the notion of melancholy at this time, a partial delirium and the action of black bile are juxtaposed, with no links other than a disordered confrontation between a group of signs and a significant denomination. But in the eighteenth century a unity would be found, or rather an exchange would be accomplished, when that cold, black humour became the dominant colour of the delirium, its full value by contrast with mania, dementia and frenzy, its essential principle of cohesion. While Boerhaave still defined melancholia as a 'long, stubborn delirium without fever, during which the patient is obsessed by a single thought',[26] within a few years Dufour had moved the weight of definition to the 'fear and sadness', which were now taken to explain the partial character of the delirium:

> This explains why melancholics prefer solitude and avoid company, which in turn increases their attachment to the object of their delirium or their dominant passion, whatever that might be, while they appear to remain indifferent to all other things.[27]

This fixing of the concept was not the result of a new rigour in observation, nor any discovery in the domain of causation, but of a qualitative transmission going from a cause implied in the name to a significant perception among the effects.

For a long time – up until the early seventeenth century – the debate on melancholy was caught up in the tradition of the four humours and their essential qualities: stable qualities inherent in a particular substance, which alone could be taken as its cause. For Fernel, the melancholic humour, associated with autumn and the earth, was 'a thick secretion, cold and dry in its temperament'.[28] But in the first half of the seventeenth century, a whole debate emerged regarding the origins of melancholy, and whether a melancholic temperament was essential in order to be affected by the condition.[29] Was a melancholic humour always dry and cold, or could it ever be warm and damp? Was it the substance that acted, or the qualities that were transmitted? The conclusions of this long-running debate can be summed up as follows:

1 The causality of substances is increasingly replaced by a movement of qualities, which, without the help of any support, are transferred immediately from the body to the soul, from the humour to the ideas, and from the organs to behaviour. So for Duncan's apologist, the best proof that melancholy was brought on by melancholic liquor was that the essential qualities of the disease were to be found there:

> The melancholic liquor has far more of the conditions necessary to produce melancholy than any burnt anger, as by its coldness it diminishes the quantity of the spirits, and by its dryness it enables them to sustain the form of a strong and stubborn imagination for much longer; and by its blackness, it deprives them of their clarity and natural subtlety.[30]

2 There is, in addition to this mechanics of qualities, a particular dynamic that analyses in each of them the force contained inside. So cold and dryness can enter into conflict with the temperament, and from that opposition signs of melancholy will appear, all the more powerful on account of the internal turmoil, creating a force that dominates, and drags along in its wake the forces that resist. This explains why women, who are little given to melancholy, suffer to a greater degree when affected: 'they suffer more cruelly and become violently agitated, because as melancholy

is more opposed to their temperament, it removes them further from their natural disposition'.[31]

3 But it is sometimes inside a quality itself that the conflict comes into being. A quality might become altered in the course of its development and become the opposite of what it was. So, when 'the entrails are inflamed, when the entire body begins to roast . . . and all the juices burn', then the excessive heat might turn into cold melancholy, producing 'almost the same effect as when a candle is overturned and wax gathers . . . This cooling of the body is the natural result of inordinate heat once it has exhausted its vigor.'[32] A sort of dialectics of quality is at work, where the qualities, free of all substantial constraints and primitive assignations, meander through reversals and contradictions.

4 Finally, qualities can undergo changes as a result of accidents, circumstances or the sufferer's way of life. A being who is cold and dry can become damp and warm, if his life style inclines him that way. This sometimes happens to women 'who remain idle too long and sweat too little (less than men), so that heat, the spirits and humours build up inside them'.[33]

Thus freed from the substantiating support within which they had been imprisoned, qualities can henceforth play an organising, integrating role in the notion of melancholy. On the one hand they will trace, among the symptoms and manifestations, a certain profile of sadness, darkness, slowness and immobility. On the other, they will sketch a causal support that will no longer be so much the physiology of a humour as the pathology of an idea, a fear or terror. The morbid unity is not *defined* on the basis of observed signs or inferred causes, but half-way between the two, above some of them, it is *perceived* as a certain qualitative coherence, which has its own laws of transmission, development and transformation. It is the secret logic of this quality that orders the future of the notion of melancholy, not medical theory. This is evident from Willis' texts onwards.

At first glance, the coherence of the analyses is assured on the level of speculative reflection. Willis' explanations are based entirely on animal spirits and their mechanical properties. Melancholy is 'a madness without frenzy or fever, accompanied by fear or sadness'. In so far as it is delirium – i.e. an essential break with the truth – its origin is to be found in the disordered motions of the spirits and in a defective state of the brain; but could these movements alone provide a sufficient explanation for the fear and worry that makes melancholics 'sad and meticulous'? Could there be a mechanism of fear and a circulation of the spirits peculiar to sadness? That was obvious to Descartes, but no longer so to Willis. Melancholy cannot be treated as a paralysis, apoplexy, vertigo or convulsion. In truth, it cannot even be analysed as simple dementia either, even though delirious melancholy supposes a similar disorder in the movement of the spirits; mechanical upsets do explain delirium (an error which is common to all forms of madness, dementia and melancholy), but not its particular quality, the colour of the sadness and fear that gives melancholy its unique landscape. It was therefore necessary to enter into the heart of the diathesis.[34] After all, it is these essential qualities, hidden in the texture of the subtle matter, which explain the paradoxical movements of the spirits.

In melancholy, the spirits are carried away by an agitation, but a weak agitation that lacks power or violence, a sort of impotent upset that follows neither a particular path nor the *aperta opercula* [open ways], but traverses the cerebral matter constantly creating new pores. Yet the spirits do not wander far on the new paths they create, and their agitation dies down rapidly, as their strength is quickly spent and motion comes to a halt: '*non longe perveniunt*' [they do not reach far].[35] A trouble of this nature, common to all delirium, does not have the power to produce on the surface of the body the violent movements or the cries to be observed in mania and frenzy. Melancholy never attains frenzy; it is a madness always at the limits of its own impotence. That paradox is explained by the secret alterations in the spirits. Ordinarily, they travel with the speed and instantaneous transparency of rays of light, but in melancholy they become weighed down with night, becoming 'obscure, thick and dark', and the images of things that they bring before consciousness are 'in a shadow, or covered with darkness'.[36] As a result they move more slowly, and are more like a dark, chemical vapour than pure light. This chemical vapour is acid in nature, rather than sulphurous or alcoholic, for in acid vapours the particles are mobile and incapable of repose, but their activity is weak and without consequence. When they are distilled, all that remains in the still is a kind of insipid phlegm. Acid vapours, therefore, are taken to have the same properties as melancholy, whereas alcoholic vapours, which are always ready to burst into flames, are more related to frenzy, and sulphurous vapours bring on mania, as they are agitated by continuous, violent movement. If the 'formal reason and causes' of melancholy were to be sought, it made sense to look for them in the vapours that rose up from the blood to the head, and which had degenerated into 'an acetous or sharp distillation'.[37] A cursory glance seems to indicate that a melancholy of spirits and a whole chemistry of humours lies behind Willis' analyses, but in fact his guiding principle mostly reflects the immediate qualities of the melancholic illness: an impotent disorder, and the shadow that comes over the spirit with an acrid acidity that slowly corrodes the heart and the thoughts. The chemistry of acids is not an explanation of the symptoms, but a qualitative option: a whole phenomenology of melancholic experience.

Some seventy years later, the animal spirits had lost their scientific prestige. The secrets of disease, it was then believed, were to be found in the body's liquid and solid elements. Robert James' *Dictionary*, published in England in 1743, contains an article on Mania, proposing a compared aetiology of mania and melancholy:

> That the brain, therefore, is the seat of all Disorders of this kind, is sufficiently obvious; for the mind is the most noble part of Body, which, tho in a manner inconceivable by us, the wise and bountiful parent of mankind Species has made the common Receptacle or Repository of the Soul, the Genius, the Fancy, the Memory, and the external Senses . . . But all these noble functions are changed, depraved, diminished, and totally destroyed, when the Blood and Humours receding from their natural Temperature and Quality are not conveyed to the Brain in a moderate of Equitable manner, but with a difficult flow, and langued motion, or with too brisk and violent an Impetus.[38]

It is the distressing combination of this languishing flow, these engorged vessels, this heavy, laden blood that the heart pumps around the organism with considerable effort, and which penetrates the fine arterioles of the brain with great difficulty, where circulation needs to be rapid to maintain the speed of thought, that serves to explain the condition. Weight, heaviness and encumbrance are still the primitive qualities that guide the analysis. The explanation is like a transfer towards the organism of the qualities perceived in the bearing, behaviour and speech of the sufferer, and the theory goes from the apprehension of quality to an explanation. But that apprehension constantly prevails, and counts for far more than theoretical coherence. In the work of Anne-Charles Lorry, the two dominant forms of medical explanation – solids and fluids – are juxtaposed, and finally intersecting, they allow two different forms of melancholy to be identified. Nervous melancholy has its origins in solids. A particularly strong vibration shakes the fibres that receive it, and consequently the tension is increased among the other fibres, which become more rigid and more prone to vibration. If the sensation continues to grow until the tension becomes such that the other fibres can vibrate no longer, the resulting rigidity immobilises the blood and stops the movement of the animal spirits. Melancholy is the consequence. In its other variety, the 'liquid form', the humours are impregnated with black bile, and become thickened, and filled with that humour the blood becomes denser and stagnates in the meninges, compressing the principal organs of the nervous system. The result again is a rigidity of the fibres, but this time as a result of a humoral phenomenon. Lorry distinguishes between two different types of melancholy, but in fact, using the same set of qualities, giving the condition its real unity, he fits them into two different systems of explanation. Only the theoretical edifice is doubled. The qualitative experiential basis remains the same.

A symbolic unity shaped by the sluggishness of the fluids, by the darkening of the animal spirits and the shadowy twilight that they spread over the images of things, by the viscosity of a blood that circulates through the vessels with difficulty, by the thickening of vapours that have blackened, acrid and deleterious, and by the slowed visceral functions, which become bogged down – more sensible than conceptual or theoretical, this unity gives melancholy its distinctive formula.

It is this elaboration, rather than any painstaking observation, that reorganises the signs and the mode of appearance of melancholy. Increasingly the theme of partial delirium disappears as the primary symptom of the condition, making way for indications of qualities such as sadness, bitterness, immobility and a taste for solitude. By the late eighteenth century, forms of madness that lacked any delirium were easily classed as melancholic. They were characterised instead by inertia, despair and a dull stupor.[39] In James' *Dictionary*, reference is already made to sufferers of an apoplectic melancholy, with no delirium:

> When they lie, they care not for erecting themselves; when they stand, they will not walk, except forc'd to it by their Friends or the By-standers. They do not shun men; but tho they seem attentive to what is said to them, yet they make no answer to it.[40]

Although in such cases the major symptoms backing up the diagnosis were immobility and silence, there were also subjects who displayed only bitterness, languor and a taste for solitude; their agitation was deceptive, and the temptation to label them as maniacs was to be resisted. They too were melancholics, for:

> [They] shun Company, love solitary Places, and know not whither they wander. The colour of the Body is yellowish; the Tongue dry, like that of a person scorched from thirst; the eyes dry, hollow, and never discharging any Tears; the whole Body dry and parched, and the Countenance overcast with Gloom, Horror and Sadness.[41]

*

Analyses of mania and their evolution in the course of the classical age follow the same principle of coherence.

Willis systematically opposes mania and melancholy. The mind of the melancholic is entirely taken up with reflection, to the extent that his imagination remains idle and at rest. In maniacs, by contrast, fancy and imagination are taken by a constant flux of impetuous thoughts. While the mind of the melancholic focuses on a single object, giving it, but it alone, unreasonable proportions, mania deforms notions and concepts. Either they lose their congruence, or their representative value becomes deformed, and the whole process of thought in its essential relationship to truth becomes warped. Melancholy is always accompanied by sadness and fear; maniacs, by contrast, invariably live with audacity and 'furor'. For both mania and melancholy, the cause of the ill is to be found in the movement of the animal spirits, although the movement of mania is quite particular. It is continuous, violent and always capable of piercing new pores in the cerebral matter, forming something like the material support for incoherent thoughts, explosive gestures and the uninterrupted flow of words that betray mania. This pernicious mobility is that of the infernal water made of sulphurous liquor, *aquae stygiae, ex nitro, vitriolo, antimonio, arsenico et similibus exstillatae* [Stygian waters, distilled from saltpetre, vitriol, antimony, arsenic and the like]. Its particles are in perpetual motion, and can open new pathways, pores and canals in any matter, and are sufficiently powerful to spread far, just as maniacal spirits can cause any part of the body to become agitated and convulsed. In the secret of its movements, infernal water contains all the images in which mania takes on a concrete form. In an indissociable manner, it constitutes both its chemical myth and in some sense its dynamic truth.

Over the course of the eighteenth century, the image of animal spirits in the nervous canals, with all their mechanical and metaphysical implications, was frequently replaced by the more strictly physical but even more symbolic image of a tension, to which all nerves, vessels and the whole system of organic fibres were subject. Mania becomes the paroxysm of tension in the fibres, and the maniac is like a musical instrument whose strings, excessively stretched, vibrate under the slightest and most remote of stimulations. Maniacal delirium is a continuous vibration of the sensibility. Through this image, differences from melancholia are more precisely perceived and are organised into a rigorous antithesis. A melancholic can no longer vibrate in harmony with the outside world because his fibres are too relaxed, or are immobilised through excessive tension (the mechanics of tension are equally useful for explaining the immobility of the melancholic and the agitation of the maniac): in a melancholic only a small number of fibres vibrate, those corresponding exactly to the point of his delirium. Maniacs, by contrast, vibrate at the slightest stimulation, and their delirium is universal. Their excitement does not die away in the stolid immobility of the melancholic, but is multiplied instead by the organism, as if the tension in the fibres of a maniac provided a supplementary form of energy. That in turn is what makes them insensible, not with the somnolent insensibility of melancholics, but with an insensibility tense with internal vibrations. That, it is supposed, is the reason for which they fear 'neither hot nor cold, tear at their clothes, and lie down naked in the depths of winter without feeling the cold'. For that reason too they replace the real world, which constantly calls out to them, with the unreal, chimerical world of their delirium: 'the essential symptoms of mania result from the fact that objects do not present themselves to sufferers in the way they really are'.[42] The delirium of the maniac is not determined by any particular vice of the judgement, but is rather a flaw in the transmission of sense impressions to the brain, a problem of information. In the psychology of madness, the old idea of truth as 'the conformity of thoughts to things' is transposed to this metaphor of resonance and vibration, a kind of musical fidelity of the fibre to the sensations that make it vibrate.

This theme of maniacal tension develops, outside this medicine of solids, in intuitions that are more qualitative still. The rigidity of the maniac's fibres is always part of a dry landscape, and mania is often accompanied by an exhaustion of the humours and a general aridity throughout the organism. The essence of mania is sandy and desert-like. Bonet, in his *Sepulchretum*, gives the assurance that according to his observations, the brains of maniacs are always dry, hard and brittle.[43] Later, Albrecht von Haller confirms that the brains of maniacs were dry, tough and broke easily.[44] Menuret recalls an observation made by Forestier which clearly demonstrates that too great a loss of humour dries out the vessels and the fibres, and can bring on a state of mania: this was the case of a young man 'who had married a woman in the summer, and become a maniac through the excessive commerce that he had had with her'.

What some only imagined or supposed, or saw in a dim quasi-perception, Dufour observed, measured and recorded. As part of a post-mortem, he cut into the medullar substance of a patient who had died of mania, and removed a six-line cube that weighed 3 drams and 3 grains, whereas the weight of a sample of the same size from a healthy brain would be 3 drams and 5 grains.

> This inequality in the weight may seem inconsequential at first, but it becomes far more important if one notes the difference between the total mass of a healthy brain and the brain of a maniac. A normal adult brain weighs three pounds: the brain of a maniac weighs about one ounce less.[45]

The desiccation and lightness of the maniac were therefore evident on the scales.

That internal dryness and heat were further proved by the ease with which maniacs could tolerate extremes of cold. It was well known that they had often been seen to walk naked in the snow,[46] and that there was no need to provide heating for them when they were locked up in asylums,[47] and that cold could even be used as a cure. Since Van Helmont, maniacs were routinely given immersions in icy water, and Menuret gave an assurance that he had known one maniacal person who, after escaping from the prison where he was held, 'travelled several leagues in a violent rainstorm without a hat and almost naked, and by that exercise returned to health'.[48] Montchau, who had cured a maniac 'by dropping icy water on him from the greatest possible height', was unsurprised by such a positive result, and his explanation gathers together all the themes of organic heat that had succeeded and been woven in and out of each other throughout the seventeenth century: 'Should we be surprised that water and ice provided a cure so promptly and completely when the blood boiled, the bile was furiously hot, and mutinous liquors carried agitation and irritation wherever they went?' The effect of the application of cold, by contrast, was that the vessels:

> Contracted more violently, releasing the liquids that engorged them. The irritation of the solid parts caused by the extreme heat of the liquors that they contain ceased, the nerves relaxed, and the passage of the spirits, which had been irregular, reverted to a normal state.[49]

The world of melancholy is damp, heavy and cold, while the world of mania is dry and ardent, made of both violence and fragility. It is a world where an imperceptible form of heat is everywhere apparent, a dry and brittle world, capable of being softened by any damp freshness. In the midst of these qualitative simplifications, mania finds its wide extension and its unity. It remained what it was in the early seventeenth century, a 'frenzy without fever', but in addition to those two characteristics, which were still only indicative, a whole perceptive theme developed, which became the real organising principle behind the clinical picture. When the explicative myths faded, and humours, spirits, solids and fluids passed from fashion, all that was left was the scheme of coherence of qualities that were no longer named. That dynamic of heat and movement had slowly formed a constellation of features characteristic of mania, which now came to be seen as a natural complex, as a truth immediately revealed by psychological observation. What had been perceived as heat, imagined as an agitation of the spirits, and dreamt of as a tension in the fibres would now be visible in the neutralised transparency of psychological notions: the exaggerated intensity of internal impressions, a rapidity in the association of ideas, and a lack of attention to the world outside. The description provided by De la Rive already possesses that clarity:

> External objects do not produce the same impression on the mind of a patient as they do on that of a healthy man: the impressions are weak, and he rarely heeds them: his mind instead is almost totally absorbed by the vivacity of the ideas produced by the altered state in his brain. These ideas have a degree of vivacity such that the patient believes that they represent real objects, and judges accordingly.[50]

But it should not be forgotten that this psychological structure of mania, such as it comes to the surface at the end of the eighteenth century and takes a stable form, is merely the visible outline of a more profound organisation which was to founder, and had come into being along the half-perceptive, half-imaginary laws of a world of qualities.

It is true that this whole universe of heat and cold, of dampness and aridity, was a reminder for medical thought, just before it turned to positivism, of the backdrop against which it had come into being. But this weight of images is more than a memory, it is also at work. To form the positive experience of mania and melancholia, what had been necessary, against a horizon of images, was a gravitational network where qualities were attracted to each other by a system of affective and sensible affinities. If mania and melancholia took on the face that we still recognise today, it is not because we have learnt to 'open our eyes' to their real nature during the course of the centuries; and it is not because we have purified our perceptive processes until they became transparent. It is because in the experience of madness, these concepts were integrated around specific qualitative themes that have lent them their own unity and given them a significant coherence, finally rendering them perceptible. We have moved from simple notional signs (frenzy without fever, a delirious or obsessional idea) to a qualitative field, which is apparently less organised, easier and less precisely defined, but which alone constitutes the perceptible, recognisable unities *genuinely present* in the overall experience of madness. The space of observation of these illnesses has been cut from landscapes that have invisibly passed on their style and structure. On the one hand we see a sodden, almost diluvian world where man is deaf, blind and insensible to all that is not his unique object of terror, a world simplified in the extreme, where a single detail becomes disproportionately large; and on the other we see a burning, deserted, panicked world where all is flight, disorder and instantaneously vanishing lines. It is the rigour of these themes in their cosmic form – not the approximations of some observational prudence – that organised the experience (already so similar to our own) of mania and melancholy.

*

It is Willis, with his fine medical sense and his spirit of observation, whom we honour as the 'discoverer' of the manic-depressive cycle, or rather of the alternation between mania and melancholy. And indeed Willis' approach was most interesting. But first for one reason: the passage from one state to the other is not perceived as an observational fact, in need of a subsequent explanation, but rather as the consequence of a profound affinity that lies in their secret nature. Willis never cites a single instance of any alternation that he has actually observed. What he deciphered was an interior affinity that prompted some strange metamorphoses: 'After melancholy, it remains for us to treat of madness, which is so far ally'd to the other, that these affects often change turns, and each passes into the other.'[51] It sometimes happened that a melancholic diathesis, if it worsened, could turn into frenzy; frenzy, on the other hand, when it eased off and lost its power sometimes became a bilious diathesis. For a strict empiricism, there would be either two adjoining conditions, or two successive symptoms for a single disease. Willis in fact never presented the problem in terms of symptoms, nor in terms of disease. What interested him was finding the link between the two states in the dynamic of the animal spirits. In the melancholic, it will be remembered, the spirits were sombre and dark, and projected their darkness over the image of things, forming a kind of twilight that crept over the light of the soul. In mania by contrast, the spirits were in perpetual, sparkling agitation, carried along by an irregular movement that constantly came and went, a movement that gnawed away and consumed them, and even in the absence of fever radiated its own heat. Between mania and melancholia the affinity was obvious: it was not the affinity of symptoms linked through experience, but a stronger unity, much more visible in the landscapes of the imagination, which fused in the same fire images of smoke and flames. 'If in Melancholy, the brain and the animal spirits are said to be darkened with fume, and thick obscurity; in Madness, they seem to be all as it were of an open or burning flame.'[52] The quick movement of the flames clears the smoke, but when the smoke returns it douses the flames and puts out their light. For Willis, the unity of melancholia and mania was not a disease, but a secret fire in which flames and smoke were in conflict, the element bearing both this light and this shadow.

Very few eighteenth-century physicians are unaware of the proximity of mania and melancholy. Yet several refuse to recognise two manifestations of a single identical illness.[53] Many note a succession, without perceiving a symptomatic unity. Sydenham prefers to divide up the domain of mania into ordinary mania, which 'proceeds from the over-richness and spirituousness of the blood', and a separate form that generally 'degenerated into ideotism'.[54] The latter 'arrives from the depressed state of the blood, occasioned by its long fermentation'. More common still is the recognition that the alternation between mania and melancholy is either a phenomenon of metamorphosis, or of remote causality. For Joseph Lieutaud, a melancholy that lasts a long time, exhausts itself and turns into delirium, loses its traditional symptoms and takes on a strange resemblance to mania: 'The final degree of melancholy has many affinities with mania.'[55] But the status of that analogy is not fully elaborated. For Dufour, the link is even looser. He sees a remote causality, with melancholy being capable of provoking mania like 'worms in the frontal sinuses, or dilated or varicose vessels'.[56] Without the support of an image, no amount of observation could transform the acknowledgement of a succession into a precise and essential symptomatic structure.

Admittedly, the image of smoke and flames disappears in the work of Willis' successors, but the organisational work is still accomplished within images. The images become more functional, and better inserted into great physiological themes like circulation and body heat, and increasingly distant from the cosmic figures where Willis found them. In Boerhaave and his commentator Van Swieten, mania naturally forms the superior degree of melancholy, not simply on account of the frequent metamorphosis, but through the effect of a necessary dynamic concatenation: the cerebral fluid, which stagnates in bilious patients, after a certain time becomes agitated, as the immobility of the black bile that engorges the viscera makes it 'more acrid and noxious'. The resulting fine acid elements are carried by the blood to the brain, bringing on the extreme agitation commonly observed in mania. Mania is therefore only distinguished from melancholy by a difference of degree, and follows on naturally, being born out of the same causes, and consequently responds to similar treatment.[57] For Friedrich Hoffmann, the unity of mania and melancholy is a natural consequence of the laws of movement and shock, but what is pure mechanics on the level of principles become dialectics in the development of life and of the illness. Melancholy is still characterised by immobility: the thickened blood causes congestion inside the brain where it begins to cause an obstruction, and where it is supposed to circulate it tends to stop, immobilised by its own weight. But if the heaviness slows down movement, it also means that the shock, when it comes, is more violent: the brain, the vessels that go through it, and its very substance, shaken with greater force, tend to oppose a stronger resistance, and hence become harder, and that hardening in turn means that the heavy blood is repulsed with ever greater force, its movement increases, and soon it is taken over by the agitation characteristic of mania.[58] There was therefore a natural progression from the image of engorgement to that of dryness, hardness and vigorous motion, by a process of concatenation where the principles of classical mechanics are bent, warped and twisted beyond recognition on account of a fidelity to imaginary themes, which are the true organising force behind this functional unity.

Later, other images too would come, but they never played quite the same constitutive role, and functioned instead as interpretative variations on the theme of a unity that had now been firmly acquired. An example is the explanation that Spengler puts forward for the alternation between madness and melancholy, whose principle is borrowed from the electric battery. First of all there is a concentration of nervous power and its fluid in a certain region of the system, and that sector alone is excited, the rest remaining in a state of sleep. This is the phase of melancholy. But when a certain degree of intensity is reached, that local charge suddenly spreads throughout the system, shaking it with considerable violence until the discharge is complete. That is the manic episode.[59] At that level of elaboration, the image is too complex and too complicated, and borrows from a model too remote to have any role in the organisation in perception of the pathological unity. It is rather a result of the perception, which in turn relies on unificatory images, but of a far more elementary nature.

These images are also a secret presence in the text of James' *Dictionary*, one of the first where the manic depressive cycle is given as a truth proven by observation, a unity easily discernible to any unprejudiced scrutiny:

> There is an absolute necessity for reducing Melancholy and Madness to the Species of disorder, and consequently considering them in one joint view, since, from daily observation, and Experience, we find, that they both arise from the same common cause and origin ... this doctrine is confirmed by daily Experience and acute Observation, since we find that melancholic patients, especially if their disorder is inveterate, easily fall into madness, which, when removed, the melancholy again discovers itself, though the madness afterwards returns at certain periods.[60]

What was constituted throughout the seventeenth and eighteenth centuries, under the influence of images, was thus a perceptual structure, and not a conceptual system or even an ensemble of symptoms. The proof of this is that, as is the case with perception, qualitative slippages could take place here without any noticeable changes in the shape of the ensemble. So Cullen, in both mania and melancholy, finds 'a prevailing object' of delirium,[61] and inversely, attributes melancholy to a 'a drier, firmer texture in the medullary substance of the brain'.[62]

The key point is that this process did not go from observation to the construction of explanatory images, but that on the contrary, images fulfilled the initial role of synthesis, and their organising force made possible a structure of perception where symptoms could finally take on their significant value, and be organised into the visible presence of the truth.

III HYSTERIA AND HYPOCHONDRIA

Two problems arose here. First, the degree to which it was legitimate to treat them as mental illnesses, or at least as forms of madness; and second whether they should be taken as a pair, as though they formed a virtual couple, similar to the early pairing of mania and melancholy.

A glance at the classifications is revealing: hypochondria does not always figure alongside dementia and mania, and hysteria is only very rarely to be found there. Plater speaks of neither as lesions of the senses, and at the close of the classical age, Cullen still classified them in a separate category to the *Vesaniae*, the other forms of madness: hypochondria is among the '*Adynamiae*, or diseases consisting in a weakness or loss of motion in the vital or natural functions', and hysteria among the 'spasmodic affections in the natural functions'.[63]

Also, it is rare to find the two grouped together in a logical manner in nosological tables, or even associated in any form of opposition. Sauvages classes hypochondria among hallucinations, the 'hallucinations that only affect the health', and hysteria among forms of convulsion.[64] Linnaeus uses the same distribution.[65] Both are probably being faithful to the teaching of Willis, who had studied hysteria in his *De Morbis convulsivis*, and hypochondria in the section of *De Anima brutorum* that dealt with diseases affecting the head, giving it the name *passio colica*. They were two quite different diseases. In the one case the overheated spirits are subjected to reciprocal pressure that may be mistaken for a minor explosion, causing the irregular and preternatural movements, whose senseless form is what is known as hysterical convulsions. By contrast, in *passio colica*, the spirits are irritated as the result of a matter that is hostile or inappropriate to them (*infesta et improportionata*); and what comes about is a disturbance and irritation, or *corrugationes*, of the sensitive fibres. Willis warned against being surprised by analogies between symptoms: it did on occasion happen that convulsions could produce pains, and the violent movements of hysteria could provoke the suffering of hypochondria. But the resemblance was deceptive. '*Non eadem sed nonnihil diversa materies est.*' (The substance is not the same, but differing in non-negligible aspects.)[66]

But below the level of the unchanging distinctions of the nosographers, a slow process was coming to fruition, where hysteria and hypochondria were increasingly associated as two forms of a disease that was one and the same. In 1725 Richard Blackmore published a *Treatise of Spleen and Vapours, or Hypochondriacal and Hysterical Affections*, where both diseases were defined as the two varieties of a single affection, either a 'morbific constitution of the spirits' or a 'disposition to leave their reservoirs and consume themselves'.[67] For Whytt, in the mid-eighteenth century, the assimilation has become complete, and the symptomatic system is henceforth identical:

> An uncommon sense of cold or heat in different parts of the body, suddenly moving from one place to another; pains in different parts of the body, hysteric faintings and convulsions, catalepsis, and tetanus, wind in the stomach and bowels, a great craving for food; a black vomiting, a sudden and great flux of pale urine; nervous atrophy; a nervous or spasmodic asthma, a nervous cough; palpitations of the heart, the pulse often varying in quickness, strength and fullness, periodical headaches, giddiness, a dimness of sight, low spirits, melancholy and mania, the incubus or nightmare.[68]

Throughout the classical age, hysteria and hypochondria slowly join the domain of diseases of the mind. Richard Mead could still write of hypochondria: *Morbius totius corporis est* (it is an illness of the whole body). Willis' text on hysteria should be restored to its full value:

> The hysterical passion is of so ill fame, among the diseases belonging to women, that like one half-damn'd, it bears the faults of many other distempers. For when at any time, a sickness happens in a woman's

body, of an unusual manner, or more occult original, so that its cause lies hid, and the curatory indication is altogether uncertain, presently we accuse the evil influence of womb (which for the most part is innocent), and in every unusual symptom, we declare it to be something hysterical, and so to this scope, which oftentimes is only the subterfuge of ignorance, the medical intentions, and use of remedies are directed.[69]

With all due respect to traditional commentators on this text, which is invariably quoted in any study of hysteria, it does not mean that Willis suspected the absence of an organic basis in cases of hysterical affection. He merely says, and in an explicit way, that the notion of hysteria is a catch-all for the fantasies, not of the person who is or believes himself to be ill, but of the ignorant doctor who feigns comprehension. Nor does the fact that hysteria is classified by Willis among diseases of the head indicate that he considered it a disorder of the mind; rather that he attributed its origins to a change in the nature, the origin and the initial course of the animal spirits.

Nonetheless, at the close of the eighteenth century, almost without dispute, hypochondria and hysteria are firmly classed as mental illnesses. In 1755, Alberti published at Halle his dissertation De morbis imaginariis hypochondriacorum; and Lieutaud, while defining hypochondria by its spasms, recognised that 'the mind is affected as much as and possibly more than the body; hence the term hypochondriac has become almost an offensive name avoided by physicians who aim to please'.[70] As for hysteria, Joseph Raulin no longer ascribed to it any organic reality, at least in its basic definition, classing it from the outset as a pathology of the imagination: 'This disease in which women invent, exaggerate and repeat all the various absurdities of which a disordered imagination is capable, has sometimes become epidemic and contagious.'[71]

There were thus two essential lines of development during the classical period for hysteria and hypochondria. One united them to form a common concept which was that of 'a disease of the nerves'; the other shifted their meaning and their traditional pathological basis – sufficiently indicated by their names – and tended to integrate them gradually into the domain of diseases of the mind, alongside mania and melancholia. But this integration was not achieved, as in the case of mania and melancholy, on the level of primitive qualities, perceived and dreamed of in their imaginative values. We are in the presence here of a new type of integration.

*

Physicians of the classical period did try to discover the qualities peculiar to hysteria and hypochondria. But they never reached the point of perceiving that particular coherence, that qualitative cohesion which gave mania and melancholy their unique identity. All qualities were contradictorily invoked, each cancelling the other, while leaving untouched the problem of the ultimate nature of these diseases.

Hysteria was often perceived as being the effect of an internal heat that spread throughout the body, an effervescence or ebullition constantly manifested in convulsions and spasms. The heat was thought to be similar to the amorous ardour with which hysteria was often linked, as in young women seeking a match or young widows who had lost their husbands. Hysteria was ardent by nature, its symptoms referring more easily to an image than a disease. The image was drawn in all its material precision in the early seventeenth century by Jacques Ferrand, in *Maladie d'amour ou mélancolie érotique*. The author notes that women are often maddened by love to a greater extent than their male counterparts, but how artful they are at disguising it!

> In which respect their appearance is like those raised stills where the fire cannot be seen from the outside. But look underneath, or place your hand on a lady's heart, and you shall find a great brazier burning brightly.[72]

This image was admirable for its symbolic weight, its affective charge and the whole range of imaginary references. Long after Ferrand, the qualitative theme of damp heat that characterised the secret distillations of hysteria continued; but slowly the image was replaced by a more abstract motif. Already in the work of Nicolas Chesneau, the flame of the feminine still had lost its colour:

> In my view hysterical passion is not a simple affliction, but what is commonly understood by the term is a grouping of several ills brought about by a malignant vapour which rises up in various ways of a corrupt nature, undergoing an extraordinary effervescence.[73]

For others, by contrast, the heat that rose up from the hypochondrium was quite dry, and hypochondriacal melancholy was a 'hot and dry' sickness caused by 'humours of the same quality'.[74] But some perceived no heat, in hysteria or in hypochondria, and considered the conditions to be characterised by langour, inertia, and the cold dampness associated with stagnant humours:

> It is my belief that hypochondriacal and hysterical affections that continue for any length of time require the nerves and the fibres of the brain to be slack and enfeebled, without action or elasticity, because the nervous fluid is impoverished and without virtue.[75]

No text demonstrates more clearly the qualitative instability of hysteria than George Cheyne's The English Malady: the unity of the condition is almost entirely abstract, and the symptoms are distributed among different qualitative regions and attributed to mechanisms specific to each of the regions in question. Anything associated with spasms, cramps and convulsions is linked to a heat-based pathology symbolised by 'saline particles' and 'noxious acrid or acrimonious steam'. By contrast, all the psychological or organic signs of weakness – 'lowness of spirits, lethargic dullness, melancholy and moping' – demonstrate that the nerves have become overly damp and flaccid, doubtless as the consequence of 'grossness, glewiness or viscidity of the animal juices, obstructing the glands, the serous pipes and the capillary blood vessels'. Paralysis is taken to signify a chilling or an immobilisation of the fibres, an 'interruption of the vibrations', which has frozen them, so to speak, into the general inertia of solids.[76]

The easier it became to organise mania and melancholia in a register of qualities, the more difficult it became to find a place there for the phenomena of hysteria and hypochondria.

Faced with them, the medicine of movement too was indecisive, and its analyses equally unstable. It is quite clear, at least to any form of perception that did not refuse its own images, that mania was linked to excessive mobility, and that in melancholy all forms of movement slowed down. For hysteria, and for hypochondria too, the choice is more difficult to make. Georg Ernst Stahl opts instead for a heaviness of the blood, which becomes so abundant and thick that it is no longer possible for it to circulate freely through the portal vein: it stagnates there, and engorges the veins, and an attack results from 'the effort required for it to find a way out, in the upper or lower regions of the body'.[77] For Boerhaave and Van Swieten by contrast, hysterical movement is the result of an excessive mobility in the fluids, which take on such lightness and such inconsistency that they are disturbed by even the tiniest movement. As Van Swieten explains:

> In weak constitutions, the blood is dissolved, and coagulates with great difficulty, so the serum lacks quality and consistency. The lymph resembles the serum and the other fluids produced by it . . . Accordingly, it is quite probable that hysterical passion and hypochondriacal sickness said to be without material foundation derive from the disposition or the particular state of the fibres.

It is to this sensibility and this mobility that the anguish, the spasms and the singular pain experienced so often 'by young women who are of a pale complexion, or people overly given to study and meditation' is to be attributed.[78] Hysteria is indifferently mobile or immobile, fluid or heavy, given to unstable vibrations or weighed down by stagnant humours. The style proper to its movements was yet to be discovered.

A similar imprecision marks chemical analogies. For Lange, hysteria is the product of fermentation, or more precisely a fermentation 'of the salts, pushed out into different parts of the body', with 'the humours to be found there'.[79] For others it is alkaline in nature. Michael Ettmüller, on the other hand, was convinced that ills of this nature were the result of an acidic reaction:

> The immediate cause is a crude acidity in the stomach; as the chyle is acidic, the quality of the blood is affected, and it no longer furnishes the spirits; the lymph becomes acidic, and the bile without virtue; the nervous stock becomes irritated, and the digestive yeast too is spoiled, becoming less volatile and excessively acidic.[80]

Viridet attempts to reconstitute a dialectics of acids and alkalis concerning 'these vapours that come upon us', whose meetings and violent movements in the brain and the nerves provoke the signs of hysteria and hypochondria. Some animal spirits, which are particularly fine, are alkaline salts that move very quickly and transform into vapours when they become too thin, while others are the vapours of volatile acids. Ether brings sufficient movement for them to be carried to the brain and the nerves, where 'coming into contact with alkalis, they cause untold suffering'.[81]

There is a strange qualitative instability in these hysterical and hypochondriacal ills, and a strange confusion between their dynamic properties and their secret chemistry. While a reading of mania and melancholia seemed simple against a qualitative horizon, the deciphering of hysteria and hypochondria seems to have been hesitant. The imaginary landscape of qualities, so decisive in the constitution of the pairing of mania and melancholy, probably remained secondary in the history of hysteria and hypochondria, where the role that it played was little more than that of a constantly changing backdrop. The path followed by hysteria did not lead through the dark qualities of the world as reflected in a medical imagination, the way it had done for mania. The space in which it took shape is of another nature altogether. It was the space of the body, in the coherence of its organic and moral values.

*

Customarily, the honour of having liberated hysteria from the ancient myths about a displacement of the uterus goes to Le Pois and Willis. Jean Liebaud, translating or rather adapting Marinello's work for the seventeenth century, still accepted (with a small number of caveats) the idea of a spontaneous movement of the womb. If it moved, it was

> to be more at ease; not that this comes about through prudence, nor is it a conscious decision or an animal stimulus, but by a natural instinct, to safeguard health and to have the pleasure of something delectable.

The idea that it could change its place and move around the body, bringing convulsions and spasms everywhere it travelled, had been abandoned, for it was now taken to be 'tightly held in place' by the cervix, ligaments, vessels and the sheath of the peritoneum; yet in some senses it could change its location.

> The womb therefore, even though it is tightly fixed to the parts that we have described and cannot easily change its place, still manages to roam, making strange, petulant movements around the woman's body. These diverse movements include ascensions and descents, convulsions, wanderings and prolapses. It can wander up to the liver, spleen, diaphragm, stomach, chest, heart, lung, throat and head.[82]

Physicians of the classical age are more or less unanimous in refusing this explanation.

In the early seventeenth century, speaking of hysterical convulsions, Le Pois wrote *Eorum omnium unum caput esse parentem, idque non per sympathiam, sed per idiopathiam*: 'Of all these the head is the sole source, and this not through sympathy, but through idiopathy.' More precisely, the origin was to be found in an accumulation of fluids in the rear section of the cranium:

> Just as a river is the result of the concourse of many smaller vessels that come together for its formation, in the same way, through the sinuses that are on the surface of the brain and come together in the rear section of the head, a liquid gathers on account of the tilt of the head. The accumulated heat causes the temperature of the liquid to rise, and in this way the origin of the nerves is affected.[83]

In his turn, Willis came up with a minute critique of the uterine explanation, and in his view it was from affections of the nervous tissue that such disturbances and irregularities were derived:

> The distemper named from the womb is chiefly and primarily convulsive, and chiefly depends on the brain and nervous stock being affected, and whatever inordination, or irregularity from thence happens, about the motion of the blood, is only secondary.[84]

Yet these analyses were not sufficient to break the theme of an essential link between hysteria and the womb. But the link is now conceived in different terms. It is no longer considered to be the trajectory of a real displacement through the body, but rather a sort of mute propagation through the paths of the organism and its functional proximities. It cannot be said that the seat of the malady has become the brain, nor that thanks to Willis a psychological explanation of hysteria was now possible. But the brain does take on the role of a relay that distributes a malady whose origins are visceral, and the womb brings it on just as the other viscera do.[85] Up until the end of the eighteenth century, and Pinel, the uterus and the womb are still present in the pathology of hysteria, but thanks to a privileged diffusion by the humours and nerves, not because of any particular prestige of their nature.[86]

Stahl justifies the parallelism between hysteria and hypochondria by a curious comparison between haemorrhoids and menstrual flux. He explains in his analysis of spasmodic movements that the hysterical sickness is a fairly violent pain 'accompanied by tension and compression, felt above all under the hypochondrium'. It is termed hypochondriacal sickness when it attacks men 'in whom nature makes an effort to get rid of an excess of blood through vomiting or haemorrhoids', and it is known as hysterical sickness when it attacks women whose 'periods are not what they should be. However, there is no essential difference between these two conditions.'[87] Hoffmann's opinion is quite similar, despite many theoretical differences. The *cause* of the hysteria is in the womb – which is loose or weakened – but as is also the case for hypochondria, the *seat* of the disease is to be looked for in the stomach and the intestines, where the blood and the vital humours have begun to stagnate 'in the nervous membranes and sheaths of the intestine'. What follows are stomach problems that gradually spread throughout the body. At the true centre of the organism, the stomach serves as a relay, and transmits the ills that originate in the interior and subterranean cavities of the body:

> There is no doubt that the spasmodic affections experienced by hypochondriacs and hysterics have their seat in the nervous tissues, and above all in the membranes of the stomach and the intestines, from where they are communicated by the intercostal nerves to the head, the chest, the kidneys, the liver, and all the principal organs of the body.[88]

The role that Hoffmann has the intestines, stomach and intercostal nerves play is significant for the manner in which the problem is posed during the classical age. It is not so much a question of getting away from the age-old uterine association as it is of discovering the principle and the paths taken by a diverse, polymorphous malady that seems to spread throughout the body. A reason is needed for this condition, which might equally affect the head or the legs, or manifest itself as a paralysis or disordered movements, catalepsy or insomnia, in short a sickness that could affect the whole corporeal space with such rapidity and cunning that it was virtually present throughout the entirety of the body.

There is no need to stress the changes in the medical horizon that had come about between Marinello and Hoffmann. Nothing remains of the infamous mobility once attributed to the uterus, which had been such a constant feature of the Hippocratic tradition. Nothing, that is, other than a certain theme that appears now more openly as it is not held within any single medical theory, but persists, identical through a succession of speculative concepts and explicative schemata. This is the theme of a dynamic upheaval of the corporeal space, and the rising up of powers from below that have been held in check for too long and become congested, and which begin to seethe and boil, until they finally spread their disorder – with or without the brain as an intermediary – throughout the whole body. The theme remains more or less unchanged until the early eighteenth century, despite the complete reorganisation of physiological concepts. And strangely, it is during the course of the eighteenth century, without there being any theoretical or experimental upheavals in pathology, that the theme suddenly changes direction and meaning. A dynamics of the corporeal space gives way to a moral theory of sensitivity. It is only at this point that the notions of hysteria and hypochondria radically alter their nature, and definitively enter the world of madness.

We must now try and reconstitute the evolution of the theme, in each of its three stages:

1 A dynamics of organic and moral penetration;
2 A physiology of corporeal continuity;
3 An ethics of nervous sensitivity.

*

If the corporeal space is seen as a solid and continuous whole, then the disordered movement brought by hysteria and hypochondria can only come from an element whose extreme fineness and incessant mobility means that it can penetrate a region occupied by the solids themselves. As Nathaniel Highmore put it, the animal spirits 'because of their igneous tenuity, can penetrate even the densest, the most compact bodies . . . and because of their activity, can penetrate the entire microcosm in a single instant'.[89] The spirits, if they are excessively mobile, and penetrate without order and in a tempestuous manner all the parts of the body where they have no business being present, bring on innumerable signs of disorder. Hysteria, for both Highmore and his adversary Willis, and also for Sydenham, is the sickness of a body that has become prey to innumerable penetrations by the spirits, where the good order of the internal organs is replaced by a disorganised space where large areas submit passively to the disordered movements of the spirits.

> Those diseases that we call hysterical in women and hypochondriacal in men, proceed from a confusion of the spirits; upon which account, too many of them in a crowd, contrary to proportion, are hurried violently upon this or that part, causing convulsions and pain, when they rush upon parts endu'd with exquisite sense; perverting the functions of the organs, both of that they thrust themselves into, and also of that whence they departed, both being much injured by this unequal distribution, which is altogether contrary to the economy of nature.[90]

The hysterical body is therefore open to a *spirituum ataxia*, an 'ataxia of the spirits', which, outside any organic law or functional necessity, might seize hold of all the available regions of the body, one after another.

The effects vary according to the region affected, and the sickness, which has no particular differentiation at the pure origin of its movement, can take on diverse appearances according to the spaces that it traverses and the places where it comes to the surface:

> The spirits are crowded in the lower belly, and violently rushing together towards the jaws, produce convulsions in every region thro which they pass, blowing up the belly like a great ball.

Above, Sydenham notes how 'rushing on the region under the Scrobiculum Cordis, it produces violent pain, very like the iliack passion'. Should it rise any higher, 'it causes so great a beating of the heart, that women who are troubled with it verily believe that those that are near may hear thumping on the ribs'. Finally, 'it seizes the outward part of the head between the pericranium and the skull, causing violent pain continually fixed in one point, which may be covered with the top of your thumb; and violent vomiting accompanies this pain'.[91]

Each part of the body determines of its own accord and through its nature the type of symptom that will be produced. Hysteria therefore becomes the most real and the most deceitful of sicknesses, real in that it has its basis in the movement of the animal spirits, but illusory too in that it brings into being symptoms that seem to be due to a disturbance inherent to the organs, but which are no more than specific configurations on the level of the organs of a problem which is central or rather general. The generalised dysfunction of internal mobility assumes the appearance of a localised symptom on the surface of the body. Genuinely suffering from the generalised, excessive movement of the spirits, the organ in question imitates its own disease, and starting out from a problem of transmission within the body, it apes a condition that would be its own. In this manner, hysteria:

> Resembles almost all the diseases that mortals are inclinable too; for whatever part it seats itself, it presently produces such symptoms as belong to it, and unless the physician is very skilful, he will be mistaken, and think those symptoms come from some essential distemper of this or that part, and not from any Hysterick Disease.[92]

Such is the cunning of a condition which, traversing the corporeal space in the homogenous form of movement, shows itself in specific guises; but the appearance of the disease has no connection to its essence, and is a feint developed by the body.

The more easily penetrable the interior space is, the more frequent hysteria will be and multiple its aspects. But if the body is firm and resistant, if the interior space is dense, well organised and solidly heterogeneous in its different regions, then the symptoms of hysteria are rare and its effects will remain simple. And here lies the difference between the feminine and masculine versions of hysteria, or rather the difference between hysteria and hypochondria. The principle that separates the two is not to be found in the symptoms, nor in fact in the causes, but in the spatial solidity of the body alone, in what might be termed the density of the interior landscape:

> For as the outward man is fram'd with parts obvious to sense, so, without doubt, the inward man consists of a due series, and, as it were, a Fabrick of the Spirits, to be viewed only by the Eye of Reason; and as this is nearly join'd, and, as it were, united with the Constitution of the Body, so much the more easily or more difficultly the Frame of it is disorder'd, by how much the Constitutive Principles that are allotted us by nature, are more or less firm. Wherefore this disease seizes many more women than men, because Nature has bestow'd them a more delicate and fine habit of body, having designed them only for an easy life, and to perform

the tender offices of Love; but she gave men robust bodies, that they might be able to delve and manure the Earth, to kill wild Beasts for food, and the like.[93]

Already, in the lines of this text, this spatial density gives up one of its secrets: this density is also moral, and the resistance of the organs to the disordered penetration of the spirits is perhaps one and the same with the strength of the soul that imposes order on thoughts and desires. After all, the interior space only becomes permeable and porous when the heart has given up the struggle. This explains why so few women accustomed to hard labour become hysterical, and why the condition is so much more common among women who lead a live of luxury and leisure, and among women whose courage is cowed by some sadness:

> Therefore, as often as women advise with me about this or that disorder of the body, the Reasons whereof cannot be deduced from the common Axioms for finding out Diseases; I always diligently enquire of them, whether they are not chiefly affected with that Indisposition which they complain of, when they have been disturbed in their Minds, and afflicted with Grief. If they confess, I am abundantly satisfy'd, that the Disease must come under this Tribe which we now discourse of.[94]

What we are faced with here is a new formulation of that ancient moral intuition which, since Hippocrates and Plato, had made the womb a sort of living, perpetually mobile animal, and which had given a spatial order to its movements. That theory saw in hysteria the uncontrollable movement of desires in those who lack the ability or the strength to satisfy or master them. This image of the feminine organ moving up to the chest or even to the head gave a mythical expression to an upheaval in the great tripartite Platonic scheme and its hierarchy, which was intended to ensure its immobility. The moral intuition is identical in Sydenham and in the disciples of Descartes, but what has changed is the spatial landscape in which it is expressed. Plato's vertical, hieratic order has been replaced with a volume which is constantly traversed by an incessant motion, bringing disorder notable not so much for its motion from bottom to top as for the uncontrollable welter it brings to what was once a well-ordered space. The inner body [or 'inward man'] that Sydenham sought to penetrate with the 'eye of reason' was not the objective body, offered to the disinterested gaze of a dispassionate observer, but a place where a certain manner of imagining the body and deciphering its inner movements met a certain manner of investing it with moral values. The transformation is accomplished here, and the work takes place at the level of this *ethical perception*. It is to fit that perception that the ever-pliable images of medical thought bend into shape; and it is here that great moral themes are formulated, and slowly come to change their initial appearance.

*

The penetrable body must however also be a continuous body. The dispersion of the disease through the organs is a reflection of a movement of propagation that allows it to pass from one organ to another and to affect them all in turn. If the body of the hypochondriac or hysterical patient is a porous body, made up of separate parts and distended by the invading force of disease, that invasion can only come about as a result of a certain spatial continuity. The body in which illness circulates must have properties different from the body in which the sufferer's dispersed symptoms appear.

This is a problem that haunts the medicine of the eighteenth century, and a problem that turns hypochondria and hysteria into diseases 'of the nervous stock'. It creates *idiopathic* diseases using the element that formed the general agent of all the *sympathies*.

Nervous fibres, it was agreed, had remarkable properties, which allowed extremely heterogeneous elements to be brought together. It was thought astonishing that nerves, throughout the body, and in all organs, were of the same nature, given that their task was to transmit such extraordinarily diverse impressions:

> the nerve whose endings in the eyeball enable it to perceive matter as delicate as rays of light, and the nerve in the ear which is sensitive to the smallest vibration of a sonorous body are no different in nature to those which serve far rougher purposes, like taste, touch and smell.[95]

That identical nature, combined with different functions, ensured the possibility of communication between the most distant organs, and the most physiologically dissimilar: 'This homogeneity in the nerves of the animal, together with the multiple communications that they serve together . . . creates a harmony between the organs, so that when one is affected, several other organs may participate in that affection.'[96] More admirable still was the fact that a nervous fibre could simultaneously carry the incitement of a voluntary movement and an impression made on an organ of sense. Tissot conceives of this double functioning in a single fibre as the combination of an *undulatory* movement for the impetus towards movement ('the movement of a fluid in a soft reservoir, like a bladder for example, which may be squeezed so that liquid passes into a tube') and a *corpuscular* movement for sensation ('like the movement of a series of ivory balls'). Thus sensation and movement can be produced at the same time in the same nerve.[97] Any tension or relaxation of the fibre alters the movements and the sensations, as is apparent in all illnesses of the nerves.[98]

And yet, despite the unifying virtues of the nervous system, it was far from certain that the cohesiveness of the very diverse disturbances that characterised hysteria and hypochondria could be explained by the real network that the fibres formed. It was difficult to imagine the link between the signs which from one end of the body to the other betrayed the presence of a nervous affection, and more difficult still to find a causal link that would explain why certain 'delicate people', when faced with a heady perfume, the vivid account of a tragic event, or with a sight of a violent struggle, were 'affected with fainting and general convulsions'.[99] The search was in vain, as there was no precise liaison between the nerves, and no predefined pathway, only a sort of remote action that was rather of the order of a physiological solidarity. It was believed that different parts of the body possessed a specific faculty that was either 'general and extended through the system, or confined in great measure to certain parts'.[100] This property, very different from 'the faculty of sensation and the faculty of motion', allowed organs to enter into communication with each other, suffering together and reacting to a remote stimulus: this was sympathy. In fact Whytt manages neither to isolate sympathy in the whole of the nervous system nor to define it strictly in relation to sensibility and movement. Sympathy only exists in organs to the extent that it is received there by the intermediary of the nerves, and the greater their mobility, the more pronounced it becomes. And at the same time it is one of the forms of sensibility: 'All sympathy or consent supposes feeling, and therefore must be owing to the nerves, which are the sole instruments of sensation.'[101] But the nervous system is no longer invoked here to explain the exact transmission of a movement or a sensation, but to justify, in its ensemble and its mass, the sensitivity of the body to its own phenomena, and the echo that it gives itself through the volume of its own organic space.

Illnesses of the nerves are essentially disorders of the sympathy. They suppose a general state of alert in the nervous system, which makes each organ susceptible to enter into sympathy with any other:

> In such a condition of the nervous system, the passions of the mind, errors in diet, and changes of heat or cold, or the weight and humidity of the atmosphere, will be apt to produce morbid symptoms; so that there will be no firm or continuous state of health, but almost a constant succession of greater or less complaints.[102]

This heightened sensibility is probably compensated for by zones of insensibility, similar to sleep. Hysterics, in general, are the group whose internal sensitivity is more acute, with hypochondriacs demonstrating the phenomenon to a lesser degree. Women, naturally, fall into the first category, as together with the brain, the womb is the organ that entertains the most sympathy with other organs throughout the body. To prove the point it is enough to note

> The vomiting that generally accompanies an inflammation of that organ, the nausea and depressed appetite after conception, the violent contractions of the diaphragm and abdominal muscles in delivery, the headache, and the heat and pain in the bowels about the time of menstruation.[103]

The whole feminine body is criss-crossed with the obscure but strangely direct paths of sympathy, and is always complicitous with itself, to the point of forming for sympathy a place of absolute privilege; from one extremity of its organic space to the other, hysteria is a perpetual possibility. The sympathetic sensibility of their organism, pervading their entire body, condemns women to the nervous illness known as the vapours. 'Women, in whom the nervous system is generally more moveable than in men, are more subject to nervous complaints, and have them to a higher degree.'[104] Whytt assures his readers that he has witnessed

> The pain of the toothach throw a young woman of weak nerves, into convulsions and insensibility, which continued for several hours, and returned, upon the pain becoming more acute.

Diseases of the nerves are sicknesses of the corporeal continuity. A body that is too close to itself, too intimate in each of its parts, is considered an organic space that is somehow strangely reduced. This becomes the new theme common to hysteria and hypochondria. This rapprochement of the body with itself is an image that becomes precise in some writers, too precise, as is clearly the case with Pomme and the 'shrivelling of the nervous system' that he describes. Such images mask the problem, but do not suppress it, and do not prevent work on the subject from continuing.

*

Is sympathy, in the final analysis, a property hidden in each organ, the 'feeling' that George Cheyne referred to, or is it a real propagation that travels through an intermediary element?[105] And is the pathological proximity that characterises nervous diseases an exasperation of that sentiment, or a greater mobility of that interstitial body?

It is a curious fact, but doubtless characteristic of the medical thought of the eighteenth century, at a time when physiologists are striving to pin down exactly the functions and role of the nervous system (sensibility and irritability, sensation and movement), that physicians use such notions in a confused manner, in the indistinct unity of pathological perception, articulating them in a scheme quite different from the one that physiology proposes.

Sensibility and movement are not distinguished. Tissot explains that children are more sensitive than others because everything inside them is lighter and more mobile.[106] Irritability, which Haller took to be a property of the nervous fibres, is confused with irritation, understood as a pathological condition in an organ brought about by prolonged excitement. It was therefore accepted that nervous diseases were states of irritation linked to an excessive mobility of the fibres:

> One sometimes comes across people in whom the smallest moving cause brings about a much greater movement than is normal in a healthy individual. The faintest sound or the tiniest ray of light can occasion extraordinary symptoms in such people.[107]

In this deliberately maintained ambiguity regarding the notion of irritation, the medicine of the late eighteenth century can demonstrate a continuity between a disposition (irritability) and a pathological event (irritation), but it can also maintain at the same time the idea of a condition particular to an organ, which experiences, in its own individual way, a generalised attack (the sensibility of each organ assuring this communication, which remains discontinuous), and the idea of a propagation inside the organism of a single condition that might attack any of its parts (the mobility of the fibres ensures that continuity, despite the different forms that it takes in different organs).

But if the notion of 'irritated fibres' maintains a concerted confusion, it also permits a decisive distinction to be made in pathology. On the one hand, nervous patients are more irritable, i.e. more sensitive, in that they have thinner fibres, a more delicate organism, and also a more impressionable soul, a worried heart and a sympathy that is overly intense for the events that go on around them. This sort of universal resonance – which is at once sensation and mobility – constitutes the first determining factor in the disease. Women who have 'weak fibres' and who are easily carried away, in their idleness, by rapid leaps of their imagination suffer from their nerves more often than men, who are 'stronger, dryer, and burnt by work'.[108] But this excessive irritation has the peculiarity that, in its intensity, it causes the sensations of the soul to diminish and sometimes disappear altogether, as though the sensitivity of the nervous organ itself were greater than the capacity of the soul to experience sensation, and confiscated for its own ends the multiplicity of sensations that its extreme mobility elicits. The nervous system is 'in such a state of irritation and reaction that it is no longer capable of transmitting to the soul all that it experiences; and all the characters being shuffled, the soul no longer reads these sensations'.[109] What takes shape is the idea of a sensibility that is not sensation, and of an inverse relation between this delicacy, which is as much of the soul as it is of the body, and of a certain sleep of sensation, preventing nervous shocks from reaching the soul. The unconsciousness of the hysteric is the converse of her sensibility. Such is the relation that the notion of sympathy cannot define, which grew out of the concept of irritability, however unelaborated and still confused in the thought of pathologists.

Consequently, the moral significance of nervous diseases is radically altered. While nervous diseases had been associated with organic movements in the lower regions of the body (even via the confused and multiple paths of sympathy), they were still situated inside a certain ethics of desire. They were the revenge of a body that was too unrefined, and it was as a result of excessive violence that people fell ill. But the new thinking was that illness was a result of excessive sensation, and patients suffered from an excessive solidarity with the beings that surrounded them. Illness was no longer a constraint brought on by one's secret nature. Rather, one became a victim of all that which, on the surface of the world, would solicit the body and soul.

As a result, people were at once more innocent and more guilty. More innocent as they were swept along by the total irritation of the nervous system into an unconsciousness whose degree was proportional to the extent of the illness. But more guilty, more guilty by far, as everything to which they were attached in the world, the life that they led, the affections that they had had, the passions and fantasies that they had nourished with excessive indulgence, all melted into an irritation of the nerves, where they found their natural effect and their moral punishment. All life ended up judged against this degree of irritation: the abuse of non-natural things,[110] the sedentary life of the city, the reading of novels, theatrical spectacles,[111] an immoderate zeal for the sciences,[112] 'an excessive passion for the sex, or for that criminal habit as repugnant to the moral as it is harmful to the physical'.[113] The innocence of the nervous patient who could no longer even feel the irritation of the nerves was actually a fair punishment for a far more serious form of guilt: that of preferring the world to nature:

> A terrible state! Such is the torture of all those effeminate souls whom inaction has precipitated into dangerous voluptuousness and who, in an attempt to elude the work that nature requires, have embraced instead the phantoms of opinion . . . thus are the rich punished for a deplorable use of their fortune.[114]

Here we find ourselves on the threshold of the nineteenth century, where the irritability of the fibres was to have its own physiological and pathological destiny.[115] But at this stage in the domain of the diseases of the nerves its legacy is already of great importance.

Part of this is the complete assimilation of hysteria and hypochondria to mental illnesses. Through this capital distinction between sensation and sensitivity, they enter the domain of unreason, which as we saw above was characterised by an essential moment of error and dream, i.e.

by blindness.[116] For as long as the vapours were convulsions or strange sympathetic communications through the body, even if they resulted in fainting and a loss of consciousness, they were not madness. But when the mind becomes blind to the very excess of its own sensibility – then madness appears.

On the other hand, it gave this madness a whole content of guilt, moral sanction and just punishment that was in no way part of the classical experience. It weighed down unreason with all these new values, and instead of making blindness the condition of possibility of all these manifestations of madness, it described it as *the psychological effect of a moral fault*. And it thereby compromised all that was essential in the experience of unreason. What had been blindness was to become unconsciousness, what had been error became fault, and all that which pointed in madness to the paradoxical manifestation of non-being became the natural punishment of a moral wrong. In short, the vertical hierarchy that constituted the structure of classical madness, from the cycle of material causes to the transcendence of delirium, was toppled over and spread on the surface of a domain first simply occupied and soon disputed by psychology and morality.

The 'scientific psychiatry' of the nineteenth century had become possible.

It was in these 'diseases of the nerves' and 'hysterias', which would soon provoke its irony, that it found its origin.

IV

DOCTORS AND PATIENTS

Medical thought and practice in the seventeenth and eighteenth centuries do not have the unity or at least the coherence that we presently associate with them. The world of the cure is organised along principles which are in a certain sense peculiar to it, and which medical theory, physiological analysis and even the observation of symptoms do not always control perfectly. We saw earlier how hospitalisation and internment were independent of medicine, but even within medicine itself, theory and therapy only communicate in an imperfect reciprocity.

In a sense the therapeutic universe remains more solid, more stable, more attached to its structures, less labile in its developments, and less open to a radical reinvention. The new physiological horizons discovered by Harvey, Descartes and Willis were not matched by inventions of a comparable order in the techniques of medication.

A prime cause for this was that the myth of the panacea had not yet completely disappeared. However, towards the end of the seventeenth century, the idea of a remedy with universal effects was beginning to change its meaning. In the quarrel about antimony, what was affirmed or denied was still a certain virtue that properly belonged to a body, capable of acting directly on the disease; in the panacea, it is nature herself that acts, effacing all that belongs to counter-nature. The dispute surrounding antimony was succeeded by discussions about opium, which was used in a great number of afflictions, particularly for 'the sicknesses of the head'. Whytt is lost for words when celebrating its merits and efficaciousness against diseases of the nerves: it lessens 'the nerves' power of feeling' and consequently brings 'sudden relief in many violent disorders of the nervous and hysteric kind, in fix'd spasms, as well as in alternate convulsions of the muscles'. It is useful for agitation of any description, and is used with great success against 'weakness, lassitude, and yawning occasioned by too great a flux of the menses', not to mention 'flatulent colics', obstructed lungs, phlegm, and 'spasmodic asthma'. In short, given that sympathetic sensibility is the great agent of communication for sicknesses inside the organic space, opium, in so far as it has a primary effect of dulling sensibility, is an antisympathetic agent, providing an obstacle to the propagation of the disease along the lines of nervous sensibility. That action becomes less effective over time, as the nerves regain their sensibility despite the opium, 'unless its dose be increased from time to time'.[1] It was clear that opium did not owe its universal value to a virtue that it contained like a secret force. Its effect is circumscribed – it brings insensibility. But as its point of application – the nervous system – is a universal agent of the sickness, it is through that anatomical and functional mediation that opium takes on its sense as a panacea. The remedy is not general in itself, but rather inserts itself into the most general forms of functioning of the organism.

The theme of the panacea in the eighteenth century is a compromise, an equilibrium more often sought than found, between a privilege of nature of this medicine and an effectiveness that allows it to intervene in the most general functions of the organism. Hecquet's 1726 study of opium, *Réflexion sur l'usage de l'opium, des calmants et des narcotiques*, is quite revealing of this compromise, a characteristic of the medical thought of the time. The physiological analysis is meticulous. Health is described as 'the just temperament' of the fluids and the 'supple springiness' of the solids, 'in short, the free and reciprocal association of the two masterful powers of life'. Inversely, 'the causes of sicknesses result from fluids and solids, from defects or alterations in their weave, their movement and so forth'.[2] But the fluids in fact have no qualities of their own, and if they are too thick or too liquid, too agitated, stagnant or corrupt, that is merely the result of a movement of solids, which alone are capable of 'expelling the liquids from their reservoirs' causing them to 'swill around inside the vessels'. The main motor of health and sickness is therefore 'the vessels that beat . . . and the membranes that squeeze', and that springy virtue that 'moves, agitates and animates'.[3] Opium is a solid with a peculiar property: when heated, 'it turns almost entirely into vapour'. There is therefore good reason to suppose that it is made up of 'an assembly of spirituous and airy parts'. These parts are quickly liberated in the organism as soon as the opium is absorbed by the body:

> The opium, once absorbed by the entrails, becomes a cloud of insensible atoms which, suddenly penetrating the blood, promptly traverse it, and with the finest elements of the lymph, infiltrate the cortical substance of the brain.[4]

Once there, opium has a threefold effect, corresponding to the physical qualities of the vapours that it liberates. These vapours are made up of spirits or 'fine, light parts, powder-like, non saline, perfectly polished, like the tiniest elements of a down feather, almost imperceptible, yet elastic, capable of penetrating any substance without violence'.[5] In that they are smooth, polished elements, they can stick to the regular surface of the membranes, leaving no discernible gap anywhere, 'just as two perfectly flat surfaces stick to one another'. Their action therefore is to reinforce the membranes and the fibres, but their suppleness also means that they resemble 'tiny spring-like elements', hardening the 'tone of the membranes' and increasing their elasticity. Finally, as they are also 'airy particles', they can blend freely with the nervous liquid, and animate it by 'rectifying' and 'correcting' it.[6]

The effect of the opium is total because the chemical decomposition that it undergoes inside the organism links it, by that metamorphosis, to the elements that in their normal state determine health, and in a decomposed state bring disease. Opium owes its value as a universal medication to the long process of chemical transformation and physiological regenerations. Yet Hecquet clings to the idea that opium cures by a virtue of nature, and that it is the repository of a secret that puts it in direct communication with the source of life. Opium is linked to sickness in two ways. There is an indirect relation, mediated and subsidiary to the concatenation of various mechanisms, and a direct, immediate relation that precedes any discursive causality, an original relation that placed in opium an essence, a spirit (it is at once spiritual and spirituous), which is the spirit of life itself:

> The spirits that are there to be found in opium are the faithful repositories
> of the spirit of life placed there by the Creator . . . for it was to a tree, the
> tree of life, that He entrusted, by choice, a vivifying spirit which, preserv-
> ing health, saved men from death, so long as they remain innocent.
> Perhaps it was also to a plant that he entrusted the spirit that can return
> sinners to health.[7]

If opium is *efficacious*, it owes that property to the extent that it has brought
well-being from the outset. It acts in accordance with a visible, *natural mechanism*, but that is because it had received *a secret gift from nature*.

Throughout the eighteenth century, the idea of the efficacy of the drug
will become increasingly linked to the theme of nature, but without ever
shaking off these ambivalences. It is understood to work following a
natural and discursive process, but the principle of its action is a proximity
of essence, an original communication with nature, an opening onto its
Principle.[8] It is against that ambiguity that the successive privileges
accorded to 'natural' medicines in the eighteenth century should be
understood. A natural medicine is one whose principle is *hidden* in nature,
but whose results are *visible* for a philosophy of nature: air, water, the ether,
and electricity. The idea of the panacea survives in each of these therapeutic themes, metamorphosed, as we have seen, but remaining an
obstacle to any search for a specific drug, whose localised effect would be
directly in relation to a particular symptom or a unique cause. The world
of the cure, in the eighteenth century, is largely linked to this space of
generalised abstraction.

But only in part. Since the Middle Ages, the privilege of the panacea had
been opposed by more localised remedies with more specific efficacies.
Between the microcosm of illness and the macrocosm of nature, a
long-established network of links established and maintained a complex
system of correspondences. The ancient idea persisted that any sickness or
disease to be found in the world could be eradicated if men were sufficiently fortunate to find the antidote, which necessarily existed, if only in
an infinitely remote corner of nature. Sickness in the pure state did not
exist, and somewhere its compensation was waiting to be found. 'In
previous times, the grass was good for madmen, and hostile to the executioner.'[9] In a short space of time the use of herbs and salts was to be
reinterpreted in a pharmacopoeia of a rationalist style, and placed in a discursive relation with the disorders of the organism that it was intended to

remedy. However, in the classical age, the one sector that resists this process is the domain of madness, which for a long time remains in a more direct communication with cosmic elements that the wisdom of the world had spread in the secrets of nature. Strangely, most of these natural antitheses to madness are not of a vegetal order, but are to be found in human or mineral realms instead. As though the disturbing power of alienation, which gave it a place apart among the different forms of pathology, could only be combated by the most subterranean secrets of nature, or by the subtlest essences that make up the visible shape of man. Here was a phenomenon of the soul and the body, a stigma that was properly human, at the limits of the world of sin, the sign of a fall that was a reminder of man's original fall, and as such madness could only be cured by men, and by their envelope as mortal sinners. But the classical imagination had not yet entirely disposed of the idea that madness was linked to dark powers, to the nocturnal forces of the world, and that it was in some fashion a force that rose up from the subterranean depths where nightmarish desires had their origins. It was therefore also linked to gems and precious stones, to all those ambiguous treasures whose sparkle was simultaneously a blessing and a curse, bright colours that enclosed a fragment of night. The lengthy persistence of these moral and imaginary themes doubtless provides some explanation of why, until well into the classical age, human and mineral medicines were still applied to madness, flying in the face of most medical concepts of the age.

In 1638, Jean de Serres retranslated the renowned *Pharmaceutical Works* of Jean de Renou, where it was noted that

> The architect of nature divinely infused a particular and admirable virtue into all precious stones, obliging kings and princes to wear them in their crowns . . . that they might use them to ward off evil spells, cure diseases and preserve good health.[10]

Lapis lazuli, for instance, 'when worn, strengthens vision, and brings good spirits; when washed and correctly prepared, it purges the melancholic humour in a harmless manner'. Of all stones, emeralds have the most numerous powers, but are also the most ambivalent. Their main virtue is to preside over Wisdom and Virtue themselves. According to Renou,

> Not only do they ward off epilepsy, in all those who wear the stone

> surrounded by gold on their finger, but also strengthen the memory and help resist the temptation of concupiscence. The story is often told of the Hungarian king who, while engaged in amorous pursuits with his queen, felt a beautiful emerald that he wore on his finger break into three pieces during their endeavours, so much does the stone favour chastity.[11]

There would be little interest in quoting this ensemble of beliefs but for the fact that they figure, quite explicitly, in pharmacopeia and medical treatises of the seventeenth and eighteenth centuries. Certain practices, however, were excluded, as their sense was too evidently magical. Lemery, in his *Dictionnaire des drogues*, refuses to allow all the properties with which emeralds are credited: 'It is claimed that they are good for epilepsy, and that they hasten childbirth when worn as an amulet, but these last qualities are imaginary.' But while their usefulness in amulet form is contested, few strip these stones of their powers altogether. They are replaced in the element of nature, where their virtues took on the appearance of an invisible juice whose secrets could be extracted by quintessence. The emerald worn on the finger had no power, but mixed with the salts of the stomach, the humours of the blood or the spirits in the nerves, its effects were guaranteed and its virtue was natural. 'Emeralds', said Lemery elsewhere, 'are excellent for sweetening the bitter humours, if delicately ground and swallowed.'[12]

At the other extremity of nature, the human body too was considered to be one of the privileged remedies for madness, right up until the mid-eighteenth century. In the complex mixture that formed the organism, there was no doubting that the wisdom of nature had hidden away secrets which alone could combat all the disorder and fantasy that human madness had invented. Here again we see the archaic theme of man the microcosm, where the elements of the world come together, which are at once the principles of life and health: Lemery notes 'in all parts of man, in his excrescences and excrement', the presence of four essential bodies, 'oil and volatile salts blended and enveloped in phlegm and earth'.[13] Using man to remedy man was using the world to combat its own disorder, turning wisdom on madness and nature against antiphysis. 'Human hair is good for defeating the vapours, if the patient is made to smell its odour when burnt . . . Fresh urine is excellent for hysterical vapours.'[14] Buchoz recommends mothers' milk, the natural food *par excellence* (Buchoz was writing after Rousseau) for any nervous illness, and urine 'for all forms of hypochondriac sickness'.[15] But it is convulsions such as hysterical spasms and epilepsy that attract the most obstinate attention from human remedies, particularly those that can be taken from the skull, which is the most precious part of a man. The violence in convulsions could only be countered with violence itself, and for that reason the long-preferred choice was the skull of a hanged man, as he had been killed by a human hand and the body was not buried in consecrated ground.[16] Lemery notes the frequent use of the powdered bone of the head, but dismisses the elixir as nothing but 'a dead head', and therefore lacking essential virtues. He preferred to use the head or brain of 'a young man who had recently died a violent death'.[17] Human blood that was still warm was also a remedy for convulsions, although excessive use of this particular cure was believed to provoke mania.[18]

With the overdetermination of the image of blood, we find ourselves here in a different region of therapeutic efficacy, in the realm of symbolic values. Here was another obstacle between the traditional pharmacopeia and the new forms of medicine and physiology. Some purely symbolic systems remained in place until the end of the classical age, and rather than recipes and secret practices, what they transmitted were images and muted, dream-like symbols whose origins were immemorial. The Serpent, the occasion of the Fall, the visible form of Temptation, the Enemy of Woman *par excellence*, was also her precious remedy in this world of compensation. The bringer of sin and death necessarily also brought healing and life. And among the snakes, it was the most poisonous ones that were the most effective against the vapours and other ills that women were prey to. 'It is to vipers,' writes Madame de Sévigné, 'that I owe my excellent health. They temper the blood, purify and refresh it.' Her desire was for real snakes, not for some bottled remedy or an apothecary's product, but the genuine article fresh from the fields:

> They must be genuine snakes in flesh and blood, and not the powdered variety. Powder brings heat, unless you take it in soup or with cooked cream or some other refreshing drink. Ask Monsieur de Boissy to procure you dozens of vipers from the Poitou region in a box, divided into groups of three or four so that they are comfortable, bedded down with moss and bran. Take two every morning. Cut off their heads, skin them, chop them into pieces and use them to stuff a chicken. Do this for a month.[19]

Against nervous illnesses, the unhinged imagination and the furies of love, symbolic values multiplied their efforts. Only ardour could extinguish ardour, and to appease the boundless appetites of madness, what was needed were lively, dense and violent bodies, which had gone to the flames of a glowing forge a thousand times. In the 'Appendix of Formulae' that follows his *Treatise on Nymphomania*, Bienville proposes seventeen remedies against the fires of love. Most are taken from traditional vegetal remedies, but the fifteenth brings a strange alchemy to these anti-love philtres. What is needed is 'quicksilver revivified with cinnabar', ground up with two drams of gold five times, heated on embers with spirit of vitriol, distilled five times and then reddened for five hours on glowing coals. The mixture is then reduced to powder, and three grains are to be given to the young girl whose imagination is inflamed with chimerical illusions.[20] There could be no doubt that these precious and violent elements, secretly animated with timeless ardours, once their truth and nature had been allowed to flare up so many times, would triumph over the passing heat of a human body, and the secret ebullition of humours and desires, thanks to the archaic magic of *similia similibus* (like curing like). Their fiery truth would be more than a match for that dull, unavowable heat. Bienville's text is from 1778.

We should not be surprised that in Lemery's very serious *Pharmacopeia* there is still to be found an electuary for chastity that is recommended for nervous illnesses, and whose therapeutic indications are thoroughly imbued with the symbolic values of a religious ritual:

> Take camphor, liquorice, the seed of the vine and henbane, waterlilly conserve and waterlilly syrup . . . take two to three drams every morning with a glass of whey, in which a piece of iron heated in the fire has been extinguished.[21]

Desire and its fantasies will be cooled in the calm of the heart, just as the strip of glowing metal will lose its ardour in that most innocent and child-like of drinks. Symbolic schemes like this one survive quite obstinately among the healing methods of the classical age. Neither the reinterpretations proposed in the style of natural philosophy nor the attempts to tone down the more ritualised elements of these cures succeeded, and madness, with all its worrying power and blameworthy moral connotation, seemed to attract this symbolic form of medicine, and to shelter it from the best efforts of positive thought.

For some time to come, asafoetida would still be used to treat hysterics and to banish the world of evil desires and forbidden appetites that were supposed to rise up to the chest, heart, head and brain from the mobile body of the uterus itself. Such a movement is considered to be quite real by Ettmüller, for whom odours had an intrinsic power of attraction and repulsion on the mobile organs of the human body, but it is a repression that becomes increasingly ideal, so that by the mid-eighteenth century the process is no longer a question of mechanics and contradictory movements but has become instead a simple effort to balance, limit and ultimately efface certain sensations. It is with that in mind that Whytt prescribes asafoetida: the disagreeable violence of its odour should diminish the irritability of the sensitive elements of the nervous tissue that it does not affect, and the hysterical pain localised above all in the organs of the stomach and chest instantly disappears:

> These medicines, by the strong and sudden impression they make on the very sensitive nerves of the nose, not only tend to excite the several organs into action, but to lessen or destroy the disagreeable sensation in that part of the body, which brought on the fit.[22]

The image of a smell whose strong effluvia revolt the body is gradually replaced by the more abstract idea of a sensibility that moves around various isolated regions of the body, but this is only a shift in the speculative interpretations of a symbolic scheme that remains unchanged – the scheme of a repression of threats from below by higher orders.

This symbolic cohesiveness around images, rites and ancient moral imperatives continued to organise, in part, medication throughout the classical age, forming cores of resistance that were difficult to conquer.

They were all the harder to conquer for the fact that most practical medicine was not carried out by physicians themselves. Even at the end of the eighteenth century there still existed a whole technical *corpus* centred on curing, over which physicians and men of medicine had no control, because these cures were the work of empirics who were faithful to their recipes, their ciphers and their symbols. The protestations of doctors multiplied right up to the end of the classical age. In 1772, a doctor from Lyon published a significant text on the subject, L'Anarchie médicinale:

> The most important branch of practical medicine is in the hands of people who are strangers to its art: ignorant women, sisters of mercy, charlatans, magi, quacks, matrons, monks, nuns, druggists, herbalists, surgeons and apothecaries treat more diseases and hand out far more remedies than do doctors themselves.[23]

This social fragmentation that separated theory and practice in medicine is notable above all where madness was concerned. Confinement meant that the insane largely escaped the clutches of doctors, and a madman at liberty, more readily than any other patient, was most commonly entrusted to an empiric. In England and France in the second half of the eighteenth century, when hospitals for the insane began to open, it was generally admitted that they should be looked after and treated by the guards rather than by the doctors. It was only with the Doublet circular in France, and the foundation of the Retreat in England, that madness was officially annexed to the realm of medical practice. Previously, in countless ways, its links to a world of extra-medical practices had been so strong and so solidly anchored that these practices were quite naturally used by physicians as well. This explains the paradoxical and heterogeneous appearance of the prescriptions of the time. In them, different modes of thinking, different degrees of technical development and levels of scientific elaboration constantly clash, while the contradiction never seems to be experienced as such.

*

And yet it was the classical age that gave full meaning to the notion of the cure.

It was, doubtless, an old idea, but it took on a new importance in that it gradually replaced the idea of the panacea. The purpose of the panacea was to suppress *all illness*, i.e. all the possible effects of all possible sicknesses, whereas the cure set out to suppress *the whole illness*, i.e. everything that determined and was determined, in a particular sickness. The different phases of the cure were therefore to be articulated around the elements that constituted the sickness. From this point onwards, sickness began to be perceived as a natural unity, which automatically defined the logic of the prescription and determined it by its own development. The different stages of the cure, the phases through which it passed and the moments that constituted it were to be articulated around the visible nature of the sickness, to match its various contradictions and pursue each of its causes. Furthermore, a cure was to pay attention to its own effects, compensate, correct and alter itself according to the different stages of the improvement, and even contradict itself if the nature of the illness and the temporary effect that it produced demanded it.

As well as being a practice, all cures were therefore a spontaneous reflection on the cure itself and on illness, and on the relation between the two. The result was not simply a report, but an experiment too, and medical theory began to come into being as a result of this process of experimentation. Something new, which was soon to become the domain of the clinic, was beginning to appear.

This was a domain where the constant and reciprocal relation between theory and practice was supplemented by an immediate confrontation between doctors and patients. Suffering and knowledge were to adjust to each other in the unity of a common experience. And this would require a common language, a communication at the very least imagined between the doctor and the patient.

It was with diseases of the nerves that eighteenth-century cures found the most varied models, and consolidated their place as the most important techniques that medicine had to offer. It is as though at last, in a particularly privileged manner, the exchange between medicine and madness, which had been so obstinately refused by the world of confinement, was finally established.

In these cures, often too hastily dismissed as fantastical, what was born was the possibility of psychiatric observation, of a confinement closer to hospitalisation, and of that dialogue with the mad which, from Pinel to Leuret and from Charcot to Freud, was to borrow such strange vocabularies.

Let us attempt to reconstitute some of the therapeutic ideas that organised the cures for madness.

1   *Consolidation.* Somewhere in madness, even in its most agitated forms, there was a whole component of weakness. If the spirits are subject to irregular movements, this is because they no longer have the force or the strength to follow the gravity of their normal course. If spasms and convulsions are common in nervous diseases, it is because the fibre is too mobile, too irritable or overly sensitive to vibrations, and above all lacking in robustness. Behind the apparent violence of madness, which sometimes

seems to multiply the strength of maniacs to an alarming degree, there is always a secret weakness, an essential lack of resistance, and the fury of the mad is ultimately no more than a passive form of violence. What should be sought is a cure that would give vigour to the spirits or the fibres, but a calm vigour, a strength that no disorder could destabilise, such would be its harmony with the natural law. More than an image of liveliness or vigour, what matters here is hardiness, joined to the idea of a new elasticity, young but already tamed. What is sought is a strength that would prevail over nature, to reinforce nature herself.

Physicians dream of remedies that 'take the side, so to speak' of the spirits, 'helping them conquer the cause that put them in a ferment'. Taking the side of the spirits means fighting the vain agitation to which they are subject despite themselves, and helping them resist the chemical processes that cause them to heat up, bringing unrest, and providing them with the solidity they need to resist the vapours that aim to suffocate them and make them inert, or carry them off in their turbulence. Against the vapours, spirits are to be reinforced 'by the most revolting odours', as disagreeable sensations strengthen spirits and in effect force them into revolt, so they rush into action to repel the assault. To that end doctors employ 'asafoetida, oil of amber, burnt feathers and leather, and anything that might bring intensely disagreeable sensations to the soul'. Against the ferment, theriac is given, as are 'antiepileptic spirits of Charras' and the legendary Queen of Hungary water; acidity disappears, and the spirits return to their normal density.[24] Finally, to restore them to the appropriate mobility, Lange recommends that the spirits be subjected to sensations and movements that are at once agreeable, measured and regular:

> When the animal spirits are dispersed and disorganised, what is required are remedies that calm their movements and return them to their natural course, such as objects that bring the soul a sweet and moderate pleasure, agreeable odours, a walk through delicious places, the sight of people who in the past have brought pleasure, and music.[25]

This firm sweetness, an agreeable heaviness and calm liveliness are to protect the body and consolidate inside the organism the fragile elements that provide the means of communication between body and soul.

But there was no better roborant than the use of the one element known both for its strength and its docility, its resistance and its capacity to be turned to any use that man required: iron was key to the success of many cures. Its privileged nature was compounded of qualities that were quickly contradictory when isolated. Nothing resisted longer than iron, and no substance was more obedient. It was to be found in nature, but it was also of use in countless human techniques. What better way could there be of assisting nature and lending it additional strength than using iron? Iron was the element closest to nature, yet most submissive to man. The example most often quoted is the ancient case of Dioscorides, who had given to the inertia of water virtues of strength alien to it, by plunging a red-hot poker into it. The ardour of the fire, the calm mobility of the water, and the rigour of a metal treated until it became malleable – all these elements, united, conferred on water a power of reinforcement, revivification, and consolidation that could be transmitted to the organism. But iron was effective even in the raw state. Sydenham recommends it in its simplest form, by the ingestion of iron filings.[26] Whytt knew a man who, to cure himself of weak stomach nerves that had brought on a permanent state of hypochondria, took as many as 230 grains a day.[27] This was because as well as all its virtues, iron has the remarkable property of transmitting its power directly and without any intermediary or transformation. What it communicates is not its substance but its strength. Paradoxically, given its resistance, it is quickly dissipated in the organism, leaving only its qualities, without rust or waste. What directed discussive thought here was the imagery of strength-bringing iron, which outweighed even observation. If experiments were carried out, it was not so that they might reveal any positive causal connection, but to isolate this immediate communication of qualities. Wright fed some Mars salts to a dog, and observed an hour later that the chyle, when mixed with tincture of oak apples, did not demonstrate the dark purple shades that would unmistakeably reveal that the iron had been absorbed. He therefore concluded that iron, without passing through the digestive processes, without passing through the blood, and without substantially penetrating the organism, directly fortified the membranes and the fibres. More than a proven effect, the consolidation of the spirits and the nerves appeared to be an operative metaphor that implied a transfer of force without any discursive dynamic. Strength passed through contact, independently of any exchange of substances, or any communication of movement.

2   *Purification.* With its associations of clogged viscera and minds bubbling with false ideas, fermentation of vapours and violence, corruption of

liquids and of spirits, madness calls for a whole series of therapeutics that can all be linked to the same purification process.

The dream was of a total purification, the simplest but also the most impossible of cures. It was to consist of the replacement of the thick, overloaded blood of melancholics, heavy with bitter humours, with light, clear blood whose fresh movement would dissipate delirium. In 1662, Moritz Hoffman had suggested blood transfusions as a remedy against melancholy. Within a few years, the idea had had sufficient success for the London Philosophical Society to plan a series of operations on subjects locked up in Bethlem hospital, but Allen, the physician in charge, refused.[28] Denis, however, did try it on one of his patients, a man stricken with amorous melancholia. He drew ten ounces of blood, which he replaced with a slightly lesser quantity drawn from the femoral artery of a calf, and repeated the operation the following day with only a few ounces. The patient's condition improved, his mind cleared day by day, and soon he was entirely back on his feet: 'all the professors at the school of surgery confirmed this'.[29] But despite further subsequent successes, the technique was quickly abandoned.[30]

Preferred methods were medications that acted against corruption. It was well known 'from experiments dating back 3,000 years that myrrh and aloes preserve corpses'.[31] It was supposed that the changes undergone by corpses were of the same nature as those that accompanied sicknesses of the humours, so products like myrrh and aloes, or better still Paracelsus' famous elixir, were highly recommended in the treatment of the vapours.[32] Corruption, however, was not simply to be prevented, it was to be destroyed as well. For that reason, there were therapeutics that attacked the changes themselves, and sought either to change the course of the corrupted matter or to dissolve the corrupting substances; techniques of diversion, and techniques of cleansing.

Among the first group were all the properly physical methods that tended to lacerate the surface of the body, creating wounds, centres of infection that freed the organism and centres of evacuation towards the exterior. Fallowes thus explains the curative mechanism of his *Oleum Cephalicum*. In madness, he says, 'the brain is disturbed by black vapours which clog the finer vessels through which the animal spirits ought freely to pass'. The blood therefore loses its direction, and clogs the veins in the brain, where it remains and stagnates, unless it is shaken up by a movement 'which causes a hurry and confusion of the mind'. *Oleum*

Cephalicum has the advantage of 'raising small pustules on the head', and once they are anointed with oil to prevent them from drying out, they can remain open for the 'black vapours fixed upon the brain'.[33] A similar effect could be achieved by burning and cauterising the body. It was even supposed that skin conditions like scabies, eczema, and smallpox could bring an end to an attack of madness, as the corruption left the viscera and the brain and spread to the surface of the body, and thence to the outside world. By the end of the century, it became customary to inoculate with scabies in the most serious cases of mania. Doublet, in his 1785 *Instruction* to hospital directors, recommends that if bleeding, purging, baths and showers fail to cure cases of mania, then recourse should be made to 'cauters, setons, superficial abscesses and inoculation with scabies'.[34]

But the principal task was the dissolution of the different fermentations in the body that brought on madness in the first place.[35] Bitters were first on the list. Bitterness had the harshness of seawater, and purified and corroded. Its corrosiveness acted on the useless, unhealthy and impure residues that sickness left in the body or in the soul. Coffee, bitter and sharp, was useful for 'fat people whose thickened humours circulate with difficulty'.[36] It brought dryness without burning, for bodies of this type dissipated superfluous humours without dangerous heat. Coffee was fire without flames, a powerful purifying substance that left no residue. It reduced impurity:

> Those who use the substance know by long experience that it restores the stomach, that it consumes superfluous dampness, that it dissipates wind, dissolves the mucus in the bowels, where it forms a mild abstersion, and of particular merit, prevents fumes from rising up to the head, and consequently dulls and sweetens the pains that we customarily feel there; lastly it brings strength, vigour and acuity to animal spirits, while leaving no great impression of heat, not even in the most burnt people who customarily use it.[37]

Bitter but tonic, the quinine that Whytt freely prescribed to people whose nervous fibres were delicate was effective against 'weakness and feebleness', and one cure that consisted of nothing but quinine (his 'tincture of the bark') 'once a day for near two years, intermitting now and then a week or ten days' was enough to cure one woman afflicted with a nervous condition.[38] Delicate patients might blend quinine with something sweeter tasting, but if the constitution was strong, nothing was more effective than quinine mixed with vitriol. Twenty or thirty drops of elixir of vitriol was a sovereign remedy.[39]

Naturally, soap and its associated products also had a privileged place in this type of purification. 'Soap dissolves almost anything concrete.'[40] Tissot was of the opinion that taken directly, soap cured many ills, but that often it was enough, first thing in the morning, to eat either alone or with bread, 'soapy fruits', i.e. cherries, strawberries, redcurrants, figs, oranges, raisins, ripe pears, 'and other fruits of that sort'.[41] But there were cases where the obstruction was sufficiently immovable for soap to be of no benefit. Soluble tartar was the next step. Muzzell was the first person to think of prescribing tartar against madness and melancholy, and published several victorious observations on the subject.[42] These were confirmed by Whytt, who also demonstrated that tartar acted as a cleansing product as it was most effective against obstructive diseases:

> As far as I have observed, the soluble tartar is more useful in maniac or melancholic disorders, proceeding from noxious vapours in the *primae viae* [primary arteries], than in those which are only due to a fault in the brain.[43]

Among other solvents, Raulin quotes honey, chimney soot, oriental saffron, woodlice, powdered shrimp claw and bezoar.[44]

Half-way between these techniques of dissolution and the externalisation of the malady there existed another series of practices, the most frequent of which was the application of vinegar. As an acid, vinegar dissolved obstructions and destroyed bodies that were in the process of fermenting. But when applied externally, it worked as a revulsive, drawing harmful liquids and humours to the surface. Curiously, but not uncharacteristically for the therapeutics of the time, no contradiction was perceived between these two modes of action. Given that by its *nature* vinegar was both revulsive and detersive, it was normal that it should act in both manners, even if one of the modalities of its action could not be analysed in a rational and discursive manner. It functioned directly, without an intermediary, by the simple contact of two natural elements. What was therefore recommended was rubbing vinegar into the head and the skull, which should be shaved whenever possible.[45] The *Gazette de médecine* quoted the case of an empiric who had managed to cure a large number of madmen by a quite prompt and simple method. His secret is as follows. After purging the upper and lower regions, he soaks the patient's feet and hands in vinegar and leaves them in that position until they fall asleep, or rather until they wake up, and the majority find themselves cured when they awaken. He also applies pounded Dipsacus leaves to the patients' skulls, or fuller's teasel.[46]

3   Immersion. Two themes meet here – the idea of ablution, with all the associations that link it to rituals of purity and rebirth, and the more physiological idea of impregnation that modifies the essential qualities of liquids and solids. Despite their different origins and the gap between their different levels of conceptual elaboration, they formed a sufficiently coherent unit up until the close of the eighteenth century for the opposition not to take on any great importance. The idea of Nature and all its ambiguities served as a cohesive element. Water, a simple, primitive liquid, belonged to all that was most pure in Nature, and the doubtful modifications that man brought to the essential bounty of Nature did nothing to alter the beneficial effects of water. When civilisation, social life, or the imaginary desires elicited by the reading of novels or theatrical spectacles brought on a nervous illness, the return to the limpidity of water had a ritual sense of purification, and through its transparent freshness innocence was reborn. But at the same time, water, which nature had included in the composition of all bodies, restored equilibrium, and was a universal physiological regulator. Tissot, who was a disciple of Rousseau, expressed all these themes, through an imagination that was as much moral as it was medical:

> Nature gave water to all Nations as their sovereign beverage; she gave it the strength to dissolve all sorts of food; it is agreeable to the palate; choose therefore water that is cold, light and soft; it fortifies and cleans the intestines; the Greeks and Romans considered it a universal remedy.[47]

The use of immersion goes back a long way in the history of madness. The baths practised at Epidaurus would be proof enough of that, but cold applications of all varieties must have been common currency in the classical world since Soranus of Ephesus protested against their abuse, if Caelius Aurelianus is to be believed.[48] During the Middle Ages, it was traditional to plunge maniacs into the water several times, 'until they had lost their strength and forgotten their fury'. Sylvius also recommended impregnations for cases of melancholy and frenzy.[49] The eighteenth-century idea that the usefulness of baths had suddenly been discovered by Van Helmont was therefore something of a reinterpretation. According to Menuret, this invention, which he dated back to the mid-seventeenth century, was the result of a fortunate coincidence. A lunatic was being transported in a cart, when suddenly he managed to slip off his chains and jumped into a lake, where he tried to swim and passed out. When he was recaptured, it was first thought that he had died, but when he came to, he had miraculously found his wits once again, and went on 'to live for a long time, suffering no more from madness'. The story was that this anecdote had been a flash of inspiration for Van Helmont, who set about plunging lunatics into baths of fresh water and sea water indiscriminately: 'the only concern is that they should be plunged suddenly and unexpect-edly into the water, and that they should be kept there a good length of time. There is no risk to life.'[50]

The truth of the story is of little importance. But one thing is certain, even when transcribed in anecdotal form: from the end of the seventeenth century onwards, the cure by baths was, or was once more, the most common form of treatment for insanity. When Doublet drew up his *Instruction* shortly before the Revolution, he prescribed for the four patho-logical forms of madness that he recognised (frenzy, mania, melancholia and imbecility) the regular use of baths, adding the use of cold showers for the first two.[51] By then, Cheyne had long since recommended that people 'who needed to fortify their temperament' should install baths in their house, and use them every second, third or fourth day, and 'those that cannot afford such conveniency, as often as they can, to go into a river or living pond, to wash their bodies'.[52]

The importance accorded to water is evident in medical practices dominated by a concern with balancing liquids and solids. For if it had powers of impregnation that placed it in the first rank of humectants, water could also transmit supplementary qualities like heat and cold, and virtues of constriction, refreshment and heat, and thus possessed the consolidating effects associated with bodies like iron. In fact, in the fluid substance of water, the game of qualities was highly labile, and just as easily as it penetrated the weave of tissues, it allowed itself to be impreg-nated with all the qualitative influences to which it was subjected. Paradoxically, the universality of its use in the eighteenth century was not a result of the widespread recognition of its effects and its mode of action, but of the ease with which the most contradictory forms could be attributed to that effectiveness. In water, all possible therapeutic themes met, forming an inexhaustible reserve of operative metaphors. It is in this fluid element that the universal exchange of qualities could take place.

Naturally, cold water cooled. For that reason it was used in mania and frenzy, sicknesses of heat where the spirits were in ebullition, solids tightened and liquids were heated to the point of evaporation, leaving the brain of the patient 'dry and brittle', as anatomists regularly demonstrated. Reasonably enough Boissieu includes cold water among his list of refreshing cures: baths were the foremost 'antiphlogistic', purifying the body of any excessive igneous particles to be found there. Taken as a drink, it was a 'dilutive procastinant' that diminished the resistance of fluids to the action of solids, thereby indirectly lowering the general heat of the body.[53]

But it was also said that cold water brought heat and that hot water cooled. Such at least was the thesis defended by Darut. Cold baths chased the blood from the periphery of the body and pushed it 'with increased vigour towards the heart'. As the heart was the seat of natural heat, the blood was warmed there, all the more so as

> the heart, which struggles alone against all the other parts, makes renewed efforts to expel the blood and overcome capillary resistance. What results is a greater intensity of circulation, the division of the blood, the fluidity of the humours, the destruction of congestions, an increase in the strength of the natural heat, of the appetite of the digestive forces, and the activity of the body and the mind.

A symmetrical paradox operated regarding hot baths: blood was attracted to the extremities of the body, as were the humours, sweat, and all forms of liquid, both beneficial and harmful. The vital centres were therefore deserted, the heart slowed and the organism thus began to cool down. This fact was confirmed by the 'fainting, lipothymia . . . weakness, nonchalance, lassitude, and lack of vigour' that generally accompanied excessive bathing with hot water.[54]

But there was more. So great was the polyvalence of water, so great was its aptitude to submit itself to the qualities that it carried, that it sometimes lost its efficacy as a liquid and acted as a desiccant instead. Water could prevent dampness. In part, this was the old principle of *similia similibus*, but in another sense, and by the intermediary of a visible mechanism. For some, it was cold water that brought dryness, as heat kept water humid. Heat dilated the pores of the organism, distended its membranes, and allowed humidity to impregnate them as a secondary effect. Liquids made their way through heat. For that reason, the hot drinks so widely used in the seventeenth century risked becoming a danger, and those who took too many risked relaxation, general dampness and a weakness of the whole organism. As these were traits commonly associated with the feminine body, as opposed to the dry, virile solidity of the male,[55] the abuse of hot drinks could lead to a general feminisation of the human race:

> Not without reason, the reproach is made to the majority of men that they have softened and degenerated, taking on the habits and inclinations of women – the only thing lacking is a physical resemblance. The abuse of humectants could accelerate the metamorphosis, and render the two sexes almost identical both physically and morally. Woe betide the human race if this prejudice ever spreads to the masses: there will be no more labourers, artisans or soldiers, as they will have lost the strength and vigour necessary for their profession.[56]

In cold water, the low temperature was more important than the power of humidity, because by forcing the tissues to contract, it prevented the possibility of impregnation: 'The manner in which our vessels and the tissue of our flesh tightens when we wash in cold water or are numbed with cold is plain to see.'[57] Cold baths therefore had the paradoxical property of consolidating the organism, and fortifying it against the softness brought by moisture, 'toning the parts', as Hoffmann said, 'and strengthening the systaltic force of the heart and the vessels'.[58]

But the relationship was reversed in other qualitative intuitions. Then it was heat that checked the humidifying properties of water, whereas cool maintained them and renewed them ceaselessly. Against diseases of the nerves due to 'shrivelling of the nervous tissue' and 'dryness of the membranes', Pomme did not recommend hot baths, as they encouraged the heat that reigned in the body; but warm or cold, they were capable of penetrating the tissues of the organism, and returning them to their natural suppleness.[59] This was the method that was practised quite spontaneously in America.[60] Its effects and even its mechanism were quite discernible to the naked eye, as the cure progressed, as when the crisis reached its highest intensity, patients floated to the top of the water in their bath, so much had the internal heat rarefied the air and the liquid in their bodies; but if they remained too long in the water, 'three, four or even six hours per day', then relaxation followed, water progressively impregnated the membranes and fibres, the body grew heavier and naturally sank down to the bottom of the water.[61]

At the end of the eighteenth century, the power of water began to wane, as a result of this excess of natural qualities. Cold, it could heat, warm, it cooled, and rather than bringing damp, it could solidify and petrify through cold, or keep a fire going simply by means of its own heat. All the beneficial and harmful values were inextricably mixed amongst its qualities, and it was prone to all forms of complicity. To medical thought, it was a therapeutic theme with infinite possibilities, whose effects could be seen in many diverse pathological and physiological situations. So varied were its modes of action, it could be used to affirm or deny almost anything. That polyvalence of course, and the discussions to which it gave rise, were ultimately its neutralisation. By the time of Pinel, water cures were still practised, but the element had become again entirely transparent. Water was cleansed of all its qualitative charges, and its action had become purely mechanical.

The shower, which until this point had been less employed than baths and drinks, then took over as the preferred technique. Paradoxically, after all the physiological variations of the preceding era, water once again reverted to its simple function of purification. The only quality it was now credited with was violence, washing away in an irresistible flow all the impurities that formed madness. Its curative force reduced individuals to their most simple expression, their purest form of existence, and so brought a kind of second birth. To Pinel's mind, this was a matter of 'destroying even the primitive traces of the eccentric ideas of the insane . . . this can only take place by reducing such ideas to a state, so to speak, close to death'.[62] This led to the infamous techniques used in asylums like Charenton at the end of the eighteenth and the start of the nineteenth centuries. In the cold shower proper, 'the lunatic was tied to a chair and placed under a reservoir filled with cold water, which poured down directly onto his head through a wide pipe'. The variant was the surprise bath, where 'the patient was taken down the corridors to the ground floor, and arrived in a square room with a vaulted ceiling, where a large bath had been constructed; he was then tipped backwards into the water'.[63] This violence promised the rebirth of a baptism.

4 *Regulation of movement.* If it was true that madness was an irregular agitation of the spirits, the disordered motion of fibres and ideas, then it was also true that it was an obstruction of the body and soul, a stagnation of the humours, an immobility of the fibres in their rigidity, a fixation of the ideas and the attention on one theme that gradually prevailed over all others. The aim then was to restore life-giving mobility to the body and soul, to the mind and the animal spirits. That mobility, however, had to be measured and controlled to ensure that it did not become an empty agitation of the fibres no longer related to stimuli from the outside world. So the idea behind this particular therapeutic theme was the restoration of a movement in harmony with the well-ordered mobility of the outside world. As madness could just as easily be dull immobility and obstinate fixation as disorder and agitation, the cure consisted in eliciting in patients a movement that was both regular and real, so that it obeyed once again the rules of movement of the world.

In this context, the solid beliefs of the ancient world concerning the salutary effects of the different forms of walking and running were often invoked. Walking brought suppleness and firmness to the body, while running in a straight line at a constantly increasing speed spread the juices and humours throughout the body, while diminishing the weight of the organs, and running fully dressed warmed and softened the tissues, restoring mobility to overly rigid fibres.[64] Sydenham recommended horseback riding above all else as a cure for hypochondria and melancholy:

> But nothing of all I have hitherto known does so much comfort and strengthen the blood and spirits, as riding much on horseback every day for a long while; for, since by this kind of exercise, the lower belly is most strongly mov'd, in which the vessels for excretion (as many as are appointed by nature to drain the impurities of the blood) are situated, what disorder of the functions, or other natural impotence of the organs, can be imagin'd so great, as not to be helped by the frequent jolting of the horse, and then too in the open air, whose innate heat is so extinguished, that it cannot be stirr'd up by this motion and ferment afresh? Or what preternatural substance, or deprav'd juices, can there be in any creek of these parts which cannot by this exercise of the body, be either reduc'd to such a constitution as is agreeable to nature, or scattered

every way, and ejected? Moreover, the blood being perpetually exagitated by this motion, and thoroughly mix'd, is as were, renewed, and grows vigorous again.[65]

Of all the movements of the world, the motion of the sea was perhaps the most natural, the most regular, and the most closely tied to the movement of the cosmos. De Lancre had judged the motion perilous for the human heart, seeing the very image of evil infinity in the hazardous temptations and improbable, unattainable dreams that it inspired. The eighteenth century considered it a privileged regulator of organic mobility, where what spoke was the rhythm of nature itself. Gilchrist wrote an entire treatise on *The Use of Sea Voyages in Medicine*. Whytt found the cure impractical for subjects suffering from melancholy:

> As we find it very difficult to prevail with any patient in this place to undertake a long sea voyage, I can say little on this from my own experience. However, . . . a young gentleman who had long been subject to epileptic fits at land, was never seized with them when at sea.[66]

Travel had the supplementary advantage of acting directly on the course of the ideas, or at least in a manner more direct that many as it passes only through the sensations. Variety in the landscape dissipated the obduracy of melancholy. This was a remedy that had been known since antiquity, but it was prescribed in the eighteenth century with renewed zeal.[67] It took many forms, and included not simply real journeys but also imaginary voyages in literature and the theatre. To 'relax the brain' in all cases of vaporous afflictions, Le Camus prescribed 'walks, journeys of all descriptions, horse riding, exercise in the open air, dance, theatrical spectacles, light-hearted reading, and any occupation to distract the mind from its central pre-occupation'.[68] The countryside, through the sweetness and variety of its landscapes, roused melancholics from their brooding, 'distancing them from the places that might recall the memory of their pain'.[69]

Inversely, the agitation brought on by mania could also be controlled by the beneficial effects of regular movement. Here it was not so much a matter of re-establishing movement as of regulating the agitation, and momentarily halting its course to arrest the attention. Travel was effective not on account of its interruptions of continuity, but because of the novelty of the objects that it proposed and the curiosity that it engendered.

It should permit the capture from the exterior of a mind without rule, lost to itself in the vibration of its inner movement:

> If it can be perceived that there are objects or persons that can call off their attention from the pursuit of their own disordered imagination, and can fix it a little upon some others; these last may be frequently presented to them; and for this reason a journey, both by its having the effect of interrupting all train of thought, and by presenting objects engaging attention, may often be useful.[70]

Used for the changes that it brought to melancholy, or the regularity that it imposed on mania, movement therapy conceals the idea that the world was establishing control over the mind of the madman. The therapy was both a forcing of the mind 'back into step' and a conversion, as movement prescribed rhythm, and also constituted in its novelty and variety a constant appeal to the spirit to emerge from its own preoccupations and re-engage with the world. If it is true to say that an ethical memory lurked in the immersion techniques, a practice redolent of religious ablution and rebirth, then it is also fair to say that a similar moral theme was also to be found in movement cures, but that this was the inverse of the former: here the call was for the mind to return to wisdom by accepting its place in the general order, thereby forgetting madness, which was the moment of pure subjectivity. We see here how the great organising structures of the experience of madness in the classical age penetrated even the empirical mechanisms of the cure. As error and fault, madness was impurity and solitude, a retreat from the world and from truth, and it was therefore an imprisonment in evil. Its double void was to be the visible form of the non-being that was evil, proffering in its brightly coloured but empty delirium the non-being of error. It was totally *pure*, as it was nothing more than the evanescent point of a subjectivity from which the presence of all truth had been removed, and it was totally *impure*, as the nothingness that constituted its being was the non-being of evil. The technique of the cure, even in its physical symbols most highly charged with imaginative intensity (the consolidation and restoration of movement on the one hand, purification and immersion on the other), is secretly structured around those two fundamental themes. The subject is to be restored to his initial purity, torn away from his pure subjectivity and reinserted in the world; the non-being that alienates him from himself is to be destroyed, that he might be opened again to the plenitude of the world and the solid truth of being.

The techniques long outlived their meaning. When madness took on a purely psychological and moral status, beyond the experience of unreason, and the relations between error and fault used by classicism to define madness were reduced to the sole notion of culpability, the techniques remained, but their meaning became much more restricted, as their only aim was a mechanical effect or a moral punishment. An example of this is the manner in which these concerns with movement degenerated into the famous 'rotatory swing', of which the mechanism and the effectiveness was demonstrated in the early nineteenth century by Mason Cox.[71] A vertical pillar was fixed between the floor and the ceiling, and the patient was tied to a chair or a bed that rotated on a horizontal arm around the pillar. An 'uncomplicated mechanism' enabled the desired speed to be set. Mason Cox quotes one of his own observations, the case of a man struck with a melancholy stupor:

> His countenance attached to saturnine blackness, the eyes, suffused with bile, were immovably fixed on the ground, the limbs seemed deprived of their locomotive powers, the action of the lungs, and the circulation, retarded, the tongue parched and silent, and the whole man resembled an automaton.[72]

He was placed on the rotatory machine, and subjected to ever increasing motion. The results surpassed all expectations, and the excessive rotation meant that the rigidity of melancholy was replaced by a manic agitation. But after the initial effects had worn off, the patient returned to his original state. The rhythm was therefore modified, and the machine was again set in rapid motion, but was stopped at regular intervals, in a quite brutal manner. The melancholy disappeared, while the rotations were too short to set off any fit of mania. This 'centrifuging' of melancholy was typical of the new use of older therapeutic ideas. Movement was no longer a means of restoring the patient to the truth of the world that surrounded him, but simply an attempt to bring about a number of internal changes of a purely mechanical and psychological variety. The cure no longer revolved around a core idea of truth, but was dominated by the idea of a behavioural norm instead. In this reinterpretation of old methods, the organism was merely brought into line with itself and its own nature, whereas in the initial version, the drive was towards repairing its relation with the world, its essential link to being and truth. Confirmation of that is to be found in the fact that from an early stage, the rotatory machine was used as a punishment threat, a clear demonstration that the rich, heavy meanings behind the therapeutic aims of the classical age were forgotten.[73] It was enough to regulate and punish, using the means that had previously served to prevent faults, and dissipate errors, restoring madness to the shining truth of the world.

*

In 1771, regarding *nymphomania*, Bienville wrote that it could on occasion be resolved 'simply by treating the imagination; but in almost no case could physical remedy alone bring about a radical cure'.[74] Later, Beauchesne came up with a similar idea:

> We try in vain to cure men of madness, if we content ourselves with physical means . . . Material remedies will never bring complete success, without the help that a fair, healthy mind will bring to a weak and feeble spirit.[75]

These texts did not discover the necessity of a psychological treatment, but rather marked the end of an era: the end of a time when the difference between physical medicine and moral treatments was not yet considered obvious by medical thought. The unity of symbols was beginning to fall apart, and techniques were beginning to detach themselves from their global significance. Their efficacy was now limited, affecting the soul or the body independently. Once again, the meaning of the cure had changed: it was no longer borne by the significant unity of the disease, and grouped around its major qualities, but segment by segment, it began to address the diverse elements that composed it. It was now to be made up of a series of partial destructions, where the psychological attack and the physical intervention were juxtaposed, and added together, but never blended.

In fact, what appears to our modern eyes as an embryonic sketch of a psychological cure was no such thing for the classical physicians who applied it. Since the Renaissance, music had regained all the therapeutic values with which it had been associated in Antiquity. Its effects were particularly noteworthy with madness. Schenck cured a man who had 'sunk into a profound state of melancholy' by making him listen to 'concerts of musical instruments of which he was particularly fond'.[76] Albrecht too cured a man suffering from delirium, when all other remedies had failed, by having a song sung during his fits, 'which woke the patient, bringing him great pleasure, and vanquishing the paroxysm for good'.[77] The literature even quotes cases of frenzy that were cured by music.[78] But these observations are never given a psychological inter-pretation. If music cured, it was because it acted on the whole human being, penetrating the body as directly and effectively as it did the soul. Diemerbroek claimed to have known plague sufferers who had been cured by music.[79] Few still believed with Porta that music, in the material reality of its sound, brought to the body the secret virtues hidden in the sub-stance of the instruments, and that lymphatic sufferers were cured by 'a lively air played on a holly flute', nor that melancholics were soothed by 'a sweet air played on a hellebore flute', nor that impotent or frigid men could be cured with 'a flute made from larkspur or iris stems'.[80] But if music no longer transported the virtues hidden in substances, it was effective on the body thanks to the qualities that it imposed upon it. Music was the most rigorous of all the mechanics of quality, as its origin was nothing other than movement, which was immediately transformed into qualitative effect once in the ear. The therapeutic value of music came from the manner in which that transformation was reversed in the body, as quality broke up once more into movement, and the pleasure of sensa-tion became once more what it had been at the outset, regular vibration and an equilibrium of tension. Man, as the unity of body and soul, walked backwards through the cycle of harmony, going from the harmonious to the harmonic. The music fell into its component parts, but health was restored. But there was another path, more direct and more effective, where man no longer played the negative role of anti-instrument, but reacted as though he himself had become the instrument:

> If one conceives of the human body as an assemblage of fibres of varying tensions, ignoring their sensibility, their life and their movement, one can easily understand that music will have the same effect on the fibres as it does on the strings of adjacent instruments.

This resonant effect had no need to follow the long and complex path of auditory sensation. The nervous fibres vibrate with the music that fills the air; the fibres are like 'deaf dancers' moving in unison to music that they cannot hear. And on this occasion it is inside the body, from the nervous fibre all the way to the soul, that the recomposition is enacted, the harmonic structure of consonance restoring the harmonious function of the passions.[81]

The use of passion in the therapeutics of madness should not be understood as a kind of psychological medication. To employ passion against dementia meant nothing more than addressing the unity of the body and soul in its most rigorous aspect, using an event in the double system of its effects, and in the immediate correspondence of their signification. Curing madness with passion meant that one placed oneself in the reciprocal symbolism of the body and the soul. Fear, in the eighteenth century, was considered to be one of the passions that it was most desirable to elicit in the insane. It was thought of as being the natural complement of the constraints imposed on maniacs and the frenzied, and the dream was of a conditioning whereby each fit of anger in a maniac would be immediately accompanied and compensated by a reaction of fear:

> It is by strength that we triumph over the frenzy of the maniac; and it is by opposing fear to anger that anger can be tamed. If the terror of a punishment and public shaming become associated in the mind with fits of anger, the one will not manifest itself without the other: the poison and the antidote will become inseparable.[82]

But fear was effective not only on the level of the effects of the illness: the sickness itself was reached and suppressed. It had the property of fixing the functioning of the nervous system, and somehow petrifying the overly mobile fibres, putting a brake on their disordered movements: 'fear, being a passion that diminishes excitement, may therefore be opposed to the excesses of it, and particularly to the irascible excitement of maniacs'.[83]

If the antithetical coupling of fear and anger was effective against manic irritation, it could also be used in the opposite manner against the ill-grounded fears of melancholics, hypochondriacs and anyone of a lymphatic temperament. Tissot, taking up the traditional idea that anger was a discharge of bile, thought that it had its uses for dissolving the phlegm that gathered in the stomach and the blood. By submitting the fibres to a higher level of tension, anger brought renewed vigour, restored the missing elasticity, and allowed the fear to be dissipated.[84] The passion cure relied on the constant metaphor of quality and movement, always implying that they should be immediately transferable in their modality from the body to the soul, and vice versa. As Scheidenmantel noted in a treatise that he devoted to this form of cure, it should be invoked 'when the cure necessitated in the body changes identical to those produced by this passion'. And in that sense, it could be a universal substitute for any other form of physical therapy, as it was simply an alternative path that would produce the same chain of effects. Between a cure that used the passions and a cure that relied on pharmaceutical ingredients, there was no difference of nature, but rather a difference in the means of access to the mechanisms common to both the body and the soul. 'We must use the passions, if the patient cannot be brought, by reason, to do all that is necessary for the reestablishment of health.'[85]

It is therefore not possible, properly speaking, to apply to the classical age a distinction, or at least a meaningful division, of the sort that is immediately apparent to us, between physical and psychological or moral medication. That difference only came into being the day fear was no longer used as a means of fixing movement, but as punishment instead, and when joy no longer meant an organic dilation but a reward, and when anger had become nothing more than a response to a process of humiliation; when, in short, the nineteenth century, through the invention of its notorious 'moral methods', had brought madness and its cure into the domain of guilt.[86] The distinction between the physical and the moral only became a practical concept in the medicine of minds when the problematics of madness were displaced towards the interrogation of a responsible subject. The purely moral space that was then defined measures exactly the psychological interiority where modern men seek both their depth and their truth. In the first half of the nineteenth century, physical therapeutics became the cure of innocent determinism, and moral treatments were used for errant liberty. From then on, psychology, as a means of cure, was organised around the idea of punishment. Before seeking to soothe, it inserted suffering within the rigour of moral necessity.

> Do not use consolation, for it is useless. Do not use reasoning, for you will not persuade. Do not be sad with melancholics, as your sadness will confirm theirs; nor should you be gay with them, or they will feel offended. What is needed is a cool head, and whenever necessary, a dose

of severity. Your reason should control their behaviour. The only string that still vibrates within them is pain; be courageous enough to pluck it.[87]

The heterogeneity of the physical and the moral in medical thought was not a result of the Cartesian distinction between thinking and extended substances: a century and a half of post-Cartesian medicine had not been sufficient to accept this separation fully, both at the level of the problems it set out to solve and at that of its methods, nor to consider the distinction between substances as an opposition between the organic and the psychological. Cartesian or anti-Cartesian, classical medicine never ventured so far as to apply his metaphysical dualism to anthropology. And when the separation was made, it was not on account of some renewed faithfulness to the *Meditations*, but rather owing to a renewed importance laid on the idea of the fault. Where the mad were concerned, only the practice of punishment separated the medicine of the body and the soul. A purely psychological medicine was only made possible when madness was alienated into guilt.

*

One aspect of the practical medicine of the classical age might provide a counter-argument to that. A psychological element, in a pure form, did have a place in some techniques. How else might we explain the importance attached to exhortation, persuasion and reasoning, and the whole dialogue that physicians of the classical age engaged in with their patients, independently of cures brought about by corporeal remedies? How else can we explain ideas like the following, which Sauvages shared with so many of his contemporaries:

> One must be a philosopher to be able to cure the sicknesses of the soul. For as the origin of such diseases is nothing other than a violent wish for a thing that the patient considers to be a good, it is the duty of the physician to come up with solid reasons showing that the thing that he desires with such force is good in appearance only, and is in fact evil in reality, thereby turning the patient away from the error that he has chosen to follow.[88]

In fact this approach to madness is no more or less psychological than all the others mentioned so far. Language, the formulation of truth or morality, has a direct effect upon the body, and Bienville, in his treatise on *Nymphomania*, had shown how the adoption or the refusal of an ethical principle could directly modify organic processes.[89] Yet there was a difference of nature between techniques that aimed to alter qualities shared by the body and the soul, and techniques that aimed to alter the course of madness through language. In the one case, what was used was a technique of metaphors, on the level of a sickness that was an alteration of nature. In the other, it was a question of linguistic techniques, on the level of a madness understood as a debate that reason had with itself. The art, in the latter form, operates in a domain where madness was 'treated' – in all senses of the word – in terms of truth and error. So it might be said that throughout the classical age, there was always a juxtaposition of two radically different types of technique in the therapeutics of madness. One, which relied on an implicit mechanics of qualities, addressed the aspects of madness that were essentially related to *passion*, i.e. demonstrated a certain mixture (of movement and quality) that belonged simultaneously to the body and the soul; while the other relied on a discursive movement of reason arguing with itself, and addressed madness as error, the double inanity of language and images associated most closely to *delirium*. The structural cycle of passion and delirium that constituted the classical experience of madness reappeared here, in the world of techniques, but in a somewhat syncopated form. Its unity is only visible from afar. All that is visible close-up, writ large, is the duality, almost an opposition, in the medicine of madness between methods for suppressing the condition, and various means of taking over unreason. These can be summed up in three essential figures.

1 *Awakening.* As delirium was the dream of people in a waking state, it was necessary to jolt the delirious out of their semi-sleep, and tear them from the dreamy wakefulness where images were all, that they might return to a genuine awakening, where the images of sleep would disappear before the figures of perception. This absolute awakening, which dispatches the various forms of illusion one after another, was what Descartes had sought at the beginning of his *Meditations*, and which he had found, paradoxically, in the consciousness of dream, in the consciousness that consciousness was deceived. But in the case of the mad, it was up to medicine to operate the awakening, transforming the solitude of Cartesian courage into the authoritative intervention by a waking person sure of his

or her wakefulness into the deceived wakefulness of the lunatic. This was a short-cut that dogmatically cut through Descartes' long path to certainty. What Descartes discovered at the end of his resolution, and in the *redoubling* of a consciousness that neither separates from itself *nor splits*, medicine in fact imposed from the outside, in the dissociation between doctor and patient. The doctor, in relation to the madman, reproduced the moment of the Cogito with relation to dreams, illusions and madness. A Cogito from the outside, foreign to cogitation itself, which could only impose itself on consciousness in the form of an irruption.

This structure of the irruption of wakefulness is one of the most constant forms in all the therapeutics of madness. Occasionally it takes on extremely simple aspects, simultaneously those most highly charged with images, and those most credited with immediate powers. Thus it was accepted that the sound of a rifle shot fired close by had cured a young girl of convulsions she suffered as the result of a violent sadness.[90] Without going quite as far as that imaginary realisation of methods of awakening, sudden, intense emotions might obtain a similar result. It was in that spirit that Boerhaave brought about a famous cure for sufferers from convulsion in Harlem. An epidemic of the disease had spread through the city hospital, and high doses of anti-spasmodic drugs had failed to have any effect. Boerhaave ordered that

> stoves filled with burning coals be brought in, and that iron hooks of a certain shape should be heated in them; he then announced that as all other methods to cure the seizures had failed, he had only one remedy left at his disposal, which was to burn to the bone a certain spot on the arm of any man, woman or child who suffered a convulsion.[91]

A slower method, but one more certain of the truth onto which it opened, was the awakening to wisdom, and its insistent, imperative passage through the landscape of madness. It was to that wisdom, in all its different forms, that Willis turned to cure madness. Imbeciles needed pedagogic wisdom, 'an assiduous and diligent master', to gradually introduce them to all that children learnt in schools. Melancholics were to be treated with a form of wisdom that took as its model the most rigorous and evident forms of truth, so that the imaginary component of their delirium evaporated in the light of incontestable truth. In their case 'mathematical or chymical studies' were recommended. Others were to be cured with the wisdom of a well ordered life, which would reduce their delirium; there was no need to impose any truth other than that of their daily life: 'they should take care of their household affairs, and [. . .] govern their family; they should build houses, plant and order gardens, orchards, or till the ground'. Maniacs, on the other hand, needed the rigour of the social order imposed from the outside, by force if necessary, to bring their minds progressively back to the light of truth:

> For the madman being placed in a house convenient for the business, must be so handled both by the physician, and also by the servants that are prudent, that he may be in some manner kept in, either by warnings, chidings, or punishments afflicted upon him, to his body, or his behaviour, or manners.[92]

Little by little, in the course of the classical age, this authoritarian awakening from madness was to lose its original meaning, and become nothing more than a reminder of the moral law, a return to order and fidelity to the law. What Willis still understood as a reopening of the self to truth was no longer entirely comprehensible to Sauvages, who spoke of lucidity in the recognition of the good: 'In this way people who have lost their reason due to erroneous principles of moral philosophy can be recalled to their senses, providing they agree to examine the true principles of the good with us, which are the ones to be preferred above the rest.'[93] It was thus not so much as an awakener that a physician was to act, but more as a moralist. Against madness, Tissot noted that 'a pure conscience beyond reproach is an excellent safeguard'.[94] Before long Pinel would believe that an awakening to reason had no meaning in the cure, and that what was required was obedience and blind submission: 'A fundamental principle for the cure of mania in a great number of cases is to first have recourse to energetic repression, and to make sure that benevolent methods only ever follow such a treatment.'[95]

2   *Theatrical Realisation.* In appearance at least this technique seems rigorously opposed to the idea of an awakening, where the vivid reality of a delirium was brought up against the patient work of reason. Reason imposed itself either through a slow form of pedagogy or as an authoritarian invasion, as though imposing the weight of its own being. The non-being of madness, the inanity of error were ultimately forced to crack under the pressure of this truth. Here the therapeutic operation was

entirely placed in the space of the imagination where unreality was complicit with itself. The imaginary had to enter into its own game, willingly calling up new images, matching the delirium on its own terms without opposition or confrontation, without even a visible dialectic paradoxically bringing a cure. Health was to invest the sickness and destroy it in the midst of the nothingness in which it was contained. Imagination, 'when sick, can only be cured by the effects of another healthy, properly employed imagination . . . it matters little whether that cure is effected by fear, by a vivid or painful impression on the senses, or by an illusion'.[96] Illusions could cure the illusory − whereas only reason could liberate the self from unreason. What then was this troubling power that the imaginary possessed?

The essence of an image is that it should be taken for reality and equally reality can ape the image, and pass itself off as having the same substance and meaning. Without disturbance or rupture, perception can continue the dream and fill in the gaps, bringing confirmation to all that is precarious in it and allowing it to accomplish its work. If illusions could appear as real as perception, then perception too could pass itself off as the truth, undeniable and visible, of the illusion. The first moment in the cure by 'theatrical realisation' was therefore the integration of the unreality of the image into the perceptive truth, without perception appearing to contradict or even contest the importance of the image. Lusitanus recounts in this fashion the cure of a melancholic who believed himself to be already damned on account of the enormity of his sins. As there was no means of convincing him by reasonable argument that he might yet be saved, his delirium was accepted, and an angel dressed in white was made to appear, sword in hand, announcing, after a severe exhortation, the remission of his sins.[97]

That example also demonstrates the second moment of the cure. *Realisation within the image* was not sufficient: it was also necessary to *continue* the *delirious discourse*. For in the senseless speech of the patient, there was a voice that spoke, obeying its own grammar, and bringing a meaning. Grammar and meaning had to be maintained in such fashion that the realisation of the fantasy in reality did not seem to involve any change of register, or the transposition into a new language with a modification in meaning. The same language should continue to be understood, bringing one new deductive element to the rigour of its discourse. That element was anything but indifferent: the idea was not simply to prolong the delirium, but to continue it until it was accomplished. It was to be led towards some form of paroxysm and crisis, where, with no intrusion from the outside, it would be confronted with itself and forced into a debate with the requirements of its own truth. The real and perception-based discourse that prolonged the delirious and image-based discourse was therefore neither to escape the laws of the delirium nor leave their sovereignty, but to exert some sort of positive function within them. It concentrated the delirium on its essential element, and while it took the risk of confirming it, it did that with a view to dramatising it to a useful end. One example quoted was the case of a patient who believed himself to be dead, and who was genuinely dying by starving himself to death:

> A troop of people, pale and dressed like the dead, entered his room, set up a table, brought food and drink, and sat down to eat. The dying man, who was ravenous, looked on, and the dead expressed surprise that he was not eating, and convinced him that they ate just as much as the living. He quickly became accustomed to the idea.[98]

Inside an unbroken discourse the elements of the delirium enter into contradiction, leading to the crisis. That crisis is ambiguously medical and theatrical. For a few years here, the tradition of Western medicine, which went all the way back to Hippocrates, was suddenly in step with one of the major forms of theatrical experience. What suddenly shaped the horizon was the theme of a great crisis that would confront the lunatic with his own insanity, reason with unreason, the lucid ruses of man with the blindness of the madman, a crisis that marked the point where illusion, turned back on itself, opened itself to the blinding nature of truth.

That opening is imminent in the crisis, and its immediate proximity is an essential component. But it is not produced by the crisis itself. For the crisis to be medical and not simply dramatic, and for it not to be a simple annihilation of the man, but rather the suppression of the illness, guaranteeing that the dramatic realisation of the delirium should have the effect of a comic purification, it was vital that the ruse be introduced at the correct moment.[99] A ruse, or at least an element that subtly altered the autonomous game of the delirium, and which while continuing to confirm it, binding it to its own truth, nonetheless only did so by tying it to the necessity of its own suppression. The simplest example of the

method was the ruse employed with delirious patients who imagined that
their body contained an object or an extraordinary animal:

> When a patient believes that he has a living animal trapped inside him,
> you must pretend to extract it. If it is in the belly, a violent purgative
> should have the desired effect, as you can feign the expulsion of the
> animal into a waiting vessel, without the patient being aware of
> the subterfuge.[100]

Acting out made the delirious object real, but at the same time exterior
and if it made it perceptible to the senses of the sufferer, it forcefully
delivered him from it. The artificial reconstruction of the delirium
constituted the real trajectory through which the patient was to recover
his liberty.

Sometimes there was no need for this distancing effect. On occasion it
was within the quasi-perception of the delirium that a perceptive element
came to take its place, silently at first, but progressively, so that its slow
affirmation gradually came to contest the whole system. It was then
within the self and within the perception that confirmed the delirium that
the patient saw the liberating reality. Trallion wrote of how a physician
cured a melancholic who imagined that he no longer had a head, but a
sort of void in its place. The doctor entered into the delirium with the
patient, and agreed to the patient's demand that he stop up the hole by
placing a large lead ball on his head. Soon the discomfort that quickly
resulted from the painful weight was enough to convince the patient that
he did indeed have a head.[101] Finally, the ruse and its function of comic
reduction could be assured with the complicity of the doctor, but without
any direct intervention on his part, through the spontaneous action of the
organism of the patient. In the case quoted above of the melancholic who
was really dying as he had lost the desire to eat on account of his belief
that he was already dead, the theatrical production of the meal of the dead
was sufficient incentive for him to eat again. The food restored his
strength, 'the use of food calmed him down', and the organic problem
disappeared; the delirium, which was both the cause and the effect of
it also vanished.[102] The real death that would have resulted from the
imaginary death was brushed aside by reality, through the very enactment
of unreal death. An exchange of non-being with itself was carried out in a
cunning fashion: the non-being of delirium was transferred to the real

being of sickness, and suppressed it by the fact of the expulsion of the delirium through the theatrical enactment. That coming-into-being of the non-being of delirium effaced it as non-being, and that by the pure mechanisms of its internal contradiction – a mechanism that is at once a game of words and a game within the deception, language game and games within the image. Delirium is suppressed as non-being in that it is perceived; but as the being of a delirium rests entirely in its non-being, it is suppressed as delirium altogether. Its confirmation in the fantastical theatre restores it to a truth which, by ensnaring it in reality, drives it out of reality, forcing it to disappear in the non-delirious discourse of reason.

What we have here is a minute rehearsal, at once theatrical and medical, of *esse est percipi* – to be is to be perceived. Its philosophical meaning is followed to the letter, and yet it is used in the opposite sense to its natural direction: it beats against the current of its own meaning. From the moment when delirium penetrates the field of *percipi*, the perceived, then despite itself it becomes a part of being, i.e. it enters into contradiction with its own being, which is *non-esse*, non-being. The theatrical and therapeutic game which is then played out consists of harmonising, inside the delirium, the demands of *this particular being* with the laws of *being* (the moment of the theatrical invention, the setting up of the comic illusion); then promoting between the two the tension and contradiction which are already inscribed there and which soon cease to be silent (the moment of the drama); and finally unveiling, and bringing out into the cruel light of day, the truth that the laws of being of delirium are nothing more than the appetites and desires of an illusion, the demands of non-being, and consequently, that the *percipi*, the 'being perceived' which gave it its being, already secretly contained the seeds of its ruin (the comedy and the dénouement). A dénouement in the strict sense that being and non-being are freed of the confusion they suffer in the quasi-reality of delirium, and are returned to the poverty of their true nature. Discernible here is a curious structural analogy during the classical age between different modes of liberation: in the artifice of medical techniques and the serious games of theatrical illusion they share the same equilibrium and the same movement.

It can now be understood why madness as such disappeared from the theatre at the end of the seventeenth century, to reappear only in the final years of the century that followed: the theatre of madness was effectively realised in medical practice, and its comic reduction was of the order of an everyday cure.

3 *The Return to the Immediate.* As madness was an illusion, the cure for madness, if it could be truly effected by the theatre, could also be brought about by even more direct means, through the suppression of theatre. Directly entrusting the vain world of madness to the plenitude of nature (which never lies, as its immediacy knows not non-being) meant giving madness over both to its own truth (since madness, as a form of sickness, was indeed a natural being), and to its closest contradiction (since delirium, as appearance without content, was also the opposite of the abundance, often secret and invisible, of nature). Nature thus appeared to be the reason of unreason, in the double sense that it both contained its causes and simultaneously concealed the principle of its suppression. It should be noted that these themes are not in evidence throughout the classical age. Although they follow the same experience of unreason, they take up where the theme of theatrical enactment left off, and their appearance indicates a moment when the interrogation of being and the lure begins to cede its place to a problematics of nature. The games of theatrical illusion lose their meaning, and the artful techniques of imaginary realisation are replaced by the simple, more ingenuous art of a natural reduction. But this replacement has an ambiguous sense, as it is both a reduction through nature and a reduction to nature.

The return to immediacy is the therapeutics *par excellence*, because it is the rigorous refusal of therapeutics, and brings a cure in that it is a forgetting of all treatments. It is in the passivity of man with regard to himself, and the silence that he imposes on his art and artifice, that nature unveils an activity that is the exact reciprocal of the renunciation. On close examination, man's passivity is revealed to be a genuine activity; when men take medication, they elude the law of work that nature imposes upon them, sliding into the world of artifice and counter-nature of which madness is but one manifestation; and it was in ignoring sickness, and retaking their place amongst the activity of natural beings, that men, in an apparent passivity which at bottom was an industrious fidelity, could finally be cured. That at least was how Bernardin de Saint-Pierre explained how he was delivered of 'a strange sickness' in which, 'like Oedipus, he saw two suns'. Medicine had come to his aid, revealing that the sickness was 'nervous in origin'. He took the most highly recommended medication to no avail, and quickly noted how physicians were killed by their own remedies. 'I owe my return to health to Jean-Jacques Rousseau,' he wrote.

> I had read in his immortal writings, among many other natural truths, that man was made to work, not to meditate. Up until that point I had always exercised my soul and rested my body, but I changed my habits, exercising my body and resting my soul. I gave up most of my books, and cast my eyes instead over the works of nature, which spoke to my senses in a language that neither time nor nations could alter. My story and my journals were the grasses of the fields and the meadows; it was not that my thoughts went painfully towards them, as in the system of men, but that their thoughts came to me in a thousand agreeable forms.[103]

Despite the formulations that certain Rousseau disciples might have proposed, this return to immediacy was neither absolute nor simple. This was because madness, even if it was brought on and fed by all that was most artificial in society, appeared in its more violent forms as the savage expression of the most primitive human desires. As we have seen, the madness of the classical age is linked to the threat of bestiality – a bestiality dominated by predatory and murderous instincts. Returning madness to nature meant abandoning it to the furies of all that was counter-natural, in a reversal that was impossible to control. The cure for madness supposed a return to all that was immediate, not in relation to desire but to the imagination – a return that removed from the lives of men and their pleasures all that was artificial, unreal and imaginary. The therapeutics of the well-considered plunge into immediacy secretly supposed a mediating wisdom that divided nature into the violent and the truthful. This was the crucial difference between the *Savage* and the *Labourer*: 'Savages . . . lead the life of a carnivorous animal, rather than that of a reasonable being.' The life of a Labourer, by contrast, 'is happier than that of a man of the world'. On the savage's side was the immediacy of desire, undisciplined, unconstrained, and devoid of real morality; on the labourer's side was unmediated pleasure, i.e. pleasure that was not vainly solicited and without imaginary excitement and accomplishments. In nature and its immediate virtues what cured madness was pleasure – but a pleasure which exposed the vanity of desire without being forced to repress it, as it offered a plenitude of satisfaction in advance, and which made imagination derisory by spontaneously providing the happy presence of reality:

The pleasures enter the eternal order of things: they exist invariably, and certain conditions are necessary to form them . . . These conditions are not arbitrary, as they have been traced out by nature. Imagination cannot create, and even the man most passionate for pleasure would be unable to increase his own other than by renouncing those that do not carry nature's imprint.[104]

The immediate world of the labourer was thus a world filled with wisdom and a sense of measure, which cured madness in that it rendered useless desire and the movements in the passions that it provoked, also in so far as it reduced along with the imaginary all the possibilities of delirium. What Tissot understood by 'pleasure' was that curative immediacy, relieved of passion and language, the two great forms of human experience from which unreason is born.

And perhaps nature, as a concrete form of the immediate, had a power more fundamental still in the suppression of madness. For it had the power of liberating man from his liberty. In nature (the nature at least that was measured by the double exclusion of the violence of desire and the unreality of fantasy), man was freed from social constraints (which obliged him to 'calculate and sum up his imaginary pleasures, those that carry the name without being such in truth'), and the uncontrollable movement of his passion. By that fact, men were subtly ensnared in a system of natural obligations from within their very lives. The pressure of their healthiest needs, the rhythm of the days and the seasons, and the non-violent necessity to find food and shelter constrained the disorder of the mad to a regular observance. Remote imaginings were dismissed, together with all that was overly urgent in desire. In the sweetness of a pleasure that does not constrain, men were linked to the wisdom of nature, and that fidelity in the form of liberty caused unreason to disappear, which juxtaposed in its paradox the extreme determinism of passion and the extreme fantasies of the image. In these mental landscapes where ethics were juxtaposed with medicine, the dream was of a liberation from madness. A liberation not to be understood in its origins as the discovery by philanthropy of the humanity of the mad, but rather as a desire to open madness to the sweet constraints of nature.

Since the end of the Middle Ages, the village of Gheel had been witness to the now forgotten association of the confinement of the mad and the exclusion of lepers, but in the last years of the eighteenth century it suddenly underwent a brusque reinterpretation. All that had previously marked there the violent and pathetic separation between the world of the mad and the world of men was reinvested with the idyllic values of a rediscovered unity between unreason and nature. For previous times, the village had been an enclosure for the insane, thereby signifying that men of reason were protected; it now demonstrated that the mad had been freed, and that in that liberty that placed them on an equal footing with the laws of nature, they readjusted to men of reason. In Gheel, according to Jouy's description,

> Four-fifths of the inhabitants are mad, but mad in the full force of the term, and yet they enjoy the same liberty as the other citizens without any problem . . . healthy food, clean air, and all the attributes of liberty is the regime that they are prescribed, and to which the majority, by the end of a year, owe their cure.[105]

Without anything in the institutions really changing, a slow modification in the meaning of exclusion and confinement was beginning to appear. It was beginning to take on positive values, and the empty, colourless and nocturnal space where unreason had previously been returned to its nothingness was slowly being peopled with a nature to which this newly liberated madness was obliged to submit. Confinement, as the separation of reason and unreason, was not suppressed, but at the heart of its intentions, the space that it occupied allowed natural powers to appear, which were more constricting to madness, and more fitted to subjugating it in its essence than all the repression and limitations of the previous system. Madness was to be liberated from this system, so that inside the space of confinement, now charged with a positive efficacy, it might be free to cast off its savage liberty, and welcome instead the commands of nature, which had the force of both truth and law. As law, nature constrained the violence of desire: as truth, it diminished and dominated the counter-natural and the fantasies of the imagination.

Pinel gave a description of this new idea of nature, when describing the hospital at Saragossa. What had been established there was:

> a sort of counterweight to the wanderings of the spirit, in the attractions and charms inspired by the cultivation of the fields, through the natural instinct that pushes men to fecundate the earth and tend the

needs of the fruits of nature with their industry. From early morning, they can be seen ... merrily wandering around the diverse parts of a vast enclosure that belongs to the hospital, dividing their labours in a pattern that follows the cycle of the seasons, cultivating wheat, vegetables and the cottage garden, taking turns to look after the harvest, the trellising, the grape harvest and the beating of the olive trees, and in the evenings, returning to the tranquillity of their solitary asylum, where they sink into a calm sleep. A lengthy experience has demonstrated at this hospital that this is the surest means of returning them to reason.[106]

Beneath the conventional images, a rigorous meaning is to be discerned. The return to the immediate is effective against unreason only in so far as it is an arranged immediate, thus separated from itself: it is an immediacy where violence is isolated from truth and savagery from freedom, and where nature can no longer be recognised in the fantastical images of the counternatural. An immediacy, in short, where nature is mediated by morality. In an arranged space such as this, madness will no longer speak the language of unreason, with all there is within it that transcends the natural phenomena of sickness. It will be entirely contained within a pathology. This was a transformation that later periods considered to be a positive step, the coming, if not of a truth, then at least of something that made the knowledge of the truth a possibility. But from the point of view of history, it should be seen for what it really was: the reduction of the classical experience of unreason to a strictly moral perception of madness, which secretly unified all the conceptions that the nineteenth century would later consider to be scientific, positive and experimental.

The metamorphosis carried out in the second half of the eighteenth century initially operated through the techniques related to the idea of the cure. But before long it was out in the open, and it quickly won over the reformers, leading to a major reorganisation of the experience of madness in the closing years of the century. Soon Pinel was able to write: 'How important it is, to prevent hypochondria, mania and melancholia, to follow the immutable laws of morality.'[107]

*

There is no sense in hunting for a distinction in the classical age between physical therapeutics and psychological medication, for the simple reason that psychology did not exist. When, for example, the absorption of bitters was prescribed, it was not simply a question of physical treatment, as the soul as well as the body was to be scoured. When the simple life of a labourer was prescribed for a melancholic, or when the comedy of his delirium was played out for him, what was being enacted was not a psychological intervention, as what was most important was still the density of the humours and the movement of the spirits inside the nerves. In one case, what was seen was the art of *the transformation of qualities*, a technique where the essence of madness was taken as nature and as sickness; and in the other it was an art of discourse, and *the restitution of truth*, where madness was considered a form of unreason.

In the years that followed, when the great experience of unreason, whose unity was characteristic of the classical age, would come apart, and when madness, restricted in its entirety to a moral intuition, would be nothing more than a sickness, then the distinction that we have just made would take on a different sense. That which was classified as sickness would be related to the domain of the organic, and all that was associated with unreason and the transcendence of its discourse would be relegated to the realm of the psychological. And it was precisely there that psychology was born, not as the truth of madness, but as a sign that madness was now detached from its truth, which was unreason, and that from now on it would be a rudderless phenomenon, *insignificant*, on the indefinite surface of nature. An enigma with no truth other than the one that could reduce it.

It is for that reason that we must do justice to Freud. Between his five *Case Histories* and Janet's scrupulous *Psychological Healing* there is more than the weight of a *discovery*: there is also the sovereign violence of a *return*. Janet enumerated the elements of a division, drew up an inventory, annexed some new territory, and perhaps conquered a few regions. But Freud took up madness at the level of its *language*, reconstituting one of the essential elements of an experience that positivism had reduced to silence. He did not set out to bring a major addition to the list of psychological treatments of madness, but restored instead the possibility of a dialogue with unreason to medical thought. We should not be surprised that the most 'psychological' of medications was so quickly paired up with its opposite and with organic confirmations. Psychoanalysis is not about psychology, but it is about an experience of unreason that psychology, in the modern world, was meant to disguise.

Part Three

INTRODUCTION

For them, I was the incarnation of the Petites-Maisons.

'One afternoon, there I was, watching carefully and speaking little, listening as little as I could, when I was accosted by one of the strangest people in this land, where God knows there is no shortage of such fellows. He was a mixture of haughtiness, baseness, good sense and unreason.'[1]

At the moment when doubt faced its greatest dangers, Descartes became aware that he could not be mad – with the understanding that for some time to come, up until the evil genius hypothesis, all the powers of unreason were watching around his thought. But as a philosopher, setting out to doubt everything in a systematic fashion, he could not be 'one of those insane persons'. But Rameau's Nephew knows very well – and it is the most permanent feature among his fleeting certitudes – that he is mad. 'Before he began, he sighed deeply and put his hands to his brow, then he regained his composure and said: "I should tell you that I am an ignoramus, a madman, an impertinent person and an idler." '

That consciousness of being mad is still quite fragile. It is not the hermetic, secret and sovereign consciousness which communicates with the deep powers of unreason: Rameau's Nephew is a subservient consciousness, open to the winds and transparent to the look of others. He is mad because that is what people tell him and because he has been treated as such: 'They wanted me to be ridiculous, so that's what I became.'[2]

Unreason in him is all on the surface, with no depth other than that of opinion, in thrall to all that is least free and betrayed by all that is most precarious in reason. Unreason is entirely on the level of the futile madness of men. It is, perhaps, nothing other than that mirage.

What then is the significance of the figure of unreasonable existence embodied in Rameau's Nephew, which was still secret for his contemporaries, but is decisive for our retrospective examination?

This is an existence that stretches far back in time, taking in very ancient figures and, among others, an idea of clowning that recalls the Middle Ages, and also announces the most modern forms of unreason, those that are the contemporaries of Nerval, Nietzsche and Antonin Artaud. To examine Rameau's Nephew and the paradox of his very public yet unperceived existence in the eighteenth century, is to move slightly out of step with a chronicle of evolution, but at the same time it allows us to perceive the great structures of unreason in their most general form – those which slumber beneath the surface of Western culture, just below the temporality of historians. *Le Neveu de Rameau* might quickly teach us, among the hurried figures of its contradictions, what was most essential in the upsets that renewed the experience of unreason in the classical age. It needs to be investigated as a shortened paradigm of history. And given that in an instant it illuminates like a bolt of lightning the great broken line that stretches from the Ship of Fools to the last words of Nietzsche and perhaps Artaud's cries of rage, we should try to understand all that this character contains, and see how reason, madness and unreason are confronted in Diderot's text, and examine the new links that grew up between them. The history that we shall write in this last part takes place inside the space opened by the words of the Nephew, although clearly much of that space will be left unexplored. The last character in whom madness and unreason are united, Rameau's Nephew is also where the moment of separation is prefigured. In the chapters that follow we shall try to retrace the movement of that separation, through its first anthropological phenomena. But it is only in the last texts of Nietzsche or in Artaud that it took on, for Western culture, its philosophical and tragic dimensions.

*

So the character of the madman reappears in *Le Neveu de Rameau*. A reappearance in clownish form. Like the fool of the Middle Ages, he lives among the forms of reason, slightly marginal no doubt in that he is not at all like the others, but still integrated in that he is there as a thing, at the disposal of reasonable people, a possession to be shown off and shunted around. He is owned like an object. But he himself immediately betrays the equivocal nature of that possession. For if for reason he is an object to be appropriated, then it must be that reason has need of him. That need is of the content and meaning of his existence. Without the madman, reason would be deprived of its reality, and would be empty monotony, bored with itself, an animal desert constantly confronted with its own contradiction: 'Now that they no longer have me, what do they do? They're as bored as dogs . . .'³ But a reason that is only itself when it possesses madness can no longer define itself as being in immediate identity with itself, and alienates itself in that appurtenance: 'A man who would be wise should have no fool, so anyone who has a fool is not wise; and if he's not wise, he's a fool; perhaps, even if he was king, he would be the fool of his fool.'⁴ Unreason becomes the reason of reason – to the exact extent that reason only recognises it as a possession.

What started out as mere clowning, in the derisory figure of the unwanted guest, reveals, in the final analysis, an imminent power of derision. The adventure of Rameau's Nephew recounts the necessary instability and the ironic reversal of any form of judgement that denounces unreason as being exterior and inessential to its workings. Unreason slowly creeps back to that which condemns it, imposing a form of retrograde servitude upon it, for a wisdom that believes it can form a pure relationship of judgement and definition with madness – 'that man is a madman' – has from the outset set up a relationship of possession and obscure belonging: 'that man is my madman', in that I am reasonable enough to recognise his madness, and that recognition is the mark, sign and almost the emblem of my reason. Reason cannot report the presence of madness without compromising itself in a relationship of ownership. Unreason is not outside reason, but precisely in it, invested and possessed by it, turned into an object: for reason, it is what is most interior and also most transparent, that which is offered to the gaze more than any other thing. Whilst wisdom and truth are always indefinitely deferred for reason, madness is only ever that which reason can possess of itself. 'For a long time there was a king's fool . . . but no king ever had a titular wise man.'⁵

Thus the triumph of madness again comes about through a double return – the flow of unreason back towards reason, which only assures its certainty through its possession of madness, and a return towards an experience where wisdom and madness are indefinitely intertwined: 'not being mad would be being mad through another trick that madness played'. Yet this implication is of a style quite different from that which threatened Western reason at the end of the Middle Ages and throughout the Renaissance. It no longer designates those obscure and inaccessible regions that transcribed for the imagination into the fantastical fusion of worlds at the end of time, but displays instead the irreparable fragility of relations of belonging, the immediate fall of reason into a possession where it searches for its own nature: *reason becomes alienated in the very movement through which it takes possession of unreason.*

In these few pages by Diderot, the relationship between reason and unreason takes on a radical new face. The destiny of madness in the modern world is strangely prefigured here, and almost enacted. From that point on, a straight line traces the improbable path that leads directly to Antonin Artaud.

*

At first sight, it is tempting to classify Rameau's Nephew among the ancient lineage of fools and clowns, and restore to him all the powers of irony with which those figures had been entrusted. Does he not also play the role of an insouciant operator of truth, long common in the theatre but profoundly forgotten by classicism? Does the truth not often shine out in the wake of his impertinence? Such madmen:

> . . . break down the fastidious conformity that our education, social convention, good behaviour and proprieties introduce. If a madman appears in company, he is like a yeast that ferments, restoring to everyone a portion of their natural identity. He shakes and stirs everything up, he brings praise and blame, he reveals who is good and he unmasks rogues.[6]

But if madness takes it upon itself to bring the light of truth to the world, it is no longer because its blindness communicates with something essential by means of strange powers, but simply because it is blind, and its power is made of nothing but error. 'If we say something worthwhile, then as with madmen and the inspired, it is by chance.'[7] We should take this as meaning that chance is the only necessary link between truth and error, the sole path of paradoxical certainty, and in that respect madness, as the glorification of chance – chance that is neither sought after nor desired, but simply results of its own accord – appears to be the truth about the truth, as well as manifest error. For error made manifest is, in the full light of day, both the being that it is, and the non-being that makes it an error. At that point, madness takes on a new meaning for the modern world.

On the one hand, unreason is all that is most immediately close to being, and that which is most deeply rooted in it: its being is made more pure and more urgent by the sacrifice of truth, reason and wisdom. Any delay or barrier that arises between being and unreason is intolerable: 'I would rather be, and even be an impertinent reasoner, than not be at all.'[8]

Rameau's Nephew is hungry and says so. All that is voracious and shameless in his character, the cynicism that is occasionally reborn in him, is not a hypocrisy that finally decides to reveal its secrets, for his secret is precisely in not being able to be hypocritical. Rameau's Nephew is not the other side of Molière's Tartuffe; he simply demonstrates the immediate pressure of being in unreason, and the impossibility of mediation.[9] But at the same time, unreason is in thrall to the non-being of illusion, and exhausts itself in the darkness. If it is reduced, by interest, to all that is most immediate in being, it also imitates all that is most distant, most fragile and least consistent in appearances. It is at once the urgency of being and the pantomime of non-being, immediate necessity and the indefinite reflection of a mirror:

> The worst of it is the contrived postures into which we are coerced by the force of necessity. A man in need doesn't walk like the others, but jumps and squirms, or crawls and drags himself along, and spends his whole life switching from one posture to another.[10]

A blend of the rigour of need and of aping the useless, unreason is in a single movement, pure, inescapable egotism, and a fascination with the outermost trappings of the inessential. Rameau's Nephew is that simultaneity, that fully conscious eccentricity, that systematic will to delirium, which is lived as a total experience of the world: 'I must say that what you call a beggar's pantomime is the hurly burly of life on Earth.'[11]

To be oneself that noise, that music, that spectacle, that comedy, to realise oneself as both a thing and an illusory thing, and thus to be not simply a thing but also void and nothingness, to be the absolute emptiness of the absolute plenitude that fascinates from the outside, to be the circular, voluble vertigo of that nothingness and that being, to be at once the total abolition that is an enslaved consciousness and the supreme glory that is a sovereign consciousness – that no doubt is the meaning of *Rameau's Nephew*, which in the mid-eighteenth century, long before Descartes' word was truly understood, offers a lesson more anti-Cartesian than anything to be found in Locke, Voltaire or Hume.

Rameau's Nephew, in his human reality, in that fragile life that only spares him anonymity by granting him a name that is not his own – the shadow of a shadow – is beyond and short of any truth, the delirium, realised as existence, of the being and non-being of the real. When one considers, on the other hand, that Descartes' project was to sustain doubt in a provisional manner until truth appeared in the reality of a self-evident idea, then one sees very well that the non-Cartesian nature of modern thought, at its most decisive, begins not in a discussion of innate ideas, or an incrimination of the ontological argument, but rather in the text of *Le Neveu de Rameau*, in the existence that it designates in a reversal that would not be understood until the time of Hölderlin and Hegel. What is called into question there is also to be found in Diderot's *Paradoxe sur le comédien*, but is now the other side of the coin: no longer that part of reality which is to be elevated to the non-being of acting by a cold heart and a lucid intelligence, but rather the aspects of the non-being of existence that can be realised in the empty plenitude of appearance, by means of a delirium reaching the furthermost degree of consciousness. After Descartes, it is no longer necessary to traverse courageously the uncertainties of delirium, dreams and illusions, and it is no longer necessary to overcome once and for all the perils of unreason: rather, it is from the depths of unreason that reason can be interrogated, and what appears once more is the possibility of regaining the essence of the world in the dizzying spin of a unifying delirium, in an illusion equivalent to the truth, that brings together the being and non-being of the real as one.

*

At the heart of madness, delirium takes on a new meaning. Until now it had been defined entirely in the space of error: as illusion, erroneous belief or ill-founded opinion, but tenaciously pursued, enveloping all that thought can produce when it is no longer placed in the domain of truth. Now delirium is the site of a perpetual, instantaneous confrontation, that of necessity and fascination, of the solitude of being and the glittering surface of appearances, of immediate plenitude and the non-being of illusion. Nothing of its previous association with dreams has disappeared, but the appearance of the resemblance has changed. Delirium is no longer a manifestation of all that is most subjective in dreams, and it is no longer the slippage to what Heraclitus had previously called ἴδιος κόσμος, 'the madness of solitary delusion'. If there is still a resemblance to dreams, it is through all that which, in dreams, is the play between luminous appearances and dull reality, the insistence of need and the servitude of fascination, all the elements that form a wordless dialogue between day and light. Dreams and delirium no longer communicate through the night of blindness, but in the light where all that is most immediate in being confronts all that is most indefinitely reflected in the mirages of appearance. It is in this tragic dimension that dreams and delirium now meet and mingle, in the uninterrupted rhetoric of their irony.

A tragic confrontation between need and illusion in an oneiric mode, presaging Freud and Nietzsche, the delirium of Rameau's Nephew is also an ironic repetition of the world, its destructive reconstitution in a theatre of illusion:

> shouting, singing, twirling like a man possessed, acting at the same time all the roles of all the male and female dancers and singers, a whole orchestra, an entire opera, dividing himself into twenty different roles, running around in circles, before suddenly stopping like a man possessed, his eyes wild, foaming at the mouth . . . he cried, shouted and sighed, he looked moved, tranquil and furious; he was a woman fainting in agony, a miserable creature filled with despair, a temple that rose up, the birds that fall silent with the setting sun . . . he was night with its darkness, he was shadows, he was silence.[12]

Unreason does not reappear as the furtive presence of the other world, but right here, in the burgeoning transcendence of any act of expression, from the source of language itself, in the initial and final moment where man is suddenly exterior to himself, gathering into his intoxication all that is most interior to the world. Unreason no longer wears the strange faces that the Middle Ages liked to recognise, but the imperceptible mask of the familiar and the identical. Unreason is at once the world itself and the same world, separated from itself by the thin surface of pantomime. Its powers are no longer that of a transport to an elsewhere, and its role is no longer to reveal the eruption of something that is radically other: instead, it forces the world to revolve around a circle of sameness.

But in this vertigo, where the truth of the world is only maintained within an absolute void, man meets also the ironic perversion of his own truth, at the moment when it passes from the dreams of interiority to the forms of exchange. Unreason then takes on the form of a new evil genius – no longer one who exiles man from the truth of the world, but one who brings mystification and clarity at the same time, who enchants to the point of extreme disenchantment the truth about the self that man has entrusted to his hand, his face and his language; an evil genius who operates not when man wishes to accede to the truth, but when he wishes to give back to the world his own truth, and when, projected into the drunkenness of the senses where he loses himself, he is left 'immobile, stupid and astonished'.[13] The possibility of the evil genius no longer lodges in *perception*, but in *expression*, and the supreme irony is to see man at the mercy of the derision of the immediate and the sensible, alienated in them through the mediation that he is.

The laughter of Rameau's Nephew prefigures and reduces in advance the whole movement of nineteenth-century anthropology: in all post-Hegelian thought, man moves from certainty to the truth through the work of the mind and of reason, and yet Diderot had long made it clear that men are constantly sent back by reason towards the non-true truth of the immediate, and this through a mediation that involves no work, a mediation that has always already been carried out since the dawn of time. This mediation without patience, which is both extreme distance and absolute promiscuity, entirely negative because its only force is subversion, but totally positive in that it is fascinated by all that it suppresses, is the delirium of unreason – that enigmatic figure in which we recognise madness. In its efforts to restore through expression the sensible drunkenness of the world and the urgent games of need and appearance, delirium finds itself ironically alone: the sufferings of hunger remain an inscrutable well of pain.

*

Half remaining in the shadows, this experience of unreason changes little from Rameau's Nephew up until Raymond Roussel and Antonin Artaud. But for that continuity to be demonstrated, it must be freed from the pathological connotations it has been assigned. The return to immediacy in the late poetry of Hölderlin and the consecration of the sensible in Nerval can offer nothing but an altered or superficial meaning so long as we set out to understand them from a positivist conception of madness. Their true meaning should be asked of the moment of unreason in which they are placed. For it is from the centre of that experience of unreason which is the concrete condition of their possibility that the two movements of poetic conversion and psychological evolution are to be understood. They are not linked to each other by a relation of cause and effect, and they proceed in what is neither a complementary nor an inverse mode. Both rest on the same base, that of submerged unreason; the experience of Rameau's Nephew already demonstrated all that it contains of the drunkenness of the sensible, the fascination with the immediate, and the painful irony where the solitude of delirium originates. What is at stake here is not the nature of madness, but the essence of unreason. If that essence could go unnoticed, it was not simply that it is hidden, but that it loses itself in all that might bring it out into the light. For – and this is perhaps one of the fundamental traits of our culture – it is not possible to occupy a place, deliberately and resolutely, at the distance offered by unreason, for any length of time. For it must be forgotten and abolished no sooner than it is measured, in the vertigo of the sensible or the confinement of madness. Van Gogh and Nietzsche in different ways were evidence of this. Fascinated by the delirium of the real, by its scintillating appearance, and by time abolished and absolutely re-found in the justice of light, ensnared by the immutable solidity of the most fragile of appearances, they thus were rigorously excluded and trapped within suffering beyond all exchange, and which figured, not only for others but for them as well, in their own truth, which had once more become immediate certitude, madness itself. The moment of the *Ja-sagen*, of the embrace of the lure of the sensible, was also the moment they retreated into the shadows of insanity.

But to us, those two moments are as distinct and distant as poetry and silence, day and night, the accomplishments of language in its manifestation and its loss in the infinity of delirium. For us, confronting unreason in all its redoubtable unity has become impossible. The nineteenth century, in all its inflexible seriousness, ripped apart the indivisible domain designated by the irony of *Rameau's Nephew*, and drew an abstract frontier through that former unity, demarcating the realm of the pathological. In the mid-eighteenth century that unity had been briefly illuminated by a bolt of lightning, but it was more than half a century again before anyone dared revisit such a region. After Hölderlin, Nerval, Nietzsche, Van Gogh, Raymond Roussel and Artaud ventured there, with tragic consequences — i.e. to the point at which the alienation of the experience of unreason pushed them into the abandonment of madness. And each of those existences, each of the words that made up those existences repeats with the insistence of time the same question, which probably concerns the essence of the modern world: why is it not possible to remain in the difference that is unreason? Why is it that unreason always has to separate from itself, fascinated in the delirium of the sensible and trapped in the retreat that is madness? How was it that it was deprived of language to such an extent? What is this power that petrifies all those who dare look upon its face, condemning to *madness* all those who have tried the test of *Unreason*?

I

THE GREAT FEAR

The eighteenth century was unable to understand the full meaning of *Le Neveu de Rameau*. And yet something did happen at the time when the text was written, promising a decisive change. Curiously, unreason, which had been put to one side in the distance that was confinement, and which had progressively found itself alienated in the natural forms of madness, suddenly reappeared, charged with new dangers, as though possessing a different power to call things into question. But what the eighteenth century perceived in it at first was not the secret interrogation, but only the social disgrace: the torn clothing, arrogance in rags, the insolence that was tolerated, and whose worrying powers were silenced with amused indulgence. The eighteenth century was incapable of recognising itself in Rameau's Nephew, but it was entirely present in the 'I' that was his interlocutor, the 'keeper' so to speak, who showed reticent amusement and harboured a deep anxiety: for this was the first time since the Great Confinement that the madman was once again a character on the social stage; it was the first time that society re-entered into conversation with him, and that he was questioned anew. Unreason reappeared as a social type, which is not saying much, but reappear it did, and it slowly took its place in the familiar social landscape once more. So it was that some ten years before the Revolution, Mercier described such a figure, without any apparent amazement:

Go into any café, and sooner or later someone will confide in you in calm, measured tones: 'You couldn't begin to imagine, sir, the ingratitude that the government has shown me, and how blind it is to its own interests. For thirty years I neglected my own affairs, and locked myself in my cabinet, in meditation, dreams and calculations, and I finally came up with a feasible scheme to pay all the debts of the State. I have another to make the king rich, and ensure that he has an income of 400 million a year, and another still to bury the English forever, may God smite their name. While I busied myself with these vast operations, which demanded the full focus of my genius, I was slightly distracted from a few domestic trifles, and my overly zealous creditors kept me in prison for three years ... Sir, you see how useless it is to be patriotic in these times, dying unknown, a martyr for the fatherland.'[1]

From afar, such characters form a circle around Rameau's Nephew: they do not have his grandeur, and they can only appear akin to him in that they share some picturesque details.

And yet they are a little more than a social type, or a caricatural silhouette. They contain something that concerns and touches upon the unreason of the eighteenth century. They shared with many a garrulousness, a worry, a vague delirium and deep-seated anguish, and they lived real lives of which the traces are still discernible. As with the libertines, the débauchés and the ruffians of the late seventeenth century, it is difficult to say if they were mad, ill or simply criminal. Mercier himself was unsure what status to confer upon them:

In Paris there are thus some totally honest men, economists or anti-economists, who have a warm heart and hold dear the interest of the public at large, but who are nonetheless *crackpots*, i.e. are very short sighted, and understand neither the century that they inhabit nor the men they must deal with; they are harder to bear than fools, because with their money and their false knowledge they start from impossible principles, reasoning wrongly from there on.[2]

Such 'planners of crackpot projects'[3] really did exist, forming a circle around the reason of the philosophers and all their reforming projects, their plans and their constitutions, providing a muffled accompaniment of unreason: the rationality of the age of Reason found in them a distorting mirror, a sort of harmless caricature. But this is a sure indication that as part of a movement of amused indulgence the figure of unreason is slowly allowed back into the light of day, precisely when it was thought to be most deeply hidden in the space of confinement. It was as though classical thought once again allowed unreason into its vicinity, in a relation of quasi-resemblance. As though at the moment of its triumph, it elicited and let loose at the edges of order a character whose mask it fashioned for derision – a sort of double in which it both recognised and repudiated itself.

*

Yet fear and anguish were not far away: like the recoil of confinement, they reappeared with redoubled strength. Previously, people had feared being confined, and that fear lived on. In the late eighteenth century, Sade would still be haunted by the fear of those he called 'the black men', who were looking for him to make him disappear.[4] But now the territory of confinement had taken on powers of its own, and had become in its turn a breeding ground of evil, which it could spread of its own accord, instituting a new reign of terror.

Suddenly, in the space of a few years in the mid-eighteenth century, a fear emerged. It was a fear formulated in medical terms, but deep down it was animated by a whole moral mythology. People were in dread of a mysterious sickness that apparently emanated from houses of confinement and was soon to spread throughout the cities. There was talk of gaol fever, and the carts transporting the condemned were blamed, as were the chain gangs who were marched through the towns, leaving a trail of disease in their wake. It was thought that scurvy was contagious, and widely believed that air contaminated by the disease was spreading through residential areas. The great image of medieval horror rose up once again, leading to a new panic among the metaphors of terror. Houses of confinement were no longer simply the lazar house on the edges of towns, but became themselves a form of leprosy that scarred the face of the town:

> A terrible ulcer on the political body, an ulcer that is wide, deep and draining, an image repugnant to the gaze. Even the air of the place, which can be smelt from half a mile away, is enough to tell you that you

are approaching a place of violence, an asylum of degradation and misfortune.[5]

Many of these high places of confinement were built on the same spot where lepers had previously been kept, and it was as though centuries later these new tenants brought a new form of contagion. They took on the emblems and the meaning of the previous inhabitants:

> This leprosy is too powerful for the capital! Bicêtre is a word that no one can utter without a feeling of repugnance, horror or scorn ... it has become a receptacle for all that is most vile and sickening in society.[6]

The evil that men had tried to exclude through confinement reappeared, and a great public fear, in a highly fantastical form, was its consequence. What came into being and spread in all directions was an evil, equally physical and moral, enveloping obscure powers of corruption and horror in that confusion. An undifferentiated image of 'rottenness' reigned, concerning the corruption of morals as much as the decomposition of flesh, compounded by a blend of pity and revulsion towards the inmates. First, evil fermented within the closed spaces of confinement. It shared the virtues of acids in the chemistry of the eighteenth century: its fine particles, sharp as needles, penetrated bodies and hearts, as easily as alkaline particles, passive and brittle. The blend then bubbled up, giving off noxious vapours and corrosive liquids: 'These wards are atrocious places where crimes ferment, spreading around them, so to speak, a contagious atmosphere which is breathed, and which seems to stick to all those who live there.'[7] The burning vapours then rose up, spread through the air and fell on the neighbourhood, impregnating bodies and contaminating souls. The idea of this evil-rot contagion was thus accomplished in images. The sensible agent of this epidemic was the air, which was described as 'spoilt', a dark intimation that the purity of its nature had been lost, and that it had become the medium through which vice was transmitted.[8] It is enough to recall here the moral and medical connotations that the air of the countryside was taking on at this time (for a healthy body and a robust soul) to understand the whole network of opposite meanings that hospitals, prisons and houses of confinement evoked. Thanks to this atmosphere heavy with ill-boding vapours, whole cities were under threat, and their inhabitants were slowly being impregnated with rotten-ness and vice.

And these were not merely reflections half-way between morality and medicine. A whole literary mechanism was at work, exploiting ill-defined fears on a pathetic and perhaps even political level. But some towns also saw moments of panic that were as real and easy to date as the mass fears periodically experienced by the Middle Ages. In 1780, an epidemic spread through Paris, and its origin was attributed to an infection at the Hôpital Général, and there was talk even of going to burn the buildings at Bicêtre. Faced with panic among the populace, the Lieutenant of Police sent in a commission of inquiry that included, along with several royal doctors, the dean of the Faculty and the physician from the Hôpital Général. It was concluded that there was indeed a 'putrid fever' there, linked to the poor quality of the air. As for the primary origin of the disease, however, the report refused to put it down to the presence of the internees, and the infection that they spread, but instead quite simply blamed the bad weather that had caused the infection to become endemic in the capital. The symptoms observed at the Hôpital Général were 'no more than was to be expected for the time of year, and differ little from anything to be observed in Paris in that period.' The aim was to reassure the population, and ensure that Bicêtre itself was not to blame: 'The rumours that began to spread about a contagious sickness emanating from Bicêtre capable of infecting the whole capital are without foundation.'[9] Evidently the report was not quite sufficient to quell all fears, as some time later the doctor in residence at the Hôpital Général published a second report repeat-ing the demonstration. He was obliged to recognise the poor sanitary conditions at Bicêtre but

> it is simply not the case that things have come to the cruel extremity where a hospice for unfortunates has become a new source of inevitable woes more serious than those whom it was set up to treat swiftly and expeditiously.[10]

The circle was therefore complete: all the forms of unreason, which in the geography of evil had taken the place of leprosy, and had been banished to the extreme margins of society, had become a visible form of leprosy, offering their corrosive wounds to the promiscuity of men. Unreason made its presence felt afresh, but it now bore the imaginary mark of a disease that lent it its power to terrorize.

It is therefore in the realm of the fantastical, and not in the rigour of medical thought, that unreason faces disease, and approaches it once more. Long before the problem of knowing to what extent the unreasonable was pathological had been formulated, what had appeared within the space of confinement, and by an alchemy that was all its own, was a blend of the horror of unreason and the ancient preoccupations about disease. The age-old confusion about leprosy came to the fore once more, and it was the vigour of those fantastical themes that formed the first agent of synthesis between the world of unreason and the medical universe. They communicated first of all through the phantasms of fear, meeting in the infernal confusion between 'corruption' and 'vice'. It is important, and decisive perhaps for the place that madness was to occupy in modern culture, that *homo medicus* had not been called to the world of confinement to *arbitrate* between sickness and evil, and decide in what measure acts were criminal or insane, but rather as a *guardian*, to protect others from the confused danger that emanated from inside the walls of confinement. It is easy to believe that this new interest in the fate of the confined was the result of some generous liberal tenderness, and that greater probity in medical attentiveness could now see sickness where previously there had only been the punishment of faults. But in fact things did not come about in an atmosphere of well-meaning neutrality. If the advice of doctors was sought, and they were asked to observe, it was simply because people were afraid. They were afraid of the strange chemistry that simmered inside the walls of the houses of confinement, afraid of the powers that formed there and threatened to spread. The men of medicine came after the imaginary conversion had been operated, and the sickness had taken on the ambiguous aspects of Fermentation, Corruption, miasma and decomposed flesh. What is traditionally regarded as 'progress' towards the acquisition of a medical status for madness was in fact only possible as the result of a strange return. In the inextricable mixture of moral and physical contagion, and by virtue of the symbolism of the Impure so familiar to the eighteenth century, antique images resurfaced in the minds of men.[11] Thanks to that imaginary reactivation, rather than a perfecting of knowledge, unreason found itself facing medical thought. Paradoxically, in the return of this fantastical life that blended with contemporary images of sickness, positivism was to get a hold on unreason, or rather find a new reason to defend itself from it.

There was no question for the moment of suppressing the houses of confinement. The concern was rather to neutralise them as possible causes of a new disease. They were to be reorganised through a process of purification. The great movement of reform that swept through the institutions in the second half of the eighteenth century had its origins there, in the desire to reduce contamination by the destruction of vapours and impurities; quelling the fermentation would prevent diseases, and evil, from permeating the air and spreading their contagion to the atmosphere of the cities. Hospitals, gaols and houses of confinement were all to be better isolated, and surrounded by purer air, and the period gave rise to a whole literature concerning the importance of proper ventilation in hospitals, which was a distant approximation to the medical problem of contagion, but which tended to focus more closely on themes of moral communication.[12] In 1776, a decree by the Council of State set up a commission that was to oversee 'the degree of improvement required in various hospitals in France'. Not long after, Viel was instructed to rebuild the wards in the Salpêtrière. The new dream was of an asylum which, while preserving its essential functions, would be set up in such fashion that disease could vegetate there without spreading, an asylum where unreason would be entirely contained and offered as a spectacle without ever threatening spectators, where it would have the power of example and none of the risks of contagion. The idea, in short, was to build asylums equal to their true nature as cages. It was this same dream of 'sterilised' confinement (if we can use such an anachronistic term in this context) that reappeared in 1789, in a pamphlet on *National Benevolence* by a priest named Desmonceaux, who proposed using asylums as tools to teach the wages of immorality:

> These guarded asylums . . . are retreats as useful as they are necessary . . . the appearance of these dark places and the guilty souls that they contain is ideal for warning licentious youths of the dangers of their ways; so much so that prudent fathers and mothers do well to ensure that their offspring are familiar with these awful, detestable places from an early age, showing them these places where shame and moral turpitude are attached to crime, and demonstrating that men who have soiled the essence of their being often lose forever the rights to which society had entitled them.[13]

Such were the dreams with which morality, with the complicity of medicine, attempted to defend itself against the notorious dangers that constantly threatened to slip the shackles of confinement. At the same time, these perils were objects of fascination for the imagination and for desires. The moral dream was to tame them, but there was something in man that dreamt of living them, or at least of getting close to them and thereby liberating fantasies. The horror that now surrounded the fortresses of confinement began to exert an almost irresistible appeal. Nights were peopled with inaccessible pleasures, and corrupt, ravaged faces suddenly took on a voluptuous countenance, and out of these dark landscapes there rose up strange combinations of pleasure and pain, recalling Hieronymus Bosch and his delirious gardens. The secrets that seeped from the castle in Sade's 120 *Jours de Sodom* were long whispered there:

> There, the most infamous excesses are carried out on the body of prisoners, and I have heard talk of certain notorious vices frequently practised there, even in public in the communal rooms of the prison, vices that the decency of modern times does not permit me to name. It is said that numerous prisoners *simillimi feminis mares stuprati et constupratores* [are men scarcely distinguishable from women, committing and submitting to debauchery], and that they return *ex hoc obscaeno sacrario cooperti stupri suis alienisque* [from these obscene ceremonies covered with the traces of their own debauchery and that of others], lost to all shame and ready to commit all manner of crimes.[14]

In his turn, La Rochefoucauld-Liancourt also spoke of women young and old in houses of correction and in the Salpêtrière who passed the same secrets and the same pleasures down the generations:

> The correctional centre, which is the punitive section of the house, contained some 47 girls when we visited, who for the most part were very young, and more thoughtless than guilty . . . but we witnessed also a terrible confusion of ages, and this shocking mix of frivolous girls with inveterate older women, who have nothing to teach them so much as the most shameful arts of corruption.[15]

Such visions persisted for a long time, deep into the night of the eighteenth century. They were dissected under a pitiless spotlight in the work of Sade, where they were subjected to the rigorous geometry of Desire. They were also to be found in the half-light of Goya's *Madhouse*, or the twilight that enveloped the *Quinta del sordo*.[16] How similar they are to the faces of the *Disparates* [*Proverbs*]! A whole imaginary landscape re-emerges, animated by the great Fear that confinement now evokes.

What classicism had locked up was not simply unreason in the abstract, where the mad, the libertine, the criminal and the sick all intermingled, but also a prodigious reserve of fantasy, a sleepy world of monsters, which were believed to have sunk back into the Bosch night from which they had first emerged. It was as though a new and totally opposed cultural role had been added to the fortresses of confinement, with their social role of segregation and purification. At the moment when on the surface of society they separated reason and unreason, they also kept, in depth, images where both seemed to mingle and fuse. They had long functioned like a great memory that had kept silent, and lurking in their shadows was the dark power of an imaginary that many hoped had been exorcised for good. Erected by the new classical order, they had preserved, against it and against the times, forbidden shapes that were transmitted intact from the sixteenth to the nineteenth century. In this timeless space, the Brocken rose beside *Dulle Griet*, and Sade's Noirceuil stands shoulder to shoulder with the great legend of Gilles de Rais.[17] Confinement permitted and even fostered this resistance of the imaginary.

But the images which broke free at the end of the eighteenth century were not identical to those which the seventeenth century had attempted to efface. Something had been worked through in the darkness, freeing them from the nether world where the Renaissance and the Middle Ages had first encountered them, and they had taken their places in the hearts, desires and imagination of men, and instead of signalling an abrupt eruption of insanity, they served instead to indicate the strange contradictions of the human appetite, the complicity of murder and desire, cruelty and the thirst for suffering, sovereignty and slavery, insult and humiliation. The great cosmic conflict of the fifteenth and sixteenth centuries, of which the Insane told the narrative, was so displaced that by the end of the classical age it had become the unmediated dialectics of the heart. Sadism is not a name finally given to a practice as old as Eros: it is a massive cultural fact that appeared precisely at the close of the eighteenth century, constituting one of the great conversions in the Western imagination – unreason transformed into the delirium of the heart, the madness of desire, and an insane dialogue between love and death in the limitless presumption of appetite. The appearance of Sadism comes at a moment when unreason, emerging from a century and a half of silence, reappears not as a figure of the world, nor as an image, but as discourse and desire. And it is no coincidence that Sadism, as an individual phenomenon that bears the name of a single man, is born from and within confinement, and that confinement figures so strongly in an *oeuvre* ordered around images of the Fortress, the Cell, the Dungeon, the Convent, the inaccessible Island that seem to be the natural places of unreason. Neither is it a coincidence that the whole fantasy literature of madness and horror contemporary with Sade's work takes place primarily in the high places of confinement. This sudden conversion in the late eighteenth century of the Western memory, and the possibility of finding familiar figures from the late Middle Ages, distorted and bearing new meanings, was authorised and enabled by the subsistence of the fantastic in the very places where unreason had been reduced to silence.

*

In the classical era, consciousness of madness and consciousness of unreason had not really been separated from each other. The experience of unreason that had guided so many of the practices of confinement smothered the consciousness of madness to such a degree that it very nearly caused it to disappear altogether, setting it off on a regressive path where it almost lost its most specific markers.

But in the anxiety of the second half of the eighteenth century, the fear of madness grew at the same rate as the dread of unreason, and for that reason these twin obsessions constantly reinforced each other. And just as the imaginary forces that accompanied unreason seemed to break loose, there came a deluge of concerns about the possible ravages of madness. We have already seen the worries that led to the birth of 'diseases of the nerves', and the belief that men became more fragile as they became more perfect.[18] As the century advanced the concern became more pressing, and the warnings ever more solemn. Soon Raulin was observing that 'since the birth of medicine, such sicknesses have multiplied, becoming more dangerous, more complicated, more thorny and difficult to cure'.[19] By the time of Tissot, that general impression had become a firmly entrenched belief, a sort of medical dogma – nervous diseases were:

previously much less common than they are today, above all for two reasons. In general men were more robust, and more rarely ill, and there were fewer diseases of all varieties. And secondly, the causes that produce nervous diseases in particular have multiplied in a greater proportion for some time now than other general causes of disease, some of which are even seeming to diminish . . . It is safe to say that if in previous times they were rarer, today they are the most frequent variety.[20]

Before long, the awareness of the fragility of reason, so common in the sixteenth century, and the knowledge that it could be definitively compromised at any moment by madness, was once again a common preoccupation. Matthey, a physician from Geneva much influenced by Rousseau, had the following warning for men of reason:

> Do not glory in your state, wise and civilised men: the so-called wisdom with which you flatter yourselves can be shattered in an instant. An unexpected event, or a sudden, intense emotion of the soul can send even the greatest or most reasonable man into a frenzy, or turn him into an idiot in a moment.[21]

The threat of madness took its place once more among the most pressing matters of the century.

And yet this consciousness was of a very specific style. The dread of unreason was affective in the extreme, and caught up almost in its entirety to this movement of resurrections of the imaginary. The fear of madness was much freer regarding that heritage, and while the return of unreason took on the appearance of a massive repetition, re-establishing its links with its previous incarnations down the ages, the consciousness of madness by contrast was accompanied by a certain analysis of modernity, which immediately placed it within a temporal, social and historical framework. In this disparity between the consciousness of madness and the consciousness of unreason, we find, in the late eighteenth century, the starting point of what was to be a decisive moment, where the experience of unreason, such as is evident in Hölderlin, Nerval and Nietzsche, always leads back to the roots of time – unreason thereby becoming the untimely within the world *par excellence* – while the knowledge of madness sought on the contrary to situate it ever more precisely within the direction of nature and history in their development. It is from this period onwards that the time of unreason and the time of madness were to be affected by two opposing vectors: unreason becoming an unconditional return, and an absolute plunge; madness developing along the chronology of a history.[22]

This acquisition of a temporal consciousness of madness did not happen all at once. It required the elaboration of a whole series of new concepts, and often the reinterpretation of some very ancient themes. Medical thought of the seventeenth and eighteenth centuries had willingly admitted an almost immediate link between madness and the world, as in the belief about the influence of the moon, or the widespread conviction that climate had a direct influence on the nature and quality of the animal spirits, and consequently on the nervous system, the imagination, the passions and all the sicknesses of the soul.[23] That dependence was neither clear in its principles, nor univocal in its effects. Cheyne admitted that the dampness of the air, swift changes of temperature and frequent rain compromise the solidity of the nervous fibre.[24] Venel, on the other hand, thought that 'cold air is heavier, thicker and more elastic, and therefore compresses solids more, increasing the firmness of their texture and making their action more efficient'. Hot air, by contrast:

> is lighter, thinner, less elastic, and therefore less compressive, so solids lose their tone, and humours stagnate and spoil; as the inner air is not counterbalanced by the outer air, fluids expand, dilate and distend the vessels that contain them, overcoming their reaction, and sometimes even breaking out of their confines.[25]

To the classical mind, madness could easily be the effect of an external 'milieu', or more exactly the stigmata of a certain solidarity with the world: just as the access to the truth of the world, after the fall, had to pass through the tortuous and often distorting medium of the senses, so the possession of reason depended to some extent on the 'physical state of the machine', and all the mechanical effects that might act upon it.[26] This we might term a naturalistic, theological take on the ancient themes of the Renaissance, where madness was linked to a whole selection of dramas and cosmic cycles.

But a new notion was to emerge from this global apprehension of a dependence. Owing to the growing concern, the link with the constants or the great circular patterns of the universe, i.e. the theme of madness as linked to the seasons of the world, was slowly supplemented with the idea of a dependence on a particular element of the cosmos. The fear was more urgent: the affective intensity of everything that reacted to madness never ceased to grow, and it is as though what emerged from the cosmic whole and its seasonal stability was an independent, relative and mobile element, subject to constant progression and continuous acceleration, whose task it was to explain this incessant multiplication, the grand contagion of madness. From the macrocosm, taken as the place where all mechanisms were complicitous, and as the general concept of their laws, something resembling that which the nineteenth century was later to term a 'milieu' starts to emerge.

Perhaps we should allow this notion, which had not yet found its equilibrium or its final denomination, to retain its unfinished nature, and speak instead, like Buffon, of 'penetrating forces', which allowed not only for the formation of an individual, but also the appearance of the different varieties of the human species: the influences of climate, of nutrition and of the way of life.[27] This negative, 'differential' notion first appeared in the eighteenth century, to explain variations and diseases rather than adaptations and convergences. It was as if the 'penetrating forces' formed the converse, or the negative, of what was later to become the positive notion of a milieu.

Paradoxically for us, we can observe the notion coming into being when men appear insufficiently constrained by social ties, and seem to float in a time where obligations have disappeared, and when they become too distant both from the true and from the sensible. 'Penetrating forces' designates a society that no longer contains desires, a religion that no longer regulates time and imagination, and a civilisation that no longer limits the errings of thought and sensibility.

1   *Madness and freedom.* For a long time, certain forms of melancholy were considered to be specifically English. This was a medical fact, and a constant in literature.[28] Montesquieu contrasted Roman suicide, a moral and political form of behaviour, the desired effect of concerted education, with English suicide, which should properly be considered an illness as 'Englishmen kill themselves for no reason we can imagine determining their actions: they kill themselves even in perfect happiness.'[29] Here the milieu had a role to play. For if in the eighteenth century happiness was linked to nature and reason, unhappiness, or at least all the factors that put an end without reason to happiness, had to be of a different order. That order was to be sought first of all in extremes of climate, and in the

deviation of nature from its own equilibrium and happy mean (temperate climates belong to the order of nature: excessive temperatures to that of the milieu). But that was insufficient to explain the English malady, and Cheyne was of the opinion that the wealth, the refined food and the general abundance that the inhabitants enjoyed, the life of leisure and laziness led by the richest society were at the origin of these nervous troubles.[30] Increasingly a political and economic explanation was sought, where riches, progress and the institutions were seen as determining factors for madness. In the early nineteenth century, Spurzheim made a synthesis of these analyses in one of the last texts on the subject. Madness, in England, was 'more frequent than elsewhere', and was no more than the price to be paid for the liberty to be found there, and for the widespread wealth of the country. Freedom of conscience brought more dangers than despotism or authoritarian rule. 'Religious sentiments . . . have no restrictions upon them; anyone can preach to anyone else who wants to listen', and the long-term effects of hearing so many different opinions are that 'minds are tormented in their search for the truth'. These were the perils of indecision, of attention not knowing where to attach itself, of a soul that vacillated. The quarrels and passions of a mind that clung firmly to the beliefs that it had chosen were another peril: 'All things find their opposition, and opposition excites the sentiments; in religion, politics, science and any other field, anyone can form a party; but they must expect also to find stiff competition.' Such an excess of liberty also meant that time could never be mastered, so the English suffered from its uncertainties, and everyone was abandoned by the state to its fluctuations: 'The English are a mercantile nation, and a mind always preoccupied with speculation is continually agitated by fear and hope. Selfishness, the soul of commerce, can quickly turn to envy, calling other faculties to its side.' In any case, such liberty was far distant from true, natural freedom; it was constrained on all sides, and constantly harried by the demands opposed to the most legitimate desires of the individuals. This was the freedom of interests, of coalitions and financial associations, not of men or their hearts and minds. For financial reasons, families were more tyrannical than elsewhere. Only rich daughters found husbands, 'the others being reduced to other means of satisfaction that ruin the body and disturb the manifestations of the soul. The same causes dispose to libertinage, and this in turn predisposes to madness.'[31] Mercantilist liberty thus appeared as the element within which opinion could never accede to the truth, where the immediate was necessarily a realm of contradiction, where time, now impossible to master, had lost the certainties of the seasons, and where men were dispossessed of their desires by the laws of interest. Freedom, in short, far from allowing men to become their own masters, drove them ever further from their essence and their world; in it, they were fascinated by the absolute exteriority of others and of money, and the irreversible interiority of passion and unfulfilled desire. Between man and the happiness of a world where he found his place, between man and a nature where he found his truth, the freedom of the mercantile state was a 'milieu', and on that account it was a determining factor in madness. At the time when Spurzheim was writing – the time of the Holy Alliance and the restoration of authoritarian monarchies – liberalism was made to bear all the sins of the madness of the world: 'It is strange to see how man's greatest desire, which is his personal freedom, has also its disadvantages.'[32] But for our purposes, the key element in such an analysis is not the critique of liberty, but the use of a notion which for Spurzheim meant the non-natural milieu, where the psychological and physiological mechanisms of madness were favoured, amplified and multiplied.

2 *Madness, religion and time.* Religious beliefs prepare a sort of imaginary landscape, an illusory milieu that encourages hallucinations and all forms of delirium. Doctors had long feared the effects of unusually intense devotion and overly strong beliefs. An excess of moral rigour or an unhealthy concentration on salvation and the life to come were often enough to push patients into melancholy. The *Encyclopédie* had many examples to offer:

> The overly strong impressions caused by certain excessive preachers, and the undue fear of the future suffering reserved by our religion for those who fail to uphold its tenets, can bring about astonishing revolutions in the feeble-minded. In the hospital at Montélimar, it is reported that several women were struck down with mania and melancholia after a mission had visited the town; they were constantly plagued by the horrible paintings they had so inconsiderately been shown, and spoke only of despair, vengeance, punishment and so forth, and among them was one who would accept no medicine, believing that she was in Hell already, and that nothing could extinguish the flames by which she claimed she was already being devoured.[33]

Pinel continued the line of these enlightened doctors, forbidding prayer books to be given to anyone 'melancholic by piety', and even recommending seclusion for 'devout women who believe themselves to be inspired, and who are constantly attempting to turn others to such proselytising'.[34] But what we find here is more a critique than a positive analysis: the religious object or themes are suspected of bringing delirium or hallucination on account of the delirious or hallucinatory character with which they are invested. Pinel recounted the case of a madwoman who had been recently cured, for whom, 'a devotional book recalled that each person had their own guardian angel; the following night, she believed that she was surrounded by a choir of angels, and claimed that she had heard celestial music and had had revelations'.[35] Here again religion was only considered to be an element through which error is transmitted. But even before Pinel, there had been analyses in a much more rigorous historical style, where religion appeared as a milieu for the satisfaction or repression of passions. In 1781, a German author evoked the distant happy times when priests were granted absolute power, and idleness was unknown; each instant was marked by 'ceremonies, religious practices, pilgrimages, visits to the poor and the sick, and feast days on the calendar'. Time was thus fully dedicated to organised happiness, leaving no leisure for empty passions, boredom or disgust with life. If someone felt guilty, a punishment was administered immediately, often in material form, to occupy the spirit and bring the certainty that the fault had been repaired. When the confessor encountered 'hypochondriac patients who went to confession too often', he either gave them as penance a severe punishment that 'diluted their thick, sluggish blood', or sent them on a long pilgrimage:

> The change of air, the long road, absence from home, distance from the objects that brought them suffering, the company of the other pilgrims, the slow energetic movements that they were forced to make by walking, all acted on them far more effectively than the comfortable journeys . . . that nowadays pass for pilgrimages.

And the sacred character of the priest gave each of his injunctions an absolute value, so no one dreamt of trying to avoid them: 'the capriciousness of patients means that they rarely have such trust and faith in their physician'.[36] For Moehsen, religion was a mediation between men and their faults, between men and punishment: in the form of an authoritarian synthesis it genuinely removed faults by carrying out a punishment; if, by contrast, religion became more lax, and was only perpetuated through idealised forms, like remorse or spiritual maceration, then it led directly to madness. Only the substantiality of the religious milieu enabled men to escape alienation in the excessive delirium of guilt. In the plenitude of its rites and its demands, it spared men the useless leisure of pre-lapsarian passions, and the empty repetition of remorse after the act; it organised all human life around the instant, in its full accomplishment. The ancient religion of happier times was the perpetual celebration of the present. But as soon as it became more idealised in the modern age, it surrounded the present with a temporal halo, an empty milieu, that of leisure and remorse, where men's hearts were given over to worry, and where passions opened time to indifference or repetition, a milieu where madness could ultimately develop freely.

3 *Madness, civilisation and sensibility.* In general terms, civilisation was a milieu favourable to the development of madness. If progress in the sciences tended to dissipate errors, it also had the effect of spreading a taste or even a mania for study. This aloofness, with its abstract speculations and a perpetual agitation of the spirit with no exercise of the body, often brought the most harmful effects. Tissot explained that in the human body, it was the parts that exercised most frequently that were the first to harden. In a labourer, the muscles and fibres of the arm hardened, giving such men their characteristic strength, and the robust health that they enjoyed until an advanced age; 'but in men of letters it is the brain that hardens, so much so that they often become incapable of stringing two ideas together', in which case dementia beckoned.[37] The more abstract or complex a science, the greater the risk of madness it presented. Forms of knowledge that remained close to the immediacy of the senses, according to Pressavin, put less strain on the inner sense and the organs of the brain, bringing nothing but a sort of physiological happiness: 'Sciences whose objects are easily perceived by the senses, and which are agreeable to the soul in the harmony of their relations . . . require only a slight effort from the whole body, which is beneficial to all its functions.' But forms of knowledge that had few direct links to the senses and no connection to the immediate brought only tension to the brain, throwing the equilibrium of the whole body out of kilter:

> The sciences of things whose relations are difficult to grasp due to the absence of any connection with the senses, or where these relations are

> excessively multiplied and oblige us to make a great mental effort in our research, present the soul with a form of exercise that fatigues the inner sense on account of the over-lengthy strain placed upon the brain.[38]

Knowledge thus forms around sensibility a whole milieu of abstract relations where men risk losing the physical happiness in which their relation to the world normally takes place. Knowledge admittedly advances and multiplies, but so does its price. It was far from certain that there were any more men of knowledge, but one thing was sure: 'there are more people who suffer the consequences'.[39] The milieu of knowledge grew more quickly than knowledge itself.

But science was not the only factor that distanced men from the sensible: sensibility itself could play that role, particularly if it was no longer commanded by the movements of nature, but ruled instead by habit or by the demands of society. Modern men, and modern women even more so, turned day into night and night into day:

> The time when our women get up in Paris bears but a distant relation to what nature intended; the best hours of the day are gone, the pure air has disappeared, and no one has benefited from it. Vapours and harmful exhalations, attracted by the heat of the sun, are already rising up through the air; and this is the time when beauty chooses to rise from her slumbers.[40]

This disorder of the senses continued at the theatre, where illusion was cultivated and vain passions were elicited by artificial means, bringing dangerous movements of the soul. Women above all love these spectacles, 'which enflame and exalt them', so that

> their soul is so strongly stirred that it produces a commotion in their nerves, which may be fleeting, but whose consequences are often most serious. The momentary loss of their senses, and the tears that they shed at a performance of one of our modern tragedies are the least of the accidents that may then befall them.[41]

Novels were a more artificial milieu still, and even more harmful for a disordered sensibility. The verisimilitude that modern writers strove to attain, and the artfulness that they deployed to imitate the truth only enhance the prestige of the violent and dangerous sentiments that they sought to awaken in their female readers:

> In the early centuries of French gallantry and manners, the less perfected minds of women were content with stories and accounts as marvellous as they were unbelievable; but now they want credible facts, and emotions so marvellous that their own are quite moved and confounded; and then they cast all around them in real life to find the marvels that so enchanted them in literature, but everything seems lifeless and devoid of sentiment, as what they seek is not to be found in nature.[42]

The novel was the milieu for the perversion of sensibility *par excellence*. It detached the soul from all that was immediate and natural in the sensible, dragging it into an imaginary world of feelings that were all the more violent for being unreal, and therefore unregulated by the sweet laws of nature:

> This plethora of authors generates a crowd of readers, and constant reading produces all the diseases of the nerves. Perhaps of all the causes that have been harmful to the health of women over the last century, the infinite multiplication of novels is the most important . . . A girl of ten who reads rather than running around will be a woman who suffers from the vapours at 20, and not a solid wet nurse.[43]

Slowly, and in a still disparate style, the eighteenth century put in place a whole new order of concepts around this consciousness of madness and its menacing increase. In the landscape of unreason where it had been placed by the seventeenth century, madness concealed a meaning and origin that were obscurely moral; its secret likened it to sin, and the imminent animality perceived in it paradoxically did nothing to make it more innocent. In the second half of the eighteenth century, it was no longer recognised in all that brought men close to their timeless fall, or to their indefinitely present animality. It was situated instead in the distance that men took from themselves, from their world, and from all that was offered to them in the immediacy of nature. Madness became possible in this *milieu* where man's relation with his feelings, with time and with others was altered, and was made possible by that rupture with immediacy in man's life and his becoming. It was no longer of the order of nature or of the fall, but bore witness instead to a new order, where history began to be felt, and where, in an obscure, shared origin, the 'alienation' of physicians and the 'alienation' of philosophers started to take shape – two configurations in which man in any case corrupts his truth, but between which, after Hegel, the nineteenth century stopped seeing any trace of resemblance.

*

This new way of apprehending madness through the determinant action of 'penetrating forces' was probably decisive – as decisive in the history of modern madness as Pinel's spectacular unchaining of the mad at Bicêtre.

What was strange and important was first of all the negative value of the concept, at this still archaic stage of its elaboration. In the analyses that we have just evoked, these forces do not designate what in nature can constitute the environment of a living being, and neither are they a place of adaptation or of reciprocal influence and regulation. They are not even the space in which a living being can deploy and impose the norms of its existence. The ensemble of these forces, if one unearths the significance that the thought of the eighteenth century obscurely placed upon them, constitutes precisely what in *cosmos* was opposed to *nature*.[44] The milieu upset time in the return of the seasons, in the alternation of day and night; it spoiled the realm of the sensible and its calm echoes in man, through the vibrations of a sensibility only attuned to the excesses of the imagination; and it distanced men from their immediate satisfactions, obliging them to submit to laws of interest that prevented him from hearing the voice of his own desire. The milieu began where nature began to die in man. Rousseau had already demonstrated how nature had ended, and how the human milieu had taken its place, with the cosmic catastrophe that was the collapse of the continents.[45] A milieu was not the positivity of nature such as it was offered to living being, but rather the negativity in which nature in its plenitude was withdrawn from the living being; and in that retreat, in that non-nature, something was substituted for nature, which was the plenitude of artifice, an illusory world of antiphysis.

And it was precisely there that the possibility of madness took on its full significance. The seventeenth century discovered it in the loss of truth: an entirely negative possibility, where the only thing in question was that faculty of waking and attention in man that was not nature but freedom. The late eighteenth century began to identify the possibility of madness with the constitution of a milieu: madness was lost nature, misplaced sensibility, the wanderings of desire, time dispossessed of its measure. It was immediacy lost in the infinity of mediations. And facing it was nature, madness abolished, a happy return of existence to its closest truth. 'Come, you lovable, sensual women,' wrote Beauchesne

> And flee the dangers of false pleasures, fleeting passions, luxury and inaction; follow your young husbands to the countryside, and on journeys; race them across grassy, flower-strewn prairies, then come back to Paris as an example to your companions, showing them the beneficial exercise and work that befits your sex. Love, and bring up your children above all, and you will learn to what degree this pleasure is greater than any other, and how it has been reserved for you by nature; you will grow old slowly, if your life is pure.[46]

Milieu therefore plays a role that is almost a mirror image of the role previously taken by animality. In earlier times there was the lurking presence of the beast, the point through which madness, in its rage, could irrupt into man; the deepest point, the ultimate point of natural existence was also the point where the counter-natural was exalted – human nature being to itself, immediately, its own counter-nature. But at the end of the eighteenth century, animality had come to be associated with the tranquillity and happiness to be found in nature, and it was by escaping from the immediacy of natural life at the moment when a milieu is constituted that man opens himself to the possibility of a counter-nature, exposing himself to the perils of madness. The animal could not be mad, or at least it was not in its animality that its madness could originate.[47] It was therefore quite natural that primitive men were the least disposed to madness:

> The order of labourers is easily superior in that respect to the social stratum that provides artisans, but unfortunately far inferior to what it was in times gone by, when the people was solely constituted of labourers; a state only found in a few savage peoples, who are strangers to

sickness and disease, and die almost exclusively in accidents or of old age.

In the early nineteenth century, Rush noted that in America 'after much inquiry, [he had] not been able to find a single instance of fatuity among the Indians, and but few instances of melancholy and madness'.[48] Similarly, Humboldt had 'never heard of a single alienated man among the wild Indians of southern America'.[49] Madness was made possible by all that the milieu repressed in man of his animal nature.[50]

From that point on, madness was linked to a certain form of becoming in man. For as long as madness was experienced as a cosmic menace or the imminence of the animal, it lurked in the shadows around man, or in the depths of his heart, as a perpetual, immobile presence; its cycles were a return, and each appearance in fact a reappearance. But now madness had a temporal starting point, even if that was only to be understood in a mythic sense; it followed a linear vector, which indicated an infinite progression. As the milieu constituted by and around man grew ever denser, the risks of madness grew. The time within which they unfolded became an infinite openness, a time of multiplication and growth. Madness then became the other side of progress: by multiplying mediations, civilisation offered men ever-increasing means to become insane. Matthey did little more than sum up a general feeling common to many men in the eighteenth century when he wrote at the time of the restoration that:

> The greatest miseries of man in society, as well as his most numerous pleasures, are born out of the excellence of his nature, of his perfectibility and the excessive development of his physical and moral faculties. The multitude of his needs, his desires and his passions are all the result of civilisation, the source of vice and virtue, of all good and all evil combined. It is from the heart of the opulence and luxury of city life that groans of misery and cries of rage and fury are heard. Bicêtre and Bethlem are proof of that.[51]

That simple dialectic of good and evil, progress and suffering, reason and unreason is a familiar feature of the eighteenth century, but its importance was decisive in the history of madness. It overturned the temporal perspective against which madness was commonly measured, and placed it within the indefinite unfolding of a time of which the point of origin was fixed but the end constantly deferred. It placed madness within an irreversible duration, breaking its cosmic cycles and obliterating the fascination with the past fault. It promised that madness would one day take over the world, not in the apocalyptic form of the triumph of the Insane the fifteenth century had imagined, but in a continuous, pernicious and progressive manner that had no foreseeable end-figure, growing ever more youthful from the very ageing of the world around it. What came into being just before the Revolution was one of the great obsessions of the nineteenth century, and before long it had a name: 'degeneration'.

Obviously, one of the most common themes in Graeco-Latin culture is the idea that children no longer uphold the values of their parents, this going hand in hand with a nostalgia for some antique wisdom, the secrets of which are lost in the madness of the modern world. But that was still a moral idea, whose only support was critical: it was less a perception than a refusal of history. But in the eighteenth century, by contrast, this empty temporality of decadence and decay began to be filled with a more concrete content. Degeneration was no longer a slippery moral slope, but was determined by the lines of force of the human milieu, or by the laws of physical heredity. It was not because they forgot time, understood as the memory of the immemorial, that men became degenerate, but rather because time grew heavy within them, becoming more pressing and more present, like a sort of material memory of the body, totalising the past and detaching existence from its natural immediacy:

> Children bear the consequences of the ills of their fathers. Our great-grandparents were the first to stray from the path of a healthy way of life, and our grandparents were weakened accordingly, bringing their own children with even less rigour, who in their turn had children who were weaker still. We, the fourth generation, now only know of the strength and health of our eighty-year-old forebears by hearsay.[52]

In what Tissot calls 'degeneration' [*dégénération*], there was little of what the nineteenth century was to term 'degeneracy' [*dégénérescence*]. It did not yet have a specific character, there was no fatal tendency to return to more rudimentary forms of life and organisation,[53] and there was as yet no hope placed in a regenerating individual.[54] Yet Morel, in his *Traité de la Dégénérescence*, begins with the teaching he received from the eighteenth century. For him, as was already the case with Tissot, men degenerated from a primitive type,[55] not as part of a spontaneous process of decay or a gravity inherent in all living matter, but more probably as the result of 'the influence of social institutions that run against nature', or even as a result of 'the decaying of the morality of nature'.[56] From Tissot to Morel, the same lesson is repeated, lending the human milieu a power of alienation, made up essentially of the memory of everything that within it mediates nature. Madness, and all its powers that were multiplied by the ages, lay not in man but in the milieu that he inhabited. We find ourselves here at a point in time when a Hegelian philosophical theme – alienation is in the movement of mediations – is still not distinguished from a biological theme best summed up by Bichat, who noted: 'all that surrounds living beings tends to destroy them'. The death of the individual is exterior to him, like his madness and his alienation; it was in that exteriority, the weighty memory of things, that men lost their truth. And how better to regain it than in another memory? A memory which could be either a reconciliation in the interiority of knowledge, or the total rupture and plunge into the absolute of time, the immediate youthfulness of barbarism: 'Either reasoned behaviour, which is perhaps too much to hope for, or a succession of barbaric centuries that no one dares desire.'[57]

In this reflection on madness,[58] and the still-nascent elaboration of the concept of the milieu, the eighteenth century strangely anticipated what were to become in the age that followed the guiding themes in all thinking about men. And in a light still dim, on the fringes of philosophy and medicine, psychology and history, with a naivety that all the disquiet of the nineteenth century and indeed our own age have yet to dispel, it proposed a very rudimentary concept of alienation, which allowed the human milieu to be defined as the negativity of man, in which the concrete *a priori* of all forms of madness were to be discerned. Madness was thus placed as close to and as far as possible from man; in the place that he inhabits, and also in the place in which he loses himself, in a strange homeland where his residency was also that which abolished his being, the accomplished plenitude of his truth and the ceaseless work of his non-being.

*

Madness therefore entered a new cycle. It was now uncoupled from unreason, which would long remain the strictly philosophical or poetic province of writers like Sade and Hölderlin, Nerval and Nietzsche, a pure plunge into a language that abolished history and caused to glitter, on the most fragile surface of the sensible, the imminence of an immemorial truth. Madness, for the nineteenth century, was to have quite a different meaning: by its nature, and through everything that opposed it to nature, it was intimately connected to history.

It is easy for us to get the impression that the positivist conception of madness is physiological, naturalist and anti-historical, and that it took psychoanalysis, sociology, and nothing less than the 'psychology of cultures' to bring to light the links that the pathology of history might secretly have with history itself.[59] But in fact this was already quite clearly established at the end of the eighteenth century: from that point on, madness was clearly inscribed in the temporal destiny of man, and was even the consequence and the price of the fact that men, unlike animals, had history. The writer who noted, in an extraordinarily ambiguous phrase, that 'the history of madness is the counterpart of the history of reason', had read neither Janet, nor Freud nor Brunschvicg; he was a contemporary of Claude Bernard, who posited what seemed to him to be an obvious equation: 'to each age its own variety of madness'.[60] Few periods had a more acute consciousness of the historical relativity of madness than the opening years of the nineteenth century; 'how many points of contact there are from this point of view', wrote Pinel, 'between medicine and the history of the human species'.[61] Pinel judged himself lucky to have had the opportunity to study diseases of the mind at a moment as propitious as the Revolution, as this era, more than any other, fostered the 'vehement passions' that were 'most commonly at the origins of alienation'. What age could be more favourable to a study of these effects than 'the tempestuous storms of revolution, which exalt human passion, or rather mania in all its forms, to the highest degree?'[62] For many years to come French medicine was to look for the traces of the Terror of 1793 in the generations that followed, as though the violence of history and madness had somehow been sedimented into the silent time of heredity:

> There is no doubt that during the Revolution, the Terror was harmful to certain individuals, even when they were at their mothers' breast . . . The individuals predisposed to madness as a result all come from the regions which suffered the horrors of the war longest.[63]

The notion of madness, such as it existed during the nineteenth century, took shape inside a historical consciousness, and that in two ways: first because madness, in its constant acceleration, forms something like a derivative of history; and second because its forms are determined by the figures of becoming. Madness, as it was then perceived or at least experienced, was relative to time, and essential to the temporality of man, more fundamentally historical, in short, than it is for us today.

Yet that relation to history was to be quickly forgotten. Freud, with difficulty, and in a manner that was perhaps not really radical, was later obliged to free it from evolutionism. This was because this relation, in the course of the nineteenth century, turned into a social and moral conception that betrayed it entirely. Madness was no longer conceived of as the counterpart of history, but as the hidden face of society. In Morel's work, we can see the clearest illustration of this reversal of historical analysis into social criticism, taking madness out of the movement of history and making it an obstacle to its normal flow and its promises of reconciliation. For him, its most fertile breeding ground is poverty, whereas for the previous century it had been riches, or progress. The milieu most favourable to its proliferation is 'dangerous or insalubrious professions, and habitations that are unhealthy or overpopulated', compounded with various intoxications.

> If one joins to these generally poor conditions the profoundly demoralising influence exerted by poverty, a lack of education, a lack of foresight, the abuse of alcohol, venereal excesses and insufficient food, one begins to have an idea of the complex circumstances that tend to modify in an unfavourable manner the temperament of the poor.[64]

Madness thus eluded all that might be historical in human becoming, and instead took on meaning in social morality. It became the stigma of a class that had abandoned the forms of bourgeois ethics, and just as the philosophical concept of alienation was taking on a historical meaning thanks to the economic analysis of work, the medical and psychological concept of insanity was severed from history to become instead a moral criticism in the name of the compromised salvation of the species. In a word, the fear of madness, which for the eighteenth century was the fear of the consequences of its own becoming, was slowly transformed in the nineteenth century, to the point that it wound up as an obsession about the contradictions that nevertheless guaranteed that its structures remained in place. Madness became the paradoxical condition of the continuation of the bourgeois order, to which from the outside it nevertheless constituted the most immediate threat. It was thus perceived both as an indispensable degeneracy – as it was the condition of the eternity of bourgeois reason – and as an accidental or contingent forgetting of the principles of morality and religion, as it was necessary to render futile, by judging it, that which is in immediate contradiction with an order whose end could not be foreseen. Towards the middle of the nineteenth century, therefore, that historical consciousness of madness, which had been kept alive in the age of 'militant positivism', fell into a deep sleep.

This passage through history, however precarious and forgotten it might be now, was nonetheless a decisive moment for the experience of madness common to the nineteenth century. What appeared was a new relation to madness, more immediate in some senses, but more external as well. In the classical experience, men communicated with madness by means of error, in other words the consciousness of madness necessarily implied an experience of the truth. Madness was error *par excellence*, the absolute loss of truth. At the end of the eighteenth century, a new outline of madness was becoming discernible, where man no longer lost the truth but lost his truth instead; it was no longer that the laws of the world were suddenly out of reach, but rather that he was severed from the laws of his own essence. Tissot described this new development in the history of madness at the end of the eighteenth century as a forgetting by man of all that had made up his most immediate truth, as men

had recourse to artificial pleasures, contrary to the customs of nature many of which are nothing more than an attempt to be different, where strangeness is sought for its own sake. For many this madness becomes their reality, saving them from the harmful feeling of an empty excitement, a feeling that no man can tolerate for any length of time, and which makes anything preferable to such emptiness. There is no doubt that this is one of the origins of luxury, which is merely to be equipped with a multitude of superfluous things ... This state is that of a hypochondriac who needs a great variety of remedies to satisfy him, and who suffers all the same.[65]

In madness, man is separated from his own truth, and exiled into the immediate presence of surroundings in which he loses himself. When men of the classical age lost the truth, it meant that they were thrown back to an immediacy where their animal nature raged, and the primitive decay that accompanied it was a sure sign of original guilt. But to talk of a madman in the nineteenth century was to single out a man who had abandoned the ground of his own immediate truth, and had lost himself.

II

THE NEW DIVISION

In the course of the eighteenth century, the position of madness began to move. First came the fear that seemed to link unreason to age-old worries, lending it once more a presence that confinement had so nearly managed to destroy. But there was more. In the very place where madness had been laid to rest, in the homogeneous space of unreason, an obscure, slow, barely formulated transformation was taking place, whose superficial effects alone are visible; a profound shift allowed madness to appear once again, as it set itself apart and began to define itself in its own terms. The new fear of the eighteenth century turned out to be not without foundation. Madness was again perceptible, as a confused presence, but one which before long began to problematise the abstraction of confinement once more.

*

Everyone agreed that madness was increasing. But it is difficult to establish with any certainty that the numbers of the mad really did grow in the course of the eighteenth century, i.e. in a greater proportion than the rest of the population. The numbers are only available to us through those of confinement, which are not necessarily representative, both because the motivation behind confinement was often obscure, and because the number who were believed to be mad but were not confined was always greater. Some numerical facts are nonetheless certain.

Looking at things overall, and comparing the figures for the late seventeenth century with those from the beginning of the Revolution, it is clear that there is a massive increase. La Salpêtrière had 3,059 inmates in 1690; one hundred years later that figure had more than doubled, rising to 6,704, according to the report that La Rochefoucauld-Liancourt made to the Committee on Begging.[1] The proportions were the same for Bicêtre. The late seventeenth century had seen slightly fewer than 2,000 inmates, and by the time of the Revolution the numbers had risen to 3,874.[2] For some religious houses, the increase was even more marked. When the Brothers of Saint John of God opened their Charité centre of confinement in Senlis in 1665, it was to have four places; by 1780 there were 91, 67 of which were occupied.[3] Château-Thierry, which was initially also very small, was home to 30 by 1783.[4] But these figures need to be studied against the curve of their evolution for their full significance to become apparent. The periods during which confinement was being introduced and organised should also be taken into account: during the early days, which stretched more or less from 1680 to 1720, growth was extremely rapid, outstripping the rate of growth of the general population. But if we concentrate solely on the seventy years that precede the Revolution, the figures are astonishingly stable, which is all the more paradoxical in the light of the sharp upturn in the demographic curve during the same period. It would appear that the number of confinements slowly reached a peak in the 1770s, and then declined in the years immediately preceding the Revolution. On 1 January 1770 there were 4,052 internees at Bicêtre; 4,277 on 1 January 1772, 3,938 on 1 January 1774, and 3,668 in 1776. When the bursar Tristan closed the accounts on 9 April 1779, inmates numbered 3,518.[5] Saint-Lazare had 62 pensioners in 1733, 72 in 1736, and attained a maximum of 77 in 1776, but by 29 October 1788 there were a mere 40. On the eve of the Revolution, Château-Thierry counted no more than 25 pensioners.

These fluctuations suffice to demonstrate that the confinement regime did not faithfully follow the demographic curve. There were definitely other influences at work: poverty, and the severity of the repressions of the last years of the reign of Louis XV caused the numbers to swell, while an economic upturn, the war in America, and the restrictions introduced by Breteuil to the *lettres de cachet* procedure and to confinement practices caused the numbers in the population of the asylums to fall.

In so far as it is possible to determine such things without a great risk of error, it appears that the numbers of the mad followed a quite particular curve, which was neither the demographic curve nor exactly that of confinement. In the early years of the Salpêtrière, adding up the numbers of women locked up in the Magdaleine, Saint-Levèze, Saint-Hilaire, Sainte-Catherine and Sainte-Elizabeth wards, as well as in the cells, a total of 479 is reached, which we can say with some certainty represented the number of inmates who were considered insane.[6]

When Tenon had an investigation carried out in 1787, he found 600 mad women. La Rochefoucauld-Liancourt found 550. The movement was of a similar order in Bicêtre; in 1726 there were 132 'mad, violent or innocent' inmates; in 1789, 187 men were found locked up in Saint-Prix, the ward reserved for madmen.[7] The highest figure had been attained in 1788: 1784 saw 110 people admitted for insanity, while there were 127 in 1786, 151 in 1788, with the years that followed seeing 132, 103, and 92.[8] We are faced therefore with a relatively slow increase in the numbers of the mad – or at least in internees who were recognised and labelled as such – throughout the eighteenth century, with a maximum being attained in the years 1785–1788, and then a swift collapse as soon as the Revolution broke out.

This pattern of development is clearly quite strange. Not only does it not exactly follow the evolution of confinement or the growth of the population, but it also fails to correspond to the rapid growth in the fear of all forms of madness and unreason that was so widespread in the eighteenth century. Naturally, the figures should not be looked at in isolation; it is probable that the consciousness of a growth in madness was not linked to the intensity of measures of confinement, but depended rather on the numbers of the mad who were not locked up, but left instead, with a mix of concern and carelessness, to move freely through society. The discovery of the vapours and of nervous diseases, and the new importance of hysterical and hypochondriac conditions perhaps contributed more towards that fear than confinement itself. But what lends the evolutionary curve of the confinement of the insane its particular inflection is the intervention of a new fact that explains the relative stagnation of the figures in comparison to the rapid increase in the fear that surrounded madness. What kept the figures of the confinement of the insane in the old asylums down was the opening, in the mid-century period, of a whole series of institutions exclusively destined for the insane.

This phenomenon was almost as sudden as the Great Confinement in the seventeenth century, but it attracted even less notice. Yet its significance is essential. Already in 1695, the town of Aix had opened a hospital for the insane, provided they were violent or dangerous (a requirement that underlined the still purely repressive nature of the institution).[9] But in the eighteenth century, confinement in houses strictly reserved for the mad became a common practice. The Picpus Brothers had one such institution in Fontaine, near Lyon. The Observantines had another in Manosque, and the Daughters of Providence had another in Saumur.[10] In Paris, twenty such private houses were opened, almost all of them in the latter half of the century, and some of them were of a considerable size, like the famous pension Belhomme, which had room for thirty-three, as did the maison Bouquelon. The pension Sainte-Colombe could take twenty-eight, and the pension Laignel twenty-nine, with the pensions Douai and Guerrois taking twenty apiece.[11] The Petites-Maisons developed a reputation for being the home of the mad *par excellence*, and it became quite common for Bicêtre or the Salpêtrière to try to pass inmates on there, arguing that they were more suited to the Petites-Maisons.[12] This was an entirely new development in comparison with the seventeenth century. Many of the insane who, fifty years earlier, would have found themselves locked up in one of the great houses of confinement, now found a land of asylum that they could properly call their own. This in part explains why their numbers grew so slowly, judging by the limited number of establishments that already existed in the seventeenth century. But more than the numbers involved, the true measure of the importance of the phenomenon was the shift in significance that it implied.

For in fact the same phenomenon can be witnessed throughout Europe. Suddenly, the mad were once more locked up in the way that they had been during the Renaissance. In 1728, for example, the ancient Dollhaus in Frankfurt was reopened.[13] Numerous private houses also sprang up in Germany. In Rockwinkel, near Bremen, a pension opened in 1764, run by a Dutchman, and the Irrenhaus of Brieg in Schleswig was set up in 1784, with space for fifty inmates, and 1791 saw the opening of the Saint George Irrenanstalt in Bayreuth. In places where no separate hospitals were built for the insane, areas were set aside inside the existing ones. In Würzburg, the Prince Bishop of Schönborn decreed in May 1743 that those who were *delirantes et simul furiosi* ('delirious and frenzied-looking') were to be kept in a special quarter of the Julius hospital, while the *placidi delirantes et non furiosi* ('the placid delirious and the non-frenzied') were to remain in the district's existing houses of confinement.[14] In Vienna, one of the biggest houses for the insane in Europe was opened, with room for 129 inmates.[15] In England, the Manchester and then the Liverpool Lunatic Hospitals came into being, and the Lunatic Ward of Guy's Hospital was set up,[16] followed in 1777 by the infamous York hospital, against which Tuke and the Quakers campaigned, not because it represented a residue of a past that they wished to obliterate, but rather on account of its novelty, since it manifested better than others a certain consciousness of madness and the status it was granted. But of all these new entities, the most important by far was clearly the Saint Luke's Hospital. Rebuilding had begun in 1782, and the plan was to house 220 inmates; when Tenon visited five years later, he found it still incomplete, and home to 130 lunatics.

> To enter here, inmates must be poor, judged to be manic, it must be less than a year since the onset of their disease, and they must not have been previously treated in another hospital for the mad. No imbeciles are admitted, nor are those who suffer from convulsions or venereal diseases, or who are senile, pregnant, or have smallpox.

If any such condition became apparent, the patient was immediately forced to leave.[17]

It is tempting to look for a connection here between these new institutions and the whole collection of reforming theories that led through Tuke, Pinel and Reil to the setting up of the great asylums of the nineteenth century. But a simple reason of chronology shows that these eighteenth-century creations are not part of the later movement of reform. The principal texts that demanded a medical status, or at least improved treatment for the mad, predate the Revolution by a very short space of time. Doublet and Colombier's instructions were only drawn up in 1785, and it was 1787 before Tenon revealed his project for a hospital for the mentally ill. Movements in that direction inside the institutions were well in advance of any theoretical effort to consider confined madmen as patients in need of treatment. And in any case the new hospitals that were opening often differed little in their structure from those that had preceded them a century earlier. The juridical conditions of confinement remained unchanged, and despite the fact that they were especially destined for the insane, there was almost no place for medicine in these new hospitals. Saint Luke's was not really 'progress' in comparison to Bethlem. Statutes fixed the period of 'treatment' at one year, and if no satisfactory result was discernible at the end of that period, subjects were dismissed. The treatment itself was extremely vague. 'Treatment is in accordance with the symptoms presented, and which seem most likely to respond. Bowel movements are to be restored to normal, and stomachs are to be kept free. Lunatics are taken to the infirmary if they are unwell.'[18] The other institutions mentioned above were no more medical than Saint Luke's, and in particular the twenty private pensions that came into existence in Paris allowed neither the presence of physicians nor even house calls from them.[19]

The key factor in the changes that were coming about in the second half of the eighteenth century was not therefore the reform of the institutions, nor the spirit of reinvention, but the spontaneous mutation that wound up creating asylums destined exclusively for the insane. Madness had not broken the circle of confinement, but it was evolving and slowly marking its distance. It was as though a new exclusion was developing within the old, as though this new exile was necessary for madness to find its place, to be on a level footing with itself at last. Madness had found its own homeland. The difference was barely perceptible, as the new style of confinement resembled the one that had preceded it so closely, but it indicated nonetheless that something essential was happening, isolating madness and granting it autonomy from the unreason with which it had been confused.

What was the nature of this homeland, now other and yet still the same? How had the location of madness shifted, placing it in a difficult position between the milieu of homogenous unreason, and the new place where it would take on its own identity? The movement was certainly not unrelated to the contemporaneous revival in the fear of madness. But to decide that this was cause rather than effect would perhaps be a little arbitrary. Is it because a society begins to be afraid of the mad that it displaces them, and ensures they are kept in isolation? Or is it rather because they have taken on an autonomous identity, and occupy an independent space, that a fear of them begins to spread? In other words, was this a resurrection of the age-old Western fear that had lingered on, despite confinement, authorising a reappearance of the *Narrtürme* and something like a new departure for the *Ship of Fools*; or is it possible to discern here the birth of new structures, the silhouette of the great asylums of the nineteenth century?

To look for causality is perhaps to cloud the issue unnecessarily. What does shift slowly in madness throughout the eighteenth century is neither what remains of the past nor a foretaste of the future, but both at once in an experience that builds its own past while planning its own future. What matters most, to understand these temporal relations and reduce their prestige, is knowing how madness was *perceived* at this time, before all conscious reflection on it and all formulation of knowledge. The fear of madness and the isolation to which it was condemned indicate a region of darkness where madness was experienced in a primitive manner – where it was recognised before it was known – and where what could be historical in its evolving truth slowly took form.

*

Unreason, under the eighteenth-century constraint of confinement, was constantly becoming ever simpler, giving up its peculiarities and fading into dull monotony. Little by little, the singular faces for which it was interned began to disappear and blend into the global apprehension of 'libertinage'.

Everyone who was confined but not labelled mad was now locked up as some kind of 'libertine'. Only the work of Sade, at the end of the century, at the moment when the structure of confinement was beginning to fall into pieces, managed to break this confused unity. Starting out from a form of libertinage reduced to its most flagrantly sexual common denominator, he re-established contact with the deepest powers of unreason, rediscovering the depths of profanation and allowing all the voices of the world where nature abolished herself to rise up within him. But even this work, and the discourse that it pursued so unrelentingly, is perhaps just another manifestation of that essential uniformity through which unreason surfaced at the end of the eighteenth century. There is there a uniformity of sexual variations, whose incessant renewal must be accepted, like a constantly repeated prayer, and which served as an invocation to a now-distant unreason.

While unreason was thus absorbed into the undifferentiated, only maintaining an obscure power of enchantment – a distant, glittering point that was perpetually out of reach – madness, by contrast, became ever more specific, probably at the same pace at which unreason retreated and unravelled into continuity. Unreason, increasingly, was just a power of fascination, while madness became an established object of perception.

On 15 July 1721, when the parliamentary commissioners were visiting Saint-Lazare, they were informed of the presence of twenty-three 'alienated', four 'feeble-minded', two 'violent' and one 'frenzied' inmate, excluding those who were serving a penal sentence ('*correctionaires*'). Twelve years later, during the course of a similar visit in July 1733, there was no significant increase in the numbers of the mad, but the world of madness was strangely more populated. We should ignore descriptions like 'libertinage', 'behaves badly', 'has no religion' or 'refuses to go to mass': these were but the ever more confused figures of unreason. Looking solely at the forms of madness that were recognised as such, we find twelve 'insane', six 'weak-minded', two 'alienated', two 'imbeciles', one man 'who had returned to childhood' and two 'frenzied'; there were also five cases of 'disturbance', one case of 'disorder', and one pensioner who suffered from 'extraordinary sentiments'. Twelve years had been sufficient time for the three or four categories into which the insane were unproblematically placed (alienation, weak-mindedness, violence and frenzy) to become insufficient to cover the whole spectrum of madness. Forms now multiplied, and doubles appeared; imbeciles were now to be distinguished from the weak-minded and the senile; disturbance, disorder and extraordinary sentiments were now no longer the same thing, and there was even a difference between the alienated (*aliénés*) and the insane (*insensés*), a division that seems enigmatic in the extreme to our eyes.

The sensibility to madness, which previously had appeared to be quite uniform, suddenly opened up, casting a new light on what until this point had been hiding within the monotony of the insane. The mad were no longer those who could be distinguished with a rapid and undiscerning glance from all the others; they became differentiated from each other, no longer concealing the secrets of their paradoxical species in the cloak of unreason that enveloped them. This intrusion of difference into the equality of madness was highly significant; reason was no longer opposed to unreason in a relation of exteriority that allowed it to do nothing other than denounce it, but it began to invade it in an extremely tenuous if decisive form: non-resemblance, which can be conceived as a first disengagement from identity. Previously, unreason had been absolute difference for reason, but a difference levelled in itself by the infinitely recommenced identity of unreason. But now the multiple faces of difference began to appear, forming a domain into which reason could venture and almost recognise itself. The day would come when all differences were to be classified and analysed objectively, and reason could claim as its own the most visible regions of unreason. For a long time, medical thought only mastered madness through the abstract analysis of these differences.[20]

This evolution is perfectly measurable, just as it can be exactly assigned to a precise moment: three or four categories are isolated on the register of Saint-Lazare in 1721, fourteen in 1728 and sixteen in 1733. In 1733, Boissier de Sauvages published *Nouvelles classes*, which multiplied the old world of the sicknesses of the mind, adding to the four or five species commonly accepted at the time of Willis or Boerhaave the long series of all the *vesaniae*. A coincidence of this nature is probably not chance; yet between the classes that Sauvages proposed and the categories indicated on the registers of institutions like Charenton or Saint-Lazare there is almost nothing in common. Excluding a few terms like 'dementia' and 'imbecility', none of the new categories of confinement coincides even approximately with those described in the nosologies of the eighteenth century. The two phenomena appear to be simultaneous, but are probably different in nature and meaning: as though the nosological analysis, following a conceptual line or a causal chain, spoke only of and for reason, and had determined nothing of what madness had to say for itself once it was situated inside the space of confinement.

The formulations were extremely simple at the outset. As we saw above, there were three or four basic categories, with the largely undifferentiated domain of alienation (*aliénation*) and the more precise figures of frenzy (*fureur*) and imbecility (*imbecillité*). The rest was only ever characterised via picturesque moral traits, or by the absurdity of errors professed.[21] It seems that the categories of 'frenzy' and 'imbecility', after many years lost among the ranks of these individual characterisations, slowly took on a more general value, forming two poles between which the whole domain of alienation spread. In 1794 for example, the register at Charenton contains mentions like the following, concerning a certain Claude Barbin:

'He seemed more eccentric (*extravagant*) than last year . . . but it would appear that his mind is still finely balanced between frenzy and imbecility.'[22] Frenzy implied all acts of violence carried out against others, death threats, and a rage that went so far as to turn against the self. D'Argenson wrote the following regarding a woman named Gohart: 'Her madness . . . often descends into frenzy, and . . . judging by appearances, would lead her either to murder her husband or to do away with herself at the earliest opportunity.'[23] Imbecility too held mortal dangers, but of a different form: imbeciles were unable to ensure their own survival, and were therefore not responsible for their lives. They were death's passive victims, not in any violent sense, but through a pure and simple incapacity to look after themselves (a refusal to eat was considered the most obvious sign of imbecility). Madness was situated and oscillated between these two points, which were its extremes, and classification was only carried out in relation to this dual urgency. Confinement distinguished above all in madness the danger of death that it involved: it was death that made the division rather than reason or nature, and the rest was a swarming individual proliferation of faults and defects. This was the first effort towards an organisation of the world of the asylums, and its prestige was of sufficient importance for Tenon to note, at the end of the eighteenth century, that it was completely valid, in that it dictated the imperatives of coercion: 'The mad are to be divided into the imbecilic and the frenzied; both need to be kept under continual surveillance.'[24]

But out of this rather rudimentary organisation where only the peril of death could obliterate the individual picturesque, newer, more coherent figures began to emerge, leading to what can best be thought of as an *asylum perception of madness*. New qualities appeared, which no longer simply signalled dangers or revolved around the threat of death. Naturally, following this work in all its meanders presents considerable difficulties, as the only clues available are the skeletal entries on the confinement registers. But even in those texts, it is clear that madness began to speak a language that was not simply related to matters of life and death, but talked of itself instead, and of all the sense and nonsense that it contained. The distinction, so frequent in the eighteenth century and so mysterious to us today, between the alienated (*les aliénés*) and the insane (*les insensés*), can probably be understood in these terms. Until the beginning of the century, the two played symmetrical and inverse roles: sometimes the 'insane' were the delirious in the wider category of the mad or alienated sometimes the alienated were those among the insane who had lost all form or trace of reason, the insane being in the most general and least precise terms 'mentally disturbed' or 'of troubled mind'. But little by little, in the course of the eighteenth century, a new division became apparent, which had quite a different meaning. An alienated person was a man who had entirely lost truth, and was given over to the illusions of all his senses and the night of the world; each of his own truths was error, and all that seemed obvious to him was mere fantasy to others, and he was therefore prey to the blindest forces of madness:

> Either he falls into a sort of dementia, where all reason and all sense of humanity is entirely absent, or he is agitated by a violent passion that torments him, and he enters into a frenzy where he breathes nothing but blood, murder and carnage, and in these moments of troubled agitation he recognises no one, and no longer knows who he is, and the world has all to fear from him.[25]

An alienated person had crossed over into inaccessible territory, and everything in his world was out of reach for other mortals and for himself. In the universe of the insane, by contrast, an observer could find his bearings, and madness there could always be identified. It either affected perception, or at least the judgement or belief that might be found in a perception: 'this is *an insane man* who believed that the Eternal Father had appeared to him, giving him the power to preach penance and to save the world',[26] or it was to be found in the intellectual apprehension of the truth, in the means by which one identified the truth as such, or in which truth was deduced or adhered to: 'He still stubbornly maintains his belief in judicial astrology, and the mysterious impieties out of which he has constructed his own system of medicine.'[27] An insane man was not like an alienated person, who gave free reign to the lifeblood of madness; he allowed unreason to circulate more or less secretly in the guise of reason. The religious brothers at Charenton had this to say on the same subject: 'What he once believed as part of his libertine principles or criminal intentions, he now believes more by eccentricity than by reason; he is now of the opinion that he is besieged by infernal spirits.' An insane man was not entirely a stranger to the world of reason, but demonstrated instead something like reason perverted, or reason that went off the rails with each new movement of the spirit. In him a perilous exchange between reason and unreason was constantly being effected, whereas alienation was more a question of the moment of rupture. An alienated person was entirely on the side of nonsense; an insane man was constantly interverting meaning.

In all probability, these distinctions remained fairly blurred for the people who used them, and nothing proves that they were rigorously applied. The organising principles however – life and death, sense and nonsense – return with sufficient frequency for the categories to remain in place for most of the eighteenth century, grouping around the major themes a number of derived notions. 'Raving' (enragé), for instance, described a mixture of frenzy and alienation, an intoxication of nonsense reaching extremes of violence. Louis Guillaume de la Formassie was first confined in Bicêtre because the 'sole use he made of his liberty was to abuse it'; but frenzy took over before long, and he fell into total nonsense, and ended up classified as 'raving': 'he can only recognise an old woman, the only person who brings him food from his family; any servant from the family would risk dying from his blows if they approached him'.[28] By contrast, the 'stubborn' were recognisable for putting their blend of frenzy and violence at the disposal of a senseless idea. One Roland Genny was locked up in the Bastille and then in Bicêtre on account of 'hallucinations that resemble the experiences of visionaries . . . the mere sight of a man of the cloth drives him to a fury'.[29] The 'deranged' mixed alienation and imbecility, their blend of good temper and incapacity revealing a great disorder in their thought. One of the registers at Bicêtre speaks of a former schoolmaster 'who had married a woman of ill repute, and had fallen into such misery that his mind had become entirely deranged'.[30]

These notions may appear quite precarious when confronted with theoretical classifications, but their consistency is proven (if only in a negative way) by the fact that they resisted the penetration of any medical influence so effectively for so long. While the asylum perception of madness became progressively more acute, medicine remained outside, or intervened in a manner that was only incidental or almost marginal. A small number of records contain medical notations, and they are picturesque in nature, like the following comments about an insane man who believed that he was possessed by evil spirits: 'The origin of his problems is to be traced to his reading of cabalistic books; the intemperance linked to his ardent and melancholic constitution has aggravated his condition considerably.' The author goes on to observe that 'his madness is increasingly accompanied by a black melancholy, and a dangerous fury'.[31] Medical classifications and confinement classifications had little in common: the former might be used for descriptive purposes, and on even rarer occasions for diagnostic purposes as well, but this was invariably in an anecdotal manner: 'His wide eyes, and his head constantly tilted over one shoulder make it clear that a cure is far from certain.'[32]

Working at the limits of the resources that we have at our disposal, we can still partially trace the evolution of a long, painstaking process of classification that moved in parallel to the theoretical model but was entirely independent from it. This simultaneity also proves, on both sides, the penetration of reason into the domain of madness, which it had attempted to banish through confinement. But on the one hand, with medicine, we find the work of a form of knowledge that treats the different forms of madness as so many natural species; on the other, an attempt at recognition that lets madness 'speak' for itself, allowing voices to be heard, which for the first time in the history of the Christian West are neither those of prophecy, nor trance or possession, nor buffoonery; voices where madness speaks for nothing or no one else, but for itself. In the silence of confinement, madness had strangely conquered a language that was its own.

For a long time to come, what is traditionally known as 'classical psychiatry' – i.e. more or less all that happens between Pinel and Bleuler – made use of concepts that were at bottom nothing more than compromises, incessant oscillations between these two domains of experience that the nineteenth century had not managed to unify: the *abstract field of a theoretical nature* within which the concepts of medical theory were constructed, and the *concrete* space of an *artificially* established confinement, where madness began to express itself. It is as if a 'medical analytics' and an 'asylum perception' never managed to overlap; and the classificatory mania of the psychiatrists of the past century probably indicates a renewed discomfort facing the duality of sources in psychiatric experience, and the impossibility of any reconciliation between them. This was not a conflict between theory and experience, between everyday familiarity and abstract knowledge, the known and the unknown: it was in a more secret manner a tear in the experience that we once had of madness, and which perhaps still exists today, a rent between madness considered by our science as mental illness, and all that it can give of itself in the space in which it has been alienated by our culture. Attentive to the mortal dangers and the meaning of language, the asylum perception probably did more than all of the nosographies of the eighteenth century to force men to finally pay attention to all that madness could say about itself. A work that was more profoundly medical than medicine itself was taking place precisely where medicine was banished and the mad were not even considered to be patients.

*

From this point on, we have a guiding thread. From the moment when, in the late eighteenth century, we see the mad almost divide themselves into groups, and take places that are theirs, we understand quite clearly how the nineteenth-century asylum and positive psychiatry became possible and how madness at last affirmed its rights. From one century to the next, everything falls into place; first of all confinement, from which the first lunatic asylums were to result, and the curiosity that was born there (soon to become pity, then humanitarianism and social concern), making Pinel and Tuke possible, eventually leading to the great movement of reform with its commissions of inquiry, and the great hospitals that emerged, leading at last to the era of Esquirol, and the felicity of a medical science of madness at last. The line is straight, and progress was easy. The Charenton of the Brothers of Saint John of God foreshadows the Charenton of Esquirol; and the Salpêtrière, doubtless, had but one possible future: the one that Charcot was to have in mind.

But a closer look reveals that this thread is broken, and in more than one place. Can we really be so sure of the meaning of the movement which, at the beginning, tends to segregate the mad? Granted, in the silence and immobility that was confinement, these early perceptions, and the movement that was sketched out, look like indications that 'we are getting closer'. It looks as though not only was a more positive form of knowledge now on the horizon, but also a more alert sensibility was coming to the fore, closer to the meaning of madness itself and more faithful to its contours. All that was alienated in man was given a voice, and for the first time these stammerings were lent an ear. Something like the prefiguration of an order was discernible in the chaos, and indifference opened up to difference, as though madness were entering the familiarity of language already most offered in a system of exchange. The idea that man, in a movement that was to compromise the whole structure of alienation, was already beginning to recognise his own image therein, would flatter our sensibilities and simplify history considerably. But what we seek is not the value that madness took for us, but the movement through which it took its place in the perceptions of the eighteenth century, the series of ruptures, discontinuities and explosions that make it what it is for us, and the opaque memories of all that it has been. If we follow events closely, the evidence is there: if the eighteenth century slowly made way for madness, and started to draw distinctions between different types of faces, it was not by examining them close up, but rather by moving at a distance. A new dimension was required, delimiting a new space and something like a new solitude, where madness from within this second silence could at last speak. If it found its place, that was largely because of the growing emptiness around it; and it owed its many faces and differences not to an increasingly attentive approach, but rather to an indifference that separated it. Which is as much to say that the maximum distance was achieved on the very eve of the day when it emerged as 'liberated' and made 'human', the day before Pinel reformed Bicêtre.[33] All that remains is to demonstrate this.

The results are well known. In the early nineteenth century, every psychiatrist, every historian yielded to the same movement of indignation, and the same scandalous reaction and virtuous indignation was heard in every corner: 'No one blushed at throwing the alienated in prison.' Esquirol drew up a list, including the Hâ fortress in Bordeaux, the gaols in Toulouse and Rennes, the 'Bicêtres' that were to be found in Poitiers, Caen and Amiens, the 'Château' in Angers:

> In fact there are few prisons that do not contain their share of raving alienated men, poor unfortunates who are chained up in cells next to common criminals. What a monstrous association! Even quiet alienated men are treated worse than criminals.[34]

The entire century echoed him. In England, the Tukes became historians and apologists for the work of their ancestors,[35] while in Germany, after Wagnitz, Reil lamented the fate of those who were 'thrown like State criminals into dungeons and cells where the eye of humanity never penetrates'.[36] For more than half a century, the positivist age relentlessly and vocally insisted that it had been the first to deliver the mad from this pitiful confusion with the condemned, and separated the innocence of unreason from criminal guilt.

But it is easy to show that these were vain pretensions. These same protestations had been doing the rounds for years. Before Reil, there was Franck:

> Anyone who has visited the lunatic asylums in Germany will remember with horror what they saw there. To enter these asylums of affliction and unhappiness is shocking: all that can be heard are cries of despair yet man lives there, distinguished by his talents and his virtues.[37]

Before Esquirol and before Pinel came La Rochefoucauld and Tenon, and they in turn had been preceded by an incessant murmur throughout the eighteenth century, made of insistent protestations repeated year after year, in particular by people one would have supposed most indifferent, or to have had perhaps the greatest interest in maintaining such confusion. Twenty-five years before Pinel's exclamations, Malesherbes could be quoted, who:

> Visited the State prisons, with the aim of breaking down their doors. Prisoners whom he considered not to be in their right mind ... were sent to houses where society, exercise, and the attention that he carefully prescribed were bound, in his opinion, to cure them.[38]

Earlier in the century came the more muted voice of a host of hospital directors, administrators and guards who from generation to generation constantly formulated and were occasionally granted the same request: the separation of the mad and the prisoners. One was the Prior of the Charité hospital in Senlis, who begged the Lieutenant of Police to send some of the prisoners away, and lock them up in a fortress somewhere;[39] another was a guard in the Brunswick gaol who asked – and this as early as 1713 – that the mad should not be mixed with the other inmates who laboured in the workshops.[40] What the nineteenth century formulated so loudly, using all the resources of pathos, the eighteenth century had murmured again and again *sotto voce* for generations. The achievement of Esquirol, Reil and the Tukes was to repeat in a higher tone what had become almost the commonplaces of asylum practice. The slow emigration of the mad of which we have spoken, from 1720 up until the Revolution, is probably nothing more than its most visible effect.

And yet we should listen carefully to all that was said in that half silence.

For what exactly did the Prior of Senlis argue, when he asked that one of his inmates be removed from the company of the insane? 'He is deserving of pity, as are one or two others who would be better suited to a citadel, because of the company of six others who are quite mad and who torment them night and day.' The meaning of the plea was clearly understood, and the Lieutenant of Police had these confined set free at once. The request of the guard at Brunswick gaol was of the same order: the good order of the workshop was disturbed by cries and disorder of the insane, their ravings were a perpetual danger, and they were better off back in their cages where they could be tied up. Evidently, the same protestations did not have quite the same value from one century to the next after all. In the early nineteenth century, the complaint was that the mad were treated no better than common criminals, or prisoners of the state; in the eighteenth century, the view was rather that criminals deserved better treatment than to be locked up alongside the insane. For Esquirol, the scandal was that convicts were merely convicts; for the Prior of Senlis, the argument was that the mad, at the end of the day, were merely insane.

The difference might not seem of great significance, and might easily have been guessed. But it is important to bear it in mind to understand how the consciousness of madness evolved during the course of the eighteenth century. It did not evolve as part of a humanitarian movement that slowly forced the human reality of the mad to be acknowledged, focusing on the familiar and pitiful face of the mad. Nor was it the result of a pressure of scientific need that forced it to be more attentive to what madness actually had to say about itself. It did change, slowly, but it was indeed in the real and artificial space of confinement, through imperceptible slippages in its structures, and occasionally through moments of violence, which slowly shaped the consciousness of madness that was contemporaneous with the Revolution. If the mad were progressively isolated, and the monotony of insanity was divided into rudimentary species, that was not thanks to medical progress or any humanitarian approach. The phenomenon was born inside confinement, and it is inside confinement that the keys to this new consciousness of madness are to be found.

This consciousness is of a political rather than philanthropic nature. For if in the eighteenth century it was noticed that among the confined, the libertine, the debauched and the prodigal there were men whose disorder was of another nature, and whose disquiet was incurable, it was precisely the confined themselves who should take the credit for that. They were

the first to protest, and theirs were the loudest voices. Ministers, Lieutenants of Police and magistrates were all harried with the same complaint,
which was taken up time and again. One man writes to Maurepas to
complain that he is 'being confused with the mad, some of whom are
constantly raving, so much so that I risk their dangerous attacks from one
moment to the next'.[41] The Abbé de Montcrif repeats the same complaint
to Lieutenant Berryer: 'for nine months now I have been locked up in a
horrible hole with fifteen or twenty raving madmen, including a number
of epileptics'.[42] As the century progressed, protestations against confinement became ever more vocal, and madness became increasingly the
obsession of the confined, the image of their humiliation, of their reason
conquered and reduced to silence. The day was soon to come when
Mirabeau would recognise in the shameful promiscuity of madness both a
subtle means of silencing those one wanted to crush and the image of
despotism, the triumph of bestiality. The mad were neither the first nor
the most innocent victims of confinement, but they were the darkest and
most visible, the most persistent symbol of the power that confined. The
dull obstinacy of power is to be found there in the midst of the confined,
the lurid presence of unreason. The struggle against the forces of the
establishment, against the family and the Church started there at the heart
of confinement, in this Saturnalia of reason. Madness was so much
a symbol of the powers that punish that it effectively played the role of a
supplementary punishment, an additional torture that maintained order
in the uniform punishments of the houses of correction. La Rochefoucauld-Liancourt bore witness to this in his report to the Committee on
Begging: 'One of the punishments inflicted on epileptics, and on the other
infirm in these chambers, even the deserving poor, is to lock them up
amongst the mad.'[43] The scandal was merely the fact that the mad were
the brutal truth about confinement, the passive instrument of all that was
worst within it. An indicator of that is to be found in the idea — a commonplace in the literature of confinement in the eighteenth century — that
a stay in a house of correction inevitably resulted in madness. To live in
that world of delirium, in the midst of the triumph of unreason, was,
through the fatality of place and things, to join the living symbols of the
institution itself:

> I would point out that most of the insane to be found in houses of
> correction and the state prisons lost their reason either as a result

of excessively poor treatment, or through a horror of the solitude where at every turn they are confronted by the illusions of an imagination sharpened by pain.[44]

The presence of the mad among prisoners was not the scandalous limit of confinement, but its truth; not an abuse, but its essence. The polemic that emerged in the eighteenth century regarding confinement did indeed touch upon the mixing that was operated between the mad and people of sound mind; but it left the fundamental relationship between confinement and the mad untouched. Whatever the attitude adopted, that at least did not enter into the question. Mirabeau, that great Friend of Man, was as severe with confinement as he was with the confined. For him, no one confined in what he termed 'the celebrated prisons of the State' was innocent, but their place was not in these costly houses, where their days were dragged out in enforced futility. Why lock up 'ladies of the night, who if sent to workshops in the provinces, could become ladies of the loom?' Similarly, 'Those rascals who are waiting for their liberty in order to get themselves hanged, as they are already in chains, why not force them to do tasks that have proved insalubrious for normal workers? They might serve as an example.' Once this whole population had been removed, what would be left in the houses of confinement? Only those who could be kept nowhere else, and who had every right to be there: 'a small number of prisoners of the State, whose crimes could not be revealed', to whom could be added 'old men burnt out by a life of debauchery and dissipation, whose only ambition had ever been to expire in the hospital, an ambition they will almost certainly attain', and finally the insane, who had to be left to rot somewhere: 'they could vegetate in any old corner'.[45] Mirabeau's son argued in the opposite direction:

> I formally defy anyone in the world to prove that prisoners of the State, rascals, libertines, madmen and ruined old men make up not the greater part, but not even a third, a quarter or a tenth of the inmates in fortresses, houses of correction and State prisons.

The scandal for him was thus not that the alienated were mixed in with other rascals, but that they did not make up with them the greater part of the population of the confined. Who then was entitled to complain about being mixed in with criminals? Certainly not those who had forever lost their reason, but rather those who were paying for the passing errors of their youth:

> I might ask . . . why libertines and rascals are mingled together . . . I might also ask why young people with a dangerous disposition are left with men who will quickly lead them to the last degree of corruption . . . if this mixing of rascals and libertines exists, as it all too clearly does, why then by this infamous, odious union do we convict ourselves of that most heinous of crimes, that of forcing men into criminality?

What other fate might be reserved for the mad? They were neither reasonable enough not to be confined, nor wise enough not to be treated like criminals: 'It is all too true that those who have lost their reason should be hidden away out of sight of society.'[46]

It now becomes clear how the political critique of confinement worked in the eighteenth century. Not at all as a liberation of madness, and in no way could it be said that it elicited a more philanthropic or medical attention to the alienated. On the contrary, the century linked confinement to insanity ever more strongly, and this by a double bind: one that made of it a symbol of the power that confined, and its derisory and obsessive representation inside the world of confinement; and the other which designated it as the object of all the measures of confinement *par excellence*. Subject and object, image and aim of repression, it was a symbol of its blind, arbitrary nature, and a justification of all that was reasonable and well founded within it. Through a paradoxical circle, madness finally appeared as the sole reason for confinement, while serving as a symbol of its deep unreason. Michelet, whose thought was still so close to that of the eighteenth century, formulated this idea with astonishing rigour, in a movement reminiscent of Mirabeau's thought when talking of his stay in the prison at Vincennes while Sade was there. First, confinement itself was a cause of alienation: 'Prison makes men mad. The people found in the Bastille and in Bicêtre were quite stupefied.' Second, all that was most unreasonable, shameful and deeply immoral about power in the eighteenth century was represented within the space of confinement, and by a madman: 'We have seen the frenzies of the Salpêtrière. A terrible madman lived in Vincennes, the poisonous Sade, who wrote in the hope of corrupting times to come.' Third, he was the only madman they should have kept

for confinement, and this was not done: 'they let him go, and kept Mirabeau instead'.[47]

*

A vacuum thus appears at the heart of confinement, a void that isolates
madness, denouncing in it all that is irreducible and unbearable to reason:
madness now appears with all that distinguishes it from the other confined forms as well. The presence of the mad seems an injustice – but only
for the others. The great envelopment that made for the confused unity of
unreason is now broken. Madness becomes individualised, strangely
twinned with crime, linked at least to it by a connection that no one had
thought to question yet. These two figures subsist alone in this confinement emptied of a part of its contents, and between them they symbolise
all that is necessary in it: from this point on, they alone are that which
merited confinement. Marking its distance, and becoming a clearly identifiable form in the confused world of unreason did not liberate madness:
instead a profound link was forged with the world of confinement, a link
that became almost its essence.

But at the same time confinement also faced a second crisis, which was
even more serious as it called into question not only its function as an
apparatus of repression, but also its very existence. This crisis came not
from within, and was unconnected to any form of political protest – but
rose up slowly from a whole economic and social horizon. No doubt
confinement never really achieved the simple, effective role that it was
supposed to have at the time of Colbert, but it answered so well a real
necessity, that it was bound to integrate into other structures, and to be
used to other ends.

It had first of all served as a relay in the demographic displacements that
the peopling of the colonies had demanded. Since the early years of the
eighteenth century, the Lieutenant of Police had traditionally presented the
minister with a list of all the confined in Bicêtre and the Salpêtrière who
were 'good enough for the Islands', asking permission for them to leave.[48]
This was another means of freeing up places occupied in the Hôpital
Général by a cumbersome but active population who could not be kept
confined indefinitely. In 1717, with the founding of the 'Compagnie
d'Occident', the exploitation of the Americas became an integral part of
the French economy. Use was made of the confined population, and the

famous departures from Rouen and La Rochelle started, with girls in carts and boys in chains. The early violent incidents of 1720 did not recur, but the custom of deportation continued, adding a new terror to the mythology of confinement.[49] Now people were sent into confinement as a prelude to being 'sent to the Islands'. The intention was to force a mobile population to move abroad and work the newly colonised lands, and confinement became a warehouse of migrants to be sent to a chosen destination when the time was ripe. From this point on the measures of confinement were not simply a function of the labour market in France, but of the state of the colonisation of the Americas: of the price of agricultural foodstuffs, the development of the plantations, the rivalry between England and France, and the maritime wars that interfered with both commerce and emigration. There were times when the confined population grew, like the Seven Years War, and there were times when demand was much higher, when the confined population was easily dispatched to the Americas.[50]

Another factor in the second half of the century was an important change in the structure of agriculture – the progressive disappearance, in both England and France, of common land. The dividing up of such land, previously a mere possibility, became obligatory in France in 1770. Directly or indirectly, it was the large landowners who profited from these measures, and small cattle farmers were often ruined. In places where the common land was equitably shared out between families or small associations, smallholdings came into existence, but their survival was precarious.[51] A whole rural population found itself cut off from its land and obliged to live the life of agricultural labourers, at the mercy of crises in production and unemployment. A double pressure was alternately brought to bear on wages, causing them to fall constantly: poor harvests caused agricultural revenues to fall, and good harvests pushed down the retail prices. A recession began, and only deepened during the twenty years preceding the Revolution.[52] Indigence and unemployment, which since the mid-eighteenth century had been mainly urban phenomena, and merely seasonal in the countryside, suddenly became rural problems as well. Workhouses and general hospitals had sprung up for the most part in regions where manufacturing and commerce had developed the fastest, and therefore where the population densities were highest. Were they now to be required too in the countryside, where a seemingly permanent crisis was taking shape?

As the century progressed, confinement became ever more closely linked to complex phenomena. It became more urgent, but also more difficult, and constantly less effective. Three serious crises followed in close succession, almost simultaneously in England and France, and the first two were greeted by an intensification in the process of confinement. By the time of the third it was clear that such simple means served no purpose. Confinement itself was questioned for the first time.

The first crisis was violent but short-lived, and resulted from the treaty of Aix-la-Chapelle, bringing an end to the War of the Austrian Succession. This was something of a surface event, as the great structures were not really affected, and an economic upturn followed shortly after the cessation of hostilities.[53] But demobilised soldiers, the confined who were waiting to be sent to the new colonies and competition from English factories combined to produce widespread unemployment, so much so that rioting or a massive exodus of the population were equally feared:

> The factories of which we thought so highly are closing everywhere: Lyon is suffering tremendously, more than 12,000 workers are now beggars in Rouen, and the same can be observed in Tours and elsewhere. More than 20,000 workers have left the kingdom in the last three months, heading for Germany, Spain or any destination that will have them.[54]

Efforts were made to halt this movement, and the order went out for all beggars to be arrested:

> An order has been given for all beggars in the kingdom to be arrested, and the police authorities are acting to that end in the provinces. The same is being done in Paris, to ensure they do not concentrate there, as they are surrounded on all sides.[55]

Confinement proved even less useful than before, and was an unpopular measure:

> The archers of Paris in charge of watching over the poor, known as the 'begging cup archers', have been arresting beggars, and either by mistake or because it suits their purposes, they have also arrested some of the sons of the bourgeoisie, which started the first rioting; there were small-scale disturbances on the 19th and 20th of this month, but the

situation grew more serious on the 23rd. The people gathered in the districts where the arrests had taken place, and between four and eight archers were killed today as a result.[56]

Eventually the hospitals were filled to breaking point, with no sign that the problem had been solved: 'In Paris, all the beggars were immediately released after they had been arrested, which had resulted in the sedition we have mentioned, and before long they were once again lining the streets and the highways.'[57] Only the economic expansion of the years that followed brought about the reduction of unemployment.

A new crisis followed in 1765, on a much larger scale. French trade collapsed, and exports were down by nearly a half; as a result of the war, trade with the colonies was brought to an abrupt halt.[58] There was widespread poverty. Summing up the whole economic history of eighteenth-century France in a single sentence, Arnould wrote: 'The state of prosperity enjoyed by France from the fall of the System until the mid-century should be remembered, and contrasted with the deep wounds inflicted on the public purse by the war of 1755.'[59] England went through a similar crisis during the same period, but with different causes and a quite different profile. Trade grew considerably as a result of colonial conquests,[60] but a succession of poor harvests (1756–1757) and the interruption of trade with the agricultural producers of Europe led to a considerable increase in the price of basic foodstuffs. Both countries responded to the crisis with an increase in the use of confinement. In 1765, Cooper published a project for the reform of charitable institutions, proposing that in each hundred, under the joint control of the clergy and the nobility, houses should be set up that would include an infirmary for sick paupers, workshops for the healthy indigent, and correctional centres for anyone who refused to work. Numerous houses were set up in the countryside on this model, which was inspired by the Carlford workhouse. In France, a Royal Ordinance of 1764 ordered the creation of centres for beggars (dépôts de mendicité), but the order only really came into force after a decree by the Council on 21 September 1767: 'That throughout the different regions of the kingdom, adequately closed houses should be created for people who have nothing . . . the inmates detained in such institutions will be fed and clothed at His Majesty's expense.'[61] The following year, eighty such centres for beggars were set up across France, all of which had more or less the same structure and purpose as the general hospitals. The regulations at the Lyon centre were typical: it was designed to receive vagabonds and beggars who had been sentenced to confinement by the local procurator, including 'loose women arrested for following troops', 'citizens sent there by order of the King', 'the insane, poor and abandoned, and those for whom a pension will be paid'.[62] Mercier's description of these *dépôts* demonstrates how closely they resembled the old houses of the Hôpital Général, and how they were filled with the same misery, the same idleness, and the same blend of inmates:

> They are a new variety of prison, dreamt up as an expeditious solution to empty the streets and lanes of beggars, so that insolent misery can no longer appear and sully the face of insolent luxury. In utter inhumanity these unfortunates are locked up in fetid, dark hovels and left to their own devices. Inactivity, bad food, and the enforced proximity of their fellow sufferers in misery will mean that they soon die, one after another.[63]

In fact few of these new *dépôts* outlasted the economic crisis.

After 1770, and throughout the period of recession that followed, the practice of confinement began to fall into decline; and rather than attempting to resolve the crisis by a persistent recourse to confinement, efforts were made to try and limit it instead.

Turgot's edict on the corn trade brought a fall in the buying price, but a steep rise in the selling price, just as the effects of dividing up the common land started expanding the ranks of an agricultural proletariat. Yet Turgot had several begging centres closed down, so much so that by the time Necker came to power, forty-seven of them had disappeared. Some, like the one in Soissons, had been reinvented as hospitals for the old and the sick.[64] A few years later, after the American War of Independence, England suffered a serious crisis in employment. In 1782, parliament voted Gilbert's Act 'for the Better Relief and Employment of the Poor', a major administrative reorganisation that stripped local authorities of their main powers where begging was concerned, and ensured that district magistrates designated directors of workhouses and 'Guardians of the Poor' in each parish. They were to appoint an inspector, whose powers of control and organisation were more or less absolute. But most important of all, besides the workhouses, poorhouses too were set up, for people who had become 'indigent through age, sickness or infirmity, incapable of meeting their own needs through their work'. Poor people who were healthy were not to be sent to either of these institutions, but were to be found a job that met their strengths and skills as soon as possible, and justly recompensed for their labours. Turgot in France and Gilbert's Act in England were not the end of confinement, but the moment when it seemed to be stripped of its essential powers. Over-use at last suddenly revealed its limits. It was now admitted that confinement could not solve an unemployment crisis, and that it had no effect on prices. If it still had a meaning, it was only with regard to an indigent population who could no longer look after their own needs. But it was now clear that it could no longer intervene in a useful manner in economic structures.

*

Traditional politics of assistance and the repression of unemployment were now called into question. The need for reform became urgent.

Poverty was gradually separated from the old moral confusions. Economic crises had shown that unemployment could not be confused with indolence, as indigence and enforced idleness spread throughout the countryside, to precisely the places that had previously been considered home to the purest and most immediate forms of moral life. This demonstrated that poverty was not always a sort of fault: 'Begging is the fruit of poverty, which in turn is the consequence of accidents in the production of the earth or in the output of factories, of a rise in the price of basic foodstuffs, or of growth of the population, etc.'[65] Indigence became a matter of economics.

But it was not contingent, nor was it destined to be suppressed forever. There would always be a certain quantity of poverty that could never be effaced, a sort of fatal indigence that would accompany all forms of society until the end of time, even in places where all the idle were employed: 'The only paupers in a well governed state must be those born in indigence, or those who fall into it by accident.'[66] This backdrop of poverty was somehow inalienable: whether by birth or accident, it formed an inevitable part of society. The state of lack was so firmly entrenched in the destiny of man and the structure of society that for a long time the idea of a state without paupers remained inconceivable: in the thought of philosophers, property, work and indigence were terms linked right up until the nineteenth century.

This portion of poverty was necessary because it could not be suppressed; but it was equally necessary in that it made wealth possible.
Because they worked but consumed little, a class of people in need allowed
a nation to become rich, to release the value of its fields, colonies and
mines, making products that could be sold throughout the world. An
impoverished people, in short, was a people that had no poor. Indigence
became an indispensable element in the state. It hid the secret but most
real life of society. The poor were the seat and the glory of nations. And
their noble misery, for which there was no cure, was to be exalted:

> My intention is solely to invite the authorities to turn part of their vigilant
> attention to considering the portion of the People who suffer . . . the
> assistance that we owe them is linked to the honour and prosperity of
> the Empire, of which the Poor are the firmest bulwark, for no sovereign
> can maintain and extend his domain without favouring the population,
> and cultivating the Land, Commerce and the Arts; and the Poor are the
> necessary agents for the great powers that reveal the true force of a
> People.[67]

What we see here is a moral rehabilitation of the figure of the Pauper,
bringing about the fundamental economic and social reintegration of his
person. Paupers had no place in a mercantilist economy, as they were
neither producers nor consumers, and they were idle, vagabond or
unemployed, deserving nothing better than confinement, a measure that
extracted and exiled them from society. But with the arrival of the industrial economy and its thirst for manpower, paupers were once again a part
of the body of the nation.

Economic theory, therefore, now constructed the notion of Poverty on
new grounds. For a whole Christian tradition, the Pauper had had a real
concrete existence, the presence of flesh, an always individual face of
need, and as such was a symbolic passage of God made man. The abstraction of confinement had brushed aside the Pauper, blending him in with
other figures, enveloping them all in one single ethical condemnation,
while never entirely destroying his identity. The eighteenth century discovered that 'the poor' did not really exist as an ultimate concrete reality,
and that in them two realities of a quite different nature had been confused.

On the one hand was *Poverty*: the scarcity of foodstuffs and money, an
economic situation linked to the state of trade, agriculture and industry.

On the other was *Population*, not a passive element that bowed to the fluctuations in riches, but a force that was a direct part of the economic situation, and the movement that produced wealth, as it was the work of men that brought it into being, or at least transmitted it, displaced it and caused it to multiply. The notion of 'Pauper' was a confused one, blending the idea of the riches that were Man, and the state of Lack seen as essential to the nature of humanity. In fact, between poverty and population, there was a rigorously inverse relation.

Physiocrats and economists agreed on this. Population itself was one of the elements of wealth, forming its certain and inexhaustible foundation. For Quesnay and his followers, man was the essential mediator between wealth and the land:

> 'The price of man is the price of land' says a well thought-out proverb. If the men are of no value, then neither is the land. With manpower, one could double the land that one possessed; land could be acquired, and fallow land put to good use. Only God could make a man from clay, but, with men, land could be had anywhere, or its product, which amounted to the same thing. It followed that manpower was the primary good, and land the second.[68]

For economists too, population was a no less vital good. All the more so for them in fact, since they considered that wealth creation was not restricted to agricultural work, but took place in any industrial transformation, and even in commercial circulation. Wealth was linked to all the work carried out by men:

> The state having no real wealth other than the annual product of its land and the industry of its inhabitants, its wealth will be at a maximum when the product of every acre of land and of the industry of each individual is as high as possible.[69]

Paradoxically, the more a population grew, the more precious it became, as it offered a supply of cheap labour, and by lowering costs allowed a greater expansion of production and trade. In this infinitely open labour market, the 'fundamental price', which for Turgot meant a subsistence level for workers, and the price determined by supply and demand ended up as the same thing. A country was all the more commercially competitive for having at its disposal the virtual wealth that a large population represented.[70]

Confinement was therefore a clumsy error, and an economic one at that: there was no sense in trying to suppress poverty by taking it out of the economic circuit and providing for a *poor population* by charitable means. To do that was merely to hide *poverty*, and suppress an important section of the *population*, which was always a given wealth. Rather than helping the poor escape their provisionally indigent situation, charity condemned them to it, and dangerously so, by putting a brake on the labour market in a period of crisis. What was required was to palliate the high cost of products with cheaper labour, and to make up for their scarcity by a new industrial and agricultural effort. The only reasonable remedy was to reinsert the population in the circuit of production, being sure to place labour in areas where manpower was most scarce. The use of paupers, vagabonds, exiles and émigrés of any description was one of the secrets of wealth in the competition between nations. Josiah Tucker wondered about the best means of weakening neighbouring states, when reflecting on the possible influx of French Protestants:

> Should we force them to remain in their countries, by refusing to welcome them and integrate them into our society, or should we try and attract them by according them the same privileges as all other citizens? [71]

Confinement was to be criticised because of the effects it had on the labour market, but also because like all other traditional forms of charity, it constituted a dangerous form of finance. As had been the case in the Middle Ages, the classical era had constantly attempted to look after the needs of the poor by a system of foundations. This implied that a section of the land capital and revenues were out of circulation. In a definitive manner too, as the concern was to avoid the commercialisation of assistance to the poor, so judicial measures had been taken to ensure that these goods never went back into circulation. But as time passed, their usefulness diminished: the economic situation changed, and so did the nature of poverty.

> Society does not always have the same needs. The nature and distribution of property, the divisions between the different orders of the people, opinions, customs, the occupations of the majority of the population,

the climate itself, diseases and all the other accidents of human life are in constant change. New needs come into being, and old ones disappear.[72]

The definitive character of a foundation was in contradiction with the variable and changing nature of the accidental needs to which it was designed to respond. The wealth that it immobilised was never put back into circulation, but more wealth was to be created as new needs appeared. The result was that the proportion of funds and revenues removed from circulation constantly increased, while that of production fell in consequence. The only possible result was increased poverty, and a need for more foundations. The process could continue indefinitely, and the fear was that one day 'the ever increasing number of foundations might absorb all private funds and all private property'. When closely examined, classical forms of assistance were a cause of poverty, bringing a progressive immobilisation that was like the slow death of productive wealth:

> If all the men who have ever lived had been given a tomb, sooner or later some of those sterile monuments would have been dug up in order to find land to cultivate, and it would have become necessary to stir the ashes of the dead in order to feed the living.[73]

*

Assistance to the poor was in need of a new meaning. In the form that it took at the time, the eighteenth century recognised that it was complicitous with poverty and contributed to its spread. The only form of assistance that would not be contradictory would be a mechanism for giving value, in a poor population, to the only potential wealth that it possessed – which was the simple fact that it was a population. Confining this population was a complete misunderstanding of what was required: it needed to be granted full liberty in the social space; providing it played its role as provider of cheap labour, other problems would gradually disappear. In places where overpopulation or poverty were the norm, the population would ensure that industry and commerce developed most rapidly.[74] The only form of assistance of any value was freedom:

All healthy men should ensure their own subsistence by their own labours, because if they are fed without working, they are fed at the expense of others who do work. What the State owes its members is the removal of hindrances that lie in their path.[75]

The social space therefore needed to be entirely empty of obstacles and barriers. Internal obstacles like duties paid to guilds were to be abolished, and social barriers like confinement removed, as they marked an absolute constraint, at the external limits of society. The policy of keeping wages low and the absence of restrictions and labour protection would remove poverty altogether, or at least integrate it into the world of wealth in a new manner.

Dozens of projects were drawn up in an attempt to define this new place for poverty.[76] All, or almost all of them, took as their starting point a distinction between the 'healthy poor' and the 'sick poor'. This was an extremely ancient division, but it had previously been quite tenuous and fluid, as it had had few uses other than as an internal classification for confinement. The distinction was rediscovered in the eighteenth century, and applied with rigour. The difference between the 'healthy poor' and the 'sick poor' was not simply the degree of their poverty, but their nature. A poor man who could work was a useful element in society, even when not put to a proper use:

Misfortune can be regarded as an instrument, and a force, for it does not affect strength, and this strength can be employed for the profit of the State, and to the profit of the individual, when he is forced to employ it.

A sick person on the other hand was an encumbrance, a 'passive, inert and negative element' who did nothing but consume what society produced:

Poverty is a weight that has a price: you can tie it to a machine, and it will make it move; sickness is a mass that one cannot get a grip on, that one has to either bear the weight of or let drop, a constant hindrance that never helps.[77]

It was therefore necessary to dissociate the two elements that had become confused in the ancient notion of hospitality – the positive element that was indigence, and the burden of disease.

The healthy poor should work, not under duress but in full freedom, i.e. under the sole pressure of the laws of economics that turned idle hands into the most precious good:

> The best assistance that can be given to a poor unfortunate is to help him to help himself through his own strength and his own work; giving alms to healthy, robust men is not charity at all, or is at best misdirected charity; it imposes a superfluous burden on society . . . this is why the government and the land owners reduce free distribution.[78]

What the seventeenth[79] century had still considered to be the 'eminent dignity' of the poor, and which had given an eternal meaning to the act of charity, now became a primordial utility. What was required was not commiseration, but acknowledgement of the riches that they represented on earth already. In the Middle Ages the rich were sanctified by the poor; in the eighteenth century they were maintained by them:

> [Without] the lower orders, the suffering sections of society, the rich would be neither lodged, dressed nor fed; it is for the rich that artisans risk their lives climbing frail ladders and raise enormous weights to the pinacles of our buildings; it is for the rich that farmers go out in all weathers, braving the endless fatigues of farming, and it is for the rich that crowds of unfortunates go down to their deaths in mines, dye factories and mineral extraction plants.[80]

The poor, after being chased out by confinement, were now brought back into the community, but they took on a new appearance. They were no longer the justification or the spiritual form of wealth; they were just its precious matter. They used to be its *raison d'être*. Now they were the condition of its existence. Through the poor, the rich no longer attained transcendence, but subsistence. As they were now essential to wealth, the poor had to be liberated from confinement and placed at its disposal.

The sick poor meanwhile became the negative element *par excellence*. They were misery without solution and no virtual wealth could be discerned within them. They, and they alone, needed total assistance. But what could such assistance be founded upon? There was no economic utility in looking after the sick, no material urgency. Only the movements of the heart could demand it. If they were to be helped, it would only ever be through the organisation of feelings of solidarity and pity, sentiments more primitive than the social body as they had surely presided over its foundation: 'Ideas of society, government and charity are to be found in nature, since the idea of compassion is natural and that primitive idea that is a basis for the others.'[81] The duty of care was outside society, as it was to be found in nature, but was social too in that society at its origins was a form of this duty, as old as the coexistence of men. The whole of human life, from the most immediate sensations to the most elaborate forms of society, was caught up in a network of duties of care: '*natural assistance*' came first, as the '*intimate feeling* innate in man, which develops to varying degrees, alerting us to the suffering and sicknesses of our fellow men'. Then came '*personal assistance*, a predilection of nature that pushes us to doing good on a personal scale'. Last of all came:

> *national assistance*, which still follows these principles of our own exist-ence, and includes an intimate sensation, a wider sentiment that causes the body of the nation to reform abuses that are brought to its attention, and listen to complaints and grievances, and to attempt to bring good wherever possible, to all classes of individuals who find themselves in poverty or afflicted with incurable diseases.[82]

Assistance becomes the foremost social duty, regardless of its recipient, as that is the basis on which societies are held together, the living bond between men, the link that is most personal and yet the most universal as well. But eighteenth-century thought hesitated over the concrete forms this assistance should take. Was a 'social duty' to be understood as an absolute obligation for society? Should the State take such welfare assist-ance in hand, building hospitals and distributing assistance? A whole polemic arose around this issue in the years that immediately preceded the Revolution. On the one side were the partisans of State control over all mechanisms of assistance, for whom *social duty* meant the *duty of society* as a whole, and finally the State. Their plan was for the creation of a permanent commission to control all the hospitals in the kingdom, to build large hospitals where the poor who fell sick were to be treated.[83] But most thinkers rejected the idea of assistance on such a massive scale. Liberals and economists considered that *social duty* meant the *duty of men in society*, and not a duty of society itself. To establish the possible forms of assistance, it was therefore necessary to define in social man the nature and the limits of feelings of pity, compassion and solidarity that might link him to the rest of mankind. The theory of assistance was to rest on a half-psychological, half-moral analysis, not on any definition of the contractual obligations of the group. Thus conceived, assistance was not a structure of the State, but a personal link from man to man.

Dupont de Nemours, a follower of Turgot, sought to define the link that joined suffering and compassion. Man, when he feels pain, first looks inside himself for some relief to his suffering; then he complains: 'and begins to beg the assistance of his parents and friends, and they each lend assistance according to the natural inclination that compassion places to varying degrees in the hearts of all men'.[84] But that inclination was doubtless similar to imagination and sympathy according to Hume: its vivacity is inconstant, its vigour indefinite; it lacks the inexhaustible strength that would enable it to react spontaneously to all men, even total strangers. The limits of compassion were quickly reached, and no man could be asked to extend his pity 'beyond the point where the care and fatigue it entailed would seem more painful than the compassion they experience'. It was therefore not possible to consider assistance as an absolute duty that would spring into action at the slightest request from misery. It could be nothing other than the result of a moral inclination, and it was in terms of forces that it should be analysed. It could be deduced from two components: one was negative, the effort or pain required of the self by the act of assistance (a function of the seriousness of the disease, and the distance travelled: the further the distance from the beneficiary and those in the vicinity, the more materially difficult giving assistance became); the other was positive, determined by the vivacity of impressions inspired by the person in need, but quickly diminishing, the further one moved from the domain of natural attachments circumscribed by family. Beyond a certain limit, which was defined by space, imagination and the vivacity of the inclination – a limit that was more or less consistent with the boundaries of the family home – only the negative element came into effect, and assistance could no longer be required: 'For that reason families lend the most assistance, as they are united most strongly by love and friendship . . . but . . . the greater the distance required, the lower its value, and the more tiresome it appears to those who assist.'

The social space in which sickness was situated was therefore entirely redefined. From the Middle Ages to the end of the classical era, it had remained more or less homogeneous. Anyone who fell into poverty or sickness was deserving of the pity of others, and could expect their care. He was universally close to everyone, and could show himself before everyone at any moment he chose. And the more distant his origins, the less familiar his face, the greater the vivacity of the symbols of universality that he bore. He was then the Poor Man, or the Sick Man *par excellence*, harbouring powers of glorification beneath his anonymity. But the eighteenth century fragmented this space, and peopled it with a world of limited figures. The Sick Man found himself within discontinuous unities, in active zones of psychological vivacity, or inactive and neutral zones of distance and inertia of the heart. The social space of sickness was fragmented into a sort of economy of dedication, so that the sick could no longer be of concern to everyone, but only to their immediate entourage, as proximity in the imagination brought closeness in sentiments. The social space of philanthropy was opposed to that of charity not only as a lay world was to a Christian world, but as a structure of moral and affective discontinuity which divided up the sick of different origins into separate domains was to a homogeneous field where each type of poverty concerned each man, on the random but always significant basis of its passage.

Yet the eighteenth century did not consider this to be a limit. On the contrary, the idea was that in such fashion the assistance given had more natural vivacity, and a sounder economic foundation. If, instead of building vast hospitals whose upkeep was extremely expensive, help was given directly to the patients' families, there was a triple advantage to be gained. It was of a sentimental nature first of all, because even if they saw patients every day, families never lost the real pity that they felt for them. It was economic, as providing food and lodging was no longer necessary if patients were kept at home. And lastly it was medical since, in addition to the meticulous care they received at home, patients were not affected by the depressing spectacle of a hospital that was generally regarded 'as a temple of death'. The melancholy of the spectacle that surrounded them, the risk of contagion and distance from loved ones, were all factors considered to aggravate a patient's condition, and result in diseases that did not occur spontaneously in nature, but seemed creations of the hospitals themselves. Patients in hospitals were exposed to unusual ills, a sort of 'hospital disease' before its time, and

> hospital doctors need to be far more able, in order to elude the dangers
> of the false experience that appears to result from these artificial dis-
> eases, which are born of the hospitals themselves. In truth no disease in
> a hospital is pure.[85]

Just as confinement was ultimately a creator of poverty, a hospital was a creator of disease.

The natural place for a cure therefore was not a hospital, but a family, or at least the immediate entourage of the patient. Just as poverty was to be absorbed by the free circulation of labour, sickness was to disappear in the midst of the care spontaneously brought by man's natural milieu: 'To create true charity, society itself should employ itself as little as possible, and use instead, whenever possible, the private strength of homes and individuals.'[86]

This 'private strength' was much solicited at the end of the eighteenth century, and efforts were made to organise it.[87] In England, a 1722 law had forbidden any form of assistance in the home; the sick poor were to be taken to hospital, where they became, in an anonymous fashion, the object of public charity. In 1796, a new law (36 Geo. III caps. 10 and 23) modified that statute, which had come to be seen as 'inconvenient and oppressive' in that it prevented worthy candidates from receiving occasional treatment that might be of considerable benefit, and robbed others of 'the comfort and domestic situation and happiness'. A guardian was to decide in each parish what assistance should be brought to indigent paupers who stayed at home.[88] Efforts were also made to encourage the system of friendly societies, and in 1786 Acland set up a project for a 'Universal Benefit or Friendly Society', to which peasants and servants subscribed, and could receive help at home in the event of sickness or accident. Each parish was to have a pharmacy to provide medicine, half of which would be paid for by the parish, with the friendly society paying the other.[89]

The Revolution, in its early days at least, abandoned the projects for a centralised reorganisation of assistance, and the construction of big hospitals. The report drawn up by La Rochefoucauld-Liancourt conforms to the liberal ideas of Dupont de Nemours and the followers of Turgot:

> If the system of help in the home were to prevail (a system that presents
> among many other precious advantages, the ability to spread the

benefits to the patient's entire family, and allows him to remain surrounded by all that is dear to him, thereby strengthening natural links and
affections with public assistance), then the resulting economies would
be considerable, as a patient cared for at home costs much less than half
a patient looked after in hospital.[90]

*

Two movements then, independent of each other.

One came into being and developed inside the space of confinement,
and led to madness gaining its independence and singularity in the confused world to which it had been consigned; and new distances meant
that it could be perceived in places where previously men had seen nothing but unreason. While all the other figures now began to emerge from
their confinement, the mad alone remained, the last remains, or witnesses
to a practice essential for the world-view of the classical age, but whose
meaning seems very enigmatic today.

And then came the other movement, born outside of confinement. This
was the new economic and social thinking concerning poverty, sickness and
social assistance. For the first time in the Christian world, sickness found
itself isolated from poverty, and all the other faces of misery.

In short, everything that previously surrounded madness began to fall
away. The circle of poverty and the circle of unreason both vanished.
Poverty became caught up instead in problems immanent to economics,
and unreason disappeared into the deep figures of the imagination. Their
destinies will no longer intertwine. And what reappears at the end of
the eighteenth century is madness itself, still condemned to the land
of exclusion, like crime, but also confronted with all the new problems
that assistance to the sick presents.

In some sense, madness was already liberated, in that it was detached
from the old forms of experience in which it had been caught. Detached
not by some philanthropic intervention, nor by any scientific or positivist
recognition of its 'truth', but rather by a long, slow process that had been
effected in the most subterranean domains of experience; not in places
where madness was sickness, but where it was tied to the life of men and
their stories, where their misery was experienced in a concrete manner,
in places haunted by the phantasms of unreason. In those dark regions,
the modern notion of madness slowly took shape. There was no new

acquisition of notions, but there was 'discovery', in that it was through a process of detachment, and thanks to the distance that was created, that its worrying presence was experienced once again. It was this 'detachment' which, a few years before the reforms of Tuke and Pinel, finally allowed it to stumble out into the light on its own, in the outrageous, ruined figure of unreason.

III

THE PROPER USE OF LIBERTY

We now find madness restored to a solitude of sorts. Not the noisy and in some respects glorious solitude that had been its lot until the Renaissance, but another, strangely silent; a solitude that slowly disengaged it from the confused community of the houses of confinement, and which came to form a neutral, empty zone around it.

What disappeared in the course of the eighteenth century was not the inhuman rigour with which the mad were treated, but the obviousness of confinement, the global unity into which the mad had been unquestioningly subsumed, and the countless threads that locked them into the unbroken weave of unreason. Madness was liberated long before Pinel, not from the material constraints that had kept it in prisons, but from a more decisive, more constricting form of servitude that had kept it under the control of that dark power. Even before the Revolution, madness had been set free. Free to a perception that individualised it, free in the recognition granted its individual faces, and the whole process that finally gave it the status of an object.

Left alone, and detached from its antique kinship, inside the tumbledown walls of confinement, madness became a problem, posing questions that it had never previously formulated.

Madness was an embarrassment above all for the legislators, who had little option but to sanction the end of confinement, and no longer knew where in the social space madness should be placed – prison, hospital, or family assistance. The measures taken immediately before and after the Revolution reflect that indecision.

In his circular on *lettres de cachet*, Breteuil asked his superintendents to indicate the nature of the detention orders in the various houses of confinement, and explain the motivation behind them. His instructions were to free, after one or a maximum of two years' confinement, inmates who 'had done nothing that required that they be exposed to the full rigour of the law, and were guilty of libertine behaviour, debauchery or dissipation'. On the other hand, those who were to be kept in the houses of confinement were:

> prisoners whose alienated mind or imbecility means that they are incapable of behaving themselves in the world, or whose ravings would make them dangerous. The nature of their condition is to be ascertained, and if it is found to be unchanging, then unfortunately it is indispensable that their detention continue, for as long as it is clear that their liberty presents a danger to society, or a benefit that is of no use to them.[1]

This was the first step: reducing as far as possible the practice of confinement where it was simply a result of a moral fault, a family conflict, the more benign aspects of libertinage, but maintaining it in its principle, and with one of its major significances to the fore: the locking up of the mad. This was the moment when madness really did take possession of confinement, just as confinement divested itself of its other forms of utility.

The second step was the great enquiries prescribed by the National and Constitutional Assemblies in the immediate aftermath of the Declaration of Human Rights:

> No man may be arrested or detained other than in cases determined by the law, and according to the forms that it prescribes ... The law should only admit of punishments that are strictly and obviously necessary, and no man shall be punished other than in virtue of a law that has been established and promulgated prior to the committing of the crime and legally applied.

The age of confinement was over. All that remained was imprisonment, where criminals convicted or awaiting trial and madmen were temporarily kept side by side. The Constituent Assembly Committee on Begging nominated five people to visit the houses of confinement in Paris.[2] The Duke La Rochefoucauld-Liancourt presented the report in December 1789. He was of the opinion that the presence of the mad gave the houses of confinement a degrading style, and risked reducing the inmates to a level that was demeaning to their humanity, and that the mix of people tolerated there showed a lack of seriousness on the part of both the authorities and the judges:

> This lack of concern is far distant from the enlightened and careful pity that palliates unhappiness, softening it and bringing all possible consolation . . . if the alleviation of misery is really the aim, how can we ever – and particularly when aiming to alleviate misery – consent to appear to degrade mankind?[3]

If the mad sullied those with whom they were imprudently mixed, then what was required for them was a special form of confinement. A confinement that was not medical by nature, but was the most effective and gentle form of assistance possible:

> Of all the misfortunes that afflict humanity, the state of madness is among those which in several ways command pity and respect the most; help should be given above all to all those in such a state, and even when there is no hope of a cure, there are still a myriad means by which their suffering may be alleviated, and good treatments that can restore these wretches to a life that is at least bearable.[4]

The status of madness appears in all its ambiguity in this text: the confined population was to be protected from its perils, and yet madness was also to be granted the advantages of a special assistance.

The third stage was the succession of decrees promulgated between 12 and 16 March 1790. The Declaration of Human Rights now found a concrete application:

> Within six weeks of the present decree, all persons detained in castles, religious houses, gaols, police houses or prisons of any other description on the strength of a *lettre de cachet* or by order of any agent of the executive power, unless they have also been sentenced or charged or

are awaiting trial for a serious crime, have been stripped of their civil rights, or have been locked up on account of madness, are to be set free.

Confinement was thus reserved in a definitive manner for limited categories of people answerable to the law, and for the mad. But there was a special provision for the latter:

> For the three-month period that follows the publication of this decree, under the responsibility of our procurators, people detained for insanity will be questioned by our judges in the usual manner, and in accordance with their decisions, visited by physicians who, under the eye of district directors, will pronounce on the true state of these patients, so that sentence may be passed on them, and they will accordingly either be set free or treated in hospitals to be designated precisely for that purpose.[5]

The decision seems to have been made at this point. On 29 March 1790, Bailly, Duport-Dutertre and an administrator from the police made a visit to the Salpêtrière to determine how the decree could be applied in practice, and followed that with a visit to Bicêtre.[6] They faced numerous difficulties, not least of which was the simple fact that there were no hospitals intended or reserved for the mad.

In the face of these material difficulties, complicated by so many theoretical uncertainties, a long period of hesitation now began.[7] Requests poured in from all sides for the Assembly to draw up a text that would protect the public from the mad, even before the promised new hospitals came into existence. A step backwards, which was of great importance for the future, was the decision that the mad fell under the jurisdiction of measures taken with immediate effect and under no control to protect the public not against known criminals but against dangerous animals. The law of 16–24 August 1790

> [entrusts] to the vigilance and authority of municipal bodies . . . the task of obviating or remedying the unfortunate consequences that might result from the insane or the raving being set free, or from the actions of dangerous and ferocious animals.[8]

The law of 22 July 1791 reinforced that measure, making families responsible for watching over the alienated, and allowing municipal authorities to take any measures necessary:

> The parents of insane people must guard them, and prevent them from wandering or committing any offences against public order. Municipal authorities are to act to prevent any problems that might result from the negligence of people involved.

This meandering on the path towards their liberation meant that once more, and this time as a result of a legal process, the mad were returned to the animal status into which confinement had alienated them. They were wild beasts once more, just as doctors were beginning to identify a benign animality in their nature.[9] Entrusting this legal disposition to the hands of the authorities did little to solve the problem. The fact was that hospitals for the alienated did not exist yet.

The Ministry of the Interior received numerous requests. De Lessart replied to one of them as follows:

> Like you, Sir, I feel that it would be most reassuring if we could immediately proceed to the creation of these establishments, designed to serve as a retreat for the unfortunate class that are the insane . . . Regarding the insane whom the lack of such establishments has by necessity placed in the various prisons of your department, I can at present see no means of extracting them from their predicament in these places so ill suited to their condition, other than their provisional transfer, if such a thing is possible, to Bicêtre. It would therefore be of assistance if the local Directoire were to write to the Paris Directoire and consult with them over the formalities of having them admitted to the establishment, where their upkeep would be paid for by your department or by their respective municipalities, if their families are not in a position to take charge of this expense.[10]

Bicêtre therefore became the main centre to which the insane were sent, particularly after the closure of Saint-Lazare. The Salpêtrière followed suit in 1792, taking in 200 mad women who had spent the previous five years living in a former noviciate of the Capucine nunnery in Rue Saint-Jacques.[11] But in the more distant provinces there was no question of sending the alienated to what had previously been the general hospitals. Most of the time they were kept in prisons, including the Hâ Fort, the Château d'Angers, and in Bellevaux. The disorder of such places was unimaginable, and continued for a long time, up until the Empire period. Antoine Nodier gave the following details about Bellevaux:

> Every day the whole neighbourhood is forced to listen to the shouting and clamour of the inmates arguing and coming to blows. Then the guards rush in. Their current state makes them a laughing stock for the inmates, and the municipal administrators are called on to inter-vene; their authority is despised, and insults rain down upon them. This is no house of justice or detention.[12]

The disorder was similar, if not greater, at Bicêtre, which was now home to political prisoners. Hunted suspects were hidden there, and poverty and scarcity meant that many went hungry. The administration protested con-stantly, requesting that criminals be segregated from the rest. Importantly, some still suggested that the mad should be thrown in together with them. On 9 Brumaire year III, the Bicêtre bursar wrote to 'citizens Grandpré and Osmond, members of the Commission for Administrations and Tribunals', saying 'I can reveal that at a time when humanity is undoubtedly the order of the day, no one could fail to feel a moment of horror on seeing crime and indigence thrust together in the same asy-lum.' Not forgetting the September massacres, continual bids for free-dom, and the manner in which many innocents were forced to watch garrotting and chain gangs leaving the asylum.[13] The poor and the old who could no longer help themselves

> have nothing but chains, bars and bolts before their eyes. Add to that the groans of other prisoners that sometimes reach their ears ... It is against this background that I once again request that the prisoners be removed from Bicêtre, leaving only the poor, or indeed that the poor be sent elsewhere so that only the prisoners remain.

That letter was written in the midst of the Revolution, long after the reports drawn up by Cabanis, and several months after Pinel is traditionally cred-ited with having 'liberated' the alienated at Bicêtre. Crucially, it continues:[14]

> If the latter is the preferred option, we could perhaps leave the mad

where they are, as they are unfortunates of a different sort, who also bring horrible suffering to humanity . . . Hasten then, you citizens who cherish humanity, and turn this beautiful dream into reality – you can be sure in advance that you will be congratulated for it.[15]

These were years of considerable confusion, and at a time when 'humanity' was being re-evaluated it was difficult to determine the status of madness within it, and, in a social space undergoing a major restructuration, where to situate it.

*

But already, in this simple chronology, we have passed the date traditionally recorded as being the start of the great reform. The measures taken between 1780 and 1793 situate the problem: the disappearance of confinement left madness without a precise point of insertion in the social space, and faced with this unchained danger, society reacted first of all with a series of measures planned for the long term, in keeping with an ideal that was coming into being – the creation of houses reserved specifically for the insane – and secondly with a series of immediate measures, which would allow madness to be mastered by force. These were regressive measures, if we wish to measure this history in terms of progress.

The situation was ambiguous, and that ambiguity reflected the difficulties that were beginning to appear, and the new forms of experience that were coming into being. To understand them, we need to liberate ourselves precisely from the idea of progress, and all the teleology and perspectival reading it implies. Only then can we discern the overall structures that carry the forms of experience in an indefinite movement, open only onto the continuity of its own prolongation, and which nothing, not even our age, can stop.

We must meticulously guard against looking for anything in the years that surround the reforms of Tuke and Pinel that looks like the beginnings of a major event, either in the positive recognition of madness or the more humane treatment of the alienated. We should give back to the events of these years, and the structures that made them possible, the liberty of their metamorphoses. Slightly below the level of the juridical measures, at the exact level of the institutions, and in the everyday debates where the mad and the non-mad were brought face to face, separating, compromising and finally recognising each other, certain structural figures came into place over a number of years. They were obviously decisive in that they formed the basis of 'positive psychiatry', and it was out of them that the myths of a finally objective and medical recognition of madness were born, bringing justification after the act by consecrating them as the discovery and liberation of the truth.

In fact these figures cannot truly be described in terms of knowledge. They are situated on its near side, where knowledge is still close to its gestures, its familiarities, and its first formulation. Three of these structures were of particular importance.

1 In one, the old space of confinement, now limited and considerably reduced, was joined to a medical space that had taken shape elsewhere, and could only adjust to it by successive modifications and refinements.
2 Another structure established a new relation between madness and those who identified it, guarded and judged it, a neutralised relation, seemingly purified of any complicity, of the order of an objective gaze.
3 In the third, the madman found himself face to face with the criminal; but neither in a space of confusion nor as a variety of irresponsibility. This was a structure that would allow madness to haunt crime without ever completely reducing it, simultaneously authorising reasonable men to judge and divide up different kinds of madness according to the new forms of morality.

These are structures to be found behind the legislative chronicle sketched out so far, and we shall now look at them in detail.

*

Medical thought and the practice of confinement had long remained strangers to each other. While a knowledge of diseases of the mind had slowly been taking shape, following its own laws, a concrete experience of madness was also being formed in the classical world, an experience that was symbolised and fixed by confinement. At the end of the eighteenth century these two figures began to come together, giving the first indication of a convergence. There was no moment of illumination, nor even a sudden realisation that revealed in a sort of conversion of knowledge that the confined were patients, but a far slower, more obscure process, in which the old homogeneous, uniform, rigorously limited space of exclusion was brought together with the social space of assistance that the eighteenth century had recently fragmented and made polymorphous, restructuring it along the lines of psychological and moral forms of devotion.

But this new space was ill suited to the particular problems of madness. If the healthy poor could be put to work, and families obliged to look after their own sick members, there was no question of allowing the mad to blend into society. The most that could be hoped for was to integrate them into a family environment, while forbidding families with dangerous madmen in their entourage to allow them to circulate freely. But that way protection was only assured from one side, and in an extremely fragile way. Inasmuch as bourgeois society felt innocent when faced with poverty, it did recognise its responsibility before madness, and felt that it should protect private citizens from it. At a time when for the first time in the Christian world sickness and poverty were becoming *private affairs*, belonging only to the sphere of individuals and families, madness, by virtue of that fact, required a *public status*, and the definition of a space of isolation that would safeguard society from its dangers.

Nothing yet determined the nature of that isolation. No one knew whether it would be closer to corrective or hospital institutions. At that time, only one thing was certain: as the world of confinement collapsed, bringing liberty to inmates and restoring the poor to their families, the mad found themselves in the same position as prisoners who were condemned or awaiting trial, together with the poor and the sick who had no family to look after them. In his report, La Rochefoucauld-Liancourt stressed that help at home could equally apply to the great majority of people hospitalised in Paris. 'Of the more than 11,000 poor affected, this form of assistance could almost certainly be applied to 8,000, i.e. to children and people of both sexes who are neither *prisoners, insane, nor lacking family*.'[16] Were the mad then to be treated simply as prisoners, and placed in a prison environment, or should they be treated as invalids who had no relatives, and who therefore needed a quasi-family environment created around them? We shall see below precisely how Tuke and Pinel combined both these approaches in defining the archetypal modern asylum.

But the common function and mixed form of these two types of confinement had not yet been discovered. On the eve of the Revolution, two series of projects found themselves in opposition. The first aimed to reinvent the old functions of confinement, with a sort of geometrical purity and almost delirious rationalism, to be used for both crime and madness; the second aimed to establish a more hospital-oriented status for madness, to take the place of the absent family. This was no struggle between philanthropy and barbarism, any more than it was a duel between tradition and the new humanism. They were rather the first stumbling steps towards a definition of madness that a whole society was once more eager to exorcise, at a time when its previous companions in misery – poverty, libertinage and sickness – had been returned to the private domain. In this entirely restructured social space, madness once more had to find a place.

There were many dreams, even as confinement was losing its meaning; ideal houses of correction, functioning unhindered with no disadvantages, in silent perfection, oneiric Bicêtres where all the mechanisms of correction operated in a pure state, where order and punishment and sentence were carefully measured, an organised pyramid of work and chastisement, the best possible of all worlds of evil. And in these ideal fortresses, the fantasy was that there would be no contact at all with the real world; they were to be entirely closed in on themselves, and would rely on the sole resources of sickness and evil, circumventing any risk of contagion and preventing terror. These independent microcosms would be an inverted mirror of society, where vice, constraint and punishment would take the place of virtue, liberty and the just rewards that made for the contentment of mankind.

Brissot for example drew up a plan for a perfect house of correction, according to the rigours of a geometry that was both architectural and moral. Every fragment of space took on the symbolic values of a meticulous social hell. Two sides of the building, which was to be square in shape, were reserved for less serious misdemeanours, with women and children on one side, and debtors on the other. They were to be given 'beds and passable food'. Their rooms would be exposed to sunlight and natural warmth. The cold and windy sides would house 'people accused of capital crimes', and they would be grouped together with libertines, the raving mad and all the insane who were 'disturbers of the public peace'. The first two classes of prisoners would do jobs that were of some use to society. The latter would carry out those indispensable tasks that were harmful to health, and which all too often honest people were forced to carry out:

Work will be proportional to strength and the delicacy of their constitution, the nature of their crimes, and so forth. Vagabonds, libertines and villains will break stones, polish marble, grind up colours and do the sort of work with chemicals that ordinarily puts the life of honest citizens in danger.

In this marvellous economy, work is doubly effective: it produces and destroys, as work necessary to society is born out of the death of workers whose disappearance is desirable. The dangerous, restive lives of men passed into the docility of objects. The irregularities of these senseless existences were all ground and polished as smooth as marble. The classic themes of confinement here reach a paroxysm of perfection: the confined are excluded until their death, but each step taken towards this death is useful to the society from which they are banished.[17]

When the Revolution began, these dreams had not yet disappeared. Musquinet's project used a fairly similar form of geometry, although the meticulousness of the symbols was even richer. His fortress was to have four sides, with each of the buildings in turn having four storeys, forming a pyramid of work. It was an architectural pyramid, with carding and weaving at its base, and at the top there was 'a platform to serve as place for warp to be stretched before it was introduced to the loom'.[18] It was a social pyramid too, as the confined were to be grouped in battalions of twelve, under the direction of a foreman. Guards would watch over their work, and a director would oversee the whole establishment. A hierarchy of merit culminated in the promise of liberation, and each week the most zealous workers 'would receive a prize of an écu of six pounds from the president, and anyone winning the prize three times would also win their liberty'.[19] Work and personal interest were therefore combined, and a fair balance was struck: the prisoners' work was an economic good for the administration, and a step towards freedom for the inmate, so a single product brought gains of two types. But there was also the world of morality, symbolised by a chapel that was to be built in the middle of the square formed by the buildings. Men and women were to attend mass every Sunday, paying particular attention to a sermon:

whose purpose will invariably be to instil feelings of repentance in the prisoners for their past life, making them understand how libertinage and idleness never bring happiness, even in this life ... and forcing them to make a firm resolution to behave better in the future.[20]

If a prisoner who had won prizes, and was only a step or two away from gaining his freedom, caused a commotion in mass, or demonstrated himself to be 'disorderly in his morals', he would immediately lose the benefits he had gained. Freedom did not simply have a market value, it had a moral value too, and was also to be acquired through virtue. Prisoners were thus placed at the intersection of two different systems. The one was purely economic, consisting of work, its product and its reward; the other was exclusively moral, and consisted of virtue, vigilance and recompense. When the two coincided, in a perfect form of work that was also pure morality, the prisoner was free. This perfected vision of Bicêtre thereby found a double justification: for the outside world, it was pure profit, as it was unremunerated work, and Musquinet reckoned that for 400 workers, it was worth precisely 500,000 pounds per year. For the interior world that it enclosed it was a gigantic moral purification:

> No man is so corrupt that he can considered incorrigible: all that is necessary is for him to understand his true interests, and for him not to be abased with unbearable punishments that are always too much for human weakness.[21]

Here we touch some of the most extreme forms of the myth of confinement. Purified into a complex scheme, its intentions are immediately visible. It becomes, in all naivety, what it always was in some obscure fashion – the moral control of inmates, and economic profit for everyone else. The product of the work accomplished can be easily broken down into the profits that go to the administration, thereby indirectly benefiting society as a whole, and the gratification awarded to workers in the form of certificates of morality. A sort of caricatural truth that indicates not only what the asylum wished itself to be, but also the style in which a whole form of bourgeois consciousness set up the relations between work, profit and virtue. It is a point at which the history of madness slides into a mythology where reason and unreason found simultaneous expression.[22]

This dream of work carried out in a purely moral environment, and this other dream of work that attains its positivity with the death of the person accomplishing it, both demonstrate that confinement attained an excessive truth. Such projects were now only determined by an overflow of psychological and social meanings, or by a system of moral symbols where madness was somehow levelled out: madness was now only disorder, irregularity and obscure faults – a disturbance in men that troubled the State and contradicted morality. Just as bourgeois society was beginning to understand the futility of confinement, and lose the unity of evidence that made unreason perceptible to the classical age, it found itself dreaming of a pure form of work – which was pure profit for this society, and death and moral submission for its outsiders – where all that was foreign in man would be snuffed out and reduced to silence.

*

In these dreams, confinement overreached itself. It became a pure form, finding its place in the network of social utilities, indefinitely fecund. These mythical elaborations were in vain, the fantastical geometry of a confinement that had already had its day. Yet purifying the space of confinement of its real contradictions, making it compatible, in the imaginary at least, with the requirements of society, it tended to give a positive significance to what had previously been pure exclusion. This region, akin to a negative zone at the limits of the State, sought to become a substantial milieu where society could recognise itself and put its own values into circulation. In that respect, the dreams of Brissot and Musquinet were complicitous with numerous other projects whose seriousness, philanthropic concerns and proto-medical preoccupations seemed to propose a meaning at the other extreme.

Although they were contemporaneous with them, these other projects were in a very different style. On the one hand was the abstraction of confinement taken in its most general terms, with no reference to the confined themselves – who were merely an opportunity and a raw material rather than the *raison d'être* of the project itself. On the other, the peculiarities of the confined, and above all the singular appearance that madness had taken on in the course of the eighteenth century as confinement lost its essential structure, were instead exalted. Alienation was treated on its own terms, not as one of the forms that necessitated confinement, but as a problem in and for itself, with confinement seen as nothing more than a solution. This was the first time that confined madness and medically treated madness were systematically brought face to face, when madness seen as unreason confronted madness seen as disease. It was, in short, the first moment of the confusion or synthesis (whichever label one prefers) that constituted mental alienation in the modern sense of the phrase.

In 1785, under the double signature of Doublet and Colombier, there appeared *Instructions Printed by Order and at the Expense of the Government on the Manner of Governing and Treating the Insane.* The madman here is located in an ambiguous manner, half-way between forms of assistance that are in the process of being reorganised, and confinement, which was in the process of disappearing. This text reflects neither a sudden discovery nor a conversion in the manner in which madness was to be treated. Rather, it points to compromises, the search for new measures, balanced positions. All the hesitations of the Revolutionary legislators are already there in embryo.

On the one hand assistance, as a manifestation of natural pity, is required by the mad, as it is for all those who are incapable of meeting their own needs: 'It is society's duty to shield the weakest and most miserable most carefully, and for that reason, children and the insane have always been the object of public concern.' But the compassion naturally felt towards children is a positive attraction, while the pity felt for the mad is quickly spent, and even replaced by a horror inspired by their foreign existence, given over to violence and fury:

> We tend to flee them, to avoid the heart-wrenching spectacle of the hideous marks on their faces and bodies and of the loss of their reason; in any case a fear of their violence is such that anyone who is not obliged to assist them remains at a distance.

What was therefore required was a middle way between the duty of assistance prescribed by an abstract pity and the legitimate fears that the real experience of this terror inspired; and the solution, naturally, was assistance *intra muros*, help that was supplied at the boundaries of the distance inspired by horror, and pity that operated inside the space prepared by more than a century of confinement, now left empty. One consequence was that the exclusion of the mad took on a whole new meaning: it no longer marked the great caesura between reason and unreason, at the furthest limits of society; but inside the group itself it drew a line of compromise between feelings and duty – between pity and horror, between assistance and security. Never again was it to have the sense of absolute limit that it had perhaps inherited from age-old terrors, and that it had confirmed in the obscure fears of men, by taking the place of leprosy in an almost geographical manner. Now it was a measure rather than a limit, and it is the obviousness of that shift in significance that meant that the 'French asylums, inspired by Roman Law' were so roundly criticised. All they relieve are

> the fears of the public, and they are unable to satisfy pity which requires not simply security, but also the care and treatment that are often neglected, and without which the madness of some is perpetual, whereas it could be cured, and the condition of others worsens, whereas it could be improved.

But this new form of confinement should also be a measure of a different sort in that it needed to reconcile the possibilities of riches and the demands of poverty; for the rich — and this was the ideal of assistance for Turgot's disciples — 'make it their duty to look after relatives stricken with madness in their own homes', and if their efforts were in vain, they had them 'looked after by trustworthy individuals'. But the poor had 'neither the necessary resources to contain the insane, nor the ability to have them looked after and treated as sick people'. What was therefore necessary was a form of treatment for the poor that resembled that of the rich — they should be watched over and guarded as carefully as the madmen of rich families were, but at no cost to the beneficiary. To that end, Colombier recommended the creation 'of a department solely destined for the poor insane in each begging centre, where madness should be treated in all its forms'.

In any case, the most significant aspect of the text was the still-hesitant search for a form of equilibrium between the exclusion of the mad pure and simple, and the medical care that was provided for them on the grounds that they were considered to be sick. To lock up the mad was in essence to protect society against the danger that they represented:

> A thousand examples have proven this danger, and the newspapers recently reaffirmed it by reporting the story of a maniac who slit the throats of his wife and children, before calmly lying down to sleep beside the bloody victims of his frenzy.

It was therefore of primary importance to lock up the mad whose needy families did not have the means to guard them at home. But they were also to benefit from the treatment they would receive either at the hands of doctors, if they were more fortunate, or in hospitals if they were not immediately confined. Doublet detailed the cures that were to be applied to different diseases of the mind – precepts that exactly summarize the treatment traditionally handed out in the eighteenth century.[23]

Despite that, the connection between confinement and medical treatment here is only of a temporal order. They did not exactly coincide, but succeeded each other: treatment was given during the short period when the disease was considered to be curable, but immediately afterwards confinement resumed its sole function of exclusion. In one sense, the 1785 Instructions did little more than take up and systematise what was already customary in hospitality and confinement; but what was essential was the manner in which it brought them together in the same institutional form, and that the treatment was to be applied in the same place as the exclusion. Previously, treatment was carried out at the Hôtel-Dieu, and confinement occurred at Bicêtre. What was now projected was a form of confinement in which the medical function and the exclusive function would alternate, but inside a single structure. Society was to be protected against the mad through a form of banishment that designated madness as irreversible alienation, and protected against disease in a recuperative space where madness, in principle at least, was considered transitory. These two types of measures, which covered two different experiences that until this point had been considered to be heterogeneous, were now superimposed, although they did not yet blend into one another.

There have been attempts to see Doublet and Colombier's text as the first great stride towards the creation of the modern asylum.[24] But however close their Instructions come to bringing medical and pharmaceutical techniques into the world of confinement, the essential step had not yet been taken. That would only happen when the space of confinement, adapted and reserved for madness, revealed values of its own, capable, with no external addition of curing madness, i.e. the day when confinement itself became the essential medication, and when the negative gesture of exclusion, by its own meaning and its intrinsic virtues, became an opening onto the positive world of the cure. Confinement was not to be supplemented by practices that were external to it, but reorganised, so that the truth that it concealed was revealed, and the loose threads that ran through it tightened at last. It would thus take on a medical value in the movement that brought madness back to reason. The space that was exclusively the domain of social division was to become a dialectical domain where the mad and the non-mad came to exchange their secret truths.

That step was taken by Tenon and Cabanis. In the work of Tenon, one can still discern the old idea that the confinement of the mad should only be decreed in a definitive manner once medical treatment had failed: 'Only after using up all possible resources is it permissible to consent to the unfortunate necessity of depriving a citizen of his liberty.'[25] But already confinement was no longer, in a rigorously negative manner, the total and absolute abolition of liberty. It was more a restrained and organised form of freedom. If the idea was to avoid all contact with the reasonable world – and in that sense it remained a form of closure – confinement was also to open, on the inside, onto an empty space where madness was free to express itself, not so that it might be abandoned to its blind rage, but so that it had the possibility of satisfaction, an opportunity for appeasement that could never result from uninterrupted constraints: 'the first remedy should be to offer the madman a certain amount of freedom, so that he can allow himself to express in some measure the desires that nature instils in him'.[26] Rather than seeking to control it entirely, confinement functioned as though it had to leave madness a certain leeway, a space in which it could be itself, a form of liberty stripped of secondary components like violence, rage, frenzy or despair, whose appearance was invariably provoked by constant oppression. The classical age, in some of its myths at least, associated the liberty of madness with the most aggressive forms of animality, and considered that predation was the basis of the resemblance between the demented and the animal. What now appeared was the idea that there could be in a madman a more gentle form of animality, which did not destroy its human truth in violence, but allowed instead one of nature's secrets to emerge: the rediscovery of the familiar but forgotten resemblance with tame animals and children. Madness was no longer an absolute perversion that went against nature, but an invasion by a neighbouring nature. To Tenon's way of thinking, the ideal form of confinement was the one practised at Saint Luke's, where a madman:

> is left to his own devices, and leaves his cell if he wishes, and roams through the gallery, or wanders off to a sandy open-air path. As he is restless, he requires covered and open walkways, so that he can yield in any weather to the impulses that overtake him.[27]

Confinement was thus to be a space of truth as much as a space of restraint, and had to be the latter only to be the former. For the first time, an idea was formulated that was to weigh heavily on the history of psychiatry up until the psychoanalytic liberation: that in these constraints, this closed-off vacuum, this 'milieu', confined madness found a privileged element in which the essential forms of its truth could surface.

Relatively free and abandoned to the paroxysms of its truth, was there not then a risk that madness might thereby gain strength and follow a sort of constant intensification? Neither Tenon nor Cabanis thought so. They thought that on the contrary, this semi-liberty, this caged freedom would be of therapeutic value. This was because for them, as for all physicians of the eighteenth century, the imagination was always responsible for all the sicknesses of the mind, because it partook of both the body and the soul and was the birthplace of error. The more men were constrained, the more their imagination tended to wander, and the stricter the rules restraining their bodies, the greater the disorder in images and dreams. So much so that freedom was therefore more effective than chains when it came to binding the imagination, as it constantly forced the imagination to confront reality, burying strange dreams under familiar gestures. Imagination was silenced by this vagabondage of liberty. Tenon praised the foresight of the administrators at Saint Luke's, where 'a madman, in general, is let loose for most of the day: that freedom, in people unaccustomed to the rule of reason, is already a remedy that brings calm to the wandering or lost imagination'.[28] In itself, without being anything other than this secluded form of liberty, confinement was thus an agent of cure: it was medical, not so much in terms of the care that it provided as in the play of imagination, liberty, silence and limits, and the movement that spontaneously organised them and brought error back to truth and madness back to reason. Confined freedom cured of its own accord, just as liberated language was soon to do for psychoanalysis, but in a movement that was its exact opposite: not by allowing fantasy to take shape in language and use it as a medium of exchange, but by forcing it instead to disappear when confronted with the insistent and heavily real silence of things.

An essential step had been taken, and confinement had at last gained a form of medical acceptability. It had become the place of cure, no longer the place in which madness kept watch and ruled until its death, but the place in which, by a sort of indigenous mechanism, it was supposed to suppress itself of its own accord.

The key fact is that this transformation of the centres of confinement into asylums was not the result of a progressive introduction of medicine – a sort of invasion coming from the outside – but was the result of an internal restructuring of a space that the classical age had designated as a place of exclusion and correction. The progressive alteration of its social significance, the political criticism of repression and the economic critique of assistance, the appropriation of the whole field of confinement by madness, at a time when all the other figures of unreason were slowly being liberated, all resulted in confinement being a doubly privileged place for madness, the place both of its truth and of its abolition. To that extent, it really did become its destiny, and the link between them became a necessary one. The twin functions that might appear quite contradictory – protection against perils that the insane represented, and the curing of sickness – were suddenly harmonised at last, as it was in the closed but empty space of confinement that madness formulated its truth and liberated its nature, and by this single operation, the danger to the public was averted and the signs of sickness removed.

Once the space of confinement was invested by these new values, and by the whole new movement that they brought, then and only then could the world of medicine take control of the asylum, bringing all the experiences of madness into its own remit at last. It was not medical thought that forced open the doors of the asylum, and if today doctors now reign in such places, it is not through any right of conquest resulting from the vital force of their philanthropy or their concern with scientific objectivity. It is because confinement itself slowly took on a therapeutic value, bringing a realignment of all the political and social gestures, and the moral and imaginary rituals that for more than a century had been used to ward off madness and unreason.

*

The appearance of confinement therefore changed. But in the complex unity between confinement and madness, where a clear division was never entirely possible, madness too underwent an alteration. It struck up new relations with the semi-liberty that it was offered, however parsimoniously, with the time within which it unfolded, with the gaze that watched over it and controlled it. Madness was at one with this closed world, a body which was by the same token its *truth* and its *home*. Through a recurrence, which is only strange if one believes that madness pre-exists the practices that designate and concern it, its situation became its nature; the constraints upon it took on the meaning of a determinism, and the language that determined it assumed the voice of a truth that spoke of itself.

The genius of Cabanis, and of the texts that he wrote in 1791, coincided with this decisive, equivocal moment, where perspectives suddenly began to lose their clarity: what had originated as a social reform of confinement became a fidelity to the deep truths of madness, and *the manner in which the mad were alienated* was forgotten, only to reappear as the *nature of their alienation*.[29] Confinement was beginning to order itself in relation to the forms to which it had given birth.

The problem of madness was no longer envisaged from the point of view of reason or order, but from the point of view of the rights of the free individual, which no coercion nor even charity could infringe. 'The liberty and safety of individuals must be protected above all other things. The rules of justice should never be violated, not even when doing good.' Liberty and reason had the same limits. Whenever reason was affected, liberty too could be constrained, but only if the attacks on reason threatened the existence of the subject or the freedom of others:

> When men enjoy the full power of their rational faculties, i.e. whenever these powers are not so altered as to compromise the safety and tranquillity of others, or expose men to genuine danger, no one, not even society as a whole, has the right to raise a hand against their independence.[30]

The ground was being prepared for a definition of madness based on the relation that freedom might have with itself. The old judicial conceptions that delivered the mad from responsibility for their actions before the law, at the cost of their civil rights, did not constitute a psychology of madness; that suspension of liberty was a purely legal consequence. But with Cabanis, freedom became man's nature, and any legitimate restriction on its exercise must necessarily have also altered the natural forms that it took in man. Locking up a madman had now to be the sanctioning of a matter of fact, a translation into juridical terms of an abolition of liberty that had already taken place on a psychological level. And in this recurrence or retroaction of law upon nature, we find the basis for the great ambiguity that causes contemporary thinking to hesitate so much when considering madness: if irresponsibility is an absence of liberty, then any form of psychological determinism is a proof of innocence. This is tantamount to saying that there is no truth in psychology that is not also a form of alienation for man.

The disappearance of liberty, once a consequence of madness, now became its foundation, secret and essence. And it was this essence that was to dictate the degree of restrictions that were to be imposed on the material liberty of the insane. A control was necessary and it had to inter-rogate madness about its own being, which given the still-ambiguous nature of this disappearance of liberty, involved a confused variety of figures, such as magistrates, jurists, doctors, and simply men of experience: 'For these reasons, the places where the mad are to be detained must be constantly inspected by the various magistrates, and carefully examined by the police.' Whenever a madman is taken to a detention centre, 'he is to be examined forthwith from all points of view. He is to be watched by health officers, and guarded by the most intelligent personnel, who are most accustomed to observing madness in all its forms.'[31] Confinement was to operate like a permanent measuring of madness, a constant series of readjustments in response to the changeable nature of its truth, restraining only inside the limits within which free-dom alienated itself: 'Humanity, justice and good medicine dictate that only the mad who risk genuinely harming others should be locked up; the only patients who should be restrained are those who otherwise risk harming themselves.' The justice that was to reign inside asylums would no longer be that of punishment, but that of truth: there was to be an exact measurement of the exercise of liberty and of its restrictions, and as rigorous a conformity as possible between constraints and the alienation of liberty. And the most concrete form of this justice, its most visible symbol, was no longer to be the chain – an absolute, punitive restriction that 'invariably wounds the flesh it rubs against' – but the new, soon-to-be-famous straitjacket, 'a close-fitting canvas shirt, which constrains and contains the arms', designed to progressively hinder movements as their violence increased.[32] The straitjacket should not be seen as the humanisation of chains, or as progress towards 'self-restraint'. A process of conceptual deduction leads to the straitjacket, showing that in madness, the experience was no longer of an absolute conflict between reason and unreason, but rather of a play – always relative, always mobile – between freedom and its limits.[33]

The draft regulations that followed the *Rapport adressé au Départment de Paris* proposed that the main ideas developed in Cabanis' text be applied in detail:

> The mad or the insane will be admitted to the different establishments that are or will be allotted to them throughout the Department of Paris on the basis of reports from legally recognised doctors and surgeons, signed by two witnesses, parents, friends or neighbours, and certified by a justice of the peace from the section or canton.

But the report gave a far wider interpretation to the regulations: even the pre-eminence of the doctor in the determination of madness was carefully controlled, precisely in the name of an experience of the asylums that was considered to be closer to the truth as it was based on a greater variety of cases, but also because it somehow allowed madness to speak more freely for itself.

> Imagine a madman being taken to hospital . . . the patient arrives, led by his family, neighbours, friends or charitable strangers. Everyone certifies that he is indeed mad; they either *are* or *are not* in possession of doctors' certificates. Appearances confirm or appear to contradict what they say. Whatever opinion one might have of the state of the patient, if, in addition, the proofs of poverty are authentic, he must be taken in provisionally.

What should then follow is a long process of observation carried out by the 'staff of the institution' and 'health officers'. And there, in the privileged environment of confinement, and under its purified gaze, the division is made: if the subject manifested obvious signs of madness,

> all doubt should disappear. He can be retained without scruples, and he should be looked after and protected from his own errors, and the use of the indicated medication should be courageously continued. But if, on the other hand, after a reasonable amount of time, no sign of madness is found, and painstaking investigations reveal nothing to arouse the suspicion that the calm is merely a lucid interval, and if the patient requests that he be allowed to leave the hospital, then it would be a crime to retain him there by force. He should immediately be returned to himself and to society.

The medical certificate issued on entry to the asylum was thus only a guarantee of doubtful value. The definitive criterion, which could not be put in doubt, was to be provided by confinement instead. Inside, madness appeared filtered of anything that might have provided an illusion, offered to an absolutely neutral gaze; for it was no longer the interest of a family that was speaking, nor power and its arbitrary nature, nor the prejudices of medicine. Confinement pronounced of its own accord, in a vocabulary that was its own, i.e. in terms of liberty and constraints that penetrated deep into the essence of madness. The guardians who watched over the limits of confinement were now the sole persons who had the possibility of a positive knowledge of madness.

By that means, Cabanis arrived at the curious idea (probably the most novel among his innovations) of an 'asylum journal'. In the classical forms of confinement, unreason was, in the strictest sense of the word, reduced to silence. We know nothing of what it was for a considerable period of time, give or take a few enigmatic inscriptions on registers of the houses of confinement: its concrete figures, its language, and its teeming, delirious existences are probably lost to us now. Madness was then without memory, and confinement was the seal on that forgetting. But from this point confinement was the space within which madness formulated its own truth; it was to mark its measure moment by moment. Within it madness would come to completion up to the point of decision:

> A journal shall be kept where a picture of each form of madness, the effects of remedies, and autopsies, are to be recorded with scrupulous exactitude. The names of all individuals in the section are to be recorded, enabling the administration to draw up a nominative report on their condition week by week, or even day by day, if that is what is judged necessary.

Madness therefore came to regions of truth that unreason had never attained: it was inserted into time, escaping the random, the purely accidental that had previously been used to mark its various episodes, and it took on an autonomous form in history. Its past and evolution became part of its truth, and what revealed madness was no longer the always-instantaneous rupture with truth that had previously been the hallmark of unreason. Madness too has a time that coincides with the calendar, not the rhythmic calendar of the seasons that would link it to the dark forces within the world, but the daily time of men, the time within which history is accounted for.

Its truth revealed by confinement, firmly installed in the time of chronicles and history, stripped of all the elements that would have made the deep presence of unreason irreducible, madness, disarmed in this fashion, could now safely enter the world of exchange. It became communicable, but in the neutralised form of offered objectivity. It could take on a public existence once more – not in the form that had once caused such scandal, when it suddenly and irrevocably called into question all that was most essential in man, and all that was most true in his truth – but as a calm object, kept at a safe distance, and yet totally visible, fully open to reveal its secrets, now no longer a cause of discomfort, but a means of instruction.

> No doubt the administration will consider the contents of the journal and its precious details to be the property of the public who provided such deplorable material. There is no doubt that it will have the results printed, and if the editor is a man of some learning and medical experience, such a compendium, providing new information year upon year, new observations, new facts, and the latest results of new and true experiments, will become an immense source of riches for all students of the physical and moral science of man.[34]

Here was madness offered up to the gaze. This had also been its position in classical confinement, when it presented the spectacle of its own animality; but the gaze that had then been cast upon it was one of fascination, in that man contemplated in that figure so foreign an animality that was his own, which he recognised in a confused manner as being indefinably close yet indefinably distant; this existence that a delirious monstrosity made inhuman and placed as far from the world as possible, he secretly felt it inside himself. The new gaze that was trained on madness was not charged with so much complicity. It was directed towards an object, which it attained by the sole intermediary of a discursive truth that had already been formulated: the madman now appeared in a purified state, madness in an abstract form. If there was anything in its spectacle that concerned reasonable individuals, it was not the extent to which madness could challenge humanity as a whole, but rather the extent to which it could bring something new to what was known about man. Madness was no longer to be inscribed in the negativity of existence, as one of its most brutal figures, but now progressively took its place in the positivity of known things.

In this new gaze, where compromises disappeared, barriers like grilles were also abolished. The mad and the non-mad were to meet face to face. The only distance between them was the one immediately measured by the gaze. It may have been almost imperceptible, but it was no less unbridgeable for that; the freedom acquired in confinement, the possibility of finding there a truth and a language were for madness no more than the other side of a movement that gave it a place as an object of knowledge. Under the gaze that now enveloped it, madness shed all the prestige that had made it until recently a figure banished on sight; it became an object of investigation, a thing invested with language, a known reality: it became, in short, an object. And if the new space of confinement brought madness and reason into closer proximity, within a mixed home it also marked off an even greater distance between them, an imbalance that could never be reversed. However free madness became in the world that reasonable men had created for it, however close it came to their spirit and their hearts, it could never be anything other than an object for them. No longer the ever-imminent converse of their existence, but a possible eventuality in the concatenation of things. This fall into objectivity was a far more effective means of mastering madness than its previous enslavement to the forms of unreason. Confinement, in the light of these developments, could offer madness the luxury of liberty – as it was now enslaved, and stripped of its deepest powers.

If this evolution was to be summed up in one sentence, we might say that the kernel of the experience of Unreason was that madness was there its own subject, but that in the experience that came into being in the late eighteenth century, madness was alienated from itself through its promotion to a new status as object.

*

What Cabanis dreamt of for madness was that half-sleep to which the asylum would consign it, and he sought to exhaust it in that problematic serenity. But strangely, at that very moment, it sprang back to life elsewhere, taking on a whole new concrete content. While it became purified for knowledge, and was freed of its ancient complicities, it also found itself engaged in a series of questions that morality began to ask itself: it penetrated everyday life, affecting everyday choices and elementary decisions, provoking archaic reactions and forcing public opinion to revise its system of values concerning madness. The clarification and puri-fication that was operated in the work of Colombier, Tenon and Cabanis as part of a continual series of reflections was immediately counteracted and compromised by this more spontaneous labour carried out on the margins of consciousness everyday. Nonetheless, it was there, in the barely per-ceptible weave of daily experience, that madness was soon to take on the moral form that was so instantly recognisable to Pinel and Tuke.

For as confinement disappeared, madness once again entered the public domain. It reappeared as though carried by a slow, silent invasion, affecting judges, families, and everyone responsible for law and order. While a status was sought for it, it posed some urgent questions: the age-old concept of the unreasonable man, in the family, society and police sense, was now beginning to disintegrate, leaving the judicial notion of irresponsibility face to face with the immediate experience of madness, with no intermediary. A whole labour now began, in which the negative concept of alienation as defined by law was slowly permeated and altered by the moral meanings that ordinary people lent to madness.

'A distinction should be made in the Lieutenant of Police between the Magistrate and the Administrator. The first is a man of the law; the latter is a man of the government.'[35] Five years later, Des Essarts had this to say about his own earlier definition:

> Re-reading, in April 1789, the article that I wrote in 1784, I must add that the nation ardently desires to diminish the influence of the administra-tor's part, or at least modify it, so that liberty of citizens should be guaranteed in the most inviolable manner.

The reorganisation of the police in the early days of the Revolution caused that power, which was both independent and mixed, to disappear, grant-ing its privileges to citizens instead, conceived of as both private individuals and the collective will of society. The electoral districts created by the decree of 28 March 1789 served as a framework for the reorganisa-tion of the police. In each district of Paris, five companies were set up, only one of which was paid (this was usually the previous police force), with the four others staffed by volunteer citizens.[36] From one day to the next, private individuals found themselves entrusted with the task of carrying out a fundamental social division that precedes the act of justice and is the work of all police. Private individuals now had to deal directly, with no intermediaries and no controls, with all the human material that was previously consigned to the houses of confinement: vagabondage, prostitution, the debauchery and immorality, and of course all the confused forms that went from violence to frenzy, from weak-mindedness to dementia. Man, as a citizen, was now called upon to exercise within the group the provisionally absolute power of police. His task was to accomplish the obscure and sovereign gesture that designates an individual as an undesirable element, a stranger to the unity that society forms; and it fell to the common citizen to judge the boundaries of order and disorder, liberty and scandal, morality and immorality. The immediate power of decision regarding the division of reason and madness was now to operate inside the citizen, and inside his conscience, before any liberation.

The citizen was universal reason, and doubly so: he was the immediate truth of human nature, the touchstone of all legislation. But he was also the person for whom unreason departed from reason: he was, in the most spontaneous forms of his consciousness, in the most immediate decisions that he took, before any theoretical or judicial elaboration, the place, the instrument and the judge of that division. Men of the classical age, as we have seen, also immediately recognised madness, without any recourse to reflection, in an immediate apprehension; but they made spontaneous use of their good sense, not of their political rights. That was man judging as man, perceiving without commentary a difference of fact. But now, when faced with madness, a citizen had a fundamental power that made him both a 'man of the law' and a 'man of the government'. As the sole sovereign of the bourgeois state, the free man became the first judge of madness. The man in the street renewed the contact with madness that had been interrupted by the classical age; but contact was renewed, without dialogue or confrontation, in the pre-existing form of sovereignty, in the absolute and silent exercise of his rights. The fundamental principles of bourgeois society allowed this private yet universal consciousness to reign over madness, before any possible contestation. And when judicial or medical experience was allowed to express an opinion on it, at trial or inside the asylums, it had already been secretly mastered.

This new reign had its primary (and highly transitory) form in what were known as the 'family tribunals'. These were an old idea, which easily predated the Revolution, and which the customs of the Ancien Régime seemed to have sketched in advance. Regarding the petitions used by families requesting *lettres de cachet*, Bertin, the Lieutenant of Police, wrote to his superintendents as follows on 1 June 1764:

> Take extreme care with the following two points: first of all, be certain that the requests are signed by the closest relatives on both the paternal and maternal sides of the family, and secondly take careful note of any signatures that are missing, and find out why they did not sign.[37]

Breteuil later considered constituting in law a special familial jurisdiction, but it was the Constituent Assembly that eventually set up family tribunals in May 1790. They were to form the most elementary cell of the civil jurisdiction, but their decisions only took on an executive force once they had been ratified by special orders from the district courts. These tribunals were to relieve the state of its duties in the innumerable procedures concerning conflicting family interests, inheritances, co-ownership and so forth. But they were also entrusted with a separate task, and were to give a proper status and juridical form to measures that courts previously asked directly of the royal authorities: spendthrift and debauched fathers, prodigal sons, inheritors who were incapable of managing their share, and all the various forms of deficiency, disorder and misdemeanour that were previously sanctioned with *lettres de cachet*, in the absence of the complete legal procedure of interdiction, all now fell into the jurisdiction of these family tribunals.

In one sense the Constituent Assembly had completed a process of evolution that had continued throughout the eighteenth century, conferring an institutional status on what was a spontaneous practice. But in fact the arbitrary power of families and their relative interests were hardly checked at all by such measures. Under the Ancien Régime, requests from families for *lettres de cachet* were followed with enquiries by the police so that the allegations might be verified,[38] whereas under the new scheme, one merely had the right to appeal against the family tribunal's decisions by going to a higher court. It is quite unlikely that these courts functioned in an effective manner, and they did not survive subsequent reorganisations of the justice system.[39] But it is quite significant that for a certain time, the family itself was elected to the status of judicial body, and that it had the prerogatives of a tribunal regarding cases of misbehaviour, disordered lifestyles and the different forms incapacity or madness could take. For this brief moment, it openly was what it was long to remain in more covert form – the most immediate instance of division between reason and madness, an archaic and simple form of justice that likened the rules of life, economics and family obligation to the norms of good health, reason and freedom. In the family, taken as an institution and defined as a court, unwritten laws took on a natural significance, and at the same time private individuals became judges, bringing their daily dialogue with unreason into the public domain. From this point onwards, there was a public and institutional grasp of private consciousness upon madness.

Numerous other transformations also bore witness to this new grasp, and foremost among them were changes in the nature of the punishments meted out. As was noted above, confinement on occasion constituted an attenuation of the punishment;[40] more often still it was used to cover up the monstrous nature of a crime, if it was the result of some form of excess, or a form of violence that seemed to reveal inhuman powers.[41] Confinement marked out a limit beyond which scandal was deemed unacceptable. For the bourgeois consciousness, on the other hand, scandal became an instrument for the exercise of its sovereignty. Its absolute power was such that this consciousness was not merely judgement, but also a punishment in and of itself. 'To know of a case' did not simply mean to instruct and to judge, but also to make public, and to make manifest in such a manner that the glaring spotlight of its own judgement was itself a punishment. In this consciousness, judgement and the execution of the sentence were unified through the ideal, instantaneous act of the gaze. Knowledge, in the organised game of scandal, was the totality of the judgement.

In his *Theory of Criminal Laws*, Brissot showed that scandal was the ideal punishment, always proportional to the crime, free of any physical stigma, and instantly adequate to the demands of moral consciousness. He took up again the old distinction between sin, which was an offence against the divine order, only punishable by God, crime, which was an act committed against one's fellow man, to be rewarded with punishment, and vice, 'a disorder that relates only to the self', which was to be punished with shame.[42] Because it was more interior, vice was also more primitive: it was crime itself, but before its accomplishment, at its roots in the human heart. Before they broke the law, criminals always infringed the silent rules present in the conscience of a man:

> Vices are to morality as crime is to law, and vice is invariably the father of crime: it is a race of monsters which, like the terrifying genealogy of sins described by Milton, seem to infinitely reproduce each other. I see a poor unfortunate on the scaffold, about to pass over to the other side . . . why is he there? Go back up the chain of his actions, and you will invariably discover that the first link was a violation of the sacred limit of morality.[43]

If crime was to be avoided, it was not through a reinforcement of the law or by the introduction of stiffer sentences, but rather by making morality more imperious, and enforcing its rules with greater force, so that scandal was the natural effect of the denunciation of vice. Such punishments seem ineffective, and were truly such in tyrannical states, where the vigilance of consciences and scandal produced nothing but hypocrisy, 'because the sinew of public opinion in such places has lost its mettle, and because, crucially, good morality is not as essential and integral a part of monarchy as it is in a republic'.[44] But when morality formed the substance of the State, and public opinion was the most solid link in the chain that held society together, then scandal became the most redoubtable form of alienation. Through it, men irreparably became outsiders to all that was most essential in society, and punishment, rather than keeping the particular character of a reparation, became a universal, present in the conscience of each man and carried out by the will of all:

> Legislators who desire to stamp out crime, take note: look at the road taken by criminals, mark the first wrong turn they take, and you shall see that it is the infringement of good morals. Block off that turning, and you will have to resort to punishment far less often.[45]

Scandal thus becomes a form of punishment that is doubly ideal, in that it is immediately fitting to the offence, and also a means of preventing it from taking a criminal form.

What confinement deliberately locked away in the shadows, the revolutionary consciousness was eager to offer to the public gaze, as manifestation became the essence of punishment. All the values relative to secrets and scandal were therefore reversed: the obscure depths of punishment that enveloped any fault were replaced with an immediately perceptible public admonition, sanctioning actions that lurked deep in the hearts of men, to prevent similar actions from rising to the surface. In a strange manner, the revolutionary consciousness rediscovered the ancient value of public punishments, which were akin to an exaltation of the dark power of unreason.[46] In appearance only: the idea was no longer to show senselessness to the world, but simply to place immorality before a scandalised public conscience.

Here a new psychology was being born, which changed the essential meaning of madness, and proposed a new description of the relations between man and the hidden forms of unreason. It is strange that the psychology of crime, in its most rudimentary aspects – or at least the desire to go back to its origins in the hearts of men – was not born of any humanisation of justice, but out of a supplementary requirement of morality, a sort of moral conversion by the state itself, and a refinement of various forms of indignation. Above all, this new psychology was a sort of reverse image of classical justice. All that was previously concealed was now converted into a manifest truth. Justice was to bear witness to those elements which, until now, had previously never had witnesses at all. As a consequence, psychology and the knowledge of all that was most interior to men were born from the fact that public conscience had been elected to the status of universal judge, as an immediately valid form of reason and morality for judging men. Psychological interiority was constituted on the basis of the exteriority of scandalised conscience. All that which had previously made up the content of the old classical unreason could now be taken up in these new forms of psychological knowledge. That world, which had been kept at an inviolable distance, suddenly became familiar to everyday conscience, since it was to be its judge; and it spread itself across the surface of a psychology that was entirely the product of the least examined and most immediate forms of morality.

*

These changes were institutionalised in the great reform of criminal justice. The jury was to represent the public conscience, and its ideal reign over all of man's secret, inhuman powers. The rule of public debate gave the sovereignty which jurors were momentarily delegated to hold an almost infinite extension: the whole body of the nation judged through them, and found itself involved in a debate with the different forms of violence, profanation and unreason that confinement had long kept out of sight. And by a paradoxical movement, ongoing even today, as the judging institution claimed greater universality for the foundation of its justice, and substituted the general norm of human rights and obligations for the particular rules of case law, and as the truth of its judgements found confirmation in a certain public consciousness, crime became interiorised, and its meaning became ever more private. Criminality lost the absolute meaning and unity that it had previously possessed in its finished gestures, in the offences that were committed, and was divided according to two measurements that were to become ever more irreducible with the passing of time: the idea of a punishment adjusted to fit the crime – a measurement borrowed from the norms of the public conscience, the requirements of scandal and the rules of the judicial attitude that assimilated punishments and manifestation; and that which defined the link between a fault and its origins – a measurement that was of the order of knowledge, and of secret, individual assignations. This dissociation suffices to prove, if proof were needed, that psychology, as knowledge of the individual, should historically be considered in a fundamental relationship with the forms of judgement that were proffered by the public conscience. The psychology of individuals would not have been possible without this entire reorganisation of scandal in the social conscience. Knowledge about the concatenations of heredity, the past and motivations only became possible when fault and crime ceased having intrinsic value and were no longer seen purely in relation to themselves, but took their meaning instead from the universal gaze of the bourgeois conscience. In this schism between scandal and secret, crime lost its real density, and took its place in a world that was half-public, half-private. To the extent that it belonged to a private world, it was error, delirium, pure imagination and therefore inexistence; and to the extent that it belonged to a public world, it manifested inhumanity and insanity, that in which the consciousness of the public was unable to recognise itself, that which was not founded in it, and which therefore had no right to exist. In both cases, crime became unreal, and in the non-being that it manifested, it discovered its own profound connection to madness.

Perhaps classical confinement had already been the sign that this relation was sealed long before. Had it also not turned any weakness of the mind and errant behaviour, any violence of word and gesture into the same monotony, enveloping them in the massive apprehension of unreason? But it was not to give them a common psychology that would denounce the same mechanism of madness in both. Neutralisation was there sought as an effect. Non-existence was now determined as an origin. And through a phenomenon of recurrence, what was obtained in confinement as a consequence was rediscovered as a principle of assimilation between madness and crime. The geographical proximity to which they were constrained in order to reduce them became a genealogical proximity in non-being.

This change is already perceptible in the first case of a crime of passion to be heard in France before a jury in a public sitting. Historians of psychology usually pay relatively little attention to this type of event, but anyone who wishes to grasp the meaning of the world of psychology that opened up to man at the end of the eighteenth century, where men have subsequently sought in ever greater depth their own truths, to the point of now trying to decipher there everything down to the last word, and anyone who wishes to know what psychology is, not as a body of knowledge but as fact and cultural expression unique to the modern world, does well to examine this trial and the manner in which it was conducted, as it is as important as the measurement of thresholds or theories of memory. A whole new relationship between man and his truth was beginning to be formulated here.

To situate it exactly, it can be compared to any other case of crime and madness that had been judged in the preceding years. The Bourgeois case, from the time during which Joly de Fleury was Minister of Justice, is typical. Bourgeois had attempted to kill a woman who refused to give him some money.[47] He was arrested, and his family immediately requested that 'it be authorised to instigate an inquiry, to prove that he had constantly shown signs of madness and dissipation, in the hope that as a consequence he would either be locked up or sent to the colonies'. Witnesses were ready to confirm that on various occasions the accused had had 'the wild look and bearing of a madman', and that he had often been 'excessively garrulous', generally giving the impression of a man who was 'losing his wits'. The procurator fiscal was inclined to grant the family's request, not out of consideration for the state of the accused, but out of respect for the honour and misery of the family:

'It is at the request of this much wronged honest family', he wrote to Joly de Fleury,

> who have only slender means, and who have six children of tender age left by Bourgeois who is now reduced to a state of atrocious poverty, that I have the honour to send your Highness the enclosed copy, so that under your protection the family might be authorised to have this man locked up, an individual who could bring dishonour upon them through the mad conduct that he has all too often demonstrated for some years now.

Joly de Fleury replied that the trial should be carried out in full, in compliance with the procedure, and that even if the madness was self-evident, confinement should never impede justice from following its course, nor prevent a sentence from being pronounced; but that part of the procedure should be an inquiry into the madness, and the accused should be 'heard and interrogated in the presence of the reporting counsel, that he should be heard and visited by the physician and surgeon of the court, in the presence of one of his deputies'. The trial took place, and on 1 March 1783 the Tournelle criminal court decreed that 'Bourgeois should be taken away to the gaol in Bicêtre, to be detained there, and to be fed, treated and given the same medication as the other insane.' After a short stay amongst the alienated, it was noted that he showed few signs of insanity, and as some form of simulation was then suspected, he was moved to a cell. Some time later he asked to return among the insane, and as he showed no signs of violence the request was granted. He was then employed to do tasks that 'brought him a minimum of comfort'. He petitioned the governor to be allowed to leave. 'The president of the courts replied that his detention was a favour, and that in any case his sentence was *ad omnia citra mortem* – for the rest of his days.'

Here we come to an essential point: being sentenced to stay with the insane was not a sign that the innocence of the criminal was recognised, but remained, simply, a favour. Which is to say that the recognition of madness, even if it was established in the course of a trial, did not form an integral part of the judgement: it was superimposed upon it, modifying the consequences, but not affecting its essential nature. The meaning of the crime, its gravity, and its absolute value as an act all remained intact; madness, even when recognised by doctors, did not penetrate to the heart of the act, making it 'any less real'; the crime remained what it was, but madness allowed the perpetrator to benefit from an attenuated form of punishment. What then came into being, in punishment, was a complex, reversible structure, a sort of oscillating sentence: if a criminal showed no obvious signs of madness, he went from the insane to the common prisoners; but if, in the cells, he showed himself to be reasonable, gave no sign that he was violent, and if his good behaviour seemed to be a step towards a pardon for his crime, then he was placed among the insane, whose regime was less harsh. Violence at the heart of the act was in turn that which indicated madness and that which justified a rigorous punishment. Alienation and crime both revolved around that unstable theme, in a confused mixture of complementarity, proximity and exclusion. But in any case the relation remained of an external nature. What was yet to be discovered, and would be formulated precisely in 1792 for the first time, was by contrast an interior relation where all the different meanings of crime began to change, becoming caught up in a system of interrogation which still has no clear answers even today.

In an appeal court in 1792, a lawyer named Bellart was called upon to defend a 52-year-old labourer named Gras who had been sentenced to death for murdering his mistress, whom he had discovered in *flagrante delicto*. For the first time, a crime of passion was to be heard at public trial before a jury, and for the first time the great debate between crime and alienation came out into the full light of day, as the public consciousness sought to establish a limit between the assignation of psychological determination and criminal responsibility. Bellart's defence brought no new knowledge to the domain of the sciences of the soul and the heart, but did more – it delineated a whole new space in which that knowledge might take meaning, and discovered one of the operations by means of which psychology in Western culture became the truth about man.

The first thing to be noted about Bellart's text is the disentanglement of psychology from the literary and moral mythology of passion, which had served it both as norm and truth throughout the eighteenth century. For the first time, the truth of passion ceased to coincide with the ethic of true passions. It was known that love had a certain moral truth, made up of verisimilitude, spontaneity and naturalness, which confusingly made up the psychological law of its genesis and the form of its validity. In the eighteenth century, no sensitive soul could fail to understand or acquit des Grieux:[48] if, instead of a 52-year-old man accused of killing a mistress of doubtful trustworthiness in a fit of jealousy, one pictured 'a young man in the full force of his age, a shining example in his beauty and his passions, then most people would be on his side . . . love belongs to the young'.[49] But beyond that form of love, which was immediately recognised by moral sensibility, there was another form, which independently of beauty and youth, could spring into being and live long in people's hearts. Its truth was to be without verisimilitude, its nature to be against nature; unlike the first form, it was not linked to man's seasons, and it was not 'the handmaid of nature, created to serve her ends and to give existence'. While the harmony of the first meant that it was promised happiness, the latter only thrived on suffering: one was 'the delights of youth, and the consolation of later years', the other was too often 'the torment of old age'.[50] The text of the passions, which the eighteenth century had indiscriminately deciphered in terms of psychology and morality, was now dissociated, and shared between two different forms of truth, revealing two different systems of natural belonging. A psychology emerged whose concern was no longer sensibility but knowledge alone, a psychology that spoke of a human nature where the figures of truth were no longer forms of moral validity.

This love no longer held in check by the wisdom of nature is entirely in thrall to its own excess: it is the rage of an empty heart, the absolute game of a passion without object; its attachment is indifferent to the truth of the love object, so violently is it controlled by the movements of its own imagination. 'It lives above all in the human breast, jealous and furious like the human heart.' This self-absorbed rage is both love as a form of naked truth, and madness in the solitude of its illusions. There comes a time when passion becomes unhinged by this excessive conformity to its mechanical truth, so much so that its momentum drags it into a state of delirium. And consequently, by the equating of a violent gesture and the violence of passion, and by the identification of some psychological truth in a pure state, it is placed in a world of blindness, illusion and insanity, which all serve to bypass its criminal reality. What Bellart unveiled for the first time in his pleading was the now fundamental relationship that establishes in any human gesture an inverse proportion between its truth and its reality. The truth of any form of behaviour necessarily makes it unreal, and has an obscure tendency to suggest that its ultimate, most secret form lies beyond any possible analysis, in the realm of madness. In the end, all that remains of Gras' murderous act is an empty gesture, accomplished 'by a hand which alone was guilty', and 'an unfortunately fatal chain of events' that took place 'in the absence of reason, in the torment of an irresistible passion'.[51] When man is liberated from all the moral myths that tended to hold his truth, what becomes apparent is that the truth of this unalienated truth is nothing other than alienation itself.

From this point onwards, what was understood by phrases like 'the psychological truth of man' took over the function and meanings that had long been the domain of unreason; and man discovered within himself, at the furthest point of his solitude, where happiness, verisimilitude and morality never reached, the age-old powers that had been banished by the classical age, and exiled on the most distant margins of society. Unreason was turned into an object by force, in what was most interior, most subjective and deepest in man. That which had so long been a manifestation of guilt now became innocence and secrecy. Unreason, which had so long exalted the forms of error where men abolished their truth, became, beyond appearances and beyond reality itself, the purest form of truth. Captured in the human heart, buried deep within it, madness could formulate all that which was most originally true in man. What then began was a slow process that has resulted today in one of the major contradictions in our moral life: anything that can be formulated as a truth about man is considered to be a form of irresponsibility, and of that innocence that has always been, in Western law, proper to madness in its ultimate degree:

> If, at the moment during which Gras killed the widow Lefèvre, he was so totally under the influence of some absorbing passion that he no longer knew what he was doing, and was therefore incapable of allowing himself to be guided by reason, then it is impossible to condemn him to death.[52]

The whole process of the calling into question of punishment, judgement, and the meaning of crime by a psychology that secretly places the innocence of madness at the heart of any form of truth that can be formulated about man was already present in a virtual form in Bellart's defence.

The word 'innocence' should not be understood here in the absolute sense. What is at stake is not a liberation of the psychological from the moral, but rather a readjustment in their equilibrium. Psychological truth only brought innocence in a sense that was extremely precise. However much it is irresponsible, this 'love that lived principally in the heart' had to be more than simply a psychological mechanism – it also had to be an indication of a different morality, a more rarefied form of morality itself. When good-looking young men in the prime of life are deceived by their mistresses, they go off and find a new one. Another man in Gras' position 'might have laughed off her infidelity by repaying the compliment'. But the passion of the accused lived only for itself – it could accept no infidelity, and the idea of change was impossible. 'Despairingly, Gras saw the last heart over which he could hope to reign disappear, and all his actions carried the imprint of that despair.'[53] He was absolutely faithful, and the blind nature of his love led him to a rare, imperious and tyrannical form of virtue that it was not possible to condemn. Must one be severe with fidelity when one is indulgent with inconstancy? When Bellart asked that his client be spared capital punishment, it was in the name of a virtue that was perhaps not so highly regarded in the eighteenth century, but had to be honoured now if people wanted to return to the virtues of earlier times.

This region of madness and frenzy where the criminal act came into being only rendered it innocent to the extent that it was not rigorously neutral morally, but rather played a role that was precise: it exalted a value that society recognised, while being unable to give it any currency. Marriage was prescribed, but society was obliged to turn a blind eye to infidelity. Madness could have the power of an excuse if it was a manifestation of jealousy, obstinacy or fidelity – even when it resulted in vengeance. Psychology was to be instilled inside guilty consciences, in the play between the values that society recognised and those it demanded. It was then and only then that the reality of a crime could be dissolved, and rendered innocent through a Quixotic valorisation of impracticable virtues.

Crime could very well be determined by the laws of psychology and the mechanisms of the heart, but if there was no indication of these inaccessible values, it warranted no indulgence, and revealed nothing but vice, perversion and wickedness. Bellart was careful to establish 'a clear distinction between crimes: some are vile, the work of a soul made of mud, like theft', and bourgeois society would obviously never find any value in such crimes, not even in an idealised form. They were to be linked to other forms of behaviour, more atrocious still, which announced 'a soul with a canker of wickedness, like assassination or premeditated murder'. But other crimes by contrast revealed 'a passionate, fiery soul, the sort to be easily carried away, like the act carried out by Gras'.[54] The degree of determination that lay behind an act did not thus fix the responsibility of the person who carried it out; on the contrary, the more distant the origins of the act, the more deeply rooted it appeared to be in 'a soul made of mud', the more guilty it became, but if it was spontaneous, carried out as though by surprise, by a pure movement of the heart towards a solitary, absurd form of heroism, then it deserved a lighter sanction. One could be guilty of having been given a perverse nature or a vicious education, but one was innocent in that immediate, violent passage from one form of morality to the other, i.e. from a common form of morality that was rarely acknowledged to an exalted form of morality that most refuse, for the greater good of others.

> Anyone who had a healthy education in his youth, and has had the good fortune to preserve those principles into a later age, should be able to tell himself that no crime like those of the first group [the cankerous, those with 'a soul of mud'] will ever be a stain on his life. But what man would be foolhardy enough to dare to claim that he would never act in the second sense, in the explosion of a great passion? Who can be certain that he will never, in the exaltation of fury or despair, soil his hands with blood, and perhaps spill the blood he considers most precious?[55]

What now came into being was a new division of madness. On the one hand was madness abandoned to the madness of its perversion, which no determinism could ever hope to excuse; on the other was a form of madness that was heroic in nature, the inverse yet complementary image of bourgeois values. That one, and that one alone, would slowly be allowed the right to belong to reason, or rather to the intermittences of reason; it was in that form of reason that responsibility could be diminished, and crime became more human and less punishable. If it was capable of being explained, that was because it was found to be secretly penetrated by moral impulses in which people recognised themselves. But there was also the other side of alienation, to which Royer-Collard was doubtless referring in his famous letter to Fouché, when he mentioned 'the madness of vice'. That madness was less than madness, as it was a total stranger to the world of morality, and its delirium spoke of nothing but evil. And while the first form of madness approached reason, mingled with it, and could be understood on its basis, the other was cast out into the external darkness; and it was there that the strange notions that succeeded one another in the course of the nineteenth century had their origins – the idea of moral madness, of degeneracy, of natural born criminals and perversion. These were the 'bad madnesses' that the modern consciousness could not assimilate, and which formed the irreducible residue of unreason, against which the only defence was an entirely negative one, in the form of refusal and absolute condemnation.

In the first great criminal trials that were held in public during the Revolutionary period, the whole ancient world of madness was once again brought out into the open on an almost daily basis. But the norms of that experience did not allow it to bear its full weight, and all that the sixteenth century had accepted into the prolix totality of an imaginary world, the nineteenth century was to divide according to the rules of moral perception: it was to recognise two forms of madness, good and bad – one whose confused presence was accepted on the margins of reason, in the play between morality and bad conscience, and responsibility and innocence, and the other that bore the full weight of the ancient anathema, and of irreparable offence.

*

The destruction of confinement was more brutal in France than anywhere else. For the few short years that preceded Pinel's reforms, the places to which madness was banished and the process of elaboration that transformed them were all out in the open. A complex work is then visible, whose different aspects we are attempting to describe here.

At first sight, the process seems to be a sort of 'realisation' [*prise de conscience*], as if madness was at last designated within a problematic proper to it. But this new realisation must be perceived in the totality of its meaning: it was less a sudden discovery than a long investment, as though in this 'realisation' the *capture* was more important than the novelty of the *illumination*. One particular historically situated form of consciousness took hold of madness, and mastered its meaning. If that new consciousness seemed to restore madness both to its liberty and to a positive truth, that was not simply owing to the disappearance of the ancient constraints, but also thanks to the equilibrium that was established between two series of positive processes. The first was of uncovering, separation, and in a sense, liberation; the second was the hasty construction of new structures of protection that allowed reason to free itself and become self-reliant, just as it was discovering madness in an immediate proximity. These two sets were not opposed, and were more than complementary; they were the same thing – the coherent unity of a gesture through which *madness was offered to knowledge in a structure that was alienating from the very first*.

And it was here that the conditions of the classical experience of madness changed definitively. The table below summarises these concrete categories, in the play of their apparent opposition:

Forms of liberation	Structures of protection
1 The suppression of a form of confinement that confused madness with all the other forms of unreason.	1 The designating for madness of a form of confinement that was no longer a place of exclusion but the privileged place where it was to regain its own truth.
2 The constitution of an asylum whose sole purpose was medical in nature.	2 The capture of madness by an inviolable space that was to be a place of manifestation and a space of cure.
3 The acquisition by madness of the right of expression, to be heard and to speak in its own name.	3 The elaboration around and above madness of a sort of absolute subject who was a pure gaze, conferring on madness the status of pure object.
4 The introduction of madness into the psychological subject as the everyday truth of passion, violence and crime.	4 The insertion of madness into a non-coherent world of values, and into the games of bad conscience.
5 The recognition of madness in its role as psychological truth, as a determinism beyond responsibility.	5 The dividing up of the different forms of madness according to the dichotomous requirements of moral judgement.

This double movement of liberation and enslavement forms the secret foundations of the modern experience of madness.

We easily believe that the objectivity we recognise in different forms of mental illness is freely offered to our knowledge as a truth that has been liberated at last. In fact, this truth is only ever available to those who are protected from it. The knowledge of madness supposes in the person who holds it an ability to distance the self from it, and to remain aloof from its dangers and its charms, a certain manner of not being mad. The historical arrival of psychiatric positivism is only linked to the promotion of knowledge in a secondary manner: at its origin, it is the fixing of a particular mode of being outside madness, a certain consciousness of non-madness that becomes a concrete situation for the subject of knowledge, the solid basis from which it is possible to know madness.

If we wish to know what happened in the course of this rapid mutation which, in the space of a few years, brought to the surface of the European world a new knowledge and new treatments for madness, there is little point in wondering what was added to the sum of previous knowledge. Tuke was not a doctor, Pinel was not a psychiatrist, and they both probably knew little more than Tissot or Cullen. What had changed, and changed quite suddenly, was the consciousness of not being mad – a consciousness which since the middle of the eighteenth century had found itself confronted once again with madness in its most vigorous forms, caught in their slow ascent, soon to be jostled with the collapse of confinement. What happened during the years that preceded and immediately followed the Revolution was a new, sudden emergence of that consciousness.

It might be imagined that this was a purely negative phenomenon, but looked at close up it reveals itself to be quite different. It could even be described as the first and the only *positive* phenomenon that accompanied the arrival of *positivism*. The disengagement was only made possible by the erection of structures of protection, designed and built successively by Colombier, Tenon, Cabanis and Bellart. And the solidity of their structures was such that they survive more or less unchanged today, even despite all the efforts of Freudian research. In the classical age, the manner of not being mad was double: it was divided between an immediate, daily apprehension of difference, and a system of exclusion that mixed madness with a whole range of other perils. That classic consciousness of unreason was therefore entirely occupied by a tension between this inner evidence that was never contested, and a more contentious arbitrary division in the social fabric. But when these two forms of experience finally joined together, and the system of social protection found itself interiorised into the forms of consciousness, and when the madness was recognised through the movement of separating from it, and measuring this distance from it in the concrete reality of institutions, the eighteenth-century tension suddenly vanished. Forms of recognition and structures of protection found themselves superimposed in a consciousness of not being mad that was henceforth sovereign. This possibility of grasping madness as something both known and mastered at a stroke, in one single act of consciousness, was at the heart of the positivist experience of mental illness. And until that possibility becomes impossible once more in a new liberation of knowledge, madness will remain for us what it was already becoming for Pinel and Tuke, and will remain mired in its age of positivity.

From this point onwards, madness was something other than an object to be feared, or an indefinitely renewed theme for scepticism. It became an object. But one with a quite singular status. In the very move-ment that objectified it, it became the first objectifying form, and the means by which man could have an objective hold on himself. In earlier times, madness had signified a vertiginous moment of dazzlement, the instant in which, being too bright, a light began to darken. Now that it was a thing exposed to knowledge – that which was most interior to man, but also that which was most exposed to the gaze of others – it operated as a great structure of transparency. This is not to say that knowledge entirely clarified it, but that starting from madness, and the status of object that had been conferred upon it, in theory at least, man could become entirely transparent to scientific investigation. It was no accident, nor the effect of a simple historical slippage, that the nineteenth century began by investigating the pathology of memory, of the will and of personality, to find out the truth of memories, volition and the individual. The order of that research remains profoundly faithful to the structures that had been elaborated at the end of the eighteenth century, which had made madness the first great figure of the objectification of man.

In the great theme of a positive knowledge of human beings, madness always occupied an uncomfortable position: it was at once objectified and objectifying, offered and held back, content and condition. For the thought of the nineteenth century, and indeed to us today, it has the status of an enigmatic thing: it may for the moment in fact be inaccessible in the totality of its truth, yet we do not doubt that one day it will split open and deliver up its secrets to our knowledge. Yet this is merely an assumption and a neglect of essential truths. This reticence that we believe to be transitory in fact camouflages the fundamental retreat of madness to a region that extends beyond the frontiers of what man can possibly know. The possibility of a positive science of man requires that somewhere, in a far distant corner, there is a space reserved for madness, in which and from which all of human existence can fall into objectivity. In its essential enigma, madness watches, always promised to a form of knowledge that will enclose it in its entirety, but always just out of reach, as it was madness that first offered objective knowledge a grasp of man. For man, the eventuality of being mad and the possibility of being an object came together in the late eighteenth century, and that meeting led directly and unambiguously (there is no chance coincidence in the dates here) to the postulates of positive psychiatry and the themes of an objective science of man.

In the work of Tenon, Cabanis, and Bellart, that conjunction, which is so essential for modern culture, only operated in the order of thought. It only became a concrete situation through Pinel and Tuke: in the asylums that they founded, which took up where the great projects for reform had left off, the danger of being mad was identified forcibly in every man, in the smallest gestures of their daily life, with the necessity to be an object. Positivism then was no longer a merely theoretical project, but the stigmata of alienated existence.

The status of object was now to be imposed immediately on any individual recognised as alienated: alienation was suddenly deposited as a secret truth at the heart of all objective knowledge of man.

IV

BIRTH OF THE ASYLUM

We know the images. They are familiar from all histories of psychiatry, where their function is to illustrate that happy age when madness was at last recognised and treated according to a truth to which everyone had been blind for too long.

> The Respectable Society of Quakers . . . has been desirous of securing to those of its members, who should have the unhappiness to lose their reason, without possessing a fortune adequate to have recourse to expensive establishments, all the resources of art, and all the comforts of life, compatible with their situation. A voluntary subscription furnished the funds; and, about two years since, an establishment, which appears to unite many advantages, with all possible economy, was founded near the city of York.
>
> If the mind shrinks for a moment at the aspect of this terrible disease, which seems calculated to humble the reason of man; it must afterwards feel pleasing emotions, in considering all that an ingenious benevolence has been able to invent, to cure and comfort the patients afflicted with this malady.
>
> This house is situated a mile from York, in the midst of a fertile and cheerful country; it presents not the idea of a prison, but rather that of a

large rural farm. It is surrounded by a garden. There is no bar or grating to the windows.[1]

The story of the deliverance of the alienated of Bicêtre is famous, with the decision taken to remove the chains from the prisoners in the cells, Couthon visiting the hospital to check that it was harbouring no suspects, and Pinel bravely going out to meet him, while everyone trembled at the sight of this 'invalid carried in men's arms'.[2] The confrontation between the wise, firm philanthropist and the paralytic monster:

> Pinel immediately led him to the section for the raving, where the view of the cells disturbed him considerably. He desired to question all the patients, but received nothing but abuse and expletives from the majority of them. There was no point in pursuing the enquiry any further. He turned to Pinel: 'So, citizen, are you not mad too, wishing to unchain such animals?' Pinel answered calmly: 'Citizen, I am convinced that these alienated are only so intractable because they are deprived of air and liberty.' 'Then do as you will, although I fear that you may become a victim of your own presumption.' And with that, Couthon was carried back to his carriage. His departure was a great relief, and everyone breathed again. The great philanthropist set to work at once.[3]

These are images, at least in so far as each of these stories takes the essential element of its power from imaginary forms: the patriarchal calm of Tuke's domain, where the passions of the heart and the disorders of the spirit are slowly appeased, and the lucid firmness of Pinel, who masters with a single word and a single gesture the twin animal furies that roar and watch him warily, and the wisdom that allowed him to recognise which was the greater danger between the raving mad and the bloodthirsty deputy of the Convention. Such images echo down the ages, carrying the full weight of legend.

It would serve little purpose to dispute them, as we have too few documents that are more trustworthy at our disposal. And then they are too dense in their naivety not to reveal much of what they do not say. In their surprising depth, one would need to identify the concrete situation that they conceal, the mythical values that they pass off as the truth, and finally the real process that took place, of which they only provide a symbolic translation.

*

First of all, Tuke was a Quaker, an active member of one of the innumerable 'Societies of Friends' that sprang up in England during the late seventeenth century.

English legislation, as we saw, increasingly favoured private initiatives in the domain of assistance in the latter half of the eighteenth century.[4] Mutual associations appeared, and friendly societies prospered. For reasons that were both economic and religious, the Quakers had played this role for a century and half, initially against the government's will. 'We don't give money to men dressed in black to help our poor, bury our dead, or to preach to the faithful. These holy duties are too precious to be shifted onto others', wrote Voltaire in his *Lettres Philosophiques*.[5] In the new conditions that prevailed in the late eighteenth century, a law was put through Parliament in 1793 'For the Encouragement and Relief of Friendly Societies'.[6] The societies in question were associations, whose model and often inspiration were those of the Quakers, based on a system of contributions and donations collected together in a mutual fund and used for members who fell into need, sickness or infirmity. The text of the law recognised that 'it is likely to be attended with very beneficial effects, by providing the happiness of individuals, and at the same time diminishing the public burthens'. Importantly, members of such societies were immune to 'Removal', the process by which a parish could and should get rid of any indigent or sick pauper who was not native to the area, sending them back to their parish of origin. It should be noted that Removal, which was the result of a clause in the Settlement Act, was abolished a few years later, in 1795, after which date parishes were obliged to take care of any sick pauper found in the region, if there was a risk that removal might present a further danger to his health.[7] Such was the juridical framework of the singular conflict that resulted in the creation of the Retreat.

It may be surmised that Quakers had long been particularly vigilant about care and assistance to the insane. From the very beginning, they had had dealings with houses of confinement. In 1649, George Fox and another of his companions had been sent, by order of a judge, to Darby prison, to be whipped and locked up for six months as blasphemers.[8] In Holland, Quakers were locked up in the Rotterdam hospital on several occasions.[9] And perhaps because he had noted down something that he had heard in their company, or because he ascribed to them a commonly held opinion concerning their beliefs, Voltaire has his Quaker say in the

Lettres Philosophiques that the breath that inspired them was not always the Word of God, but sometimes the senseless verbiage of unreason: 'We cannot tell whether a man who rises to speak will be inspired by the Spirit or by folly.'[10] In any case, the Quakers, like many religious sects in the late seventeenth and early eighteenth centuries, found themselves caught up in the great debate between religious experience and unreason.[11] To outsiders, and perhaps even in their own eyes, some forms of that experience were situated in the grey area that lay between sense and madness, and decisions were constantly required about which was which, while they were continually forced to confront the constant accusations of insanity that were made against them. This led quite understandably to the slightly guarded interest that the Societies of Friends took in the treatment of the mad in the houses of confinement.

In 1791, 'a female of the Society of Friends was placed at an establishment for insane persons in the vicinity of the City of York'. Her family, who lived far away, asked the Friends to look after her fate. But the administration of the asylum refused any visiting rights, on the pretext that the patient's condition would not permit it. The woman died a few weeks later.

> The circumstance was affecting, and naturally excited reflections on the situation of insane persons, and on the probable improvements which might be adopted in establishments of this nature. In particular, it was conceived that peculiar advantage would be derived to the Society of Friends, by having an Institution of this kind under their own care, in which a milder and more appropriate system of treatment, than usually practised, might be adopted.[12]

That was how Samuel Tuke presented the story, twenty years after the events took place.

It is quite possible that this was merely one of numerous incidents provoked by the Settlement Act. If a person without means fell ill far from home, the law required that the person be sent home. But their condition, and perhaps the cost of transportation often meant that they were forced to stay. This partly illegal situation could only be justified by the immediate danger to health, and in this particular case it must have been resolved by a confinement order signed by a Justice of the Peace. But besides the asylum to which the patient was sentenced, no charitable

organisation other than one in the patient's parish of origin had the right
to intervene. In other words, the poor who fell seriously ill outside their
parish found themselves at the mercy of the arbitrariness of a confinement
that nothing could control. It was this situation that the friendly societies
were protesting against when they demanded the right to care for any of
their brethren who fell sick when away from home, regardless of the
parish of origin, a right they obtained with the 1793 law, two years after
the events described by Samuel Tuke. This project for a private, collective
house destined for the insane should thus be understood as one of
the extremely numerous protests against the old legislation regarding the
poor and the sick. The chronology makes that clear, even if Tuke is careful
not to stress it, in his concern to lay all the merits of the enterprise at the
door of private generosity. In 1791, the York Quakers came up with
their project, and in early 1793 a law came into force encouraging the
growth of friendly societies, which exempted them from Removal. The
responsibility for assistance thus moved from the parish to private
enterprise. Also in 1793, the York Quakers launched the subscription, and
voted in the regulations of the society. Land was acquired the following
year. The Settlement Act was repealed in 1795, and work began on the
construction of the Retreat, which opened in 1796. Tuke's enterprise
fits neatly into the great legal reorganisation of assistance in the late
eighteenth century, a series of measures that allowed the bourgeois State
to invent, for its own requirements, private welfare.

The event in France that sparked the liberation of those 'in chains at
Bicêtre' is of a different nature, and the historical circumstances are
considerably more difficult to determine. The law of 1790 had planned
the creation of large hospitals for the insane, but by 1793 none had yet
materialised. Bicêtre had been converted into a '*Maison des pauvres*' and, as
had been the case before the Revolution, contained a confused mixture
of the poor, the old, the criminal and the mad. That traditional population was supplemented by all those placed there by the Revolution. First
of all there were the political prisoners. On 28 Brumaire Year III, i.e.
during Pinel's time there, Piersin, who had charge of the mad at Bicêtre,
wrote to the Civil Administration Commission, saying: 'I still have in
my employ here even people who are detained for the Revolutionary
Tribunal'.[13] There were also suspects who were in hiding. Like the
Belhomme pension, and the Douai and Vernet houses, Bicêtre too was
used as a refuge for suspects.[14] Under the Restoration, when it became

important to forget the fact that Pinel had been the physician at Bicêtre under the Terror, he was credited with having protected aristocrats and priests:

> Pinel was the physician at Bicêtre during those dark days when men came asking for its tribute to death. The Terror had filled the house with priests and émigrés who had returned. Mr Pinel opposed the extradition of a great number of them, claiming that they had lost their wits. The requests were repeated, and he redoubled his opposition; his will was soon of such strength that it impressed the executioners, and the energy of this normally quiet, even-tempered man saved the life of many victims, including a prelate who currently occupies one of the highest positions in France.[15]

But another factor should also be borne in mind: during the Revolution, Bicêtre did become the main centre for the hospitalisation of the insane. From the earliest attempts to apply the 1790 law, the mad who had been freed from the gaols were sent there, as were the alienated patients who were too numerous at the Hôtel-Dieu.[16] So much so that by force of circumstance rather than as part of any great scheme Bicêtre inherited the medical function that had subsisted through the classical age, without ever being confused with confinement, and had made the Hôtel-Dieu the only Parisian hospital where any systematic attempts were made to cure the mad. What the Hôtel-Dieu had done uninterruptedly since the Middle Ages, Bicêtre was now ordered to do, in the framework of a form of confinement that was more confused than ever, and for the first time it became a hospital where the alienated received treatment until they were cured:

> Since the Revolution, the administration of public establishments only confines the mad in free hospices for the period during which they are judged to be harmful and a menace to society, so they only stay so long as they are ill, and as soon as it becomes apparent that a cure has been effected, they are sent back to the bosom of their families or friends. The proof of this is the large number who have left after recovering their wits, even including some who had been confined for life by the previous Parliament. The current administration considers it its duty to lock up only the mad who are unable to enjoy their liberty.[17]

The medical function was clearly introduced to Bicêtre, and a general revision of all the confinements for madness that had been decreed in the past was now begun.[18] And for the first time in the history of the General Hospital, in the infirmaries of Bicêtre, a man who already had a certain reputation for being well versed in the sicknesses of the mind was appointed head physician.[19] Pinel's appointment in itself is proof that the presence of the mad in Bicêtre had *already* become a medical problem.

But there is no doubt that it was also something of a political problem. The certainty that there were innocents confined together with the guilty, and that there were men of reason locked up among the insane, had long been part of the mythology of the Revolution:

> Bicêtre is sure to contain criminals, brigands, and ferocious men . . . but it is doubtless also home to a host of victims of arbitrary power, of the tyranny of families and of paternal despotism . . . the cells conceal men, our brothers and equals, to whom the air is refused, and who see no light other than through narrow skylights.[20]

Bicêtre, the prison of innocence, came to haunt the public imagination as the Bastille had done before:

> During the massacre of the prisons, brigands broke into the hospice at Bicêtre, on the pretext of delivering some of the innocent victims of the ancient tyranny that had sought to mix them with the insane. Armed, they went from cell to cell, interrogating the inmates and leaving them there if their alienation was plain. But one of the detainees in chains caught their attention on account of the clarity of his reasoning and the bitterness of his complaints. Was it not odious that he had been bound in chains, and locked up with the other inmates? The brigands became quite incensed, and they started threatening the hospital controller, who was forced to account for his actions.[21]

Under the Convention, a new fear emerged. Bicêtre was still an immense reservoir of fears, but now it was seen as the haunt of suspects – aristocrats dressed as paupers who had taken refuge there, and scheming agents from abroad who merely simulated insanity. The concern was still with denouncing madness so that innocence appeared, but now also while unmasking duplicity. In the great fear associated with Bicêtre throughout the Revolutionary period, which turned it into a dark, menacing force on the outskirts of the city where the Enemy was inextricably mixed with unreason, madness had two alienating roles to play. It alienated anyone who had been wrongly adjudged to be mad, but it could also alienate those who thought they were protected against its grip. It tyrannised or it deceived, and was a perilous intermediary between men of reason and the mad, threatening to alienate them both and deprive them of their liberty. In any case, it needed to be foiled, so that truth and reason might be restored to their natural relation.

In this slightly confused situation – a tight network of real conditions and imaginary forces – it is difficult to be sure about the exact role played by Pinel. He took up his duties on 25 August 1793. It is to be supposed, given that his reputation as a doctor was already considerable, that he had been chosen precisely in the hope that he would 'foil' madness, determining its exact medical form, and that he would then free victims and denounce suspects, and finally provide a rigorous justification for the confinement of the mad, the necessity of which was recognised, but whose perils were also feared. In addition, Pinel had republican feelings and would not allow the prisoners of the Ancien Régime to remain confined there, or show any favouritism towards those hunted by the new regime. In a sense, Pinel found himself invested with an extraordinary moral power. In classical unreason, there was no incompatibility between madness and simulation, nor between madness recognised from without and madness objectively assigned; it was rather the case that there was something of an essential link from madness to the illusory forms and the guilt hidden beneath it. Pinel's political task was to unravel the knot, and operate a division so that a single rigorous unity emerged for discursive knowledge: madness, its objective truth and its innocence. It was to be shorn of all the fringes of non-being where the games of unreason unfolded, and where it was accepted both as persecuted non-madness and as hidden non-madness, without ever ceasing to be madness on that account.

What then was the exact meaning of freeing 'the enchained'? Was it the pure and simple application of ideas that had been formulated several years previously, which were part of the reorganisation process of which Cabanis was the best example, one year before Pinel's arrival at Bicêtre? Removing the fetters of the madmen in the cells meant opening for them a domain of liberty that was also the domain of verification, allowing them to appear in an objectivity that was no longer veiled by persecution or the frenzy that it provoked in return; it was the invention of the asylum in its pure state, just as Cabanis had defined it, and which the Convention wanted to see established for political reasons. But there are perhaps also grounds for believing that in doing what he did, Pinel was dissimulating a political operation of the opposite tenure: when he liberated the mad, they blended in with the whole population of Bicêtre, engendering further, inextricable confusion, abolishing the criteria that might have permitted a division. Was it not the constant concern of the Bicêtre administration at this time to prevent the separation that the political authorities were demanding?[22] Whatever the truth, Pinel was moved to la Salpêtrière on 13 May 1795, several months after Thermidor, as the political climate was relaxing.[23]

It is probably impossible to know exactly what Pinel was intending to do when he decided to free the alienated. It matters little – for the key point is precisely that ambiguity that was to mark the rest of his work, and the meaning it was to take on for the modern world: the constitution of a domain in which madness appears in its pure truth, both objective and innocent, but a constitution indefinitely delayed, each of the figures of madness blending in with non-madness in an inextricable proximity. What madness gained in precision through its scientific outline, it lost in the vigour of concrete perception; the asylum, where it was to rejoin its truth, was not a place from which it could be distinguished from that which was not its truth. The more objective it became, the less certain it was. The gesture that set it free in order to investigate it was also the operation that disseminated it, and hid it in all the concrete forms of reason.

*

Tuke's work was carried along by the readjustment of English social welfare legislation that took place at the end of the eighteenth century; Pinel's by the ambiguity of the situation of the mad at the moment of the Revolution. But that in no way diminishes their originality. There was a decisiveness in their work that cannot be reduced, and which comes through quite clearly – barely transposed – in the myths that have transmitted its sense.

It was important that Tuke was a Quaker. Just as important was the fact that the Retreat was a country house. 'The air also is healthy, and much more free from smoke than situations near manufacturing towns.'[24] The house opened through unbarred windows onto a garden:

> The Retreat is situate on an eminence, at the distance of about half a mile from the eastern gate of the city of York. It commands a very delightful prospect, extending, on the south, as far as the eye can reach, over a wooded, fertile plain.

The neighbouring land was given over to livestock and arable farming, and the garden 'furnishes abundance of fruit and vegetables. It also affords an agreeable place for recreation and employment, to many of the patients.'[25] Exercise in the open air, regular walks and work in the garden were thought to be of great benefit:

> the general effects of fine air upon the animal spirits, would induce us to expect especial benefit from it, in cases of mental depression … Several instances have occurred, in which melancholy patients have been much improved by their journey to the Retreat.[26]

All the imaginary powers of the simple life, the happiness of the countryside and the return of the seasons were called together here to preside over the curing of different forms of madness. Madness, in the view of the eighteenth century, was a disease, not of nature nor of man himself, but of society. Emotions, uncertainties, agitation and artificial food were all causes of madness for Tuke, and his contemporaries shared those beliefs. Madness was only ever of the order of a consequence, the product of a life that had strayed from the path of nature; it never called into question what was fundamental in man, his immediate belonging to nature. It left intact man's nature, which was also his reason, like a secret that had been forgotten. That secret could reappear under strange conditions, just as it could reappear by ruse or fraud, the result of a chance disturbance. Tuke quotes the case of a young woman in a state of 'perfect idiocy'; she remained in the state for many years, with no alteration in her condition, until one day she was attacked by a typhus fever. As the fever mounted, her mind

4. William Hogarth (1697– 1764), *Scene in a Madhouse, from A Rake's Progress,*
1735

5. Francisco Jose de Goya y Lucientes (1746–1828), *The Madhouse*, 1812–1815 (oil on canvas). Real Academia de Bellas Artes de San Fernando, Madrid

6. Tony Robert-Fleury (1837–1912), *Philippe Pinel Freeing the Insane from their Chains at the Salpêtrière in Paris in 1795* (colour lithograph [or oil painting]), Bibliothèque des Arts Décoratifs, Paris, France

became clearer, more limpid and lively. Throughout the acute period during which patients normally suffer from delirium, the patient was entirely reasonable, recognising her entourage and recalling events to which she had seemed to pay no attention at the time. 'But, alas! it was only the gleam of reason; as the fever abated, clouds again enveloped the mind; she sunk into her former deplorable state, and remained in it until her death, which happened a few years afterwards.'[27]

What we have here is a whole mechanism of compensation. In madness, nature is forgotten, not abolished, or rather it migrates from the mind to the body, in such manner that dementia is in some sense a guarantee of solid health; but if illness strikes, nature is shaken from the body and returns to the spirit, purer and clearer than it has ever been. So much proof that one should not consider 'the mad as absolutely deprived of reason', but rather evoke in them, through the play of resemblances and proximities, that part of nature that invariably slept beneath the agitation of their madness. The seasons and the days, the great plain of York and the wisdom of gardens, where nature coincides with the order of men, were to recall reason and awaken it from its momentary slumber. Inside this life of tending the vegetable patch that was imposed on patients at the Retreat, under the sole guidance of an unshakeable confidence, a magical operation was concealed, where nature helped nature triumph by a process of resemblance, *rapprochement* and mysterious penetration, while the anti-nature that society had infused into man was simultaneously exorcised. Behind such images a new myth was beginning to take shape, which was to become one of the great organising forms of the psychiatry of the nineteenth century – the myth of the three natures: Nature as Truth, Nature as Reason, and Nature as Health. It was in this space that the movement of alienation and its cure were developed: if Nature as Health could be abolished, Nature as Reason could only ever be obscured, while Nature as the Truth of the world always remained adequate to itself, and it was from the last that Nature as Reason could be woken and restored; and the exercise of reason, when it coincided with truth, permitted the restoration of Nature as Health. And it was in that sense that Tuke preferred the French term 'mental alienation' to the English word 'insane': 'I adopt this term from an opinion, that the *aliéné*, of the French, conveys a more just idea of this disorder, than those expressions which imply, in any degree, the "abolition of the thinking capacity".'[28]

The Retreat placed patients in a simple dialectic with nature, but it also

built up a social group at the same time. It did that by strangely contradictory means. It was founded by subscription, and it had to function as
an insurance system like the many friendly societies that came into being
at that time; each subscriber could designate a patient whom he would
follow and who would pay a reduced rate, while other patients paid the
amount in full. The Retreat was a contractual coalition, a convergence of
interests organised along the lines of a simple society.[29] But at the same
time it took its place in the myth of the patriarchal family: it aimed to be a
great fraternal community of patients and helpers, under the authority of
the directors and the administration. It was a rigorous family, without
weakness or complacency, but fair, in accordance with the great image of
the biblical family. 'The study of the superintendents to promote [the
comfort of the patients] with all the assiduity of parental, but judicious
attention, has been, in numerous instances, rewarded by an almost filial
attachment.'[30] And in this common affection, without indulgence
but without injustice, patients were reunited once more with the calm
happiness and security of a family in its pure state; they were the children
of the family in its primitive ideality.

With its contracts and families, its unstated interests and its natural
affection, the Retreat combined the two great myths through which the
eighteenth century had sought to define the origin of societies and
the truth about man in the state of society. It was both individual interest
renouncing itself in order to regain itself and the spontaneous affection
that nature creates among the members of a family, thereby proposing a
sort of immediate and affective model to all possible society. At the
Retreat, the human group was brought back to its original, purest form;
men were put back into elementary social relations, which conformed
absolutely to their origins, which was to say that they had to be both
rigorously founded and rigorously moral. Patients were taken back to
the point at which society had freshly emerged from nature, where it
accomplished itself with an immediacy that the whole history of mankind
had subsequently clouded. The idea was that here all the artifice, the vain
worries, the unnatural links and obligations that society had instilled in
man would be effaced from the alienated mind of the patient.

Such were the mythical powers of the Retreat: powers that mastered
time, contested history, led men back to their essential truths, and identified them to the First Natural Man and the First Social Man in an
immemorial space. The distance that separated them from this primitive

being was abolished, and the thick layers of society cut away, and at the end of their 'retreat', the inalienable beneath the alienation at last appeared – nature, truth, reason and pure social morality. Tuke's work seemed to be carried, as well as explained, by a long process of reforms that had preceded it. It actually was, but what made it both a rupture and an initiation was the mythical landscape in which it was set from its inception, and which it managed to inject into the old world of madness and confinement. In place of the simple linear division that confinement had operated between reason and unreason, it brought a dialectic, whose movement could only originate in the mythic space that had been constituted. In this dialectic, madness became alienation, and its cure was the return to the inalienable; but at its core was a new power that was invested in confinement for the first time, at least in the manner in which it was dreamt of by the founders of the Retreat. Thanks to that power, at the very moment when madness revealed itself to be alienation, and as a result of that discovery, men were brought back to the inalienable. The myth of the Retreat makes it possible to establish both the imaginary procedure of the cure as it was then obscurely conceived, and the essence of madness, such as it was to be implicitly transmitted in the nineteenth century:

1 The role of confinement is to reduce madness to its truth.
2 The truth of madness is what it is, minus the world, minus society, and minus the anti-natural.
3 This truth of madness is man himself, in all that can be most primitively inalienable in him.
4 All that is most inalienable in man is a blend of Nature, Truth and Morality: i.e. Reason itself.
5 The Retreat has the power to heal because it brings madness back to a truth that is both the truth of madness and the truth of man, and to a nature that is both the nature of sickness and the serene nature of the world.

We can now see how positivism was able to take root in this dialectic, despite the fact that nothing seemed to herald its coming, as the talk was all of moral experiences, philosophical themes and dream-like images of man. But positivism was really the contraction of this movement, the reduction of this mythical space. From the outset, it took for granted, as objectively obvious, that the truth of madness was man's reason, entirely reversing the classical scheme where the experience of unreason in madness called into question the possibility that man might bear any kind of truth. Henceforth, any objective grasp of madness, all knowledge and all truth formulated about it was to be reason itself, reason restored and triumphant, the undoing of alienation.

*

In the traditional telling of the liberation of the prisoners in chains at Bicêtre, one point has never been established with any certainty – the presence of Couthon. Some have claimed that his visit could not have taken place, and that there must have been confusion with a member of the Paris Commune who was also paralysed, and his infirmity coupled with Couthon's sinister reputation meant that the one was taken for the other.[31] Leaving that aside, what is more important is that the confusion happened and has been passed on, and the fact that the image that came to dominate with such force was that of an invalid retreating in horror before the mad, abandoning 'such animals' to their fate. At the heart of the scene is a paralytic carried by other men; and it was preferable that this paralytic was a fearsome figure of the Convention, known for his cruelty and infamous for condemning so many to their death. Consequently it was Couthon who visited Bicêtre, and who for a moment was the master of the fate of the mad. The imaginary force of history wills it so.

What this strange tale hides is a decisive chiasm in the mythology of madness. Couthon visited Bicêtre to see if the mad that Pinel wished to liberate were in fact suspects. He hoped to find reason in hiding, but what he found was animality, which displayed the full force of its violence. He gave up looking for signs of intelligence and simulation there, and decided to leave the mad to their own devices, and allow madness to resolve itself in its essential savagery. It was precisely here that the metamorphosis was operated: Couthon, the paralytic Revolutionary, the sick man who cut off heads, just as he was treating the mad as animals, through the double stigmata of his sickness and his crimes, unknowingly became the incarnation of all that was most monstrous in humanity. For that reason, it was his presence that the myth required, and not the presence of someone less infirm or less cruel, so that he could pronounce the last words which, for the last time in the Western world, consigned madness to its own animality. When he left Bicêtre, carried by his helpers, he thought that he had consigned the insane to their bestial nature, but in fact he was the one who carried the charge of animality, while the freedom that the mad were offered allowed them to demonstrate that they had lost nothing of all that was essential in man. When he had formulated the animality of the mad, and given them the freedom to move around in it, he liberated them from it but revealed his own, and enclosed himself within it. His rage was more insane, more inhuman than the madness of the demented. Madness had thus emigrated to the side of its keepers; those who locked up the mad like animals were now possessed by the animal brutality of insanity, and it was in them that the beast raged, while the beast that showed its face in the demented was no more than a cloudy reflection of that rage. A secret was revealed: animality was not to be found in the animal, but in its taming; the latter, by its rigour alone, was enough to bring it into being. The mad were thus purified of their animality, or at least of that part of animality which is violence, predation, anger and savagery; and what remained was a docile animality, which did not respond to constraints and attempts to tame it by violence. The legend of the meeting of Couthon and Pinel recounts this process of purification, or more exactly, demonstrates that the purification had already taken place when the legend was written.

Once Couthon had left, 'the philanthropist immediately set to work'. He decided to unchain twelve patients who were kept in irons. The first was an English captain who had been locked up in a Bicêtre dungeon for forty years: 'He was considered the most terrifying of all the alienated; . . . in a rush of frenzy, he had once hit an attendant on the head with one of his handcuffs, who had fallen down dead.' Pinel approached him, requested that 'he be reasonable, and harm no one'; if he complied, his chains would be removed and he would be granted the right to walk around the courtyard: 'Take my word. Be calm and confident, and I shall restore your liberty.' The captain listened to the speech, and remained calm when his irons were removed. As soon as he was free, he rushed out to admire the sunlight, crying out ecstatically, 'How beautiful! How beautiful!' Throughout this first day of recovered liberty, 'he constantly ran around, rushing up and down the stairs, exclaiming "How beautiful! How beautiful!" again and again.' That evening, he returned to his cell and slept peacefully:

During the two further years that he remained at Bicêtre, he never again suffered from frenzy, and even became useful around the house, exercising a certain degree of authority over the other inmates whom he controlled as he wished, almost taking on the status of a guard.

Another liberation, equally well known in the chronicles of medical hagiography, was that of the soldier Chevingé. He was a drunkard with delusions of grandeur, who took himself for a general, but Pinel had seen 'an excellent nature behind the irritation'. He undid his chains, declaring that he was taking him into his service, and that he would require of him all the fidelity that a 'good master' should expect from a grateful servant. The miracle happened, and the virtues of a faithful valet were awoken in that troubled soul: 'Never was a revolution operated more quickly nor more completely in a human intelligence . . . as soon as he was delivered, he was attentive to his every gesture.' Bad-tempered, but tamed by so much generosity, he took it upon himself to face and appease the fury of others for his new master; 'he spoke the language of reason and goodness to the alienated, he who had been on their level until so recently, but above whom he now felt elevated by the height of his liberty.'[32] In the legend that grew up around Pinel, this good servant was to play his role to the full; he devoted himself body and soul to his master, and he protected him when the people of Paris came to break down the doors of Bicêtre to mete out justice on the 'enemies of the nation: he shielded him with his body, exposing himself to the blows to save Pinel's life'.

So the chains came off and the mad were free. And at that moment, they recovered their reason. Or rather, they did not: it was not so much that reason reappeared in and for itself, but rather fully-fledged social species that had slept for so long in madness were suddenly awakened, and stood up straight, in perfect conformity with all that they represented, without alteration or grimaces. As though the madman, freed from the animality to which his chains confined him, could only rejoin humanity as a recognised *social type*. It would not have sufficed for the first man delivered to have become a normal healthy man; he had to become an officer, an English captain, loyal to the man who set him free, like a man kept in bondage to a conqueror by his word, a figure of authority for others on whom he exercised his prestige as an officer. His health was only restored in the social values that were both its sign and its concrete presence. His reason was not of the order of knowledge or happiness, nor of the good functioning of his mind. Here, reason was honour. For the soldier, it was to be fidelity and sacrifice: Chevingé became not a reasonable man but a manservant. In his story, there are more or less the same mythical meanings as there are between Man Friday and Robinson Crusoe. The relationship that Defoe set up between the white man isolated in nature and the good savage is never a man-to-man relationship, totally comprised in its immediate reciprocity, but an instance of the master–servant relation, of intelligence versus devotion, of wise strength against brute force, of reflective courage versus heroic unconsciousness: a social relation, in short, with its literary status and all its ethical coefficients, is transposed to a natural state, and becomes an immediate truth in that two-man society. The same values are to be found in the story of the soldier Chevingé; his encounter with Pinel was less the meeting of two like forms of reason than of two clearly defined social characters who instantiate their type perfectly and strike up a rapport in accordance with pre-ordained social structures. It is quite clear here that the force of the myth is far more important than any psychological truth or rigorous medical observation; if the subjects freed by Pinel were really madmen, it is clear that they were not cured by the simple gesture of liberation – their conduct must have long been marked by traces of alienation. But that was unimportant to Pinel. What mattered to him was that reason be signified by crystallised social types very early on, from the very moment when the mad were no longer treated as Outsiders, Animals, figures that were absolutely foreign to men and the relations that existed between them. What constituted the curing of the mad for Pinel was their installation in a recognised social type that was morally recognised and approved.

What is most important then is not the fact that the chains were removed – that measure had been taken on many occasions in the eighteenth century, and particularly so at Saint Luke's – but the myth that gave meaning to this liberation, opening it onto a reason peopled by social and moral themes and figures long recognised in literature, thereby creating in the imaginary an idealised form of the asylum. An asylum that was no longer a cage for man abandoned to his savagery, but a dream republic where relations were only ever established in a virtuous transparency. Honour, fidelity, courage and sacrifice reign here in a pure state, and designate both the ideal forms of society and the criteria of reason. And the myth takes its strength from the fact that it is more or less explicitly opposed – and here again the presence of Couthon is indispensable – to the myths of the Revolution, such as they were formulated after the Terror: the republic of the Convention is a republic of violence, passion and savagery – and it was that republic, without even being aware of it, that harboured the various forms of insanity and unreason. The republic that spontaneously came into being among the mad who were left to their own violence was pure of passion, and was the city of essential obedience. Couthon was the symbol of this 'bad liberty' that had unleashed passions in the people, bringing the tyranny of the Committee of Public Safety, a liberty in whose name the mad were left in chains; Pinel was the symbol of 'good liberty', which delivered the most insane and violent of men, taming their passions and introducing them to the calm world of traditional virtue. Between the people of Paris who came to Bicêtre on a hunt for the enemies of the nation, and Chevingé, the soldier who saved Pinel's life, the more insane and the less free was not the one who had been locked up for years for drunkenness, delirium and violence.

The myth of Pinel, like that of Tuke, hides a whole discursive movement that holds good both as a description of alienation and as an analysis of its suppression:

1 In the inhuman, animal relation that classical confinement imposed, madness did not reveal its moral truth.
2 That truth, when it was allowed to appear, revealed itself to be a human relation filled with virtuous idealism, such as heroism, fidelity, sacrifice, etc.
3 But madness was vice, violence and wickedness, as the rage of the revolutionaries made all too clear.
4 Liberation within confinement, to the extent that it is a reconstruction of society along the lines of conformity to types, could not fail to bring a cure.

The myth of the Retreat and that of the deliverance of men in chains correspond exactly to each other in an immediate opposition. The one brings out all the themes of primitivism, and the other puts transparent images of social virtues into circulation. One looks for the truth and the suppression of madness in a place where man is barely emerging from nature; the other requires a sort of social perfection, and an ideal functioning of human relations. But the two themes were still too close and had been too often blended together in the eighteenth century for them to have radically different meanings for Pinel and Tuke. Here and there, traces of a single effort to integrate certain confinement practices into the great myth of alienation can be found, as in the work of Hegel writing a few years later, which rigorously filled out the conceptual lesson of all that had happened at the Retreat and at Bicêtre:

> The right psychical treatment therefore keeps in view the truth that insanity is not an abstract *loss* of reason (neither in intelligence nor in will and responsibility), but a simple derangement, a contradiction in a reason that still survives – just as physical disease is not an abstract or total loss of health (that would be death), but a contradiction in it. The humane treatment, benevolent and reasonable in equal measure . . . [the services of Pinel here deserve the highest acknowledgement] presupposes the patient's rationality, and that assumption provides a sound basis for dealing with him on this side.[33]

Classical confinement had created a state of alienation, which only existed from the outside, for those who interned and only recognised the interned as an Outsider or an Animal; Pinel and Tuke, in those simple gestures that were to provide its paradoxical origin to positive psychiatry, interiorised alienation, and installed it inside confinement, delimiting it as the distance from a madman to himself, and thereby invented the myth of alienation. For it is indeed of myth that we must speak when attempts are made to pass off concepts as nature, the reconstitution of a whole moral system as the liberation of truth, and to present as a spontaneous cure for madness what is perhaps no more than its secret insertion into a deceitful reality.

*

The legends of Tuke and Pinel transmit mythical values, which the psychiatry of the nineteenth century came to accept as natural truths. But beneath the myths themselves was an operation, or rather a whole series of operations that silently organized the world of the asylum, the methods of cure, and the concrete experience of madness.

First of all, Tuke's action. Because he was a contemporary of Pinel, and because he was known to be part of a 'philanthropic' movement, his gesture was always seen as a 'liberation' of the mad. In fact it was something quite different:

> there has also been particular occasion to observe the great loss, which individuals of our Society have sustained, by being put under the care of those, who are not only strangers to our principles; but by whom they are frequently mixed with other patients, who may indulge themselves in ill language, and other exceptionable practices. This often seems to leave an unprofitable effect upon the patients' minds, after they are restored to the use of their reason, alienating from those religious attachments which they had before experienced; and, sometimes, even corrupting them with vicious habits, to which they had been strangers.[34]

The Retreat was to act as an instrument of segregation: moral and religious segregation, which sought to rebuild around madness an atmosphere that resembled a Quaker community as closely as possible. And that for two reasons. First of all because the spectacle of evil was a source of suffering for any sensitive soul, and the origin of harmful passions like horror, hatred and spite, which engendered or perpetuated madness:

> It was thought, very justly, that the indiscriminate mixture, which must occur in large public establishments, of persons of opposite religious sentiments and practices; of the profligate and the virtuous; the profane and the serious; was calculated to check the progress of returning reason, and to fix, still deeper, the melancholy and misanthropic train of ideas.[35]

But the main reason was elsewhere: religion could play the double role of nature and rule, as it had taken on, in its ancestral habits, education and everyday exercise, the depth of nature, while remaining at the same time a constant principle of coercion. It was both spontaneity and constraint, and to that extent, it was the only means of counteracting the limitless violence of madness during the eclipse of reason:

> Where these [its precepts] have been strongly imbued in early life, they become little less than principles of our nature; and their restraining power is frequently felt, even under the delirious excitement of insanity. To encourage the influence of religious principles over the mind of the insane, is considered of great consequence, as a means of cure.[36]

In this dialectic of alienation, where reason hid without ever disappearing, religion was the concrete form of that which cannot be alienated; it contained all that was invincible in reason, which subsisted beneath madness as a quasi-nature, and around it was a constant invitation from the milieu: 'During lucid intervals, or the state of convalescence, the patient might enjoy the society of those who were of similar habits and opinions.'[37] It assured the secret watch of reason over madness, making nearer and more immediate the constraints that had already been operative inside classical confinement. There, the religious and moral milieu was imposed from without, so that madness, without ever being cured, had a restraint placed upon it. At the Retreat, religion was part of the movement that indicated that despite appearances there was reason in madness, and it brought people back from alienation to health. Religious segregation had a quite precise meaning: it was not there to preserve the sick from the profane influence of non-Quakers, but placed the alienated in a moral environment where they entered into debate with themselves and their surroundings; the aim was to constitute a milieu in which, far from being protected, he was maintained in a state of perpetual unease, constantly threatened by Law and Guilt.

'The principle of fear, which is rarely decreased by insanity, is considered as of great importance in the management of the patients.'[38] Fear appears as an essential character of the asylum. It was probably a familiar figure already, if one considers the terrors of confinement. But confinement imposed fear on madness from without, marking the boundary between reason and unreason, and playing on a double power – on the violence of frenzy, in order to contain it, and on reason itself, in order to keep it outside. The result was a fear that was a surface phenomenon. Fear at the Retreat was a much deeper affair. It was a mediating link between reason and madness, the evocation of a nature that was still shared, which could be used to solder the connection between the two. The terror that reigned was the most visible sign of the alienation of madness in the classical world; fear now was granted the power of disalienation, restoring a sort of primitive complicity between the mad and men of reason. Fear was to renew the solidarity between the two. Madness was no longer to strike fear into people's hearts, nor would it be able to – it was itself *to be afraid*, helplessly, irrevocably afraid, entirely in thrall to the pedagogy of good sense, truth and morality.

Samuel Tuke recounts the arrival of a maniac at the Retreat, a young man of prodigious strength, whose attacks brought panic to his entourage and even among his guards. He arrived at the Retreat handcuffed and in chains, with his clothes tied on with ropes. As soon as he entered, his fetters were removed, and he was allowed to eat with the superintendents, and his agitation disappeared immediately. 'His attention appeared to be arrested by his new situation.' He was led to his room, and the superintendent explained how the house was set up for the greater freedom and comfort of all, and that he would never be restrained unless he broke the rules of the house, or went against the general principles of human morality. The superintendent assured him that he had no desire ever to use the means of coercion that he had at his disposal. 'The maniac was sensible of the kindness of his treatment. He promised to restrain himself.' On occasion he still became agitated, raising his voice and frightening his companions. The superintendent then repeated the threats and promises of the first day, saying that unless he calmed down, they would be forced to return to older means of punishment. The patient's agitation would increase slightly, and then rapidly decline: 'he would listen with attention to the persuasions and arguments of his friendly visiter. After such conversations, the patient was generally better for some days or a week.' After four months, he was released from the Retreat, entirely cured.[39] Fear here was directed straight at the patient, not through any instrument but purely by means of discourse. There was no question of limiting a raging liberty, but of defining and exalting a region of simple responsibility, where any manifestation of madness would be linked to a punishment. The obscure guilt that in the past had linked transgression and unreason was thus displaced, and the madman, as a human being originally blessed with the faculty of reason, was no longer guilty of being mad; but the madman, as an insane person, and within the sickness for which he was no longer to feel guilty, was forced to feel responsible for all within it that could trouble morality and good society, and only blame himself for any punishment that he received. The assignation of guilt was no longer the mode of relation between the mad and the man of reason in purely general terms: it became instead at the same time the form of the concrete coexistence of each madman and his guardian, and the form of consciousness that an alienated man was to have of his own madness.

A re-evaluation of the significance usually attributed to Tuke's work is therefore necessary. The liberation of the alienated, the abolition of constraints, and the constitution of a human milieu were mere justifications. The real operations were quite different. In fact, Tuke created an asylum where he substituted the stifling responsibility of anguish for the free terror of madness; the fear was no longer of what lay on the other side of the prison door, but what raged instead beneath the seals of conscience. The secular terrors in which the alienated found themselves caught up were transferred by Tuke to the heart of madness. True, the asylum no longer sanctioned the guilt of the madman, but it did more: it organised it. It organised it for the madman as self-consciousness, in a non-reciprocal relation with his keeper, and it organised it for men of reason as a consciousness of the other, and a therapeutic intervention into the madman's existence. Through this guilt, the madman became an object of punishment always offered to himself and the other; and from that recognition of his status as object, and his consciousness of his own guilt, the madman was to return to his consciousness as a free, responsible subject, thereby regaining reason. This movement where, by becoming an object for an other, the alienated person returned to his own freedom, was a process to be found in Work as well as in the Gaze.

It must be remembered that this was a Quaker universe, where God blessed men with the signs of their prosperity. Work was of primary importance in the 'moral treatment' that was practised at the Retreat. In itself, work has a power to constrain which was superior to all other forms of physical coercion, as the regularity of the hours, the demands it made on attention, and the obligation to achieve a result removed what would otherwise have been a harmful liberty of thought, fixing patients in a system of responsibility:

> Of all the modes by which the patients may be induced to restrain them-selves, regular employment is perhaps the most generally efficacious; and those kinds of employment are doubtless to be preferred, both on a moral and physical account, which are accompanied by considerable bodily action; that are most agreeable to the patient, and which are most opposite to the illusions of his disease.[40]

By such means man entered once more the order of God's command-ments; he submitted his liberty to laws that were both those of reality and those of morality. For the same reasons mental work was not discouraged, although all exercise of the imagination was to be banned, as it always involved complicity with passion, desire, and all forms of delirious illu-sion. On the other hand, the study of all that is eternal in nature, and conforms most closely to the wisdom and bounty of Providence, was tremendously efficacious when it came to limiting the excessive freedom of the mad and helping them to discover the different forms of their responsibility. 'The various branches of the mathematics and natural science, furnish the most useful class of subjects on which to employ the minds of the insane.'[41] In the asylum, work was stripped of any production value; it was only imposed as a moral rule. It was a limitation of liberty, submission to order, an engagement to responsibility, of which the only goal was the tethering of a spirit that roamed too freely in the excess of a liberty which physical constraints only limited in appearance.

More useful still than work was the gaze of others, which Tuke termed the 'desire of esteem': 'This principle in the human mind, which doubtless influences, in a great degree, though often secretly, our general manners; and which operates with peculiar force on our introduction to a new circle of acquaintance.'[42] In classical confinement too the madman had been exposed to the gaze, but it had little power of penetration, going no deeper than the monstrous surface of his visible bestiality; and it had a degree of reciprocity, as healthy men could read there, as in a mirror, the imminent movement of their own fall. The gaze that Tuke instituted as one of the primary components of life in the asylums was at once more profound and less reciprocal. It was to track the least perceptible indications of madness in patients, hunting for the point where madness was secretly attached to reason, and barely began to drift apart from it; and it was a gaze that the madman could never return in any form, for he was only ever the observed; he was like a newcomer, the last settler in the world of reason. Tuke organised a whole ceremony articulated around the processes of the gaze. These were English-style evenings, where everyone was to observe the minutiae of social conduct in the strictest possible terms, and where the only object in circulation was an inquisitorial gaze on the lookout for any infringement of the codes, any disorder, incongruity or ineptness that betrayed a sign of madness. The directors and the keepers at the Retreat would thus regularly invite some of the patients to tea-parties:

> All who attend, dress in their best clothes, and vie with each other in politeness and propriety. The best fare is provided, and the visiters are treated with all the attention of strangers. The evening generally passes in the greatest harmony and enjoyment. It rarely happens that any

unpleasant circumstance occurs; the patients control, in a wonderful degree, their different propensities; and the scene is at once curious, and affectingly gratifying.[43]

Curiously, this ritual is not one of intimacy, of dialogue or of mutual knowledge; it is the organisation around the madman of a whole world where everything seems similar and accessible, but to which he is a perpetual outsider, the Stranger *par excellence* judged not only on appearances, but on all that they might reveal and betray despite themselves. Constantly recalled to this empty role of the unknown visitor, and challenged in everything that can be known of him, attracted to his own surface by the social type whose form and mask are silently imposed upon him by the gaze, the madman was invited to turn himself into an object for the eyes of reasonable reason, as the perfect stranger, i.e. he whose foreignness is never perceptible. The city of reasonable men only welcomes him to the extent that he conforms to that anonymous type.

We can see that the partial suppression of physical constraint at the Retreat was part of a whole, of which the essential element was the constitution of 'self-restraint', where the freedom of the mad, checked by work and by the gaze of others, was constantly threatened by an acknowledgement of guilt.[44] What at first glance seemed to be a simple negative operation that loosened bonds and freed the profound nature of madness turned out to be a positive operation that enclosed madness in a system of rewards and punishments, including it into the movement of moral consciousness. It was the passage from a world of Censure to a universe of Judgement. But at the same time a psychology of madness became possible, for before the gaze, on its own surface, madness is constantly made to deny its own dissimulation. It is judged on its actions alone; its intentions are not put on trial, and no attempt is made to plumb its secret depths. It is only answerable for the part of itself that is visible. All the rest is reduced to silence. Madness no longer exists except as that which is seen. The proximity that comes into being in the asylum, in the absence of chains and bars, does not encourage reciprocal interaction. It is simply that of a piercing gaze, observing, scrutinizing, moving pitilessly close the better to see, while remaining sufficiently distant to avoid any contamination by the values of the Stranger. The science of mental illness, such as it was to develop in the asylums, was only ever of the order of observation and classification. It was never to be a dialogue. That could only begin once psychoanalysis had exorcised the phenomenon of the gaze, so essential to the nineteenth-century asylum, substituting its silent magic with the powers of language. Or perhaps it would be more accurate to say that psychoanalysis doubled the absolute gaze of the watcher with the indefinite monologue of the surveyed – thus keeping in place the old asylum structure of a non-reciprocal gaze, but balancing it out, in a non-symmetrical reciprocity, with the new structure of a language without response.

Surveillance and Judgement: a new type of personage was coming into being, who would be essential for the functioning of the nineteenth-century asylum. Tuke himself outlined his profile, when he told the story of a maniac who was subject to fits of irrepressible violence. One day, when he was walking with the superintendent in one of the gardens of the house, the patient suddenly had an attack, and ran off to pick a large stone, which he 'held up as in the act of throwing it at his companion'. The superintendent stopped in his tracks, and stared the patient in the eye, advanced a few paces and, 'in a resolute tone of voice, commanded him to lay down the stone'. As he approached, the patient lowered his arm, and dropped the weapon. 'He then submitted to be quietly led to his apartment.'[45] Something was born here, which was not repression but authority. Until the end of the eighteenth century, the world of the mad had been peopled only by the abstract, faceless power that kept patients locked up. Inside these limits, it was a void, a world empty of anything that was not madness itself, where even the keepers were often recruited among the patients. What Tuke instituted was a mediating element between guardians and patients, between reason and madness. The space reserved by society for alienation was now haunted by figures 'from the other side', representing both the prestige of the authority that confined, and the rigours of the reason that judged. The superintendent intervened unarmed, with no instruments of constraint at his disposal other than the gaze and language. He advanced towards madness, stripped of anything that might protect him or turn him into a figure of menace, risking an immediate confrontation with no possible retreat. And yet it was not as a concrete person that he confronted madness, but rather as the incarnation of reason, bearing the full force of the authority invested in him by the fact of his not being mad. In previous times, the victory of reason over unreason was assured only by material force, in a combat of sorts that was quite genuine. But now the battle was always won in advance, and the defeat of unreason was already inscribed in the concrete situation where the mad and the non-mad met. The absence of constraint in the asylums of the nineteenth century was not the liberation of unreason, but madness mastered in advance.

For this new reason that reigned in the asylums, madness was less an absolute form of contradiction than a minority status, an aspect of itself that had as yet no right to autonomy, which could only exist grafted onto the world of reason. Madness was childhood, and at the Retreat, everything was organised so that the alienated might be treated as minors. They were considered

> as children, who have too much strength, and who make a dangerous use of it. Their punishments and rewards must be immediate, since that which is distant has no effect on them. A new system of education must be adopted to give a fresh course to their ideas. Subject them at first; encourage them afterwards, employ them, and render their employment agreeable by attractive means.[46]

In the eyes of the law, the alienated had long been considered minors, but that was a legal situation, abstractly defined by interdiction and trusteeship; it was not a concrete means by which men related to each other. For Tuke, that minority status became a style of existence for the mad, and a mode of sovereignty for their guardians. Much was made of the 'big family' atmosphere formed by the community of the insane and their keepers at the Retreat. The belief was that the 'family' placed the patient in a milieu that was both normal and natural; the reality was that it alienated them still further. The mad were accorded the legal status of minors to protect them as subjects before the law; but when this ancient structure became a form of coexistence, it meant that they were entirely controlled, as psychological subjects, by men of reason, who became for them the incarnation of adulthood, i.e. both domination and destination.

In the great reorganisation of relations between madness and reason, the family, at the end of the eighteenth century, played a decisive role – it was both an imaginary landscape and a real social structure. The family was both the origin and the destination of Tuke's work. Lending it the prestige of primitive values not yet compromised in the social, Tuke had it play a role of disalienation: in its mythology, it was the antithesis of the 'milieu' in which the eighteenth century saw the origin of all madness. But he also introduced it in a very real way to the world of the asylum, where it appeared as both truth and norm for all the relations that could be struck up between madmen and men of reason. Thus minority under family tutelage, a juridical status in which the civil rights of the mad were alienated, became a psychological situation where their concrete liberty was alienated. The whole existence of madness, in the world that was now being prepared for it, was enveloped in what we might describe by anticipation as a 'parental complex'. The privileges of patriarchy were revived once more around it in the bourgeois family unit. It was this historical sedimentation that psychoanalysis would later bring up to date, with the institution of a new myth that gave it the meaning of a destiny, traceable through the civilization of the West, and perhaps all civilization, whereas the process had in fact been much more gradual, and its bedrock had only recently solidified, during this fin-de-siècle period when madness found itself twice alienated inside the family – by the myth of a disaliena-tion in the purity of patriarchy, and then again by a genuinely alienating situation in asylums closely modelled on the family unit. From this point onwards, and for a period whose end is still impossible to see, the discourses of unreason became inextricably linked to the half-real, half-imaginary dialectic of the Family. And in the place where, in their violence, we previously saw profanation and blasphemy, we must now decipher endless attacks against the Father. All of which means that in the modern world, what was once the great, irreparable confrontation between reason and unreason has become instead the dull thud of instincts repeatedly coming up against the solidity of the institution of the family and its most archaic symbols.

There is an astonishing convergence between the development of the basic institutions and this evolution of madness in the world of confine-ment. As we have seen, the liberal economy tended to place the onus on the family rather than the State when it came to assistance to the poor and the sick, so that the family became the place of social responsibility. But if a sick patient could be entrusted to a family, a madman could not, as he was too foreign and inhuman. Tuke's innovation was to create a simu-lacrum of the family around the mad, an institutional parody that was nonetheless a real psychological situation. Where family was lacking, he substituted a fictitious familial décor through signs and attitudes. But by a curious crossover, the day was to come when the family was discharged of its role in assisting the poor and alleviating the suffering of the sick, but still kept its fictitious values regarding madness; and long after the sickness of the poor had again become an affair of the State, asylums maintained the insane in a fictional family imperative. The mad remained minors, and for a long while to come reason bore for them the attributes of a Father.

With these fictitious values locked up inside it, the asylum was sheltered from the forces of history and social change. Tuke's intention was to create a milieu that imitated the most ancient, pure, and natural forms of coexistence: the milieu was to be as human as possible, while remaining as un-social as possible. What he did in practice was to copy the structure of a bourgeois family, symbolically recreate it inside the asylum and set it adrift in history. Always oriented towards anachronistic symbols and structures, the asylum was outside time and ill adapted *par excellence*. And in this place where animality manifested a presence without history, constantly beginning anew, the immemorial signs of ancient hatreds and ancient familial profanations, the forgotten signs of punishment and incest, would slowly surface once more.

*

There was no such religious segregation in the work of Pinel. Or rather, the segregation went in the opposite direction to everything practised by Tuke. The benefits of the new model asylums were open to all, or almost all, with the exception of fanatics 'who believe that they are inspired, and constantly search for new adherents to spread their gospel'. Bicêtre and the Salpêtrière, as Pinel saw them, formed a kind of complementary figure to the Retreat.

Religion was not to be a moral substratum of life in the asylum, but purely and simply an object of medicine:

> Religious opinions, in a hospital for the alienated, should only ever be examined from the point of view of medicine, so any considerations related to public cults or to politics should be swept aside, and all that should be considered is whether it is important to oppose the exalted ideas or feelings that derive from such sources, in order to help cure certain patients.[47]

Catholicism, a source of powerful emotions and haunting images born of the terrors of an afterlife, often provoked insanity, giving birth to delirious beliefs and hallucinations, leading people into despair and melancholy. Pinel was not surprised that 'looking down the list of alienated patients at Bicêtre, we find the names of many priests and monks, as well as country folk frightened out of their wits by terrifying paintings of the future'.[48] And he was even less surprised to see how the figures for religious madness varied down the ages. Under the Ancien Régime and during the Revolution, the strength of superstitious beliefs and the violence of the struggles that pitted the Republic against the Catholic Church caused melancholia of religious origin to multiply. With the return of peace, the Concordat smoothed over the differences, and such forms of delirium disappeared: in Year X of the revolutionary calendar, 50 per cent of the melancholics at the Salpêtrière were still diagnosed as suffering from religious madness; the following year that number had fallen to 33 per cent, and by the year XII they were a mere 18 per cent.[49] The asylum was thus to be freed of religion and its imaginary correlates. Those who were 'melancholic by devotion' had their pious books removed, as experience had shown that allowing them 'was the surest way of perpetuating their alienation, and even rendering it incurable. The more such permission is granted, the less their worries and scruples can be calmed.'[50] Nothing could be further from Tuke and his dreams of a religious community that would also be a privileged place for the curing of the mind than this idea of a neutral asylum, purified of all the images and passions that Christianity had brought into existence, and which led the mind to error, delusion, and ultimately delirium and hallucinations.

But Pinel's aim was to reduce the imaginary forms, not the moral content of religion. For once such images had been filtered, religion had a power of 'disalienation', dissipating images, calming passions and restoring to man all that was immediate and essential in his being: it could help him approach his moral truth. And for that reason it was often capable of bringing about a cure. Pinel tells several stories that are reminiscent of Voltaire. He writes of one young 25-year-old woman, 'of a strong constitution, united in marriage to a man who was weak and delicate'. She suffered from 'violent crises of hysteria, and imagined that she was possessed by a demon which, she claimed, took on a variety of forms, sometimes imitating the singing of birds, or making low, lugubrious sounds, and sometimes uttering piercing cries'. Luckily, the local priest preferred natural religion to exorcism, and put his trust in the benevolence of nature to cure her:

This enlightened man, of a calm, persuasive disposition, gained some sway over the mind of the patient, and managed to convince her to leave her bed, so that she returned once more to her domestic chores, and even to digging her garden . . . this was followed by even more successful results, and a cure that lasted three years.[51]

Brought back to the extreme simplicity of its moral content, religion invariably went hand in hand with philosophy, medicine, and all the forms of wisdom and knowledge that could restore reason to the wandering mind. There were even cases where religion could serve as a preliminary treatment and prepare what was to be done at the asylum. One example was a young girl 'of an ardent temperament, although well behaved and very pious', who was torn between 'the inclinations of her heart and the severe principles of her conduct'. Her confessor, after advising her in vain to attach herself to God, showed her cases of firm, measured saintliness, counselling her 'to trust in the traditional remedies to the great passions – patience and time'. Taken to the Salpêtrière, she was treated under Pinel's orders, using 'the same moral principles', and her sickness was 'of short duration'.[52] The asylum thus took on not the social theme of a religion where men felt like brothers in one communion and one community, but a moral power of consolation, confidence and docile faithfulness to nature. It was to do the moral work of religion, ignoring the fantastical text and concentrating on the levels of virtue, work and social life.

The asylum was thus a religious domain stripped of religion, a domain of pure morality and ethical uniformity. All that retained the imprint of the old differences was slowly effaced, and the last memories of the sacred were gradually extinguished. Previously, houses of confinement had inherited, in the social space, the almost absolute limits of the lazar houses, and had been foreign territory. The asylum was now to figure the great continuity of social morality, and was ruled by the values of family and work and all recognised virtues. And that in two ways. First, they reigned in fact, at the heart of madness itself: under the violence and disorder of alienation, the solid nature of essential virtues remained unbroken. A primitive form of morality remained, ordinarily untouched even by the most extreme forms of dementia, and it was this that both appeared and operated during the cure:

> I must state my unstinting admiration for the pure virtues and severe principles that invariably come to light in the course of the cure. Nowhere else, other than in novels, have I come across husbands more worthy of being cherished, fathers and mothers more tender, lovers more passionate, or people more attached to their duties than most of the alienated who are happily brought to the period of convalescence.[53]

This inalienable virtue is both the truth and the resolution of madness. For that reason, if it reigned in fact, it also *had to do so*. The asylum was to reduce difference, repress vice, and eliminate irregularity. It denounced anything that was opposed to the essential virtues of society, like celibacy:

> The number of young girls who fell into idiocy is seven times greater than the number of married women between year XI and year XIII; for dementia, the proportion is a factor of two or four times. It can therefore be presumed that for women, marriage offers considerable protection against the two most inveterate (and often incurable) forms of alienation.[54]

Debauchery, bad behaviour and 'extreme perversity of morals' got the same treatment: 'the habit of vice, like that of drunkenness, unrestrained and promiscuous lechery, bad behaviour and general apathetic insouciance can slowly chip away at reason, and often result in a clear case of alienation'.[55] Laziness was 'the most constant and unanimous result of the experience that in public asylums, as in prisons and hospices, the most certain and perhaps the sole guarantor of health, good morals and social order is the law of a mechanical work, rigorously executed'.[56] The asylum's aim was the homogeneous reign of morality, and its rigorous extension to all those who attempted to escape it.

But by that fact, it allowed difference to creep in: if the law did not reign universally, then that was because there were men who did not recognise it, a social class that lived in disorder, negligence, and something approaching illegality:

> If on the one hand we see families prospering for many years in peace and harmony, how many others do we also see, particularly in the lower strata of society, offending our sight with a repugnant vision of debauchery, dissent and shameful distress! Day after day, my notes indicate that

this is the most common source of alienation that we are called upon to treat in the hospices.[57]

In a single movement, the asylum, in the hands of Pinel, becomes an instrument of moral uniformity and social denunciation. The intention was to erect one form of morality as universal, which was to be imposed from within on other forms of morality that were foreign to it, and which contained the alienation that would inevitably affect people in the end. In the first case, the asylum was to act as an awakening and a reminder, invoking a forgotten nature; in the second, it was to act as social displacement, to uproot individuals from their condition. The operation as practised at the Retreat was still simple: a religious segregation for the purposes of moral purification. What Pinel practised was relatively complex, as he tried to operate moral syntheses, assuring an ethical continuity between the worlds of madness and reason, but enacting a form of social segregation all the while that guaranteed bourgeois morality a *de facto* universality, enabling it to impose itself as a system of law over all forms of alienation.

In the classical age, poverty, laziness, vice and madness all blended into a single culpability inside unreason; the mad were locked up in the great confinement of poverty and unemployment, but all were promoted to the vicinity of sin, close to the essence of the Fall. But madness now became more of a social fall, confusedly perceived as its cause, model and limit. Within the space of half a century, mental illness would be treated as a form of degeneration. And from then on, the essential madness, and the real threat, was something that floated up from the lower depths of society.

Pinel's asylum was not to be a retreat from the world, a space of nature and immediate truth like that of Tuke, but a uniform domain of legislation, a place of moral syntheses where the nascent alienation that came into being on the fringes of society was to be eliminated.[58] The lives led by the internees, and their behaviour towards doctors and guards, were organised by Pinel in such manner that these moral syntheses should be carried out. This he did by three principal means.

1   *Silence.* The fifth chained prisoner freed by Pinel was a defrocked priest whose madness had caused him to be expelled from the church. He suffered delusions of grandeur, and imagined himself to be Jesus Christ: this was 'the sublime of human arrogance in delirium'. He had been

admitted to Bicêtre in 1782, and had been in chains for twelve years. His proud bearing and grandiloquent speeches meant that he was one of the best appreciated spectacles in the hospital, but as he knew that he was in the midst of reliving Christ's Passion, 'he patiently endured his martyrdom and the constant sarcasm, to which he was exposed'. Pinel chose him to be among the first dozen delivered from their chains, despite the fact that his delirium was as strong as ever. But he did not act with him in the same way as with the others: there were no exhortations, and no promises were extracted. He removed his chains without uttering a word, and

> expressly ordered that everyone imitate his reserve, so that not a word was said to this poor unfortunate. This rigorously observed prohibition had a more tangible effect on this man so imbued with himself than either the irons or his cell; he felt humiliated by the abandonment, and by this new form of isolation within his full liberty. Finally, after a long period of hesitation, he was seen of his own accord to mingle with the society of the other patients; and from that day on, he slowly returned to more reasonable and correct ideas.[59]

Deliverance here takes on a paradoxical meaning. In the patient's delirium, the cell, the chains, the continual spectacle and the sarcasm were the element of his liberty. Thus recognised, through his very bondage, and fascinated from without by so much complicity, he could not be dislodged from his immediate truth. But the removal of the chains, the indifference and the silence of all around him confined him in the limited use of an empty liberty; he was delivered in silence to a truth without recognition, which he would demonstrate in vain since he was no longer observed, and from which he could no longer extract any form of exaltation as his humiliation had come to an end. It was the man himself, and no longer his projection into delirium, who now found himself to be humiliated, and instead of physical constraints he now had a liberty that showed him the limits of his solitude every instant. Where there had previously been a dialogue between insult and delirium, there was now a monologue that exhausted itself in the silence of others, and his parade of presumption and outrage was met with indifference. From that moment on, more genuinely confined than he could be in a dungeon or in chains, a prisoner of nothing but himself, the patient was trapped in a relation to the self that was of the order of guilt, and in a non-relation to others that was of the order of shame. The others were made innocent, and were no longer persecutors; guilt was displaced to within, demonstrating to the madman that he was fascinated by nothing other than his own presumption. The faces of the enemy disappeared, and he no longer experienced their presence as a gaze, but rather as a refusal to pay any attention to him, a gaze averted; for him others were now nothing but a limit that constantly retreated as he advanced. Freed from his chains, he was now truly a prisoner, by virtue of silence, in sin and shame. Before, he felt himself to be punished, and saw there the signs of his innocence; now, free of any physical punishment, he had no option but to consider himself guilty. His torture had been his glory: his deliverance was his humiliation.

In comparison to the incessant dialogue between reason and madness that had marked the Renaissance, classical confinement had been a silencing. But that silence was not total, and language was now engaged in things rather than totally suppressed. Confinement, prisons, dungeons, and even torture had set up a silent dialogue between reason and unreason, which was of the order of a struggle. That dialogue itself was now undone, and the silence was absolute; there was no longer any common language between madness and reason, and all that answered the language of delirium was an absence of language, for delirium was not a fragment of dialogue with reason, but no language at all; its only reference, in the consciousness finally silenced, was guilt. And it was only from that point on that a common language was once more possible, after guilt had been recognised and acknowledged. 'Finally, after a long period of hesitation, he was seen of his own accord to mingle with the society of the other patients . . .' The absence of language, as a fundamental structure of life in the asylums, had as its correlative the renewal of the act of confession. When Freud cautiously reinstituted the exchange in psychoanalysis, or rather began to listen once more to this language, now eroded into monologue, was it any wonder that the formulations he heard were always a reference to guilt? In this inveterate silence, guilt had taken over the very source of language.

2 *Recognition as mirror.* At the Retreat, the mad were observed, and made aware of it; but, for madness, that direct gaze was only a sideways glance and it had no immediate grasp on itself. With Pinel, by contrast, the gaze only worked inside the space defined by madness, without surface

or exterior limits. It saw itself and was seen by itself – as both pure object of spectacle and absolute subject.

> Three alienated men, who each believed themselves to be sovereigns, and had all taken the title of Louis XVI, were arguing one day about their rights to royalty, which they were seeking to assert with slightly excessive enthusiasm. The guard approached one of them and took him to one side: 'Why', she said, 'are you bothering to argue with those people, who are obviously mad? Doesn't everyone know that you should clearly be recognised as Louis XVI?' The patient was flattered by this treatment, and withdrew, looking down his nose at the other two with considerable disdain. The same tactic worked with the second patient. And from that point on there were no more arguments.[60]

This was the first moment, the period of exaltation. Madness is called upon to examine itself, but in others, and it appears in them as unfounded pretension, i.e. as derisory madness; and yet in this gaze that condemns others, the madman assures his own justification, and the certainty of being equal to his own delirium. The cleavage between presumption and reality can only be recognised in the object. It remains entirely veiled in the subject, who becomes immediate truth and absolute judge; an exalted sovereignty denounces the fake sovereignty of the others and dispossesses them, thereby confirming the unbroken surface of its own presumption. Madness, as simple delirium, is projected onto others, and as perfect unconsciousness is entirely accepted.

But at that moment the complicitous mirror becomes a means of demystification. Another Bicêtre patient still believed himself to be king, and still expressed himself 'with the commanding tone of supreme authority'. One day when he was less agitated, the guard approached him and asked him, if he was king, why he didn't bring his detention to an end, and how it was that he allowed himself to be kept together with the other inmates. Repeating this speech day after day,

> he gradually caused him to see the ridiculous nature of his exaggerated pretensions, showing him another alienated patient who had also long been convinced that he was invested with supreme power and yet had become an object of derision. The maniac felt shaken at first, and soon began to doubt his own title as sovereign, and finally managed to

recognise the chimerical nature of his imaginings. This highly unexpected moral turnaround happened in about two weeks, and after a few months of tests, this dutiful father was returned to his family.[61]

This then was the stage of abasement; presumptuously identified with the object of his delirium, the madman recognised himself in the mirror of the madness whose ridiculous pretension he had already denounced; the solidity of his sovereign subjectivity crumbled in the object that he had demystified by taking it as his own identity. He found himself the unpitied object of his own gaze, and faced with the silence of those who represented reason and did nothing other than hold out a dangerous mirror, he recognised himself as objectively mad.

We have already seen the means – and the mystifications – employed in the therapeutic practices of the eighteenth century to persuade the mad of their insanity, the better to free them from it.[62] Here the movement is of a quite different nature. It is not that error is dissipated by the imposing spectacle of truth, or its counterfeit; the aim is to attack the arrogance of madness rather than its aberration. The classical mind condemned in madness a certain blindness to the truth; from Pinel onwards, it recognised in it an impulse from the depths which exceeded the juridical limits of the individual, ignoring fixed moral limits and tending towards an apotheosis of the self. For the nineteenth century, the initial model of madness was to believe oneself to be God, whereas for preceding centuries it had been to turn one's back on God. Madness was thus to find its salvation in the spectacle of itself as unreason humiliated, when, fascinated by the absolute subjectivity of its delirium, it glimpsed its derisory and objective image in an identical madman. The truth insinuated itself as though by surprise (not by violence, as had been the case during the eighteenth century) into this game of reciprocal glances, where it only ever saw itself. But the asylum, in this community of madmen, ensured that mirrors were positioned in such fashion that eventually the mad could not fail to see themselves for what they were. Freed from the chains that had ensured it was a pure object of the gaze, madness was paradoxically stripped of its essential liberty, which was that of solitary exaltation; it became responsible for what it knew of its truth, and was imprisoned in its own gaze, which was constantly turned back on itself, finally chained to the humiliation of being an object for itself. Realisation, or gaining consciousness was now linked to the shame of being identical to that other, compromised in him and scorned by oneself even before reaching recognition and knowledge of oneself.

3 *Perpetual judgement*. In that mirror game, as with silence, madness was constantly called upon to become its own judge. But in addition, it was at each moment judged from without; judged not by a moral or scientific consciousness, but rather by a sort of invisible court that was permanently in session. The asylum Pinel dreamt of, and which he realised in part at Bicêtre, and even more so at the Salpêtrière, was a judicial microcosm. In order to be effective, this justice needed a fearsome aspect. All the imaginary paraphernalia of judge and executioner needed to be present in the mind of the alienated, so that they understood completely the universe of judgement in which they found themselves. The ceremony of justice, the full terror of its implacability, was therefore to be a part of the treatment. One of the inmates at Bicêtre suffered from a religious delirium that revolved around a panicked fear of Hell, and he believed that the only manner in which he would escape eternal damnation was by observing a rigorous abstinence. It was necessary for that fear of a distant justice to be compensated by the presence of an immediate form of justice that was more redoubtable still: 'Could the irresistible course of his sinister ideas be counterbalanced other than by an intense, deep-seated impression of fear?' One night, the director turned up at the patient's door:

> with an appearance designed to terrify him, his eyes aflame, and with a thundering tone of voice, surrounded by a group of men carrying heavy chains, which they shook loudly. They placed some soup in front of the alienated patient, and ordered him to eat it during the night, unless he wished to experience the most terrible treatment. Then they retreated, leaving the patient painfully oscillating between the fear of an immediate punishment and the terrifying prospect of eternal torment in the life to come. After an inner struggle that went on for several hours, the first idea carried the day, and he decided to eat the food.[63]

As a judicial instance, the asylum recognised no other. It judged immediately, and there was no appeal. It had its own instruments of punishment, and it used them as it saw fit. The old confinement, on the whole, had taken place outside of the normal juridical forms. But it imitated the punishments of those on whom sentence was passed, using the same prisons and dungeons, the same physical punishments. The justice that reigned in Pinel's asylum owed nothing to other forms of repression, and invented its own instead. Or rather it employed the therapeutic means that had become more widespread during the eighteenth century, reinventing them as forms of punishment. This conversion of medicine into justice, and therapeutics into repression ranks not lowest among the paradoxes in the achievements of this 'liberator' and 'philanthropist'. In the medicine of the classical age, baths and showers were used as remedies, as a result of physicians' dreams about the nature of the nervous system. The idea had been to refresh the system, relaxing the burning, desiccated fibres;[64] and it was doubtless true that among the fortunate consequences of the cold shower there was also the psychological effect of a disagreeable surprise, which broke the chain of thoughts and changed the nature of feelings; but here we are still in the domain of medical dreams. With Pinel, the use of the cold shower became openly judicial, and a shower was the usual punishment meted out by the simple police tribunal that permanently sat in the asylums:

> Considered as a means of repression, they are often enough to force an alienated woman to submit to the general law of manual labour, and will also conquer refusals to take food, and calm alienated women who are carried away by a sort of turbulent and reasoned humour.[65]

Everything is organised so that the mad recognise themselves in the world of judgement that envelops them from all sides: they are to know that they are observed, judged and condemned. The link between the crime and its punishment was to be clear, and guilt was to be acknowledged by all:

> Advantage is taken of the circumstances surrounding the bath, and the fault that has been committed or the omission of the important duty is recalled, and with the help of a tap a quick burst of cold water is directed at the head, often disconcerting the alienated patient, or freeing her from a dominant idea with this strong and unexpected sensation. If she is obstinate, the cold shower is repeated, but care is taken to avoid a harsh tone or words that might shock or offend; she is made to understand that it is for her good and that recourse is regretfully made to measures of such violence; sometimes a joke is made of it, although care must be taken that it does not go too far.[66]

The almost arithmetical obviousness of the punishment, repeated as often as necessary, and the recognition of fault by the repression that was exerted were all intended to bring about an interiorisation of the judicial instance, leading to the beginnings of remorse in the patient's mind. Only then did the judges agree to bring the punishment to an end, as they were sure that it would continue indefinitely inside the patient's conscience. One maniac was in the habit of tearing at her clothes and breaking any object within her reach. She was given the cold water treatment, and then tied up in a straitjacket, and appeared at last 'humiliated and deeply concerned'; but fearing that her feelings of shame were merely transitory and her remorse too superficial, 'the director spoke to her in the strongest terms to ensure that she experienced a feeling of real terror; he did not show anger, but he informed her that henceforth she would always be treated as severely as possible'. The expected result was not long in coming: 'Her repentance began in a torrent of tears, which she shed for nearly two hours.'[67] The cycle was doubly complete: the fault was punished, and its author had acknowledged her guilt.

There were, however, alienated patients who escaped this movement and resisted the moral synthesis it operated. Such people were to be locked away inside the asylum, making a new confined population that was even out of the reach of justice. When people speak of Pinel and the liberation he initiated, this second form of incarceration is too often ignored. We have already seen him refusing the benefits of asylum reform to

> religious fanatics who believe themselves to be inspired, and who constantly seek to convert others to their cause, and take a perfidious pleasure in fomenting dissent amongst other alienated patients, on the pretext that they should obey God rather than man.

But reclusion and the dungeon were equally obligatory for those 'who refuse to cooperate with the general law of work and who, in malicious activity, enjoy tormenting the other inmates, provoking them and inciting them to revolt', and for women who 'during their attacks, have an irresistible propensity to steal anything that comes into their grasp'.[68] Disobedience on account of religious fanaticism, resistance to work, and theft, the three great sins against bourgeois society, three major attacks on its essential values, were all inexcusable, even in the mad. Such faults demanded imprisonment pure and simple, and exclusion in the most

rigorous form possible, as all three crimes demonstrated the same resistance to moral and social uniformity, which were the *raison d'être* of the
asylum such as it was conceived by Pinel.

In previous times, unreason was placed outside judgement, to be
arbitrarily handed over to the powers of reason. Now, it was judged, and
not just once, on entry to the asylum, to be recognised, classified and
declared innocent forever; instead it was caught in a perpetual judgement,
which never ceased to hound it and apply sanctions, proclaiming faults
and demanding a frank admission of wrongdoing, banishing anyone
whose errant ways risked compromising the social order for a long time.
Madness escaped arbitrariness only to fall into a sort of endless trial, for
which the asylum provided the police, the prosecutors, the judges and the
executioners. This was a trial where any error in life, by a virtue proper
to life in the asylum, became a social crime, observed, sentenced and
punished; a trial that had no issue other than in a perpetual recommence-
ment in the interiorised form of remorse. The mad who were 'delivered'
by Pinel, and, in their wake the madmen of the modern confinement, are
characters on trial; if they have the privilege of no longer being locked up
or confused with other prisoners, they are still condemned at each instant
to be the subject of a process of accusation which never takes place in
public, for it is formulated by their whole asylum life. The asylum of the
positivist age, which Pinel is credited with having founded, is not a free
domain of observation, diagnosis and therapeutics: it is a judicial space
where people are accused, judged, and sentenced, from which they can
only be freed by a translation of this judicial process into the depths of
psychology, i.e. through repentance. Madness was to be punished in
asylums, even if its innocence was proclaimed outside. For a long time to
come, and at least until today, it was imprisoned in a moral world.

*

A fourth structure, proper to the world of the asylum as it came into being
at the close of the eighteenth century, should also be added to silence, the
recognition in a mirror and perpetual judgement. This is the apotheosis
of the medical character ('*personnage médical*'). This is perhaps the most
important of all, as it was to authorise not only new contacts between
doctors and patients, but also a new relation between alienation and medical thought, which was finally to take command of the whole modern

experience of madness. Until now, what had been found in the asylum was essentially a repetition of the structures of confinement, although displaced and deformed. With the new status of the medical character, it was the deepest meaning of confinement that was abolished; mental illness, with all the connotations that are familiar to us today, then became possible.

The works of Tuke and Pinel, which were so different in spirit and values, come together in this transformation of the medical character. As we saw above, physicians had no role to play in the life of confinement. But they became essential figures in the asylum. They presided over entry, as the rules of the Retreat made clear:

> On the admission of patients, the Committee should, in general, require a certificate signed by a medical person. It should also be stated, whether the patient is afflicted with any complaint independent of insanity. It is also desirable, that some account should be sent, how long the patient has been disordered; whether any, or what sort of medical means have been used.[69]

Since the end of the eighteenth century, a medical certificate had been more or less obligatory for the confinement of the mad.[70] But inside the asylum, the doctor took pride of place, since it was he who transformed the space into a medical institution. Despite that, and this was the key point, the intervention of the doctor was not done on the basis of some skill or medical power as such that he alone possessed, justified by a body of objective knowledge. It was not as a scientist that homo medicus gained authority in the asylum, but as a wise man. If medical practitioneers were required, then it was not for the knowledge that they brought, but rather as a moral and juridical guarantee of good faith.[71] Any man of good conscience and unquestionable virtue, providing he had a long experience of the asylum, could just as well take his place.[72] For medical duties were only one part of the immense moral task to be accomplished inside the asylum, and which alone could guarantee the insane a cure:

> Must it not be an inviolable law in the administration of any public or private establishment for the alienated that maniacs should be given the maximum of liberty that their safety and that of others permits, so that repression should be proportional to any danger that their behaviour

might pose . . . and that any facts that might aid the doctor in his choice of treatment should be carefully recorded, and particular differences in behaviour or temperament studied precisely so that gentleness or firmness, conciliatory terms or an imposing, authoritative tone and inflexible severity should be used accordingly?[73]

According to Samuel Tuke, the first doctor who was assigned to the Retreat was to be commended on his 'indefatigable perseverance'; admittedly, he had no particular experience of mental illness when he arrived at the institution, but he 'entered on his office with the anxiety and ardour of a feeling mind, upon the exertion of whose skill, depended the dearest interests of many of his fellow-creatures'.[74] He tried the remedies that his good sense and the experience of his predecessors suggested. But he was quickly disappointed, although not because the results were bad or because the number of cures was minimal:

> [Although the proportion of cures, in the early part of the Institution, was respectable;] yet the medical means were so imperfectly connected with the progress of recovery, that he could not avoid suspecting them, to be rather concomitants than causes.

He then realised that the known medical methods of the time were of little use. A concern with humanity was of much greater importance, and he decided to forego any form of medicine that patients found disagreeable. But this was not to say that the doctor had only a minor role to play at the Retreat: the regular visits that he made to patients, the authority that he exercised in the house, which placed him above the guards, meant that 'The physician, from his office, sometimes possesses more influence over the patients' minds, than the other attendants.'[75]

It is generally believed that Tuke and Pinel opened up the asylum to medical knowledge. But it was not science that they introduced so much as a new character, who borrowed little more than the disguise offered by that knowledge, or at best used it as a justification. These powers, by their nature, were of an order that was moral and social. They had their roots in the status of the mad as minors, and in the alienation of their character rather than their minds. If the medical character could circumscribe madness, it was not because he knew it but because he mastered it; and what positivism came to consider as objectivity was nothing but the converse, the effects of this domination:

> It should be the great object of the superintendent to gain the confidence of the patient, and to awaken in him respect and obedience; but it will readily be seen, that such confidence, obedience and respect can only be procured by superiority of talents, discipline of temper, and dignity of manners. Imbecility, misconduct and empty consequence, although enforced with the most tyrannical severity, may excite fear, but this will always be mingled with contempt.
>
> In speaking of the management of insane persons, it is to be understood that the superintendent must first obtain an ascendancy over them. When this is once effected, he will be enabled, on future occasions, to direct and regulate their conduct, according as his better judgement may suggest. He should possess firmness, and when occasion may require, should exercise his authority in peremptory manner. He should never threaten, but execute; and when the patient has misbehaved, should confine him immediately.[76]

The doctor could only exert his absolute authority over the world of the asylum in so far as he was, from the beginning, Father and Judge, Family and Law, and for a long time his medical practice did little more than offer a commentary on the ancient rites of Order, Authority and Punishment. Pinel recognised very well that doctors cure when, outside modern therapeutics, they bring these immemorial figures into play.

He quotes the case of a young 17-year-old girl who had been brought up by her parents in 'a most indulgent fashion'; she had fallen into a 'gay, dreamy delirium, for no reason that could be determined'. In hospital she had been treated with the utmost gentleness, but she had always had a slightly 'haughty air' that could not be tolerated inside the asylum, and she only ever spoke 'of her parents with bitterness'. It was decided that she should be submitted to a regime of strict authority:

> In order to break her inflexible character, the keeper chose his moment at bath time, and expressed himself quite forcibly about certain unnatural people who dared go against their parents and question their authority. He warned her that she was to be treated henceforth with all the severity that she deserved, since she had clearly set herself against a cure and

was seeking to disguise the original cause of her malady with
insurmountable obstinacy.

Faced with the rigours of this new threat, the patient felt herself to be

deeply moved . . . and wound up admitting the error of her ways, and
made a frank confession that she had fallen into her unreasoned state as
a result of heartbreak, even naming the person who had been its object.

After that first confession, the cure became easy: 'A most favourable
change came over her . . . and she was quite relieved, and filled with
gratitude towards the keeper who had put a term to her suffering, restoring tranquillity and calm to her heart.' Every moment of this story could
be readily transposed into a psychoanalytical narrative, so true is it that the
medical character in Pinel's definition was to act not in accordance with
an objective definition of the sickness or a diagnosis based on a classification, but rather by using the sort of prestige that envelopes the secrets of
Family, Authority, Punishments and Love. By bringing these powers into
play, and taking on the mantle of the Father and Lord of Justice, the doctor,
by one of those sudden short-cuts that bypass medical competence,
became the almost magical practitioner of the cure, taking on the appearance of a worker of miracles. It was enough for him to look and talk for
secret faults to appear, insane presumptions to vanish, so that madness
would finally tow the line of reason. His presence and his language
possessed that power of disalienation, which at a stroke revealed faults and
restored the moral order.

It is a curious paradox to see medical practice enter the uncertain
domain of the quasi-miraculous just as the science of mental illness was
trying to assume a sense of positivity. On the one hand madness is placed
at a distance in an objective field where the threats of unreason disappear;
but at the same moment the madman and the doctor begin to form a
strange sort of couple, an undivided unity where complicity is forged
along very ancient lines. Life in the asylums, such as it was constituted by
Tuke and Pinel, enabled the growth of this subtle structure that was like
the root cell of madness – a structure forming a microcosm where all
the great, massive structures of bourgeois society and its values had their
own symbol: the relationship between Family and Children structured
around the theme of paternal authority; the relationship between Fault

and Punishment around the theme of immediate justice; and the links between Madness and Disorder around the theme of social and moral order. It was here that the origins of the doctor's power to cure were to be found, and it was in so far as the patient found himself, through so many ancient links, already alienated in the doctor, inside the doctor–patient couple, that the doctor had an almost miraculous ability to cure him.

There was nothing extraordinary about that power in the days of Pinel and Tuke, as it could be explained and demonstrated by the sole efficacy of moral conduct; it was no more mysterious than the power of an eighteenth-century physician when he diluted fluids or relaxed fibres. But very quickly, the meaning of this moral practice escaped doctors, as they began to wrap up their knowledge in the norms of positivism. By the early nineteenth century, psychiatrists no longer understood the nature of the power that they had inherited from the great reformers, whose effectiveness seemed so distant from the idea that they had of mental illness, and the medical practice of all other doctors.

This dense mystery that surrounds psychiatric practice, which is obscure even to those who used it, is largely responsible for the strange situation of the mad inside the medical world. First, because mental medicine, for the first time in the history of Western science, was to take on almost complete autonomy. Since the Greeks, it had only been one chapter in medicine, and as we saw above, physicians like Willis studied madness under the rubric 'diseases of the head'; after Pinel and Tuke, psychiatry was to become medicine of a particular style: even those most determined to find the origins of madness in organic causes or in hereditary dispositions would not escape this style. All the more so as this particular style – involving the use of continuously more obscure moral powers – was at the origin of a sort of bad conscience: the more they felt that their practice escaped the confines of positivism, the more rigorously they attempted to pursue it.

As positivism imposed itself on medicine, and above all on psychiatry, the practice became more obscure, the power of the psychiatrist more miraculous, and the doctor–patient couple sank ever deeper into a strange world. In the eyes of the patient, the doctor was a miracle worker, and the authority that he borrowed from order, morality and the family he now seemed to derive from himself. It is as a doctor that he is believed to have such powers, and whereas both Pinel and Tuke underlined quite clearly that their moral actions were not necessarily linked to any scientific competence, it came to be believed, above all by patients, that it was some esoteric, almost demoniacal secret in his knowledge that gave him the power to undo alienation. Patients increasingly accepted this abandonment in the hands of a doctor who was both divine and satanic, or in any case beyond human measure; the more they were alienated in the doctor, accepting entirely in advance all his prestige, and submitting immediately to a will that they felt to be magical and to a form of science which seemed endowed with prescience and divination, the more such patients became the ideal and perfect correlate of the powers that were projected onto the physician, pure objects with no resistance other than inertia, ripe to become precisely the hysterical woman in whom Charcot exalted the marvellous powers of the doctor. Anyone who wants to pursue an analysis of the deep structures of objectivity in the knowledge and the psychiatric practice of the nineteenth century, from Pinel to Freud,[77] needs to show that, from the very beginning, objectivity was a reification of a magical type, which could only be accomplished with the complicity of the patients themselves, starting out from a transparently clear moral framework which was slowly forgotten as positivism imposed its myth of scientific objectivity. The origins and the meaning of the practice were forgotten, but its use persisted and it was always present. What we call psychiatric practice is a certain moral tactic contemporaneous with the late eighteenth century, which is preserved in the rituals of life in asylums, covered over by the myths of positivism.

But if doctors soon became miracle workers in the eyes of patients, to their own eyes they could never be anything other than positivist physicians. A status still had to be found for this dark power whose origins had disappeared, where the complicity of the patient could not be deciphered, as doctors refused to recognise the ancient powers that lent it its strength. As there was nothing in positive knowledge that could justify such a transfer of will, or these operations that seemed to take place at a distance, the moment would soon come when madness itself was to be held responsible for these anomalies. Cures without any solid basis, yet whose reality was undeniable, were quickly transformed into real cures of false illnesses. Madness was not what one thought, nor what it claimed to be; it was infinitely less than itself, a blend of persuasion and mystification. We can see here the genesis of Babinski's pithiatism.[78] And by a strange return, thoughts went back nearly two centuries to the time when the distinctions between madness, false madness and simulated madness were far from clear, and all that held them together was the knowledge that they were all linked to guilt in some manner. Going back further still, medical thought finally operated a process of assimilation that all Western medicine had refused since the Greeks: the assimilation of madness and madness, i.e. of the medical and the critical concepts of madness. During the late nineteenth century, in the thought of Babinski's contemporaries, we find the first daring formulation of the idea that medical thought had so long refused – that madness, after all, was perhaps just madness.

Thus, while the mentally ill person is wholly alienated in the real person of his doctor, the doctor dissipates the reality of mental illness in the critical concept of madness. So much so that beyond the empty forms of positivist thought, all that remains is a single concrete reality: the doctor–patient couple, in which all alienations are summed up, formed and resolved. It is in that respect that all the psychiatry of the nineteenth century really does converge on Freud, who was the first to accept the seriousness of the reality of the doctor–patient couple, and who consented never to avert his gaze and his research from this link, and who sought not to mask it in a psychiatric theory merely attempting to keep in harmony with the rest of medical knowledge: he was the first to have followed the rigour of these consequences very closely. Freud demystified all the other asylum structures: he abolished silence and the gaze, and removed the recognition of madness by itself in the mirror of its own spectacle, and he silenced the instances of condemnation. But, on the other hand, he exploited the structure that enveloped the medical character: he amplified his virtues as worker of miracles, preparing an almost divine status for his omnipotence. He brought back to him, and to his simple presence, hidden behind the patient and above him, in an absence that was also a total presence, all the powers that had been shared out in the collective existence of the asylum; he made him the absolute Gaze, the pure, indefinitely held Silence, the Judge who punishes and rewards in a judgement that does not even condescend to language; and he made him the mirror in which madness, in an almost immobile movement, falls in and out of love with itself.

Freud made sure that all the structures integrated by Pinel and Tuke into confinement were appropriated by the doctor. He freed the patient from that asylum existence to which his 'liberators' had condemned him, but he failed to spare him the essential components of that existence. He concentrated its powers, stretched them to the limit, and placed them in the hands of the doctor. He created the psychoanalytic situation, where, in the short circuit of a stroke of genius, alienation became disalienating because, in the doctor, it became subject.

The doctor, as an alienating figure, remains the key to psychoanalysis. Perhaps because it has never suppressed that ultimate structure, but included all the others in it instead, psychoanalysis cannot and will never be able to hear the voices of unreason nor decipher on their own terms the signs of the insane. Psychoanalysis can untangle some forms of madness, but it is a perpetual stranger to the sovereign work of unreason. It cannot liberate or transcribe, and *a fortiori* explain, what is essential in that work.

Since the late eighteenth century, the life of unreason has only manifested itself in the incendiary work of a small number of writers such as Hölderlin, Nerval, Nietzsche and Artaud – works that could never be reduced to these alienations that cure, resisting, through their own strength, that gigantic moral imprisonment that became known, ironically perhaps, as Pinel and Tuke's liberation of the mad.

V

THE ANTHROPOLOGICAL CIRCLE

There is no question here of concluding. The work of Pinel and Tuke is not a destination. All that becomes manifest there – a sudden new figure – is a restructuring, whose origins were hidden in an unbalance inherent to the classical experience of madness.

The liberty of the mad, that liberty which Pinel, like Tuke, thought he had given to the mad, had long belonged to the domain of their existence. True, it was never given, nor offered, in any positive gesture. But it quietly wove its way round certain practices and concepts – a truth that was glimpsed, a faltering request, on the margins of what was said, thought and done about the mad, a stubborn presence that never allowed itself to be entirely grasped.

And yet was it not solidly implied in the very notion of madness, if the will had been to push it to its limits? Was it not linked, and necessarily so, to that great structure that stretched from the excesses of a passion always complicitous with itself to the rigorous logic of delirium? In that affirmation which, transforming the images of dreams into the non-being of error, *made* madness, how could it be denied that there was an element of liberty? Madness, at bottom, was only possible in so far as it had that latitude around it, the leeway that allowed the subject to speak the language of his own madness, and constitute himself as mad. Sauvages described this fundamental liberty of the madman in the naivety of a marvellously fecund tautology: 'how little we care to seek out the truth and cultivate our judgement'.[1]

And what of the liberty that confinement denounced in the act of suppressing it? Liberating individuals from the infinite tasks and consequences of their responsibility, it certainly did not place them in a neutralised environment where everything was flattened out in the monotony of a single determinism. It is true that people were often confined so that they might escape judgement, but they were confined to a world where all was a matter of evil and punishment, libertinage and immorality, penitence and correction. A whole world where, beneath those shadows, liberty is hidden.

Doctors first came across this freedom when they began to engage with the insane for the first time, in the mixed world of body images and organic myths, where they discovered, engaged in so many mechanisms, the dull, insistent presence of guilt: here was passion, disorder, laziness, the complacent life of cities, over-eager reading, the complicity of the imagination, sensibility overly curious for excitement and excessive concerns for the self – so many dangerous games for liberty, where reason ventures at its peril into madness.

This was an obstinate but precarious form of liberty. It always remained on the horizon of madness, but vanished as soon as one attempted to pin it down. It was only present and possible in the form of an imminent abolition. Glimpsed in the extreme regions where madness could speak for itself, when fixed by the gaze it only ever reappeared as engaged, constrained and reduced. The liberty of the madman is only ever in that instant, that imperceptible distance that makes a man free to abandon his liberty and chain himself to his madness: it is there only in that virtual point of choice, where we elect to 'put ourselves in the impossibility of using our freedom and correcting our mistakes'.[2] Thereafter it becomes no more than a mechanism of the body, a sequence of fantasies, the necessities of delirium. Saint Vincent de Paul, who darkly acknowledged that freedom in the very gesture of confinement, was still careful to make a distinction between responsible libertines, 'children of pain . . . the opprobrium and ruin of their houses', and the mad, who were 'properly deserving of compassion . . . not being the masters of their will, and having neither judgement nor liberty'.[3] The freedom which made classical madness possible was suffocated inside this madness itself, and collapses in that which manifested its contradictions most cruelly.

This must be the paradox of that constitutive freedom: the means through which the mad become mad are also the means through which, madness having not yet come into being, the mad can communicate with non-madness. From the outset, the madman escapes himself and his madman's truth, approaching, in a region that is neither truth nor innocence, the risk of wrongdoing, crime, or comedy. The freedom that causes the mad, in this originary and obscure moment of departure and separation which is so difficult to pin down and identify, to renounce the truth, nevertheless prevents them from ever becoming prisoners of their own truth. A madman is only mad to the extent that his madness is never exhausted in his own truth as a madman. For that reason, in the classical experience, madness can at the same time be *slightly* criminal, *slightly* faked, *slightly* immoral and *slightly* reasonable too. This is not a confusion of thought, or a lesser degree of elaboration, but only the logical effect of a very coherent structure: madness is only possible as a result of a very distant but very necessary moment where it splits from itself in the free space of its non-truth, constituting itself by that very process as truth.

This is exactly where the operations of Pinel and Tuke fit into the classical experience. That liberty, a constant horizon for the concepts and practices at stake, a demand that disguised its own being and abolished itself as though of its own accord, that ambiguous liberty that was at the heart of the madman's existence, was now actually demanded in facts themselves as the framework of his real life and the element necessary for the appearance of his truth as a madman. The effort was made to ensnare it in an objective structure. But just when people believed they could grasp it, affirm it and proclaim its value, all that was actually harvested was the irony of contradictions:

- the liberty of the madman was given a free reign, but in a space that was more enclosed and more rigid, less free than the always slightly indecisive space of confinement;
- the madman was freed from his association with crime and evil, only to be locked into the rigorous mechanisms of a determinism. He was only completely innocent in the absolute of a non-freedom;
- the chains that hindered the exercise of his free will were removed, but

only so that he could be stripped of that will itself, which was transferred to and alienated in the doctor's will.

The madman was henceforth completely free, and completely excluded from freedom. Previously he was free in that tenuous instant in which he began to abandon his liberty; now he was free in the open space where his liberty had already been lost.

What the late eighteenth century witnessed was not a *liberation* of the mad but an *objectification of the concept of their liberty*. That objectification had three consequences.

First of all, it meant that liberty now became the key issue where madness was concerned. Not the sort of liberty that might be glimpsed on the horizon of the possible, but a freedom that was to be hunted down in things and through mechanisms. In thinking on madness, and even in the medical analyses that were carried out, it would no longer be a question of error and non-being but of freedom in its real determinations: desire and will, determinism and responsibility, automatisms and spontaneity. From Esquirol to Janet, as from Reil to Freud or from Tuke to Jackson, the madness of the nineteenth century would tirelessly recount the winding journeys of freedom. The night of the modern madman was no longer that oneiric night ablaze with the false truths of images – it was a night of impossible desires and the savagery of a will, less free than any other to be found in nature.

On the level of facts and observations, this objective freedom found itself exactly divided between a determinism that denied it completely and specific guilt that exalted it. The ambiguity of classical thought about the relationship between fault and madness was now to come apart, and the psychiatric thought of the nineteenth century was both to search for a total determinism and to attempt to pin down the point at which culpability could enter the process. Discussions about criminal forms of madness, the prestige of general paralysis, the great theme of degeneracy and the criticism of hysterical phenomena, the themes that drove medical research from Esquirol to Freud, all reflected these twin concerns. The mad of the nineteenth century were to be both subject to determinism and guilty: their non-freedom was more infused with guilt than the freedom in which the mad of the classical age were able to escape from themselves.

Once free, the mad were face to face with themselves, i.e. they could no longer escape their own truth; they were thrown into it, and it confiscated them entirely. Classical freedom had situated the madman in relation to his own madness, in an ambiguous, unstable relation that was always coming apart, but which prevented the madman from making one identical, single thing of his madness. The freedom that Pinel and Tuke imposed on the mad locked them into a certain truth about madness that they could only passively escape if they were liberated from their madness. From that point on madness no longer indicated a certain relation between men and the truth – a relation which, silently at least, always implied freedom; what it indicated instead was a relationship between man and his own truth. In madness, men fell into their own truth, which was a manner of being entirely their own truth, but also of losing it. Madness was no longer to speak of non-being, but of the being of man, of the content of what he is, and the forgetting of that content. While previously he was a Stranger to Being – a man of nothingness, of illusion, *Fatuus* (the void of non-being and the paradoxical manifestation of that void) – now he was trapped in his own truth and thus exiled from it. A Stranger from himself, *Alienated*.

Madness now spoke an anthropological language: denoting, in an equivocal process that gave it its worrying power for the modern world, the truth of man and the loss of that truth, and consequently, the truth of this truth.

An uncompromising language, rich in promise and ironic in its reductiveness. The language of madness rediscovered for the first time since the Renaissance. Let's listen to its first utterances.

*

Classical madness belonged to the realms of silence. This language that sang its own praises had long been gagged. While it is true that numerous texts from the seventeenth and eighteenth centuries talked about madness, it was merely cited as an example, as a medical species, or because it illustrated the dull truth of error; madness was attacked at an angle, in its negative dimension, because it was an *a contrario* proof of what, in its positive nature, reason was. Its meaning could only appear to doctors and philosophers, i.e. to those who were capable of understanding its deep nature, who could master it in its non-being and move beyond it towards the truth. In itself, it was a silent thing: there was no place in the classical age for a literature of madness, in that there was no autonomous language for madness, and no possibility that it might express itself in a language that spoke its truth. The secret language of delirium was recognised, and these were true discourses concerning it. But it had no power, no original right to operate of its own accord a synthesis of its language and its truth. Its truth could only ever be enveloped in a discourse to which it remained a stranger. After all, 'such people are insane' . . . Descartes, in his movement towards truth, made impossible the lyricism of unreason.

Le Neveu de Rameau and the whole literary fashion that followed it indicated a reappearance of madness in the domain of language, a language where madness was permitted to speak in the first person, uttering in the midst of the empty verbiage and the insane grammar of its paradoxes something that bore an essential relation to the truth. That relationship now began to unfold and clarify and offer itself in its whole discursive development. What madness says of itself was, for the thought and the poetry of the early nineteenth century, what dreams say in the disorder of their images; a truth of man, very archaic and very near, very silent and very threatening, a truth that underlies all truth, the truth closest to the birth of subjectivity, and the most widely spread at the very level of things; a truth that is the deep retreat of man's individuality, and the inchoate form of the cosmos:

> That which dreams is the Spirit during the instant at which it descends into Matter, and Matter the instant that it rises up to the level of the Spirit . . . Dreams are the revelation of man's very essence, the most peculiar and intimate process that life has to offer.[4]

Thus, in the discourse common to delirium and dreams, the possibility of a lyricism of desire and the possibility of a poetry of the world are bound together; as madness and dreams are both the moment of extreme subjectivity and the moment of ironic objectivity, there is no contradiction; the poetry of the heart, in the final, exasperated solitude of its lyricism, through an immediate reversal, finds itself to be the original song of things; and the world, so long silent in the face of the tumults of the heart, finds its voice once more: 'I question the stars and they fall silent; I address the day and the night but they do not reply. From the depths of myself, when I interrogate myself, there come strange, inexplicable dreams.'[5]

What is specific to the language of madness in Romantic poetry is the language of the ultimate end, and that of the absolute beginning; the end

of man, who sinks into the night, and the discovery, at the end of the
night, of a light which is that of things as they first come into being:

> It is an underground cavern that slowly becomes illuminated, where the
> pale, gravely immobile figures who live in this limbo gradually begin to
> emerge from the shadows and night. Then the picture takes shape, and a
> new clarity becomes apparent.[6]

Madness speaks the language of the great return: not the epic return from
long odysseys, in the undefined path traced out by the myriad roads of the
real, but a lyrical return in one lightning instant, which matures at
a stroke the tempest of completeness, illuminating and pacifying it in a
rediscovered origin. 'The thirteenth one returns, and it's still the first.'[7]
Such was the power of madness, announcing man's senseless secret – that
the lowest point of his fall is also his first morning, and that his evening
finishes in his first light, and that in him the end is a beginning.

After the long silence of the classical age, madness therefore found its
voice once more. But this was a language pregnant with a new significance: the old tragic discourses of the Renaissance, which had spoken of a
tear in the fabric of the world, the end of time, and man devoured by his
own animality, were forgotten. This language of madness was reborn, but
as a lyrical explosion: the discovery that in man, the interior was also the
exterior, that the extremity of subjectivity blended into the immediate
fascination of the object, and that any ending was the promise of an
obstinate return. A language in which what transpired were no longer the
invisible figures of the world, but the secret truths of man.[8]

What lyricism said, the stubbornness of discursive thought also taught;
and what was known about the mad (independently of all the possible
advancements of learning in the objective content of scientific knowledge) took on a significance that was quite new. The gaze that was cast on
the madman – which was also the concrete experience on the basis of
which medical or philosophical experience was to be elaborated – could
no longer be the same. At the time of the public visits to Bicêtre and
Bethlem hospital, when looking at the mad, men measured from the
outside the whole distance that separated the truth of man from his
animality. Now the mad were examined with both more neutrality and
more passion. More neutrality, as it was in them that the deep truths of
man were to be discovered, sleeping forms in which what they are come

into being. And more passion too, as to recognise the mad was to recognise oneself, feel the same forces, hear the same voices and see the same strange lights rise up within. This gaze, which could promise itself the spectacle of a naked truth of man, at last (this is what Cabanis had in mind when talking about the ideal asylum), could no longer avoid contemplating an immodesty that was its own. This gaze could no longer see without seeing itself. And the mad thereby found their power of attraction and fascination increased twofold, as they bore more truth than their own truths. 'I believe,' said Cyprien, the protagonist of a Hoffmann novel,

> I firmly believe that through abnormal phenomena, Nature allows us to peer into the most fearsome abysses, and in fact at the very heart of the terror that has often overcome me through this strange commerce with the mad, intuitions and images have often risen up in my spirit, lending it an extraordinary new life, vigour and energy.[9]

In a single movement, the madman is given both as an object of knowledge offered in his most exterior determinations, and as a theme of recognition, investing in return all those who apprehend him with all the insidious familiarities of their common truth.

But while this recognition may have been welcome in lyrical experience, it could find no place in reflective thought. It protected itself, affirming with growing insistence that the mad were nothing but objects, medical things. Refracted in such fashion on the surface of objectivity, the immediate content of this recognition was dispersed in a multitude of antinomies. But we should not be deceived: beneath the speculative seriousness, what was really at stake was the relationship between man and the mad, and these faces, so long unfamiliar, now took on the virtues of a mirror.

1   Madness unveiled the elementary truth about man: it reduced him to his primitive desires, to his simple mechanisms, to the most pressing determinations of his body. Madness was a sort of chronological and social, psychological and organic childhood of man. 'So many analogies between the art of directing the alienated and that of bringing up young people!' remarked Pinel.[10]

– But the madman unveiled the terminal truth of man: he showed how far he could be pushed by the passions, life in society and everything that distanced him from a primitive nature that knew no madness. Madness was always linked to society and its discontent. 'According to reports from travellers, savages are not subject to disorders of the intellectual functions.'[11] Madness began when the world began to age; and every face that madness took over the course of time spoke of the shape and truth of that corruption.

2   Madness operated in man a sort of atemporal caesura, sectioning not time but space. It neither advanced nor retreated in the course of human liberty, but showed an interruption, a sinking within the determinism of the body. It was the triumph of the organic, the sole truth about man that could be objectified and scientifically perceived. Madness was a 'disturbance of the cerebral functions . . . the cerebral parts are the seat of madness, as the lungs are the seat of dyspnoea, and the stomach is the seat of dyspepsia'.[12]

– But madness differs from diseases of the body in that it manifests a truth not found in the latter: it reveals an inner world of bad instincts, perversity, suffering and violence, which until then had lain sleeping. It reveals a depth that gives the freedom of man its full meaning, and this depth revealed by madness is wickedness in its wild state. 'Evil is always latent in the heart, because the heart as immediate is natural and selfish. It is the evil genius of man that gains the upper hand in insanity.'[13] Heinroth said something similar when he stated that madness was *das Böse überhaupt* – 'mostly evil'.

3   The innocence of the mad was guaranteed by the intensity and the strength of this psychological content. Imprisoned by the strength of his passions, carried away by the vividness of desires and images, the madman was therefore beyond responsibility, and his irresponsibility was a matter for medical appreciation, in that it resulted from an objective determinism. The madness of an action was to be gauged by the number of reasons that had determined it.

– But the madness of an action was precisely determined by the fact that no reason could ever exhaust it. The truth of madness was in an automatism that had no logic behind it, and the more an action was empty of reason, the greater the chances that it was solely the result of a determinism of madness, the truth of madness being in man the truth of all that was without reason, of all that resulted, as Pinel said, from 'an unreflected determination, devoid of any concern for self-interest and any motivation'.

4   As man discovered his truth in madness, it was from that truth and from the depths of that madness that a cure was possible. The non-reason of madness contains the reason for a return, and if there was still a secret in the unfortunate objectivity in which the madman was lost, that secret was the one that made a cure possible. Just as sickness was never a total loss of health, so madness was 'not an abstract loss of reason', but 'a contradiction in the reason that remained', and consequently, 'humane treatment, no less benevolent than reasonable (the services of Pinel to this end deserve the highest acknowledgement), presupposes the patient's rationality, and in that assumption has the sound basis for dealing with him on this side'.[14]

– But the human truth that madness reveals is the immediate contradiction of the moral and social truth of man. The initial moment of any treatment is thus the repression of that inadmissible truth, the abolition of the evil that reigns there, and the forgetting of this violence and these desires. The cure for madness is in the reason of the other – the madman's reason being only the truth of his madness: 'Let your reason be the rule for their conduct. One string alone still resonates inside them, which is the string of pain. Have the courage to pluck it'.[15] Man will thus not speak the truth of his truth other than in the cure that will lead him from his alienated truth to the truth of man: 'By these soft, conciliatory means, even the most violent and fearsome alienated man has become most docile, and most worthy of interest for his touching sensitivity.'[16]

Tirelessly repeated, these antinomies accompany all nineteenth-century thinking on madness. In the immediate totality of poetic experience, and in the lyrical recognition of madness, they were already there, in the undivided form of a duality reconciled with itself as soon as it was given. They were indicated, in the brief happiness of a language not yet shared, as a knot linking the world and desire, sense and nonsense, the night of completion and the primitive dawn. But for reflective thought on the other hand, these antinomies only offer themselves in the extremities of dissociation; there they take on measure and distance, to be experienced in the slowness of the language of contradictions. All that was ambiguous in the *fundamental* and *constitutive experience* of madness was soon lost in a network of *theoretical conflicts* about the *interpretation* of the phenomena of madness.

A conflict between a historical, sociological and relativist view of madness (Esquirol and Michéa), and an analysis of a structural type that looked at mental illness as involution, degeneracy and a progressive slide to the vanishing point of human nature (Morel); a conflict between a spiritualist theory that defined madness as an alteration in the mind's relation to itself (Langerman and Heinroth), and materialist efforts to localise madness in a differentiated organic space (Spurzheim and Broussais); a conflict between the requirement for a medical judgement that measured the degree of irresponsibility of the mad against the degree of determinism of the mechanisms at work within them, and the immediate appreciation of the insane character of their behaviour (the polemic between Elias Régnault and Marc); and a conflict between the humanitarian conception of therapeutics witnessed in the methods used by Esquirol and the infamous 'moral treatment' that used confinement as the major means of submission and repression (Guislain and Leuret).

*

We shall reserve the detailed exploration of these antinomies for another study, as that could only be done in a meticulous inventory of the totality of the nineteenth-century experience of madness, i.e. in the totality of its scientifically explicated forms and its silent aspects. Such an analysis would show with no difficulty that this system of contradictions conceals a deeper coherence, the coherence of an anthropological thought that ran permanently underneath the diversity of scientific formulations. It would show that it was the constitutive but historically mobile bedrock that made possible the developments of concepts from Esquirol and Broussais to Janet, Bleuler and Freud. And this anthropological structure had three terms – man, his madness and his truth – which replaced the binary structure of classical unreason (truth and error, world and fantasy, being and non-being, Day and Night).

For the moment, our intention is simply to maintain the structure against the still ill-differentiated horizon where it appears, to grasp it in some examples of diseases that reveal what the experience of madness in the early part of the nineteenth century might have been. It is easy to understand the extraordinary prestige of general paralysis, and the value as a model that it took on for the nineteenth century and the general extension that it was given for a general comprehension of psycho-pathological symptoms: guilt in the form of a sexual fault was clearly designated, and the traces that it left prevented all escape from accusation, as it was inscribed inside the organism itself. In addition to that, the dark power of attraction of the fault itself, and the familiar ramifications that stretched into the soul of those who diagnosed the condition meant that this knowledge implied the worrying ambiguity of recognition; deep in men's hearts, before all contamination, the blame was shared between patients and their families, between the patient and his entourage, and between patients and their doctors. The great complicity between the sexes meant that the disease was strangely close, and lent it the old lyricism of guilt and fear. But at the same time, the threats within this subterranean communication between the mad and those who recognised, judged and condemned them diminished, as the illness became more rigorously objectified, circumscribed inside the space of a body and invested in a purely organic process. Medicine thereby put an end to that lyrical recognition, hiding its moral accusations behind the objectivity of observation. Seeing this evil, this fault, this age-old complicity between men as clearly situated in exterior space, reduced to the silence of things, and punished only in others gave knowledge the inexhaustible satisfaction of being found innocent once justice had been done, and it was protected from its own accusations by serene, distant observation. In the nineteenth century, general paralysis was 'the right madness', in the same way that we speak of 'the right shape'. The great structure that commanded all perceptions of madness was perfectly represented in the analysis of the psychiatric symptoms of nervous syphilis.[17] Culpability, its condemnation and its recognition, acknowledged and hidden in equal parts in an organic objectivity: this was the most felicitous expression of everything that the nineteenth century understood and wanted to understand about madness. Everything that was 'philistine' in its attitude towards mental illness can be found there perfectly represented, and until Freud or thereabouts it was in the name of 'general paralysis' that this philistine medical expression was to defend itself against any other form of access to the truth of madness.

The scientific discovery of general paralysis was not prepared by that anthropology that had come into being some twenty years earlier, but the very precise origin of the intense significance that it took and the fascination that it exerted for more than half a century are both to be found there.

But general paralysis had still another importance as well. Guilt, and all that might be hidden and interior within it, immediately found its punishment and its objective side in the organism. This theme was very important for the psychiatry of the nineteenth century: madness locked men into their objectivity. Throughout the classical period, the transcendence of delirium granted madness, regardless of how manifest it was, a sort of interiority that never spread to the outside, and which locked it into an irreducible relationship to itself. Now all madness, and madness in its entirety, were to have an external equivalent; or rather, the very essence of madness was to turn men into objects, chasing them to the outside of themselves, ultimately reducing them to the level of a nature pure and simple, to the level of things. The fact that madness could be that, an objectivity with no relation to a central, hidden, delirious activity, was so opposed to the spirit of the eighteenth century that the idea of 'madness without delirium' or 'moral madness' was something of a conceptual scandal.

Pinel had observed several alienated women at the Salpêtrière who 'at no point showed any damage to their understanding, and who were dominated by a sort of instinct of frenzy, as though the affective faculties alone had been damaged'.[18] Among such 'partial madnesses', Esquirol had a particular place for those 'whose character was not an alteration in the intelligence', and in which there was scarcely anything to observe other than 'a disorder in their actions'.[19] According to Dubuisson, people suffering from this sort of madness:

> judge, reason and behave themselves well, but are carried away by the most trivial subject, often for no occasional cause and only by an irresistible urge, and by a sort of perversion of the moral affections, leading to maniacal tantrums, acts inspired by violence, and explosions of fury.[20]

This is the notion that English authors, after Prichard in 1835, termed 'moral insanity'. The name under which this notion was to achieve its definitive success already signals the strange ambiguity of its structure quite clearly: on the one hand, it indicates a form of madness none of whose signs appear in the sphere of reason, and in that sense is entirely hidden, a form of madness that makes the absence of all unreason almost invisible, a transparent, colourless form of madness that subtly circulates inside the soul of the madman, interiority inside interiority – 'they do not seem mad to superficial observers, and for that reason are all the more harmful and dangerous'[21] – but on the other hand, this secret madness only exists on account of its explosive objective existence, demonstrated in violence, wild gestures and occasionally murderous acts. At bottom it only exists in the imperceptible virtuality of a free fall towards the most visible and worst of objectivities, towards the mechanical concatenation of irresponsible gestures: it is the always internal possibility of being entirely projected onto the surface of the self, and of no longer existing, at least for a certain lapse of time, other than in a total absence of interiority.

Like general paralysis, 'moral insanity' has an exemplary value. Its longevity in the course of the nineteenth century, and the obstinate return of the same discussions around similar themes, can be explained by its proximity to the essential structures of madness. More than any other mental illness, it manifested that curious ambiguity that made madness an element of interiority in the form of an exteriority. In that sense, it was like a model for all possible psychology: it showed, at a perceptible level, bodies, modes of behaviour, mechanisms and objects, the inaccessible moment of subjectivity, and just as that subjective moment could only have a concrete existence for knowledge in objectivity, that objectivity could only be acceptable and have meaning through what it expressed of the subject. The suddenness, properly insane, of the switch from the subjective to the objective in moral insanity encouraged everything that psychology could possible desire, far exceeding its promises. It formed a sort of spontaneous psychologisation of man. And that in itself revealed one of the obscure truths that dominated all nineteenth-century thinking about man: the essential moment of objectification, in man, is nothing less than the passage into madness. Madness is the purest, the principal and the primary form of the movement through which the truth of man is transferred to the side of the object and becomes accessible to scientific perception. Man only becomes *nature* for himself to the extent that he is capable of *madness*. Madness, like the spontaneous passage into objectivity, is a constitutive moment in man's becoming an object.

Here we find ourselves at the opposite pole to the classical experience. Madness, which was nothing but an instantaneous contact between the non-being of error and the nothingness of the image, always maintained a dimension that enabled it to elude an objective grasp; and when the attempt was made to seize it in its most intimate structure, hunting it down in the innermost recesses of its essence, the only language found to formulate it was the language of reason deployed in the impeccable logic of delirium; and that which made it accessible ensured that it also eluded any firm grasp as madness. Now, by contrast, it was through madness that man, even in his reason, could become a concrete truth and an object for his own gaze. The path from *man* to the *true man* passed through the *madman*. The exact geography of this path was never clearly mapped out by the thought of the nineteenth century, but it was constantly travelled, from Cabanis to Ribot and Janet. The paradox of 'positive' psychology in the nineteenth century was to have only been possible from the moment of negativity: the psychology of the personality through an analysis of its splitting, the psychology of memory by amnesia, of language by aphasia, of intelligence by mental deficiency. The truth of man was only spoken during the moment of its disappearance: it only showed itself when it had already become something other than itself.

A third notion that also appeared in the early nineteenth century had the origins of its importance here. The idea of a form of madness localised in one point and only developing its delirium around a single subject was already present in the classical analysis of melancholy, and for medicine was a specific form of delirium rather than a contradiction.[22] The notion of *monomania* by contrast was entirely constructed around the scandal represented by an individual who was mad in respect of one particular point but reasonable regarding everything else. The scandal was multiplied by the crimes that monomaniacs carried out, and the problem of the responsibility that was to be imputed to them. A man, who seemed normal in all other aspects of his being, suddenly committed a crime of extraordinary savagery, and no cause or reason could be found to explain his action as no profit, interest or passion was involved; and once the act had been committed, the criminal returned to normal.[23] Could this be said to be the action of a madman? Was the complete absence of any visible form of determinism, the total absence of *reasons*, enough to infer *non-reason* here? Irresponsibility was identified with the impossibility of making use of one's will, and therefore with a determinism. But as the act was determined by nothing at all, it could not indicate irresponsibility. Inversely, could it be normal that an action could be accomplished for no reason, beyond any possible motivation or usefulness for a particular interest, with nothing that could provide the sort of motive that was indispensable for passion? An action that had no roots in any determinism was insane.

These questions, which came to the fore in the great criminal trials of the early part of the nineteenth century, and which had a lasting effect on the juridical and medical consciousness of the age, touch perhaps the very heart of the experience of madness that was beginning to come into being.[24] The case-law of earlier times had only seen crises and intervals, i.e. chronological successions and phases of responsibility inside a given illness. The problem here became more complicated: could there be such a thing as a chronic disease which only manifested itself in a single gesture – or could it be the case that a man could become suddenly other, losing the liberty by which he was defined, becoming momentarily alienated from himself? Esquirol attempted to define the nature of this invisible disease that would exonerate the perpetrator of a monstrous crime, grouping together the symptoms: the subject always acted without an accomplice, and with no motive, his crime did not necessarily concern a person that he already knew, and once it had been carried out, 'everything was over for him, the goal was attained; after the murder he is calm, and no longer thinks of hiding'.[25] Such was 'homicidal monomania'. But these symptoms were only signs of madness in that they indicated the isolated nature of the gesture, and its solitary improbability; there was a kind of madness that was reason in all things except in the one thing that was to be explained by it.[26] But if this sickness and this sudden alterity were not accepted, if the subject was to be considered to be responsible, then that was because there was a continuity between him and his gesture, a whole world of dark reasons that provided its foundation, explaining it and ultimately removing any blame.

In short, either the subject was to be found guilty, in which case he had to be the same in his act and outside of it, so that an unbroken circuit of determinism linked him to his crime (but this supposed that he was not free, and was thus other than himself when he acted); or he was to be found innocent, in which case the crime had to be an exterior element, irreducible to the subject. What was then assumed was an originary alienation that constituted a sufficient determination, and therefore a continuity, and therefore an identity between the subject and himself.[27]

The madman therefore found himself in the eternally recommenced dialectic of the *Same* and the *Other*. Whereas previously, in the classical experience, he was identified instantly, without speech, by the simple fact of his presence, in the visible (luminous and nocturnal) division between being and non-being, he was from now on the bearer of a language, wrapped in a language that was never exhausted and constantly started up again, reflected in a game of contrasts and opposites, where man appeared in his madness as being other than himself; but in that alterity, he revealed the truth that he was himself, and endlessly so, in the verbose movement of *alienation*. The madman was no longer the *insane* person who had occupied the divided space of classical unreason: he was *alienated*, in the modern form of the disease. In this madness, man was no longer considered in a sort of absolute retreat from truth; he was there its truth and the opposite of that truth — he was himself and something other than himself. He was caught in the objectivity of truth, but was true subjectivity; he was trapped in that which caused him to lose his way, but he only gave away what he wanted to reveal; he was innocent because he was not what he was, and guilty of being what he was not.

The great critical division of unreason was now replaced by the proximity, always lost and always rediscovered, of man and his truth.

*

General paralysis, moral insanity and monomania did not of course cover the whole field of psychiatric experience in the first half of the nineteenth century, but they took over a major part of it.[28]

Their extension does not simply signal a reorganisation of the nosographical space, but, underlying the medical concepts, the presence and the workings of a new structure of experience. The institutional form that Pinel and Tuke designed, the constitution around the mad of a containing asylum space where they were to admit their guilt and rid themselves of it, allowing the truth of their sickness to appear and then suppressing it, rediscovering their freedom by alienating it in the will of doctors — all this now became an *a priori* of medical perception. Throughout the nineteenth century, the mad would only be known and recognised against the backdrop of an implicit anthropology that spoke of the same guilt, the same truth, and the same alienation.

But it was also necessary that the mad, now situated in the problematics of the truth of man, dragged in the true man and linked him to this new fate. If madness in the modern world has a meaning other than being a night in the face of the light of truth, if, in the depths of the language that it speaks, what is at stake is the truth of man, and of a truth that precedes it, founds it and has the power to destroy it, then that truth is only available to man in the disaster of madness, and it evaporates at the first sign of any reconciliation. It is only in the night of madness that light is possible, a light that disappears when the shadow that it forces to flee begins to vanish. Man and madmen are perhaps more closely linked in the modern world than they could ever have been in the powerful animal metamorphoses illuminated by the burning mills of Bosch: they are joined by the impalpable link of a reciprocal and incompatible truth; they murmur to each other this truth of their essence, which evaporates from having been said by one to the other. Each light is extinguished by the light that it has brought into being, and is thereby returned to the light that it tore, yet which had summoned it, and which it had so cruelly exposed. Today, the only truth that men possess is the enigma of the mad that they both are and are not; each madman both does and does not carry within him this truth about man, which he bares in the fall of his humanity.

The asylum scrupulously constructed by Pinel served no purpose, and has not protected the contemporary world from the great rise of madness. Or rather it did serve, and it served well. If it freed the madman from the inhumanity of his chains, it also chained the mad to man and his truth. From that day on, men had access to themselves as true beings; but true being was only given to them in the form of alienation.

In our naivety, we perhaps imagined that we had described a psychological type, the madman, across 150 years of his history. But we are forced to admit that in writing the history of the mad, what we have done – not on the level of a chronology of discoveries, or a history of ideas, but by following the links in the chain of the fundamental structures of experience – is to write the history of the things that made possible the very appearance of a psychology. And by that we understand a cultural fact peculiar to the Western world since the nineteenth century: this massive postulate defined by modern man, but which also defines him in return – *human beings are not characterised by a certain relationship to truth; but they contain, as rightly belonging to them, a truth that is simultaneously offered and hidden from view.*

Here we should allow language to follow its inclination: *homo psychologicus* (psychological man) is descended from *homo mente captus* (insane man).

As the only language it can speak is that of alienation, psychology is therefore only possible in the criticism of man or the criticism of itself. It is always, by its very nature, at a crossroads: one path explores man's negativity to the furthest point, where love and death, day and night, the atemporal repetition of things and the haste of the passing seasons all belong to each other without division – and end up philosophising with a hammer. The other means becoming involved in the game of incessant resumptions, adjustments between the subject and the object, between within and without, between lived experience and knowledge.

Given its origins, it was quite necessary that psychology should be more of the latter, while refusing to admit it. It is an inexorable part of the dialectics of modern man and his tussle with his truth, which is tanta-mount to admitting that it will never exhaust its being on the level of true knowledge.

Faced with these wordy dialectical struggles, unreason remains mute, and forgetting comes from the great silent wounds [déchirements] within man.

*

And yet there are others, who, 'losing their way, prefer to remain lost for ever'.[29] This end of unreason, elsewhere, is transfiguration.

There is a region where unreason, if it breaks the near-silence and the murmur of the implicit where classicism was so convinced that it belonged, it is to collect itself once more in a silence punctuated by cries: the silence of interdiction, watchfulness and revenge.

The Goya who painted The Madhouse, in all probability, faced with that flesh swarming in the void, and those naked forms on naked walls, must have felt something that resembled a contemporary pathos: the symbolic faded finery on the heads of mad kings showed begging bodies, bodies offered to whips and chains, and contradicted the delirium of their faces not so much by the misery of their nudity as by the human truth that radiates from their intact flesh. The man with the three-pointed hat is not mad because he has stuck that battered headgear atop his total nakedness, but from the madman in the hat leaps out, by virtue of the silent language of his well-muscled form and the wild, marvellous freedom of his youth, a free human presence who affirms his birthright as though this were the beginning of a new era. The Madhouse speaks less of the madness of those strange figures to be found in the Caprichos than the great monotony of those new bodies, brought into the light in all their vigour, and whose gestures, if they call up their dreams, sing above all of their dark liberty: its language is close to the world of Pinel.

The Goya of the Disparates and the Quinta del sordo addresses another madness altogether: not that of the mad who were thrown in prison, but that of man cast into his own night. He renews a connection, beyond memory, with the old worlds of enchantment, of fantastical rides, of witches perched on the branches of dead trees. The monster who whispers secrets into the ear of the Monk is surely related to the gnome who fascinated Bosch's *Saint Anthony*. In a sense, Goya rediscovered these great forgotten images of madness. But they mean something else to him, and their prestige, which is spread through all of his late work, comes from a different strength. In Bosch or Breughel, these forms were born of the world itself; through the fissures of a strange poetry, they rose up out of minerals and plants, or sprang from gaping animal jaws, and the whole complicity of nature was necessary to form their supernatural round. Goya's forms are born of nothing. They are bottomless, in the double sense that they only stand out against the most monotonous of nights, and that nothing can assign them their origin, their term and their nature. The *Disparates* have no landscape, no walls and no décor, and there lies another difference from the *Caprichos*: no star lights up the night of the great human bat-like creatures to be seen in the *Way of Flying*. What tree supports the branch where the witches cackle? Does it fly? And if so, to what Sabbath or what clearing? Nothing in that speaks of any recognisable world, neither this one nor any other. We are clearly in the realm of what he had labelled the *Sleep of Reason* back in 1797, describing it as the first aspect of the 'universal language'. This indeed is the night of classical unreason, the triple night into which Oreste was locked. But in that dark night, man communicates with his deepest being, and all that is most solitary within him. The desert of Bosch's *Saint Anthony* was infinitely peopled; and even if it was the work of her imagination, the landscape through which *Dulle Griet* ran was still criss-crossed by human language. Goya's *Monk*, with that hot beast on his back, its paws on his shoulders and its snout panting in his ear, is alone, and no secret is told. All that is present is the most interior, and at the same time the most savagely free of all forces: the one that dismembers bodies in the *Gran Disparate*, the one that runs wild and gouges out eyes in *Raging Madness*. From that point on, even the faces themselves begin to decompose, and what is left is no longer the madness of the *Caprichos*, which drew masks more true than the truth of faces; a madness from beneath the mask, a madness that bites faces and gnaws features; there are no eyes and no mouths, but only gazes that come from nowhere and stare at nothing (as in the *Witches' Sabbath*), or cries that echo out from black holes (as in the *Pilgrimage of Saint Isidore*). Madness has become the possibility in man of abolishing both man and the world – and even these images that challenge the world and deform humanity. It lies deeper than dreams, well below the nightmare of animality, a last resort: the end and the beginning of all things. Not because it was a promise, as in German lyricism, but because it is the ambiguity of chaos and apocalypse: the *Idiot* who screams and twists his shoulder to escape from the nothingness that surrounds him – is that the birth of the first man, and his first movement towards liberty, or the last spasm of the last dying man?

This madness, which knots and divides time, which curves the world in the loop of night, this madness so foreign to the experience contemporaneous with it, does it not utter to those who can hear them, like Nietzsche and Artaud, the scarcely audible words of classical unreason, where all was nothingness and night, but now amplified into screams and fury? Giving them for the first time expression, a *droit de cité* ['right of abode'], and a grasp on Western culture, a point from which all contestation becomes possible, as well as the contestation of all things? By restoring them to their primitive savagery?

The calm, patient language of Sade also gathers up the last words of unreason, and it too lends them a more distant meaning for the future. Between the broken lines of Goya and the unbroken line of words that stretches from the first volume of *Justine* to the 10th volume of *Juliette*, there is perhaps little in common, other than a certain movement which, doubling back on the course of contemporary lyricism, dries up its source and rediscovers the secret of the nothingness of unreason.

In the castle where Sade's heroes lock themselves away, in the convents, forests and dungeons where the indefinite agony of their victims is played out, a first glance seems to indicate that what is made possible is the totally free play of nature. As though what man refound there was a truth that he had forgotten despite its obviousness: what desire could go against nature, when it was nature herself that instilled the desire in man, reinforcing it with the great lesson about life and death that endlessly echoes around the world? The madness of desire, insane murders and the most unreasonable passions were wisdom and reason as they were of the order of nature. Everything that morality, religion and a badly organised society had managed to snuff out in man came back to life in the murderous castle. Here at last man was in tune with his nature; or rather by an ethic consistent with this strange confinement, here man was to take care to remain unflinchingly faithful to nature: a strict task, and a task inexhaustible in its totality. 'Until you have experienced everything, you will know nothing; and if your timidity causes you to pull up short before nature, then she will escape you forever.'[30] Inversely, when man has wounded or altered nature, it is up to man to make good the damage by plotting a sovereign vengeance: 'Nature made us all born equal; so if it pleases chance to upset this scheme of the general laws, it falls to us to correct its caprices, and use all our skill to make up for the most grievous usurpations.'[31] The slowness of the revenge, like the insolence of desire, belongs to nature. There is nothing in all that the madness of men has invented that is not either nature manifested or nature restored.

But that, in Sade's thought, is merely the beginning: a rational and lyrical ironic justification, a gigantic pastiche of Rousseau. On the basis of this *reductio ad absurdum* of the inanity of contemporary philosophy, and all its verbiage about man and nature, the true decisions were to be taken – decisions that were so many ruptures where the link between man and his natural being was abolished.[32] The infamous Society of the Friends of Crime, the programme for a Constitution for Sweden, stripped of their caustic references to the *Social Contract* and the projected constitutions for Poland and Corsica, only ever establish the sovereign rigour of subjectivity in their refusal of all natural freedom and equality: uncontrolled use of one person by another, an excessive use of violence, an unlimited application of the right to kill – this whole society, whose sole bond is the refusal of any bond, appears to be a radical dismissal of nature – and the only cohesion demanded of the individuals who make up the group is to protect not natural existence, but the free exercise of sovereignty over and against nature.[33] The relationship established by Rousseau is thus exactly reversed: sovereignty no longer transposes natural existence. Natural existence becomes merely an object for the sovereign, allowing him to take the measure of his absolute freedom. Taken to its logical extreme, desire leads to a rediscovery of nature in appearance only. In fact, in Sade, there is never any return to the native land, no hope that the primary refusal of the social surreptitiously changes into the re-established order of happiness, in a dialectical process where nature renounces itself, thereby confirming itself. The solitary madness of desire, which for Hegel still, as for the philosophers of the eighteenth century, plunged man into a natural world only to be instantly reclaimed by a social world, for Sade casts man into a void that dominates nature from afar, in a total absence of proportion or community, in the endlessly recommenced non-existence of satisfaction. The night of madness then has no limits: what was previously understood to be the violent nature of man turns out to be only the infinity of the non-natural.

Here, the great monotony of Sade finds its source: as he advances, backgrounds fade away, and surprises, incidents, and pathetic or dramatic links between the scenes disappear. The twisting plot of *Justine*, where events were endured, and therefore new, becomes a sovereign, ever-triumphant game in *Juliette*, where there is no negativity, and whose perfection is such that novelty can only ever be similarity to itself. As in Goya, these meticulous *Disparates* have no backdrop. And yet in this absence of décor, which might equally be total darkness or bright daylight (there are never any shadows in Sade), we do advance inexorably towards a term: the death of Justine. Her innocence exhausts even the desire to torment it. It cannot be claimed that crime fails to overcome her virtue: what should be said instead is that her natural virtue finally leads to the point where it has exhausted all the possible ways in which it can be an object for crime. At that point, when the only thing left for crime to do is expel virtue from the domain of its sovereignty (Juliette expelling her sister from the Château de Noirceuil), then nature, which has so long been dominated, trampled and profaned,[34] entirely submits to that which contradicted it; in its turn it enters madness, and there, in an instant, but only for an instant, it restores its omnipotence. The storm that is unleashed, the lightning that strikes Justine and consumes her, is nature made criminal subjectivity. This death that seems to escape from the insane reign of Juliette belongs to her more profoundly than any other. The night of the storm, the lightning and the thunder are proof enough that nature is beginning to tear itself apart, that it is reaching the extremes of its violent division, and that what she is revealing in this golden flash is a sovereignty that is both her own and something totally other than herself: the sovereignty of a maddened heart which in its solitude has found the limits of the world, which lacerate it, turn it against itself and abolish it at the moment when the fact of having mastered it so entirely gives it the right to identify totally with it. That instantaneous lightning bolt that nature extracts from itself to strike down Justine is at one with the lengthy existence of Juliette, who will also vanish into nothingness, leaving no body and no mortal remains which nature could then claim back for itself. The nothingness of unreason, where the language of nature was silenced forever, has become a violence of nature and against nature, and that to the point of the sovereign abolition of itself.[35]

In Sade, as in Goya, unreason still watches in its night; but through that watchfulness it connects with younger powers. The non-being that it was becomes the power to destroy. Through Sade and Goya, the Western world rediscovered the possibility of going beyond its reason with violence, and of rediscovering tragic experience beyond the promises of dialectics.

*

After Goya and Sade, and since them, unreason belongs to all that is most decisive in the modern world in any œuvre: anything that the œuvre contains which is murderous or constraining.

The madness of Tasso, Swift's melancholy and Rousseau's delirium were all part of their œuvre, in the same way that those œuvres belonged to them. In these texts, and in the lives of these men, the same violence spoke, or the same bitterness; visions were exchanged for sure, and language and delirium intertwined. But there is more: in the classical experience, œuvre and madness were more profoundly linked, on a level that was altogether different – paradoxically, in the place where they limited each other. For there also existed a region in which madness called the œuvre into question, ironically reducing it, and turning its imaginary landscape into a pathological world of fantasy: language that was delirium was in no sense an œuvre. Conversely, delirium wrenched itself away from its meagre truth as madness if it was certified as an *œuvre*. But in that contestation itself, there was no reduction of the one by the other, but rather (as in Montaigne), the discovery of a central uncertainty where the œuvre was born, at the moment where it ceased being born to truly become a work. In that confrontation, which Tasso and Swift witnessed after Lucretius – and which men attempted in vain to understand in terms of a succession of crises and intervals of lucidity – what was revealed was a distance where the truth of an œuvre became problematic: was it madness or art? Inspiration or fantasy? The spontaneous chattering of words, or the pure origin of a language? Was its truth to be identified as predating its entry into the impoverished truth of man, or was it to be discovered, well beyond its origins, in the being of which it was an intimation? For others, the madness of writers was an opportunity to witness the birth, and the endless rebirth, in the discouragements of repetition and disease, of the truth of a work of art.

Nietzsche's madness, and the madness of Van Gogh or Artaud, belong to their œuvre, perhaps no more or no less profoundly, but in a totally different way. The frequency in the modern world of these œuvres that explode into madness no doubt proves nothing about the reason of this world, the meaning of these œuvres, nor even about the relationships that are made and unmade between the real world and the artists who produce such an œuvre. And yet that frequency must be taken seriously, like the insistence of a question; since Hölderlin and Nerval, the number of writers, painters and musicians who have 'lapsed' into madness has multiplied, and yet we should not be deceived – between madness and œuvre there has been no arrangement, no more constant exchange, and no communication between languages. The confrontation now is far more perilous than before, and their competition allows no quarter: their game is one of life and death. The madness of Artaud does not slip into the interstices in his œuvre: it is precisely the *absence of an œuvre*, the constantly repeated presence of that absence, the central void that is experienced and measured in its never-ending dimensions. Nietzsche's last cry, as he proclaimed himself to be both Christ and Dionysus, is not at the limits of reason and unreason, the vanishing point of their œuvre, their common dream, reached at last and instantly evaporating, a reconciliation between 'the shepherds of Arcady and the fishermen of Tiberias'; but it is rather the destruction of the œuvre itself, the point at which it becomes impossible, and where it must begin to silence itself: the hammer falls from the philosopher's hand. Van Gogh, who did not want to 'ask the doctors' permission to paint', knew very well that his œuvre and his madness were incompatible.

Madness is an absolute rupture of the œuvre: it is the constitutive moment of an abolition, which founds the truth of the œuvre in time; it delineates the outer limit, the line of its collapse, its outline against the void. Artaud's *œuvre* experiences in madness its own absence, but the ordeal, and the eternally recommenced courage of this ordeal, all those words hurled at a fundamental absence of language, that whole space of physical suffering and terror that surrounds the void or rather coincides with it, that is the œuvre itself – a cliff-top over the abyss of the œuvres absence. Madness is no longer the space of indecision where the truth of the origin of the œuvre threatened to transpire, but the decision from which it irrevocably ceases, forever suspended above history from that point onwards. It matters little exactly what day in the autumn of 1888 Nietzsche went definitively mad, and from which point his texts were suddenly more the concern of psychiatry than of philosophy; all those texts, including the postcard to Strindberg, belong to Nietzsche, and all are connected in a common parentage to *The Birth of Tragedy*. But that continuity should not be thought of as being on the level of a system, or a thematics or even an existence: Nietzsche's madness, i.e. the collapse of his thought, is the way in which that thought opens onto the modern world. It is that which made it impossible that makes it present to us: we are offered it by all that wrenched it from his grasp. That is not to say that madness is the only language common to an œuvre and the modern world (we must be wary of the emotional appeal of the accursed artist, or the inverse and symmetrical danger of psychoanalysis); but it does mean that through madness, an œuvre that seems to sink into the world and reveal there its non-sense, and to acquire these purely pathological features, ultimately engages with the time of the world, mastering it and taking the lead. By the madness that interrupts it, an œuvre opens a void, a moment of silence, a question without an answer, opening an unhealable wound that the world is forced to address. By it everything that is necessarily blasphemous in an œuvre is reversed and, in the time of the œuvre that has slumped into madness, the world is made aware of its guilt. Henceforth and through the mediation of madness, it is the world that becomes guilty (for the first time in the history of the West) in relation to the œuvre: it is now arraigned by the œuvre, constrained to speak its language, and obliged to take part in a process of recognition and reparation, to find an explanation for this unreason, and *explain itself* before it. The madness where an œuvre plunges into a void is the space of our work, the infinite path to understanding it at last, our confused vocation as apostles and interpreters. For that reason it matters little when the voice of madness first whispered within Nietzsche's pride or Van Gogh's humility. There is only madness as the last instant of the œuvre – for the œuvre indefinitely repels madness to its outer limits. *Where there is an œuvre, there is no madness*: and yet madness is contemporaneous with the œuvre, as it is the harbinger of the time of its truth. The instant in which, together, madness and an œuvre come into being and reach fulfilment is the beginning of the time when the world first finds itself summoned by the œuvre, and is responsible for all that it is in the face of it.

That ruse is a new triumph for madness. The world believes that madness can be measured, and justified by means of psychology, and yet it must justify itself when confronted by madness, for its efforts and discussions have to measure up to the excess of the œuvres of men like Nietzsche, Van Gogh and Artaud. And nothing within itself, and above all nothing that it can know of madness, serves to show that these œuvres of madness prove it right.

Appendices

I

MADNESS, THE ABSENCE OF AN ŒUVRE

One day, perhaps, we will no longer know what madness was. Its form will have closed up on itself, and the traces it will have left will no longer be intelligible. To the ignorant glance, will those traces be anything more than simple black marks? At most, they will be part of those configurations that we are now unable to form, but which will be the indispensable grids that will make our culture and ourselves legible to the future. Artaud will then belong to the foundation of our language, and not to its rupture; neuroses will be placed among the forms that are constitutive of (and not deviant from) our society. All that we experience today as limits, or strangeness, or the intolerable, will have joined the serenity of the positive. And that which for us now designates this Exterior might come, one day, to designate us.

All that will remain will be the enigma of that Exteriority. What, they will wonder, was that strange delimitation that was in force from the early middle ages until the twentieth century, and perhaps beyond? Why did Western culture expel to its extremities the very thing in which it might just as easily have recognised itself – where it had in fact recognised itself in an oblique fashion? Why, since the nineteenth century, but also since the classical age, had it clearly stated that madness was the naked truth of man, only to place it in a pale, neutralised space, where it was almost entirely cancelled out? Why had it accepted the words of Nerval and Artaud, and recognised itself in their words but not in them?

In this way the vivid image of reason in flames will fade. The familiar game of gazing at the furthest part of ourselves in madness, of lending an ear to those voices which, from far away, tell us most clearly what we are, that game, with its rules, its tactics, its inventions, its ruses, its tolerated illegalities, will forever be nothing more than a complex ritual whose meanings will have been reduced to ashes. Something like those grand ceremonies of exchange and rivalry in archaic societies. Something like the ambiguous attention that Greek reason paid to its oracles. Or that twin institution, since the Christian fourteenth century, of the practices and trials of witchcraft. For civilisations of historians there will be nothing more than the codified measures of confinement, the techniques of medicine, and on the other side the sudden, irruptive inclusion in our language of the words of the excluded.

*

What will the technical substratum of such a mutation be? The possibility of medicine mastering mental illness like any other organic condition? The precise pharmacological control of all psychical symptoms? Or a definition of behavioural deviancies sufficiently rigorous for society to be able to provide, for each one, the appropriate mode of neutralisation? Or other modifications still, none of which perhaps will really suppress mental illness, but whose meaning will be to remove the face of madness from our culture?

I am well aware that by formulating that last idea, I am contesting something that is ordinarily admitted: that medical progress might one day cause mental illness to disappear, like leprosy and tuberculosis; but that one thing will remain, which is the relationship between man and his fantasies, his impossible, his non-corporeal pain, his carcass of night; that once the pathological is nullified, the obscure belonging of man to madness will be the ageless memory of an ill whose form as sickness has been effaced, but which lives on obstinately as unhappiness. Truth be told, such an idea supposes that that which is most precarious, far more precarious than the constancies of the pathological, is in fact unalterable: the relationship of a culture to the very thing that it excludes, and more precisely the relationship between our own culture and that truth about itself which, distant and inverted, it uncovers and covers up in madness.

That which will be not be long in dying, that which is already dying in us (and whose death bears our current language) is *homo dialecticus* – that being of the outset, of the return and of time itself, the animal that loses its truth and finds it again illuminated, a stranger to himself who becomes familiar once more. That man was the sovereign subject and the dominated object of all the discourses on man, and especially alienated man, that have been in circulation for a long time. Luckily, their chatter is killing him.

So much so that we will no longer know how man was able to cast at a distance this figure of himself, how he could push beyond the limit the very thing that depended on him, and on which he depended. No thought will be able to think that movement where still very recently Western man found its bearings. It is that relationship to madness (and not any know-ledge about mental illness, or a certain attitude in the face of alienated man) that will be lost forever. All that will be known is that we, Western men five centuries old, were, on the surface of the earth, those people who, among many other fundamental characteristics, had one that was stranger than all the others: we had a deep and pathos-filled relationship to mental illness, one that we ourselves found difficult to formulate, but which was impenetrable to anyone else, and in which we experienced the most vivid of all our dangers, and what was perhaps our closest truth. It will be said not that we were *distant from* madness, but that we were *in the distance of* madness. In the same way that the Greeks were not distant from hubris because they condemned it, but rather were in the distancing of that excess, in the midst of the distance at which they kept it confined.

These people – who will no longer be us – will still have to consider this enigma (a little the way we do ourselves, when we try to understand today how Athens managed to fall in and out of love with the unreason of Alcibiades): how could men have searched for their truth, their essential words and their signs in a risk that made them tremble, and from which they could not avert their gaze, once it had caught their eye? This will seem even stranger to them than asking death about the truth of man; for death at least says what all men will be. Madness, on the other hand, is that rare danger, a chance that weighs little in relation to the fears that it engenders and the questions it is asked. How, in a culture, could so slim an eventuality come to hold such a power of revelatory dread?

To answer that question, these people who will be looking back at us over their shoulders will have little to go on. Only a few burnt clues: a fear that came back repeatedly over the centuries that madness would rise up and swamp the world; the rituals surrounding the exclusion and inclusion of the madman; that careful attention, from the nineteenth century onwards, that tried to surprise in madness something that would reveal the truth of man; the same impatience that rejected and accepted the words of madness, a hesitancy to recognise their inanity or their decisiveness.

As for the rest: that single movement with which we go to meet the madness from which we are distancing ourselves, that terrified recognition, that will to fix the limit and to make up for it immediately through the weave of a single meaning, all that will be reduced to silence, just as for us today the Greek trilogy of mania, hubris and alogia, or the posture of shamanic deviancy in a particular primitive society, are silent.

We are at that point, that fold in time, where a certain technical control of sickness hides rather than designates the movement that closes the experience of madness in on itself. But it is precisely that fold that allows us to unfurl that which has been curled up for centuries: mental illness and madness – two different configurations, which came together and became confused from the seventeenth century onwards, and which are now moving apart before our eyes, or rather inside our language.

*

To say that madness is disappearing today is to say that the implication that included it in both psychiatric knowledge and a kind of anthropological reflection is coming undone. But that is not to say that the general form of transgression of which madness has been the visible face for centuries is disappearing. Nor that transgression, just as we are beginning to ask what madness is, is not in the process of giving birth to a new experience.

There is not a single culture anywhere in the world where everything is permitted. And it has been known for some time that man does not begin with freedom, but with limits and the line that cannot be crossed. The systems that forbidden acts obey are familiar, and every culture has a distinct scheme of incest prohibitions. But the organisation of prohibitions in language is still little understood. The two systems of restriction are not superimposed the one on the other, as though one were merely the verbal version of the other: that which must not appear on the level of speech is not necessarily that which is forbidden in the order of acts. The

Zuni, who forbid the incest of a brother and a sister nevertheless narrate it, and the Greeks told the legend of Œdipus. Inversely, the 1808 code abolished the old penal laws against sodomy, but the language of the nineteenth century was far more intolerant of homosexuality (at least in its masculine form) than the language of previous ages had been. And it is quite probable that psychological concepts such as compensation and symbolic expression are totally inadequate to account for such a phenomenon.

One day it will be necessary to study the field of prohibitions in language in all its autonomy. Perhaps it is still too soon to know exactly how such an analysis might be done. Could the divisions that are currently permitted in language be used? First of all, at the border between taboo and impossibility, we should identify the laws that govern the linguistic code (the things that are called, so clearly, *language faults*); and then, within the code, and among the words or existing expressions, those whose articulation is forbidden (the religious, sexual, magic series of *blasphemous words*); then the statements that are authorised by the code, licit in the act of speech, but whose meaning is intolerable for the culture in question at a given moment: here a metaphorical detour is no longer possible, for it is the meaning itself that is the object of *censorship*. Finally, there is a fourth form of excluded language: this consists of submitting speech that apparently conforms to the recognised code to a different code, whose key is contained within that speech itself, so that the speech is doubled inside itself; it says what it says, but it adds a mute surplus that silently states what it says and the code according to which it is said. This is not a question of coded language, but of a language that is structurally esoteric. Which is to say that it does not communicate, while hiding it, a forbidden meaning; it sets itself up from the very first instant in an essential fold of speech. A fold that mines it from the inside, perhaps to infinity. What is said in such a language is of little importance, as are the meanings that are delivered there. It is this obscure and central liberation of speech at the heart of itself, its uncontrollable flight to a region that is always dark, which no culture can accept immediately. Such speech is transgressive, not in its meaning, not in its verbal matter, but in its *play*.

It is quite probable that every culture, of whatever nature, knows, practises and tolerates (to a certain degree) but equally represses and excludes these four forms of forbidden speech.

In Western history, the experience of madness has shifted along this scale. Truth be told, it long occupied an undecided region, which is difficult for us to define, between the prohibition of action and that of language: hence the exemplary importance of the *furor-inanitas* pairing which practically organised, according to the registers of action and speech, the world of madness until the end of the Renaissance. The time of the Great Confinement (the Hôpitaux généraux, Charenton, Saint-Lazare, which were organised in the seventeenth century) marks a migration of madness towards the region of the insane: madness henceforth keeps little more than a moral relationship to forbidden acts (it remains essentially linked to sexual taboos), but it is included in the universe of language prohibitions; with madness, classical confinement encloses libertinage of thought and speech, obstinacy in impiety or heterodoxy, blasphemy, witchcraft, alchemy – everything in short that characterises the *spoken* and forbidden world of unreason; madness is the excluded language – the one which against the code of language pronounces words without meaning (the 'insane', the 'imbeciles', the 'demented'), or the one which pronounces sacred words (the 'violent', the 'frenzied'), or the one which puts forbidden meanings into circulation ('libertines', the 'obstinate'). Pinel's reform was far more the most visible consecration of the repression of madness as forbidden speech than a modification of it.

That modification only really came about with Freud, when the experience of madness shifted towards the last form of language prohibition mentioned above. At that point, it stopped being a language fault, a blasphemy spoken out loud, or an intolerable meaning (and in that sense, psychoanalysis is indeed the great lifting of prohibitions that Freud himself defined); it appeared as speech wrapped up in itself, saying, below everything that it says, something else, for which it is at the same time the only possible code: an esoteric language perhaps, since its language is contained inside a speech that ultimately says nothing other than this implication.

Freud's work should be taken for what it is; it does not discover that madness is caught up in a network of meanings that it shares with everyday language, thereby authorising us to speak of it with the everyday platitudes of psychological vocabulary. It displaces the European experience of madness to situate it in the perilous, still transgressive region (and therefore still forbidden, but in a particular manner), which is that of languages that imply themselves, i.e. which state in their statement the language with which they state it. Freud did not discover the lost identity of a meaning; he identified the irruptive figure of a signifier that is *absolutely unlike* the others. That alone should have sufficed to protect his work

from all the psychologising intentions that our half-century has employed
to smother it in the name (the derisory name) of the 'human sciences'
and their asexual unity.

By that very fact, madness appeared, not as the ruse of a hidden meaning, but as a prodigious *reserve* of meaning. But 'reserve' here should be
understood less as a stock than as a figure that contains and suspends
meaning, which furnishes a void where all that is proposed is the still-
unaccomplished possibility that a certain meaning might appear there, or
a second, or a third, and so on to infinity. Madness opens a lacunary
reserve, which designates and demonstrates this hollow where language
and speech imply each other, forming the one on the basis of the other,
and speaking of nothing other than their still-mute relationship. Since
Freud, Western madness has become a non-language because it has
become a double language (a language which only exists in this speech, a
speech that says nothing but its language) – i.e. a matrix of the language
which, strictly speaking, says nothing. A fold of the spoken which is an
absence of work.

One day, it will have to be acknowledged that Freud did not make *speak* a
madness that had genuinely been a language for centuries (a language that
was excluded, garrulous inanity, speech which ran indefinitely outside
the reflective silence of reason); what he did was silence the unreasonable
Logos; he dried it out; he forced its words back to their source, all the way
back to that blank region of auto-implication where nothing is said.

*

We perceive things that are currently going on around us in a light that is
still dim; and yet, in our language, a strange movement can be discerned.
Literature (and this probably since Mallarmé), in its turn, is slowly becoming a language [*un language*] whose speech [*parole*] states, at the same time as
what it says and as part of the same movement, the langage [*la langue*] that
makes it decipherable as speech. Before Mallarmé, writing was a matter of
establishing one's speech inside a given language, so that a work made
of language was of the same nature as any other language, but for the
signs (and they were majestic) of Rhetoric, the Subject, or Images. At the
close of the nineteenth century (at the time of the discovery of psychoanalysis, or thereabouts), it had become a speech that inscribed inside
itself the principle of its own decoding; or in any case, it supposed,

beneath each of its sentences, each of its words, the sovereign power to modify the values and meanings of the language to which despite every-thing (and in fact) it belonged; it suspended the reign of language in the present of a gesture of writing.

One consequence is the necessity for these secondary languages (what we call criticism, in short): they no longer function as external additions to literature (judgements, mediation, relays that were thought useful between a work examined in the psychological enigma of its creation and the act of consumption that is reading). Now they are a part, at the heart of literature, of the void that it creates in its own language; they are the necessary, but necessarily unfinished, movement whereby speech is brought back to its language, and whereby language is established in speech.

Another consequence is that strange proximity between madness and literature, which must not be interpreted as a psychological kinship that has been laid bare at last. Discovered as a language silencing itself in its superimposition on itself, madness neither demonstrates nor recounts the birth of an œuvre (or something that, by genius or by chance, might have become an œuvre); it designates the empty form from which such an œuvre comes, i.e. the place from which it is unceasingly absent, where it will never be found because it has never been there. There, in that pale region, beneath that essential cover, the twin incompatibility of an œuvre and madness is unveiled; it is the blind spot of each one's possibility, and of their mutual exclusion.

But since Raymond Roussel, since Artaud, it is also the place where language approaches literature most closely. But it does not approach it as though its task were to formulate what it has found. It is time to understand that the language of literature is not defined by what it says, nor by the structures that make it signify something, but that it has a being, and that it is about that being that it should be questioned. But what is that being at the present time? Something, no doubt, that is related to auto-implication, to the double and the void that is hollowed out within it. In that sense the being of literature, such as it has been created since Mallarmé and still is today, attains the region where, since Freud, the experience of madness has been enacted.

In the eyes of I know not which future culture – and perhaps it is already very near – we shall be the people who brought most closely together two sentences that are never really uttered, two sentences as contradictory and impossible as the famous 'I am lying' and which both designate the same empty self-reference: 'I write' and 'I am delirious'. In this way we find ourselves beside a thousand other cultures that grouped together 'I am mad' with 'I am an animal', or 'I am a God' or 'I am a sign', or even 'I am a truth', as was the case for the nineteenth century up until Freud. And if that culture has a taste for history, it will recall that Nietzsche, going mad, proclaimed (in 1887) that he was the truth (why I am so wise, why I know so many things, why I write such good books, why I am a fatality); and that less than fifty years later Roussel, on the eve of his suicide, wrote in *Comment j'ai écrit certains de mes livres*[1] the story, systematically twinned, of his madness and his writing techniques. And they will no doubt be surprised that we were able to recognise such a strange kinship between that which, for so long, was feared as a cry, and that which, for so long, was awaited like a song.

*

But perhaps this mutation will not appear to merit any astonishment. We, after all, are the ones who, today, are surprised to see two languages (that of madness and that of literature) communicate, when their incompatibility was built by our own history. Since the seventeenth century, madness and mental illness have occupied the same space in the field of excluded languages (roughly speaking, that of insanity). When it enters another region of excluded language (one that is circumscribed, held sacred, feared, erected vertically above itself, reflecting itself in a useless and transgressive Fold, and is known as literature), madness releases itself from its kinship (ancient or recent, according to the scale we choose) with mental illness.

The latter, in all certainty, is set to enter a technical region that is increasingly well controlled: in hospitals, pharmacology has already transformed the rooms of the restless into great tepid aquariums. But below the level of these transformations, and for reasons which seem external to them (at least to our current glance), a *dénouement* is beginning to come about: madness and mental illness are undoing their belonging to the same anthropological unity. That unity itself is disappearing, together with man, a passing postulate. Madness, the lyrical halo of sickness, is ceaselessly dimming its light. And far from pathology, in language, where it folds in on itself without yet saying anything, an experience is coming into being where our thinking is at stake; its imminence, visible already but absolutely empty, cannot yet be named.

II

MY BODY, THIS PAPER, THIS FIRE

On pages 44–47 of the *History of Madness*, I said that dreams and madness did not at all have the same status nor the same role in the development of Cartesian doubt: dreaming allows me to doubt the place where I am, the paper that I see, and the hand that I stretch out; but madness is in no sense an instrument or a stage of doubt; because 'I, who think, cannot be mad'.[1] Exclusion, therefore, for madness, whereas the sceptical tradition, by contrast, had made it one of the reasons for doubting.

To resume the objection that Derrida makes to this thesis,[2] it is probably best to quote the passage where he gives, in the most vigorous manner, his reading of Descartes:

> Descartes has just said that all knowledge derived from the senses may deceive him. He pretends to address to himself the astonished objection of the imaginary non-philosopher who is frightened by such a bold step, and who tells him: no, not the totality of sensible knowledge, or you would be mad, and it would be unreasonable to measure ourselves by the mad, and to offer ourselves a madman's discourse. Descartes *makes himself the echo* of that objection: since I am here, since I am writing and you understand me, I am not mad, neither are you, and we are both

sane people here. The example of madness is therefore not revelatory of the fragility of ideas derived from the senses. Perhaps. Descartes agrees with this natural point of view, or rather he pretends to take refuge in this natural comfort, the better and the more radically and the more definitively to abandon it and worry his interlocutor. Agreed, he says, you think that I would be mad to doubt that I am seated by the fire, etc., and that I would be eccentric to base my conduct on the example of madmen. I will therefore propose a hypothesis that you will find much more natural, which will not seem foreign to you because it is a matter of a more common experience, more universal than that of madness: that of sleep and dreams. Descartes then develops this hypothesis, which will ruin *all* the *sensible* foundations of knowledge, and will only lay bare the *intellectual* foundations of certainty. This hypothesis, above all, will not flee the possibility of eccentricities – epistemological ones in particular – that are much more serious than those of madness.

This reference to dreams is not, therefore, far from it, less radical than the possibility of a madness that Descartes might have kept at bay or even excluded. It constitutes, in the methodical order that is our own here, the hyperbolic exasperation of the hypothesis of madness. This hypothesis only affected, in a contingent and partial manner, certain regions of sensible perception. In any case, Descartes' concern here is not with determining the concept of madness, but with using the contemporary notion of eccentricity [*extravagance*] to juridical and methodological ends, in order to ask questions of principle that only concern *the truth* of ideas.[3] What must be retained here is that *from this point of view*, the sleeper or the dreamer is madder than the madman. Or at least that in relationship with the problem of knowledge that interests Descartes here, the dreamer is further from true perception than the madman. It is in the case of sleep, and not of eccentricity, that the absolute totality of ideas derived from the senses becomes suspect, and is stripped of 'objective value', in the words of M. Guéroult. The hypothesis of eccentricity was therefore not a good example, a revelatory example; it was not a good instrument of doubt. And that for at least two reasons:

(a) it does not cover the *totality* of the field of sensible perception. The madman is not always wrong about everything; he is never wrong enough, he is never mad;

(b) it is an ineffective and unfortunate example in pedagogical terms, for it is resisted by the non-philosopher, who is not daring enough to follow the philosopher when the latter admits that he might well be mad at the moment he is speaking.

*

Derrida's argumentation is remarkable. For its depth, and even more so for its frankness. What is at stake in the debate is indicated clearly: is it possible that there might be something anterior or exterior to philosophical discourse? Could it have its condition in an exclusion, a refusal, a risk eluded, and, why not, in a fear? A suspicion that Derrida rejects with passion. *Pudenda origo* (shameful origin!), said Nietzsche of religious people and their religion.

Let us confront the analyses of Derrida and the texts of Descartes.

1 THE PRIVILEGES OF DREAM OVER MADNESS

Derrida: 'Dreaming is an experience more common, and also more universal than that of madness' 'The madman is not always wrong about everything'. 'Madness only affects in a contingent and partial manner certain regions of sensible perception'.

Now Descartes does not at all say that dreaming is 'more common and also more universal than madness', and neither does he say that madmen are only mad from time to time and regarding particular points. Let us listen instead to his reference to people who 'constantly claim to be kings'.[4] Is the madness of these people who take themselves for kings, or who believe that they have a body of glass, more intermittent than dreaming?

And yet it is a fact: Descartes, along the path of doubt, privileges dreaming over madness. Let us put to one side for a moment the problem of knowing whether madness is excluded, solely neglected, or taken up again later in a wider and more radical experiment.

Immediately after he has mentioned, in order to abandon it, the example of madness, Descartes evokes the case of dreams:

> In any case, I must consider here that I am a man, consequently that I am in the habit of dreaming, and of seeing the same things in my dreams, and sometimes seeing things more improbable than the waking visions of these insane people.[5]

A double advantage therefore of the dream. On the one hand, it is capable of creating eccentricities that equal, or sometimes surpass madness; on the other, it has the property of producing itself in an habitual manner. The first advantage is of a logical and demonstrative order: everything of which madness (the example of which I have just set aside) could make me doubt, dreams too could make uncertain for me; as a power of uncertainty, dreaming has nothing to fear from madness, and none of the demonstrative force of madness is lost by dreaming when I have to convince myself of everything that I must revoke in doubt. The other advantage of the dream is of a different order: it is frequent, it often happens; I have recent memories of it, and it is not difficult to draw on the extremely vivid memories that it leaves. A practical advantage, in short, when what is at stake is no longer demonstrating, but carrying out an exercise and calling up a memory, a thought, a state, in the very movement of meditation.

The extravagance of the dream guarantees its *demonstrative* character as *example*: its frequency assures its *accessible* character as *exercise*. And it is certainly this accessible character that worries Descartes here, certainly more so than its demonstrative character, which is signalled once and for all, as though he were assuring himself that the hypothesis of madness could be abandoned without regrets. The theme that dreams happen quite often, by contrast, returns several times. We can find: 'I am a man, and consequently, I am in the habit of dreaming', 'how often at night have I not dreamt', 'what happens during sleep', 'considering the matter carefully, I remember often being deceived while sleeping'.[6]

My fear is that Derrida may have confused these two aspects of dreaming. Everything happens as though he had covered them with a word that forcibly joins them together: 'universal'. As 'universal', dreaming would happen to everyone and regarding everything. The dream: a dubiousness of all things for all men. But this is forcing words, and going well beyond what the Cartesian text says: or rather, stopping well short of its singularities, effacing the quite distinct character of the eccentricity of dreaming and its frequency, erasing the specific role of these two characteristics in the Cartesian discourse (demonstration and exercise) and omitting the greater importance accorded to custom over extravagance.

But why is it so important that dreaming should be familiar and accessible?

2   MY EXPERIENCE OF DREAMING

Derrida: 'The reference to dreaming constitutes, in the methodical order that is our own here, the hyperbolic exasperation of the hypothesis of madness.'

Before rereading the paragraph about dreaming[7] let us keep in our ears the sentence that has just been spoken: 'But so what? Such people are insane, and I would be no less eccentric if I modelled myself on their example.'[8]

And then the discourse goes on as follows: a resolution in the meditating subject to take into consideration the fact that he is a man, that he often sleeps and dreams; the appearance of a memory (or rather of a multitude of memories), of dreams which coincide exactly, trait for trait, with today's perception (being seated here in this place, fully dressed, beside the fire); the feeling that somehow there is a difference between the perception and the memory, a difference that is not simply noted, but effected by the subject in the very movement of his meditation (I look at this paper, I shake my head, I stretch out my hand, so that the difference between wakefulness and sleeping appears quite vividly); but new memories, on a second level (the vividness of this impression has often been a part of my dreams); with these memories, the vivid feeling that I am awake begins to disappear; it is replaced by the clear vision that there is no certain indication that might separate sleeping and wakefulness: a conclusion that provokes an astonishment in the meditating subject such that the indifference between sleep and wakefulness provokes the quasi-certainty that one is sleeping.

And so we can see it: the resolution to think about dreams does not merely have the consequence of turning sleep and wakefulness into a theme for reflection. This theme, in the movement that proposes it and causes it to vary, *takes effect* in the meditating subject in the form of memories, vivid impressions, voluntary movements, differences experienced, memories again, clear vision, astonishment, and an indifferentiation which is close to the feeling of sleeping. To think of dreaming is not at all to think of something exterior, of which I would know the effects and the causes; it is not simply to evoke a whole strange phantasmagoria, or the movements of the brain that might provoke it; thinking of dreaming is such, when one applies oneself to it, that its effect is to scramble for the meditating subject, and at the very heart of his meditation, the perceived limits of sleeping and wakefulness. The dream *troubles the subject* who thinks about it.

Turning one's mind to dreams is not an indifferent task: it is perhaps at first a theme that one proposes to oneself, but it quickly reveals itself to be a risk to which one exposes oneself. The risk for the subject that he might be modified, the risk that he may no longer be at all certain of being awake, the risk of *stupor*, says the Latin text.

And it is here that the example of the dream reveals another of its privileges. However much it modifies the meditating subject on this matter, it does not prevent him, at the very heart of this stupor, from continuing to meditate, and to meditate in a valid fashion, and to see clearly a certain number of things or principles despite the indistinction, however profound it might be, between sleeping and wakefulness. Even if I am not sure of being awake, I remain certain of what my meditation allows me to see; and that is what is demonstrated by the passage that follows, beginning precisely with a sort of hyperbolic resolution: 'Suppose then that we are dreaming', or as the Latin text says even more forcibly, *Age somniemus*. The thought of dreaming had led me to uncertainty; the latter, by the astonishment that it provokes, to the quasi-certainty of sleep; that quasi-certainty is now turned by my resolutions into a systematic feint. This is the artful putting to sleep of the meditating subject: *Age somniemus*, and from that point on, the meditation, once again, may be pursued.

We can now see all the possibilities that are given by the character, certainly not 'universal', but modestly customary, of dreaming.

1 It is a possible experience, immediately accessible, of which the model is proposed by a thousand memories.
2 This possible experience is not simply a theme for meditation; it is really and presently produced in meditation, according to the following series: thinking about dreaming; remembering dreaming; seeking to make the distinction between dreaming and waking; no longer knowing if one is dreaming or not, and voluntarily acting as though one were dreaming.
3 Through this meditative exercise, the thought of the dream has an effect on the subject himself: it modifies him by filling him with *stupor*.
4 But by modifying him, by turning him into a subject uncertain of his waking state, it does not disqualify him as a meditating subject: even transformed into a 'subject supposed to be dreaming', the meditating subject can pursue, in a sure fashion, the path of his doubt.

But we must go further back, and compare this experience of dreaming with the example of madness that immediately precedes it.

3   THE 'GOOD' EXAMPLE AND THE 'BAD' ONE

Derrida: 'What must be retained here is that from this point of view, the sleeper or the dreamer is more mad than the madman.'

For Derrida, madness is not excluded by Descartes; it is simply neglected. Neglected for a better, more radical example. The example of the dream prolongs, completes and generalises what the example of madness indicated in such unsuitable fashion. To go from madness to the dream is to go from a 'bad' to a 'good' instrument of doubt.

But I believe that the opposition between dreaming and madness is of a quite different type. We must compare step by step the two paragraphs of Descartes, and follow in detail the system of their opposition.

(1) The *nature* of the meditative exercise. It appears clearly in the *vocabulary* employed. In the paragraph on madness, there is the vocabulary of comparison. If I want to deny that 'these hands and this whole body are mine' I must 'liken myself to madmen' (*comparare*); but I would be quite eccentric 'if I took anything from them as a model' (*si quod ab iis exemplum ad me transferrem*). The madman is an exterior term to which I compare myself.

In the paragraph on dreams there is the vocabulary of memory. 'I am in the habit of dreaming', 'How often have I not', 'Considering the matter carefully, I remember'.[9] The dreamer is what I recall having been myself; from the depths of my memory rises up the dreamer that I myself have been, and that I will be again.

(2) The *themes* of the meditative exercise. They appear in the examples that the meditating subject proposes to himself.

For madness: to take oneself for a king when one is poor; to believe oneself dressed in gold when one is naked; to imagine that one has a body of glass, or that one is a water pitcher. Madness is when all is other, it deforms and transports, it evokes a different scene.

For the dream: to be seated (as I am now); to feel the heat of the fire (as I feel it today); to stretch out my hand (as I decide to do, right now). Dreams do not transport the scene; they reproduce demonstratives that point towards the scene where I am (this hand? Perhaps a picture of another hand. This fire? Perhaps a different fire, in a dream). The oneiric imagination matches the current perception exactly.

(3) The *central test*[10] of the exercise. It is to be found in the search for difference: will I be able to incorporate the themes proposed into my meditation? Can I seriously ask myself if I have a body of glass, and if I am not quite naked in my bed? If so, I will be obliged to doubt even my own body. But it will be spared if, on the other hand, my meditation remains quite distinct from madness and from dreaming.

From dreaming? I try the test: I remember having dreamt that I was nodding my head. I will therefore nod it again here, right now. Is there a difference? Yes. A certain clarity, a certain distinctiveness. But, and this is the second part of the test, can that clarity and distinctiveness be found in dreams? Yes, I have a clear memory of that. Therefore what I thought to be the criterion of difference (clarity and distinctiveness) belongs indifferently to dreaming and wakefulness. It cannot therefore make the difference.

From madness? The test is immediately done. Or rather, when one looks closely, one sees that it does not take place, in the manner that it is carried out for the dream. There is in fact no question of me trying to take myself for a madman who takes himself for a king; and neither is there any question of me wondering if I am a king (or a captain from Touraine) who thinks himself to be a philosopher who has locked himself away to meditate. The difference from madness does not have to be tested: it is noted. No sooner are the themes of eccentricity evoked than the distinction bursts out like a cry: *sed amentes sunt isti.*

(4) The *effect* of the exercise. It appears in the sentences, or rather in the sentence-decisions that finish each of the two passages.

The paragraph about madness: 'But so what? Such people are insane' (third person plural, they, the others, isti); 'I would be no less eccentric if I modelled myself on their example';[11] it would be (note the conditional) madness even to try the test, to want to imitate all these delights, and to play the madman with the mad, like the mad. It is not by imitating madmen that I will be persuaded that I am mad (just as, a moment ago, the thought of dreaming convinced me that perhaps I am asleep); it is the very project of imitating them that is eccentric. The eccentricity relates to the very idea of putting it to the test, and for that reason it is absent, replaced by a mere acknowledgement of difference.

The paragraph about dreaming: the phrase, '*such people* are insane' is answered exactly by 'I begin to feel dazed' (*obstupestere*: to the cry of difference corresponds the stupor of indistinction); and the phrase 'I would be no less eccentric if ...' corresponds to 'my astonishment (*stupor*) is such that it is almost enough to persuade me that I am sleeping'. The test that has been tried out has 'worked' so well that I am now (note the present indicative) in the uncertainty of my own wakefulness. And it is in that uncertainty that I decide to continue my meditation.

It would be mad to want to play the madman (and I give up); but to think of dreaming is to already have the impression that one sleeps (and that is what I am going to meditate).

It is extremely difficult to remain deaf to the echo between these two paragraphs. And difficult not to be struck by the system of complex oppositions that underlies them. Difficult not to recognise there two exercises that are at once parallel and different: the exercise of the *demens* and that of the *dormiens*. Difficult not to understand the words and the phrases that confront each other on either side of this 'In any case'[12] of which Derrida has so profoundly underlined the importance, but of which he is wrong, I feel, not to analyse the function in the play of discourse. Difficult, truly, to say simply that madness is an insufficient and pedagogically clumsy example among the reasons for doubting, because the dreamer is in any case madder than the madman.

The whole discursive analysis demonstrates it; the acknowledgement of non-madness (and the rejection of the test) is not in continuity with the sleep test (and the acknowledgement that one might be sleeping).

But why this rejection of the test of the *demens*? Can we conclude from the fact that it has not happened that it is excluded? After all, Descartes speaks so little, and so quickly, of madness.

4   THE DISQUALIFICATION OF THE SUBJECT

Derrida: 'What is significant is that Descartes, at bottom, never actually speaks of madness itself in this text ... this text does not speak of madness, it is not in question, not even to be excluded.'

Several times Derrida wisely remarks that in order to understand Descartes' text properly, we must refer to the original Latin version. He recalls – and he is quite right – the words used by Descartes in the famous phrase: 'But such people are insane (*sed amentes sunt isti*), and I would be [thought] equally mad (*demens*) if I took anything from them as a model for myself.' Unfortunately, his analysis does not go beyond this simple recollection of the words.

Let us return to the passage itself: 'How could it be denied that these hands or this whole body are mine? Unless perhaps I were to liken myself to madmen' (the term employed here is *insani*). But what are these *insani* who take themselves for kings or earthenware? They are *amentes*; and I would be no less *demens* if I applied their example to myself. Why these three terms, or rather why employ first of all the term *insanus*, and then the couple *amens–demens*? When it is a question of characterising them by the improbability of their imaginings, the mad are called *insani*: a word that belongs as much to everyday vocabulary as it does to medical terminology. To be *insanus* is to take oneself for what one is not, it is to believe in chimeras, to be the victim of delusions; these at least are the signs. The cause is a brain swollen with vapours. But when Descartes wishes not to characterise madness, but to affirm that I should not take my example from the mad, he employs the terms *demens* and *amens*, terms that are legal before being medical, and which designate a whole category of people who are incapable of certain religious, civil and legal acts; the *dementes* do not have all their rights in matters of speaking, promising, committing themselves, signing, bringing legal actions, etc. *Insanus* is a term of characterisation; *amens* and *demens* are disqualifying terms. The first refers to signs; the other two to capability.

The two sentences, in order to doubt my body, I must 'liken myself to madmen' and 'but such people are insane', are not proof of an impatient and irritated tautology. In no sense is it a matter of saying 'one should be or act like madmen', but 'they are mad, and I am not'. To summarise the text as Derrida does, 'Since I am here, I'm not mad, neither are you, and we are among sane people here', is singularly to flatten it. The development of the text is quite different: to doubt one's body is to be like those of deranged mind, the sick, the *insani*. Can I follow their example, and on my own account at least feign madness, and become in my own eyes uncertain whether I am mad or not? I neither can nor should. For those *insani* are *amentes*; and I would be no less *demens* than them, and juridically disqualified if I followed their example.

Derrida obscurely sensed the juridical connotation of the word. He returns to it several times, insistent and hesitating. Descartes, he says, 'treats [madness] like an index for a point of law and epistemological value'.[13] Or again, 'For Descartes here it is not a matter of determining the concept of madness, but of using the contemporary notion of eccentricity to juridical and methodological ends, to ask legal questions that solely concern the truth of ideas.' Derrida is correct to underline that at this point it is indeed a question of law. And he is right again to say that Descartes did not want to 'determine the concept of madness' (who ever claimed that anyway?). But he is wrong not to have seen that Descartes' text plays on the gap between two types of determination of madness (the medical ones and the juridical ones). And more than anything he is wrong to conclude hastily that the question of law that is posed here concerns 'the truth of ideas', while as the words clearly state, it concerns the qualification of the subject.

The problem can then be posed thus. Can I doubt my own body, can I doubt my own actuality? The example of the mad, the *insani*, invites me to do so. But comparing myself to them, doing as they do, implies that I too will become like them, demented, incapable and disqualified from my meditative enterprise: I would be no less *demens* if I followed their example. But if, on the other hand, I take the example of dreams, if I pretend that I am dreaming, then, however *dormiens* I am, I will still be able to meditate, reason, and see clearly. *Demens*, I would be unable to continue: I have to stop with the very hypothesis, and envisage something else, and see if another example might allow me to doubt my own body. *Dormiens*, I can continue my meditation: I am still qualified to think; and so I make my resolution: *Age somniemus*, which introduces a new moment of the meditation.

It would take quite a distant reading to conclude that 'it is not a question of madness in this text'.

Perhaps, you might say. Let us admit, despite Derrida, that we should pay such detailed attention to the text, and to all its little differences. For all that, have you demonstrated that madness is well and truly excluded from the path of doubt? Will Descartes not refer to it again with reference to imagination? Is it not to that that he refers when talking of the eccentricity of painters, and all those fantastical chimera that they invent?

5 THE ECCENTRICITY OF PAINTERS

Derrida: 'What Descartes seemed to exclude as eccentricity above is here admitted as a possibility . . . but in these representations, these images, these ideas in the Cartesian sense, everything can be false and fictitious, like the representations of these painters whose imagination, Descartes explicitly says, 'manages to think up something so new that nothing remotely like it has been seen before'.

Granted, madness is dealt with several times elsewhere in the Cartesian *oeuvre*. And its disqualifying role for the meditating subject in no way prevents meditation from bearing upon it, for it is not for the content of such eccentricities that madness is removed from the game: it is removed for the subject who would at once 'play the madman' and meditate, when it is a question of knowing whether the subject can assume madness for himself, imitate it, feign it, and risk no longer really knowing if he is reasonable or not. As I think I have said quite clearly, madness is excluded by the subject who doubts, in order that he may qualify himself as a doubting subject. But it is in no sense rejected as an object of reflection and knowledge. Is it not typical that the madness of which Descartes speaks in the paragraph studied above should be defined in medical terms, the result of 'brains . . . damaged by the persistent vapours of melancholia'?

But Derrida could insist and underline that madness is still to be found in the movement of the doubt, mixed with the imagination of the painters. It is clearly present in the French text, as indicated by the word '*extravagant*' (eccentric), used to describe the imagination of painters; 'if perhaps their imagination is sufficiently eccentric to invent something so new that we have never seen anything like it before . . . at least the colours they use must be true to life', Derrida has understood perfectly what was singular in the expression 'if their imagination is sufficiently eccentric'. He understands it so well that he underlines it in his quotation probably as the point on which his demonstration is to hang. I subscribe entirely to the necessity of sufficiently isolating these few words.

But for a different reason: quite simply because *they are not to be found in* the original text. They are an addition by the French translator. The Latin text simply says '*si forte aliquid ex cogitent ad eo novum ut nihil*', 'if perhaps they manage to think up something so new'. It is curious that Derrida, to demonstrate the validity of his thesis, has spontaneously chosen, retained and underlined that which can *only* be found in the French translation of the *Meditations*; curious too that he insists, and claimed, that the word 'eccentric' was used 'on purpose' [*expressément*] by Descartes.

It does not therefore seem that the example of the dream is simply for Descartes a generalisation or a radicalisation of the case of madness. It is not as a feeble, less good, insufficient, insufficiently 'revealing', 'ineffective' example that madness is to be distinguished from dreaming. And it is not at all for its lesser value that it is to be left aside after being evoked. The example of madness faces that of dreams; they are confronted and placed in opposition to each other according to a system of differences that are clearly articulated in the Cartesian discourse.

But the analysis of Derrida neglects, I fear, many of these differences. Literal differences between words (*comparare/reminscerere*; *exemplum transferre/* to persuade; conditional/indicative). Thematic differences of images (to be beside the fire; to stretch out one's hand and open one's eyes/to take oneself for a king, to be covered with gold, to have a body made of glass); textual differences in the arrangement and the opposition of the paragraphs (the first plays on the distinction between *insanus* and *demens*, and on the *juridical implication of demens* by *insanus*; the second plays on the distinction 'remembering one has slept/convincing oneself that one is asleep', and on the *real passage* from the one to the other in a mind that applies itself to such a memory). But differences above all on the level of what is happening in the meditation, on the level of *events* that succeed one another; *acts* carried out by the meditating subject (comparison/remembering); *effects* produced inside the meditating subject (sudden and immediate perception of a difference/astonishment-stupor-experience of an indistinction); qualification of the meditating subject (invalidity if he is *demens*; validity even if he is *dormiens*).

We can see it quite clearly: this last group of differences commands all the others; it refers less to the signifying organisation of the text than to the series of events (acts, effects, qualifications) that the discursive practice of the meditation brings in its wake; it concerns the modification of the subject through the very exercise of the discourse. And I have the impression that if a reader, even a reader as remarkably assiduous as Derrida, has missed so many literary, thematic or textual differences, it is because he has misunderstood those that are their principle, i.e. the 'discursive differences'.

*

We must keep in mind the title itself of 'Meditations'. Any discourse, whatever its nature, is made up of a group of enunciations which are produced in their space and in their time, as so many discursive events. If they form a pure demonstration, these enunciations can be read as a series of events, linked to each other according to a certain number of formal rules; the subject of the discourse is in no sense implied in the demonstration; it remains, in relation to it, fixed, invariant and as though neutralised. A 'meditation', by contrast, produces, as so many discursive events, new enunciations that bring in their wake a series of modifications in the enunciating subject: through what is said in the meditation, the subject passes from darkness to light, from impurity to purity, from the constraint of passions to detachment, from uncertainty and disordered movements to the serenity of wisdom, etc. In the meditation, the subject is ceaselessly altered by his own movement; his discourse elicits movements inside which he is caught up; it exposes him to risks, subjects him to tests [*épreuves*] or temptations, produces in him states, and confers a status or a qualification upon him which he in no sense possessed at the initial moment. A meditation implies, in short, a subject who is mobile and capable of being modified by the very effect of the discursive events that take place. We can see from this what a demonstrative meditation would be: a set of discursive events that form at the sime time groups of enunciations linked to each other by formal rules of deduction, and series of modifications in the enunciating subject, modifications that continually follow on from each other; and more precisely, in a demonstrative meditation, enunciations which are formally linked modify the subject as they develop, and liberate him from his convictions or induce systematic doubts, provoke illuminations or resolutions, free him from his attachments or his immediate certainties, induce new states, but inversely the decisions, fluctuations, displacements, primary or acquired qualifications of the subject make possible sets of new enunciations, which are regularly deduced from the others.

The *Meditations* require such a double reading: a group of propositions, forming a *system*, which each reader must run through if he wishes to experience their truth; and a group of modifications forming an *exercise*, which each reader must carry out, and by which each reader must be affected, if he wishes in his turn to be the subject enunciating this truth on his own account. And while it is true that there are certain passages in the *Meditations* which can be deciphered, in an exhaustive manner, as a systematic concatenation of propositions – moments of pure deduction – there are also sorts of 'chiasms' where the two forms of discourse intersect, and where the exercise modifying the subject orders the succession of propositions, or commands the junction of distinct demonstrative groups. It would appear that the passage on madness and dreaming is of that order.

Let us take it up again in its entirety, and as an intersection of the demonstrative and the ascetic threads.

1   The passage that immediately precedes it has the appearance of a practical syllogism:

> *I must be wary of anything that has deceived me once*
> *But in my senses, which have given me all that I hold most true and*
> *   most certain, have deceived me, and more than once*
> *Therefore I must no longer trust them.*

We can see it quite clearly: this section is a deductive fragment whose implications are quite general – *everything* that we have held to be most true is suddenly in doubt, together with the senses that brought it. *A fortiori*, there is therefore nothing that remains which does not become at least as doubtful. Is there any need to generalise any further? Derrida's hypothesis, that the (ineffective) example of madness and the (effective) example of dreaming are called upon to operate this generalisation, and to lead on the syllogism of doubt, cannot therefore be retained. By what, then, are they summoned?

2   They are summoned less by an objection or a restriction than by a resistance; there are sensible things about which 'doubt is quite impossible' [in French, 'dont on ne peut pas *raisonnablement* douter', which we cannot *reasonably* doubt']. It is the word '*plane*' that Descartes' French translator renders by '*raisonnablement*'. What then is this 'impossibility', when we have just established a totally compelling syllogism? What is the obstacle that prevents us from doubting 'entirely', 'wholly', 'completely', (reasonably?), when we have just presented a rationally unassailable reasoning? It is the impossibility for the subject of really carrying out, in the exercise that modifies his self, a doubt so general. It is the impossibility of constituting oneself as a universally doubting subject. What presents a problem, following a syllogism of such general import, is the conversion of a counsel of prudence into effective doubt, the transformation of a subject 'knowing that he must doubt all things' into a subject who is 'applying to all things his resolution to doubt'. We can see very well why the translator rendered '*plane*' by '*raisonnablement*'; in attempting to carry out this rationally necessary doubt, I expose myself to losing the qualification of '*raisonnable*' that I brought into play from the very beginning of the meditations (and in at least three forms: having a mind that is sufficiently mature, having a mind that is free of cares and passions, and being sure of a peaceful retreat). In order to take the resolution to doubt everything, should I disqualify myself as reasonable? If I wish to

maintain my qualification as reasonable, should I give up attempting to effect this doubt, or at least to effect it in its generality?

The importance of the words 'to be able to doubt completely' comes from the fact that they mark a point of overlap of the two discursive forms – that of the system and that of the exercise: on the level of the ascetic discursivity, we cannot yet reasonably doubt. It is thus the latter that will command the following development, and what finds itself engaged there is not the panoply of doubtful things, but the status of the doubting subject, the qualificatory elaboration which permits him at once to be 'omnidoubting' and reasonable.

But what then is the obstacle, the point of resistance in the exercise of the doubt?

3   Is it my body, and the immediate perception that I have of it? Or more exactly the domain that can be defined as that of the 'vivid and near' (as opposed to all those things that are 'faint and distant' which I can unproblematically put in doubt): I am here, wearing a dressing gown, seated near the fire, in short the whole system of actuality that characterises this particular moment of my meditation. It is capital that Descartes here does not evoke the certainty that one can have in general of one's own body, but clearly all that which, in this precise *instant* of the meditation, resists in *fact* the effectuation of the doubt by the subject who is *actually* meditating. We see clearly that it is not at all certain things which in themselves (their nature, their universality, their intelligibility) might resist doubt; but, rather, that which characterises the actuality of the meditating subject (the place of his meditation, the action that he is carrying out, the sensations that strike him). If he really doubted this system of actuality, would he still be reasonable? Would he not precisely renounce all those guarantees of a reasonable meditation he gave himself by choosing, as was said above, the moment of his enterprise (quite advanced in years, but not excessively so; the moment has come which must not be passed up), its conditions (to be seated quietly, without any care that might form a distraction), its place (a peaceful retreat)? If I am to start doubting the place where I am, the attention I am paying to this paper, and the heat of the fire that marks my present instant, how will I be able to remain convinced of the reasonable character of my undertaking? Would I not, by doubting this actuality, by the same token, make reasonable meditation impossible, and deny any value in my resolution to finally discover the truth?

Two examples are called up, both of which make it necessary to put into doubt the system of the actuality of the subject.

4   First example: madness. The mad, in effect, entirely delude themselves about what constitutes their actuality: they believe they are dressed when they are naked, they believe themselves to be kings when they are poor. But can I use this example for myself? Is it by such means that I will be able to transform into an effective resolution the proposition that I must doubt everything that comes to us in dreams? Impossible: *isti sunt dementes*, which is to say that they are juridically disqualified as reasonable subjects, and to qualify myself as them, in the same fashion as them ('if I took anything from them') would disqualify me in turn and I could no longer be a reasonable subject for meditation ('I would be [thought] equally mad'). If one uses the example of madness to pass from systems to ascesis, from proposition to resolution, one can effectively constitute oneself as a subject ready to put everything in doubt, but one cannot remain qualified as a subject reasonably leading his meditation through doubt towards a possible truth. The resistance of actuality to the exercise of doubt is reduced by an example that is too strong: with it the possibility of meditating in a valid fashion disappears; the two qualifications 'doubting subject' and 'meditating subject' are not in this case simultaneously possible.

That madness be posited as disqualifying in any search for the truth, that it should not be 'reasonable' to call it to oneself to carry out the necessary doubting, that one cannot feign it even for an instant, and that the impossibility appears immediately in the very assignation of the term 'demens'; this is indeed the decisive point where Descartes departs from all those for whom madness may be in some way or other a bearer or a revealer of truth.

5   Second test [*épreuve*]: dreams. Madness has thus been excluded, not at all as an insufficient example but as an excessive and impossible test. Dreaming is then invoked: not that it renders the actuality of the subject less doubtful than madness (one believes that one is seated at one's table while one is naked in bed); but it presents a number of differences in relation to madness — it is part of the virtualities of the subject (I am a man), of his frequently actualised virtualities (it is my custom to sleep and to dream), his memories (I remember very well having dreamt), and his memories that can be called up most vividly (to the point that I can validly compare my actual impression and my memory of a dream). On the basis of these properties of dreaming, it is possible for the meditating subject to

carry out the exercise of doubting his own actuality. The first moment (which defines the test): I remember having dreamt what I currently perceive as my actuality. Second moment (which seems for an instant to invalidate the test): the movement that I make in the very instant of my meditation to know if I am sleeping, seems to have the clarity and distinctiveness of waking. The third moment (which validates the test): I remember not only the images of my dream, but their clarity, which is equal to that of my actual impressions. The fourth moment (which concludes the test): at the same time I *see manifestly* that there is no certain mark to allow a distinction between dreaming and reality; *and* I no longer know, in this precise moment, *so astonished* am I, if I am in the process of dreaming or not. These two sides of the successful test (an uncertain stupor and a manifest vision) constitute very well the subject as *effectively doubting* his own actuality, and as *validly continuing a meditation* which disregards all that which is not manifest truth. The two qualifications (doubting everything that comes from the senses, and validly meditating) are carried out in reality. The syllogism had required their simultaneous enactment: the consciousness of actuality of the meditating subject was an obstacle to the accomplishment of that requirement. The attempt to follow the example of the mad had confirmed that incompatibility; on the other hand the effort to actualise the vividness of dreaming showed that that incompatibility was not insurmountable. And the meditating subject finds himself a doubting subject at the issue of two tests that are opposed to each other: the one that composed the subject as reasonable (as opposed to the disqualified madman), and the other that constituted the subject as doubting (in the indistinction of dreaming and wakefulness).

Once this qualification of the subject is at last acquired (*Age somniemus*), the systematic discursivity will then be able once more to intersect with the discourse of the exercise and take the upper hand, to begin to call intelligible truths into question, until a new ascetic moment constitutes the subject as threatened by falling into universal error by the 'great deceiver'. But even in that moment of the meditation, the qualification of 'non-mad' (like the qualification of 'possible dreamer') will remain valid.

*

It seems to me that Derrida felt, vividly and in depth, that this passage on madness had a unique place in the development of the *Meditations*. And he transcribes this feeling in his text, at the very moment he is trying to master it.

1   To explain the discussion of madness here, and at this particular point of the *Meditations*, Derrida invents an alternation of voices which would displace, push to the exterior and banish from the text itself the difficult exclamation: 'Mais quoi, ce sont des fous'.

Derrida found himself faced with a difficult problem here. If it is the case, as he supposes, that the whole movement of the First Meditation operates a generalisation of doubt, why should it stop, even if only for a moment, at madness or even at dreaming? Why take pains to demonstrate that vivid and immediate sensations are no less doubtful than the faintest and most distant ones, when it has been established, *in a general manner*, that one should not trust what comes from the senses? Why this detour via a particular point of my body, this paper, this fire, why a detour through the singular deceptions of madness and dream?

Derrida gave this inflection the status of a rupture. He imagined a foreign intervention, the scruple or reticence of a simpleton worried by the movement that surrounds him, and who fights a rearguard action at the last minute. No sooner has Descartes said that the senses cannot be trusted, than a voice protests, that of a peasant who is a stranger to any philosophical urbanity; in his simple manner, he would like to breach or at least to limit the thinker's resolve: 'Fine, I understand that you doubt some of your perceptions, but . . . that you are sitting here, near the fire, talking like this, holding this paper in your hand, and things like that',[14] one would have to be mad to doubt them, or more exactly, only madmen can commit errors regarding things that are so certain. And mad is one thing that I most certainly am not. At that point Descartes takes over again, and says to this rustic, to this stubborn person: yes, I am happy to admit that you are not mad, as you are resolved not to be so; but you should remember that you dream every night, and that your nightly dreams are no less mad than this madness that you are refusing. And the naive reticence of the objector who cannot doubt the existence of his own body because he does not want to be mad would be conquered by the example of the dream, which is so much 'more natural', 'more common', 'more universal'.

Derrida's hypothesis is seductive. It solves his problem most neatly, showing that the philosopher goes straight to the questioning of the 'totality of being-ness'[15] and that the philosophical form and mark of his method is to be found precisely here: if it is the case that he stops for a moment at a 'Being' as singular as madness, it can only be because some naive person has tugged his sleeve and posed the question; of his own accord, he would never have lingered on these stories of naked kings and water jugs. In this way, the rejection of madness, the abrupt exclamation 'mais quoi, ce sont des fous' are themselves rejected by Derrida and three times confined *outside* the philosophical discourse: because it is another subject who is speaking (no longer the philosopher of the *Meditations*, but this gruff-voiced objector); because it speaks from a place which is that of non-philosophical naivety; and because the philosopher then begins to speak again, and by quoting the 'stronger' and 'more convincing' example of the dream, disarms the objection and imposes something much worse than madness on the person who refuses it.

But we can now see the price that Derrida must pay for his clever hypothesis. The omission of a certain number of *literal* elements (which appear as soon as one makes the effort to compare the Latin text and the French translation); the elision of *textual* differences (the whole play of semantic and grammatical oppositions between the paragraph on dreaming and the paragraph on madness); finally, and above all, the effacing of essential *discursive* determination (the double weave of the exercise and the demonstration). Curiously, Derrida, by imagining this other objecting and naive voice behind Descartes' writing, has swept away all the differences in the text; or rather, by effacing all these differences, by bringing together so closely the test of madness and the test of dreaming, making the one the pale and failed draft of the other, and by reabsorbing the insufficiency of the first into the universality of the second, Derrida was pursuing the Cartesian exclusion. The meditating subject, for Descartes, was to exclude madness by qualifying himself as not mad. But that exclusion in its turn is perhaps too dangerous for Derrida: no longer because of the disqualification with which it risks tarring the philosophising subject, but by the qualification with which it would mark the philosophical discourse; it would thus determine it as 'other' than the mad discourse, it would establish between them a relation of exteriority, and it would force philosophical discourse into the 'other side', into the pure presumption of not being mad. A division, an exteriority and a determination that the discourse of the philosopher must be spared if it is to be the 'project of exceeding all finished and determined totality'. It is therefore necessary to exclude, because it is determining, this Cartesian exclusion.

And to do this, Derrida, as we can see, is obliged to carry out three operations: to affirm, against the whole visible economy of the text, that the power of doubt proper to madness is included, *a fortiori*, in the dream; to imagine (to admit that it is, despite everything, a question of madness) that it is an other who excludes madness, on his own account and according to the diagonal of an objection; and finally to remove any philosophical status from this exclusion by denouncing its naive rusticity. To turn the Cartesian exclusion into inclusion; to exclude the one who excludes by giving his discourse the status of an objection; to exclude the exclusion by rejecting it into pre-philosophical naivety: Derrida needed all of that to master the Cartesian text, and to reduce to nothing the question of madness. We can see the results: the elision of the differences in the text and the compensatory invention of a difference of voices lead the Cartesian exclusion to a second level; in the end, it is excluded that philosophical discourse should exclude madness.

2   But perhaps madness does not allow itself to be reduced in this fashion. If we suppose that Descartes 'did not speak' of madness, there in his text where it is a question of *insani* and *dementes*, if we suppose that he made way for a moment for a rustic to raise such a clumsy question, could we not say that he proceeded, although in an insidious and silent manner, towards the exclusion of madness?

Could we not say that, in fact and constantly, he avoided the question of madness?

To this objection Derrida replies in advance: the risk of madness is indeed well and truly confronted by Descartes, not as you claim in a prior and almost marginal manner, regarding some business with water jugs and naked kings, but at the very heart of his philosophical enterprise; there precisely where his discourse, wrenching itself away from natural considerations about errors of the senses or swellings of the brain, takes, in the hyperbolic doubt and the hypothesis of the evil genius, its most radical dimension. It is precisely there that madness is put to the test and confronted; with the evil genius, I suppose I am deceived even more radically than those who believe they have a body made of glass; I go as far as to persuade myself that perhaps 2 and 3 do not make 5; then, with the *cogito*, I reach that extreme point, that excess in relation to all determination, which allows me to say that mad or not, deceived or not, I am. The evil genius would be the point where philosophy single-handedly, and in

the excess which is its own, risked madness; and the *cogito*, the moment
when madness disappeared (not at all because it was excluded, but
because its determination in the face of reason would cease to be relevant).
In no way, according to Derrida, should one attach too much importance
to the farce of the peasant who interrupts at the beginning of the text,
with his village idiots; despite their caps and bells, they would never
manage to raise the issue of madness. On the other hand, all the threats
of Unreason would play beneath the incarnations, which are so much
more worrying and dark, of the evil genius. Equally, the taking up again
by dream of the worst eccentricities of the madmen would be, at the
beginning of the text, an easy victory; on the other hand, after the great
maddening that is the evil genius, what is required is nothing less than
the point of the *cogito* (and its excess on the 'totality of being-ness') for the
determinations of madness and reason to appear as not radical. The great
solemn theatre of the universal deceiver and the 'I think' would repeat, but
this time in philosophical radicality, the still-natural fable of the madman
[*dément*] and the sleeper.

For such an interpretation, Derrida needed first of all to deny that
madness was in question in the place where it was named (and in specific
terms, carefully differentiated), then he needed to demonstrate that it is in
question in the place in which it is not named. Derrida operates this
demonstration by two series of semantic derivations. Let's recall them:

Evil genius: 'total madness', 'a total maddening', 'disorder of the body'
and 'subversion of pure thought', 'eccentricity', 'a maddening I am
unable to master'.

Cogito: 'mad audacity', 'mad project', 'project that recognises madness as its liberty', 'disorder and excess of hyperbole', 'unheard of and
unique excess', 'excess towards Nothingness and Infinity', 'hyperbolic
extreme which should be, like all pure madness in general, silent'.

All these derivations are necessary surrounding Descartes' text for the
evil genius and the *cogito* to become, as Derrida wishes, the true scene of
the confrontation with madness. But even more is required: it is necessary
to remove from Descartes' texts themselves everything which shows that
the episode of the evil genius is a voluntary exercise, controlled, mastered,
and carried out from beginning to end by a meditating subject who never
allows himself to be surprised. If it is true that the hypothesis of the evil
genius pushes the suspicion of error well beyond the errors of the senses,
of which certain madmen provide the example, the person who makes

this fiction (and by the very fact that he voluntarily performs it as an exercise) escapes the risk of 'assenting to any falsehoods', as is the case and the misfortune of the mad. He is deceived, but he is not imposed upon. Everything is perhaps illusion, but with no credulity. The evil genius, no doubt, deceives more effectively than a swollen brain; he can conjure up the illusory backdrop of madness, but he is something quite different from madness. It could even be said that he is its contrary: in madness I *believe* that an illusory robe covers my nudity and my poverty, whereas the hypothesis of the evil genius allows *me not to believe* that this body and these hands exist. As for the scope of the trap, the evil genius, it is true, differs not from madness; but regarding the positioning of the subject in relation to the trap, the evil genius and madness are rigorously opposed. The evil genius takes over the power of *madness*, but only after the exercise of the meditation has excluded the risk of *being mad*.

Let us return to Descartes' text. 'I shall think that the sky, the earth, colours, shapes, sounds and all external things are merely the delusions of dreams' (whereas the madman believes that his illusions and dreams really are the sky, the air and an external things). 'I shall consider myself as not having hands or eyes . . . but as falsely believing that I have all these things' (whereas the madman wrongly believes that his body is made of glass, but *does not* consider himself to be believing it wrongly). 'I shall at least do what is in my power, that is, resolutely guard against assenting to any falsehoods' (whereas the madman assents to them all).

We can now see quite clearly: when faced with the cunning deceiver, the meditating subject behaves not at all like a madman ruled by universal error, but like an adversary who is no less cunning and always on the lookout, constantly reasonable, remaining in the position of a master in relation to his fiction: 'I shall resolutely guard against assenting to any falsehoods, so that the deceiver, however cunning or powerful he might be, will be unable to impose on me in the slightest degree.' How far we are from the themes so prettily varied by Derrida: 'Total madness, a total maddening I *would be unable to master*, since it was *inflicted* upon me by hypothesis and I *am not responsible for it.*' How could it be imagined that the meditating subject was no longer responsible for what he himself terms 'this arduous undertaking'?

*

It might well be asked how an author as meticulous as Derrida, and one so attentive to texts, managed not only to allow so many omissions, but also to operate so many displacements, interventions and substitutions. But perhaps we should do that while remembering that Derrida is recalling an old tradition in his reading. He is well aware of this, of course; and this faithfulness seems, quite rightly, to comfort him. He is reluctant, in any case, to think that classical commentators missed, through inattentiveness, the importance and singularity of the passage on madness and dreaming.

I am in agreement on one fact at least: that it was not at all on account of their inattentiveness that classical scholars omitted, before Derrida and like him, this passage from Descartes. It is part of a system, a system of which Derrida is today the most decisive representative, in its waning light: a reduction of discursive practices to textual traces; the elision of events that are produced there, leaving only marks for a reading; the invention of voices behind the text, so as not to have to examine the modes of implication of the subject in discourses; the assignation of the originary as said and not-said in the text in order to avoid situating discursive practices in the field of transformation where they are carried out.

I would not say that it is a metaphysics, metaphysics *itself*, or its closure, that is hiding behind this 'textualisation' of discursive practices. I would go much further: I would say that it is a historically well-determined little pedagogy, which manifests itself here in a very visible manner. A pedagogy which teaches the student that there is nothing outside the text, but that in it, in its interstices, in its blanks and silences, the reserve of the origin reigns; that it is never necessary to look beyond it, but that here, not in the words of course, but in words as crossings-out, in their *lattice*, what is said is 'the meaning of being'. A pedagogy that inversely gives to the voice of the masters that unlimited sovereignty that allows it indefinitely to re-say the text.

Father Bourdin[16] supposed that, according to Descartes, it was not at all possible to doubt things that were certain, even if one was asleep or mad. In relation to a well-founded certainty, the fact of dreaming or being delirious was not at all relevant. But Descartes replied to this interpretation in a quite explicit manner. 'I have no recollection of having said any such thing, nor even dreamt it while sleeping.' Quite so: nothing that is perceived clearly and distinctly can be untrue (and on that level, the problem of knowing if the person who is conceiving, dreams or is delirious is not actually posed). But, Descartes immediately adds, who then can distinguish 'that which is clearly conceived, and that which merely seems and appears to be so'? Who then, as a thinking and meditating subject, can know if he knows clearly or not? Who then is capable of not deluding himself about his own certainty, and not letting himself be impressed? If not precisely those who are not mad? Those who are 'wise'? And Descartes retorts, targeting Father Bourdin, 'But as it is clearly only people who are wise who can distinguish between that which is clearly conceived, and that which merely seems and appears to be so, I am not surprised that that good man takes the one for the other.'

III

REPLY TO DERRIDA

('MICHEL FOUCAULT DERRIDA E NO KAINO') FROM *PAIDEIA*, NO. 11: *MICHEL FOUCAULT*, 1 FEBRUARY 1972, pp. 131–147

Derrida's analysis[1] is undoubtedly remarkable for its philosophical depth and the meticulousness of his reading. I will not try to respond to it; what I would simply like to do is add a few remarks, remarks which will probably seem quite exterior, and which will be so, to the extent that the History of Madness and the texts that have followed it are exterior to philosophy, as it is practised and taught in France.

Derrida thinks that he can capture the meaning of my book or its 'project' from the three pages, the only three pages that are given over to the analysis of a text that is recognised by the philosophical tradition. With his admirable honesty, he himself recognises the paradoxical nature of his enterprise. But he believes that he will be able to surmount it, no doubt, because fundamentally he admits three postulates.

1   He supposes first of all that all knowledge, or in an even broader sense all rational discourse, entertains a fundamental relation with

philosophy, and that it is in this relationship that this rationality or this knowledge have their foundation. To free the implicit philosophy of a discourse, to reveal its contradictions, its limits, or its naivety, is to operate *a fortiori* and by the shortest possible route a critique of all that is said within it. Consequently, there is no point arguing about the 650 pages of a book, no point analysing the historical material that is brought to bear therein, and no point criticising the choice of this material, its distribution and its interpretation, if one has been able to denounce a defect in the founding relationship to philosophy.

2   In relation to this philosophy, which eminently holds the 'law' of all discourse, Derrida supposes that one commits 'faults' of a singular nature: not so much faults of logic or reasoning, which bring errors that might be isolated in a material fashion, but rather faults that are something like a blend of Christian sin and Freudian slip. One sins in Christian fashion against this philosophy by averting one's eyes from it, by refusing its blinding light and attaching oneself to the singular positivity of things.

In relation to it, genuine slips are also made: we betray it without realising it, we reveal it by resisting it, and we allow it to appear in a language that only a philosopher is in a position to decode. The fault *par excellence* against philosophy is naivety, naivety that only ever thinks at the level of the world, and which ignores the law of that which thinks in it and despite it. Because the fault against philosophy is close to the slip, it will be 'revelatory' in the same way: the smallest 'snag' will suffice for the whole apparatus to be laid bare. But because the fault against philosophy is of the order of Christian sin, it suffices for there to be one, a mortal one, for salvation to be no longer possible. For that reason Derrida supposes that if he shows an error regarding Descartes in my text, on the one hand he will have shown the law that unconsciously rules everything that I could say about police regulations in the seventeenth century, unemployment in the classical era, Pinel's reform and psychiatric asylums of the nineteenth century; and on the other hand, as it is a matter of sin as much as it is of a slip, he will not have to show the precise effect of this error in the field of my study (how it affects the analysis that I make of the institutions or of medical theories): one single sin is enough to compromise a whole life . . . without one having to show all the major and minor faults that developed from it.

3   Derrida's third postulate is that philosophy is on the far side and the near side of any event. Not only can nothing happen to it, but everything

that can happen is already anticipated or enveloped by it. In itself, philosophy is only the repetition of an origin that is more than originary, and which infinitely exceeds, in its retreat, anything that it could say in any of its historical discourses. But as it is a repetition of that origin, any philosophical discourse, provided it is authentically philosophical, exceeds in its excess anything that can happen in the order of knowledge, of institutions, of societies, etc. The excess of this origin, which philosophy alone (and no other form of discourse or practice) can repeat beyond any forgetting, denies all pertinence to the event. So much so that, for Derrida, there is no sense in discussing the analysis that I propose of this series of events which, for two centuries, constituted the history of madness; and, truth be told, my book is quite naive, in his view, in wanting to write history on the basis of the derisory events that are the confinement of a few tens of thousands of people, or the setting up of an extra-judiciary State police; it would have been sufficient, more than amply so, to rehearse once again the repetition of philosophy by Descartes, who himself repeated the Platonic excess. For Derrida, what happened in the seventeenth century could only ever be a 'sample' (i.e. a repetition of the identical) or a 'model' (i.e. the inexhaustible excess of origin). He does not know the category of the singular event; it is therefore pointless for him – and probably impossible – to read that which occupies the essential part, if not the totality of my book: the analysis of an event.

These three postulates are considerable and highly respectable: they form the framework of the teaching of philosophy in France. It is in their name that philosophy presents itself as the universal criticism of all knowledge (the first postulate), without any real analysis of the content or the forms of this knowledge; as a moral injunction to awaken only by its own light (the second postulate), as a perpetual reduplication of itself (the third postulate) in an infinite commentary of its own texts and without any relation to any exteriority.

Of all the people who currently philosophise in France, sheltered by these three postulates, Derrida, without a shadow of a doubt, is the most profound and the most radical. But it is perhaps these postulates themselves that should be called into question: I, for my own account, try to free myself of them, in so far as it is possible to free oneself of that which, for so long, the institutions have imposed upon me.

What I have tried to show (but it was probably not clear to my own eyes when I was writing the *History of Madness*) is that philosophy is neither historically nor logically a foundation of knowledge; but that there are conditions and rules for the formation of knowledge to which philosophical discourse is subject, in any given period, in the same manner as any other form of discourse with rational pretension.

What I tried to show, moreover, in the *History of Madness* and elsewhere, is that the systematicity which links together forms of discourse, concepts, institutions, and practices is not of the order of a forgotten radical thought that has been covered over and hidden from itself, nor is it a Freudian unconscious, but that knowledge has an unconscious that has its own specific forms and rules. This is to say that I set out to study and analyse the 'events' that can come about in the order of knowledge, and which cannot be reduced either to the general law of some kind of 'progress', or the repetition of an origin.

It should now be clear why my book inevitably appeared quite exterior and superficial compared to the profound philosophical interiority of Derrida's work. For me, the most essential part of the work was in the analysis of these events, these bodies of knowledge, and those systematic forms that link discourses, institutions and practices, and these are all things about which Derrida has not a word to say in his text. But I had not yet managed to free myself sufficiently from the postulates of philosophical teaching, as I was unable to resist placing at the head of one chapter, and therefore in quite a privileged place, the analysis of a text by Descartes. This was no doubt the most expendable part of my book, and I willingly admit that I should have omitted it, had I been more consistent in my casual indifference towards philosophy.

But, after all, this passage exists: it is the way it is, and Derrida claims that it contains an important series of errors which contain and compromise the total meaning of the book.

I believe, however, that Derrida's analysis is inexact. In order to be able to show that these three pages of my text would carry away with them the 650 other pages, in order to be able to criticise the totality of my book without saying a word about its historical content, its methods, its concepts, its hypotheses (where there would undoubtedly be ample room for criticism), it seems to me that Derrida was forced to falsify his own reading of Descartes, and also the reading that he made of my text.

Derrida remarks that, in the passage from the *First Meditation* which deals with madness, it is not so much Descartes who speaks as a fictive interlocutor who makes a naive objection: all the senses do not deceive us all the time, this objector apparently says; I cannot doubt for example that I am here by the fire; to deny it would be to 'liken oneself [*se comparer*]' to certain insane people; but, the naive person apparently continues, I am not mad, therefore there are things that I could not doubt. To this, in Derrida's reading, Descartes replies by quoting the case of dreams which produce eccentricities [*extravagances*] as great as those of madness, but to which we are all, each one of us, exposed. Derrida then concludes:

- that it is not Descartes who states 'But so what? Such people are insane' [*mais quoi, ce sont des fous*];
- that in any case the eccentricities of madness are implicated in the dream that follows. To Derrida's analysis one might reply as follows:

1   If it is true that it is another voice that appears to interrupt the text and voice this objection, then why not travel a little further in the same direction, along the lines of the objection that I had advanced, i.e. that Descartes does not allow madness to enter the process of his doubt? If it is in that way that Descartes' text should be read, then Derrida is saying that I was even more right than I thought.

2   The hypothesis of another voice seems to me (despite all the advantages that it might present to me) useless and arbitrary. We should keep in mind the title of the text itself, *Meditations*. That means that the speaking subject ceaselessly moves, changes, modifies his convictions, and advances in his certainties, taking risks and constantly trying new things. Unlike deductive discourse, where the speaking subject remains fixed and invariable, the meditative text supposes a mobile subject who tries out on himself the hypotheses that he envisages. Derrida imagines a 'rhetorical' or 'pedagogical' fiction, where what should be understood is a meditative episode. One need only, as Derrida recommends, refer back to the Latin text of the *Meditations* to see that it is punctuated throughout by expressions like *at tamen* (but however), *sed contra* (but on the other hand), moments which mark 'peripeteia', turning points, events in the meditation, rather than the emergence of a different voice.

We should therefore read Descartes' trajectory in the following manner: a resolution not to trust the senses (as it has been the case that they have deceived me); an attempt to save nonetheless a domain of sensible certainty (my present situation, with the things around me). How could that domain in fact be attacked? Who is mistaken about what he is, about what he is doing, and about the place where he is? Only the mad and people who are sleeping.

Let us try the first hypothesis. We are immediately stopped, because 'Such people are insane, and I would be no less eccentric . . .' Let us now try the second hypothesis. This time there is no more resistance; the possibility reveals itself to be a frequent reality: 'how often at night have I not dreamt that I was in this place, that I was dressed, that I was by the fire', and, as though to show that the possibility of dreaming might provoke doubt about this region of sensible things which the hypothesis of madness was unable to reach, Descartes takes up again here, as an example of dreaming, the same perceptive elements that, a few moments earlier, he had tried to save. Let us resume this path, not in terms of a 'pedagogical fiction', but as a meditative experience:

- the resolution to be wary of everything that comes from the senses;
- the temptation nonetheless to salvage a part of that (that which is near me);
- the first test for that temptation: madness. The temptation resists because the test disappears of its own accord;
- the second test: dreaming. This time the test is a success and the temptation disappears; the certainty of that which is near me no longer has any reason to block and 'seduce' the resolution to doubt.

3   Descartes insists on the fact that dreaming is often even more unlikely than madness. Derrida is quite right to underline this point. But what does this insistence mean for Descartes? Derrida thinks that, for Descartes, madness is but an attenuated and relatively uneccentric form of dreaming, and that for that reason, he did not have to pay it too much heed. Derrida goes so far as to write that dreaming – still for Descartes – is a 'more universal' experience than madness: 'the madman is not always wrong, nor about everything'.

Descartes, however, does not say that: he does not say that a madman is only mad from time to time; it is, on the contrary, dreaming which happens from time to time, when one sleeps, and as 'I am a man', 'it is my custom to dream'.

If dreaming for Descartes has one privilege that madness does not have, if it can take its place in the meditating experience of doubt, it is because, while producing imaginings that are at least as extravagant as madness, and perhaps even more so, it can happen to me. Let us read the section of Descartes that immediately follows his rejection of the hypothesis of madness: 'However, I must consider here that I am a man, and that consequently it is my custom to dream and to see in my dreams.' Dream has the double power of producing sensible eccentricities (like madness, and to a greater extent) and of happening to me on a regular basis (which is not at all the case with madness). The extreme imaginative richness of dreaming means that, from the point of view of logic and reasoning, the experience of the dream will be, in order to doubt the totality of the sensible domain, at least as convincing as madness; but the fact that it can happen to me enables it to enter the very movement of the meditation, and to become a test in its own right, and an effective one, whereas madness is an experience that is immediately impossible.

Derrida only saw the first aspect of dreaming (its greater eccentricity), whereas for Descartes, that only meant that the experiment he accepted and included is no less demonstrative than the one that he excluded. Derrida completely omits the second characteristic of dreaming (the fact that it can happen to me, and that it does in fact happen quite often). Or rather, Derrida, with his ever-sharp sense for texts, has a presentiment of this, as he says at one point that, for Descartes, dreaming is more 'natural'; but he moves on swiftly without realising that he has just touched the essential and misrepresented it; Descartes of course does not speak of dreaming as something that is 'natural and universal'; he says that he is a man, and that consequently, it is his custom to dream and to sleep. And he returns several times to the fact that dreaming is a frequent thing, which happens countless times; 'how often at night have I not dreamt', 'what happens during sleep', 'considering the matter carefully, I remember often being deceived while sleeping'.

Now while it is important for Descartes that sleeping is a customary thing, this is not at all to demonstrate that it is more 'universal' than madness, it is to be able to take up again, to be able to imitate and feign in the meditation the experience of dreaming, it is in order to pretend or to act as though we were dreaming; it is so that the experience of dreaming can take its place in the effective movement carried out by the meditating subject. There again, it is enough to go back to Descartes' text: it happens that I dream, that I dream that I am by the fire, that I stretch out my hand; if I apply myself to this thought (which is a memory); and the vivacity of this memory, the current form of this thought makes me see (in this precise moment of the meditation) 'that there is no sure indication allowing a clear distinction to be made between waking and sleeping'. And this indistinction is not simply a logical inference, it is genuinely inscribed at this precise moment of the meditation; it has its immediate effect on the subject who is meditating; it makes him abandon, or almost, the certainty that he possessed up until that point, that as a meditating and speaking subject, he was awake; it genuinely places him inside the possibility that he is actually asleep: 'I am quite astonished by this, and my astonishment is such that it is nearly sufficient to convince me that I am asleep'.

That sentence is not there for stylistic effect: it is neither 'rhetorical' nor 'pedagogical'. On the one hand it enables all the movement of the meditation that follows, which opens out into the possibility of sleeping. The following sentences should be read as instructions that are made possible by the 'astonishment' that has just come into being: 'Let us now suppose then [Supposons donc maintenant] that we are asleep . . . let us think that perhaps neither our friends nor our body are as we imagine them to be.' And on the other hand, it answers, almost exactly, a sentence from the preceding paragraph: 'But so what? Such people are insane,' said the first paragraph; 'I see so clearly . . . I am quite astonished by this', says the second. 'I would be no less eccentric if I modelled myself on their example', says the paragraph of the mad; 'my astonishment is such that it is nearly sufficient to convince me that I am asleep,' says, in response, the paragraph about dreaming.

It is extraordinarily difficult not to hear the symmetry of the two sentences here, and not to recognise that madness plays the role of the impossible possibility, while dreaming in its turn appears like a possibility that is so possible, so immediately possible, that it is already here, now, at the moment when I am speaking.

4   For Derrida, the most important word in the text is the word 'eccentric' [extravagant], which is used to characterise both the imagination of the mad and the fantasy of dreamers. And as dreamers are even more eccentric than the mad, madness dissolves quite naturally into dreaming.

I will pass quickly over the fact that the same word is used in the French version, but that this was not the case in the Latin text. I will simply point out that, in the paragraph about the mad, Descartes uses the word dementes, a technical, medical and legal term to designate a category of people who were statutorily incapable of a certain number of religious, civil and legal acts; the *dementes* were disqualified whenever it was a question of acting, going to court or speaking. That Descartes used the word at this point in the text, where the speaking and meditating subject claims that he cannot be mad, is probably not down to chance. I would perhaps not even have thought of it if Derrida had not tempted me into it with a sentence I find quite enigmatic: 'For Descartes here it is not a matter of determining the concept of madness, but of using the contemporary notion of eccentricity for legal and methodological ends, to ask questions of law[2] [*pour poser des questions de droit*] about the truth of ideas.' Indeed, Derrida is right to remark on the legal connotation of the term, but he is wrong not to note that the legal term is no longer used in the Latin when it is a question of dreaming; and he is wrong above all to add hastily that it is a question of law regarding the truth of ideas, whereas the question of law concerns the qualification of the speaking subject. Can I play the *demens* in a valid manner in the path of my meditation, as I played the *dormiens* [the sleeper] a moment ago? Is there not a risk that I might disqualify myself in my meditation? Would I not risk no longer meditating at all, or carrying out nothing more than an eccentric meditation, instead of meditating in a valid manner about eccentricity, if I started to play the madman? The answer is formulated in the text, in an extremely explicit manner: 'Such people are insane, and I would be no less eccentric if I modelled myself on their example.' If I play the madman, I will be no less *demens* than they are, no less disqualified than they are, no less external to any legitimacy of action or speech than they are. On the contrary, if I play the sleeping person, if I suppose that I am sleeping, I continue to think and I can even perceive the things that are represented before me 'like pictures and paintings'.

But despite the importance, which is indeed legal, of the word *demens*, it seems to me that the key terms in the text are expressions like 'here', 'now', 'this paper', 'I am beside the fire', 'I stretch out my hand', in short all the expressions that refer to the system of actuality of the meditating subject. They indicate those impressions which, in the first instance, one would be quite tempted not to doubt. They are the same impressions that can be found identically in dreaming. Curiously – and Derrida omits to note it – Descartes, who spoke of the unlikelinesses of dreaming, of its fantasies which are no less great than those of madness, gives in this paragraph no other example than that of dreaming that one is 'in this place, dressed, beside the fire'. But the reason for this quite paradoxical example of oneiric extravagance is easily discovered in the paragraph that follows, when it is a question, for the meditating person, of playing the sleeper: he will act as though the eyes that he opens on his paper, the hand that he stretches out, the head that he shakes, were nothing more than images in a dream. The same scene is given three times over the three paragraphs: I am seated, I have my eyes open on a piece of paper, the fire is beside me, I stretch out my hand. The first time it is given as the immediate certainty of the meditating subject; the second time it is given as a dream which, quite frequently, has just happened; the third time it is given as the immediate certainty of the meditating subject who is pretending, in the full application of his thought, to be a man who is dreaming, so that inside his resolution he persuades himself that it is of no matter, for the progress of his meditation, to know whether he is awake or sleeping.

If we accepted Derrida's reading, we would not understand the repetition of this scene. It would be necessary, on the contrary, for the example of madness to be in retreat in relation to the examples of oneiric phantasmagoria. But it is the opposite that happens. Descartes, while affirming the great power of dreams, can give no other example than the one which exactly redoubles the current situation of the subject who is meditating and speaking; and that, so that the experience of feigned dreaming can come and take exactly its place between the markers of the here and now. On the other hand, the insane are characterised as those who take themselves for kings, as those who imagine themselves to be dressed in gold, or that they have a body of glass or that they are water pitchers. More or less eccentric than dreaming, it matters little, the images of madness that Descartes chooses as an example are, unlike those of dreaming, incompatible with the system of actuality that the individual who is speaking signals of his own accord. The madman is elsewhere, in a different moment, with another body and other clothes. He is on a different stage. The person who is there beside the fire, looking at his paper, cannot be mistaken. Descartes has loaded the dice: if the meditating subject were to have pretended to be a madman, just as he was to pretend a moment later that he was dreaming, it would have been necessary to propose to him the tempting image of a madman believing in his madness that he is actually sitting here beside the fire, looking at his paper and taking himself for a man who is meditating about a man who is sitting here right now, beside the fire, etc.

Descartes' *coup de force* is easily discernible at this point. While proclaiming the great freedom of dreaming, he constrained it to confining itself to the actuality of the meditating subject; and while asserting that madness is perhaps less eccentric, he gave it the liberty to take a shape as distant as possible from the meditating subject, so that the impossibility of pretending, of doubling, of indifferentiation immediately appears in an exclamation. But so what? Such people are insane. . . It is this dissymmetry between dreaming and madness that allows Descartes to reconstitute after the act an appearance of symmetry, and to present them in turn as two tests to gauge the solidity of immediate certainties.

But, as we can see, this dissymmetry in the contents quoted as an example buries a much more important dissymmetry: one that concerns the meditating subject, who would disqualify himself and no longer be able to meditate if he took it upon himself to pretend, to play or to be the madman, but who loses nothing of his qualification when he resolves to feign sleep.

5   Let us take up again the two most characteristic sentences of Derrida regarding our passage: 'the hypothesis of eccentricity seems at this moment in the Cartesian order not to receive any privileged treatment and not to be subject to any particular exclusion', and the hypothesis of eccentricity is 'an ineffective and unfortunate example in the pedagogical order, because it comes up against the resistance of the non-philosopher who dares not follow the philosopher when he notes that he might well be mad at the moment at which he is speaking'.

Both the first and the second of these sentences contain a major error:
–   the inexactness of the first appears when one follows the meditation as a series of resolutions that are immediately put into practice: 'I shall first tackle', 'it is prudent never to trust', and 'Let us now imagine'. Three resolutions, then. The first resolution concerns the putting in doubt of the principles 'on which all my previous opinions were founded'; the second concerns that which has been learned by the senses; the third concerns dreaming. Now, although there are three resolutions, there are four themes: the principles behind the opinions, knowledge that can be derived from the senses, madness, and dreaming. No particular resolution corresponds to the theme of 'madness'.
–   Derrida's second sentence seems moreover to recognise this exclusion, as he sees in the hypothesis of extravagance an 'ineffective and unfortunate example'. But he immediately adds that it is the non-philosopher who refuses to follow the philosopher in his acknowledgement that he might be mad. However, nowhere in this passage

does the 'philosopher', or let us say more precisely the person who is meditating, accept that he might be mad, whereas he accepts and even imposes upon himself the acknowledgement that he might be dreaming.

If I recall these two sentences by Derrida, it is not at all because they sum up the manner in which he has falsified the Cartesian text (to the point of being almost in contradiction with himself in his commentary), but because they allow a question to be asked: how could a philosopher as attentive as Derrida, as preoccupied with the rigour of texts, have been able to read this Descartes passage in a manner so vague, so distant, so unsuited to its overall disposition, its concatenations and its symmetries, and to all that is said there?

I believe that the reason is indicated by Derrida himself in the two sentences in question. In each one, it should be noted, he employs the word 'order': 'at this moment in the Cartesian order', and 'pedagogical order'. We shall pass over the fact that it is slightly strange to speak of a 'pedagogical order' regarding the movement of the *Meditations*, unless one gives a very narrow and strong sense to 'pedagogical'. Let us simply examine the word 'order'. There is indeed a rigorous order in the *Meditations*, and no sentence in the text can be detached with impunity from the moment at which it is placed. But what is this order? Is it an architectural order, whose elements are retained in a visible permanence, and may be read in any direction? Is it a spatial order that any anonymous and distant gaze may take in without itself being enveloped by it? Is it, in other words, an 'architectonic' order?

It seems to me that the order of the *Meditations* is of a different sort. First, because it is not made up of the elements of a figure, but of the moments in a series; and latterly (or rather at the same time) because it is in fact an exercise during which the meditating subject is slowly modified, and starting as a subject of opinions becomes qualified as a subject of certainty. The *Meditations* should be read as a temporal series of transformations that qualify the subject. It is a series of events that are proposed to the reader as events that are repeatable both by and for himself. In this series, where the resolution to doubt occurred as an event, and the resolution to be wary of the senses as another, and where the decision to act as though one were sleeping will take place, there is a moment where madness is indeed envisaged, but as an eventuality that one cannot assume, and to which one cannot grant access to the game of qualifying transformations (precisely because it would be disqualifying); this moment is by that very action a certain manner of qualifying the meditating subject as being unable to be mad – a manner therefore of transforming him by exclusion, by the exclusion of any possibility of madness. And, once this qualifying exclusion has been acquired (which enables me to avoid feigning and risking madness), then, and only then, can madness with its images and its eccentricities appear; a justification after the act will appear: in any case, I was not so wrong to avoid the test of madness, as the images that it gives me are often less fantastical than those that I find every night while sleeping. But, at the moment when this theme appears, the moment of the exclusion has already been passed, and madness presents itself in all its oddities, as an object of which one speaks, and no longer as a test which is possible for the subject. It would appear that one misses the essential part of the Cartesian text if one does not place at the forefront of the analysis the relations between the moment and subject in the order of the tests.

At the moment when he was most distant from the letter of the Cartesian text, and at the moment when his reading is the most inexact, Derrida – and this is indeed a sign of his rigorous concern – is unable to prevent himself from using the decisive word 'order', as though he were dimly aware that it is indeed order that is in question here, that it is order that presents a problem to him, and an objection. But he immediately hastens to attenuate the import of that which Descartes' text nonetheless constrains him to mention: in one case he speaks without dwelling on it, and as though to limit the rip that the word represents in the fabric of his own text, of a 'pedagogical order'; in the other case he totally reverses the value of what happens at this moment in the order he discerns: he denies that madness is excluded, a negation to which he returns two pages later, saying that madness is an example that is not retained by Descartes because it is 'ineffective and unfortunate'. If the word 'order' is such a problem for Derrida that he cannot use it without disarming it or blurring its meaning, that is because he uses it regarding this moment about madness in the manner in which historians of philosophy employ it when they speak of the ordering, of the architecture, or of the structure of a system. But, it might be objected, what is the matter with that? Have there not been architectonic studies of the Cartesian system, and are they not perfectly convincing? Of course.

It is of course possible to identify as elements of a system all the moments of the *Meditation*; the test of the doubt for the perceptions received from the senses and the tests of dreaming and sleeping may all be re-read from the inside of the system when it is laid out, in so far as they are positive tests which the subject who is slowly becoming qualified as a subject of certainty did indeed pass through; what the system will have to say about the foundations of sensible certainty, about the divine guarantee, about the functioning of the senses will then come to coincide with that which is revealed in the meditation test. It is because he will have pretended to dream or believe that all his senses are deceiving him that the meditating subject becomes capable of perfectly founded certainty regarding the functioning of his senses, of images, of the brain, and of the trust that can be put in them. Systematic truth includes the moment of the test. This moment can therefore be understood on the basis of the systematic truth, and of the ordering which is its own.

On the other hand, as far as madness is concerned, and madness alone, the same cannot be said. Madness is not a qualifying test for the subject, it is a test which is on the contrary excluded. So that what can be known with founded certainty before madness, inside the system, will not later have to take into account a test that has not taken place. Inside the system, the mechanisms of madness do indeed have their place (and precisely beside those of dreaming); but the moment of the exclusion of madness cannot be found if one sets out from there, as, to understand in a valid manner the mechanisms of the brain, of the vapours and of madness, it was necessary for the meditating subject not to expose himself to the hypothesis of being mad. The moment of the exclusion of madness in the subject who seeks the truth is necessarily hidden from the point of view of the architectonic ordering of the system. And, as he places himself at that vantage point, which is probably legitimate for all the other moments of the *Meditations*, Derrida was necessarily condemning himself to not seeing the exclusion of madness.

If, however, he had paid a little more attention to the text of which he speaks, he would no doubt have perceived a very strange fact. In this first *Meditation*, Descartes, when he speaks of errors of the senses or of dreaming, obviously never proposes any explanation for them, but only takes them at the level of their eventuality and of their most obvious effects. It is only in the unfolding of founded truths that we will understand why the eyes can deceive, and why images can present themselves to the mind during sleep. Regarding madness, by contrast, Descartes mentions those mechanisms from the very first steps in the test of doubt ('a brain so

troubled and shrouded in the black vapours of the bile'): an explanation
whose general principles we will find again later on; but this explanation is given as though the system were already bursting in, and was
beginning to speak before it had even been founded. What we should see
here, I believe, is the proof that at 'this moment of the Cartesian order',
madness appears in all its impossibility for the subject who is meditating;
it appears from within the element of constituted knowledge like a process
that can happen to the brains of others, according to mechanisms that are
already known, and which knowledge has already localised, defined, and
mastered. At the moment at which the risk of the mad philosopher
is rejected – both to mask and to justify this refusal – what appears is
madness as mechanism, madness as disease. An anticipated fragment of
knowledge comes to take the place of the rejected test.

Therefore, by wrongly placing what he already knows at the moment
when all knowledge is put to the test, Descartes signals that which he is
masking, and reintroduces in advance into his system that which for his
philosophy is simultaneously a condition of its existence and pure exteriority: the refusal really to suppose that he is mad. For this second reason,
one cannot perceive, from inside the system, the exclusion of madness. It
can only appear in analysis of the philosophical discourse, not as an architectural remnant, but as a series of events. But how could a philosophy of
traces, following the tradition and the maintaining of the tradition, be
sensible to an analysis of the event? How can a philosophy that is so
preoccupied with remaining inside the interiority of philosophy recognise this external event, this limit event, this primary division, through
which the resolution to be a philosopher and to attain the truth excludes
madness? How could a philosophy which places itself under the sign of
origin and repetition think the singularity of the event? What status and
place could it give to an event that really happened (even if in Descartes'
writing the personal pronoun 'I' allows anyone to repeat it), an event
which meant that a man sitting by the fire, his eyes fixed on his paper,
accepted the risk of dreaming that he was a man asleep, who was dreaming that he was seated by the fire, his eyes fixed on a piece of paper, but
refused the risk of seriously imagining that he was a madman imagining
that he was seated by the fire, reading or writing?

On the external margins of Cartesian philosophy, the event is still so
legible that Derrida, from the inside of the philosophical tradition that he
assumes with such depth, was unable to avoid recognising that it was still

there, restlessly roaming. It is probably for that reason that he decided to give this event the imaginary face of a fictive interlocutor, who is totally exterior, in the naivety of his discourse, to philosophy. Through this voice that he superimposes on the text, Derrida guarantees that the Cartesian discourse remains closed to any event that would be outside the great interiority of philosophy. And, as the messenger of this insolent event, he imagined a naive fellow with his stupid objections, coming to knock on the door of philosophical discourse, and being thrown out without having been able to come in.

It is indeed in such manner, in the form of the naive interlocutor, that philosophy represented to itself all that which was external to it. But where is the true naivety?

ENDNOTES

FOREWORD

1 'Pierre Menard, Author of Don Quixote', in J. L. Borges, *Ficciones*, Grove Press, 1962, pp. 45–55 (original Spanish of 1939).

INTRODUCTION

1 The French edition was abridged by Foucault himself. There is evidence that Foucault was consulted on the English edition since a chapter missing in the abridged French edition was reinserted in the English one. On the impact of this abbreviation on the reception of the book in the English-speaking world, see Colin Gordon, '*Histoire de la folie*, an unknown book by Michel Foucault', in A. Still and I. Velody, eds., *Rewriting the History of Madness*, London: Routledge, 1992.

2 At the end of the 1961 preface, Foucault places the whole book 'beneath the sun of the great Nietzschean quest'. An extensive discussion of Nietzsche on history is to be found in 'Nietzsche, la généalogie, l'histoire', an essay Foucault published in 1971 in a festschrift offered to the great historian of Hegelianism, Jean Hyppolite (translation in Paul Rabinow, ed., *The Foucault Reader*, London: Penguin Books, 1991).

3 This is still the point of view of Pascal, in the seventeenth century, but from a purely theological point of view. In an association still marked by existentialism, he opens, together with Dostoevsky, Foucault's 1961 Preface.

4 In a debate of 1979 with John Searle, Foucault stressed that he was not 'claiming that there is no such thing as truth but that [he] only wanted to describe its

rules'. One of the main tasks of the research described in *The Archaeology of Knowledge* (1969, trans. A. M. Sheridan Smith, London: Routledge, 1972) is to analyse the rules followed by discourses seen as practices that systematically form the objects of which they speak (p. 49). It thus does not place itself at the epistemological level, the level of the type of history of science developed by G. Bachelard and G. Canguilhem which aims at determining how a science has detached itself from pre-scientific conceptions, and therefore starts from an assumption of scientificity and concerns itself with 'the opposition of truth and error, the rational and the irrational, the obstacle and fecundity, purity and impurity, the scientific and the non-scientific'. Foucault's *Archaeological History* targets an earlier stage where: 'what one is trying to uncover are discursive practices in so far as they give rise to a corpus of knowledge, in so far as they assume the status and role of a science', knowing that they may very well not have succeeded in becoming sciences (p. 190). In the first edition of his first book, *Maladie mentale et personnalité* (Paris: Presses Universitaires de France, 1954) Foucault still defines his project as 'to show from what postulates mental medicine must free itself in order to become rigorously scientific' (p. 2). On this, see Frédéric Gros, *Foucault et la folie* (Paris: Presses Universitaires de France, 1997).

5   The great precursor to this historicisation of what has come to be considered natural and of the genealogical method is, before Nietzsche, Rousseau (in particular in the *Discourse on the Origin and the Foundations of Inequality Among Men* of 1754). Curiously, Foucault fails to acknowledge it even when he refers (p. 372) to the passages where Rousseau asserts the contingent origin of what human beings take to be their nature.

6   In the Introduction to *The Archaeology of Knowledge*, Foucault indicated that the book was still too close to 'admitting an anonymous and general subject of history'. He specifically marked his distance from this perspective: 'We are not trying to reconstitute what madness itself might be, in the form in which it first presented itself to some primitive, fundamental, obscure, scarcely articulated experience.' He added in a footnote: 'This is written against an explicit theme of my book *The History of Madness*, and one that recurs particularly in the Preface' (p. 47). In fact Foucault started to move away from phenomenology in his 1954 Introduction to Ludwig Binswanger's *Dream and Existence* (edited by Keith Hoeller, Atlantic Highlands, NJ: Humanities Press, 1993).

7   He was shortly, but apparently unknowingly, followed by Harry Frankfurt, who published in 1970 his *Demons, Dreamers and Madmen: The Defense of Reason in Descartes' 'Meditations'*. The earliest commentator on the question was probably the author of the Seventh Objections to Descartes' *Meditations*, the Jesuit priest Pierre Bourdin, to whom Foucault alludes as anticipating Derrida's criticism of his own thesis.

8   Reprinted in Jacques Derrida, *Writing and Difference*, London: Routledge, 1979, pp. 31–63. This text originates in a talk given by Derrida at a meeting of the Collège Philosophique in March 1963, and attended by Foucault at his invitation. It was first published in the *Revue de Métaphysique et de Morale* in 1964.

9   In 1992, in a commemorative volume for the thirtieth anniversary of the first
    edition of *History of Madness*, Derrida published a long reflexion on the impos-
    sible exchange with Foucault, under the title ' "Être juste avec Freud". L'histoire
    de la folie à l'âge de la psychanalyse' (' "Being fair to Freud". The history of
    madness in the age of psychoanalysis') in E. Roudinesco, ed., *Penser la folie.
    Essais sur Michel Foucault* (Paris, Galilée 1992). An English translation of
    this essay was published in Arnold Davidson, *Foucault and his interlocutors*,
    (Chicago University Press, 1997, 57–96). Here he tries to fold Foucault upon
    himself and write an archaeology of the book.
10 Foucault could have added that Descartes did rewrite the *Meditations* in the
    form of a dialogue, *La Recherche de la vérité*. In this dialogue, the objection
    against the argument from madness does not seem to come from the 'hon-
    nête homme', Poliandre, but from the philosopher, Descartes-Eudoxe, who
    objects it to himself.

PREFACE TO THE 1961 EDITION

1   'Les hommes sont si nécessairement fous que ce serait être fou par un autre
    tour de folie de n'être pas fou' Pascal, *Pensées*, 414 (412 Lafuma). Usually
    translated by the simpler approximation 'Men are so necessarily mad that not
    to be mad would amount to another form of madness', this formulation has
    been preferred as Foucault makes great play with the idea of the 'tour' (literally
    'trick'). But, laden with all the Pascalian ideas about the different levels at
    which illusion can occur and double up, it could equally be translated as 'turn'
    and 'detour'. [Translators' note, henceforth abbreviated as TN.]
2   In French, *'conjuration'* – a word that hovers between the English 'expulsion'
    and 'exorcism'.
3   'Tear' (*déchirure*) here as in a rip in the fabric of society.
4   Bibliothèque de l'Arsenal: mss no. 12023 and 12024.
5   Yves Bonnefoy, *Vrai nom*, from *Du mouvement et de l'immobilité de Douve*, in
    Poèmes (Paris: Mercure de France, 1978).
6   René Char, *Suzerain*, in *Poèmes et prose choisis* (Paris: Gallimard, 1957), p. 87.
7   Ibid.
8   René Char, *Partage formel*, in *Poèmes et prose choisis*, pp. 220–221.

PART ONE

I *STULTIFERA NAVIS*

1   Quoted in Collet, *Vie de saint Vincent de Paul*, I, Paris, 1818, p. 293.
2   See J. Lebeuf, *Histoire de la ville et de tout le diocèse de Paris*, Paris, 1754–1758.
3   Quoted by H. M. Fay, *Lépreux et cagots du Sud-Ouest*, Paris, 1910, p. 285.
4   P.-A. Hildenfinger, *La Léproserie de Reims du XIIe au XVIIe siècle*, Reims, 1906,
    p. 233.

5   N. de La Mare, *Traité de police*, Paris, 1738, vol. I, pp. 637–639. Foucault refers to Nicolas de La Mare (1639–1723, Procureur du Roi), as Delamare, we have adopted the Bibliothèque Nationale de France international scientific spelling. [TN]

6   Valvonnais, *Histoire du Dauphiné*, vol. II, p. 171.

7   L. Cibrario, *Précis historique des ordres religieux de Saint-Lazare et de Saint-Maurice*, Lyon, 1860.

8   J. Rocher, *Notice historique sur la maladrerie de Saint-Hilaire-Saint-Mesmin*, Orléans, 1866.

9   J.-A. Ulysse Chevalier, *Notice historique sur la maladrerie de Voley près Romans*, Romans, 1870, pp. 12–13.

10 John Morrisson Hobson, *Some Early and Later Houses of Pity*, London, 1926, pp. 12–13.

11 Ch. A. Mercier, *Leper Houses and Medieval Hospitals*, p. 19.

12 Virchnow, *Archiv zur Geschichte des Aussatzes*, vol. XIX, pp. 71 and 80; vol. XX, p. 511.

13 Ritual from the diocess of Vienne, printed under Archbishop Gui de Poissieu, around 1478. Quoted in Charret, *Histoire de l'Eglise de Vienne*, p. 752.

14 J. Pignot, *Les Origines de l'Hôpital du Midi*, Paris, 1885, pp. 10 and 48.

15 From a manuscript in *Archives de l'Assistance publique* (Petites-Maisons dossier, bundle 4).

16 Trithemius, *Chronicon Hisangiense*, quoted by Potton in his translation of Ulrich von Hutten's *Sur la maladie française et sur les propriétés du bois de gaïac*, Lyon, 1865, p. 9.

17 The earliest mention of venereal disease in France is at the Hôtel-Dieu, quoted by Brièle, *Collection de documents pour servir à l'histoire des hôpitaux de Paris*, Paris, 1881–1887, III, fascicule 2.

18 See the report on a visit to the Hôtel-Dieu in 1507 quoted by Pignot, p. 125.

19 According to R. Goldhahn, *Spital und Arzt von Einst bis Jetzt*, p. 110.

20 Béthencourt reports this treatment as superior to all others, in *Nouveau carême de pénitence et purgatoire d'expiation*, 1527.

21 Béthencourt's book for example is a rigorous medical textbook, despite its title.

22 In the translations of vocabulary relating to madness, we have tried to remain as close to the French as possible: 'mad', 'madman' or 'madwoman' for *fou, folle*, 'insane' for *insensé*, 'unreason' for *déraison*, etc. (the word 'folly' has been avoided wherever possible, on account of its literary or pejorative over-tones). It should be remembered, however, that while some forms translate quite well, this is not always the case. Even for writers who, like Willis and Descartes, published their work in Latin, and shared a common vocabulary, some of the more technical divisions (like *vesaniae*) are more problematical. Here, where the equivalence between French and English presents difficulties, the original French is presented in square brackets. [TN]

23 'Les fous avaient alors une existence facilement errante.' This sentence was the basis for a lengthy polemic among Foucault's English-language readers, as it was originally translated as 'Madmen then led an easy wandering existence.'

Another possible translation is: 'The existence of the mad might easily be a wandering one.' The mistranslation was used in an influential essay by H. C. Erik Midelfort as evidence of Foucault's 'poor scholarship'. [TN]

24 T. Kirchhoff, *Geschichte der Psychiatrie*, Leipzig, 1912.

25 Cf. Kriegk, *Aerzte, Heilanstalten und Geistkranke im mittelälterliche* Frankfurt a.M., 1863.

26 See the Hôtel-Dieu accounts, XIX, 190 and XX, 346. Quoted in Coyeque, *L'Hôtel-Dieu de Paris au Moyen Age*, Paris, 1889–1891. Histoire et Documents, vol. I, p. 109.

27 *Archives hospitalières de Melun*. Fonds Saint-Jacques, E, 14, 67.

28 A. Joly, *L'Internement des fous sous l'Ancien Régime dans la généralité de Basse-Normandie*, Caen, 1868.

29 Cf. Eschenburg, *Geschichte unserer Irrenanstalten*, Lübeck, 1844, and von Hess, *Hamburg topographisch, historisch und politik beschreiben*, vol. I, pp. 344–345.

30 For example, in 1461 the city of Hamburg gave 14 th. 85 s. to a woman, for her to look after the mad (Gernet, *Mitteilungen aus der ältereren Medizine-Geschichte Hamburgs*, p. 79). In Lübeck, there is the will left by one Gerd Sunderberg leaving money for 'den armen dullen Luden' ['poor stupid idiots'] in 1479. Quoted in Laehr, *Gedenktage der Psychiatrie*, Berlin, 1887, p. 320.

31 Sometimes even replacements were paid for: 'Paid to a man who was sent to Saint-Mathurin de Larchant for the novaine of the aforementioned sister Robine, who is ill and suffering from frenzy, VIII., s.p.' (Hôtel-Dieu Accounts, XXIII; Coyeque, loc. cit., ibid.).

32 In Nuremberg, in the years 1377–1378 and 1381–1397, thirty-seven madmen were imprisoned, seventeen of whom were foreigners from Regensburg, Weissenberg, Bamberg, Bayreuth, Vienna and from Hungary. In the period that followed, for reasons that are unknown, Nuremberg abandoned this role as rallying point and scrupulously chased out madmen who were not originally from the city (cf. Kirchhoff, loc. cit.).

33 One boy in Nuremberg was imprisoned for three days for bringing a madman into a church in 1420. Cf. Kirchhoff, loc. cit.

34 The council of Carthage in 348 had decreed that communion could be given to a madman, even if he was not in a state of remission, providing there was no risk of irreverence. Aquinas was of the same opinion. Cf. Pontas, *Dictionnaire des cas de conscience*, 1741, vol. I, p. 785.

35 A man who had stolen his cloak was punished with seven days in prison (Kirchhoff, loc. cit.).

36 Cf. Kriegk, loc. cit.

37 These themes are strangely close to those found in stories of illegitimate or cursed children, who are placed in a basket and entrusted to the waters to be taken to another world, but in this one there is a return to truth at the end.

38 *Tristan et Iseut*, ed. Bossuat, pp. 219–222. NB: Foucault's reference here is to a twentieth-century prose retelling that homogenizes all the versions of the myth. The relevant original sources are the Berne and Oxford manuscripts, consultable in *Tristan et Iseut* (Paris: Gallimard, Bibliothèque de la Pléiade,

2004), pp. 217–224 (Oxford *Folie Tristan*, p. 222) and pp. 245–261 (Berne *Folie Tristan*, p. 245). [TN]

39 See among others Tauber, *Prediger*, XLI.

40 De Lancre, *De l'Inconstance des mauvais anges*, Paris, 1612.

41 George Cheyne, *The English Malady*, London, 1733.

42 *Lunacy* too was part of this same theme. The moon, whose influence on madness was commonly admitted throughout the centuries, is the most aquatic of all celestial bodies. The links between madness and the sun and fire are a much later occurrence (Nerval, Nietzsche, Artaud).

43 Cf. for example *Des six manières de fols*, Arsenal, ms. 2767.

44 In the *Sottie de Folle Balance*, four characters are fools: the Gentleman, the Merchant, the Labourer (i.e. the whole of society) and Folle Balance itself.

45 Which is still the case in *Moralité nouvelle des enfants de maintenant*, or in *Moralité nouvelle de Charité*, where the Fool is one of twelve characters.

46 As in the *Farce de Tout Mesnage*, where the fool apes the doctor to cure a lovesick chambermaid.

47 In the *Farce des cris de Paris*, the fool intervenes in a discussion between two young people to explain the nature of marriage.

48 The Sot, in the *Farce du Gaudisseur*, speaks the truth whenever the Braggart boasts.

49 Heidelberg, 1480.

50 Strasbourg, 1489. These discourses are a serious version of the sermons and clownish speeches declaimed in theatres, like the *Joyous Sermon of Great Value to the Mad to Show Them the Path to Wisdom*.

51 Cf. for instance a feast of the mad reproduced in Bastelaer's *Les Estampes de Brueghel*, Brussels, 1908, or the *Nasentanz* visible in Geisberg' *Deutsche Holzsch*, p. 262.

52 According to the *Journal d'un Bourgeois de Paris*, 'The Danse Macabre in the Innocents' cemetery dates from 1424', quoted in Emile Mâle's *L'Art religieux de la fin du Moyen Age*, p. 363.

53 In this sense, the experience of madness has a rigorous continuity with that of leprosy. The ritual exclusion of the leper showed that he was, in life, the presence of death itself.

54 Eustache Deschamps, *Œuvres*, ed. Saint-Hilaire de Raymond, vol. I, p. 203.

55 See below, Part II, chapter 3.

56 Even if the Lisbon *Temptation* is not one of Bosch's last works, as Baldass believes, it certainly postdates the *Malleus Maleficarum* [Kramer and Sprenger's infamous witch-hunting manual, 'The Hammer of Witches'. TN], which was published in 1487.

57 A thesis put forward by Desmonts in 'Deux primitifs Hollandais au musée du Louvre', *Gazette des Beaux-Arts*, 1919, p. 1.

58 As Desmonts does with regard to Bosch and Brant: even if it is the case that Bosch's picture was painted within a few years of the publication of the book, which also enjoyed considerable success itself, there is no proof that Bosch

intended it as an illustration of the *Narrenschiff*, still less the whole of the *Narrenschiff*.

59 Cf. Emile Mâle, pp. 234–237.

60 Cf. C.-V. Langlois, *La Connaissance de la nature et du monde au Moyen Age*, Paris, 1911, p. 243.

61 There is a possibility that the face in the 'head with legs' in the centre of Hieronymus Bosch's Lisbon *Temptation* is a self-portrait. (Cf. Brion, *Jérôme Bosch*, p. 40).

62 In the mid-fifteenth century, René d'Anjou's *Livre des Tournois* is still a moral bestiary.

63 J. Cardan, *Ma Vie*, trans. Dayré, p. 170.

64 The fifteenth century resurrected Bede's text and the description of the fifteen signs.

65 It should be noted that Madness appears neither in the *Psychomachia* of Prudentius, nor in the *Anticlaudianus* of Alain de Lille, nor in the work of Hugues de Saint-Victor. Might its presence date only from the thirteenth century?

66 The list of twelve dichotomies Foucault alludes to also comprises Fortitude and Cowardice, Humility and Pride.

67 Hugues de Saint-Victor, *De fructibus carnis et spiritus. Patrol*, CLXXVI, col. 997.

68 Desiderius Erasmus, *The Praise of Folly*, translated by Clarence H. Miller (Yale University Press, New Haven and London, 2nd edition, 2003), p. 17.

69 Louise Labé, *Débat de folie et d'amour*, Lyon, 1566. p. 98.

70 Ibid., pp. 98–99.

71 Erasmus, p. 85 seq.

72 Brant, *Stultifera Navis*, Latin translation of 1497, fo. 11.

73 Erasmus, p. 75.

74 Ibid., p. 76.

75 Ibid., p. 68.

76 Brant, *Stultifera Navis*, Prologues, Jacobi Locher, 1497 ed., ix.

77 Erasmus, p. 58.

78 Ibid., p. 78.

79 Ronsard, *Discours des Misères de ce temps*.

80 Brant, *Narrenschiff*, canto 117, particularly verses 21–22, and 57 seq., which make a precise reference to the *Apocalypse* (13 and 20).

81 Joseph de Siguença, *Tercera parte de la Historia de la orden de S. Gerónimo*, 1605, p. 837. Quoted in Tolnay, *Hieronimus Bosch*, Appendix, p. 76.

82 Ibid.

83 A later study will show how experience of the demonic and its waning between the sixteenth and the eighteenth centuries should not be understood as a victory of humanitarian or medical theory over the old, wild universe of super-stition, but as a taking up again, within a critical experience, of the forms that had previously borne the threat of a tear in the fabric of the world.

84 Foucault uses the adjective 'positive', and the noun 'positivity', extensively in this work, and the terms are important for an understanding of the text. 'Positive' in his sense is not a sign of approval, but essentially means 'having

its basis in fact'. The difference between this and 'Positivism', the idea that sensory phenomena and facts are the only possible basis for knowledge, that philosophy should be scientific and that metaphysical speculation is meaningless, is central to the development of his argument in the later stages of his study (cf. Part III, chapter 3 below). [TN].

85   Artaud, *Vie et mort de Satan le Feu*, Paris, 1949, p. 17.

86   Calvin, John, *Institutes of the Christian Religion*, a new translation by Henry Beveridge (Edinburgh: T. & T. Clark, 1863), book I, chapter I, part 2.

87   Sébastien Franck, *Paradoxes*, ed. Ziegler, nos. 57 and 91.

88   Erasmus, pp. 42–43. Cases carved to resemble an ugly Silenus, Bacchus' boon companion, could be opened to reveal beautiful objects within. Erasmus repeats the idea in the *Adages* and in his letter to Martin Dorp [TN].

89   The Platonism of the Renaissance, particularly after the sixteenth century, is ironic and critical.

90   II Corinthians, 11, 23.

91   Tauler, *Predigter*, XLI. Quoted in Gandillac, *Valeur du temps dans la pédagogie spirituelle de Tauler*, p. 62.

92   Calvin, John, *Second Sermon on the Epistle to the Ephesians*.

93   Erasmus, p. 128 seq.

94   Nicholas of Cusa, *The Layman on Wisdom and the Mind*, trans. M.L. Führer (Canada: Dovehouse editions, 1989), book I, pp. 24–25.

95   Montaigne, *Essays*, trans. M. A. Screech, Book 2, Chapter XII, p. 505.

96   Erasmus, p. 45.

97   Ibid., p. 10.

98   Charron, *De la sagesse*, book I, chapter 15, ed. Amaury Duval, 1827, vol. 1, p. 130.

99   Montaigne, p. 548.

100 Charron, p. 130.

101 In the same spirit, see Saint-Evremond, *Sir Politick would be* (Act V, scene II).

102 *Pensées*, ed. Brunschvicg, no. 414 (Lafuma 412).

103 It was a common belief in the eighteenth century, particularly in the wake of Rousseau, that novels and theatre shows could drive people mad. See below, part II, chapter 4.

104 Saint-Evremond, *Sir Politick would be* (act V, scene II).

105 Miguel de Cervantes Saavedra, *The Ingenious Hidalgo Don Quixote de la Mancha*, translated with an Introduction and Notes by John Rutherford (London: Penguin books, 2000), Part II, chapter 1, p. 492.

106 In *Les Visionnaires*, a cowardly Captain takes himself for Achilles, a pompous Poet believes he is a master of the epic, a Versifier believes himself to be a man of great learning, a poor man believes he is rich, a young girl thinks that everyone is in love with her, a pedant believes that he is a great judge of the dramatic art and another character mistakes herself for a heroine in a novel.

107 *Macbeth*, Act V, scene 1.

108 Ibid.

109 Cervantes, pp. 977–978.

110 Cervantes, p. 981.

111 There is an important structural study waiting to be done on the links between dreams and madness in the theatre of the seventeenth century. Their proximity had long been a philosophical and medical theme (see Part II, chapter 3); yet dreaming seems to come slightly later as a key element in dramatic structure. In any case its meaning is quite other, as the reality that it inhabits is no longer that of reconciliation, but rather one of tragic endings. Its trompe-l'œil delineates the true perspective of the drama, and does not lead to *error*, unlike madness, which in the irony of its apparent disorder, indicates a false conclusion.

112 G. De Scudéry, *La Comédie des comédiens*, Paris, 1635.

113 Gazoni, *L'Ospedale de' passi incurabili*, Ferrara, 1586. Translated into French and edited by F. de Clavier (Paris, 1620). Cf. Beys, *L'Ospital des fous* (1635), later reworked and re-edited as *Les Illustres fous* in 1653.

114 François Colletet, *Le Tracas de Paris*, 1665.

115 Cf. Peleus, *La Deffence du Prince des Sots* (n.d.): *Plaidoyer sur la Principauté des Sots*, 1608. See also *Surprise et fustigation d'Angoulevent par l'archiprêtre des poispillés*, 1603. *Guirlande et réponse d'Angoulevent*.

116 *Intitulation et Recueil de toutes les oeuvres que (sic) Bernard de Bluet d'Arbères, comte de permission*, 2 volumes, 1601–1602.

117 Régnier, Satire VI, line 72.

118 Brascambille, (*Paradoxes* 1622, p. 45). Cf. a similar indication in Desmarin, *Défense du poème épique*, p. 73.

119 Régnier, Satire XIV, lines 7–10.

II THE GREAT CONFINEMENT

1 René Descartes, *First Meditation*, in *The Philosophical Writings of Descartes*, tr. John Cottingham, Robert Stoothoff, Dugald Murdoch (Cambridge: Cambridge University Press, 1985) vol. II, p. 13. (AT, IX, 14).

2 Ibid. The 1647 French translation, by the Duc de Luynes, authorised by Descartes and used by Foucault simply says: 'Je ne serais pas moins extravagant' [TN].

3 Montaigne, *Essays*, trans. Screech, book 1, chapter 27, p. 201. [Foucault quoted this as chapter 26. TN]

4 Ibid.

5 A *lettre de cachet* was 'a letter written by order of the King, countersigned by his secretary of State, and sealed with the King's seal' (Guyot, *Répertoire de jurisprudence*, 1785, vol. X). What it commonly meant under the Ancien Régime was the removal of liberty without any judicial process for a family member, in response to a petitioning of the King or of the Lieutenant of Police by other family members. Foucault later published and studied such documents in *Le Désordre des familles, lettres de cachet des archives de la Bastille presenté par Arlette Farge et Michel Foucault* (Paris: Gallimard, 1982).) [TN]

6 Esquirol, *Des établissements consacrés aux aliénés en France* (1818) in *Des maladies mentales*, Paris, 1838, vol. 2, p.134.

7 Cf. Louis Boucher, *La Salpêtrière*, Paris, 1883.

8 Cf. Paul Bru, *Histoire de Bicêtre*, Paris, 1890.

9 Edict of 1656, article 4. See documents in Annex I. Saint-Esprit and Les Enfants-Trouvés would be later additions, while La Savonnerie would be removed.

10 Article 11.

11 Article 13.

12 Article 12.

13 Article 6.

14 The project presented to Anne of Austria had been signed by Pomponne de Bellièvre.

15 Report by La Rochefoucauld Liancourt in the name of the Committee on Begging of the Constitutive Assembly (*Procès-verbaux de l'Assemblée nationale*, vol. XXI).

16 Cf. *Statuts et règlements de l'hôpital général de la Charité et Aumône générale de Lyon*, 1742.

17 *Ordonnances de Monseigneur l'archevêque de Tours*, Tours, 1681. Cf. Mercier, *Le Monde médical de Touraine sous la Révolution*.

18 Aix, Albi, Angers, Arles, Blois, Cambrai, Clermont, Dijon, Le Havre, Le Mans, Lille, Limoges, Lyon, Mâcon, Martigues, Montpellier, Moulins, Nantes, Nîmes, Orléans, Pau, Poitiers, Reims, Rouen, Saintes, Saumur, Sedan, Strasbourg, Saint-Servan, Saint-Nicolas (Nancy), Toulouse, Tours. Cf. Esquirol vol. 2, p. 157.

19 The pastoral letter from the Archbishop of Tours quoted above demonstrates that the Church resisted this exclusion, and took credit for being the inspiration behind the movement and having proposed the earliest models.

20 Cf. Esquirol, *Mémoire historique et statistique sur la Maison royale de Charenton*, in *Des maladies mentales*, vol. 2.

21 Hélène Bonnafous-Sérieux, *La Charité de Senlis*, Paris, 1936.

22 R. Tardif, *La Charité de Château-Thierry*, Paris, 1939.

23 The hospital in Romans was built with stones taken from the demolished Voley leprosarium. See J.-A. Ulysse Chevalier, *Notice historique sur la maladrerie de Voley près Romans*, Romans, 1870, p. 62, and appendices, no. 64.

24 Such was the case for instance at the Salpêtrière, where the 'sisters' were to be recruited among 'women or young widows, who are childless and have no ties'.

25 In Orléans, the Bureau was composed of 'The Bishop, the Lieutenant Général, and 15 others, i.e. 3 men of the cloth, and 12 prominent inhabitants of the city, being officers, merchants and bourgeois.' *Règlements et statuts de l'hôpital général d'Orléans*, 1692, pp. 8–9.

26 Answers to questions from the Department of Hospitals, regarding La Salpêtrière, 1790, Archives Nationales, F 15, 1861.

27 1693–1695. Cf. above, chapter 1.

28 The Charité in Romans for example was initially set up by the Royal Almonry, then ceded to the Brothers of Saint John of God, and finally attached to the General Hospital in 1740.

29 The founding of Saint-Lazare is one good example of this. Cf. Collet, *Vie de saint Vincent de Paul*, vol. I, pp. 292–313.

30 The date is uncertain, but the first regulations were published in 1622.

31 Cf. Wagnitz, *Historische Nachrichten und Bemerkungen über die merkwürdigsten Zuchthäuser in Deutschland*, Halle, 1791.

32 Nicholls, *History of the English Poor Law*, London, 1898–1899, vol. I, pp. 167–169.

33 39 Eliz. c.5.

34 Nicholls, p. 228.

35 John Howard, *State of the Prisons in England and Wales* (3rd edition: Warrington: William Ayres, 1784), p. 8.

36 Nicholls, *History of the Scotch Poor Law*, pp. 85–87.

37 Although the creation of workhouses was provided for far earlier by an act from 1624 (21 James I. c. 1).

38 Nicholls, *History of the English Poor Law*, I, p. 353.

39 Ibid., pp. 35–38.

40 According to a statement of 12 June 1662, directors of the Paris hospital 'gave food and lodgings in the 5 houses of the aforementioned hospital to more than 6,000 people'. Quoted in Lallemand, *Histoire de la Charité*, Paris, 1902–1912, vol. 4, p. 262. The population of Paris at the time was more than half a million, and that proportion remained more or less constant throughout the classical period for the geographical area in question.

41 Calvin, *Institutes of the Christian Religion*, book 1, chapter 16.

42 Ibid.

43 Ibid.

44 The Augsburg Confession.

45 Calvin, *Justifications*, book 3, chapter 12, note 4.

46 Calvin, *The Catechism of the Church of Geneva*, trans. Elijah Waterman (Hartford: Sheldon and Goodwin, 1815), p. 82.

47 J. Janssen, *Geschichte des deutschen Volkes seit dem Ausgang des Mittelalters, III, Allgemeine Zustände des deutschen Volkes bis 1555*, p. 46.

48 Laehr, *Gedenktage der Psychiatrie*, Berlin, 1893, p. 259.

49 Laehr, p. 320.

50 18 Eliz. c.3. Cf. Nicholls, I, p. 169.

51 Published six years after the author's death, in 1683.

52 Sir Matthew Hale, *Discourse touching provision for the poor* (reprinted in London by Peter Davies, 1927), p. 44.

53 Session 23.

54 There is an almost undeniable influence of Vives' thought on Elizabethan legislation. He had taught at Corpus Christi College, Oxford, where he wrote *De Subventione*. He defined poverty as follows, linking it not to any mystical conception of poverty but to the politics of virtuous assistance: 'those who are poor lack far more than money: they are all those who lack strength in their body, their health, their spirit or their senses'.

55 In F. Watson, *Luis Vives, El Gran Valenciano* (Oxford: Oxford University Press, 1922), p. 62.

56 *De la orden que en algunos pueblos de Espana se ha puesto en la limosna para remedio a los verdaderos pobres*, 1545.

57 *Discursos del Amparo de los legítimos pobres*, 1598.

58 In Lallemand, IV, p. 15, note 27.

59 This request was made by municipality of Ypres, which had just legislated against begging and all private forms of charity. BNR 36–215, quoted in Lallemand, IV, p. 25.

60 Letter of March 1657, in *Correspondance de Saint Vincent de Paul*, ed. Coste, volume 6, p. 245.

61 Pastoral letter of 10 July 1670, ibid.

62 'Here the serpent and the dove must go hand in hand, and pride of place must not be given to simplicity at the expense of prudence. Only thus will we learn to make the distinction between the sheep and the goats.'

> (Camus, *De la mendicité légitime*, Douai, 1634, pp. 9–10).

Camus goes on to explain that there are important differences between individual acts of charity, and that the spiritual significance of an action differs in accordance with the moral value of the person affected by the gesture: 'there being of necessity a relation between the Alm and the Beggar, it follows that the only true Alm is that given to men who are just and truthful in their begging.' (ibid.).

63 Dom Guevarre, *La mendicità provenuta* (1693).

64 At the Salpêtrière, and at Bicêtre, the mad were placed either among the 'deserving poor' (which in the former meant the Madeleine quarter), or among the 'bad poor' (the House of Correction, or the Atonement).

65 In Lallemand, IV, pp. 216–226.

66 It is our modern perspective that considers the 'possessed' as mad (this is a postulate on our part), and that supposes that the mad were all treated as though they were possessed (which is simply wrong). This error and this postulate are common in many writers on the subject, such as Zilboorg.

67 *Tristan et Isolde*, p. 232 (Oxford), p. 250 (Berne).

68 Voltaire, ed. Moland, *Œuvres complètes* (Paris: Garnier, 1877–1885), vol. XXIII, p. 477. (Not p. 377, as Foucault indicated. [TN])

69 From a spiritual point of view, in the late sixteenth and early seventeenth centuries, poverty was seen as the threat of an impending apocalypse.

'One of the clearest signs of the imminent coming of the Son of God and the end of time is the extremely widespread temporal and spiritual poverty to which the world is currently reduced. Now times are truly bad, and misery multiplies in response to so many faults, our pains being the inseparable shadows of guilt.'

> (Camus, *De la mendicité légitime des pauvres*, pp. 3–4)

70 La Mare, *Traité de police*, loc. cit.

71 Cf. Thomas Platter, *Description de Paris*, 1559, published in *Mémoires de la société de l'Histoire de Paris*, 1899.

72 Similar measures were taken in the provinces. The city of Grenoble employed a 'beggar-chaser', who patrolled the streets on the lookout for vagabonds.

73 This was notably the case for paper and print workers. Cf., for example, the text

in the Hérault departmental archives published by G. Martin in *La Grande Industrie sous Louis XIV*, Paris, 1900, p. 89, note 3.

74 According to Earl Hamilton, *American Treasure and the Price Revolution in Spain* (1934), the difficulties experienced by the whole of Europe in the seventeenth century were due to a halt in production in the mines in South America.

75 I James I, c. 6: 'justices of the peace are to fix wages for any labourers, weavers, spinners and any workmen and workwomen whatsoever, either working by the day, week, month or year'. Cf. Nicholls, I, p. 209.

76 Quoted in Nicholls, I, p. 245. [Foucault omitted the passages in square brackets. TN]

77 Nicholls, I, p. 212.

78 Sir Frederic Morton Eden, *State of the Poor* (London: J. Davis, 1797), I, p. 160.

79 Order issued by the Lord Mayor, 1655, King's Pamphlets, 669, fo. 20, no. 21 (23 January 1655/6), quoted in E.M. Leonard, *The Early History of English Poor Relief* (Cambridge: Cambridge University Press, 1900), p. 270 (reprinted in 1965 in London by Frank Cass & Co.).

80 Marquis d'Argenson, *Journal et Mémoires* (Paris, 1867), vol. VI, p. 80 (30 November 1749).

81 In typically characteristic conditions: 'A famine had brought several boatloads of paupers from neighbouring provinces, which they could no longer afford to feed.' The great industrial families, notably including the Halincourt, made donations. (*Statuts et règlements de l'Hôpital général de la Charité et Aumône générale de Lyon*, 1742, pp. vii and viii.)

82 Howard, pp. 72–73.

83 Howard, pp. 66–136.

84 Nicholls, I, p. 353.

85 The Worcester workhouse was forced to agree to export all wares not worn by the inmates as far away as possible.

86 In Nicholls, I, p. 367.

87 Howard, p. 4.

88 He advised the abbey at Jumièges to give wool to its needy so that they could spin: 'wool and stocking factories can be an admirable means of putting beggars to work' (G. Martin, p. 225, note 4).

89 Forot, pp. 16–17.

90 Cf. Lallemand, vol. IV, p. 544, note 18.

91 In 1733, Germain Boffrand, an architect, drew up a plan for a deep well. It soon turned out to be useless, but work continued to keep the inmates occupied.

92 Musquinet de la Pagne, *Bicêtre réformé ou établissement d'une maison de discipline*, 1789, p. 22.

93 As had been the case in England, this was a source of friction in France. In Troyes, for example, the guild of hosiers took the hospital administrators to court (*Archives du département de l'Aube*).

94 Bossuet, *Élévations sur les mystères*, 6th week, 12th élévation (*Bossuet, Textes choisis par Henri Bremond*, Paris, 1913, vol. III, p. 285).

95 Calvin, *The Sermons of M. John Calvin upon the fifth booke of Moses called*

Deuteronomy (London: Henry Middleton, 1583) 'Sermon 155', 12 March 1556. (Reprinted in Facsimile by the Banner of Trust Trust, Edinburgh, 1987, p. 598.)

96 Bossuet, p. 285.

97 Calvin, 'Sermon 49', 3 July 1555, p. 292.

98 'Wee wil needs have God served after our own fond liking, and make him as it were subject unto us' (Calvin, ibid.).

99 Huizinga, *Le Déclin du Moyen Age*, Paris, 1932, p. 35.

100 Bourdaloue, *Dimanche de la Septuagésime, Œuvres*, Paris, 1900, I, p. 346.

101 Typical examples are the problems faced by the house of correction at Brunswick: see below, Part Three, chapter 2.

102 Cf. Nicholls, I, p. 352.

103 Articles 12 and 13 of the regulations of the Hôpital Général.

104 Quoted in *Histoire de l'Hôpital général*, an anonymous brochure published in Paris in 1676.

105 Arsenal, ms 2566, fos. 54–70.

106 *Discours sur les sciences et les arts*, translated as *Discourse on the Sciences and Arts*, in Rousseau, Jean-Jacques, *The Discourses and Other Philosophical Writings*, edited and translated by Victor Gourevitch (Cambridge: Cambridge University Press, 1977), p. 19.

107 Howard, p. 73.

108 Nicholls, vol. II, p. 367 (not Howard, as Foucault indicated. TN).

109 A sermon quoted in Collet, *Vie de saint Vincent de Paul*.

110 Cf. Tardif, p. 22.

111 Howard, p. 136.

112 La Mare, *Traité de police*, vol. I, pp. 287–288.

III THE CORRECTIONAL WORLD

1 The man behind this interpretation of events was Sérieux (see among other texts Sérieux and Libert, *Le Régime des aliénés en France au XVIIIe siècle*, Paris, 1914). In the same spirit was Philippe Châtelain (*Le Régime des aliénés et des anormaux aux XVIIe et XVIIIe siècles*, Paris, 1921), Marthe Henry (*La Salpêtrière sous l'Ancien Régime*, Paris, 1922), Jacques Vié (*Les Aliénés et correctionaires à Saint-Lazare aux XVIIe et XVIIIe siècles*, Paris, 1930), Hélène Bonnafous-Sérieux (*La Charité de Senlis*, Paris, 1936), René Tardif (*La Charité de Château-Thierry*, Paris, 1939). The goal, backed up by the ideas of Funck-Brentano, was to 'rehabilitate' the confinement practised under the Ancien Régime, and destroy the myth of the Revolution delivering the mad, a myth that had been put in place by Pinel and Esquirol, which was still discernible at the close of the nineteenth century in the work of Sémelaigne, Paul Bru, Louis Boucher and Émile Richard.

2 Strangely, this rather naïve methodological presupposition, common to all the authors in question, is also to be found in Marxist authors when they touch on the history of the sciences.

3 Cf. Marthe Henry, op. cit., *Cassino*.
4 Cf. Bru, *Histoire de Bicêtre*, Paris, 1890, pp. 25–26.
5 Howard, p. 100.
6 See the appendix: *State of Persons Detained in Saint-Lazare, and Table of the Orders of the King for Incarceration in the Hôpital Général*. [This text never actually figured among the annexed documents of any of the different editions of the book. TN]
7 Minutes of deliberations of the Hôpital Général; *Histoire de l'Hôpital général*.
8 Thierry de Héry, *La Méthode curative de la maladie vénérienne*, 1569, pp. 3 and 4.
9 To which should be added the Hôpital du Midi. Cf. Pignot, *L'Hôpital du Midi et ses origines*, Paris, 1885.
10 Cf. *Histoire de l'Hôpital général*.
11 Bossuet: *Traité de la concupiscence*, chapter 5, in *Bossuet, Textes choisis par Henri Bremond*, Paris, 1913, vol. III, p. 183.
12 In particular where the moral sedatives of Guislain were concerned.
13 *État abrégé de la dépense annuelle des Petites-Maisons*. 'The Petites-Maisons contain 500 poor and old people, 120 paupers with scabies, 100 paupers afflicted with the pox, and 80 insane paupers.' Dated 17 February 1664, for Mgr de Harlay (B.N. MS 18606).
14 Pinel, *Traité médico-philosophique*, p. 207.
15 Arsenal, MS 10918, fo. 173.
16 There were other sentences handed out in similar fashion. The *Mémoires* of the Marquis d'Argenson read 'two peasants were burnt for sodomy today' (*Journal et Mémoires*, vol. VI, p. 227).
17 Voltaire, *Philosophical Dictionary*, trans. Theodore Besterman (Harmondsworth: Penguin, 1971), p. 34, note 2; *Dictionnaire philosophique* in *Œuvres complètes*, ed. Moland, vol. XVII, p. 183, note 1.
18 At the Arsenal, 14 dossiers – i.e. some 4,000 cases – are devoted to these minor police matters, shelfmarks 10254–10267.
19 Cf. Chauveau and Helie, *Théorie du Code pénal*, vol. IV, no. 1507.
20 In trials of the fifteenth century, the accusation of sodomy was always accompanied by that of heresy (the heresy *par excellence* being Catharism). See for example the trial of Gilles de Rais. The same accusation was also to be found in trials for witchcraft. Cf. De Lancre, *Tableau de l'inconstance des mauvais anges*, Paris, 1612.
21 The case of Mme Drouet and Mlle de Parson is a typical example where the added complication of homosexuality made the accusation of sodomy all the worse. Arsenal, ms. 11183.
22 This new levelling out was demonstrated by the fact that the ordinance of 1670 classed sodomy together with other 'royal cases', not in fact a sign of the gravity of the offence but of the wish to withdraw such cases from the remit of the parliaments, who still tended to apply the old rules of medieval law.
23 La Mare, *Traité de police*, vol. I, p. 527.
24 After 1715, it was possible to appeal to Parliament against a sentence passed by the Lieutenant of Police, but the possibility remained largely theoretical.

25 For example, a woman called Loriot was imprisoned because 'the unfortunate Chartier has almost abandoned his wife, his family and his duties to give himself up to this unsavoury character, who had already cost him the greater part of his worldly goods.' *Notes de René d'Argenson*, Paris, 1866, p. 3.

26 The brother of the bishop of Chartres was interned at Saint-Lazare: 'he was of a cast of mind so base, and born with inclinations so unworthy of his birth, that the worst was to be expected. It is said that he desired to marry the wet-nurse of Mgr his brother' (BN, Clairambault, 986).

27 Saint-Évremond, *Le Cercle*, in *Œuvres*, 1753, vol. II, p. 86.

28 *Les Précieuses ridicules*, scene V.

29 Bossuet, *Traité de la concupiscence*, chapter IV (textes choisis par H. Bremond, vol. III, p. 180).

30 *Le Bourgeois Gentilhomme*, Act III, scene 3 and Act IV, scene 4.

31 Balzac, *L'Interdiction. La Comedie humaine*, ed. Conard, vol. VII, pp. 135 sq.

32 One petition for confinement among many reads as follows: 'All the family of Noël Robert Huet ... have the honour of bringing to the attention of His Lordship that they have the misfortune to be related to the man in question, and that he has never been worth a jot, nor ever shown any desire to make good, and is wholly given to debauchery and frequents bad company, all of which could be the ruin of his family, all the more so as his sister is still unmarried.' Arsenal, ms. 11617, fo. 101.

33 Quoted in Pietri, *La Réforme de l'État au XVIIIe siècle*, Paris, 1935, p. 263.

34 A Breteuil circular, quoted in Funck-Brentano, *Les Lettres de cachet*, Paris, 1903.

35 Arsenal, ms. 10135.

36 Ordinance of 10 November 1617 (La Mare, *Traité de la Police*, I, pp. 549–550).

37 Cf. Pintard, *Le Libertinage érudit*, Paris, 1943, pp. 20–22.

38 An ordinance of 7 September 1651, renewed on 30 July 1666, reiterated the hierarchy of punishments, which according to the frequency of the offence went from the iron collar to being burnt at the stake.

39 The case of the Chevalier de la Barre should be considered an exception, as is demonstrated by the uproar that it provoked.

40 B.N. Clairambault, 986.

41 Customary laws in Brittany stated that 'anyone who knowingly took their own life should be hung by the feet and dragged like a murderer'.

42 Le Brun de la Rochette, *Les Procès civils et criminels*, Rouen, 1663. Cf. Locard, *La Médecine judiciaire en France au XVIIe siècle*, pp. 262–266.

43 1670 ordinance, section XXII, article 1.

44 'Providing that the plan had not been put into action, and his will accomplished, unless he be driven to such action by intractable pain, violent illness, despair or a sudden frenzy.' Le Brun de la Rochette, loc. cit.

45 There was also a new clemency for those who succeeded: 'People who were persecuted after their death by inept laws are now no longer dragged through the city after their demise. It was in any case a repugnant spectacle, with possibly grave consequences for the many pregnant women in this city, who might have caught sight of it.' Mercier, *Tableau de Paris*, 1783, III, p. 195.

46 Cf. Heinroth, *Lehrbuch der Störungen des Seelenleben*, 1818.

47 Cf. Casper, *Charakteristik der französischen Medizin*, 1865.

48 I intend to return to this problem in a later work.

49 Perhaps on account of the recent poisoning scandals.

50 La Mare, *Traité de Police*, I, p. 562.

51 A few examples. Witchcraft: in 1706, a widow named Matte was transferred from the Bastille to the Salpêtrière, 'a fake witch, who used abominable sacrileges to support her preposterous divinations'. The following year she fell ill, and it was hoped 'that death would purge the public of her presence' (Ravaisson, *Archives Bastille*, XI, p. 168). Alchemy: 'Aulmont the younger brought Madame Lamy to the Bastille today, after she was found to be one of five implicated in an affair of secrets about metals; three of the others have already been arrested and sent to Bicêtre, with the women going to the Hôpital général' (*Journal de Du Junca*, quoted by Ravaisson, XI, p. 165). Another example was Marie Magnan, who worked at 'distilling and freezing mercury to make gold' (Salpêtrière, *Archives préfectorales de Police*, Br. 191). Magic: a woman called Mailly was sent to the Salpêtrière for brewing a love philtre 'for a widow much taken with a younger man' (*Notes de R. d'Argenson*, p. 88).

52 La Mare, p. 562.

53 'By an unfortunate chain of commitments, those who are most strongly under the sway of these seducers may have been driven to criminal extremes, adding spells and poison to impiety and sacrilege' (La Mare, ibid.).

54 There is a manuscript copy of the text of *Doutes sur la religion* at the Bibliothèque de l'Arsenal, ms. 10515.

55 BN Fonds Clairambault, 986.

56 Cf. Frédéric Lachèvre, *Mélanges*, 1920, pp. 60–81.

57 La Bruyère, *Les Caractères*, ed. Benda (Paris: Gallimard, 1951), *Des esprits forts*, chapter 11, p. 453.

58 La Mothe Le Vayer, *Dialogues d'Orasius Tubero*, 1716 edition, vol. I, p. 5.

59 *Justine*, 1797 edition, vol. VII, p. 37.

60 *Justine*, p. 17.

61 A famous example of confinement for libertinage was the case of the Abbot of Montcrif:

> He is extravagant in carriages, horses, meals, lottery tickets and buildings, all of which led him into a debt of 70,000 pounds . . . he loves the confessional, and puts such passion into the spiritual direction of women that some husbands have become suspicious . . . he loves legal machinations, and has several prosecutors in the courts . . . such behaviour demonstrates all too clearly the general derangement of his mind, and shows that his head has been quite turned.
>
> (Arsenal, ms. 11811. Cf. also 11498, 11537, 11765, 12010, 12499)

62 Arsenal, ms. 12692.

63 The broad outlines of correctional existence could be drawn up on the basis of lives like those of Henri-Louis de Loménie (cf. Jacobé, *Un internement sous le*

grand roi, Paris, 1929), or the Abbot Blache, whose dossier can be consulted at the Arsenal, ms. 10526; cf. 10588, 10592, 10599, 10614.

IV EXPERIENCES OF MADNESS

1   This proportion remained more or less constant from the end of the seventeenth century to the middle of the eighteenth century. See *Tableaux des ordres du roi pour l'incarcération à l'Hôpital général*.
2   Cf. M. Fosseyeux, *L'Hôtel-Dieu de Paris au XVIIe et au XVIIIe siècle*, Paris, 1912.
3   They are mentioned in the accounts. 'For making the base of a closed couchette, the trestles, and for making two holes for observation and food, XII, sp.' Hôtel-Dieu Accounts, XX, 346. Quoted by Coyecque, *L'Hôtel-Dieu de Paris*, Paris, 1889–1891, p. 209, note 1.
4   Tenon, *Mémoires sur les hôpitaux de Paris, 4e Mémoire*, Paris, 1788, p. 215.
5   Daniel Hack Tuke, *Chapters on the History of the Insane* (London: Kegan Paul, Trench and Co, 1882), p. 70. These twin statues, representing a maniac and a melancholic, were the work of Caius Gabriel Cibber. Foucault attributes them to 'Gibber'. [TN]
6   In a note from 1675, the Bethlehem directors asked that a distinction be made between patients kept in the hospital so that they might receive treatment, and those who were merely beggars and vagabonds.
7   Tuke, pp. 79–80.
8   The first of these physicians was Raymond Finot, who was followed by Fermelhuis until 1725, then l'Epy (1725 to 1762), Gaulard (1762–1782) and finally Philip (1782 to 1792). They were provided with assistants in the course of the eighteenth century. Cf. Delaunay, *Le Monde médical parisien au XVIIIe siècle*, pp. 72 to 73. In Bicêtre, during the late eighteenth century, there was a student surgeon who visited the infirmary once a day, with two companions and several pupils. (*Mémoires de P. Richard*, ms. in the Bibliothèque de la Ville de Paris, fo. 23).
9   Audin Rouvière, *Essai sur la topographie physique et médicale de Paris. Dissertation sur les substances qui peuvent influer sur la santé des habitants de cette cité*, Paris, Year II, pp. 105–107.
10   Title XIII, in Isambert, *Recueil des anciennes lois*, Paris, 1821–1833, X, VIII, p. 393.
11   In the eighteenth century, it was believed that the whole of the small town of Axminster, in Devon, had been contaminated in such fashion.
12   Howard, p. 7.
13   The case of Claude Rémy, Arsenal, ms. 12685.
14   The rubric 'treated and given medication like the other insane' begins to appear in the late eighteenth century, as in the case of Louis Bourgeois in 1784: 'Transferred from the Conciergerie prison by virtue of a Parliamentary decree, to the secure section of Bicêtre, to be detained there, fed, treated and given medication like the other insane.'

15 Arsenal, ms. 11396, fos. 40 and 41.

16 Arsenal, ms. 12686.

17 Cf. Tuke, p. 117. The real figures were almost certainly much higher, as a few weeks later, Andrew Halliday counted 112 madmen locked up in Norfolk, where the Committee had found only 42.

18 Howard, p. 8.

19 Esquirol, 'Des établissements consacrés aux aliénés en France' in *Des maladies mentales*, vol. II, p. 138.

20 Ibid., vol. II, p. 137.

21 These notations are from *Tableaux des ordres du roi pour l'incarcération à l'Hôpital général;* and from *États des personnes détenues par ordre du roi à Charenton et à Saint-Lazare* (Arsenal).

22 One example is Hélène Bonnafous-Sérieux, *La Charité de Senlis.*

23 Cf. *Journal of Mental Science*, vol. X, p. 256.

24 Cf. *Journal of Psychological Medicine*, 1850, p. 426. But a contrary opinion has been expressed by Ullersperger, *Die Geschichte der Psychologie und Psychiatrie in Spanien*, Würzburg, 1871.

25 Sandwith, F.M., 'The Cairo Lunatic Asylum', *Journal of Mental Science*, vol. XXXIV, pp. 473–474.

26 The King of Spain, followed by the Pope on 26 February 1410, both gave their permission. Cf. Laehr, *Gedenktage der Psychiatrie*, p. 417.

27 Pinel, *Traité médico-philosophique*, pp. 238–239.

28 Like that of St Gergen. Cf. Kirchhoff, *Deutsche Irrenärzte*, Berlin, 1921, p. 24.

29 Laehr, *Gedenktage der Psychiatrie.*

30 Krafft Ebing, *Lehrbuch der Psychiatrie*, Stuttgart, 1879, vol. I, p. 45. Anm.

31 To be seen in *Pey der spitallpruck das narrhewslein gegen dem Karll Holtzschmer uber*, a book by the architect Tucker. Cf. Kirchhoff, p. 14.

32 Kirchhoff, p. 20.

33 Cf. Beneke, loc. cit.

34 Cf. Esquirol, 'Mémoire historique et statistique sur la maison royale de Charenton', in *Traité des maladies mentales*, vol. II, pp. 204 and 208.

35 Cf. Collet, *Vie de saint Vincent de Paul* (1818), vol. I, pp. 310–312. 'He had for them the tenderness that a mother feels for her son.'

36 B.N. Coll. Joly de Fleury, ms. 1309.

37 Quoted in J. Vié, *Les Aliénés et correctionaires à Saint-Lazare aux XVIIe et XVIIIe siècles*, Paris, 1930.

38 *Une relation sommaire et fidèle de l'affreuse prison de Saint-Lazare*, coll. Joly de Fleury, 1415. Petites-Maisons also became a place of confinement after starting out as a hospital, as the following text from the late sixteenth century demonstrates: 'This hospital still admits the poor who have lost their worldly possessions as well as their wits, and run the streets like madmen and the insane; some such patients recover their senses and health with time and the good treatment they receive.' Quoted in Fontanou, *Édits et ordonnances des rois de France*, Paris, 1611, vol. I, p. 921.

39 Hélène Bonnafous-Sérieux, p. 20.

40 Ned Ward, *London Spy*, 1700, reprinted in East Lansing in 1993 by Colleagues' Press, p. 54.

41 Quoted in Tuke, p. 90.

42 Zacchias (1584–1659) was First Physician in Rome, and was often consulted by the Rota tribunal when an expert opinion was required for civil and religious cases. He published his *Quæstiones medico-legales* from 1624 to 1650.

43 *Von der Macht des Gemüths durch den blossen Vorsatz seiner krankhaften Gefühlen Meister sein*, 1797.

44 Heinroth, *Lehrbuch der Störungen des Seelenlebens*, 1818. Elias Régnault, *Du degré de compétence des médecins*, Paris, 1828.

45 Zacchias, book II, title 1.

46 Cf. Falret, *Des maladies mentales et des asiles d'aliénés*, Paris, 1864, p. 155.

47 'Formalités à remplir pour l'admission des insensés à Bicêtre' (quoted by Richard, *Histoire de Bicêtre*, Paris, 1889).

48 In which case, mentions such as 'Transferred from the Conciergerie prisons by virtue of a Parliamentary decree to be taken to . . .' are to be found in the register.

49 That ordinance was complemented in 1692 by another that provided for two experts in all towns that had a court, a bishopric, an appeals court or bailiwick. Smaller towns had only one expert.

50 A post that an ordinance of 1699 generalised to 'all towns and places in the kingdom where it is necessary'.

51 Cf. for example a letter from Bertin to La Michodière concerning a woman named Rodeval (Archives Seine-Maritime, C 52), or a letter from a sub-delegate in the district of Saint-Venant regarding a certain Roux (Archives Pas-de-Calais, 709, fo. 165).

52 'It is impossible to be too careful regarding two points: firstly in ensuring that the statements have been signed by the closest relatives on both the paternal and the maternal sides of the family, and secondly in taking careful note of those who did not sign and the reasons that prevented them, all of which is to be done independently of the verification of the truth of their statement.' Quoted in Joly, *Lettres de cachet dans la généralité de Caen au 18e siècle*.

53 Cf. the Case of Lecomte, Archives Aisne, C 677.

54 Cf. a memoir regarding Louis François Soucanye de Moreuil. Arsenal, ms. 12684.

55 Cf. for instance the attestation quoted in Locard, p. 172.

56 *Interdiction* was a judicial measure introduced in 1690, removing the right of an individual to look after his own affairs, after he was judged to be imbecile, mad or frenzied. [TN.]

57 Cf. the article 'Interdit' in Cl.-J. de Ferrière's *Dictionnaire de droit et de pratique*, Paris 1769, vol. II, pp. 48–50.

58 Zacchias, book II, title 1, question 7, Lyon, 1674, pp. 127–128.

59 Quoted in Bonnafous-Sérieux, p. 40.

60 Arsenal, ms. 10928.

61 Quoted in Devaux, *L'Art de faire les rapports en chirurgie*, Paris, 1703, p. 435.

62 But he did go on to add: 'Unless the families have absolutely no means to pay for the procedure that precedes interdiction. But in that case the dementia must be notorious, and verified by exact clarifications.'

V THE INSANE

1 BN Fonds Clairambault, 986.
2 Cf. Letter to Fouché, see above Chapter 3, p. 147.
3 *Notes de René d'Argenson*, Paris, 1866, pp. 111–112.
4 *Archives de la Bastille*, ed. Ravaisson, vol. XI, p. 243.
5 Ibid., p. 199.
6 Cl.-J. de Ferrière, *Dictionnaire de droit et de pratique*, entry on 'Folie', vol. I, p. 611. Cf. heading XXVIII, article 1 of the criminal ordinance of 1670: 'The frenzied or insane cannot be punished as they have no will of their own: their derangement is punishment enough.'
7 Arsenal, ms. 12707.
8 *Notes de René d'Argenson*, p. 93.
9 Cl.-J. de Ferrière, *Dictionnaire de droit et de pratique*, entry on 'Folie', vol. I, p. 611, our emphasis.
10 *Archives de la Bastille*, ed. Ravaisson, vol. XIII, p. 438.
11 Ibid., pp. 66–67.
12 *Dictionnaire de droit et de pratique*, entry on 'Folie', p. 611.
13 *Bibliothèque de droit français*, entry on 'furiosus'.
14 René Descartes, 'Discours de la Méthode', part IV. Pléiade, p. 147, translated as *Discourse on the Method* in *The Philosophical Writings of Descartes*, translated by John Cottingham, Robert Stoothoff and Dugald Murdoch (Cambridge: Cambridge University Press, 1985) vol. I, p. 126.
15 René Descartes, *First Meditation*, in *The Philosophical Writings of Descartes*, translated by John Cottingham, Robert Stoothoff, Dugald Murdoch (Cambridge: Cambridge University Press, 1985) vol. II, p. 15 (AT, IX, 14).
16 Baruch Spinoza, *Treatise on the Emendation of the Intellect*, in *The Ethics; Treatise on the Emendation of the Intellect; Selected Letters* translated by Samuel Shirley, edited by Seymour Feldman (Indianapolis: Hackett, 1992), pp. 233–235.
17 In French, 'les insensés, les esprits aliénés, ou dérangés, les extravagants, les gens en démence.'
18 Article 41 of the act of accusation, French translation quoted by Hernandez in *Le Procès inquisitorial de Gilles de Rais*, Paris, 1922.
19 Sixth session of the trial (in *Procès de Gilles de Rais*, Paris, 1959, p. 232).
20 *Archives de la Bastille*, ed. Ravaisson, XIII, pp. 161–162.
21 BN Fonds Clairambault, 986.
22 Quoted in Pietri, *La Réforme de l'Etat*, p. 257.
23 BN Fonds Clairambault, 986.
24 Very late on, probably under the influence of the practice that concerned the mad, sufferers from venereal diseases were also put on public show. Père

Richard, in his *Mémoires*, tells of a visit paid by the Prince de Condé and the Duke d'Enghien, 'that he might be filled with a horror of vice' (fo. 25).

25 Ned Ward, in *London Spy*, quotes a figure of tuppence. The entrance fee may have fallen over the course of the eighteenth century.

26 'In those days anyone could visit Bicêtre, and when the weather was fine at least 2,000 visitors would flock to the hospital every day. Money in hand, you were led by a guide to the special section where the insane were kept' (*Mémoires de Père Richard*, loc. cit., fo. 61). The visit included an Irish priest who 'slept on straw', a ship's captain who flew into a rage at the sight of men 'for it was the injustice of men that had driven him mad', and a young man 'who sang in exquisite fashion' (ibid.).

27 Mirabeau, *Observations d'un voyageur anglais*, 1788, p. 213, note 1.

28 See above, chapter 1.

29 Esquirol, 'Mémoire historique et statistique de la Maison Royale de Charenton', in *Des maladies mentales*, vol. II, p. 222.

30 Pascal, *Pensées*, ed. Brunschvicg, no. 339 (Lafuma, 111).

31 D.H. Tuke, *Chapters on the History of the Insane*, p. 151.

32 Coguel, *La Vie parisienne sous Louis XVI*, Paris, 1882.

33 Esquirol, *Des maladies mentales*, vol. II, p. 481.

34 Fodéré, *Traité du délire appliqué à la medicine, à la morale, à la legislation*, Paris, 1817, vol. I, pp. 190–191.

35 This moral relation with animality, established within man, not as a power of metamorphosis but as the limit of his being, is well summed up in a text by Mathurin Le Picard:

> Man is a wolf in his rapaciousness, a lion in his subtlety, a fox in his cunning and deceitfulness, a monkey in his hypocrisy, a bear in his envy, a tiger in his vengeance, a dog in his blasphemy, slander and criticism, a serpent that feeds on earth in his miserliness, a chameleon in his inconstancy, a panther in his heresy, a basilicum in the lasciviousness of his eyes, a dragon dying of thirst in his drunkenness, and a piglet in his luxury.
>
> (*Le Fouet des Paillards*, Rouen, 1623, p. 175)

36 Pinel, *Traité médico-philosophique*, vol. I, pp. 60–61.

37 A different expression of this theme is to be found in the diet that was fed to the mad in Bicêtre (in the Saint-Prix division). 'Six quarters of bread twice a day, soup to go with the bread, a quarter of meat on Sunday, Tuesday and Thursday, a third of a litre of peas or beans on Monday and Friday, one ounce of butter on Wednesday, and one ounce of cheese on Saturday.' (Archives de Bicêtre, 1781 regulations, chapter V, article 6.)

38 Pinel, p. 312.

39 Ibid.

40 A study of the notion of nature in Sade and his relationship to the philosophy of the eighteenth century would reveal a movement in that direction, taken to its purest extremes.

41 Bossuet, 'Panégyrique de saint Bernard'. Introduction. *Œuvres complètes*, 1861, vol. I, p. 622.

42 Sermon quoted in Abelly, *Vie du vénérable serviteur de Dieu Vincent de Paul*, Paris, 1664, vol. I, p. 199.

43 Cf. ibid., p. 198. Saint Vincent is here alluding to I Corinthians, I, 23: *Judaeis quidem scandalum, Gentibus autem stultitiam*, 'we preach Christ crucified, unto the Jews a stumbling block, and unto the Greeks foolishness'.

44 *Correspondance de saint Vincent de Paul*, ed. Coste, vol. V, p. 146.

PART TWO

INTRODUCTION

1 Régnier, Satire XIV, *Œuvres complètes*, ed. Railaud, v. 9.

2 Ibid., v. 13–14.

3 Ibid., v. 7–8.

4 William Blake, *The Marriage of Heaven and Hell*, in *William Blake – The Complete Poems*, ed. W.H. Stevenson (London and New York: Longman, 1989), 2nd edition, p. 110.

5 Blake, p. 108.

6 Régnier, v. 155.

7 By writing of an 'age of the understanding', as opposed to an 'age of reason', Foucault adopts the terminology Hegel, after Kant, used to characterise a taxonomic (or 'divisive') mode of knowledge (Understanding) as opposed to a dialectical mode (Reason), where categories of the world are also perceived as acts or practices of the mind. TN

I THE MADMAN IN THE GARDEN OF SPECIES

1 *Pygmalion, prince de Tyr*, Prologue, *Œuvres* by Fontenelle (Paris, 1790), vol. IV, p. 472.

2 Bayle, quoted in Delvolvé, *Essai sur Pierre Bayle*, Paris, 1906, p. 104.

3 Fontenelle, *Dialogues des morts modernes*, Dialogue IV, *Œuvres*, 1790, vol. I, p. 278.

4 Cf. Mandeville, *La Fable des abeilles*, and Montesquieu on the madness of honour among the nobility (*Esprit des lois*, book III, chapter VII.)

5 *Histoire de l'Académie des sciences*. Year 1709, edition of 1733, pp. 11–13, *Sur le délire mélancolique*.

6 *Dialogues des morts modernes*. Dialogue IV, *Œuvres*, I, p. 278. In the same manner, regarding liberty, Fontenelle explained that the mad were neither more nor less subject to determinant causes than anyone else. If man is capable of resisting a moderate disposition of the brain, he should also be capable of resisting a much more powerful one: 'It can also be the case that a man be quite intelligent despite a moderate disposition towards stupidity.' By the same logic, if a man was incapable of resisting a violent impulse, he would be equally powerless in the face of a more innocuous desire. (*Traité de la liberté de l'âme* – attributed to Fontenelle in the Depping edition, vol. III, pp. 611–612.)

7 Boissier de Sauvages, *Nosologie méthodique*, trad. Gouvion, Lyon, 1772, vol. VII, p. 33.

8 Ibid.

9 Voltaire, *Philosophical Dictionary*, trans. Theodore Besterman, p. 211. (Colney Hatch being the British equivalent of Paris' Petites-Maisons, to which Voltaire refers). Foucault quotes Voltaire, *Dictionnaire philosophique*, article on 'Folie', Benda edition, Paris, 1935, vol. I, p. 286. Voltaire, *Œuvres complètes*, ed. Moland (Paris: Garnier, 1879) vol. XVII (iii), p. 160.

10 Boissier de Sauvages, vol. VII, p. 34.

11 Voltaire, *Philosophical Dictionary*, trans. Theodore Besterman, p. 210; Voltaire, *Dictionnaire philosophique*, ed. Benda, vol. I, p. 285. *Œuvres complètes*, p. 159.

12 Cicero, *Tusculan Disputations*, book III, i, 1.

13 Cicero, ibid., book III, iv, 8.

14 Cicero, ibid., book III, iii, 5.

15 Cicero, ibid., book III, v, 11.

16 Ibid.

17 Also in the *Tusculan Disputations*, one can find an effort to bypass the *furor/insania* divide in a single moral attribution:

> a strong soul cannot be attacked by madness, whereas the body can; but the body can fall ill without it being in any sense our fault, which is not the case for the soul, where the fundamental cause of all sicknesses and passions is a disdain for reason.
>
> (Cicero, ibid., book IV, xiv, 31)

18 Plater, *Praxeos medicæ ires tomi*, Basel, 1609.

19 Sauvages, *Nosologie méthodique*, French translation, I, p. 159.

20 Sauvages, p. 160.

21 Sauvages, p. 159.

22 Sauvages, p. 129.

23 Sauvages, p. 160.

24 Willis, Thomas, *Of Convulsive Diseases*, in *The Remaining Works of that Famous and Renowned Physician, Dr Thomas Willis, Englished by S. Pordage* (London: T. Dring, 1681), p. 12. [Hereafter, *Works*]

25 Sauvages, I, pp. 121–122.

26 Cf. also Thomas Sydenham, 'An Epistolary Discourse to the learned Dr William Cole, concerning some Observations of the Confluent Small-Pox, and of Hysterick Diseases', in *The Whole Works of that excellent Practical Physician Thomas Sydenham*, 8th edition, translated from the Latin by John Pechey (London: Darby & Poulson, 1772). [Hereafter, *Works*]

27 Sauvages, vol. I, pp. 91–92. Cf. also A. Pitcairn, *The Whole Works done from the Latin Original* by G. Sewel and I.T. Desaguliers, 2nd edition, 1777, pp. 9–10).

28 Sydenham, preface, p. vi.

29 Gaubius, *Institutiones pathologiae medicinales*, quoted by Sauvages.

30 *Les Nouvelles Classes des maladies* dates from 1731 or 1733. On this subject, see Berg's *Linné et Sauvages: les rapports entre leurs systèmes nosologiques* (Uppsala: Lychnos, 1956).

31 Sydenham, preface, viii–ix. [The sentence in square brackets is not in the

English version, but was included by Jault, his French translator, in *Médecine pratique* (Paris, 1784; preface, pp. xxiv–xxv), and in the Boisser de Sauvages *Nosologie méthodique* (Lyon, 1772, 10 vols, vol. I, pp. 124–125) that Foucault quotes from here (a text misquoted by Foucault, who repeated 'diseases' in place of 'animals' at the end). TN.]

32   Sydenham, preface, xi.

33   Linnaeus, Letter to Boissier de Sauvages, quoted by Berg, *Linné.*

34   This problem seems to be the counterpart of another to be found in Part One, when we tried to understand how the hospitalisation of the mad could coincide with their confinement. It is merely one of the numerous examples of structural analogies between the domain explored on the basis of practices and the domain discernible through scientific or theoretical speculation. In both domains, the experience of madness is contradictory and singularly dissociated from itself; but our task is to find in the depths of that experience the foundation and unity behind that dissociation.

35   Paracelsus, *Sämtliche Werke*, Munich, Südhoff, 1923, I Abteilung, vol. II, pp. 391 seq.

36   Foucault's translation omits 'and the ratiocination'. [TN]

37   Joannes Jonstonus, *The Idea of Practical Physick, written in Latin by John Johnston, and Englished by Nich. Culpeper* (London: Peter Cole, 1657), Book 8, 'Head Diseases'.

38   Arnold, Thomas, *Observations on the nature, kinds, causes and prevention of insanity, lunacy and madness*, Leicester, vol. I, 1702, vol. II, 1786, reprinted in London in 1806 by Richard Philips. [Foucault reproduces here the contents page TN].

39   Foucault wrote Wieckhard but probably meant Boissier de Sauvages (cf. p. 193 above).

40   Vitet, *Matière médicale réformée ou pharmacopée médico-chirurgicale*; Pinel, *Dictionnaire des Sciences médicales*, 1819, vol. XXXVI, p. 220.

41   Sauvages, VII, p. 43 (see also vol. I, p. 366).

42   Sauvages, p. 191.

43   Sauvages, p. 1.

44   Sauvages, pp. 305–334.

45   Willis, *De anima brutorum: two Discourses on the Soul of Brutes, Englished by S. Pordage* (London: Thomas Dring, 1683), p. 201.

46   Ibid.

47   Pinel, *Nosographie philosophique*, Paris, 1798.

48   Esquirol, *Des maladies mentales*, Paris, 1838.

49   Cullen, *First Lines of the Practice of Physic* (Edinburgh: Bell and Bradfute, 1791), vol. I, p. 134.

50   Daniel de Laroche, *Analyse des fonctions du système nerveux*, Genève, 1778, vol. I, preface, p. 8.

51   Viridet, *Dissertation sur les vapeurs*, Yverdon, 1726, p. 32.

52   Beauchêne, *De L'influences des affections de l'âme dans les maladies nerveuses des femmes, avec le traitement qui convient à ces maladies*, Paris, 1783, pp. 65–182 and pp. 221–223.

53   Pressavin, *Nouveau Traité des vapeurs*, Lyon, 1770, pp. 7–31.

II THE TRANSCENDENCE OF DELIRIUM

1 Voltaire, *Philosophical Dictionary*, trans. Theodore Besterman, p. 210; Voltaire, *Dictionnaire philosophique*, ed. Benda, vol. I, p. 285. *Œuvres complètes* p. 159.

2 Sainte-Beuve, *Résolution de quelques cas de conscience*, Paris, 1689, vol. I, p. 65. This rule also applied to the deaf and dumb.

3 Cf. a decision by the Paris Parliament of 30 August 1711. Quoted in Parturier, *L'Assistance à Paris sous l'Ancien Régime et la Révolution*, Paris, 1897, p. 159 and note 1.

4 *L'Ame matérielle, ou nouveau système sur les purs principes des philosophes anciens et modernes qui soutiennent son immatérialité*. Arsenal, ms. 2239, p. 139.

5 Ibid.

6 Voltaire, trans. Besterman, p. 211. *Œuvres complètes*, pp. 160–161.

7 This for instance was the view of the contributors to James' *Dictionary*.

8 Sauvages, vol. VII, pp. 130, 141, and pp. 14–15.

9 Voltaire, trans. Besterman, ibid. *Œuvres complètes*, p. 160.

10 Tissot, *Avis aux gens de lettres*, French translation, 1767, pp. 1–3.

11 Assuming, of course, that these people have read Diemerbroek.

12 Zacchias, *Quæstiones medico-legales*, Lyon, 1657, book II, title I, q. II, p. 114. Regarding the joint implication of the body and soul in madness, definitions proposed by other authors are much in the same style. Willis speaks of 'distempers of the brain, in which reason is hurt, as well as the other animal functions' (*De anima brutorum*, p. 179); Lorry notes: *Corporis ægrotantis conditio illa in qua judicia a sensibus orienda nullatenus aut sibi inter se aut rei representatæ responsant.* [The reason of the sick body is at the mercy of the faculty of judgement, which in turn is dependent on physical sensations; but the faculty no longer responds to such sensations, or anything that resembles them.]

(*De Melancholia*, 1765, vol. I. p. 3)

13 Willis, *De anima brutorum*, p. 188.

14 Generally speaking, animal spirits were considered to be imperceptible. Diemerbroek (*Anatomia*, book VIII, chapter 1) states their invisibility against Bartholin, who states that he has seen them (*Institutions anatomiques*, book III, chapter 1). Haller (*Elementa physiologiae*, vol. IV, p. 371) claims that they have no discernible taste, in contrast to Jean Pascal, who claimed that he had tasted them and discerned an acidic flavour (*Nouvelle découverte et les admirables effets des ferments dans le corps humain*).

15 Sydenham, *Epistolary Discourse to the learned Dr William Cole concerning some observations of the Confluent Small-Pox, and of Hysterick Diseases*, in *Works*, p. 312. [Jault's French translation is more detailed, and is worth quoting in full: 'La force de l'âme, tandis qu'elle est enfermée dans ce corps mortel dépend principalement de la force des esprits animaux qui lui servent comme d'instruments dans l'exercice de ses functions, et qui sont la plus fine portion de la matière, et la plus approchante de la substance spirituelle. Ainsi la

faiblesse et le désordre des esprits cause nécessairement la faiblesse et le désordre de l'âme, et la rend le jouet des passions les plus violentes, sans qu'elle soit en aucune façon maîtresse d'y résister.' (p. 407). TN]

16 A note by the translator in Sydenham, *Dissertation sur l'affection hystérique* (*Médecine pratique*, trad. Jault, p. 407).

17 There is an interesting study waiting to be done on what *seeing* is in the medicine of the eighteenth century. It is notable in the *Encyclopédie* that the entry on the physiology of nerves, *Nerfs*, written by Jaucourt, criticises the tension theory of nerves, while it serves as an explanatory principle in most of the entries on pathology (see, for example, the entry on *Démence*).

18 Pomme, *Traité des affections vaporeuses des deux sexes*, Paris, 3rd edition, 1767, p. 94.

19 Bonet, *Sepulchretum*, Geneva, 1700, vol. I, section VIII, pp. 205 and f., and section IX, pp. 221 and f. In the same manner, Lieutaud noted in melancholics that 'most of the vessels of the brain are engorged with thick, black blood, and there is water in the ventricles; the heart sometimes seems dried out and empty of blood' (*Traité de médecine pratique*, Paris, 1759, vol. I, pp. 201–203).

20 A line was $1/12$ of an inch, while a dram was $1/8$ of an ounce. A grain was the weight of one seed. [TN].

21 'Nouvelles observations sur les causes physiques de la folie, lues à la dernière assemblée de l'Académie royale de Prusse' (*Gazette salutaire*, XXXI, 2 August 1764).

22 Quoted by Cullen *First Lines of the Practice of Physic* (Edinburgh: Bell and Bradfute), 1791, vol. 1, p. 141–142.

23 Ibid.

24 M. Ettmüller, *Pratique de la médecine spéciale*, Lyon, 1691, pp. 437 sq.

25 Robert Whytt, *Observations on the Nature, Causes and Cure of those Disorders which have been commonly called Nervous, Hypochondriac, or Hysteric* (Edinburgh: T. Becket, 1765), p. 188.

26 *Encyclopédie*, entry on *Manie*.

27 Cf. the anonymous pamphlet entitled *Observations de médecine sur la maladie appelée convulsion*, Paris, 1732, p. 31.

28 Cf. Tissot, *Traité des Nerfs*, II, 1, pp. 29–30: 'The true homeland for delicacy of the nervous fibre is between 45 and 55 degrees latitude.'

29 An anonymous article in the *Gazette salutaire*, XL, 6 October 1768.

30 Cf. Daquin, *Philosophie de la folie*, Paris, 1792, pp. 24–25.

31 J.-Fr. Dufour, *Essai sur les opérations de l'entendement humain et sur les maladies qui les dérangent*, Amsterdam, 1770, pp. 361–362.

32 William Black, *A Dissertation on Insanity* (London: Ridgway, second edition, 1811), p. 15, quoted by Matthey, p. 365. [Matthey (a retranslation of his French version appears in the text above, as that was the text used by Foucault) does considerable injustice to Black's text, which included the numbers of the insane, and listed them as follows:

misfortunes, troubles, disappointments, grief: 206; religion and Methodism: 90; love: 74; jealousy: 9; pride: 8; study: 15; fright: 51; drink and intoxication: 58;

fevers: 110; childbed: 79; obstruction: 10; family and hereditary: 115; contusions and fractures of the skull: 12; venereal: 14; small pox: 7; ulcers and scabs dried up: 5.

TN]

33 Quoted in Esquirol, vol. II, p. 219.

34 At the same time, Dumoulin, in *Nouveau traité du rhumatisme et des vapeurs*, 2nd edition, 1710, criticised the idea that the moon had an influence on the regularity of convulsions, p. 209.

35 R. Mead, *A Treatise Concerning the Influence of the Sun and the Moon*, London, 1748.

36 *Philosophie de la folie*, Paris, 1792.

37 Leuret and Mitivé, *De la fréquence de pouls chez les aliénés*, Paris, 1832.

38 Guislain, *Traité des phrénopathies*, Brussels, 1835, p. 46.

39 Daquin, *Philosophie de la folie*, Paris, 1792, pp. 82, 91; see also Toaldo, *Essai météorologique*, translated by Daquin, 1784.

40 Sauvages, *Nosologie méthodique*, vol. VII, p. 12.

41 Bayle and Grangeon, *Relation de l'état de quelques personnes prétendues possédées faite d'autorité au Parlement de Toulouse*, Toulouse, 1682, pp. 26–27.

42 Malebranche, *Recherche de la vérité*, book V, chapter III, in *Œuvres complètes*, vol. I, ed. Geneviève Rodis-Lewis (Paris: Gallimard, Pléiade, 1979), pp. 502–3.

43 Sauvages, *Nosologie méthodique*, vol. VII, p. 291.

44 Whytt, p. 212.

45 Whytt, p. 212. The theme of an excessive movement that leads to immobility and death is a frequent one in classical medicine. There are examples in *Le Temple d'Esculape*, 1681, vol. III, pp. 79–85, and in Pechlin's *Observations médicales*, book III, observation 23. The case of Chancellor Bacon, who fell into a faint whenever he saw an eclipse of the moon, was a commonplace of the medicine of the time.

46 Lancisi, *De nativis Romani cœli qualitatibus*, chapter XVII.

47 Cf., among others, Tissot's *Observations sur la santé des gens du monde*, Lausanne, 1760, pp. 30–31.

48 Sauvages, *Nosologie méthodique*, vol. VII, pp. 21–22.

49 Dufour, in his *Essai sur l'entendement*, pp. 366–367, sides with the *Encyclopédie* and states that fury is nothing more than a specific degree of mania.

50 De la Rive, *Sur un établissement pour la guérison des aliénés*. Bibliothèque Britannique, VIII, p. 304.

51 Encyclopédie, entry on *Manie*.

52 *L'Ame matérielle*, p. 169.

53 Zacchias, *Quæstiones medico-legales*, book II, vol. I, question 4, p. 119.

54 Sauvages, *Nosologie*, vol. VII, p. 15.

55 Sauvages, p. 20.

56 Cf. Daquin, *Philosophie de la Folie*, p. 30.

57 Zacchias, *Quæstiones medico-legales*, book II, title I, question 4, p. 120.

58 Diemerbroek, *Disputationes practicæ, de morbis capitis*, in *Opera omnia anatomica et medica*, Utrecht, 1685, *Historia*, III, pp. 4–5.

59 Bienville, *De la nymphomanie*, Amsterdam, 1771, pp. 140–153.

60 James, Robert, *A Medicinal Dictionary, including Physic, Surgery, Anatomy, Chymistry and Botany, and all their Branches relative to Medicine* (London, T. Osborne, 1745), vol. II, (unpaginated) entry on 'Delirium'.

61 Ibid.

62 Sauvages considers that hysteria is not just a *vésanie*, but 'a sickness characterized by an access of convulsions of a general or particular nature, either external or internal'; but on the other hand he did class tinnitus, hallucinations and vertigo as *vésanies*.

63 Du Laurens, *Discours de la conservation de la vue, des maladies mélancoliques, des catarrhes, de la vieillesse*, Paris, 1597, in *Toutes les Œuvres de Me André Du Laurens*, Rouen, 1661, p. 29.

64 Zacchias, *Quæstiones medico-legales*, book I, title II, question 4, p. 118.

65 Ibid.

66 Cf. Dufour for example: 'I consider that what is common to all these illnesses is the error of the understanding which makes a wrong judgement regarding things on which everyone agrees, *in the waking state*' (*Essai*, p. 355, our underlining); or Cullen:

> I apprehend that Delirium may be defined to be – 'In a person awake, a false or mistaken judgment of those relations of things, which as occurring most frequently in life, are those about which the generality of men form the same judgment.'
>
> (p. 122)

67 Pitcairn, quoted in Sauvages, VII, p. 33 and p. 310. See also Kant's *Anthropology*.

68 Zacchias, p. 118.

69 *Encyclopédie*, entry on *Folie*.

70 Sauvages, VII, p. 33.

71 Zacchias, p. 118.

72 The French *vésanie* – from the Latin *vesania* – has no direct equivalent in English, and covers various forms of mental disturbance from hallucination to foolishness, depending on the writer and the time. The Latin term is occasionally used in English nosologies, as for example in the Crichton reference that follows here, where it covers an order containing delirium, hallucinations and amentia (a diminishing of the faculties). [TN]

73 Crichton, Alexander, *An Enquiry into the Nature and Origins of Mental Derangement* (1798), 2 vols, vol. II, recapitulative table.

74 *Encyclopédie*, entry on *Folie*.

75 [In French, '*Eblouissement*'. TN] Taken in the sense that Nicolle gave the word, when he wondered whether the heart took part in the 'dazzlement of the mind' (*Essais*, vol. VIII, part II, p. 77).

76 This is a Cartesian theme that Malebranche often took up: to think nothing is not to think; to see nothing is not to see.

77 We should also add Andromaque, widowed, married and widowed again, dressed in mourning and in the regalia of the celebration, clothes that

eventually fuse and come to mean the same thing; and the glory of her royal nature illuminating the darkness of her slavery.

78 In that sense, a definition of madness such as the one proposed by Dufour (essentially no different from any others proposed by his contemporaries) can also pass for a *theory* of confinement, as it designates madness to be an oneiric error, a double non-being immediately perceptible in its difference from the universal nature of men: 'An error of the understanding which makes a wrong judgement regarding things on which everyone agrees, in the waking state' (*Essai*, p. 355).

79 Cf. for example annotations like the following, regarding a madman who had been confined in Saint-Lazare for seventeen years: 'His health is greatly weakened, and it is to be hoped that he will soon die' (BN Clairambault, 986, fo. 113).

III FIGURES OF MADNESS

1 *Examen de la prétendue possession des filles de la paroisse de Landes*, 1735, p. 14.
2 Willis, *De anima brutorum*, p. 179. [The translation of the terminology is complex here. Foucault's *démence*, translated into English as 'dementia' here, was in fact what Willis termed 'delirium.' TN]
3 Willis, p. 209.
4 Willis' translator speaks of the 'middle of the brain' for the corpus callosum, and the 'cortical marrows' for the white matter. [TN]
5 Ibid.
6 Ibid.
7 Dufour, pp. 358–359.
8 Cullen, vol. I, p. 317.
9 *Apologie pour Monsieur Duncan*, pp. 113–115.
10 Fem, *De la nature et du siège de la phrénésie et de la paraphrénésie*. Thesis defended in Göttingen under the presidence of M. Schroder; reviewed in the *Gazette salutaire*, 27 March 1766, no. 13.
11 James, entry on 'Phrenitis'.
12 Cullen, p. 315.
13 Ibid.
14 James, entry on 'Phrenitis'.
15 As in the following example: 'I have reported to Mgr le duc d'Orléans what you were good enough to tell me about the state of imbecility and dementia in which you found the woman called Dardelle.' Bastille Archives (Arsenal 10808, fo. 137).
16 Willis, p. 209.
17 Dufour, p. 357.
18 Dufour, p. 359.
19 Sauvages, vol. VII, pp. 334–335.
20 In practice, imbecility was long considered to be a mixture of madness and

sensorial infirmity. An order dated 11 April 1779 required that the Superior at La Salpêtrière receive Marie Fichet, following signed reports by physicians and surgeons 'confirming that Fichet was born a demented deaf-mute.' (BN, Joly de Fleury collection, ms. 1235, fo. 89).

21 An anonymous article in the *Gazette de médecine*, vol. III, no. 12, 10 February 1762, pp. 89–92.

22 Pinel, *Nosographie philosophique*, 1818, vol. III, p. 130.

23 J. Weyer, *De præstigiis dæmonum*, French translation, p. 222.

24 Sydenham, *Dissertation on Hysterical Affections* in *Works*, p. 306.

25 Weyer, loc. cit.

26 Boerhaave, *Aphorismes*, 1089.

27 Dufour, *Essai*.

28 Fernel, *Physiologia*, in *Universa medica*, 1607, p. 121.

29 Behind the debate lay the question as to whether the possessed could be considered as suffering from melancholia. The protagonists in France were Duncan and La Mesnardière.

30 *Apologie pour Monsieur Duncan*, p. 63.

31 Ibid., pp. 93–94.

32 La Mesnardière, *Traitté de la mélancholie*, 1635, p. 10.

33 *Apologie pour Monsieur Duncan*, pp. 85–86.

34 Willis, *De anima brutorum*, pp. 188–189.

35 Foucault notes 'ibid.' for the last two Latin references, although he adapts them for his purposes [TN].

36 Willis, p. 188.

37 Ibid.

38 James, article on 'Mania'. [The French edition adds references to 'the Creator' and 'the seat of the soul'. TN]

39 One soldier became melancholic on account of a refusal from the parents of a girl he loved madly. He became dreamy, complained constantly of severe headaches, and of a continual numbing of that part of his anatomy. Weight fell off him, his face grew pale, and he became so weak that he was unaware of his bodily functions . . . there was however no delirium, although the patient never gave a positive answer to anything and seemed quite lost in his own thoughts. He never asked to eat or drink.

(*Observation de Musell*, *Gazette salutaire*, 17 March 1763)

40 James, entry on 'Melancholy'.

41 Ibid.

42 *Encyclopédie*, entry on *Manie*.

43 Bonet, *Sepulchretum*, p. 205.

44 A. von Haller, *Elementa Physiologiæ*, book XVII, section 1, no. 17, vol. V, Lausanne, 1763, pp. 571–574.

45 Dufour, pp. 370–371. Dufour uses ancient units of measurement, the grain, dram, ounce, pound and 'gros', which has no direct equivalent in English. A *gros* was ⅛ of an ounce. [Translator's note.]

46 *Encyclopédie*, article on *Manie*.

47 This idea is to be found in Daquin (pp. 67–68) and in Pinel. It was common practice in confinement. On the register at Saint-Lazare, concerning Antoine de la Haye Monbault, one can read 'Cold, however biting, makes no impression on him at all.' (BN Clairambault, 986, p. 117.)

48 *Encyclopédie*, entry on *Manie*.

49 Montchau, in an observation sent to the *Gazette salutaire*, no. 5, 3 February 1763.

50 De la Rive, *Sur un établissement pour la guérison des aliénés*, Bibliothèque britannique, VIII, p. 304.

51 Willis, *De anima brutorum*, chapter 12, p. 201. [In Latin, the chapter was entitled 'De Mania'; Pordage, Willis' English translator, never employs the word 'mania', and systematically uses the word 'madness' instead. The French uses *manie*. [TN]

52 Ibid.

53 Aumont is an example, in the article *Mélancolie* in the *Encyclopédie*.

54 Sydenham, *Works*, pp. 653–654.

55 Lieutaud, *Précis de médecine pratique*, p. 204.

56 Dufour, *Essai sur l'entendement*, p. 369.

57 Boerhaave, *Aphorismes*, 1118 and 1119; Van Swieten, *Commentaria*, vol. III, pp. 519–520.

58 Hoffmann, *Medicina rationalis systematica*, vol. IV, p. 188 ff.

59 Spengler, *Briefe, welche einige Erfahrungen der elektrischen Wirkung in Krankheiten enthalten*, Copenhagen, 1754.

60 James, entry on 'Mania' [Foucault wrongly attributes this to Cullen. TN].

61 Cullen, vol. IV, p. 148.

62 Cullen, vol. IV, p. 183.

63 Cullen, vol. IV, p. 94.

64 Sauvages' hysteria is in class IV (spasms) and hypochondria in class VIII ('*vesaniæ*').

65 Linnaeus, *Genera Morborum*. Hypochondria belongs to the 'imaginary' category of mental illnesses, epilepsy to the 'tonic' category of convulsive diseases.

66 Cf. the polemic with Highmore, *Exercitationes duæ, prior de passione hysterica, altera de affectione hypochondriaca*, Oxford, 1660, and *De Passione hysterica, responsio epistolaris ad Willisium*, London, 1670.

67 These are literal translations from the French. Blackmore mentions 'an inordinate firmness and activity of the animal spirits' (p. 30), and 'their proneness to excessive rarification, dissipation and convulsive contradictions' (p. 33), but Foucault seems to quote here from a translation he does not refer to. [TN]

68 Whytt, pp. 224–327. Cf. a similar enumeration in Revillon, *Recherches sur la cause des affections hypocondriaques*, Paris, 1779, pp. 5–6.

69 Willis, *Of Convulsive Diseases*, in *Works*, p. 69.

70 Lieutaud, *Traité de médecine pratique*, 1761, p. 127.

71 Raulin, *Traité des affections vaporeuses*, Paris, 1758, discours préliminaire, p. xx.

72 J. Ferrand, *De la maladie d'amour ou mélancolie érotique*, Paris, 1623, p. 164.

73 N. Chesneau, *Observationum Nicolai Chesneau*, Paris, 1672, book III, chap. xiv.

74 T.A. Murillo, *Novissima hypochondriacæ melancholiæ curatio*, Lyon, 1672, chapter IX, p. 88 ff.

75 M. Flemyng, *Neuropathia sive de morbis hypochondriacis et hystericis*, Amsterdam, 1741, pp. L–LI.

76 George Cheyne, *The English Malady*, 1733, edited with an introduction by Roy Porter (London and New York: Tavistock/Routledge, 1991), pp. 16–17.

77 Stahl, *Theoria medica vera, de malo hypochondriaco*, p. 447 ff.

78 Van Swieten, *Commentaria in Aphorismos Boerhaavii*, 1752, I, p. 22 ff.

79 Lange, *Traité des vapeurs*, Paris, 1689, pp. 41–60.

80 *Dissertatio de malo hypochondriaco*, in *Pratique de médecine spéciale*, p. 571.

81 Viridet, *Dissertation sur les vapeurs*, Yverdon, 1716, pp. 50–62.

82 Liébault, *Trois livres des maladies et infirmitez des femmes*, 1649, p. 380.

83 C. Piso, *Observationes*, 1618, reedited in 1733 by Boerhaave, section II, no 2, chapter VII, p. 144.

84 Willis, *Of Hysterical Affections* in *Works*, p. 78.

85 Willis, *Of Convulsive Diseases* in *Works*, p. 69.

86 Pinel classes hysteria among the reproduction-related neuroses (*Nosographie philosophique*).

87 Stahl, p. 453.

88 Hoffmann, *Medicina rationalis systematica*, vol. IV, *pars tertia*, p. 410.

89 Highmore, loc. cit.

90 Sydenham, p. 308.

91 Ibid.

92 Ibid.

93 Ibid.

94 Ibid.

95 Pressavin, *Nouveau traité des vapeurs*, Lyon, 1770, pp. 2–3.

96 Ibid.

97 Tissot, *Traité des nerfs*, vol. I, part II, pp. 99–100.

98 Tissot, pp. 270–292.

99 Whytt, pp. 9–11.

100 Ibid.

101 Whytt, pp. 29–30.

102 Whytt, p. 89.

103 Whytt, pp. 27–28

104 Whytt, pp. 118.

105 Cheyne, p. 71.

106 Tissot, *Traité des nerfs*, vol. 1, part II, p. 274.

107 Tissot, p. 302.

108 Tissot, pp. 278–279.

109 Tissot, pp. 302–303.

110 I.e. the air, food and drink, sleep and waking, movement and rest; excretion

and retention, the passions. (Cf., amongst others, Tissot, *Traité des nerfs*, II, I, p. 3–4.)

111 Cf. Tissot, *Essai sur les maladies des gens du monde*, Lausanne, 1770.
112 Pressavin, *Nouveau traité des vapeurs*, pp. 15–55, pp. 222–224.
113 Pressavin, p. 65.
114 Mercier, *Tableau de Paris*, Amsterdam, 1783, III, p. 199.
115 Cf. Broussais, *De l'irritation et de la folie*, 2nd edition, 1839.
116 In French 'aveuglement' [TN].

IV DOCTORS AND PATIENTS

1 Whytt, p. 359.
2 P. Hecquet, *Réflexion sur l'usage de l'opium, des calmants et des narcotiques*, Paris, 1726, p. 11.
3 Hecquet, pp. 32–33.
4 Ibid., p. 84.
5 Ibid., p. 86.
6 Ibid., p. 87.
7 Ibid., pp. 87–88.
8 Critics of the drug use the same principles as its apologists. James' *Dictionary* claims that opium can bring on mania: 'we consider that these remedies abound with a certain volatile and fetid sulphur, highly unfriendly to nature' (James entry on 'Mania').
9 A line from René Char's prose poem *Jacquemard et Julia* in *Poèmes et prose choisis* (Paris: Gallimard, 1957, p. 83) unidentified by Foucault [TN].
10 Jean de Renou, *Œuvres pharmaceutiques*, translated by de Serres, Lyon, 1638, p. 405.
11 Ibid., pp. 406–413. Previously, Albert de Bollsdat had said of chrysolite that it 'brought wisdom and warded off madness', while Barthélemy (*De proprietatibus rerum*) credited topaz with the ability to cure frenzy.
12 Lemery, *Dictionnaire universel des drogues simples*, 1759 ed., p. 821. See also Madame de Sévigné, *Œuvres*, vol. VII, p. 411.
13 Lemery, entry on 'Homo', p. 429. See also Moïse Charas, *Pharmacopée royale*, 1676 ed., p. 771: 'It may be said that there is no part, no excrement or superfluity in men or women that chemistry cannot prepare and use as a cure or for the soothing of most of the ills to which both sexes are subject.'
14 Ibid., p. 430.
15 Buchoz, *Lettres périodiques curieuses*, 2 and 3. They are summarised in the *Gazette salutaire*, XX and XXI, 18 and 25 May 1769.
16 Cf. Raoul Mercier, *Le Monde médical de Touraine sous la Révolution*, p. 206.
17 Lemery, *Pharmacopée universelle*, p. 124, p. 359 and p. 752.
18 Buchoz, op. cit.
19 Madame de Sévigné, letter of 8 July 1685, *Œuvres*, vol. VII, p. 421.
20 Bienville, pp. 171–172.
21 Lemery, op. cit.
22 Whytt, p. 472.

23 T.-E. Gilibert, *L'Anarchie médicinale*, Neufchâtel, 1772, vol. II, pp. 3–4.

24 Madame de Sévigné was a great user of Queen of Hungary water, finding it 'excellent against sadness'. Cf. the letters of 16 and 20 October 1675, *Œuvres*, vol. IV, p. 186 and 193. The recipe is given by Mme Fouquet, *Recueil de remèdes faciles et domestiques*, Paris, 1678, p. 381.

25 Lange, *Traité des vapeurs*, pp. 243–245.

26 Sydenham, *Dissertation on Hysterical Affection*, p. 318.

27 Whytt, p. 343.

28 Laehr, *Gedenklage der Psychiatrie*, p. 316.

29 Zilboorg, *History of Psychiatry*, pp. 275–276. Ettmüller strongly recommended transfusion in cases of delirious melancholy (*Chirurgia transfusoria*, 1682).

30 Transfusion was again cited as a cure for madness by Dionis, in *Cours d'opération de chirurgie* (Demonstration VIII, p. 408) and by Manjet, *Bibliothèque médico-pratique*, III, book IX, pp. 334 and seq.

31 Lange, *Traité des vapeurs*, p. 251.

32 Lieutaud, *Précis de médecine pratique*, pp. 620–621.

33 Fallowes, *The Best Method for the Cure of Lunatics with some Accounts of the Incomparable Oleum Cephalicum*, London, 1705, quoted in Tuke, *Chapters on the History of the Insane*, pp. 93–94.

34 Doublet, *Traitement qu'il faut administrer dans les différentes espèces de folie*. In *Instruction* by Doublet and Colombier (*Journal de médecine*, July, 1785).

35 James' *Dictionary* proposes the following genealogy of insanity: 'Melancholy is a symptom very frequently attending hysteric and hypochondriacal disorders; for it is certain that a want of a due tone in the viscera, and a slow circulation of a thick and abundant blood through them, produce in the abdomen spasms and flatulences . . . from which all the symptoms may be derived and accounted for.' Entry on 'Mania', in James, *Dictionary*.

36 Thirion, *De l'usage et de l'abus du café*, a thesis defended in Pont-à-Mousson in 1763 (cf. the *compte rendu* in the *Gazette salutaire*, no. 37, 15 September 1763).

37 Consultation by La Closure, Arsenal, ms. no. 4528, fo. 119.

38 Whytt, pp. 339–340.

39 Ibid.

40 Raulin, *Traité des affections vaporeuses du sexe*, Paris, 1758, p. 339.

41 Tissot, *Avis aux gens de lettres sur leur santé*, p. 76.

42 Muzzell, quoted in the *Gazette salutaire*, 17 March 1763.

43 Whytt, p. 518.

44 Raulin, p. 340.

45 F.H. Muzzell, *Medizin und Chirurgie*, Berlin, 1764, vol. II, pp. 54–60.

46 *Gazette de médecine*, 14 October 1761, no. 23, vol. II, pp. 215–216.

47 Tissot, *Avis aux gens de lettres sur leur santé*, p. 90.

48 Aurelianus, *De morbis acutis*, I, 11. Asclepiades frequently used baths as a treatment for mental illnesses. Pliny reports that he invented hundreds of different types of baths (*Natural History*, book XXVI).

49 Sylvius, *Opera medica* (1680), *De methodo medendi*, book I, chapter XIV.

50 Menuret, *Mémoires de l'Académie royale des sciences*, 1734. *Histoire*, p. 56.

51 Doublet, *Traitement*.
52 Cheyne, *De infirmorum sanitate tuenda*, quoted in Rostaing, *Réflexions sur les affections vaporeuses*, pp. 73–74. [The English version quoted here is from Cheyne's *An Essay of Health and Good Life* (London: George Strahan, 1725), 4th edition, p. 102. TN]
53 Boissieu, *Mémoire sur les méthodes rafraîchissantes et échauffantes*, Dijon 1770, pp. 37–55.
54 Darut, *Les bains froids sont-ils plus propres à conserver la santé que les bains chauds?* A thesis from 1763 (*Gazette salutaire*, no. 47).
55 Cf. Beaugresne, *De l'influence des affections de l'âme*, p. 13.
56 Pressavin, *Nouveau traité des vapeurs*, unpaginated foreword. See also Tissot's *Avis aux gens de lettres*, p. 85: 'most illnesses are a consequence of the teapot'.
57 Rostaing, *Réflexions sur les affections vaporeuses*, p. 75.
58 Hoffmann, *Opera*, II, section ii, no. 5. See also Chambon de Montaux, 'les bains froids dessèchent les solides', *Des maladies des femmes*, vol. II, p. 469.
59 Pomme, *Traité des affections vaporeuses des deux sexes*, 3rd edition, 1767, pp. 20–21.
60 Lionet Chalmers, *Journal de médecine*, November 1759, p. 388.
61 Pomme, note to p. 58.
62 Pinel, *Traité médico-philosophique*, p. 324.
63 Esquirol, *Des maladies mentales*, vol. II, p. 225.
64 Burette, *Mémoire pour servir à l'histoire de la course chez les Anciens*, Mémoires de l'Académie des Belles-Lettres, vol. III, p. 285.
65 Sydenham, *Epistolary Discourse*, pp. 324–325.
66 Whytt, p. 356.
67 According to Lieutaud, the treatment of melancholy is not so much a matter of medicine as 'dissipation and exercise' (*Précis de médecine pratique*, p. 203). Sauvages recommends horse riding because of the variety of images. (*Nosologie*, vol. VIII, p. 30).
68 Le Camus, *Médecine pratique* (quoted by Pomme, *Nouveau recueil de pièces*), p. 7.
69 Chambon de Montaux, *Des maladies des femmes*, vol. II, pp. 477–478.
70 Cullen, vol. IV, p. 175. The techniques of the cure by work relied on the same idea, and justified, in the eighteenth century, the workshops which were already present in hospitals.
71 There is some dispute whether the inventor of the machine was Maupertuis, Darwin, or the Danish physician Katzenstein.
72 Joseph Mason Cox, *Practical Observations on Insanity* (London: C. & R. Baldwin, 1804), p. 110.
73 Esquirol, *Des maladies mentales*, vol. II, p. 225.
74 Bienville, *De la nymphomanie*, p. 136.
75 Beauchesne, *De l'influence des affections de l'âme*, pp. 28–29.
76 J. Schenck, *Observationes*, 1654 edition, p. 128.
77 W. Albrecht, *De effectu musicæ*, no. 314.
78 *Histoire de l'Académie royale des sciences*, 1707, p. 7 and 1708, p. 22. Cf. also

J.-L. Royer, *De vi soni et musicæ in corpus humanum* (a thesis in Montpellier); Desbonnets, *Effets de la musique dans les maladies nerveuses* (notice in the *Journal de médecine*, vol. LIX, pp. 556); Roger, *Traité des effets de la musique sur le corps humain*, 1803.

79 Diemerbroek, *De peste*, book IV, 1665.

80 Porta, *De magia naturali* (quoted in the *Encyclopédie* in the article *Musique*). Xenocrates, it was said, previously used hellebore flutes to cure the insane, and poplar wood flutes to cure sciatica. Cf. Roger, *Traité*.

81 *Encyclopédie*, article *Musique*. Cf. also Tissot (*Traité des nerfs*, vol. II, pp. 418–419), where music is 'one of the most primitive forms of medicine, as it has its perfect model in birdsong'.

82 Crichton, *On Mental Diseases* (quoted in Elias Regnault, *Du degré de compétence des médecins*, Paris, 1828, pp. 187–188).

83 Cullen, vol. IV, p. 156.

84 Tissot, *Traité des nerfs*, vol. II.

85 Scheidenmantel, *Die Leidenschaften, abs Heilemittel betrachtet*, Hildburgh, 1787. Quoted in Pagel-Neuburger, *Handbuch der Geschichte der Medizin*, vol. III, p. 610.

86 Guislain listed moral sedatives as follows: the feeling of dependence, threats, harsh words, wounds inflicted on the self-esteem, isolation, seclusion, punishments (such as the rotatory chair, cold showers, or Rush's 'tranquilizing chair'), and occasionally hunger and thirst (*Traité des phrénopathies*, pp. 405–433).

87 Leuret, *Fragments psychologiques sur la folie*, Paris, 1834. See also 'Un exemple typique', pp. 308–321.

88 Sauvages, *Nosologie méthodique*, vol. VII, p. 39.

89 Bienville, *De la nymphomanie*, pp. 140–153.

90 Histoire de l'Académie des sciences, 1752. A report read by Lieutaud.

91 Quoted in Latin in Whytt.

92 Willis, *De anima brutorum*, chapter 12, in Willis, *Works*, p. 206.

93 Sauvages, *Nosologie méthodique*, vol. VII, p. 28.

94 Tissot, *Avis aux gens de lettres sur leur santé*, p. 117.

95 Pinel, *Traité médico-philosophique*, p. 222.

96 Hulshorff, *Discours sur les penchants*, read in the Academy at Berlin. Quoted in the *Gazette salutaire*, 17 August 1769, no. 33.

97 Z. Lusitanus, *Praxis medica*, 1637, obs. 45, pp. 43–44.

98 *Discours sur les penchants*, M. Hulshorff, read at the Academy of Berlin. Extracts quoted in *Gazette salutaire*, 17 August 1769, no. 33.

99 *Hic omnivarius morbus ingenio et astutia curandus est* (Lusitanus, p. 43).

100 *Encyclopédie*, article *Mélancolie*.

101 Ibid.

102 *Gazette salutaire*, 17 August 1769, no. 33.

103 Bernardin de Saint-Pierre, *Préambule de l'Arcadie*, in *Œuvres*, Paris, 1818, vol. VII, pp. 11–14.

104 Tissot, *Traité sur les maladies des gens de lettres*, pp. 90–94.

105   Quoted by Esquirol, *Des maladies mentales*, vol. II, p. 294.
106   Pinel, *Traité médico-philosophique*, pp. 238–239.
107   Ibid.

PART THREE

INTRODUCTION

1   *Le Neveu de Rameau*, Diderot, *Contes et romans*, ed. Michel Delon (Paris: Gallimard, 2004), p. 585.
2   Diderot, p. 627.
3   Diderot, p. 597.
4   Diderot, p. 626.
5   Ibid.
6   Diderot, pp. 586–587.
7   Diderot, p. 591. In place of *des inspirés* (in Diderot's text), Foucault wrote *des philosophes*. [TN]
8   Diderot, p. 593.
9   Interest, in *Le Neveu de Rameau*, precisely indicates this pressure exerted by being and this absence of mediation. The same thought process can be found in Sade. Beneath the apparent proximity, it is the opposite of the philosophy of 'interest' (as mediation towards truth and reason) commonly found in the eighteenth century.
10   Diderot, p. 657.
11   Diderot, p. 658.
12   Diderot, p. 643.
13   Ibid.

I THE GREAT FEAR

1   Mercier, *Tableau de Paris*, vol. I, pp. 233–234.
2   Ibid., pp. 235–236.
3   The phrase *faiseur de projets à tête fêlée* – 'planner of crackpot projects' – was common on confinement registers.
4   Letter to his wife, quoted in Lély's *Vie de Sade* (Paris, 1952), vol. I, p. 105.
5   Mercier, vol. VIII, p. 1.
6   Ibid. p. 2.
7   Musquinet de la Pagne, *Bicêtre réformé*, Paris, 1790, p. 16.
8   This theme is linked to the problems of chemistry and hygiene posed by breathing such as they were studied at the time. See Hales, *A Description of Ventilators*, London, 1743, or Lavoisier, 'Altérations qu'éprouve l'air respiré', 1785, in *Œuvres*, 1862, vol. II, pp. 676–687.
9   A manuscript copy of this report can be found in the Bibliothèque Nationale Joly de Fleury Collection, 1235, fo. 120.

10 Ibid, fo. 123. The whole affair is treated on folios 117–126. For more on 'gaol fever' and the threat of contagion for cities, see Howard, pp. 2 and 8.

11 'I knew, like everyone, that Bicêtre was both a hospital and a prison: but I did not know that the hospital had been built to engender diseases, and the prison to engender crime' (Mirabeau, *Observations d'un voyageur anglais*, p. 6).

12 Cf. Hanway, 'Réflexions sur l'aération' (*Gazette salutaire*, 25 September and 9 October 1766, nos. 39 and 41); Genneté, *Purification de l'air dans les hôpitaux*, Nancy, 1767. In 1762, the Academy of Lyon announced a competition on the question: 'What is the harmful quality that corrupts the air of hospitals and prisons? And what is the best means of counteracting this?' For a more general view, see Coqueau, *Essai sur l'établissement des hôpitaux dans les grandes villes*, Paris, 1787.

13 Desmonceaux, *De la bienfaisance nationale*, Paris, 1789, p. 14.

14 Mirabeau, *Observations d'un voyageur anglais*, p. 14. [The Latin quote is a slight reworking of the description of the Bacchanalia in Livy's *History of Rome*, Section 39, chapter 15. TN]

15 A report in the name of the Committee on Begging at the National Assembly. Procès-verbal, vol. XLIV, pp. 80–81.

16 The 'Deaf Man's Estate' – Goya's final house in Madrid, whose walls he covered with the 'Black paintings' of 1820–1823. The *Disparates* are engravings from the same period. [TN]

17 The Brocken is the highest mountain in the Harz region, where Goethe set the witches' sabbath of Walpurgis Night; Pieter Bruegel's c. 1562 oil painting *Dulle Griet* (*Mad Meg* in English), who runs through a nightmare landscape towards the mouth of Hell with a sword and basket of loot in her hand (now in the Mayer van der Bergh Museum, Antwerp); Noirceuil, the persecutor in Sade's *Juliette*; Gilles de Rais, Joan of Arc's companion in arms, burnt at the stake in 1440 for his multiple crimes and impiety. [TN]

18 See Part Two, chapter V.

19 Raulin, *Traité des affections vaporeuses*, Preface.

20 Tissot, *Traité des maladies des nerfs*, Preface, vol. I, pp. iii–iv.

21 Matthey, *Nouvelles recherches sur les maladies de l'esprit*, Paris, 1816, Part I, p. 65.

22 In nineteenth-century evolutionism, madness is indeed a return, but along a chronological *path*: it is not the absolute *defeat* of time. What is at stake is the idea of returning, of going back against time, and not repetition, strictly speaking. Psychoanalysis, which tried once again to confront madness and unreason, found itself faced with precisely this problem of time; fixation, the death instinct, the collective unconscious and archetypes are more or less successful attempts at isolating the heterogeneity of these two temporal structures, the one being proper to the experience of Unreason and the knowledge that it envelops, the other being proper to the knowledge of madness and the science that it authorises.

23 See above, Part Two, chapter II.

24 George Cheyne, *The natural method of cureing the diseases of the body: and the disorders of the mind depending on the body*. Montesquieu was of the

same opinion (see *Esprit des lois*, Part III, book XIV, chapter 2, Pléiade vol. II, pp. 474–477).

25 Venel, *Essai sur la santé et l'éducation médicinale des filles destinées au mariage*, Yvernon, 1776, pp. 135–136.

26 Cf. Montesquieu, *Causes qui peuvent affecter les esprits et les caractères*, in *Œuvres complètes*, Paris, Pléiade, vol. II, pp. 39–40.

27 Buffon, *Histoire naturelle*, in *Œuvres complètes*, 1848 ed., vol. III, 'De l'homme', pp. 319–320.

28 Sauvages spoke of '*Melancolia anglica or tædium vitæ*', vol. VII, p. 366.

29 Montesquieu, *Causes* . . ., Part III, book XIV, chapter XII, Pléiade vol. II, pp. 485–486.

30 Cheyne, *The English Malady*, London, 1733.

31 Spurzheim, *Observations sur la folie*, 1818, pp. 193–196.

32 Ibid., pp. 193–196.

33 *Encyclopédie*, article *Mélancolie*.

34 Pinel, *Traité médico-philosophique*, p. 268.

35 Pinel, p. 291, note 1.

36 Moehsen, *Geschichte der Wissenschaften in der mark Brandenburg*, Berlin and Leipzig, 1781, p. 503.

37 Tissot, *Avis aux gens de lettres sur leur santé*, p. 24.

38 Pressavin, *Nouveau traité des vapeurs*, pp. 222–224.

39 Tissot, *Traité des nerfs*, II, p. 442.

40 Beauchesne, *De l'influence des affections de l'âme dans les maladies nerveuses des femmes*, Paris, 1783, p. 31.

41 Ibid., p. 33.

42 Ibid., pp. 37–38.

43 'Causes physiques et morales des maux de nerfs' (*Gazette salutaire*, no. 40, 6 October 1768. Anonymous).

44 Here medical analyses depart from the analyses of Buffon. For him, penetrating forces included natural factors like air and sky, as well as all that was clearly separate from it, like society or epidemics.

45 Jean-Jacques Rousseau, *Discours sur l'origine de l'inégalité*, in *Œuvres* (Paris, 1852), vol. I, p. 553, translated as *Discourse on the Origin and Foundation of Inequality among Men* in *The Discourses and Other Philosophical Writings*, ed. Victor Gourevitch (Cambridge: Cambridge University Press, 1977), p. 165.

46 Beauchesne, *De l'influence des affections de l'âme*, pp. 39–40.

47 The madness of animals was seen either as an effect of their domestication and their enforced life in society (the melancholy of a dog for example was an effect of the absence of its master), or as the effect of an injury to their superior, quasi-human faculties. (Cf. the observation of an imbecile dog which lacked any *sensorium commune*, in the *Gazette de médecine*, vol. III, no. 13, 10 February 1762, pp. 89–92.)

48 Benjamin Rush, *Medical Inquiries and Observations*, vol. I, p. 119 [Not p. 19 as Foucault noted. TN]

49 Quoted in Spurzheim, *Observations sur la folie*, p. 183.

50   Raulin quotes a curious analysis of the appearance of madness in the passage from animal consumption to the human alimentary milieu:

Men distanced themselves from the simple life by their habit of listening ever more closely to their passions. First of all they made the pernicious discovery of food that flattered the taste buds, then they adapted such findings, and these fatal discoveries slowly multiplied; their use augmented the passions, and passions demanded ever greater luxury; the discovery of the Indies then brought the means to nourish such passions bringing them to the point that they have reached in our century. The first appearance of such sicknesses is almost exactly contemporaneous with this change in the combination of foods and the excesses that followed.

(Raulin, pp. 60–61)

51   Matthey, *Nouvelles recherches sur les maladies de l'esprit*, p. 67.
52   'Causes physiques et morales des maladies de nerfs' (*Gazette salutaire*, 6 October 1768).
53   'All living matter descends by degrees from more elevated types to ever lower variants, the last of which is a return to an inorganic state' (article *Dégénerescence* by Bœkel in Jaccoud's *Dictionary*).
54   'Certain individuals will always avoid such hereditary alteration, and by the exclusive use of such specimens to perpetuate the species, we can swim against this fatal tide' (Prosper Lucas, *Traité physiologique et philosophique de l'hérédité naturelle*, Paris, 1847).
55   'The existence of a primitive type, which the human mind considers to be the masterpiece and the summary of creation, is a fact that conforms so closely to our beliefs that the idea of a degeneracy of our nature is inseparable from the idea of a deviation from that primitive type that contained within it the elements of the continuity of the species.'

(Morel, *Traité des dégénérescences physiques, intellectuelles et morales de l'espèce humaine*, Paris, 1857, pp. 1–2)

56   Cf. Morel, *Traité des dégénérescences physiques, intellectuelles et morales de l'espèce humaine*, Paris, 1857, pp. 50 f., describing the struggle between individuals and 'the artificial nature that social conditions impose upon their existence.'
57   *Causes physiques et morales des maux de nerfs* (*Gazette salutaire*, 6 October 1768, no. 40).
58   Buffon also speaks of *dégénération*, meaning either a general weakening of nature (pp. 120–121), or individuals who degenerate in relation to their species (p. 311).
59   The strictest form of positivist biology is preformationist; positivism impregnated with evolutionism appeared much later.
60   Michea, article 'Démonomanie' in Jaccoud's *Dictionnaire*, vol. 11, p. 125.
61   Pinel, *Traité médico-philosophique*, Introduction, p. xxii.
62   Ibid., p. xxx.
63   Esquirol, *Des maladies mentales*, vol. II, p. 302.

64 Morel, p. 50.
65 *Essai sur les maladies des gens du monde*, pp. 11–12.

II THE NEW DIVISION

1 La Rochefoucauld-Liancourt, Report to the Committee on Begging. Procès-verbal de l'Assemblée nationale, vol. XLIV, p. 85.
2 Ibid., p. 38. The *Gazette nationale* of 21 December 1789, no. 121, gives the figure of 4,094. These variations were often due to the inclusion or exclusion of employees in the figures, as many of them were also confined (in Bicêtre in 1789 for example, 435 of the confined were employed in minor posts, and as such were listed on the register).
3 Bonnafous-Sérieux, p. 23.
4 Tardif, p. 26.
5 Cf. The report drawn up by Tristan, the bursar at Bicêtre, BN Joly de Fleury Collection, 1235, fo. 238.
6 As these quarters were reserved for women who had a low mental age, were feeble-minded, or were intermittently or violently insane.
7 *Gazette nationale*, 21 December 1789, no. 121.
8 Ibid.
9 *Règlement de l'hôpital des insensés de la ville d'Aix* (Aix, 1695), Article XVII: 'Inmates must be natives of the town or have lived here for at least five years.' Article XVIII: 'Only individuals liable to cause a public nuisance if they are not confined are admitted.' Article XXVII: 'No simple fools, innocents or imbeciles.'
10 Cf. Tenon, *Papiers sur les hôpitaux*, II, fos. 228–229.
11 A complete list can be consulted in Annex I.
12 The Bicêtre bursar wrote to Joly de Fleury on 1 April 1746 about one particular imbecile:

> For as long as he remains in this state, there is no hope of him ever recovering his wits, and the harsh conditions (those of Bicêtre) are most likely to cause his condition to worsen, and perhaps become incurable. In the Petites-Maisons he would be better lodged, bedded and fed; there would be more hope.
>
> (BN Joly de Fleury collection, 1238, fo. 60)

13 Laehr, *Gedenktage den Psychiatrie*, p. 344.
14 Cf. Sérieux, 'Notice historique sur le développement de l'assistance des aliénés en Allemagne', *Archives de neurologie* (November, 1895), vol. II, pp. 353 f.
15 Laehr, p. 115.
16 D.H. Tuke, *Chapters on the History of the Insane*. Appendix C, p. 514.
17 Tenon, 'Journal d'Observations sur les principaux hôpitaux et prisons d'Angleterre', *Papiers sur les hôpitaux*, III, fos. 11–16.
18 Ibid.

19 There was, however, one exception, but it was clearly experimental in nature. In 1749, the Duke of Brunswick published a decree that stated that 'There are examples that demonstrate that through medical intervention and other similar measures, the alienated have sometimes been cured.' He therefore instructed a doctor to visit the madmen in the town hospital twice a week, offering five thalers for any cure (Sérieux).

20 For a long period in the nineteenth century, much of the psychiatry in the asylums consisted of taxonomic work. The endless analyses of monomania are a case in point.

21 One example was Mathurin Milan, who was confined in Charenton on 31 August 1707:

> His madness has always been to hide from his family, and to live an obscure life both in Paris and in the country, and to be constantly involved in court cases; he also lends out money at usurious rates, and with no security; he is forever getting lost on unknown highways, and believes himself worthy of the greatest positions.
>
> (BN fonds Clairambault, 985, p. 403)

22 Clairambault, 985, p. 349. See also Pierre Dugnet: 'His madness continues, and is closer to imbecility than frenzy' (ibid., p. 134), or Michel Ambroise de Lantivy: 'His madness is more characterised by disturbance and imbecility than stubbornness and frenzy' (Clairambault, 986, p. 104).

23 R. d'Argenson's *Notes*, p. 93. See also:

> This l'Amoureux is a frenzied specimen, quite capable of killing his parents and extracting revenge even at the cost of his own life. He has been involved in all the rebellions that have taken place in the hospital, and played a major role in the one when the Brigadier of the Archers of the Poor unfortunately lost his life.
>
> (Ibid., p. 66)

24 Tenon, 'Projet du rapport sur les hôpitaux civils', *Papiers sur les hôpitaux*, vol. II, fo. 228.

25 BN Joly de Fleury, ms 1301, fo. 310.

26 BN Clairambault, ms. 985, p. 128.

27 Ibid., p. 384.

28 Ibid., p. 1.

29 Ibid., pp. 38–39.

30 Ibid., p. 129.

31 Ibid., pp. 377 and 406.

32 Ibid., p. 347. It should be noted that such remarks only ever appeared on the register at Charenton, a house kept by the Brothers of Saint John of God, i.e. a hospital order that claimed expertise in medicine.

33 Naturally, we have no intention here of becoming embroiled in the debate between Pinel's hagiographers (like Sémelaigne) and others, like Sérieux and Libert who aim to reduce his originality by finding in classical confinement all

the loci of nineteenth-century humanitarianism. From our point of view this is not a question of individual influence, but of historical structure, the structure of the experience a culture has of insanity. The polemic between Sémelaigne and Sérieux is a political and also familial matter. Sémelaigne, who is an ally of the descendents of Pinel, is a radical [i.e. a secular republican reformer during the Third Republic – TN]. There is no hint of a concept in these discussions.

34   Esquirol, *Des maladies mentales*, vol. II, p. 138.

35   Tuke, Samuel, *Description of the Retreat*, York: 1813; D.H. Tuke, *Chapters on the History of the Insane*, London, 1882.

36   Quoted by Esquirol, pp. 134–135.

37   Ibid.

38   Mirabeau, *Des lettres de cachet*, Chapter XI, *Œuvres*, ed. Merilhou, I, p. 269.

39   Arsenal, ms. 11168. Cf. Ravaisson, *Archives de la Bastille*, vol. XIV, p. 275.

40   Kirchhoff, pp. 110–111.

41   Bourges de Longchamp, Arsenal ms. 11496.

42   Quoted in Bonnafous-Sérieux, p. 221.

43   La Rochefoucauld-Liancourt, Report to the Committee on Begging, p. 47.

44   Mirabeau, p. 264.

45   Mirabeau, *L'Ami des hommes*, 1758, vol. II, p. 414 f.

46   Ibid, p. 264.

47   *Histoire de France*, 1899 edition, pp. 293–294. The facts are inaccurate. Mirabeau was confined in Vincennes from 8 June 1777 to 13 December 1780. Sade was kept there from 15 February 1777 until 29 February 1784, apart from a thirty-nine-day interval in 1778. And he only left Vincennes for the Bastille.

48   Cf. Arsenal, ms. 12685 and 12686 for Bicêtre and 12692–12695 for the Salpêtrière.

49   The violence was committed above all by the special companies set up to recruit colonisers, like 'the Mississippi Bandoliers'. For a detailed description, see Levasseur, *Recherches historiques sur le système de Law*, Paris, 1854.

50   'In those days, there was a constant hunt for young people who were willing to volunteer for the colonies' (Abbé Prévost, *Histoire du Chevalier des Grieux et de Manon Lescaut*, ed. Frédéric Deloffre et Raymond Picard (Paris: Garnier, 1965, p. 183).

51   Laverdy, the 'contrôleur général', ordered the dividing up of common land with a Royal Decree on 5 July 1770. (Cf. Sagnac, *La Formation de la société française moderne*, pp. 256 f.) The phenomenon was more widespread in England than in France. English landlords were usually granted the right of enclosure quite easily, while in France *Intendants* (the local representatives of the crown) often resisted the process.

52   Cf. Labrousse, *La Crise de l'économie française à la fin de l'Ancien Régime*, Paris, 1944.

53   Arnould gives the following figures for the volume of external trade: for the period 1740 to 1748, 430 trading operations totalling one million pounds; for 1749 to 1755, 616 for seven million pounds. Exports alone rose by 103 million

pounds. (*De la balance du commerce et des relations commerciales extérieures de la France*, Paris, Year III [1795], second edition).

54 Argenson, *Journal et Mémoires*, vol. VI, p. 228, 19 July, 1750.

55 Ibid., p. 80, 30 November 1749.

56 Ibid., pp. 202–203, 26 May 1750.

57 Ibid., pp. 228, 19 July 1750.

58 Total exports for the period 1749 to 1755 had been 341, totalling two million pounds; for 1756 to 1763 the figure was 148, for a value of nine million pounds. Cf. Arnould, see note 53.

59 Ibid.

60 Exports for the year 1748 had been 11,142,202 pounds; in 1760 the figure stood at 14,693,270 pounds. Cf. Nicholls, *English Poor Laws*, vol. II, p. 54.

61 A commission had been set up in 1763 to study ways of putting an end to begging. This was the commission that ordered the decree of 1764.

62 Article 1 of the Regulations at the Dépôt de Lyon, 1783, quoted in Lallemand, vol. IV, p. 278.

63 Mercier, *Tableau de Paris*, 1783, vol. IX, p. 120.

64 Cf. Sérieux: 'Le Quartier d'aliénés du dépôt de Soissons' (*Bulletin de la Société historique de Soissons*, 1934, vol. V, p. 127). 'The Soissons Dépôt is clearly one of the most beautiful, best directed establishments to be found in France' (Récalde, *Traité sur les abus qui subsistent dans les hôpitaux du Royaume*, p. 110).

65 Brissot de Warville, *Théorie des lois criminelles* (1781), vol. I, p. 79.

66 The *Encyclopédie* entry on *Hôpital*.

67 Ibid. Récalde, preface, p. II, III.

68 Mirabeau, *L'Ami des hommes*, 1758, vol. I, p. 22.

69 Turgot, 'Eloge de Gournay', *Œuvres*, ed. Schelle, vol. I, p. 607.

70 Cf. Turgot, Letter to David Hume, 25 March, 1767, *Œuvres*, ed. Schelle, vol. II, pp. 658–665.

71 Tucker, Josiah, 'Reflections on the expediency of a law for the naturalization of foreign Protestants' (London: T. Trye, 1752), translated as *Questions importants sur le commerce*, by Turgot, in *Œuvres*, ed. Schelle, vol. I, pp. 442–470. For reasons that are unclear, this sentence does not exist in English: Tucker's original version, and subsequent reprints of the essay, jump from point 5 to point 7, and this point 6 only exists in the French translation. It is therefore translated here literally from the French.

72 Turgot, article on *Fondation* in the *Encyclopédie*, *Œuvres*, ed. Schelle, vol. I, pp. 584–593.

73 Cf. Turgot, 'Lettre à Trudaine sur le Limousin', *Œuvres*, ed. Schelle, vol. II, pp. 478–495.

74 Turgot, ibid.

75 Article on *Fondation* in the *Encyclopédie*.

76 A selection of some of the texts: Savarin, *Le Cri de l'humanité aux États généraux* (Paris, 1789); Marcillac, *Hôpitaux remplacés par des sociétés physiques* (no place or date); Coqueau, *Essai sur l'Établissement des hôpitaux dans les grandes villes* (Paris, 1787); Récalde, *Traité sur les abus qui subsistent dans nos hôpitaux* (Paris,

1786). There were numerous anonymous writings too: *Précis des vues générales en faveur de ceux qui n'ont rien* (Lons-le-Saulnier, 1789), followed by *Un moyen d'extirper la mendicité* (Paris, 1789); *Plaidoyer pour l'héritage du pauvre* (Paris, 1790). In 1777, the academy at Châlons-sur-Marne offered a prize for the best essay on 'Causes of Begging and Means of Making Them Disappear'. They received more than 100 memoirs, and published a resumé. Means suggested included the following: sending beggars back to their original communities and obliging them to work there; abolishing public alms; decreasing the number of hospitals; reforming the remainder; setting up public pawn shops; setting up workshops, and reducing the number of feast days; opening correction centres for 'anyone who troubled the harmony of society'. Cf. Brissot de Warville, *Théorie des lois criminelles*, vol. I, p. 261, note 123.

77 Coqueau, pp. 23–24.
78 Coqueau, p. 7.
79 The French original indicates the eighteenth century here, which is probably a typographical error.
80 Coqueau, p. 7.
81 Ibid.
82 Desmonceaux, *De la bienfaisance nationale*, Paris, 1789, pp. 7–8.
83 Récalde's request was that a committee should be set up 'for the general reform of hospitals', then 'a permanent commission, invested with the authority of the King, which would work ceaselessly to maintain order and equity in the use of the funds allocated to the welfare of the poor' (p. 129). Cf. Claude Chevalier, *Description des avantages d'une maison de santé* (1762). Dulaurent, *Essai sur les établissements nécessaires et les moins dispendieux pour rendre le service dans les hôpitaux vraiment utile à l'humanité*, Paris, 1787.
84 Dupont de Nemours, *Idées sur les secours à donner aux pauvres malades dans une grande ville*, 1786, pp. 10–11.
85 Ibid.
86 Ibid., p. 113.
87 At the request of Turgot, Brienne opened an inquiry into assistance in the region of Toulouse. He drew up his findings in 1775, and read them in Montigny. He recommended help in the home, but also the creation of hospices for certain categories like the mad. (BN, Fonds français 8129, fos. 244–287.)
88 Nicholls, *The English Poor Laws*, vol. II, pp. 115–116.
89 F. Eden, *State of the Poor*, vol. I, p. 373.
90 La Rochefoucauld-Liancourt (Procès-verbal de l'Assemblé nationale, vol. XLIV, pp. 94–95).

III THE PROPER USE OF LIBERTY

1 A circular to all superintendents from March 1784, quoted in Funck-Brentano, *Les Lettres de cachet à Paris*, p. XLII.
2 They were the Duke de Liancourt, the curé de Sergy, and the curé de Cretot,

who were all deputies, and Montlinot and Thouret, who were *agrégés externes au travail du Comité*. Cf. *Rapport au Comité de mendicité*, p. 4.

3   *Rapport au Comité de mendicité*, p. 47.

4   Ibid., p. 78. Summing up its work at the end of the Constituent Assembly, the Committee requested the creation of 'two hospitals reserved for the curing of madness' (Cf. Tuetey, *L'Assistance publique à Paris pendant la Révolution*, vol. I, Introduction, p. xv).

5   Article IX of the decree.

6   Cf. the *Moniteur* of 3 April 1790.

7   There were numerous discussions about what should be done with the mad in the hospitals. In the hospice in Toulouse for example, the Minister of Police refused to free the mad for safety reasons, despite the fact that the Minister of the Interior had granted them their freedom because of the poverty of the hospital, and because 'assistance was very costly and difficult to provide' (Archives nationales, F 15, 339).

8   Title XI, article 3.

9   These dispositions were also to found in the Penal Code. Portalis refers to them in a circular of 30 Fructidor Year XII (17 September 1804).

10 Letter from the Minister of the Interior (5 May 1791) to M. Chalan, *Procureur Général* and *Syndic* of the Seine-et-Oise department. (Manuscript quoted by Lallemand, vol. IV, ii, p. 7, note 14.)

11 Cf. Pignot, *Les Origines de l'hôpital du Midi*, pp. 92–93.

12 Report of the Government Commissioner Antoine Nodier to the Tribunals, 4 Germinal Year VIII. Quoted in Léonce Pingaud, *Jean de Bry*, Paris, 1909, p. 194.

13 The *Mémoires du Père Richard* note that 400 political prisoners once arrived at Bicêtre on the same day (fos. 49–50).

14 Pinel, who had taken up office at Bicêtre on 11 September 1793, was later nominated to the Salpêtrière, on 13 May 1795 (24 Floréal Year III).

15 Letter from Létourneau, the bursar of the House of the Poor in Bicêtre, to citizens Osmond and Grand Pré. Quoted in Tuetey, *L'Assistance publique à Paris pendant la Révolution*, vol. III, pp. 360–362.

16 La Rochefoucauld-Liancourt, p. 95. Our emphasis.

17 Brissot de Warville, pp. 183–185. It is worth noting that Sade wrote or made a plan to write 'a dissertation on the death penalty, followed by a project on the useful employment of criminals for the good of the State'. *Portefeuille d'un homme de lettres*, quoted by G. Lély, *Vie du marquis de Sade*, vol. II, p. 343).

18 Musquinet de la Pagne, *Bicêtre réformé, où l'établissement d'une maison de discipline*, Paris, 1790, pp. 10–11.

19 Musquinet de la Pagne, p. 26.

20 Ibid., p. 27.

21 Ibid., p. 11.

22 It should not be forgotten that Musquinet himself had been confined in Bicêtre under the Ancien Régime, and was sentenced and locked up again during the

Revolution – at one time because he was considered a madman, and at the other as he was thought to be a criminal.

23 *Journal de médecine*, August 1785, pp. 529–583.

24 Cf. Sérieux et Libert, 'L'Assistance et le Traitement des maladies mentales au temps de Louis XVI', *Chronique médicale*, 15 July–1 August 1914.

25 Tenon, *Mémoires sur les hôpitaux de Paris*, Paris, 1788, fourth Mémoire, p. 212.

26 Tenon, *Projet de rapport au nom du comité de secours*, ms. BN fo. 232.

27 Ibid. Cf. in the same perspective *Mémoires sur les hôpitaux*, fourth Mémoire, p. 216.

28 Ibid.

29 1791: 'Report submitted to the department of Paris by one of its members on the state of the mad women in the Salpêtrière, and adoption of draft regulations for the admission of the insane.' The text is quoted in full, without the author's name, in Tuetey, *L'Assistance publique à Paris pendant la Révolution. Documents inédits*, vol. III, pp. 489–506. Much of it was repeated in *Vues sur les secours publics*, 1798.

30 *Vues sur les secours publics*, in Cabanis, *Œuvres philosophiques*, Paris, 1956, part II, p. 49.

31 Cabanis, p. 51.

32 Ibid., p. 58.

33 Tenon had nothing but praise for the straitjacket, which he had seen at Saint Luke's: 'if there is a risk that the madman might harm himself or others, his arms are restrained with long sleeves that knot behind the back' (*Projet de rapport au nom du comité des secours*, fo. 232).

34 Cabanis, 'Report submitted to the department of Paris by one of its members on the state of the mad women in the Salpêtrière, and adoption of draft regulations for the admission of the insane' (quoted by Tuetey, vol. III, pp. 492–493).

35 Des Essarts, *Dictionnaire universel de police*, Paris, 1786, vol. VIII, p. 526.

36 The decrees of 21 May–7 June 1790 replaced the seventy districts with forty-eight sections.

37 Quoted in Joly, *Les Lettres de cachet dans la généralité de Caen au XVIIIe siècle*, Paris, 1864, p. 18, note 1.

38 Bertin's text, quoted above, stipulates the precautions to be taken: 'Such measures should be taken in addition to an exact verification of their statement.'

39 Cf. the report presented by the Justice Minister to the Legislative Assembly (*Archives parlementaires*, supplement to the session of 20 May 1792, vol. XLIII, p. 613). Between 11 December 1790 and 1 May 1792, the court in Saint-Germain-en-Laye ratified a mere forty-five judgments by the family tribunal.

40 See above, Part One, chapter IV.

41 See above, Part One, chapter V.

42 Brissot de Warville, *Théorie des lois criminelles*, vol. I, p. 101.

43 Ibid., p. 49–50.

44 Ibid., p. 114.

45 Ibid., p. 50.

46 An example: on 30 August 1791, a woman was condemned for a sex crime

to be led by the high justice executioner to all the usual public crossroads, and particularly to the place du Palais-Royal, mounted on a donkey, facing backwards, with a straw hat on her head and a panel on her front and her back reading 'corrupter of the youth', and to be beaten and whipped with sticks, naked, and branded with a hot iron in the shape of a fleur-de-lys.

(*Gazette des tribunaux*, I, no. 18, p. 284. Cf. ibid, II, no. 36, p. 145)

47 BN collection Joly de Fleury, 1246, fos. 132–166.
48 The hero of Prévost's *Manon Lescaut* (1731), whose overwhelming passion for the heroine leads him to crime. [TN]
49 Bellart, *Œuvres*, Paris, 1827–28, vol. I, p. 103.
50 Ibid.
51 Ibid., pp. 76–77.
52 Ibid., p. 97.
53 Ibid., p. 103.
54 Ibid., p. 90.
55 Ibid., pp. 90–91.

IV BIRTH OF THE ASYLUM

1 Dr Delarive, Letter to the editors of the *Bibliothèque britannique*. Quoted in S. Tuke, *Description of the Retreat, an Institution near York for Insane Persons*, York, 1813, (reprinted in facsimile, London: Process press, 1996), p. 221. Delarive visited the Retreat in 1798.
2 Georges Couthon (1755–1794), a member of the Convention and part of the triumvirate of the Committee of Public Safety (with Robespierre and Saint-Just), who died on the guillotine in 1794. [TN]
3 Scipion Pinel, *Traité complet du régime sanitaire des aliénés*, Paris, 1836, p. 56.
4 See above, Part Three, chapter 2.
5 Voltaire, *Lettres philosophiques*, ed. Droz, vol. I, p.17, translated as *Letters on England*, with an introduction by Leonard Tancock (Harmondsworth: Penguin books, 1980), p. 27.
6 33. George III, cap. V.
7 35. George III, cap. 101. On the repeal of the Settlement Act, see Nicholls, vol. II, pp. 112–113.
8 Sewel, *The History of the Rise, Increases and Progress of Christian People*, 3rd edition, p. 28. [Fox's autobiography claims that the Darby imprisonment was in 1650; 1649 found him in prison in Nottingham. TN]
9 Sewel, p. 233.
10 Voltaire, *Lettres philosophiques*.
11 Like the Protestant mystics of the late seventeenth century, and the last Jansenists.
12 Samuel Tuke, *Description of the Retreat, an Institution near York for Insane Persons*, York, 1813, pp. 22–33. [Foucault omitted the word 'milder'. TN]

13 Quoted in Tuetey, vol. III, p. 369.

14 It was in the Pension Vernet, in rue Servandoni, that Pinet and Boyer had found a hiding place for Condorcet, when a warrant was issued for his arrest on 8 July 1793.

15 Dupuytren, *Notice sur Philippe Pinel*. Excerpt from the *Journal des Débats*, 7 November 1826, p. 8. Dupuytren was probably alluding to the Abbé Fournier, who had protested from the pulpit against the execution of Louis XVI, and who, after being confined to Bicêtre due to 'an attack of madness', went on to become Napoleon's chaplain, and then the Bishop of Montpellier.

16 Cf. for example the decree from the General Safety Committee ordering the transfer to Bicêtre of a madman who could not be kept 'in the great hospice of humanity' (Tuetey, vol. III, pp. 427–428).

17 Letter from Piersin to the Civil Administration Commission, 19 Frimaire Year III (Tuetey, vol. III, p. 172).

18 Piersin calculated that there were 207 madmen in Bicêtre, on 10 Frimaire Year III (Tuetey, p. 370).

19 Pinel had been the editor of the *Gazette de Santé* before the Revolution, and had written several articles about mental illness, including in particular, 'Are fits of melancholy not more common and more to be feared in the first months of winter?' (1787), and 'Observations on the moral regime most fitting for the restoration of reason in maniacs' (1789). In *La Médecine éclairée par les Sciences physiques*, he had published an article 'about a particular variety of melancholy that leads to suicide' in 1791.

20 *Gazette nationale*, 12 December 1789.

21 Quoted in Sémelaigne, *Philippe Pinel et son œuvre*, pp. 108–109.

22 Cf. the correspondence between Létourneau and the Public Works Commission quoted in Tuetey, vol. III, pp. 397–476.

23 In his concern to portray Pinel as a victim of the Terror, Dupuytren recounts that he was 'arrested, and was about to be dragged before the Revolutionary Tribunal; luckily the authorities were made to understand the necessity of his work with the poor at Bicêtre, and he was set free' (Dupuytren, p. 9).

24 Report to the Society of Friends, 5 April 1793, quoted in Tuke, p. 36.

25 Tuke, pp. 93–95.

26 Ibid., pp. 130–131. [Foucault ends this section by quoting 'et les premiers jours de repos qu'ils avaient l'occasion d'y prendre', '[and by] the first days of rest that they took there', although there is no such line in Tuke's text. TN]

27 Tuke, p. 137, note.

28 Ibid.

29 Share-based systems had been common among the Quakers since the seventeenth century. Anyone who contributed a minimum of £20 to the Retreat got an annual return of 5% on their investment. From a financial point of view, the Retreat appears to have been a considerable success, as can be seen from the profits in its early years: £268 in June, 1798; £245 in 1799; £800 in 1800; £145 in 1801; £45 in 1802; £258 in 1803; £449 in 1804; £521 in 1805. (See Tuke, pp. 72–75).

30 Tuke, p. 178.

31 In fact only a member of the Commune could be designated to inspect

a hospital. But Couthon was never a member of that particular assembly. (See Emile Richard, *Histoire de l'Hôpital de Bicêtre*, Paris, 1889, p. 113, note).

32 Scipion Pinel, *Traité complet du régime sanitaire des aliénés*, Paris, 1836, pp. 56–63.

33 Hegel, *Encyclopaedia of the Philosophical Sciences*, no. 408, note. [Foucault removed the reference to Pinel here. TN]

34 Tuke, p. 50.

35 Ibid., p. 23.

36 Ibid., pp. 160–161.

37 Ibid., p. 23.

38 Ibid., p. 141.

39 Ibid., pp. 146–147.

40 Ibid., p. 156.

41 Ibid., p. 183.

42 Ibid., p. 157. [Foucault translated desire as need here, the '*desire* for esteem' becoming 'le *besoin* d'estime'. TN]

43 Tuke, p. 178.

44 There were plenty of physical constraints still in use at the Retreat. To force patients to eat, Tuke recommended the use of a simple door key forced between the patient's jaws and slowly turned as necessary. In his view, patients' teeth were broken less often this way (Tuke, p. 170).

45 Tuke, pp. 172–173.

46 Delarive, quoted in Tuke, pp. 223.

47 *Traité médico-philosophique*, p. 265.

48 Ibid., p. 458.

49 Ibid. All of the statistics drawn by Pinel can be found on pp. 427–437.

50 Ibid., pp. 268.

51 Ibid., pp. 116–117.

52 Ibid., pp. 270–271.

53 Ibid., p. 141.

54 Ibid., p. 417.

55 Ibid., pp. 122–123.

56 Ibid., p. 237.

57 Ibid., pp. 29–30.

58 Pinel invariably privileged legislation over the advancement of knowledge. In a letter to his brother, written on 1 January 1799, he notes:

> If you glance at the systems of legislation that have flourished around the world, you soon see that in the institution of society, laws always precede the light of science and art, which presupposes a well-policed people, led by circumstances and the passage of time to a form of authority that allows the seeds of letters to germinate . . . No one will say that the English owe their laws to the flourishing state of the arts and the sciences, as that legislation predates it by several centuries. When those proud islanders began to stand out for their genius and their talent, their laws were already all they could be.
>
> (Quoted in Sémelaigne, *Aliénistes et philanthropes*, pp. 19–20)

59   Scipion Pinel, *Traité du régime sanitaire des aliénés*, p. 63.
60   Quoted in Sémelaigne, *Aliénistes et philanthropes*, appendix, p. 502.
61   Philippe Pinel, p. 256.
62   See Part Two, chapter V.
63   Pinel, *Traité médico-philosophique*, pp. 207–208.
64   Cf. above, Part Two, chapter IV.
65   Pinel, *Traité médico-philosophique*, p. 205.
66   Ibid., p. 205.
67   Ibid., p. 206.
68   Ibid., p. 291, note 1.
69   Rules of the Retreat, Section III, article 5, quoted in Tuke, pp. 89–90.
70   'The admission of the mad or the insane to establishments that are or will be reserved for them anywhere in the department of Paris will be done on the recommendation of a physician or a legally recognised surgeon.' (*Projet de Règlement sur l'admission des insensés*, adopted by the department of Paris, quoted in Tuetey, vol. III, p. 500.)
71   For the same reasons, Langermann and Kant preferred that this essential role be played by a 'philosopher'. This is not in opposition to the beliefs of either Tuke or Pinel, rather the reverse.
72   Cf. what Pinel said of Pussin and his wife, whom he appointed as his assistants at the Salpêtrière (Sémelaigne, *Aliénistes et philanthropes*, Appendix, p. 502).
73   Pinel, pp. 292–293.
74   Tuke, pp. 110–111.
75   Ibid., p. 115.
76   John Haslam, *Observations on Insanity with practical remarks on this disease*, London, 1798, pp. 122–123, quoted by Pinel, pp. 253–254.
77   These structures still persist in non-psychoanalytic psychiatry, and in many ways still inside psychoanalysis as well.
78   Joseph Babinski (1857–1932), a French neurologist who coined the term in 1901 for conditions he described as 'caused by suggestion, cured by persuasion'. [TN]

V THE ANTHROPOLOGICAL CIRCLE

1   Boissier de Sauvages, *Nosologie méthodique*, VII, p. 4.
2   Ibid.
3   Abelly, *Vie de saint Vincent de Paul*, Paris, 1813, II, chapter XIII.
4   Troxler, *Blicke in Wesen des Menschen*, quoted in Béguin, *L'Âme romantique et le rêve*, Paris, 1939, p. 93.
5   Hölderlin, *Hyperion* (quoted in Béguin, p. 162).
6   Nerval, *Aurélia*, Paris, 1927, p. 25.
7   The first line of Nerval's mystic sonnet *Artémis*, from *Les Chimères*. [TN]
8   It is in Zarathustra that this laughter will finally come together, in a single midday intoxication: a *tragic* rip in the fabric of the *world*, which each instant

wrenches its truth from its appearance, and the *lyrical* promise that any end in *man* is a new beginning. Shimmering noon promises *tragic man* the *lyrical return* of the world. Both experiences come into contact in a poetic language where both fundamental expressions of madness meet. [This footnote appeared in the first edition, *Folie et Déraison: Histoire de la folie à l'âge classique* (Paris: Plon, 1961), p. 435, and was deleted from subsequent editions. It contains allusions to Paul Valéry's poem: 'Le Cimetière marin'. TN]

9   Hoffmann, quoted by Béguin, p. 297.
10 Pinel, quoted without a reference in Sémelaigne, *Philippe Pinel et son œuvre*, p. 106.
11 Matthey, p. 67.
12 Spurzheim, *Observations sur la folie*, pp. 141–142.
13 Hegel, *Encyclopaedia of the Philosophical Sciences*, no. 408.
14 Ibid. [Foucault omits the reference to Pinel here. TN]
15 Leuret, *Du traitement moral de la folie*, Paris, 1840.
16 Pinel, *Traité médico-philosophique*, p. 214.
17 In the face of general paralysis, hysteria was 'bad madness': there was no fault that could be identified, nothing organic to be blamed, no possible communication. The general paralysis/hysteria duality marks the extremes of the domain of psychiatric experience in the twentieth century, the perpetual object of a double and constant preoccupation. It could and should be demonstrated that explanations for hysteria (up to and excluding Freud) were all taken from the model of general paralysis, but that the model was purified, made more psychological and more transparent.
18 Pinel, *Traité médico-philosophique*, p. 156
19 Esquirol, *Des maladies mentales*, II, p. 335.
20 As late as 1893, the Medico-psychological Association devoted its 35th annual conference to the problems of 'Moral Insanity'.
21 U. Trélat, *La Folie lucide*, Avant-propos, p. x.
22 See above, Part Two, chapter IV.
23 Some of these affairs generated an immense medical and juridical literature. See the case of Léger, who ate the heart of a young girl, Papavoine, who, in the presence of their mother, slit the throat of two children that he was seeing for the first time, or Henriette Cornier, who cut off the head of a child that she did not know. England had the Bowler case, and Germany had the Sievert affair.
24 Cf. Élias Régnault, *Du degré de compétence des médecins*, 1828; Fodéré, *Essai médico-légale*, 1832; Marc, *De la folie*, 1840; see also Chauveau and Hélie, *Théorie du code pénal*. And a whole series of communications by Voisin to the Académie de médecine (*Sur le sentiment du juste*, 1842, *Sur la peine de mort*, 1848).
25 Esquirol, *De la monomanie homicide*, in *Des maladies mentales*, chap. II.
26 This led Régnault to note: 'In homicidal monomania, it is only the will to kill that overpowers the will to obey laws' (p. 39). A magistrate said to Marc, 'If monomania is a disease, when it leads to capital crimes, it should also lead to public execution in place de Grève' (vol. I, p. 226).

27 Dupin, who had understood the urgency and the danger of the problem, said of monomania that it could be 'too convenient, either to spare the guilty the full rigour of the law, or to deprive the citizen of his freedom. When it was impossible to say, "he is guilty", men would say "he is mad", and the Bastille would simply be replaced by Charenton' (quoted by Sémelaigne, *Aliénistes et philanthropes*, Appendix, p. 455).

28 Mania, one of the most solid pathological forms of the eighteenth century, lost much of its importance. Between 1801 and 1805, Pinel noted that maniacs accounted for some 60% of mad women at the Salpêtrière (624 out of 1,002); Esquirol counted 545 maniacs out of 1,557 patients in Charenton between 1815 and 1826 (35%); in the same hospital, for the period 1856 to 1866, Calmeil found only 624 out of 2,524 admissions (25%); during the same period, at the Salpêtrière and at Bicêtre, Marcé diagnosed 779 out of 5,481 (14%); and slightly later, Achille Foville the younger found only 7% at Charenton.

29 Another quote from René Char's *Jacquemard et Julia* unidentified by Foucault. (cf. p. 300) [TN]

30 *Cent vingt journées de Sodome* (quoted in Blanchot, *Lautréamont et Sade*, Paris, 1949, p. 235).

31 Quoted by Blanchot, p. 225.

32 Infamy should go as far as 'dismembering nature, and dislocating the universe' (*Cent vingt journées . . .*, Paris, 1935, vol. II, p. 369).

33 This cohesion imposed on the fellows of the society implies a refusal to exercise their right to kill on other fellows (a right they can exercise outside), but the recognition between fellows of an absolute right of free disposal: each must be able to *belong* to the other.

34 As in the episode with the volcano at the end of *Juliette*, ed. J.-J. Pauvert, Sceaux, 1954, vol. VI, pp. 31–33.

35 'It was as though nature, bored with her own creations, were ready to blend all the elements together, forcing them into some new shape' (Ibid., p. 270).

APPENDICES

I MADNESS THE ABSENCE OF AN ŒUVRE

1 Raymond Roussel, *Comment j'ai écrit certains de mes livres* (Paris: Lemerre, 1935), translated into English by Trevor Winkfield as *How I Wrote Certain of My Books* (Boston: Exact Change, 1996).

II MY BODY, THIS PAPER, THIS FIRE

1 In this text Foucault mostly refers to the *Méditations métaphysiques*, the French translation (by the Duc de Luynes) of *Renati Descartes Meditationes de prima philosophia in qua Dei existentia et animæ immortalitas demonstratur* (Paris, 1641) read and approved by Descartes. This translation is sometimes signifi-

cantly different from the Latin text. Quotes here are therefore translated from the French, with the standard English translation from the original Latin text (*The Philosophical Writings of Descartes*, tr. John Cottingham, Robert Stoothoff, Dugald Murdoch (Cambridge: Cambridge University Press, 1985) given in the footnotes. [TN]

2 Derrida, Jacques, '*Cogito et Histoire de la Folie*' in *L'Écriture et la différence* (Paris: Seuil, 1967), pp. 61–97, translated as '*Cogito and The History of Madness*' in *Writing and Difference*, trans. Alan Bass (Chicago: University of Chicago Press, 1980) pp. 31–63.

3 *Madness – a theme or an index*: what is significant is that Descartes, at bottom, never actually speaks of madness itself in this text. It is not his theme. He treats it like an index for a question of principle *(question de droit)* and of epistemological value. And that, it might be said, is a sign of a deeper exclusion. But this silence regarding madness itself simultaneously means the opposite of exclusion, because this text *does not speak of madness*, it is not in question, not even to be excluded. It is not in the *Meditations* that Descartes speaks of madness itself.

4 '[F]irmly maintain they are kings.' Descartes, *First Meditation*, in *The Philosophical Writings of Descartes*, tr. John Cottingham, Robert Stoothoff, Dugald Murdoch (Cambridge: Cambridge University Press, 1985) vol. II, p. 13 (AT, IX, 14).

5 'A brilliant piece of reasoning! As if I were not a man who sleeps at night, and regularly has all the same experiences while asleep as madmen do when awake – indeed sometimes even more improbable ones.'

6 'A man who sleeps at night, and regularly has all the same experiences', 'how often, asleep at night, am I convinced of just such familiar events', 'this would not happen . . . to someone asleep', 'As if I did not remember other occasions when I have been tricked by similar thoughts while asleep'.

7 I employ the term paragraph out of commodity, amusement and faithfulness to Derrida. Derrida says, in an imaged and rather amusing manner, 'Descartes va à ligne' – Descartes starts a new paragraph. Whereas we know very well that this is not the case.

8 'But such people are insane, and I would be thought equally mad if I took anything from them as a model for myself.' Descartes' text in French begins with an interjection: 'Mais quoi? Ce sont des fous, et je ne serais pas moins extravagant si je me réglais sur leurs exemples'. At issue is the colloquial interjection, 'Mais quoi', rendered here as 'But so what?' but absent from the Latin original. TN

9 'A man who regularly has the same experiences', 'how often am I convinced', 'as if I did not remember'.

10 In French, '*épreuve*', importantly, has two meanings: not just a tool for verification, but also a difficult experience undergone by the subject. TN

11 'I would be thought equally mad if I took anything from their example.'

12 'A brilliant piece of reasoning!' In French, 'Toutefois'.

13 Foucault takes Derrida's text literally here, assuming that 'question de droit'

has only a juridical meaning (hence its translation here as 'point of law'), whereas Derrida uses the phrase in the Kantian sense of a question of principle (as opposed to an empirical one). [TN]

14 I am quoting Derrida. As we know, in Descartes' text, these things, which it is so difficult to doubt, are not characterised by their 'nature', but by their proximity and their vividness. By their relation to the meditating subject.

15 In French, 'Etantité' – the Heideggerian characteristic of being a specific being. TN

16 Pierre Bourdin, a Jesuit priest whose objections to Descartes were included in the second (1642) edition (in Latin) of the *Meditationes*. TN

III REPLY TO DERRIDA

1 A lecture given on 4 March 1963 at the Collège Philosophique, published in *Revue de métaphysique et de morale*, 1964, nos. 3–4, republished in Derrida, Jacques, *L'Ecriture et la différence* (Paris: Seuil, 1967).

2 See note 13 to Appendix II regarding the studied ambiguity of this phrase.

Annexes

I

DOCUMENTS

HISTORY OF THE HÔPITAL GÉNÉRAL

From *L'Hôpital Général*, anonymous brochure, 1676

Despite numerous measures,

the vast majority of beggars remained at liberty in the city and faubourgs of Paris; they came here from all the provinces of the kingdom, and all the States of Europe, and their numbers grew every day, so that they became an independent people who were strangers to both law and religion, superiors and police; impiety, sensuality and libertinage were all that reigned amongst them; and most murders, thefts, and acts of violence both by day and by night were the work of their hands, and these people, whose poverty made them an object of compassion for the faithful, became the least worthy of public assistance on account of their corrupt morals, their blasphemy and their insolent discourse.

This extraordinary disorder continued until the year 1640 without too much thought being expended upon it. But then a group of virtuous individuals were touched by the deplorable state in which the souls of these poor Christians were to be found. However afflicted they appeared, their bodies were not true objects of compassion; for the alms that they begged were more than enough to meet their needs, and even the needs of their debauchery; but their souls, which foundered in total ignorance of our mysteries, and in the extreme corruption of their morals, were a great source of pain to persons concerned with the well-being and salvation of these paupers.

(p. 2)

The first efforts, and their initial success (the charitable storehouses set up in 1651) made it believable

that it was not impossible to find the necessary subsistence to confine and contain in duty a lazy, libertine people who had never known any rules.

(p. 3)

It was then announced in sermons and in all the Parishes of Paris that the Hôpital Général would open on 7 May 1657 for all the poor who wished to enter of their own accord, and the magistrates ordered the town criers to announce that it was henceforth illegal to beg for alms in Paris; and rarely was an order so well executed.

On the 13th, the high mass of the Holy Spirit was sung in the church of the Pitié, and on the 14th the Confinement of the Poor was carried out without any emotion.

On that day, Paris underwent a change of face; the vast majority of beggars returned to the Provinces, and the wisest among them thought of leaving of their own accord. Doubtless the protection of God smiled on these great works, for few would have believed that the operation would be executed with such ease, and that success would be so complete.

the foresight of the directors had been so exact, and their calculations so precise that the number of the confined coincided almost exactly with their projections, and the 40,000 beggars reduced to 4,000–5,000 who were happy to find a retreat in the Hôpital; their number however has since increased; it soon passed 6,000 and is now around 10,000; for this reason it has been necessary to augment the size of the buildings to circumvent the extreme discomfort that the Poor suffer, when they are too numerous in their rooms and in their beds.

(p. 5)

Edict of the King for the establishment of the Hôpital Général for the Confinement of the poor beggars of the city and Faubourgs of Paris

Paris, April 1657, approved by Parliament on 1 September (Paris, the Royal Printworks, 1661).

Louis, by the grace of God King of France and of Navarre, salutes all those present and those who are yet to come. Since the last century, our Royal predecessors passed several Police ordinances regarding the Poor in our fair city of Paris, and zealously used their full authority to prevent begging and idleness, which are the source of all unrest. Although our sovereign companies have executed these ordinances to the best of their abilities, the passage of time has seen them have little effect, either through a lack of funds required for continuing the execution of so great a design, or by deviation from a well established and appropriate direction of action. So much so that in recent times, and even under the reign of my father, our highly honoured Lord and Father, may he rest in peace, the ill had grown still further, due to public licentiousness and loose morals, and it was recognised that the implementation of that Policy was hampered by the freedom beggars had to beg wherever they chose, and the relief available was not sufficient to prevent secret begging, or to convince them to abandon their idle ways. With that in mind, a new and praiseworthy project was put forward, to confine beggars to the house of the Pitié, and other centres dependent upon it, and patent letters were issued to that effect in 1612, and this recorded in the Paris Parliament, so that the Poor were henceforth to be confined; their control was assigned to worthy and notable Burghers, whose best efforts and good actions were successively applied to achieve this end. Their actions, however, were only effective for five or six years, and even imperfectly so, on account of the lack of employment for the Poor in public Works and factories, and because these directors did not enjoy the support from the public Powers and authorities necessary for the importance of the enterprise, and also because owing to the unfortunate sufferings and disorders of war, the numbers of the Poor increased well beyond expectations, so that the ill far exceeded the remedy. So much so, that the libertinage of the beggars grew to embrace all manner of those crimes which bring down the wrath of God on the State, when they remain unpunished. The experience of those who worked with such people has shown that many of them of both sexes, as well as their children, are unbaptised, and live in an almost complete ignorance of religion, contempt for the Sacraments and the continual habit of vices of all varieties. For this reason, as we owe so much to the divine pity for so many graces, and for the visible protection that it extends over our conduct, from the coronation and during the happy course of our reign through the success of our armies, and the good fortune of our victories, we believe ourselves to be obliged to bear witness to our gratitude through a Royal and Christian application to things which regard his honour and service; we consider these beggars to be the living members of Jesus Christ, and not useless members of the State, and act here in the accomplishment of so great a work not through any concern with Policing, but motivated solely by Charity.

Article 1

We desire and decree that all poor beggars, both able and unable, of both sexes, be employed in a hospital for manufacturing and other works, according to their ability, and in accordance with the Regulations signed by our hand, which are attached to the seal of this edict and which we desire to be executed both in form and content.

4

And for the confinement of all the Poor who are in a condition to be confined, according to the regulations, we have given, and hereby give the House and Hospital, of both the large and the small Pitié, and the Refuge in the faubourg Saint-Victor, the House and the Hospital of Scipion, and the House of the Savonnerie, with all its dependent places, Squares, Gardens and Houses and Buildings, as well as the Houses and Plots at Bicêtre.

6

It is our intention to be both the curator and protector of this Hôpital Général, and of all the places that depend upon it, as a royal foundation; and nevertheless they will depend in no fashion on the grand Almoner nor on any of our other officers; they will be totally exempt from the superiority, visit and jurisdiction of the Officers of the general Reformation, or of the grand Almonry, or of any other, to which we forbid any knowledge or jurisdiction in these matters, in any way conceivable.

9

We forbid most formally any person of either sex, regardless of their age and origin, quality or birth, and whatever their condition, be they able or unable, ill or convalescent, curable or incurable, to beg in the city and the faubourgs of Paris, or in the churches, or at church doors, or at the doors of houses, or in the streets, or anywhere else, publicly or in secret, by day or by night, without excluding the solemn feasts, pardons, jubilees, Assemblies, Fairs or Markets, nor any other cause or pretext imaginable, on pain of whipping for the first offence, and galleys for the second, for men and boys, and with banishment for men and women.

17

We prohibit any person of any condition or quality whatsoever to hand out alms to beggars in the streets or any other place, regardless of any motive of compassion, pressing need or other pretext whatsoever, on pain of a fine of four Paris pounds, which will go to the coffers of the Hospital.

23

As our concern is with the salvation of the Poor who must be confined, as well as with their lodging and subsistence, and we have recognised for many years the blessing that God has given to the work of the Missionary priests of Saint-Lazare, and the great fruits of their labours for the assistance of the Poor, and in the hope that we have that they may continue and will in future increase, we desire and will that they may have charge of the care and spiritual instruction for the assistance and consolation of the Poor of the Hôpital Général, and all places dependent upon it, and that they administer the sacraments, under the authority and spiritual jurisdiction of the Archbishop of Paris.

53

We hereby permit and give to the Directors power to make and manufacture throughout this Hospital and its dependencies, any sort of manufactured goods, and to have them sold for the benefit of the Poor in said hospital.

Regulations to be observed in the Hôpital Général in Paris, by order of the King

19 To encourage the confined Poor to work more assiduously and with more affection in the factory, those of both sexes who have reached the age of 16 may keep one third of the profit of their work, without anything else being taken away from them.

22 The Directors may order all punishments and sentences both public and private in the Hôpital Général and all places dependent upon it for the poor if they contravene any order that has been given to them, or any thing that may have been entrusted to them, even, in cases of disobedience, insolence or other scandals, expel them and forbid them from begging.

Declaration by the King for the establishment of a *Hôpital Général* in all the cities and major towns of the realm, following the ordinances of King Charles IX and King Henri III

The great desire that we have always had to provide for the needs of beggars as the most abandoned, and to procure their salvation by Christian instruction, and to abolish begging and idleness by bringing up their children in trades they could practise, had led us to found the Hôpital Général in our fair city of Paris . . .

Nonetheless, the surcharge of beggars who have come from diverse provinces of our kingdom has reached such a point that the directors, who have half the revenue they need for the ordinary subsistence of 4,000–5,000 paupers, must also feed 3,000 other married paupers in 6 different parts of the city. In addition, there are still a great number of beggars at large in the city . . .

It is therefore our pleasure and desire to order that in all cities and large faubourgs of our Kingdom where no Hôpital Général has yet been founded, such a Hospital should immediately be set up, with all its attendant Regulations, to house, confine and feed sick pauper beggars who are native to the place or who are born to pauper parents. All beggars are to be instructed in piety and the Christian religion, and in trades they will be able to master . . .

Done at Saint-Germain-en-Laye, June 1662.

Rules for the order of the day in the House of Saint-Louis de la Salpêtrière

1. Reveille will be sounded at five o'clock. All officers male and female, domestics and all the poor will rise, with the exception of the infirm or children aged under five years.

2. Prayers will begin in the dormitories at quarter past five. Female officers will do the rounds, to ensure that the necessary order is maintained among the poor.

3. At half-past five the poor will make their beds, comb their hair, and perform all ablutions until six o'clock . . .

4. At six o'clock each female officer will join the youth officers in her dormitory, and will alternate schooling and religious instruction on a daily basis until seven o'clock. The other female officers will supervise the poor entrusted to their care and, with the governesses, lead them to church to hear mass.

6. At seven o'clock, children and any sick patients who are able will go to church to hear mass.

8. At eight o'clock, the officer in charge of works in the house will sound the bell to notify all inmates that it is time to begin work . . . the officers will then do their rounds among the workers, ensuring that the poor are occupied and not suffering any form of idleness.

13. At nine o'clock, the hymn *Veni Creator* shall be sung in all dormitories, and in the children's dormitories the Commandments of God and the Church, and various acts of faith shall also be read out, as is the normal custom, and then the whole house will be silent. In each dormitory, the supervisor or governess will read the *Imitation of Christ* or some other religious books without interruption of work, for a quarter of an hour.

14. At ten o'clock, silence will end with the hymn *Ave Maris Stella* and the litanies of the holy name of Jesus Christ, and on Thursdays *Pange Lingua* will be sung together with the litanies of the holy sacrament.

(Rules 15, 16, 17 and 18 concern the midday meal)

19. At half-past one, work will begin again; if any of the officers find paupers unwilling to work, they will have them locked up for three or four hours with the permission of the supervisor as an example so the others keep to the rule.

20. At two o'clock, there will be silence in all the dormitories and the workshops as in the morning, without work being interrupted.

21. At three o'clock, in the women's dormitory, there will be readings or religious instruction that will last five quarters of an hour.

22. At a quarter after four, the rosary will be said, together with the litanies of the Holy Virgin; the poor will then be allowed to converse with each other without leaving their dormitories or interrupting their work until six o'clock.

26. At half-past five the women will be served supper (six o'clock for those who are working in the workshops).

27. At six o'clock, evening prayers will begin in each dormitory . . . when prayers are over, the poor may go out into the courtyard or go to church, and the sick will be allowed to return to their beds.

29. At eight o'clock . . . the officers will do their rounds to ensure that all the poor are abed.

32. On Sundays and holidays, officers both male and female, the shop-keeper, the governesses and the poor, after hearing the first mass, which as on other days will be said at a quarter after six, will remain in the church to hear the sermon that follows the mass.

33. Three women officers will be in charge of keeping order among the poor, and ensuring that they behave with modesty at all times.

36. The poor, the workers and the domestics will attend confession at least once a month and before all major feasts.

38. At half-past nine all the poor will return to church to hear the high mass.

39. At eleven o'clock there will be dinner, followed by a walk around the parlour.

41. At one o'clock, the poor will return to church to hear Vespers, the Sermon, Compline and Benediction; all of which must be finished by four o'clock.

(Rules 42 and 44 concern walks or the parlour, followed by supper and recreation)

Certified copy of the original, 8 August 1721.
Arsenal, ms. 2566, fos. 54–70

The four classes of diseases of the mind, according to Doublet

1 Frenzy

Frenzy is a furious and continuous delirium, accompanied by fever; either it is an alarming symptom that develops in acute diseases, or it is produced by a primary affection of the brain, and in itself is an essential disease. Regardless of its type however, it is often the source from which all other diseases of the head will flow, such as mania and imbecility, which are its frequent consequences.

(pp. 552–553)

2 Mania

Mania is a constant delirium without fever. If fever occurs in maniacs, it does not depend on any affection of the brain, but on some other circumstance that chance has brought into being. The symptoms of mania are an extraordinary strength, the ability to resist hunger, sleep and cold to an unusual degree, much longer than other men, healthy or sick; their look is threatening, their face dark and dry and hungered, they often suffer from ulcers on the legs, their stools are often rare; they sleep little but deeply; their waking is agitated, turbulent, and filled with visions and uncontrolled behaviour which is often dangerous for the people around them. Some have fairly tranquil interludes; others suffer from continuous or frequent intensified bouts.

The brain of maniacs is dry, hard and brittle, sometimes the cortex is yellow, at other times there are abscesses; the blood vessels are swollen with black blood, which is varicose, thick in some parts and more dilute in others.

(pp. 558–559)

3 Melancholy

Melancholy is a continuous delirium that differs from mania in two ways; first of all, the delirium revolves around a single object, which is termed the *melancholic point*; secondly, whether the delirium is gay or serious, it is always pacific; so melancholy only differs from mania in degree, and while it is true that some melancholics become maniacal, several maniacs who are half-cured or in between attacks also suffer from accesses of melancholy.

(p. 575)

4 Imbecility

Imbecility appears to be the least frightening and the least dangerous of all the forms of madness; and yet in truth it is the most dangerous condition of the mind, as it is the most difficult to cure. Imbeciles are neither agitated nor frenzied, and they are rarely sombre; they have a stupidly happy face, and change little, regardless of whether they are happy or suffering. Imbecility is the consequence of frenzy, mania or melancholy that is prolonged too long. It is produced by a dryness of the brain in old people; softness or an infiltration into this viscera cause it in children; blows, falls, the abuse of strong liquor, masturbation or a communicated virus are the more ordinary causes, and it is also a quite common consequence of apoplexy.

(p. 580)

Instructions sur la manière de gouverner les insensés, et de travailler à les guérir dans les asiles qui leur sont destinés, in Journal de médecine, 1785, pp. 529–583.

Ideal plan for a prison for the insane

1 The air must be pure and the water must be clean. These precautions are all the more essential given that most madmen eat relatively little solid food and survive so to speak mainly on air and water.

2 The practice of walks is important for these patients to give them the pleasure and freedom of breathing fresh air . . .

(p. 542)

3 The section will be divided into various sets of buildings, each having their own courtyard.

Each set of buildings will form a square, whose centre will be a courtyard, and whose four sides will be one-storey buildings. A covered gallery will run around the inside walls of the inside of the square, and the gallery and the buildings will be on the same level, but raised three feet above the courtyard.

The bedrooms or the dormitories where the insane will be kept during the day are to form the four corners of the square; the rest of the building will be divided into cells of eight square feet, which will be lit by a skylight grill, placed in the roof.

Each cell will have one solid bed, cemented into the wall, covered with a mattress filled with oat straw, a bolster of the same quality, and one cover; the bed should also be fitted with iron rings in case they are required.

Near the door will be a stone bench cemented into the wall, with a smaller one inside the cell itself.

In the centre of the courtyard there will be a building containing several stone baths, supplied with running water, both hot and cold.

(pp. 542–544)

One department or section of the buildings will be reserved for imbeciles, the second and the third for violent madmen, and the fourth for those who have lucid intervals of some duration, and whose condition seems to be improving.

(p. 544)

Instructions sur la manière de gouverner les insensés et de travailler à leur guérison dans les asiles qui leur sont destinés, in *Journal de médecine*, August 1785, pp. 529–583.

Medications recommended for the various illnesses of the mind

1 Frenzy

This terrible illness is the least difficult to cure of all the affections of the brain . . . Considerable bleeding is required at the outset, which should begin with the foot two or three times, and then pass to the temporal artery and the jugular, with each bloodletting being larger and more copious.

(p. 555)

The patient should be given abundant cold drinks, which are thinning and anti-phlogistical; between each bloodletting, whenever possible, two enemas should be administered, one purgative and the other emollient.

As soon as the illness strikes, the head should be shaved or the hair cut, a bandage known as a Hippocrates bonnet should then be applied, and this should always be kept wet, by the use of sponges dipped in a mixture of water and cold vinegar.

(p. 556)

2 *Mania*

Although bleeding should be used copiously for mania, it should be more restricted than with frenzy, which is an acute and initiating disease; this restriction is more important if the disease is of long date.

(p. 560)

The use of purgatives is even more essential than bleeding, for many types of mania can be cured without bleeding, whereas very few of them can be cured without the use of purges, which are repeated to combat the thinning of the blood, and to attenuate and expel sticky and thick humours.

(p. 561)

Baths and showers could be continued for a long time with maniacs; they are most efficacious when alternated with purgatives, i.e. one day of purgatives should be alternated with one day of bathing.

(p. 564)

Cauters, setons and artificial ulcers will always be useful, as no evacuation is easy in these cases.

(p. 565)

3 *Melancholy*

When the attacks are violent and the subject is plethoric or subject to circumstances that mean a flow of blood may be feared, they should be bled boldly, but after the bloodletting, time should pass before any purgative at all should be employed . . . Before purging, efforts must be made to liquefy the viscous humour that is at the origin of this disease; and for that, the means are well known. Lightly aperitive herbal infusions, curds, extracts of cream of tartar, warm baths and a liquefying regime; recourse should then be made to more active liquefying agents such as grass juices, bowls of soapy water, and pills with ammomoque gum, cream of tartar and sweet mercury; when the humour has at last become mobile again, purging may begin.

(pp. 577–579)

4 *Imbecility*

When this state is the consequence or the last stage of a different disease there is little hope . . . The first thing to be done is to ensure that the patient eats well, then they should take artificial thermal water; they can be purged with bryony root and jalap infused in brandy; cold baths and showers should also be tried.

(pp. 580–581)

Imbecility that results from masturbation can only be cured by means of analeptics, tonics, thermal waters and dry friction.

(p. 581)

If one suspects that a communicated virus is the cause of the imbecility, try inoculating scabies, and this method could be tried on all imbeciles, if other treatments do not prove effective.

(p. 582)

Instructions sur la manière de gouverner les insensés et de travailler à leur guérison dans les asiles qui leur sont destinés, in *Journal de médecine*, August 1785, pp. 529–583.

Inventory of the *Pensions de force* in Paris on the eve of the Revolution

Pension du Sieur Massé in Montrouge:
7 madmen, 9 feeble-minded men, 2 feeble-minded women, 2 women who are subject to attacks of madness. In total, 20. No raving mad in this house.

Pension du Sieur Bardot, rue Neuve Sainte-Geneviève:
4 mad women, 5 mad men. Total 9. No raving mad in this pension.

Pension de la femme Roland, route de Villejuif:
8 feeble-minded women, 4 feeble-minded men. Total 12. No raving mad in this house.

Pension de la Demoiselle Laignel, Cul-de-sac des Vignes:
29 mad women, 7 feeble-minded women. Total 36. No raving mad women in this house.

Pension du Sieur de Guerrois, rue de Notre-Dame:
17 demented women, no raving mad women in this house.

Pension du Sieur Teinon, rue Coppeau:
1 feeble-minded woman, 3 feeble-minded men, 2 mad men, total 6. No raving mad in this house.

Maison de la Dame Marie de Sainte-Colombe, place du Trône, rue de Picpus:
28 male boarders, demented and imbecilic; no women, no raving madmen.

Maison du Sieur Esquiros, rue du Chemin vert:
12 demented men, 9 demented women, 2 epileptics, one of whom is occasionally demented on account of his illness.

Maison de la veuve Bouquillon, au petit Charonne:
10 demented men, 20 demented women, 3 raving women.

Maison du Sieur Belhomme, rue de Charonne:
15 demented men, 16 demented women, 2 raving men.

Maison du Sieur Picquenot, au petit Bercy:
5 demented men, 1 raving woman, 1 raving man.

Maison de la femme Marcel, au petit Bercy:
2 demented men, 2 demented women, 1 epileptic, no raving mad.

Maison du Sieur Bertaux, au petit Bercy:
2 demented men, 1 demented woman, 3 raving men.

Maison des religieux Picpus, in Picpus:
3 demented men.

Maison du Sieur Cornilliaux, in Charonne:
1 demented man, 1 demented woman.

Maison du Sieur Lasmezas, rue de Charonne:
Only boarders at the present time, and no madmen.

Maison Saint-Lazare, faubourg Saint-Denis:
17 mad women.

Pension de la Demoiselle Douay, rue de Bellefond:
15 mad women, 5 raving women.

Pension du Sieur Huguet, rue des Martyrs:
6 mad men, 3 mad women.

From Tenon, *Papiers sur les hôpitaux*, vol. II, fos. 70–72 and 91. These figures
were transcribed by Tenon from reports by commissioners Gallet for the
Faubourgs Saint-Jacques, Saint-Marcel et d'Enfer, Joron for the Faubourg
Saint-Antoine, and Huguet for the Montmartre quarter.

Assistance and punishment

One of the first texts, and one of the most characteristic ones dedicated to
the reform of the hospitals, was written by Baudeau in 1765. Here, in the
pure state, we find a dissociation between help for the sick, which is to be
done at home, and is therefore a matter for private charity, and confinement as punishment, for which Baudeau proposes a rigorous, almost
mathematical equilibrium between death and work.

> We no longer hesitate in totally refusing the system of public
> infirmeries. Control of their revenues and buildings should be handed
> over to the common Fund of the universal Almonry in each diocese,
> under the direction of the General Charity Bureau; then the sick poor will
> no longer be obliged to go and seek humiliating, painful and often
> detrimental assistance; patriotic good works will bring help into
> their houses, by their fellow men, in line with the system of *bureaux de
> miséricorde*, which is infinitely preferable to that of the hospitals.

For the houses of correction,

> the Dutch have invented an excellent method; which consists of tying to
> a pump people who they wish to train to work. They teach them to wish
> to cultivate the land, and prepare them by far more difficult work, which
> however unpleasant must be carried out.
>   The person who is to be taught to become accustomed to work is
> locked up alone in a hole, which canals fill in such a way that he will
> drown unless he continuously turns the handle of a pump. He is given as
> much water and as many hours as his strength will allow for the first few
> days, but this is gradually increased.
>   This is the first task that we inflict on the guilty who are locked up in

our house of correction. It is clear that they become quite bored with this continuous work and from being continually alone, occupied with such hard work; knowing that they could also spade the earth of the enclosure in the company of others, they quickly desire to return to labouring like the others. This grace is granted them sooner or later, in accordance with their fault and their current disposition.

Baudeau, *Idée d'un citoyen sur les besoins et les devoirs des vrais pauvres*, printed in Amsterdam and Paris in 1765, vol. I, pp. 64–65, vol. II, pp. 129–130.

Confinement among the mad considered as a punishment

In the course of a discussion on the project to reform criminal legislation, Le Pelletier de Saint-Fargeau proposes that any man who fought a duel be exposed to the public eye for two hours, dressed entirely in a suit of armour; and then be locked in a house for madmen for two years.

> Duelling was an abuse of chivalry, and Knights Errant were the ridiculous culmination of it. Using this ridicule to make of it a punishment of this abuse is a means more repressive than capital punishment, which is used in vain against the crime, and which has never prevented anyone from duelling, and has been very rarely employed.

Le Pelletier's proposition was rejected.

Rapport sur le projet du code pénal présenté à l'assemblée nationale au nom des Comités de Constitution et de Législation criminelle, p. 10.

II

FOUCAULT'S ORIGINAL BIBLIOGRAPHY

GENERAL STUDIES

Bernier, J., *Histoire chronologique de la médecine*, Paris, 1717.
Brett, G. S., *A History of Psychology*, London, 1912.
Flemming, C., *Geschichte der Psychiatrie*, Leipzig, 1859.
Kirchhoff, T., *Geschichte der Psychiatrie*, Leipzig, 1912.
Leclerc, D., *Histoire de la médecine*, Amsterdam, 1723.
Neuberger, M. and Pagel, J., *Handbuch der Geschichte der Medizin*, Jena, 1902.

PART ONE

Abelly, L., *Vie du vénerable Vincent de Paul*, Paris, 1664.
Adnès, A., *Shakespeare et la folie*, Paris, 1935.
Alboize de Pujol, J. E., et Maquet, A. *Histoire des prisons de Paris*, 8 volumes, Paris, 1846.
Argenson, R.-L., d', *Journal et Mémoires*, 9 volumes, Paris, 1867.
Argenson, R. d', *Notes de René d'Argenson*, Paris, 1891.
Berghauser, W., *Die Darstellung des Wahnsinns im englischen Drama bis zum Ende des 18. Jahrdunderts*, Frankfurt, 1863.
Bézard, L., and Chapon, J., *Histoire de la prison de Saint-Lazare du Moyen Age à nos jours*, Paris, 1925.

Blégny, N. de, *La Doctrine des rapports*, Paris, 1684.

Boislisle, A. de, *Lettres de Monsieur de Maréville, lieutenant général de police au ministre Maurepas*, Paris, 1896.

Bonnafous-Sérieux, H., *La Charité de Senlis*, Paris, 1936.

Boucher, L., *La Salpêtrière*, Paris, 1883.

Brièle, L., *Collection de documents pour servir à l'histoire des hôpitaux de Paris*, 4 volumes, Paris, 1881–1887.

Bru, P., *Histoire de Bicêtre*, Paris, 1890.

Brunet, E., *La Charité paroissiale à Paris sous l'Ancien Régime et sous la Révolution*, Paris, 1897.

Burdett, H. C., *Hospitals and Asylums of the World*, London, 1891.

Burns, J., *History of the Poor Law*, London, 1764.

Camus, J.-P., *De la mendicité légitime des pauvres*, Douai, 1634.

Chassaigne, M., *La Lieutenance de police à Paris*, Paris, 1906.

Chatelain, P., *Le Régime des aliénés et des anormaux au XVIIe et XVIIIe siècle*, Paris, 1921.

Chevalier, J.-A. Ulysse, *Notice historique sur la maladrerie de Voley près Romans*, Romans, 1870.

Collet, P., *Vie de saint Vincent de Paul*, 3 volumes, Paris, 1818.

Coste, P., *Les Détenus de Saint-Lazare aux XVIIe et XVIIIe siècles* (Revue des Etudes historiques, 1926).

Delannoy, A., *Note historique sur les hôpitaux de Tournay*, 1880.

Delaunay, P., *Le Monde médical parisien au XVIIIe siècle*, Paris, 1906.

Devaux, J., *L'Art de faire des rapports en chirurgie*, Paris, 1703.

Eden, F., *State of the Poor*, 2 volumes, London, 1797.

Eschenburg, *Geschichte unserer Irrenanstalten*, Lübeck, 1844.

Esquirol, J., *Des établissements consacrés aux aliénés en France*, 1818.

—— *Mémoire historique et statistique sur la Maison Royale de Charenton* (1824); in *Des maladies mentales*, vol. II, Paris, 1838.

Fay, H.-M., *Lépreux et cagots du Sud-Ouest*, Paris, 1910.

Ferrière, Cl.-J. de, *Dictionnaire de droit et de pratique*, Paris, 1769.

Fosseyeux, M., *L'Hôtel-Dieu à Paris au XVIIe et au XVIIIe siècle*, Paris, 1912.

Freguier, H. A., *Histoire de l'administration de la police à Paris depuis Philippe-Auguste jusqu'aux États généraux de 1789*, 2 volumes, Paris, 1850.

Funck-Brentano, F., *Les Lettres de cachet*, Paris, 1903.

Gazoni, T., *L'Ospital des fols incurables*, French translation, Paris, 1620.

Gendry, R., *Les Moyens de bien rapporter en justice*, Angers, 1650.

Gernet, H. B., *Mitteilungen aus alterer Medizin-Geschichte Hamburgs*, Hamburg, 1882.

Golhahn, R., *Spital und Arzt von Einst bis Jetzt*.

Guevarre, Dom, *De la Mendicità provenuta*, Aix, 1693.

Henry, M., *La Salpêtrière sous l'Ancien Régime*, Paris, 1922.

Hildenfinger, P.-A., *La Léproserie de Reims du XIIe au XVIIe siècle*, Reims, 1906.

Histoire de l'Hôpital général, An., Paris, 1676.

Hôpital général, (L'), An., Paris, 1682.

Howard, J., *État des prisons, hôpitaux et maisons de force*, French translation, 2 volumes, Paris, 1788.

Institutions et règlements de Charité aux XVIe et XVIIe siècles, réimprimés par Biencourt, Paris, 1903.

Jacobé, P., *Un internement sous le Grand Roi: H. Loménie de Brienne*, Paris, 1929.

Joly, A., *L'Internement des fous sous l'Ancien Régime dans la généralité de Basse-Normandie*, Caen, 1868.

Kriegk, G., *Aerzte, Heilanstalten und Geisteskranke im mittelalterlichen Frankfurt*, Frankfurt am Main, 1863.

Lallemand, L., *Histoire de la Charité*, five volumes, Paris, 1902–1912.

La Mare, N. de, *Traité de police*, 4 volumes, Paris, 1738.

Langlois, C. V., *La Connaissance de la nature et du monde au Moyen Age*, Paris, 1911.

Lautard, J.-B., *La Maison de fous de Marseille*, Marseille, 1840.

Le Brun de la Rochette, C., *Les Procès civils et criminels*, Rouen, 1663.

Legier-Desgranges, H., *Hospitaliers d'autrefois; Hôpital général*, Paris, 1952.

Legrand, L., 'Les Maisons-Dieu et léproseries du diocèse de Paris au milieu du XIVe siècle', *Mémoires de la société d'histoire de Paris*, volume XXIV, 1897, and volume XXV, 1898.

Leonard, E. M., *The Early Story of English Poor Relief*, Cambridge, 1900.

Locard, E., *La Médecine judiciaire en France au XVIIe siècle*.

Louis, 'Questions de jurisprudence du suicide', *Journal de médecine*, volume XIX, p. 442.

Loyac, J. de, *Le Triomphe de la Charité ou la vie du bienheureux Jean de Dieu*, Paris, 1661.

Muyart de Vouglans, P. F., *Les Lois criminelles de France dans leur ordre naturel*, 2 volumes, Paris, 1781.

Nicholls, G., *History of the English Poor Law*, two volumes, London, 1898.

O'Donoghue, E. G., *The Story of Bethlehem Hospital*, New York, 1915.

Parturier, L., *L'Assistance à Paris sous l'Ancien Régime et sous la Révolution*, Paris, 1897.

Paultre, Chr., *De la répression de la mendicité et du vagabondage en France sous l'Ancien Régime*, Paris, 1906.

Petit, J.-B., 'Consultation médico-légale sur un homme qui s'était pendu', *Journal de médecine*, volume XXVII, p. 515.

Peuchet, J., *Collections de lois, ordonnances et règlements de police depuis le XIIIe jusqu'au XVIIIe siècle*, second series, Paris, 1818–1819.

Pignot, L., *Les Origines de l'hôpital du Midi*, Paris, 1885.

Pintard, R., *Le Libertinage érudit*, Paris, 1943.

Pontas, J., *Dictionnaire des cas de conscience*, Paris, 1741.

Ravaisson, Fr., *Les Archives de la Bastille*, 19 volumes, Paris, 1866–1904.

Règlements de l'hôpital des insensés de la ville d'Aix, Aix, 1695.

Règlements et statuts de l'Hôpital général d'Orléans, Orléans, 1692.

Rocher, J., *Notice historique sur la maladrerie de Saint-Hilaire-Saint-Mesmin*, Orléans, 1866.

Sainte-Beuve, J., *Résolution de quelques cas de conscience*, Paris, 1680.

Sérieux, P., *L'Internement par ordre de justice des aliénés et des correctionnaires*, Paris, 1932.

Sérieux P. et Libert, L., *Le Régime des aliénés en France au XVIIIe siècle*, Paris, 1914.

Sérieux P. et Trénel, M., *L'Internement des aliénés par voie judiciaire*, Recueil Sirey, 1931.

Tuke, D. H., *Chapters on the History of the Insane*, London, 1882.

Statuts et règlements de l'Hôpital général de la Charité de Lyon, Lyon, 1742.

Verdier, F., *La Jurisprudence de la médecine en France*, two volumes, Paris, 1723.

Vié, J., *Les Aliénés et correctionnaires à Saint-Lazare aux XVIIe et XVIIIe siècles*, Paris, 1830.

Vincent de Paul, *Correspondance et Sermons*, ed. Coste, 12 volumes, Paris, 1920–1924.

Vives, J.-L., *L'Aumônerie*, French translation, Lyon, 1583.

PART TWO

Andry, C.-L., *Recherches sur la mélancolie*, Paris, 1785.

Apologie pour Monsieur Duncan (An.)

Arnold, Th., *Observations on the Nature, Kinds, Causes and Preventions of Insanity, Lunacy and Madness*, 2 volumes, Leicester, 1782–1786.

—— *Observations on the Management of the Insane*, London, 1792.

Baglivi, G., *Tractatus de fibra motrice*, Pérouse, 1700.

Bayle, F., and Grangeon, H., *Relation de l'état de quelques personnes prétendues possédées*, Toulouse, 1682.

Beauchêne, E.-P. Ch., *De l'influence des affections de l'âme dans les maladies nerveuses des femmes, avec le traitement qui convient à ces maladies*, Paris, 1781.

Bienville, J.-D. T., *De la nymphomanie*, Amsterdam, 1771.

Blackmoore, A., *A Treatise of the Spleen and Vapours*, London, 1726.

Boerhaave, H., *Aphorismes*, French translation, Paris, 1745.

Boissier de Sauvages, F., *Nosologie méthodique*, French translation, 10 volumes, Lyon, 1772.

Boissieu, B.-C., *Mémoire sur les méthodes rafraîchissantes et échauffantes*, Dijon, 1772.

Bonet, Th., *Sepulchretum anatomicum*, 3 volumes, Paris, 1700.

Brisseau, P., *Traité des mouvements sympathiques*, Paris, 1692.

Chambon de Montaux, N., *Des maladies des femmes*, 2 volumes, Paris, 1784.

—— *Des maladies des filles*, 2 volumes, Paris, 1785.

Chesneau, N., *Observationum Nicolai Chesneau, . . . libri quinque*, Paris, 1672.

Cheyne, G., *The English Malady, or a Treatise on Nervous Diseases of all kinds*, London, 1733.

—— *Méthode naturelle de guérir les maladies du corps et les dérèglements de l'esprit*, French translation, 2 volumes, Paris, 1749.

Clerc, N.-G., *Histoire naturelle de l'homme dans l'état de maladie*, 2 volumes, Paris, 1767.

Cox, J.-M., *Practical Observations on Insanity*, London, 1804.

Crugeri, *Casus medicus de morbo litteratorum*, Zittaviae, 1703.

Cullen, W., *Institutions de médecine pratique*, French translation, 2 volumes, Paris, 1785.

Daquin, J., *Philosophie de la folie*, Paris, 1792.

Diemerbroek, I., *Opera omnia anatomica et medica*, Utrecht, 1685.

Dionis, P., *Dissertation sur la mort subite*, Paris, 1710.

Dufour, J.-F., *Essai sur les opérations de l'entendement humain et sur les maladies qui les dérangent*, Amsterdam and Paris, 1770.

Dumoulin, J., *Nouveau Traité du rhumatisme et des vapeurs*, Paris, 1710.

Ettmüller, M., *Opera medica*, Frankfurt, 1696.

Examen de la prétendue possession des filles de la paroisse de Landes, An. 1735.

Fallowes, S., *The Best Method for the Cure of Lunatics*, London, 1705.

Faucett, H., *Ueber Melancholie*, Leipzig, 1785.

Fernel, J., *Universa Medica*, Frankfurt, 1607.

Ferrand, J., *De la maladie d'amour ou mélancolie érotique*, Paris, 1623.

Flemyng, M., *Neuropathia sive de morbis hypochondriacis et hystericis*, Amsterdam, 1741.

Forestus, P., *Observationes et curationes*, Rotterdam, 3 volumes, 1653.

Fouquet, F., *Recueil de remèdes faciles et domestiques*, Paris, 1678.

Friedreich, N., *Historisch-kritische Darstellung der Theorien über das Wesen u. den Sitz der psychischen Krankheiten*, 1836.

Gaubius, D., *Institutiones pathologiae medicinales*, Leyden, 1758.

Haller, Alb. Von, *Eléments de physiologie*, French translation, Paris, 1769.

Haslam, J., *Observations on Insanity*, London, 1794.

Hecquet, P., *Réflexions sur l'usage de l'opium, des calmants et des narcotiques, pour la guérison des maladies, en forme de lettre*, Paris, 1726.

Highmore, N., *Exercitationes duæ, prior de passione hysterica, altera de affectione hypochondriaca*, Oxford, 1660.

—— *De passione hysterica, responsio epistolaris ad Willisium*, London, 1670.

Hoffmann, F., *Dissertationes medicæ selectiores*, Halle, 1702.

—— *De motuum convulsivorum vera sede et indole*, Halle, 1733.

—— *De morbi hysterici vera indole*, Halle, 1733.

—— *De affectu spasmodico-hypochondriaco-inveterato*, Halle, 1734.

Hunauld, P., *Dissertation sur les vapeurs et les pertes du sang*, Paris, 1716.

James, R., *Dictionnaire universel de médecine*, French translation, 6 volumes, 1746–1748.

Jonston, D., *Idée universelle de la médecine*, French translation, Paris, 1644.

Lacaze, L., *Idée de l'homme physique et moral*, Paris, 1755.

Lancisius, J.-M., *Opera omnia*, 2 volumes, Geneva, 1748.

Lange, *Traité des vapeurs*, Paris, 1689.

Laroche, D. de, *Analyse des fonctions du système nerveux*, 2 volumes, Geneva, 1778.

Laurens, A. du, *Toutes les Œuvres de M. André Du Laurens*, French translation, Rouen, 1661.

Le Camus, A., *La Médecine de l'esprit*, 2 volumes, Paris, 1769.

Lemery, J., *Dictionnaire universel des drogues simples*, Paris, 1769.

Liébaut, J., *Trois livres des maladies et infirmitez des femmes*, Paris, 1649.

Lieutaud, J., *Traité de médecine pratique*, 2 volumes, Paris, 1759.

Linné, K, *Genera morborum*, Upsala, 1763.

Lorry, A. C., *De melancholia et morbis melacholicis*, 2 volumes, Paris, 1765.

Mead, R., *A Treatise Concerning the Influence of the Sun and the Moon*, London, 1748.

Meckel, J.-F., *Recherches anatomo-physiologiques sur les causes de la folie*, Academic memoir, Berlin, volume XX, 1764, p. 65.

Mesnardière, H.-J. La, *Traité de la mélancholie, sçavoir si elle est la cause des effets que l'on remarque dans les possédées de Loudun*, La Flèche, 1635.

Morgagni, J. B., *De sedibus et causis morborum*, 2 volumes, Venice, 1761.

Mourre, M., *Observations sur les insensés*, Toulon, 1791.

Murillo, T. A., *Novissima hypochondriacæ melancholiæ curatio*, Lyon, 1672.

Perfect, W., *Methods of Cure in Some Particular Cases of Insanity*, London, 1778.

La Philosophie des vapeurs, ou lettres raisonnées d'une jolie femme sur l'usage des symptômes vaporeux, Paris, 1774. [This text is attributed to Abbé C.-J. de B. de Paumerelle. TN]

Pinel, P., *Nosographie philosophique*, 2 volumes, Paris, Year VI.

Piso, C., *Selectiorum observationum et consiliorum liber singularis*, Lyon, 1650.

Pitcairn, A., *The Whole Works*, London, 1777.

Plater, F., *Praxeos medicae tres tomi*, Basel, 1609.

Pomme, P., *Traité des affections vaporeuses des deux sexes*, Paris, 1760.

Pressavin, J.-B., *Nouveau traité des vapeurs*, Lyon, 1770.

Raulin, J., *Traité des affections vaporeuses du sexe, avec l'exposition de leurs symptômes, de leurs différentes causes, et la méthode de les guérir*, Paris, 1758.

Renou, J. de, *Oeuvres pharmaceutiques*, French translation, Lyon, 1638.

Revillon, C., *Recherches sur la cause des affections hypochondriaques*, Paris, 1779.

Rostaing, A., *Réflexions sur les affections vaporeuses*, Paris, 1778.

Scheidenmantel, F. C. G., *Die Leidenshaften als Heilmittel betrachtet*, Hildburgh, 1787.

Schenkius, A., and Grafenberg, J., *Observationes medicorum variorum libri VII*, Frankfurt, 1665.

Schwarz, A., *Dissertation sur les dangers de l'onanisme et les maladies qui en résultent*, Strasbourg, 1815.

Spengler, L., *Briefe, welche einige Erfahrungen der elektrischen Wirkung in Krankheiten enthalten*, Copenhagen, 1754.

Stahl, G. E., *Dissertatio de spasmis*, Halle, 1702.

—— *Theoria medica vera*, 2 volumes, Halle, 1708.

Swieten, G. Van, *Commentaria in Hermanni Boerhaave Aphorismos de cognoscendis et curandis morbis*, Paris, 1753.

Sydenham, T, *Médecine pratique*, French translation, Paris, 1784.

Tissot, S.-A., *Avis aux gens de lettres sur leur santé*, Lausanne, 1767.

—— *Observations sur la santé des gens du monde*, Lausanne, 1770.

—— *Traité des nerfs et de leurs maladies*, Paris, 1778–1780.

Venel, J.-A., *Essai sur la santé et l'éducation médicinale des filles destinées au mariage*, Yverdon, 1776.

Vieussens, R., *Traité nouveau des liqueurs du corps humain*, Toulouse, 1715.

Viridet, J., *Dissertation sur les vapeurs*, Yverdon, 1726.

Weickard, M. A., *Der philosophische Arzt*, 3 volumes, Frankfurt, 1790.

Whytt, R., *Traité des maladies nerveuses*, French translation, 2 volumes, Paris, 1777.

Willis, T., *Opera omnia*, 2 volumes, Lyon, 1681.

Zacchias, P., *Quæstiones medico-legales*, 2 volumes, Avignon, 1660–1661.

Zacutus Lusitanus, A., *Opera omnia*, 2 volumes, Lyon, 1657.

Zilboorg, G., *The Medical Man and the Witch during the Renaissance*, Baltimore, 1935.

PART THREE

Alletz, P.-A., *Tableau de l'humanité et de la bienfaisance*, Paris, 1769.

Ariès, Ph., *L'Enfant et la vie familiale sous l'Ancien Régime*, Paris, 1960.

Baudeau, N., *Idées d'un citoyen sur les devoirs et les droits d'un vrai pauvre*, Paris, 1765.

Bellart, N.-F., *Œuvres*, 6 volumes, Paris, 1827–28.

Bixler, E., 'A forerunner of psychiatric nursing: Pussin', *Annals of Medical History*, 1936, p. 518.

Bloch, C., *L'Assistance à l'Etat à la veille de la Révolution*, Paris, 1908.

Brissot de Warville, J.-P., *Théorie des lois criminelles*, 2 volumes, Paris, 1781.

Cabanis, P. J. G., *Œuvres philosophiques*, 2 volumes, Paris, 1956.

Clavareau, N.-M., *Mémoires sur les hôpitaux civils de Paris*, Paris, 1805.

Coqueau, C.-P., *Essai sur l'établissement des hôpitaux dans les grandes villes*, Paris, 1787.

Daignan, G., *Réflexions sur la Hollande, où l'on considère principalement les hôpitaux*, Paris, 1778.

Desmonceaux, A., *De la bienfaisance nationale*, Paris, 1789.

Détails sur l'établissement du Docteur Willis pour la guérison des aliénés, Bibliothèque britannique, vol. I, p. 759.

Doublet, F., *Rapport sur l'état actuel des prisons de Paris*, Paris, 1791.

Doublet, F., and Colombier, J., 'Instructions sur la manière de gouverner et de traiter les insensés', *Journal de médecine*, August 1785, p. 529.

Dulaurent, J., *Essai sur les établissements nécessaires et les moins dispendieux pour rendre le service dans les hôpitaux vraiment utile à l'humanité*, Paris, 1787.

Dupont de Nemours, P.-S., *Idées sur les secours à donner aux pauvres malades dans une grande ville*, Philadelphia and Paris, 1786.

Dreyfus, F., *L'Assistance sous la Législative et la Convention*, Paris, 1905.

Essarts, N. des, *Dictionnaire universel de police*, 7 volumes, Paris, 1785–1787.

Francke, A.-H., 'Précis historique sur la vie des établissements de bienfaisance', *Recueil de mémoires sur les établissements d'humanité*, no. 39, Paris, 1804.

Genil-Perrin, G., 'La Psychiatrie dans l'oeuvre de Cabanis', *Revue de Pyschiatrie*, October 1910.

Genneté, L., *Purification de l'air dans les hôpitaux*, Nancy, 1767.

Gruner, J.-C., 'Essai sur les vices et les améliorations des établissements de sûreté publique', *Recueil de Mémoires sur les établissements d'humanité*, no. 39, Paris, 1804.

Hales, S., *A Description of Ventilators*, London, 1743.

Imbert, J., *Le Droit hospitalier de la Révolution et de l'Empire*, Paris, 1954.

Mac Auliffe, L., *La Révolution et les hôpitaux*, Paris, 1901.

Marsillac, J., *Les Hôpitaux remplacés par des sociétés civiques*, Paris, 1792.

Matthey, A., *Nouvelles recherches sur les maladies de l'esprit*, Paris, 1816.

Mercier, J.-S., *Tableau de Paris*, 12 volumes, Amsterdam, 1782–1788.

Mirabeau, H., *Observations d'un voyageur anglais*, Paris, 1788.

Mirabeau, V., *L'Ami des hommes*, 6 volumes, Paris, 1759.

Moehsen, J. C. N., *Geschichte der Wissenschaften in der Mark Brandeburg*, Berlin and Leipzig, 1781.

Moheau, M., *Recherches sur la population de la France*, Paris, 1788.

Morel, A., *Traité des dégénérescences*, Paris, 1857.

Musquinet de la Pagne, L. M., *Bicêtre réformé*, Paris, 1790.

Pinel, P., *Traité médico-philosophique*, Paris, Year IX.

Pinel, S., *Traité complet du régime sanitaire des aliénés*, Paris, 1836.

Plaidoyer pour l'héritage du pauvre à faire devant les représentants de la nation, Paris, 1790.

Précis des vues générales en faveur de ceux qui n'ont rien, Lons-le-Saulnier, 1789.

Rapports du comité de mendicité. Procès-verbaux de l'Assemblée nationale, 1790, volumes XXI, XXII and XLIV.

Récalde, Abbé de, *Traité sur les abus qui subsistent dans les hôpitaux du royaume*, Paris, 1786.

Régnault, É., *Du degré de compétence des médecins*, Paris, 1828.

Rive, C. G. de la, 'Lettre sur un nouvel établissement pour la guérison des aliénés', *Bibliothèque britannique*, volume VIII, p. 308.

Robin, A., *Du traitement des insensés dans l'hôpital de Bethléem (suivi d'observations sur les insensés de Bicêtre et de la Salpêtrière)*, Amsterdam, 1787.

Rumford, 'Principes fondamentaux pour le soulagement des pauvres', Bibliothèque britannique, volume I, p. 499, and II, p. 137.

Rush, B., *Medical Inquiries*, 4 volumes, Philadelphia, 1809.

Sémelaigne, R., *Aliénistes et philanthropes*, Paris, 1912.

—— *Philippe Pinel et son oeuvre*, Paris, 1927.

Spurzheim, J.-G., *Observations sur la folie*, Paris, 1818.

Table alphabétique, chronologique et analytique des règlements relatifs à l'administration des hôpitaux, Paris, 1815.

Tenon, J., *Mémoires sur les hôpitaux de Paris*, 1788.

Tuetey, A., *L'Assistance publique à Paris pendant la Révolution*, 4 volumes, Paris, 1895–1897.

Tuke, S., *Description of the Retreat*, York, 1813.

Turgot, A. J., *Œuvres*, ed. Schelle, 5 volumes, Paris, 1913–1919.

Wagnitz, H. B., *Historische Nachrichten und Bemerkungen Zuchthaüser in Deutschland*, 2 volumes, Halle, 1791–1792.

Wood, 'Quelques détails sur la maison d'industrie de Shrewsbury', Bibliothèque britannique, volume VIII, p. 273.

A complete bibliography of the medical texts on sicknesses of the mind from the fifteenth to the eighteenth centuries can be found in Laehr, H., *Die Literatur der Psychiatrie von 1459 bis 1799*, 4 volumes, Berlin, 1900.

Under the title *Gedenktage der Psychiatrie* (Berlin, 1893), the same author published a chronology in the form of a calendar, which, unlike the bibliography, is not entirely trustworthy.

III

BIBLIOGRAPHY OF ENGLISH WORKS QUOTED IN THIS TRANSLATION

Arnold, *Observations on the nature, kinds, causes and prevention of insanity, lunacy and madness*, (Leicester, vol. I, 1702, vol. II, 1786, reprinted in London in 1806 by Richard Philips).

Black, William, *A Dissertation on Insanity* (London: Ridgway, 1811), second edition.

Blake, William, *The Complete Poems*, ed. W. H. Stevenson (London and New York: Longman, 1989) second edition.

Calvin, John, *The Catechism of the Church of Geneva*, trans. Elijah Waterman (Hartford: Sheldon and Goodwin, 1815).

—— *Institutes of the Christian Religion, a new translation by Henry Beveridge* (Edinburgh: T. and T. Clark, 1863).

—— *Upon the fifth booke of Moses called Deuteronomy* (London: Henry Middleton, 1583). Reprinted in facsimile by the Banner of Truth Trust, Edinburgh, 1987.

Cervantes, Miguel de Saavedra, *The Ingenious Hidalgo Don Quixote de la Mancha*, trans. with an Introduction and Notes by John Rutherford (London: Penguin books, 2000).

Cheyne, George, *An Essay of Health and Good Life* (London: George Strahan, 1725), 4th edition.

—— *The English Malady* (Dublin: G. Risk, 1733), reprinted with an introduction by Roy Porter (London and New York: Tavistock/Routledge, 1991).

Crichton, Alexander, *An Enquiry into the Nature and Origins of Mental Derangement* (1798).

Cullen, William, *First Lines of the Practice of Physic* (Edinburgh: Bell and Bradfute, 1791).

Nicholas of Cusa, *The Layman on Wisdom and the Mind*, trans. M. L. Führer (Canada: Dovehouse editions, 1989).

Descartes, René, *The Philosophical Writings of Descartes*, trans. John Cottingham, Robert Stoothoff, Dugald Murdoch (Cambridge: Cambridge University Press, 1985).

Eden, Sir Frederic Morton, *State of the Poor* (London: J. Davis, 1797).

Erasmus, Desiderius, *The Praise of Folly*, trans. Clarence H. Miller (New Haven and London: Yale University Press, 2nd edition, 2003).

Hale, Sir Matthew, *Discourse Touching Provision for the Poor* (London: Peter Davies, 1927).

Haslam, John, *Observations on Insanity, with Practical Remarks on this Disease* (London: F. and C. Rivington, 1798).

Howard, John, *State of the Prisons in England and Wales* (3rd edition, Warrington: William Ayres, 1784).

James, Robert, *A Medicinal Dictionary, including Physic, Surgery, Anatomy, Chymistry and Botany, and all their Branches relative to Medicine* (London, T. Osborne, 1745).

Jonstonus, Joannes, *The Idea of Practical Physick, written in Latin by John Johnston, and Englished by Nich. Culpeper* (London: Peter Cole, 1657).

Leonard, E. M., *The Early History of English Poor Relief* (Cambridge: Cambridge University Press, 1900, reprinted in 1965 in London by Frank Cass & Co.).

Montaigne, *The Complete Essays*, trans. by M. A. Screech (Harmondsworth: Penguin Books, 1991).

Nicholls, George, *History of the English Poor Law* (London: 1898–1899), 2 vols.

Rousseau, Jean-Jacques, *The Discourses and Other Philosophical Writings*, ed. and trans. Victor Gourevitch (Cambridge: Cambridge University Press, 1977).

Rush, Benjamin, *Medical Inquiries and Observations* (Philadelphia, 1809), 4 vols.

Spinoza, Baruch, *Treatise on the Emendation of the Intellect*, in *The Ethics; Treatise on the Emendation of the Intellect; Selected Letters*, trans. Samuel Shirley, ed. Seymour Feldman (Indianapolis: Hackett, 1992).

Sydenham, Thomas, *The Whole Works of that excellent Practical Physician Thomas Sydenham*, 8th edition, trans. from the Latin by John Pechey (London: Darby & Poulson, 1772).

Tucker, Josias, *Reflections on the expediency of a law for the naturalization of foreign protestants; the first being historical remarks on the late naturalization bill; the second, queries occasioned by the same* (London: T. Trye, 1751–52).

Tuke, Samuel, *Description of the Retreat, an Institution near York for Insane Persons*, York, 1813 (reprinted in facsimile, London: Process Press, 1996).

Voltaire, *Philosophical Dictionary*, trans. Theodore Besterman (Harmondsworth: Penguin Books, 1984).

—— *Letters on England*, trans. with an introduction by Leonard Tancock (Harmondsworth: Penguin Books, 1980).

Watson, F., *Luis Vives. El Gran Valenciano* (Oxford: Oxford University Press, 1922).

Whytt, Robert, *Observations on the Nature, Causes and Cure of those Disorders which have been commonly called Nervous, Hypochondriac, or Hysteric* (Edinburgh: T. Becket, 1765).

Willis, Thomas, *The Remaining Works of that Famous and Renowned Physician, Dr Thomas Willis, Englished by S. Pordage.* (London: T. Dring, 1683), 8th edition.

IV

CRITICAL BIBLIOGRAPHY ON FOUCAULT'S *HISTORY OF MADNESS*

PRIMARY TEXTS

Foucault, M. (1954a) 'Introduction', in L. Binswanger, *Le Rêve et l'existence*, Paris: Desclée de Brouwer.

—— (1954b; 2nd edn 1995) *Maladie mentale et psychologie*, Paris: Quadrige/ Presses Universitaires de France.

—— (1961a) *Folie et Déraison: histoire de la folie à l'âge classique*, Paris: Plon.

—— (1961b) 'La folie n'existe que dans une société', interview with J.-P. Weber, *Le Monde*, 5135, 22 July: 9; reprinted in *Dits et écrits, 1954–1988* (1994), vol. I, Paris: Gallimard.

—— (1961c) 'Préface' in *Folie et Déraison: histoire de la folie à l'âge classique*, Paris: Plon; reprinted in *Dits et écrits, 1954–1988* (1994), vol. I, Paris: Gallimard.

—— (1963) 'L'eau et la folie', *Médecine et Hygiène*, 613: 901–6; reprinted in *Dits et écrits, 1954–1988* (1994), vol. I, Paris: Gallimard.

—— (1964) 'La folie, l'absence d'œuvre', *La Table Ronde*, 196: Situation de la psychiatrie: 11–21; reprinted in *Dits et écrits, 1954–1988* (1994), vol. I, Paris: Gallimard.

—— (1967) *Madness and Civilization: a History of Insanity in the Age of Reason*, trans. R. Howard, London: Tavistock Publications.

—— (1972a; 2nd edn 1989) *Histoire de la folie à l'âge classique*, Paris: Gallimard.

—— (1972b) 'Mon corps, ce papier, ce feu', in *Histoire de la folie*, Paris: Gallimard; reprinted in *Dits et écrits* (1994), vol. II, Paris: Gallimard.

—— (1973) *Moi, Pierre Rivière, ayant égorgé ma mère, ma sœur et mon frère . . . Un cas de parricide au XIXᵉ siécle*, Paris: Gallimard/Julliard.

—— (1976; 2nd edn 1987) *Mental Illness and Psychology*, trans. A. Sheridan, Berkeley: University of California Press.

—— (1980) *Power/knowledge: selected interviews and other writings 1972–1977*, ed. C. Gordon, trans. C. Gordon et al., Brighton: Harvester Press.

—— (1981) 'Truth and Power', in C. C. Lemert (ed.) *French Sociology: rupture and renewal since 1968*, New York: Columbia University Press.

—— (1983) 'Comment on "Madness" by Lawrence Stone', *New York Review of Books*, 30, (5) 42–44; reprinted in B. Smart (ed.) (1994–95) *Michel Foucault: critical assessments*, vol. IV, Section 1: *History of Forms of Rationality*, London: Routledge.

—— (1984a) 'The Birth of the Asylum', from *Madness and Civilization*, in *The Foucault Reader*, ed. P. Rabinow, Harmondsworth: Penguin.

—— (1984b; 2nd edn 1991) *The Foucault reader*, ed. P. Rabinow, Harmondsworth: Penguin.

—— (1984c) 'The Great Confinement', from *Madness and Civilization*, in *The Foucault Reader*, ed. P. Rabinow, Harmondsworth: Penguin.

—— (1990) 'La psychologie de 1850 à 1950', *Revue internationale de philosophie*, 44 (173): 159–76.

—— (1991) 'Experiences of Madness', trans. A. Pugh, *History of the Human Sciences*, 4 (1): 1–25.

—— (1993) 'About the Beginning of the Hermeneutics of the Self: Two Lectures at Dartmouth', *Political Theory*, 21 (2): 198–227.

—— (1994) *Dits et écrits, 1954–1988*, Paris: Gallimard.

—— (1997; 2nd edn 2000) *The essential works of Michel Foucault, 1954–1984*, trans. R. Hurley and others, London: Allen Lane, The Penguin Press.

—— (1999) *Les Anormaux. Cours au Collège de France (1974–1975)*, Paris: Gallimard/Seuil.

—— (2003) *Le Pouvoir psychiatrique. Cours au Collège de France (1973–1974)*, Paris: Gallimard/Seuil.

Foucault, M. and Binswanger, L. (1993) *Dream and Existence*, K. Hoeller (ed.), New Jersey: Humanities Press.

SECONDARY TEXTS

(1961) 'The Story of Unreason', *Times Literary Supplement*, 3 (100): 653–654; reprinted in B. Smart (ed.) (1994–1995) *Michel Foucault: critical assessments*, vol. IV Section 1: *History of Forms of Rationality*, London: Routledge.

(1968) 'Social process and the perimeters of psychiatry', *Canadian Medical Association Journal*, 99 (15): 767–769.

Adams, J. W. (1981) 'Consensus, Community, and Exoticism', *Journal of Interdisciplinary History*, 12 (2): 253–265.

Alvarez-Uria, F. (1979) 'Contra el poder, el saber y la verdad', *RS, Cuadernos de Realidades Sociales*, 14–15 (Jan.): 181–186.

Alves, A. A. (1989) 'The Christian Social Organism and Social Welfare: The Case of Vives, Calvin and Loyola', *The Sixteenth Century Journal*, 20 (1): 3–22.

Appleby, J. (1998) 'The Power of History', *American Historical Review*, 103 (1): 1–14.

Arac, J. (ed.) (1988) *After Foucault: humanistic knowledge, postmodern challenges*, New Brunswick: Rutgers University Press.

Armstrong, D. (1985a) 'Review essay – Madness and Civilization', *Sociology of Health and Illness*, 7 (1): 108–117.

—— (1985b) 'The Subject and the Social in Medicine: An Appreciation of Michel Foucault', *Sociology of Health and Illness*, 7 (1): 108–117.

—— (1997) 'Foucault and the Sociology of Health and Illness: A Prismatic Reading', in A. Petersen and R. Bunton (eds) *Foucault, Health and Medicine*, London: Routledge.

Bachhuber, U. (1992) 'Vom Tater zum Opfer – Der "Selbst-Mord"', *Österreichische Zeitschrift fur Soziologie*, 17 (2): 32–45.

Baker, H. A. J. (1987) 'Modernism and the Harlem Renaissance', *American Quarterly*, 39 (1): 84–97.

Barker, P. (1993) *Michel Foucault: subversions of the subject*, New York, London: Harvester Wheatsheaf.

—— (1998) *Michel Foucault: an introduction*, Edinburgh: Edinburgh University Press.

Barthes, R. (1961) 'Savoir et folie', *Critique*, 17: 915–922.

—— (1972) 'Taking Sides', in *Critical Essays*, Evanston: Northwestern University Press; reprinted in B. Smart (ed.) (1994–1995) *Michel Foucault: critical assessments*, vol. IV Section 1: History of Forms of Rationality, London: Routledge.

Bernauer, J. W. (1992) *Michel Foucault's force of flight: toward an ethics for Thought*, Atlantic Highlands, NJ: Humanities Press International.

Bevis, P., et al. (1993) 'Archaeologizing genealogy. Michel Foucault and the economy of austerity', in M. Gane and T. Johnson (eds) *Foucault's new domains*, London: Routledge.

Blanchot, M. (1969) 'L'Oubli, la Déraison', in *L'Entretien Infini*, Paris: Gallimard; reprinted in B. Smart (ed.) (1994–1995) *Michel Foucault: critical assessments*, vol. IV Section 1: History of Forms of Rationality, London: Routledge.

Boyne, R. (1990) *Foucault and Derrida: the other side of reason*, London: Unwin Hyman.

Brain, D. (1990) 'Madness and Civilization: A History of Insanity in the Age of Reason' (Richard Howard's Translation) (A review of Michel Foucault), *Contemporary Sociology*, 19 (6): 902–906.

Braudel, F. (1962) 'Note', *Annales*, 17: 771–72; reprinted in B. Smart (ed.) (1994–95) *Michel Foucault: critical assessments*, vol. IV Section 1: History of Forms of Rationality, London: Routledge.

Braudy, L. (1970) 'Fanny Hill and Materialism', *Eighteenth Century Studies*, 4 (1): 21–40.

Broustra, J. (1973) 'Quelques questions à Michel Foucault', *Nouvel Observateur*, 2 April, 10.

Brown, B. and Cousins, M. (1986) 'The Linguistic Fault: The Case of Foucault's Archaeology', in M. Gane (ed.) *Towards a critique of Foucault*, London: Routledge & Kegan Paul.

Brown, P. (1995) 'Naming and Framing: The Social Construction of Diagnosis and Illness', *Journal of Health and Social Behavior*, 35: 34–52.

Brown, R. H. (1990) 'Rhetoric, Textuality, and the Postmodern Turn', *Sociological Theory*, 8 (2): 188–197.

Bull, M. (1990) 'Secularization and Medicalization', *British Journal of Sociology*, 41 (2): 245–261.

Burke, P. (ed.) (1992) *Critical Essays on Michel Foucault*, Aldershot: Scolar Press.

Cadoret, M. (ed.) (1989) *La Folie raisonnée*, Paris: Presses Universitaires de France.

Carroll, D. (1987) *Paraesthetics: Foucault, Lyotard, Derrida*, London: Methuen.

Céard, J. (ed.) (1985) *La Folie et le corps*, Paris: Presses de l'École Normale Supérieure.

Chambon, A. S. et al. (eds) (1999) *Reading Foucault for social work*, New York: Columbia University Press.

Chebili, S. (1999) *Figures de l'animalité dans l'œuvre de Michel Foucault*, Paris: L'Harmattan.

Chesler, P. (1971) 'Women as Psychiatric and Psychotherapeutic Patients', *Journal of Marriage and the Family*, 33 (4): 746–759.

Chesney, E. (1977) 'The Theme of Madness in Rabelais and Ariosto', *Journal of Medieval and Renaissance Studies*, 7: 67–93.

Clark, M. (1982) *Michel Foucault, an annotated bibliography: tool kit for a new age*, New York: Garland.

Clausen, J. A. and Huffine, C. L. (1975) 'Sociocultural and Social-Psychological Factors Affecting Social Responses to Mental Disorder', *Journal of Health and Social Behavior*, 16 (4): 405–420.

Collins, R. (1974) 'Three Faces of Cruelty: Towards a Comparative Sociology of Violence', *Theory and Society*, 1 (4): 415–440.

Colombel, J. (1994) *Michel Foucault : la clarté de la mort*, Paris: O. Jacob.

Connolly, W. E. (1983) 'Discipline, Politics, and Ambiguity', *Political Theory*, 11 (3): 325–341.

Conrad, P. (1992) 'Medicalization and Social Control', *Annual Review of Sociology*, 18: 209–232.

Cook, D. (1990) 'Madness and the Cogito: Derrida's critique of "Folie et Déraison"', *Journal of the British Society for Phenomenology*, 21 (2): 164–74.

—— (1993) 'Madness and the Cogito: Derrida's Critique of "Folie et Déraison"', *The Subject Finds a Voice: Foucault's turn toward subjectivity*, New York: P. Lang.

Cravens, H. (1985) 'History of the Social Sciences', *Osiris, Historical Writing on American Science*, 1 (2): 183–207.

Crocker, L. G. (1985) 'Interpreting the Enlightenment: A Political Approach', *Journal of the History of Ideas*, 46 (2): 211–230.

Crossley, N. (1994) *Politics of subjectivity: between Foucault and Merleau-Ponty*, Aldershot: Avebury.

Danaher, G. et al. (2000) *Understanding Foucault*, London: Sage.

Daumézon, G. (1969) 'Lecture historique de "L'histoire de la folie"', paper presented at La conception idéologique de 'L'histoire de la folie' de Michel Foucault: Journées Annuelles de L'Évolution psychiatrique, Toulouse, 6 and 7 December 1969; reprinted in *Évolution psychiatrique: cahiers de psychologie clinique et de psychopathologie générale* (1971), 36 (2): 227–242.

David-Ménard, M. (1992) 'Le laboratoire de l'œuvre', in L. Giard (ed.) *Michel Foucault: lire l'œuvre*, Grenoble: J. Millon.

Davidson, A. I. (ed.) (1997) *Foucault and his interlocutors*, Chicago: University of Chicago Press.

Dean, M. (1994) *Critical and Effective Histories: Foucault's methods and historical sociology*, London: Routledge.

De George, R. T. (ed.) (1972) *The Structuralists: from Marx to Lévi-Strauss*, Garden City, NY: Anchor Books.

Deleuze, G. (1999) 'A New Cartographer', in K. Racevskis (ed.) *Critical essays on Michel Foucault*, New York: G. K. Hall.

Deleuze, G. and Guattari, F. (1997) *Anti-Oedipus: capitalism and schizophrenia*, trans. R. Hurley et al., London: Athlone.

Derrida, J. (1978) 'Cogito and the History of Madness', in *Writing and Difference*, London: Routledge & Kegan Paul; reprinted in B. Smart (ed.)

(1994–1995) *Michel Foucault: critical assessments*, vol. IV Section 1: History of Forms of Rationality, London: Routledge.

—— (1994) ' "To Do Justice to Freud": The History of Madness in the Age of Psychoanalysis', *Critical Inquiry*, 20 (2): 227–266.

—— (1998) *Resistances of psychoanalysis*, trans. P. Kamuf et al., Stanford: Stanford University Press.

Dews, P. (1986) 'The Nouvelle Philosophie and Foucault', in M. Gane (ed.) *Towards a critique of Foucault*, London: Routledge & Kegan Paul.

Digby, A. (1983) 'Changes in the Asylum: The Case of York, 1777–1815', *Economic History Review*, 36: 2.

Dols, M. W. (1983) 'The Leper in Medieval Islamic Society', *Speculum: A Journal of Mediaeval Studies*, 58 (4): 891–916.

Donnelly, M. (1986) 'Foucault's genealogy of the human sciences', in M. Gane (ed.) *Towards a critique of Foucault*, London: Routledge & Kegan Paul.

Dreyfus, H. L. (1987) 'Foucault's Critique of Psychiatric Medicine', *The Journal of Medicine and Philosophy*, 12 (4): 313–333; reprinted in B. Smart (ed.) (1994–95) *Michel Foucault: critical assessments*, vol. IV, Section 1: History of Forms of Rationality, London: Routledge.

Dreyfus, H. L. and Rabinow, P. (1983) *Michel Foucault: beyond structuralism and hermeneutics*, Chicago: University of Chicago Press.

—— (1992) *Michel Foucault: un parcours philosophique: au-delà de l'objectivité et de la subjectivité*, trans. F. Durand-Bogaert, Paris: Gallimard.

Droit, R.-P. (2004) *Michel Foucault, entretiens*, Paris: Odile Jacob.

During, S. (1992) *Foucault and literature: towards a genealogy of writing*, London: Routledge.

Duvivier, R. (1970) 'La mort de Don Quichotte et l'Histoire de la folie', *Marche Romaine*, 20: 69–83.

Eisenstein, E. L. (1968) 'Some Conjectures about the Impact of Printing on Western Society and Thought: A Preliminary Report', *The Journal of Modern History*, 40 (1): 1–56.

Ellul, J. (1971) 'The Sociology of the Opposition to Science and Technology: With Special Reference to the Work of Sklair, Leslie', *Comparative Studies in Society and History*, 13 (2): 217–235.

Eribon, D. (1992) *Michel Foucault*, trans. B. Wing, London: Faber.

—— (1994) *Michel Foucault et ses contemporains*, Paris: Fayard.

Ernst, W. (1997) 'Idioms of Madness and Colonial Boundaries: The Case of the European and "Native" Mentally Ill in Early Nineteenth-Century British India', *Comparative Studies in Society and History*, 39 (1): 153–181.

Ey, H. (1969a) 'Introduction aux débats', paper presented at La conception idéologique de 'L'histoire de la folie' de Michel Foucault: Journées Annuelles de l'Evolution psychiatrique, 6 and 7 December 1969; reprinted in *Evolution psychiatrique: cahiers de psychologie clinique et de psychopathologie générale* (1971), 36 (2): 225–226.

Ey, H. (1969b) 'Commentaires critiques sur "L'histoire de la folie de Michel Foucault", paper presented at La conception idéologique de 'L'histoire de la folie' de Michel Foucault: Journées Annuelles de l'Évolution psychiatrique, 6 and 7 December 1969; reprinted in *Évolution psychiatrique: cahiers de psychologie clinique et de psychopathologie générale* (1971), 36 (2): 243–258.

Felman, S. (1972) 'Aurélia ou "le livre infaisable": de Foucault à Nerval', *Romantisme*: 43–55.

—— (1975) 'Madness and Philosophy or Literature's Reason', *Yale French Studies, Graphesis: Perspectives in Literature and Philosophy*, 52: 206–228.

Fine, B. (1979) 'Struggles Against Discipline: The Theory and Politics of Michel Foucault', *Capital and Class*, 9: 75–96; reprinted in B. Smart (ed.) (1994–1995) *Michel Foucault: critical assessments*, vol. IV, Section 1: History of Forms of Rationality, London: Routledge.

Flaherty, G. (1986) 'The Stage-Struck Wilhelm Meister and 18th-Century Psychiatric Medicine', *MLN, German Issue*, 101 (3): 493–515.

Flaherty, P. (1986) '(Con)textual Contest: Derrida and Foucault on Madness and the Cartesian Subject', *Philosophy of the Social Sciences*, 16 (2): 157–175.

Flax, J. (1981) 'Why Epistemology Matters: A Reply to Kress', *The Journal of Politics*, 43 (4): 1006–1024.

Flynn, B. (1989) 'Derrida and Foucault: Madness and Writing', in H. Silverman (ed.) *Derrida and Deconstruction*, New York: Routledge.

Flynn, T. R. (1997) *Sartre, Foucault, and historical reason*, vol. 1, *Toward an existentialist theory of history*, Chicago: University of Chicago Press.

Fowler, B. (1979) '"True to Me Always": An Analysis of Women's Magazine Fiction', *British Journal of Sociology*, 30 (1): 91–119.

Gane, M. (1986) 'Introduction', in M. Gane (ed.) *Towards a critique of Foucault*, London: Routledge & Kegan Paul.

Gane, M. and Johnson, T. (1993) *Foucault's new domains*, London: Routledge.

Gardiner, J. K. (1977) 'Elizabethan Psychology and Burton's Anatomy of Melancholy', *Journal of the History of Ideas*, 38 (3): 373–388.

Gauchet, M. (1994) 'À la recherche d'une autre histoire de la folie', in G. Swain, *Dialogue avec l'insensé*, Paris: Gallimard.

Geisenhanslüke, A. (1997) *Foucault und die Literatur: eine diskurskritische Untersuchung*, Opladen: Westdeutscher Verlag.

Giard, L. (ed.) (1992) *Michel Foucault: lire l'œuvre*, Grenoble: J. Millon.

Gill, C. (1985) 'Ancient Psychotherapy', *Journal of the History of Ideas*, 46 (3): 307–325.

Gilman, S. (1985) 'The Mad Man as Artist: Medicine, History and Degenerate

Art', *Journal of Contemporary History, Medicine, History and Society*, 20 (4): 575–597.

Goldstein, J. (1984) 'Foucault among the Sociologists: The "Disciplines" and the History of the Professions', *History and Theory*, 23 (2): 170–192.

—— (1993) 'Framing Discipline with Law: Problems and Promises of the Liberal State', *The American Historical Review*, 98 (2): 364–375.

—— (ed.) (1994) *Foucault and the writing of history*, Oxford: Blackwell.

Gordon, C. (1990) 'Histoire de la Folie: An Unknown Book by Michel Foucault', *History of the Human Sciences*, 3: 3–26; reprinted in B. Smart (ed.) (1994–1995) *Michel Foucault: critical assessments*, vol. IV, Section 1: *History of Forms of Rationality*, London: Routledge.

Greenbaum, L. S. (1993) 'Thomas Jefferson, the Paris Hospitals, and the University of Virginia', *Eighteenth Century Studies*, 26 (4): 607–626.

Gros, F. (1997) *Foucault et la folie*, Paris: Presses Universitaires de France.

Guédez, A. (1972) *Foucault*, Paris: Éditions universitaires.

Gutting, G. (1989) *Michel Foucault's archaeology of scientific reason*, Cambridge: Cambridge University Press.

—— (ed.) (1994) *The Cambridge companion to Foucault*, Cambridge: Cambridge University Press.

—— (1999) 'Reason and Philosophy', in K. Racevskis (ed.) *Critical essays on Michel Foucault*, New York: G. K. Hall.

Hacking, I. (1979) 'Michel Foucault's Immature Science', *Nous*, 13 (1): 39–51.

Halperin, D. M. (1995; 2nd edition 1997) *Saint Foucault: towards a gay hagiography*, Oxford: Oxford University Press.

Hampton, T. (1991) 'Introduction: Baroques', *Yale French Studies, Baroque Topographies: Literature/History/Philosophy*, 80: 1–9.

Hansen, L. (1998) 'Metaphors of Mind and Society: The Origins of German Psychiatry in the Revolutionary Era', *Isis*, 89 (3): 387–409.

Harsin, J. (1992) 'Gender, Class, and Madness in Nineteenth-Century France', *French Historical Studies*, 17 (4): 1048–1070.

Harth, E. (1973) 'Classical Innateness', *Yale French Studies, Science, Language, and the Perspective Mind: Studies in Literature and Thought from Campanella to Bayle*, 49: 212–230.

Hayes, T. (1996) 'Diggers, Ranters, and Women Prophets: The Discourse of Madness and the Cartesian Cogito in Seventeenth-Century England', *CLIO*, 26 (1): 29–50.

Hewitt, M. (1982) *Social policy and the politics of life: Foucault's account of welfare*, Hatfield: School of Social Sciences, the Hatfield Polytechnic.

Hirst, P. (1994) 'Foucault and Architecture', *Architectural Association Files*, 26: 52–60; reprinted in B. Smart (ed.) (1994–1995) *Michel Foucault: critical assessments*, vol. IV, Section 1: *History of Forms of Rationality*, London: Routledge.

Hooke, A. E. (1987) 'The Order of Others: Is Foucault's Antihumanism against Human Action?', *Political Theory*, 15 (1): 38–60.

Horowitz, A. (1979) 'Models, Muddles, and Mental Illness Labeling', *Journal of Health and Social Behavior*, 20 (3): 296–300.

Horrocks, C. and Jevtic, Z. (1997) *Introducing Foucault*, ed. R. Appignanesi, Cambridge: Icon Books.

Hoskin, K. (1990) 'Foucault under examination: the crypto-educationalist unmasked', in S. J. Ball (ed.) *Foucault and education: disciplines and knowledge*, London: Routledge.

Howe, M. (1974) 'Open Up a Few Corpses: Review of "The Birth of the Clinic", by Michel Foucault', *The Nation*, 117–19, 26 January; reprinted in B. Smart (ed.) (1994–95) *Michel Foucault: critical assessments*, vol. IV, Section 1: *History of Forms of Rationality*, London: Routledge.

Hug, J.-C. (1985) *Michel Foucault: une histoire de la vérité*, Paris: Syros.

Huot, S. (2003) *Madness in Medieval French Literature: Identities Found and Lost*, Oxford: Oxford University Press.

Hutton, P. H. (1981) 'The History of Mentalities: The New Map of Cultural History', *History and Theory*, 20 (3): 237–259.

Ignatieff, M. (1984) 'Anxiety and Asceticism', *Times Literary Supplement*, 28 September, 1071; reprinted in P. Burke (ed.) (1992) *Critical essays on Michel Foucault*, Aldershot: Scolar Press.

Imershein, A. W. and Simons, R. L. (1976) 'Rules and Examples in Lay and Professional Psychiatry: An Ethnomethodological Comment on the Scheff-Gove Controversy', *American Sociological Review*, 41 (3): 559–563.

Johnston, J. (1990) 'Discourse as Event: Foucault, Writing, and Literature', *MLN, French Issue*, 105 (4): 800–818.

Juarrero, A. (1992) 'The Message Whose Message It Is That There is No Message', *MLN, Comparative Literature*, 107 (5): 892–904.

Keller, H. (1987) 'Narrativity in History: Post-Structuralism and Since', *History and Theory*, 26 (4): 1–29.

Kelly, M. (ed.) (1994) *Critique and power: recasting the Foucault/Habermas debate*, Cambridge, MA.: MIT Press.

Kemper, R. (1996) *Il était un petit navire – zur Archäologie der Narrenschiff-Phantasien Michel Foucaults*, Frankfurt am Main: P. Lang.

Kennedy, D. (1979) 'Michel Foucault: The Archaeology and Sociology of Knowledge', *Theory and Society*, 8 (2): 269–290.

Kenway, K. (1990) 'Education and the Right's Discursive Politics. Private versus state school', in S. J. Ball (ed.) *Foucault and education: disciplines and knowledge*, London: Routledge.

Keskin, F. (1997) 'Foucault'da oznellik ve ozgurluki', *Toplum ve Bilim/Science & Society*, 73: 30–44.

Kirp, D. L. (1982) 'Professionalization as a Policy Choice: British Special Education in Comparative Perspective', *World Politics*, 34 (2): 137–174.

Kögler, H. H. (1996) *The Power of dialogue: critical hermeneutics after Gadamer and Foucault*, trans. P. Hendrickson, Cambridge, MA.: MIT Press.

Kurzweil, E. (1977) 'Michel Foucault: Ending the Era of Man', *Theory and Society*, 4 (3): 395–420.

—— (1980a) *Age of structuralism: Lévi-Strauss to Foucault*, New York; Guildford: Columbia University Press.

—— (1983) 'Michel Foucault and Culture', *Current Perspectives in Social Theory*, 4: 143–179.

Laboucarie, J. (1969) 'Allocution', paper presented at La conception idéologique de 'L'histoire de la folie' de Michel Foucault: Journées Annuelles de l'Évolution psychiatrique, Toulouse, 6 and 7 December 1969; reprinted in *Évolution psychiatrique: cahiers de psychologie clinique et de psychopathologie générale* (1971), 36 (2): 223–224.

Lacombe, D. (1996) 'Reforming Foucault: A Critique of the Social Control Thesis', *British Journal of Sociology*, 47 (2): 332–352.

Laing, R. D. (1987) 'The Invention of Madness', *New Statesman*, 16 June, 843; reprinted in B. Smart (ed.) (1994–1995) *Michel Foucault: critical assessments*, vol. IV, Section 1: *History of Forms of Rationality*, London: Routledge.

Lamont, M. (1987) 'How to Become a Dominant French Philosopher: The Case of Jacques Derrida', *American Journal of Sociology*, 93 (3): 584–622.

Lardet, P. (1992) 'La désinvolture de se présenter comme discours', in L. Giard (ed.) *Michel Foucault: lire l'œuvre*, Grenoble: J. Millon.

Larsen, D. (2001) 'South Park's Solar Anus, or, Rabelais Returns: Cultures of Consumption and the Contemporary Aesthetic of Obscenity', *Theory, Culture & Society*, 18 (4): 65–82.

Lasch, C. (1974) 'After the Church the Doctors, After the Doctors Utopia: The Birth of the Clinic', *The New York Times Book Review*, 24 February, 6; reprinted in B. Smart (ed.) (1994–1995) *Michel Foucault: critical assessments*, vol. IV, Section 1: *History of Forms of Rationality*, London: Routledge.

Lash, S. (1985) 'Postmodernity and Desire', *Theory and Society*, 14 (1): 1–33.

Lears, T. J. J. (1985) 'The Concept of Cultural Hegemony: Problems and Possibilities', *The American Historical Review*, 90 (3): 567–593.

Le Brun, J. (1992) 'Une œuvre classique', in L. Giard (ed.) *Michel Foucault: lire l'œuvre*, Grenoble: J. Millon.

Lecourt, D. (1972) *Pour une critique de l'épistémologie: (Bachelard, Canguilhem, Foucault)*, Paris: F. Maspero.

Lemert, C. C. and Gillan, G. (1982) *Michel Foucault: social theory and transgression*, New York: Columbia University Press.

Levin, M. R. (1993) 'Democratic Vistas-Democratic Media: Defining a Role for Printed Images in Industrializing France', *French Historical Studies*, 18 (1): 82–108.

Levinson, S. (1983) 'Law', *American Quarterly*, 35 (1/2): 191–204.

Levy, J. E. (1969) 'Some Comments upon the Ritual of the Sanni Demons', *Comparative Studies in Society and History*, 11 (2): 217–226.

Liska, A. E. (1997) 'Modeling the Relationships Between Macro Forms of Social Control', *Annual Review of Sociology*, 23: 39–61.

Liska, A. E. et al. (1999) 'Modeling the Relationship Between the Criminal Justice and Mental Health Systems', *American Journal of Sociology*, 104 (6): 1744–1775.

Macdonald, M. (1992) 'Mystical Bedlam', in P. Burke (ed.) *Critical essays on Michel Foucault*, Aldershot: Scolar Press.

Macey, D. (1993) *Lives of Michel Foucault*, London: Hutchinson.

Macherey, P. (1986) 'Aux sources de "L'Histoire de la Folie": Une Rectification et ses Limites', *Critique*, August/September: 753–774; reprinted in reprinted in B. Smart (ed.) (1994–95) *Michel Foucault: critical assessments*, vol. IV, Section 1: *History of Forms of Rationality*, London: Routledge.

Mandrou, R. (1962) 'Trois clefs pour Comprendre la Folie à l'Époque Classique', *Annales*, 17: 761–771; reprinted in B. Smart (ed.) (1994–1995) *Michel Foucault: critical assessments*, vol. IV, Section 1: *History of Forms of Rationality*, London: Routledge.

—— (1967) 'L'Historiographie française des XVIe et XVIIe siècles: Bilans et perspectives', *French Historical Studies*, 5 (1): 57–66.

Mannoni, O. (1973) 'The Antipsychiatric Movement(s)', *International Social Science Journal*, 25 (4): 489–503.

Marcus, S. (1975) 'Madness, Literature, and Society', in *Representations: Essays on Literature and Society*, New York: Random House.

Margolin, J.-C. (1967) 'Tribut d'un anti-humaniste aux études d'Humanisme et Renaissance – Note sur l'œuvre de M. Foucault', *Bibliothèque d'Humanisme et de Renaissance*, 29 (3): 701–711.

Martin, W. (1971) 'On the Road with the Philosopher and the Profiteer: A Study of Hugh Henry Brackenridge's Modern Chivalry', *Eighteenth Century Studies*, 4 (3): 241–256.

Matza, D. (1966) 'Review of Madness and Civilization: A History of Insanity in the Age of Reason, by Michal Foucault', *American Sociological Review*, 31: 551–552; reprinted in B. Smart (ed.) (1994–1995) *Michel Foucault: critical assessments*, vol. IV, Section 1: *History of Forms of Rationality*, London: Routledge.

Mazlish, B. (1971) 'Seventeenth-Century Attitudes toward Deviant Sex: Comment', *Journal of Interdisciplinary History*, 1 (3): 468–472.

—— (1992) 'The Question of the Question of Hu', *History and Theory*, 31 (2): 143–152.

Mccarthy, T. (1990) 'The Critique of Impure Reason: Foucault and the Frankfurt School', *Political Theory*, 18 (3): 437–469.

McHoul, A. W. and Grace, W. (1993; 2nd edn 1995) *A Foucault primer: discourse, power and the subject*, London: UCL Press.

McKinlay, A. and Starkey, K. (eds) (1998) *Foucault, management and organization theory: from panopticon to technologies of self*, London: Sage.

McLaren, A. (1974) 'Some Secular Attitudes toward Sexual Behavior in France: 1760–1860', *French Historical Studies*, 8 (4): 604–625.

McMenamin, D. J. (1999) 'The Critic's Cartographer', in K. Racevskis (ed.) *Critical essays on Michel Foucault*, New York: G.K. Hall.

Megill, A. (1979) 'Foucault, Structuralism, and the Ends of History', *The Journal of Modern History*, 51 (3): 451–503.

—— (1987) 'The Reception of Foucault by Historians', *Journal of the History of Ideas*, 48 (1): 117–141.

Merquior, J. G. (1985) *Foucault*, London: Fontana.

—— (1986) *Foucault ou le nihilisme de la Chaire*, trans. M. Azuelos, Paris: Presses Universitaires de France.

Michael, M. and Still, A. (1992) 'A Resource for Resistance: Power-Knowledge and Affordance', *Theory and Society*, 21 (6): 869–888.

Midelfort, H. C. E. (1980) 'Madness and Civilization in Early Modern Europe: A Reappraisal of Michel Foucault', in B. Malament (ed.) *After the Reformation*, Philadelphia: University of Pennsylvania Press; reprinted in B. Smart (ed.) (1994–1995) *Michel Foucault: critical assessments*, vol. IV, Section 1: *History of Forms of Rationality*, London: Routledge.

Miller, J. (1981) *French structuralism: a multidisciplinary bibliography*, London: Garland.

—— (1993) *The Passion of Michel Foucault*, New York: Simon & Schuster.

Milner, M. J. (1987) 'Theories of Inequality: An Overview and a Strategy for Synthesis', *Social Forces*, 65 (4): 1053–1089.

Minson, J. (1988) *Genealogies of morals: Nietzsche, Foucault, Donzelot and the eccentricity of ethics*, Basingstoke: Macmillan.

Moore, S. D. (1994) *Poststructural-ism and the New Testament: Derrida and Foucault at the foot of the Cross*, Minneapolis: Fortress.

Moreno, B. (1986) 'La naturaleza de la locura según M. Foucault: "La historia de la locura" como tesis', *Clínica y Analisis Grupal*, 10 (42): 628–656.

Morris, M. and Patton, P. (1979) *Michel Foucault: power, truth, strategy*, Sydney: Feral Publications.

Moss, J. (ed.) (1998) *The Later Foucault: politics and philosophy*, London: Sage.

Muldoon, M. S. (1995) 'Foucault: Madness and Language', *International Studies in Philosophy*, 27 (4): 51–68.

Munro, R. (1998) 'Masculinity and Madness', in J. Hassard and R. Holliday (eds) *Organization-representation: work and organization in popular culture*, London: Sage.

Nalli, M. A. G. (2001) 'Figuras da loucura em "Histoire de la Folie"', *Psicologia em Estudo*, 6 (2): 39–47.

Neely, C. T. (1991) 'Recent Work in Renaissance Studies: Psychology Did Madness Have a Renaissance?', *Renaissance Quarterly*, 44 (4): 776–791.

Nehamas, A. (2000) *Art of living: Socratic reflections from Plato to Foucault*, Berkeley; London: University of California Press.

Neto, A. d. F. P. (1998) 'Foucault, Derrida e a historia da loucura: notas sobre uma polemica', *Cadernos de Saude Publica*, 14 (3): 637–641.

Nilson, H. (1998) *Michel Foucault and the games of truth*, trans. R. Clark, Basingstoke: Macmillan.

Nola, R. (ed.) (1998) *Foucault*, London: Frank Cass.

Norris, C. (1994) '"What is Enlightenment?". Kant according to Foucault', in R. Miguel-Alfonso and S. Caporale-Bizzini (eds) *Reconstructing Foucault: essays in the wake of the 8os*, Amsterdam: Rodopi.

O'Farrell, C. (1989) *Foucault: historian or philosopher?*, Basingstoke: Macmillan.

O'Hara, D. T. (1994) 'Why Foucault no Longer Matters', in R. Miguel-Alfonso and S. Caporale-Bizzini (eds) *Reconstructing Foucault: essays in the wake of the 8os*, Amsterdam: Rodopi.

Olivier, L. (1988) 'La Question du pouvoir chez Foucault: espace, stratégie et dispositif', *Canadian Journal of Political Science/Revue canadienne de science politique*, 21 (1): 83–98.

Olson, C. (1999) 'Rationality and Madness: The Post-modern Embrace of Dionysus and the Neo-Vedanta Response of Radhakrishnan', *Asian Philosophy*, 9 (1): 39–50.

Olssen, M. (1999) *Michel Foucault: materialism and education*, London: Bergin & Garvey.

Pace, D. (1978) 'Structuralism in History and the Social Sciences', *American Quarterly*, 30 (3): 282–897.

Paden, R. (1987) 'Foucault's Anti-Humanism', *Human Studies*, 10 (1): 132–141.

Palombini, A. d. L. (1999) 'O louco e a rua: a clinica em movimento mais alem das fronteiras institucionais', *Educação, Subjetividade & Poder*, 6: 25–31.

Pasquino, P. (1986) 'Michel Foucault (1926–84): The Will to Knowledge', *Economy and Society*, 15: 97–109; reprinted in B. Smart (ed.) (1994–1995) *Michel Foucault: critical assessments*, vol. IV, Section 1: *History of Forms of Rationality*, London: Routledge.

Peet, R. (1994) 'Discourse, Text, Location Theory', *Economic Geography*, 70 (3): 297–302.

Pelorson, J.-M. (1970) 'Michel Foucault et l'Espagne', *La Pensée*, 152 (August): 88–89.

Peñalver, P. (1994) 'Archaeology, History, Deconstruction: Foucault's Thought and the Philosophical Experience', in R. Miguel-Alfonso and S. Caporale-Bizzini (eds) *Reconstructing Foucault: essays in the wake of the 80s*, Amsterdam: Rodopi.

Petersen, C. R. (1985) 'Time and Stress: Alice in Wonderland', *Journal of the History of Ideas*, 46 (3): 427–433.

Pigeaud, J. (2001) *Aux portes de la psychiatrie: Pinel, l'Ancien et le Moderne*, Paris: Aubier.

Porot, M., et al. (1969) 'Discussion', paper presented at La conception idéologique de 'L'histoire de la folie' de Michel Foucault: Journées Annuelles de l'Évolution psychiatrique, Toulouse, 6 and 7 December 1969; reprinted in *Évolution psychiatrique: cahiers de psychologie clinique et de psychopathologie générale* (1971), 36 (2): 279–298.

Porter, R. (1990) 'Foucault's Great Confinement', *History of the Human Sciences*, 3: 47–54; reprinted in B. Smart (ed.) (1994–1995) *Michel Foucault: critical assessments*, vol. IV Section 1: *History of Forms of Rationality*, London: Routledge.

Poster, M. (1989) *Critical theory and poststructuralism: in search of a Context*, Ithaca: Cornell University Press.

Powell, J. L. (2002) 'An Enlightenment Madness', *Human Studies*, 25 (3): 311–316.

Prado, C. G. (1995) *Starting with Foucault: an introduction to genealogy*, Boulder: Westview Press.

Racevskis, K. (1983) *Michel Foucault and the subversion of intellect*, Ithaca: Cornell University Press.

—— (ed.) (1999) *Critical essays on Michel Foucault*, New York: G. K. Hall.

Rajchman, J. (1999) 'Foucault's Art of Seeing', in K. Racevskis (ed.) *Critical essays on Michel Foucault*, New York: G. K. Hall.

Ramazanoglu, C. (ed.) (1993) *Up against Foucault: explorations of some tensions between Foucault and feminism*, London: Routledge.

Ransom, J. S. (1997) *Foucault's discipline: the politics of subjectivity*, Durham, NC: Duke University Press.

Revel, J. (1992) 'Sur l'introduction à Binswanger (1954)', in L. Giard (ed.) *Michel Foucault: lire l'œuvre*, Grenoble: J. Millon.

Rickes, S. M. (1996) 'A loucura (e/in)scrita: um ensaio', *Educação, Subjetividade & Poder*, 3: 84–87.

Ritzer, G. (1988) 'Sociological Metatheory: A Defense of a Subfield by a Delineation of its Parameters', *Sociological Theory*, 6 (2): 187–200.

Robinson, B. S. (1977) 'Some Fragmented Forms of Space', *Annals of the Association of American Geographers*, 67 (4): 549–563.

Rose, N. (1990) 'Of Madness Itself: Histoire de la folie and the Object of Psychiatric History', *History of the Human Sciences*, 3 (3): 373–380.

Rosemann, P. (1999) *Understanding scholastic thought with Foucault*, Basingstoke: Macmillan.

Rosenberg, M. (1984) 'A Symbolic Interactionist View of Psychosis', *Journal of Health and Social Behavior*, 25 (3): 289–302.

Rotenberg, M. (1975) 'The Protestant Ethic against the Spirit of Psychiatry: The Other Side of Weber's Thesis', *British Journal of Sociology*, 26 (1): 52–65.

Roth, M. (1988) 'Nobly wild, not mad?', *British Medical Journal*, 296: 1165–1168.

Roudinesco, É. (ed.) (1992) *Penser la folie: essais sur Michel Foucault*, Paris: Galilée.

Rousseau, G. S. (1969) 'Science and the Discovery of the Imagination in Enlightened England', *Eighteenth Century Studies*, 3 (1): 108–135.

—— (1981) 'Literature and Medicine: The State of the Field', *Isis*, 72 (3): 406–424.

Rubino, C. A. (1973) 'Le Clin d'Œil Échangé avec un Chat', *Comparative Literature*, 88 (6): 1238–1261.

Russ, J. (1979) *Histoire de la folie: Foucault*, Paris: Hatier.

Scalzo, J. (1990) Scalzo, Joseph, 'Campanella, Foucault, and Madness in Late-Sixteenth Century Italy', *The Sixteenth Century Journal*, 21 (3): 359–372.

Schäfer, T. (1995) *Reflektierte Vernunft: Michel Foucaults philosophisches Projekt einer antitotalitären Macht- und Wahrheitskritik*, Frankfurt am Main: Suhrkamp.

Schmidt, P. (1975) 'La psychose et l'autre réalité', *Annales médico-psychologiques*, 133 (2): 683–702.

—— (1977) 'Une introduction à l'étude des rapports de la psychose et de la réalité du langage', *Annales médico-psychologiques*, 135 (1): 43–55.

Schnittker, J. et al. (2000) 'Nature, Nurture, Neither, Nor: Black-White Differences in Beliefs about the Causes and Appropriate Treatment of Mental Illness', *Social Forces*, 78 (3): 1101–1132.

Scott, C. E. (1984) 'Speech and the Unspeakable in the "Place" of the Unconscious', *Human Studies*, 7 (1): 39–54.

—— (1990) *Question of Ethics: Nietzsche, Foucault, Heidegger*, Bloomington: Indiana University Press.

Scott, J. W. (1998) 'Border Patrol', *French Historical Studies*, 21 (3): 383–397.

Scull, A. (1990) 'Michel Foucault's History of Madness', *History of the Human Sciences*, 3: 57–67; reprinted in B. Smart (ed.) (1994–1995) *Michel Foucault: critical assessments*, vol. IV, Section 1: *History of Forms of Rationality*, London: Routledge.

Seigel, J. (1990) 'Avoiding the Subject: A Foucaultian Itinerary', *Journal of the History of Ideas*, 51 (2): 273–299.

Serres, M. (1968) 'D'Erehwon à l'Antre du Cyclope', in *Hermès ou la Communication*, Paris: Éditions de Minuit; reprinted in B. Smart (ed.) (1994–1995) *Michel Foucault: critical assessments*, vol. IV, Section 1: *History of Forms of Rationality*, London: Routledge.

Sheridan, A. (1980; 2nd edn 1994) *Michel Foucault: the will to truth*, London: Routledge.

Shiner, L. (1982) 'Reading Foucault: Anti-method and the Genealogy of Power-Knowledge', *History and Theory*, 21 (3): 382–398.

Shumway, D. R. (1989) *Michel Foucault*, Boston: Twayne Publishers.

Simons, J. (1995; 2nd edn 1996) *Foucault & the political*, London: Routledge.

Smart, B. (1985) *Michel Foucault*, Chichester: Ellis Horwood.

—— (1994–1995a) 'Introductory Essay: The Government of Conduct – Foucault on Rationality, Power and Subjectivity', in B. Smart (ed.) *Michel Foucault: critical assessments*, vol. IV Section 1: *History of Forms of Rationality*, London: Routledge.

—— (ed.) (1994–1995b) *Michel Foucault: critical assessments*, vol. IV Section 1: *History of Forms of Rationality*, London: Routledge.

Smith, J. M. (1993) '"Our Sovereign's Gaze": Kings, Nobles, and State Formation in Seventeenth-Century France', *French Historical Studies*, 18 (2): 396–415.

Sohlich, W. F. (1974) 'Genet's Drama: Rites of Passage of the Anti-Hero: From Alienated Existence to Artistic Alienation', *MLN, French Issue*, 89 (4): 641–653.

Sonntag, O. (1974) 'Albrecht Von Haller on the Future of Science', *Journal of the History of Ideas*, 35 (2): 313–322.

Still, A. and Velody, I. (eds) (1992) *Rewriting the history of madness: studies in Foucault's Histoire de la folie*, London: Routledge.

Stone, L. (1982) 'Madness', *New York Review of Books*, 29: 28–31, 34–36; reprinted in B. Smart (ed.) (1994–1995) *Michel Foucault: critical assessments*, vol. IV Section 1: *History of Forms of Rationality*, London: Routledge.

Swain, G. (1977; 2nd edn 1997) *Le Sujet de la folie*, Paris: Calmann-Lévy.

—— (1994) *Dialogue avec l'insensé*, Paris: Gallimard.

Swanson, G. E. (1986) 'Phobias and Related Symptoms: Some Social Sources', *Sociological Forum*, 1 (1): 103–130.

Swidler, A. and Arditi, J. (1994) 'The New Sociology of Knowledge', *Annual Review of Sociology*, 20: 305–329.

Szakolczai, Á. (1998) *Max Weber and Michel Foucault: parallel life-works*, London: Routledge.

Sztulman, H. (1969) 'Folie ou maladie? Étude critique, psychopathologique et épistemologique des conceptions de Michel Foucault', paper presented at La conception idéologique de 'L'histoire de la folie' de Michel Foucault: Journées Annuelles de l'Évolution psychiatrique, Toulouse, 6 and 7 December 1969; reprinted in *Évolution psychiatrique: cahiers de psychologie clinique et de psychopathologie générale* (1971), 36 (2): 259–277.

Tardits, A. (1992) 'Partage, séparation, aliénation', in L. Giard (ed.) *Michel Foucault: lire l'œuvre*, Grenoble: J. Millon.

Townsend, M. M. (1975) 'Cultural Conceptions, Mental Disorders and Social Roles: A Comparison of Germany and America', *American Sociological Review*, 40 (6): 739–752.

Turkel, G. (1990) 'Michel Foucault: Law, Power, and Knowledge', *Journal of Law and Society*, 17 (2): 170–193.

Turner, B. S. (1984) 'The Disciplines', in *The Body and Society: explorations in social theory*, Oxford: Blackwell; reprinted in B. Smart (ed.) (1994–1995) *Michel Foucault: critical assessments*, vol. IV, Section 1: *History of Forms of Rationality*, London: Routledge.

—— (1987; 2nd edn 1995) *Medical power and social knowledge*, London: Sage Publications Ltd.

Valadez, J. J. and Clignet, R. (1984) 'Household Work as an Ordeal: Culture of Standards Versus Standardization of Culture', *American Journal of Sociology*, 89 (4): 812–835.

Vázquez García, F. (2002) 'La tension infinie entre l'histoire et la raison: Foucault et Bourdieu', *Revue Internationale de Philosophie*, 56 (220): 343–365.

Visker, R. (1995) *Michel Foucault: genealogy as critique*, trans. C. Turner, London: Verso.

Volek, J. (1994) 'Pojem silenstvi v kontextu dila Michela Foucaulta', *Sbornik Praci Filosoficke Fakulty Brnenske University: Rada Socialnevedna/Series Sociologica*, 43 (G36): 47–73.

Watts, S. (1991) 'The Idiocy of American Studies: Poststructuralism, Language, and Politics in the Age of Self-Fulfilment', *American Quarterly*, 43 (4): 625–660.

Weber, E. (1982) 'Introduction: Decadence on a Private Income', *Journal of Contemporary History, Medicine, History and Society*, 17 (1): 1–20.

Whitton, B. J. (1992) 'Universal Pragmatics and the Formation of Western Civilization: A Critique of Habermas's Theory of Human Moral Evolution', *History and Theory*, 31 (3): 299–313.

Wiener, M. J. (1994) 'The Unloved State: Twentieth-Century Politics in the Writing of Nineteenth-Century History', *Journal of British Studies*, 33 (3): 283–308.

Wolpert, J. (1976) 'Opening Closed Spaces', *Annals of the Association of American Geographers*, 66 (1): 1–13.

Wright, R. A. (1980) 'Geosociology: A Geological Analogy for Social Structural Theory', *Quarterly Journal of Ideology*, 4 (3): 3–8.

Wuthnow, R. (1985) 'State Structures and Ideological Outcomes', *American Sociological Review*, 50 (6): 799–821.

Yapa, L. (1996) 'What Causes Poverty? A Postmodern View', *Annals of the Association of American Geographers*, 86 (4): 707–728.

[This bibliography was compiled by Alice Wilson]

Index

n. indicates that the entry is to be found in a note

eBooks – at www.eBookstore.tandf.co.uk

A library at your fingertips!

eBooks are electronic versions of printed books. You can store them on your PC/laptop or browse them online.

They have advantages for anyone needing rapid access to a wide variety of published, copyright information.

eBooks can help your research by enabling you to bookmark chapters, annotate text and use instant searches to find specific words or phrases. Several eBook files would fit on even a small laptop or PDA.

NEW: Save money by eSubscribing: cheap, online access to any eBook for as long as you need it.

Annual subscription packages

We now offer special low-cost bulk subscriptions to packages of eBooks in certain subject areas. These are available to libraries or to individuals.

For more information please contact webmaster.ebooks@tandf.co.uk

We're continually developing the eBook concept, so keep up to date by visiting the website.

www.eBookstore.tandf.co.uk

Related titles from Routledge

The Order of Things
Michel Foucault

'Michel Foucault is a very brilliant writer ... he has a remarkable angle of vision, a highly disciplined and coherent one, that informs his work to such a degree as to make the work *sui generis* original.' – *Edward W. Said*

In this virtuoso history of thought, Foucault takes us far beyond the limits of our usual categories into a realm of what he calls 'exotic charm', taking in literature, art, economics and even biology along the way. This work, which offers an insight into the early development of postmodernism, established Foucault as an intellectual giant and remains one of the most significant works of the twentieth century. A must.

ISBN10: 0–415–26736–6 (hbk)
ISBN10: 0–415–26737–4 (pbk)

ISBN–13: 978–0–415–26736–6 (hbk)
ISBN–13: 978–0–415–26737–3 (pbk)

Available at all good bookshops
For ordering and further information please visit:
www.routledge.com

Related titles from Routledge

The Birth of the Clinic
An archaeology of medical perception
Michel Foucault

'Foucault's importance is that he has boldly attempted to create a new method of historical analysis and a new framework for the study of the human sciences as a whole. . . . The homage that is paid to Foucault as commentator on medical history is fully justified.' – Theodore Zeldin, *New Statesman*

In this remarkable book, Michel Foucault calls us to look critically at specific historical events in order to uncover new layers of significance and analyses the methods of observation that underpin the origins of modern medical techniques. The scope of such an undertaking is vast, but it is Foucault's skill that, by means of his uniquely engaging narrative style, his penetrating gaze is able to confront our own.

ISBN10: 0–415–30772–4
ISBN13: 978–0–415–30772–7

Available at all good bookshops
For ordering and further information please visit:
www.routledge.com